An Elizabeth Prentiss Treasury

Stepping Heavenward

&

The Life and Letters of Elizabeth Prentiss

By Elizabeth Prentiss and George L. Prentiss

A Woodbine Cottage Publication

WC

A Woodbine Cottage Publication
PO Box 211
Lakehurst, NJ 08733-0211
awcpublications@aol.com

Edited by Thomas Adamo
Copyright 2013

All rights reserved, including the right to reproduce this book or portions thereof in any form whatsoever.

Cover Illustration: "View of Arles with Irises in the foreground" by Vincent Van Gogh

ISBN: 1-4818-1518-0

EAN-13: 978-1-4818-1518-5

An Elizabeth Prentiss Treasury

Stepping Heavenward

&

The Life and Letters of Elizabeth Prentiss

WC

CONTENTS

STEPPING HEAVENWARD
BY ELIZABETH PRENTISS

Chapter 1	1
Chapter 2	5
Chapter 3	9
Chapter 4	12
Chapter 5	17
Chapter 6	20
Chapter 7	23
Chapter 8	27
Chapter 9	29
Chapter 10	35
Chapter 11	38
Chapter 12	42
Chapter 13	46
Chapter 14	49
Chapter 15	52
Chapter 16	55
Chapter 17	59
Chapter 18	62
Chapter 19	66
Chapter 20	69
Chapter 21	72
Chapter 22	75
Chapter 23	78

Chapter 24	82
Chapter 25	85
Chapter 26	88
Chapter 27	92

THE LIFE AND LETTERS OF ELIZABETH PRENTISS
BY GEORGE L. PRENTISS

CHAPTER 1 - THE CHILD AND THE GIRL - 1818-1839.	97
CHAPTER 2 - THE NEW LIFE IN CHRIST - 1840-1841.	110
CHAPTER 3 - PASSING FROM GIRLHOOD INTO WOMANHOOD - 1841-1845.	124
CHAPTER 4 - THE YOUNG WIFE AND MOTHER - 1845-1850.	137
CHAPTER 5 - IN THE SCHOOL OF SUFFERING - 1851-1858.	149
CHAPTER 6 - IN RETREAT AMONG THE ALPS - 1858-1860.	163
CHAPTER 7 - THE STRUGGLE WITH ILL-HEALTH - 1861-1865.	179
CHAPTER 8 - THE PASTOR'S WIFE & DAUGHTER OF CONSOLATION - 1866-1868.	191
CHAPTER 9 - STEPPING HEAVENWARD - 1869.	203
CHAPTER 10 - ON THE MOUNT - 1870.	217
CHAPTER 11 - IN HER HOME.	229
CHAPTER 12 - THE TRIAL OF FAITH - 1871-1872.	245
CHAPTER 13 - PEACEABLE FRUIT - 1873-1874.	261
CHAPTER 14 - WORK AND PLAY - 1875-1877.	278
CHAPTER 15 - FOREVER WITH THE LORD - 1878.	298
APPENDIX	320

More Love to Thee

Elizabeth Payson Prentiss (*Proprior Deo* 6. 4. 6. 4. 6. 6. 4) Sir Arthur Sullivan

1. More love to Thee, O Christ! More love to Thee! Hear Thou the pray'r I make On bend-ed knee; This is my ear-nest plea, More love, O Christ, to Thee, More love to Thee, More love to Thee! A-MEN.

2. Once earth-ly joy I craved, Sought peace and rest; Now Thee a-lone I seek; Give what is best: This all my pray'r shall be, More love, O Christ, to Thee, More love to Thee, More love to Thee! A-MEN.

3. Then shall my la-test breath Whis-per Thy praise; This be the part-ing cry My heart shall raise, This still its pray'r shall be, More love, O Christ, to Thee, More love to Thee, More love to Thee! A-MEN.

STEPPING HEAVENWARD

Chapter 1

January 15, 1831.

How dreadfully old I am getting! Sixteen! Well, I do not see as I can help it. There it is in the big Bible in father's own hand: "Katherine, born Jan. 15, 1815."

I meant to get up early this morning, but it looked dismally cold out of doors, and felt delightfully warm in bed. So, I covered myself up, and made ever so many good resolutions.

I determined, in the first place, to begin this Journal. To be sure, I have begun half a dozen, and got tired of them after a while. Not tired of writing them, but disgusted with what I had to say of myself. But this time I mean to go on, in spite of everything. It will do me good to read it over, and see what a creature I am.

Then I resolved to do more to please mother than I have done.

And I determined to make one more effort to conquer my hasty temper. I thought, too, I would be self-denying this winter, like the people one reads about in books. I fancied how surprised and pleased everybody would be to see me so much improved!

Time passed quickly amid these agreeable thoughts, and I was quite startled to hear the bell ring for prayers. I jumped up in a great flurry and dressed as quickly as I could. Everything conspired together to plague me. I could not find a clean collar, or a handkerchief. It is always just so. Susan is forever poking my things into out-of-the-way places! When at last I went down, they were all at breakfast.

"I hoped you would celebrate your birthday, dear, by coming down in good season," said mother.

I do hate to be found fault with, so I fired up in an instant.

"If people hide my things so that I cannot find them, of course I have to be late," I said. And I rather think I said it in a very cross way, for mother sighed a little. I wish mother would not sigh. I would rather be called names out and out.

The moment breakfast was over I had to hurry off to school. Just as I was going out mother said, "Have you your overshoes, dear?"

"Oh, mother, do not hinder me! I shall be late," I said. "I do not need overshoes."

"It snowed all night, and I think you do need them," mother said.

"I do not know where they are. I hate overshoes. Do let me go, mother," I cried. "I do wish I could ever have my own way."

"You shall have it now, my child," mother said, and went away.

Now what was the use of her calling me "my child" in such a tone, I should like to know.

I hurried off, and just as I got to the door of the schoolroom, it flashed into my mind that I had not said my prayers! A nice way to begin on one's birthday, to be sure! Well, I had not time. And perhaps my good resolutions pleased God almost as much as one of my rambling stupid prayers could. For I must own I cannot make good prayers. I cannot think of anything to say. I often wonder what mother finds to say when she is shut up by the hour together.

I had a pretty good time at school. My teachers praised me, and Amelia seemed so fond of me! She brought me a birthday present of a purse that she had knit for me herself, and a net for my hair. Nets are just coming into fashion. It will save a good deal of time my having this one. Instead of combing and combing and combing my old hair to get it glossy enough to suit mother, I can just give it one twist and one squeeze and the whole thing will be settled for the day.

Amelia wrote me a dear little note, with her presents. I do really believe she loves me dearly. It is so nice to have people love you!

When I got home mother called me into her room. She looked as if she had been crying. She said I gave her a great deal of pain by my self-will and ill temper and conceit.

"Conceit!" I screamed out. "Oh, mother, if you only knew how horrid I think I am!"

Mother smiled a little. Then she went on with her list until she made me out the worst creature in the world. I burst out crying, and was running off to my room, but she made me come back and hear the rest. She said my character would be essentially formed by the time I reached my twentieth year, and left it to me to say if I wished to be as a woman what I was now as a girl. I felt sulky, and would not answer. I was shocked to think I had got only four years in which to improve, but after all a good deal could be done in that time. Of course, I do not want to be always exactly, what I am now.

Mother went on to say that, I had in me the elements of a fine character if I would only conquer some of my faults. "You are frank and truthful," she said, "and in some things conscientious. I hope you are really a child of God, and are trying to please Him. And it is my daily prayer that you may become a lovely, loving, useful woman."

I made no answer. I wanted to say something, but my tongue would not move. I was angry with mother, and angry with myself. At last, everything came out all in a rush, mixed up with such floods of tears that I thought mother's heart would melt, and that she would take back what she had said.

"Amelia's mother never talks so to her!" I said. "She praises her, and tells her what a comfort she is to her. But just as I am trying as hard as I can to be good, and making resolutions, and all that, you scold me and discourage me!"

Mother's voice was very soft and gentle as she asked, "Do you call this 'scolding,' my child?"

"And I do not like to be called conceited," I went on. "I know I am perfectly horrid, and I am just as unhappy as I can be."

"I am very sorry for you, dear," mother replied. "But you must bear with me. Other people will see your faults, but only your mother will have the courage to speak of them. Now go to your own room, and wipe away the traces of your tears that the rest of the family may not know that you have been crying on your birthday." She kissed me but I did not kiss her. I really believe Satan himself hindered me. I ran across the hall to my room, slammed the door, and locked myself in. I was going to throw myself on the bed and cry till I was sick. Then I should look pale and tired, and they would all pity me. I do like so to be pitied! But on the table, by the window, I saw a beautiful new desk in place of the old clumsy thing I had been spattering and spoiling so many years. A little note, full of love, said it was from mother, and begged me to read and reflect upon a few verses of a tastefully bound copy of the Bible, which accompanied it every day of my life. "A few verses," she said, "carefully read and pondered, instead of a chapter or two read for mere form's sake." I looked at my desk, which contained exactly what I wanted, plenty of paper, seals, wax, and pens. I always use wax. Wafers are vulgar. Then I opened the Bible at random, and lighted on these words:

"Watch, therefore, for ye know not what hour your Lord doth come." There was nothing very cheering in that. I felt a real repugnance to be always on the watch, thinking I might die at any moment. I am sure I am not fit to die. Besides, I want to have a good time, with nothing to worry me. I hope I shall live ever so long. Perhaps in the course of forty or fifty years I may get tired of this world and want to leave it. And I hope by that time I shall be a great deal better than I am now, and fit to go to heaven.

I wrote a note to mother on my new desk, and thanked her for it I told her she was the best mother in the world, and that I was the worst daughter. When it was done I did not like it, and so I wrote another. Then I went down to dinner and felt better. We had such a nice dinner! Everything I liked best was on the table. Mother had not forgotten one of all the dainties I like. Amelia was there too. Mother had invited her to give me a little surprise. It is bedtime now, and I must say my prayers and go to bed. I have got all chilled through, writing here in the cold. I believe I will say my prayers in bed, just for this once. I do not feel sleepy, but I am sure I ought not to sit up another moment.

JAN. 30. -Here I am at my desk once more. There is a fire in my room, and mother is sitting by it, reading. I cannot see what book it is, but I have no doubt it is Thomas A Kempis. How she can go on reading it so year after year, I cannot imagine. For my part, I like something new. But I must go back to where I left off.

That night when I stopped writing, I hurried to bed as fast as I could, for I felt cold and tired. I remember saying, "Oh, God, I am ashamed to pray," and then I began to think of all the things that had happened that day, and never knew another thing till the rising bell rang and I found it was morning. I am sure I did not mean to go to sleep. I think now it was wrong for me to be such a coward as to try to say my prayers in bed because of the cold. While I was writing, I did not once think how I felt. Well, I jumped up as soon as I heard the bell, but found I had a dreadful pain in my side, and a cough. Susan says I coughed all night. I remembered then that I had just such a cough and just such a pain the last time I walked in the snow without overshoes. I crept back to bed feeling about as mean as I could. Mother sent up to know why I did not come down, and I had to own that I was sick. She came up directly looking so anxious! And here I have been shut up ever since only today, I am sitting up a little. Poor mother has had trouble enough with me I know I have been cross and unreasonable, and it was my own entire fault that I was ill. Another time I will do as mother says.

JAN. 31. -How easy it is to make good resolutions, and how easy it is to break them! Just as I had got so far, yesterday, mother spoke for the third time about my exerting myself so much. And just at that moment, I fainted away, and she had a great time all alone there with me. I did not realize how long I had been writing, nor how weak I was. I do wonder if I shall ever really learn that mother knows more than I do!

Feb. 17. -It is more than a month since I took that cold, and here I still am, shut up in the house. To be sure, the doctor lets me go down stairs, but then he won't listen to a word about school. Oh, dear! All the girls will get ahead of me.

This is Sunday, and everybody has gone to church. I thought I ought to make a good use of the time while they were gone, so I took the Memoir of Henry Martyn, and read a little in that.

I am afraid I am not much like him. Then I knelt down and tried to pray. But my mind was full of all sorts of things, so I thought I would wait till I was in a better frame. At noon, I disputed with James about the name of an apple. He was very provoking, and said he was thankful he had not got such a temper as I had. I cried, and mother reproved him for teasing me, saying my illness had left me nervous and irritable. James replied that it had left me where it found me, then. I cried a good while, lying on the sofa, and then I fell asleep. I do not see as I am any the better for this Sunday, it has only made me feel unhappy and out of sorts. I am sure I pray to God to make me better, and why doesn't He?

Feb. 20.-It has been quite a mild day for the season, and the doctor said I might drive out. I enjoyed getting the air very much. I feel just well as ever, and long to get back to school. I think God has been very good to me in making me well again, and wish I loved Him better. But, oh, I am not sure I do love Him! I hate to own it to myself, and to write it down here, but I will. I do not love to pray. I am always eager to get it over with and out of the way so as to have leisure to enjoy myself. I mean that this is usually so. This morning I cried a good deal while I was on my knees, and felt sorry for my quick temper and all my bad ways. If I always felt so, perhaps praying would not be such a task. I wish I knew whether anybody exactly as bad as I am ever got to heaven at last. I have read ever so many memoirs, and they were all about people who were too good to live, and so died or else went on a mission. I am not at all like any of them.

March 26.-I have been so busy that I have not said much to you, you poor old journal, you, have I? Somehow, I have been behaving quite nicely lately. Everything has gone on exactly to my mind. Mother has not found fault with me once, and father has praised my drawings and seemed proud of me. He says he shall not tell me what my teachers say of me lest it should make me vain. And once or twice when he has met me singing and frisking about the house he has kissed me and called me his dear little Flibbertigibbet, if that's the way to spell it. When he says that I know he is very fond of me. We are all very happy together when nothing goes wrong. In the long evenings, we all sit around the table with our books and our work, and one of us reads aloud. Mother chooses the book and takes her turn in reading. She reads beautifully. Of course, the readings do not begin till the lessons are all learned. As to me, my lessons just take no time at all. I have only to read them over once, and there they are. So I have a good deal of time to read, and I devour all the poetry I can get hold of. I would rather read "Pollok's Course of Time" than read nothing at all.

April 2.-There are three of mother's friends living near us, each having lots of little children. It is perfectly ridiculous how much those creatures are sick. They send for mother if so much as a pimple comes out on one of their faces. When I have children, I do not mean to have such goings on. I shall be careful about what they eat, and keep them from getting cold, and they will keep well of their own accord. Mrs. Jones has just sent for mother to see her Tommy. It was so provoking. I had coaxed her into letting me have a black silk apron they are all the fashion now, embroidered in floss silk. I had drawn a lovely vine for mine entirely out of my own head, and mother was going to arrange the pattern for me when that message came, and she had to go. I do not believe anything ails the child! A great chubby thing!

April 3.-Poor Mrs. Jones! Her dear little Tommy is dead! I stayed at home from school today and had all the other children here to get them out of their mother's way. How dreadfully she must feel! Mother cried when she told me how the dear little fellow suffered in his last moments. It reminded her of my little brothers who died in the same way, just before I was born. Dear mother! I wonder I ever forget what troubles she has had, and is not always sweet and loving. She has gone now, where she always goes when she feels sad, straight to God. Of course, she did not say so, but I know mother.

April 25.-I have not been down in season once this week. I have persuaded mother to let me read some of Scott's novels, and have sat up late and been sleepy in the morning. I wish I could get along with mother as nicely as James does. He is late far oftener than I am, but he never gets into such scrapes about it as I do. This is what happens. He comes down when it suits him.

Mother begins.-"James, I am very much displeased with you."

James.-"I should think you would be, mother."

Mother, mollified.-"I do not think you deserve any breakfast."

James, hypocritically.-"No, I do not think I do, mother."

Then mother hurries off and gets something extra for his breakfast. Now let us see how things go on when I am late.

Mother.-"Katherine" (she always calls me Katherine when she is displeased, and spells it with a K), "Katherine, you are late again how can you annoy your father so?"

Katherine.-"Of course I do not do it to annoy father or anybody else. But if I oversleep myself, it is not my fault."

Mother.-"I would go to bed at eight o'clock rather than be late as often as you. How should you like it if I were not down to prayers?"

Katherine, muttering.-"Of course that is very different. I do not see why I should be blamed for oversleeping any more than James. I get all the scoldings."

Mother sighs and goes off.

I prowl round and get what scraps of breakfast I can.

May 12.-The weather is getting perfectly delicious. I am sitting with my window open, and my bird is singing with all his heart. I wish I was as gay as he is.

I have been thinking lately that it was about time to begin on some of those pieces of self-denial I resolved on upon my birthday. I could not think of anything great enough for a long time. At last, an idea popped into my head. Half the girls at school envy me because Amelia is so fond of me, and Jane Underhill, in particular, is just crazy to get intimate with her. But I have kept Amelia all to myself. Today I said to her, Amelia, Jane Underhill admires you above all things. I have a good mind to let you be as intimate with her as you are with me. It will be a great piece of self-denial, but I think it is my duty. She is a stranger, and nobody seems to like her much."

"You dear thing, you!" cried Amelia, kissing me. "I liked Jane Underhill the moment I saw her. She has such a sweet face and such pleasant manners. But you are so jealous that I never dared to show how I liked her. Do not be vexed, dearie if you are jealous it is your only fault!"

She then rushed off, and I saw her kiss that girl exactly as she kisses me!

This was in recess. I went to my desk and made believe I was studying. Pretty soon, Amelia came back.

"She is a sweet girl," she said, "and only to think! She writes poetry! Just hear this! It is a little poem addressed to me. Isn't it nice of her?"

I pretended not to hear her. I was as full of all sorts of horrid feelings as I could hold. It enraged me to think that Amelia, after all her professions of love to me, should snatch at the first chance of getting a new friend. Then I was mortified because I was enraged, and I could have torn myself to pieces for being such a fool as to let Amelia see how silly I was.

"I do not know what to make of you, Katy," she said, putting her arms round me. "Have I done anything to vex you? Come, let us make up and be friends, whatever it is. I will read you these sweet verses I am sure you will like them."

She read them in her clear, pleasant voice.

"How can you have the vanity to read such stuff?" I cried.

Amelia colored a little.

"You have said and written much more flattering things to me," she replied. "Perhaps it has turned my head, and made me too ready to believe what other people say." She folded the paper, and put it into her pocket. We walked home together, after school, as usual, but neither of us spoke a word. And now here I sit, unhappy enough. All my resolutions fail but I did not think Amelia would take me at my word, and rush after that stuck-up, smirking piece.

May 20.-I seem to have got back into all my bad ways again. Mother is quite out of patience with me. I have not prayed for a long time. It does not do any good.

May 21.-It seems this Underhill thing is here for health, though she looks as well as any of us. She is an orphan, and has been adopted by a rich old uncle, who makes a perfect fool of her. Such dresses and such finery as she wears! Last night she had Amelia there to tea, without inviting me, though she knows I am her best friend. She gave her a bracelet made of her own hair. I wonder Amelia's mother lets her accept presents from strangers. My mother would not let me. On the whole, there is nobody like one's own mother. Amelia has been cold and distant to me of late, but no matter what I do or say to my darling, precious mother, she is always kind and loving. She noticed how I moped about today, and begged me to tell her what the matter was. I was ashamed to do that. I told her that it was a little quarrel I had had with Amelia.

"Dear child," she said, "how I pity you that you have inherited my quick, irritable temper."

"Yours, mother!" I cried out "what can you mean?"

Mother smiled a little at my surprise.

"It is even so," she said.

"Then how did you cure yourself of it? Tell me quick, mother, and let me cure myself of mine."

"My dear Katy," she said, "I wish I could make you see that God is just as willing, and just as able to sanctify, as He is to redeem us. It would save you so much weary, disappointing work. But God has opened my eyes at last."

"I wish He would open mine, then," I said, "for all I see now is that I am just as horrid as I can be, and that the more I pray the worse I grow."

That is not true, dear," she replied "go on praying-pray without ceasing.

I sat pulling my handkerchief this way and that, and at last rolled it up into a ball and threw it across the room. I wished I could toss my bad feelings into a corner with it.

"I do wish I could make you love to pray, my darling child," mother went on. "If you only knew the strength, and the light, and the joy you might have for the simple asking. God attaches no conditions to His gifts. He only says, 'Ask!'"

"This may be true, but it is hard work to pray. It tires me. And I do wish there was some easy way of growing good. In fact, I should like to have God send a sweet temper to me just as He sent bread and meat to Elijah. I do not believe Elijah had to kneel down and pray for them."

Chapter 2

June 1.

LAST Sunday Dr. Cabot preached to the young. He first addressed those who knew they did not love God. It did not seem to me that I belonged to that class. Then he spoke to those who knew they did. I felt sure I was not one of those. Last of all he spoke affectionately to those who did not know what to think, and I was frightened and ashamed to feel tears running down my cheeks, when he said that he believed that most of his hearers who were in this doubtful state did really love their Master, only their love was something as new and as tender and perhaps as unobserved as the tiny point of green that, forcing its way through the earth, is yet unconscious of its own existence, but promises a thrifty plant. I do not suppose I express it very well, but I know what he meant. He then invited those belonging to each class to meet him on three successive Saturday afternoons. I shall certainly go.

July 19.-I went to the meeting, and so did Amelia. A great many young people were there and a few children. Dr. Cabot went about from seat to seat speaking to each one separately. When he came to us, I expected he would say something about the way in which I had been brought up, and reproach me for not profiting more by the instructions and example I had at home. Instead of that he said, in a cheerful voice,

"Well, my dear, I cannot see into your heart and positively tell whether there is love to God there or not. But I suppose you have come here today in order to let me help you to find out?"

I said, "Yes" that was all I could get out.

"Let me see, then," he went on. "Do you love your mother?"

I said "Yes," once more.

"But prove to me that you do. How do you know it?"

I tried to think. Then I said,

"I feel that I love her. I love to love her, I like to be with her. I like to hear people praise her. And I try—sometimes at least—to do things to please her. But I do not try half as hard as I ought, and I do and say a great many things to displease her."

"Yes, yes," he said, "I know."

"Has mother told you?" I cried out.

"No, dear, no indeed. But I know what human nature is after having one of my own fifty years, and six of my children's to encounter."

Somehow, I felt more courage after he said that.

"In the first place, then, you feel that you love your mother? But you never feel that you love your God and Savior?"

"I often try, and try, but I never do," I said.

"Love won't be forced," he said, quickly.

"Then what shall I do?"

"In the second place, you like to be with your mother. But you never like to be with the Friend who loves you so much better than she does?"

"I do not know, I never was with Him. Sometimes I think that when Mary sat at His feet and heard Him talk, she must have been very happy."

"We come to the third test, then. You like to hear people praise your mother. And have you ever rejoiced to hear the Lord magnified?"

I shook my head sorrowfully enough.

"Let us then try the last test. You know you love your mother because you try to do things to please her. That is to do what you know she wishes you to do? Very well. Have you never tried to do anything God wishes you to do?" "Oh yes often. But not so often as I ought."

"Of course not. No one does that. But come now, why do you try to do what you think will please Him? Because it is easy? Because you like to do what He likes rather than what you like yourself?"

I tried to think, and got puzzled.

"Never mind," said Dr. Cabot, " I have come now to the point I was aiming at. You cannot prove to yourself that you love God by examining your feelings towards Him. They are indefinite and they fluctuate. But just as far as you obey Him, just so far, depend upon it, you love Him. It is not natural to us sinful, ungrateful human beings to prefer His pleasure to our own, or to follow His way instead of our own way, and nothing, nothing but love to Him can or does make us obedient to Him."

"Couldn't we obey Him from fear ?"Amelia now asked. She had been listening all this time in silence.

"Yes and so you might obey your mother from fear, but only for a season. If you had no real love for her you would gradually cease to dread her displeasure, whereas it is in the very nature of love to grow stronger and more influential every hour."

"You mean, then, that if we want to know whether we love God, we must find out whether we are obeying Him?" Amelia asked.

"I mean exactly that. 'He that keepeth my commandments he it is that loveth me.' But I cannot talk with you any longer now. There are many others still waiting. You can come to see me some day next week, if you have any more questions to ask."

When we got out into the street, Amelia and I got hold of each other's hands. We did not speak a word till we reached the door, but we knew that we were as good friends as ever.

"I understand all Dr. Cabot said," Amelia whispered, as we separated. But I felt like one in a fog. I cannot see how it is possible to love God, and yet feel as stupid as I do when I think of Him. Still, I am determined to do one thing, and that is to pray, regularly instead of now and then, as I have got the habit of doing lately.

July 25.- School has closed for the season. I took the first prize for drawing, and my composition was read aloud on examination day, and everybody praised it. Mother could not possibly help showing, in her face, that she was very much pleased. I am pleased myself. We are now getting ready to take a journey. I do not think I shall go to see Dr. Cabot again. My head is so full of other things, and there is so much to do before we go. I am having four new dresses made, and I cannot imagine how to have them trimmed. I mean to run down to Amelia's and ask her.

July 27.-I was rushing through the hall just after I wrote that, and met mother.

"I am going to Amelia's," I said, hurrying past her.

"Stop one minute, dear. Dr. Cabot is downstairs. He says he has been expecting a visit from you, and that as you did not come to him, he has come to you."

"I wish he would mind his own business," I said.

"I think he is minding it, dear," mother answered. "His Master's business is his, and that has brought him here. Go to him, my darling child I am sure you crave something better than prizes and compliments and new dresses and journeys."

If anybody but mother had said that, my heart would have melted at once, and I should have gone right down to Dr. Cabot to be molded in his hand to almost any shape. But as it was, I brushed past, ran into my room, and locked my door. Oh, what makes me act so! I hate myself for it, I do not want to do it!

Last week I dined with Mrs. Jones. Her little Tommy was very fond of me, and that, I suppose, makes her have me there so often. Lucy was at the table, and very fractious. She cried first for one thing and then for another. At last, her mother in a gentle, but very decided way put her down from the table. Then she cried louder than ever. But when her mother offered to take her back if she would be good, she screamed yet more. She wanted to come and would not let herself come. I almost hated her when I saw her act so, and now I am behaving ten times worse and I am just as miserable as I can be.

July 29.- Amelia has been here. She has had her talk with Dr. Cabot and is perfectly happy. She says it is so easy to be a Christian! It may be easy for her everything is. She never has any of my dreadful feelings, and does not understand them when I try to explain them to her. Well, if I am fated to be miserable, I must try to bear it.

Oct. 3.-Summer is over, school has begun again, and I am so busy that I have not much time to think, to be low-spirited. We had a delightful journey, and I feel well and bright, and even gay. I never enjoyed my studies as I do those of this year. Everything goes on pleasantly here at home. But James has gone away to school, and we miss him sadly. I wish I had a sister. Though I dare say I should quarrel with her, if I had.

Oct 23.-I am so glad that my studies are harder this year, as I am never happy except when every moment is occupied. However, I do not study all the time, by any means. Mrs. Gordon grows more and more fond of me, and has me there to dinner or to tea continually. She has a much higher opinion of me than mother has, and is always saying the sort of things that make you feel nice. She holds me up to Amelia as an example, begging her to imitate me in my fidelity about my lessons, and declaring there is nothing she so much desires as to have a daughter bright and original like me. Amelia only laughs, and goes and purrs in her mother's ears when she hears such talk. It costs her nothing to be pleasant. She was born so. For my part, I think myself lucky to have such a friend. She gets along with my odd, hateful ways better than anyone else does. Mother, when I boast of this, says she has no penetration into character, and that she would be fond of almost any one fond of her and that the fury with which I love her deserves some response. I really do not know what to make of mother. Most people are proud of their children when they see others admire them but she does say such pokey things! Of course, I know that having a gift for music, and a taste for drawing, and a reputation for saying witty, bright things isn't enough. But when she doesn't find fault with me, and nothing happens to keep me down, I am the gayest creature on earth. I do love to get with a lot of nice girls, and carry on! I have got enough fun in me to keep a houseful merry. And mother needn't say anything. I inherited it from her.

Evening.-I knew it was coming! Mother has been in to see what I was about, and to give me a bit of her mind. She says she loves to see me gay and cheerful, as is natural at my age, but that levity quite upsets and disorders the mind, indisposing it for serious thoughts.

"But, mother," I said, "didn't you carry on when you were a young girl?"

"Of course I did," she said, smiling. "But I do not think I was quite so thoughtless as you are."

"Thoughtless" indeed! I wish I were! But am I not always full of uneasy, reproachful thoughts when the moment of excitement is over? Other girls, who seem less trifling than I, are really more so. Their heads are full of dresses and parties and beaux, and all that sort of nonsense. I wonder if that ever worries their mothers, or whether mine is the only one who weeps in secret? Well, I shall be young but once, and while I am, do let me have a good time!

Sunday, Nov. 20.-Oh, the difference between this day and the day I wrote that! There are no good times in this dreadful world. I have hardly courage or strength to write down the history of the past few weeks. The day after I had deliberately made up my mind to enjoy myself, cost what it might, my dear father called me to him, kissed me, pulled my ears a little, and gave me some money.

"We have had to keep you rather low in funds," he said laughing. "But I recovered this amount yesterday, and as it was a little debt I had given up, I can spare it to you. For girls like pin-money, I know, and you may spend this just as you please."

I was delighted. I want to take more drawing-lessons, but did not feel sure he could afford it. Besides-I am a little ashamed to write it down-I knew somebody had been praising me or father would not have seemed so fond of me. I wondered who it was, and felt a good deal puffed up. "After-all," I said to myself, "some people like me if I have got my faults." I threw my arms around his neck and kissed him, though that cost me a great effort. I never like to show what I feel. But, oh! How thankful I am for it now.

As to mother, I know father never goes out without kissing her good-by.

I went out with her to take a walk at three o'clock. We had just reached the corner of Orange Street, when I saw a carriage driving slowly towards us it appeared to be full of sailors. Then I saw our friend, Mr. Freeman, among them. When he saw us, he jumped out and came up to us. I do not know what he said. I saw mother turn pale and catch at his arm as if she were afraid of falling. But she did not speak a word.

"Oh! Mr. Freeman, what is it?" I cried out. "Has anything happened to father? Is he hurt? Where is he?"

"He is in the carriage," he said. We are taking him home. He has had a fall."

Then we went on in silence. The sailors were carrying father in as we reached the house. They laid him on the sofa, we saw his poor head…

Nov. 23.-I will try to write the rest now. Father was alive but insensible. He had fallen down into the hold of the ship, and the sailors heard him groaning there. He lived three hours after they brought him home. Mr. Freeman and all our friends were very kind. But we like best to be alone, we three, mother and James and I. Poor mother looks twenty years older, but she is so patient, and so concerned for us, and has such a smile of welcome for every one that comes in, that it breaks my heart to see her.

Nov. 25.-Mother spoke to me very seriously today, about controlling myself more. She said she knew this was my first real sorrow, and how hard it was to bear it. But that she was afraid, I should become insane some time, if I indulged myself in such passions of grief. And she said, too, that when friends came to see us, full of sympathy and eager to say or do something for our comfort, it was our duty to receive them with as much cheerfulness as possible.

I said they, none of them, had anything to say that did not provoke me.

"It is always a trying task to visit the afflicted," mother said, "and you make it doubly hard to your friends by putting on a gloomy, forbidding air, and by refusing to talk of your dear father, as if you were resolved to keep your sorrow all to yourself."

"I cannot smile when I am so unhappy," I said.

A good many people have been here today. Mother has seen them all, though she looked ready to drop. Mrs. Bates said to me, in her little, weak, watery voice:

"Your mother is wonderfully sustained, dear. I hope you feel reconciled to God's will. Rebellion is most displeasing to Him, dear."

I made no answer. It is very easy for people to preach. Let me see how they behave when they their turn to lose their friends.

Mrs. Morris said this was a very mysterious dispensation. But that she was happy to see that Mother was meeting it with so much firmness. "As for myself," she went on, "I was quite broken down by my dear husband's death. I did not eat as much as would feed a bird, for nearly a week. But some people have so much feeling then again, others are so firm. Your mother is so busy talking with Mrs. March that I won't interrupt her to say goodbye. I came prepared to suggest several things that I thought would comfort her but perhaps she has thought of them herself."

I could have knocked her down. Firm, indeed! Poor mother.

After they had all gone, I made her lie down, she looked so tired and worn out.

Then, I could not help telling her what Mrs. Morris had said.

She only smiled a little, but said nothing.

"I wish you would ever flare up, mother," I said.

She smiled again, and said she had nothing to "flare up" about.

"Then I shall do it for you!" I cried. To hear that namby-pamby woman, who is about as capable of understanding you as an old cat, talking about your being firm! You see what you get by being quiet and patient! People would like you much better if you refused to be comforted, and wore a sad countenance."

"Dear Katy," said mother, "it is not my first object in life to make people like me."

By this time, she looked so pale that I was frightened. Though she is so cheerful, and things go on much as they did before, I believe she has got her deathblow. If she has, then I hope I have got mine. And yet I am not fit to die. I wish I was, and I wish I could die. I have lost all interest in everything, and do not care what becomes of me.

Nov. 23.-I believe I shall go crazy unless people stop coming here, hurling volleys of texts at mother and at me. When soldiers drop wounded on the battlefield, they are taken up tenderly and carried "to the rear," which means, I suppose, out of sight and sound. Is anybody mad enough to suppose it will do them any good to hear Scripture quoted sermons launched at them before their open, bleeding wounds are staunched?

Mother assents, in a mild way, when I talk so and says, "Yes, yes, we are indeed lying wounded on the battle-field of life, and in no condition to listen to any words save those of pity. But, dear Katy, we must interpret aright all the well-meant attempts of our friends to comfort us. They mean sympathy, however awkwardly they express it."

And then she sighed, with a long, deep sigh, which told how it all wearied her.

Dec. 14.-Mother keeps saying I spend too much time in brooding over my sorrow. As for her, she seems to live in heaven. Not that she has long prosy talks about it, but little words that she lets drop now and then show where her thoughts are, and where she would like to be. She seems to think everybody is as eager to go there as she is. For my part, I am not eager at all. I cannot make myself feel that it will be nice to sit in rows, all the time singing, fond as I am of music. And when I say to myself, "Of course we shall not always sit in rows singing," then I fancy a multitude of shadowy, phantom-like beings, dressed in white, moving to and fro in golden streets, doing nothing in particular, and having a dreary time, without anything to look forward to.

I told mother so. She said earnestly, and yet in her sweetest, tenderest way,

"Oh, my darling Katy! What you need is such a living, personal love to Christ as shall make the thought of being where He is so delightful as to fill your mind with that single thought!"

What is "personal love to Christ?"

Oh, dear, dear! Why need my father have been snatched away from me, when so many other girls have theirs spared to them? He loved me so! He indulged me so much! He was so proud of me! What have I done that I should have this dreadful thing happen to me? I shall never be as happy as I was before. Now I shall always be expecting trouble. Yes, I dare say mother will go next. Why shouldn't I brood over this sorrow? I like to brood over it I like to think how wretched I am I like to have long, furious fits of crying, lying on my face on the bed.

Jan. I, 1832.-People talk a great deal about the blessed effects of sorrow. But I do not see any good it has done me to lose my dear father, and as to mother she was good enough before.

We are going to leave our pleasant home, where all of us children were born, and move into a house in an out-of-the-way street. By selling this, and renting a smaller one, mother hopes, with economy, to carry James through college. And I must go to Miss Higgins' school because it is less expensive than Mr. Stone's. Miss Higgins, indeed! I never could bear her! A few months ago, how I should have cried and stormed at the idea of her school. But the great sorrow swallows up the little trial.

I tried once more, this morning, as it is the first day of the year, to force myself to begin to love God.

I want to do it I know I ought to do it but I cannot. I go through the form of saying something that I try to pass off as praying, every day now. But I take no pleasure in it, as good people say they do, and as I am sure mother does. Nobody could live in the house with her, and doubt that.

Jan. 10.-We are in our new home now, and it is quite a cozy little place. James is at home for the long vacation and we are together all the time I am out of school. We study and sing together and now and then, when we forget that dear father has gone, we are as full of fun as ever. If it is so nice to have a brother, what must it be to have a sister! Dear old Jim! He is the very pleasantest, dearest fellow in the world!

Jan. 15.-I have come to another birthday and am seventeen. Mother has celebrated it just as usual, though I know all these anniversaries, which used to be so pleasant, must be sad days to her now my dear father has gone. She has been cheerful-and loving, and entered into all my pleasures exactly as if nothing had happened. I wonder at myself that I do not enter more into her sorrows, but though at times the remembrance of our loss overwhelms me, my natural elasticity soon makes me rise above and forget it. And I am absorbed with these school days, which come one after another, in such quick succession that I am all the time running to keep up with them. And as long as I do that, I forget that death has crossed our threshold, and may do it again. But tonight I feel very sad, and as if I would give almost anything to live in a world, where nothing painful could happen. Somehow, mother's pale face haunts and reproaches me. I believe I will go to bed and to sleep as quickly as possible, and forget everything.

Chapter 3

July 16. - My school days are over! I have come off with flying colors, and mother is pleased at my success. I said to her today that I should now have time to draw and practice to my heart's content.

"You will not find your heart content with either," she said.

"Why, mother!" I cried, "I thought you liked to see me happy!"

"And so I do," she said, quietly. "But there is something better to get out of life than you have yet found."

"I am sure I hope so," I returned. "On the whole, I haven't got much so far."

Amelia is now on such terms with Jenny Underhill that I can hardly see one without seeing the other after the way in which I have loved her, this seems rather hard. Sometimes I am angry about it, and sometimes grieved. However, I find Jenny quite nice. She buys all the new books and lends them to me. I wish I liked more solid reading but I do not. And I wish I were not so fond of novels but I am. If it were not for mother, I should read nothing else. And I am sure I often feel quite stirred up by a really good novel, and admire and want to imitate every high-minded, noble character it describes.

Jenny has a miniature of her brother "Charley" in a locket, which she always wears, and often shows me. According to her, he is exactly like the heroes I most admire in books. She says she knows he would like me if we should meet. But that is not probable. Very few like me. Amelia says it is because I say just what I think.

Wednesday.-Mother pointed out to me this evening two lines from a book she was reading, with a significant smile that said they described me:

"A frank, unchastened, generous creature, whose faults and virtues stand in bold relief."

"Dear me!" I said, "So then I have some virtues after all!"

And I really think I must have, for Jenny's brother, who has come here for the sake of being near her, seems to like me very much. Nobody ever liked me so much before, not even Amelia. But how foolish to write that down!

Thursday.-Jenny's brother has been here all evening. He has the most perfect manners I ever saw. I am sure that mother, who thinks so much of such things, would be charmed with him but she happened to be out, Mrs. Jones having sent for her to see about her baby. He gave me an account of his mother's death, and how he and Jenny nursed her day and night. He has a great deal of feeling. I was going to tell him about my father's death, sorrow seems to bring people together so, but I could not. Oh, if he had only had a sickness that needed our tender nursing, instead of being snatched from us in that sudden way!

Sunday, Aug. 5.-Jenny's brother has been at our church all day. He walked home with me this afternoon. Mother, after being up all night with Mrs. Jones and her baby, was not able to go out.

Dr Cabot preaches as if we had all got to die pretty soon, or else have something almost as bad happen to us. How can old people always try to make young people feel uncomfortable, and as if things couldn't last?

Aug. 25.-Jenny says her brother is perfectly fascinated with me, and that I must try to like him in return. I suppose mother would say my head was turned by my good fortune, but it is not. I am getting quite sober and serious. It is a great thing to be—to be—well—liked. I have seen some verses of his composition today that show that he is all heart and soul, and would make any sacrifice for one he loved. I could not like a man who did not possess such sentiments as his.

Perhaps mother would think I ought not to put such things into my journal.

Jenny has thought of such a splendid plan! What a dear little thing she is! She and her brother are so much alike! The plan is for us three girls, Jenny, Amelia, and myself, to form ourselves into a little class to read and to study together. She says "Charley" will direct our readings and help us with our studies. It is perfectly delightful.

September 1.-Somehow I forgot to tell mother that Mr. Underhill was to be our teacher. So when it came my turn to have the class meet here, she was not quite pleased. I told her she could stay and watch us, and then she would see for herself that we all behaved ourselves.

Sept. 19.-The class met at Amelia's to-night. Mother insisted on sending for me, though Mr. Underhill had proposed to see me home himself. So he stayed after I left. It was not quite the thing in him, for he must see that Amelia is absolutely crazy about him.

Sept. 28-We met at Jenny's this evening. Amelia had a bad headache and could not come. Jenny idled over her lessons, and at last took a book and began to read. I studied awhile with Mr. Underhill. At last, he said, scribbling something on a bit of paper:

"Here is a sentence I hope you can translate."

I took it, and read these words:

"You are the brightest, prettiest, most warm-hearted little thing in the world. And I love you more than tongue can tell. You must love me in the same way."

I felt hot and then cold, and then glad and then sorry. But I pretended to laugh, and said I could not translate Greek. I shall have to tell mother, and what will she say?

Sept. 29.-This morning mother began thus:

"Kate, I do not like these lessons of yours. At your age, with your judgment quite unformed, it is not proper that you should spend so much time with a young man.

"Jenny is always there, and Amelia," I replied.

"That makes no difference. I wish the whole thing stopped. I do not know what I have been thinking of to let it go on so long. Mrs. Gordon says—"

"Mrs. Gordon! Ha!" I burst out, "I knew Amelia was at the bottom of it! Amelia is in love with him up to her very ears, and because he does not entirely neglect me, she has put her mother up to coming here, meddling, and making—"

"If what you say of Amelia is true, it is most ungenerous in you to tell of it. But I do not believe it. Amelia Gordon has too much good sense to be carried away by a handsome face and agreeable manners."

I began to cry.

"He likes me," I got out, "he likes me ever so much. Nobody ever was so kind to me before. Nobody ever said such nice things to me. And I do not want such horrid things said about him."

"Has it really come this!" said mother, quite shocked. "Oh, my poor child, how my selfish sorrow has made me neglect you."

I kept on crying.

"Is it possible," she went on, "that with your good sense, and the education you have had, you are captivated by this mere boy?"

"He is not a boy," I said. "He is a man. He is twenty years old or at least he will be on the fifteenth of next October."

"The child actually keeps his birthdays!" cried mother. "Oh, my wicked, shameful carelessness."

"It's done now," I said, desperately. "It is too late to help it now."

"You do not mean that he has dared to say anything without consulting me?" asked mother. "And you have allowed it! Oh, Katherine!"

This time my mouth shut itself up, and no mortal force could open it. I stopped crying, and sat with folded arms. Mother said what she had to say, and then I came to you, my dear old Journal.

Yes, he likes me and I like him. Come now, let's out with it once for all. He loves me and I love him. You are just a little bit too late, mother.

Oct 1.-I never can write down all the things that have happened. The very day after I wrote that mother had forbidden my going to the class, Charley came to see her, and they had a regular fight together. He has told me about it since. Then, as he could not prevail, his uncle wrote, told her it would be the making of Charley to be settled down on one young lady instead of hovering from flower to flower, as he was doing now. Then Jenny came with her pretty ways, and cried, and told mother what a darling brother Charley was. She made a good deal, too, out of his having lost both father and mother, and needing my affection so much. Mother shut herself up, and I have no doubt prayed over it. I really believe she prays over every new dress she buys. Then she sent for me and talked beautifully, and I behaved abominably.

At last, she said she would put us on one year's probation. Charley might spend one evening here every two weeks, when she should always be present. We were never to be seen together in public, nor would she allow us to correspond. If, at the end of the year, we were both as eager for it as we are now, she would consent to our engagement. Of course we shall be, so I consider myself as good as engaged now. Dear me! How funny it seems.

Oct. 2.-Charley is not at all pleased with mother's terms, but no one would guess it from his manner to her. His coming is always the signal for her trotting down stairs he goes to meet her and offers her a chair, as if he was delighted to see her. We go on with the lessons, as this gives us a chance to sit pretty close together, and when I am writing my exercises and he corrects them, I rather think a few little things get on to the paper that sound nicely to us, but would not strike mother very agreeably. For instance, last night Charley wrote:

"Is your mother never sick? A nice little headache or two would be so convenient to us!"

And I wrote back.

"You dear old horrid thing How can you be so selfish?"

Jan. 15, 1833.-I have been trying to think whether I am any happier today than I was at this time a year ago. If I am not, I suppose it is the tantalizing way in which I am placed in regard to Charley. We have so much to say to each other that we cannot say before mother, and that we cannot say in writing, because a correspondence is one of the forbidden things. He says he entered into no contract not to write, and keeps slipping little notes into my hand but I do not think that quite right. Mother hears us arguing and disputing about it, though she does not know the subject under discussion, and today she said to me:

"I would not argue with him, if I were you. He never will yield."

"But it is a case of conscience," I said, "and he ought to yield."

"There is no obstinacy like that of a f——," she and stopped short.

"Oh, you may as well finish it!" I cried. "I know you think him a fool."

Then mother burst out,

"Oh, my child," she said, "before it is too late, do be persuaded by me to give up this whole thing. I shrink from paining or offending you, but it is my duty, as your mother, to warn you against a marriage that will make shipwreck of your happiness."

"Marriage!" I fairly shrieked out. That is the last thing I have ever thought of. I felt a chill creep over me. All I had wanted was to have Charley come here every day, take me out now and then, and care for nobody else.

"Yes, marriage!" mother repeated. "For what is the meaning of an engagement if marriage is not to follow? How can you fail to see, what I see, oh! So plainly, that Charley Underhill can never, never meet the requirements of your soul. You are captivated by what girls of your age call beauty, regular features, a fair complexion, and soft eyes. His flatteries delude, and his professions of affection gratify you. You do not see that he is shallow, and conceited, and selfish and-"

"Oh mother! How can you be so unjust? His whole study seems to be to please others."

"Seems to be—that is true," she replied. "His ruling passion is love of admiration the little pleasing acts that attract you are so many traps set to catch the attention and the favorable opinion of those about him. He has not one honest desire to please because it is right to be pleasing. Oh, my precious child, what a fatal mistake you are making in relying on your own judgment in this, the most important of earthly decisions!"

I felt very angry.

"I thought the Bible forbade back-biting," I said.

Mother made no reply, except by a look that said about a hundred and forty different things. And then I came up here and wrote some poetry, which was very good (for me), though I do not suppose she would think so.

Oct. 1.-The year of probation is over, and I have nothing to do now but to be happy. But being engaged is not half so nice as I expected it would be. I suppose it is owing to my being obliged to defy mother's judgment in order to gratify my own. People say she has great insight into character, and sees, at a glance, what others only learn after much study.

Oct. 10.-I have taken a dreadful cold. It is too bad. I dare say I shall be coughing all winter, and instead of going out with Charley, be shut up at home.

Oct. 12.-Charley says he did not know that I was subject to a cough, and that he hopes I am not consumptive, because his father and mother died of consumption, and it makes him nervous to hear people cough. I nearly strangled myself all the evening trying not to annoy him with mine.

Chapter 4

Nov. 2. - I really think I am sick and going to die. Last night I raised a little blood. I dare not tell mother, it would distress her so, but I am sure it came from my lungs. Charley said last week he really must stay away till I got better, for my cough sounded like his mother's. I have been very lonely, and have shed some tears, but most of the times have been too sorrowful to cry. If we were married, and I had a cough, would he go and leave me, I wonder?

Sunday, Nov 18-Poor mother is dreadfully anxious about me. But I do not see how she can love me so, after the way I have behaved. I wonder if, after all, mothers are not the best friends there are! I keep her awake with my cough all night, and am mopey and cross all day, but she is just as kind and affectionate as she can be.

Nov. 25.-The day I wrote that was Sunday. I could not go to church, and I felt very forlorn and desolate. I tried to get some comfort by praying, but when I got on my knees, I just burst out crying and could not say a word. For I have not seen Charley for ten days. As I knelt there I began to think myself a perfect monster of selfishness for wanting him to spend his evenings with me, now that I am so unwell and annoy him so with my cough, and I asked myself if I ought not to break off the engagement altogether, if I was really in consumption, the very disease Charley dreaded most of all. It seemed such a proper sacrifice to make of myself. Then I prayed-yes, I am sure I really prayed as I had not done for more than a year, the idea of self-sacrifice grew every moment more beautiful in my eyes, till at last I felt an almost joyful triumph in writing to poor Charley, and tell him what I had resolved to do. This is my letter:

My Dear, Dear Charley -I dare not tell you what it costs me to say what I am about to do but I am sure you know me well enough by this time believe that it is only because your happiness is far more precious to me than my own, that I have decided to write you this letter. When you first told me that you loved me, you said, and you have often said so since then, that it was my "brightness and gayety" that attracted you. I knew there was something underneath my gayety better worth your love, and was glad I could give you more than you asked for. I knew I was not a mere thoughtless, laughing girl, but that I had a heart as wide as the ocean to give you-as wide and as deep.

But now my "brightness and gayety" have gone I am sick and perhaps am going to die. If this is so, it would be very sweet to have your love go with me to the very gates of death, and beautify and glorify my path thither. But what a weary task this would be to you, my poor Charley! And so, if you think it best, and it would relieve you of any care and pain, I will release you from our engagement and set you free. Your Little Katy.

I did not sleep at all that night. Early on Monday I sent off my letter and my heart beat so hard all day that I was tired and faint. Just at dark, his answer came I can copy it from memory.

Dear Kate: -What a generous, self-sacrificing little thing you are! I always thought so, but now you have given me a noble proof of it. I will own that I have been disappointed to find your constitution so poor, and that it has been very dull sitting and hearing you cough, especially as I was reminded of the long and tedious illness through which poor Jenny and myself had to nurse our mother. I vowed then never to marry a consumptive woman, and I thank you for making it so easy for me to bring our engagement to an end. My bright hopes are blighted, and it will be long before I shall find another to fill your place. I need not say how much I sympathize with you in this disappointment. I hope the consolations of religion will now be yours. Your notes, the lock of your hair, etc., I return with this now. I will not reproach you for the pain you have cost me I know it is not your fault that your health has become so frail. I remain your sincere friend,

Charles Underhill

Jan. I, 1834.-Let me finish this story if I can.

My first impulse after reading his letter was to fly to mother, and hide away forever in her dear, loving arms.

But I restrained myself, and with my heart beating so that I could hardly hold my pen, I wrote:

Mr.. Underhill Sir-The scales have fallen from my eyes, and I see you at last just as you are. Since my note to you on Sunday last, I have had a consultation of physicians, and they all agree that my disease is not of an alarming character, and that I shall soon recover. But I thank God that before it was too late, you have been revealed to me just as you are-a heartless, selfish, shallow creature, unworthy the love of a true-hearted woman, unworthy even of your own self-respect. I gave you an opportunity to withdraw from our engagement in full faith, loving you so truly that I was ready to go trembling to my grave alone if you shrank from sustaining me to it. But I see now that I did not dream for one moment that you would take me at my word and leave me to my fate. I thought I loved a man, and could lean on him when strength failed me I know now that I loved a mere creature of my imagination. Take back your letters loathe the sight of them. Take back the ring, and find, if you can, a woman who will never be sick, never out of spirits, and who never will die. Thank heaven it is not Katherine Mortimer.

These lines came to me in reply:

"Thank God it is not Kate Mortimer. I want an angel for my wife, not a vixen. C. U."

Jan. 15-What a tempest-tossed creature this birthday finds me. But let me finish this wretched, disgraceful story, if I can, before I quite lose my senses.

I showed my mother the letters. She burst into tears and opened her arms, and I ran into them as a wounded bird flies into the ark. We cried together. Mother never said, never looked, "I told you so." All she did say was this,

"God has heard my prayers! He is reserving better things for my child!"

Dear mother's are not the only arms I have flown to. But it does not seem as if God ought to take me in because I am in trouble, when I would not go to him when I was happy in something else. But even in the midst of my greatest felicity I had many and many a misgiving many a season when my conscience upbraided me for my willfulness towards my dear mother, and my whole soul yearned for something higher and better even than Charley's love, precious as it was.

Jan. 26.-I have shut myself up in my room today to think over things. The end of it is that I am full of mortification and confusion of face. If I had only had confidence in mother's judgment I should never have get entangled in this silly engagement. I see now that Charley never could have made me happy, and I know there is a good deal in my heart he never called out. I wish, however, I had not written him when I was in passion. No wonder he is thankful that he free from such a vixen. But, oh, the provocation was terrible!

I have made up my mind never to tell a human soul about this affair. It will be so high-minded and honorable to shield him thus from the contempt he deserves. With all my faults, I am glad that there is nothing mean or little about me!

Jan. 27.-I cannot bear to write it down, but I will. The ink was hardly dry yesterday on the above self-laudation when Amelia came. She had been out of town, and had only just learned what had happened. Of course, she was curious to know the whole story.

And I told it to her, every word of it! Oh, Kate Mortimer, how "high-minded" you are! How free from all that is "mean and little"! I could tear my hair if it would do any good?

Amelia defended Charley, and I was thus led on to say every harsh thing of him I could think of. She said he was of so sensitive a nature, had so much sensibility, and such a constitutional aversion to seeing suffering, that for her part she could not blame him.

"It is such a pity you had not had your lungs examined before you wrote that first letter, she went on. "But you are so impulsive! If you had only waited you would be engaged to Charley still!"

"I am thankful I did not wait," I cried, angrily. "Do, Amelia, drop the subject forever. You and I shall never agree upon it. The truth is, you are two-thirds in love with him, and have been, all along."

She colored, and laughed, and actually looked pleased. If anyone had made such an outrageous speech to me, I should have been furious.

"I suppose you know," said she, "that old Mr. Underhill has taken such a fancy to him that he has made him his heir and he is as rich as a Jew."

"Indeed!" I said, dryly.

I wonder if mother knew it when she opposed our engagement so strenuously.

Jan. 31.-I have asked her, and she said she did. Mr. Underhill told her his intentions when he urged her consent to the engagement. Dear mother! How unworldly, how unselfish she is!

Feb. 4.-The name of Charley Underhill appears on these pages for the last time. He is engaged to Amelia! From this moment, she is lost to me forever. How desolate, how mortified, how miserable I am! Who could have thought this of Amelia! She came to see me, radiant with joy. I concealed my disgust until she said that Charley felt now that he had never really loved me, but had preferred her all along. Then I burst out. What I said I do not know, and do not care. The whole thing is so disgraceful that I should be a stock or a stone not to resent it.

Feb. 5.-After yesterday's passion of grief, shame, and anger, I feel perfectly stupid and .languid. Oh, that I was prepared for a better world, and could fly to it and be at rest!

Feb. 6.-Now that it is all over, how ashamed I am of the fury I have been in, and which has given Amelia such advantage over me! I was beginning to believe that I was really living a feeble and fluttering, but real Christian life, and finding some satisfaction in it. But that is all over now. I am doomed to be a victim of my own unstable, passionate, wayward nature, and the sooner I settle down into that conviction, the better. And yet how my very soul craves the highest happiness, and refuses to be comforted while that is wanting.

Feb. 7.-After writing that, I do not know what made me go to see Dr. Cabot. He received me in that cheerful way of his that seems to promise the taking one's burden right off one's back.

"I am very glad to see you, my dear child," he said.

I intended to be very dignified and cold. As if I was going to have any Dr. Cabot's undertaking to sympathize with me! But those few kind words just upset me, and I began to cry.

"You would not speak so kindly," I got out at last, "if you knew what a dreadful creature I am. I am angry with myself, and angry with everybody, and angry with God. I cannot be good two minutes at a time. I do everything I do not want to do, and do nothing I try and pray to do. Everybody plagues me and tempts me. And God does not answer any of my prayers, and I am just desperate."

"Poor child!" he said, in a low voice, as if to himself. "Poor, heart-sick, tired child, that cannot see what I can see, that its Father's loving arms are all about it?"

I stopped crying, to strain my ears and listen. He went on.

"Katy, all that you say may be true. I dare say it is. But God loves you. He loves you."

"He loves me," I repeated to myself. "He loves me! Oh, Dr. Cabot, if I could believe that! If I could believe that, after all the promises I have broken, all the foolish, wrong things I have done and shall always be doing, God perhaps still loves me!"

"You may be sure of it," he said, solemnly. "I, minister, bring the gospel to you today. Go home and say over and over to yourself, 'I am a wayward, foolish child. But He loves me! I have disobeyed and grieved Him ten thousand times. But He loves me! I have lost faith in some of my dearest friends and am very desolate. But He loves me! I do not love Him, I am even angry with Him! But He loves me! '"

I came away, and all the way home, I fought this battle with myself, saying, "He loves me!" I knelt down to pray, and all my wasted, childish, wicked life came and stared me in the face. I looked at it, and said with tears of joy, "But He loves me!" Never in my life did I feel so rested, so quieted, so sorrowful, and yet so satisfied.

Feb 10.-What a beautiful world this is, and how full it is of truly kind, good people! Mrs. Morris was here this morning, and just one squeeze of that long, yellow old hand of hers seemed to speak a bookful! I wonder why I have always disliked her so, for she is really an excellent woman. I gave her a good kiss to pay her for the sympathy she had sense enough not to put into canting words, and if you will believe it, dear old Journal, the tears came into her eyes, and she said:

"You are one of the Lord's beloved ones, though perhaps you do not know it"

I repeated again to myself those sweet, mysterious words, and then I tried to think what I could do for Him. But I could not think of anything great or good enough. I went into mother's room and put my arms round her and told her how I loved her. She looked surprised and pleased.

"Ah, I knew it would come!" she said, laying her hand on her Bible.

"Knew what would come, mother?"

"Peace," she said.

I came back here and wrote a little note to Amelia, telling her how ashamed and sorry I was that I could not control myself the other day. Then I wrote a long letter to James. I have been very careless about writing to him.

Then I began to hem those handkerchiefs mother -asked me to finish a month ago. But I could not think of anything to do for God. I wish I could. It makes me so happy to think that all this time, while I was caring for nobody but myself, and fancying He must almost hate me, He was loving and pitying me.

Feb. 15.-I went to see Dr. Cabot again today. He came down from his study with his pen in his hand.

"How dare you come and spoil my sermon on Saturday?" he asked, good-humoredly.

Though he seemed full of loving kindness, I was ashamed of my thoughtlessness. Though I did not know, he was particularly busy on Saturdays. If I were a minister, I am sure I would get my sermons done early in the week.

"I only wanted to ask one thing," I said. "I want to do something for God. And I cannot think of anything unless it is to go on a mission. And mother would never let me do that. She thinks girls with delicate health are not fit for such work."

"At all events I would not go today," he replied. Meanwhile do everything you do for Him who has loved you and given Himself for you."

I did not dare to stay any longer, and so came away quite puzzled. Dinner was ready, and as I sat down to the table, I said to myself:

"I eat this dinner for myself, not for God. What can Dr. Cabot mean?" Then I remembered the text about doing all for the glory of God, even in eating and drinking but I do not understand it at all.

Feb. 19. It has seemed to' me for several days that it must be that I really do love God, though ever so little. But it shot through my mind today like a knife, that it is a miserable, selfish love at the best, not worth my giving, not worth God's accepting. All my old misery has come back with seven other miseries more miserable than itself. I wish I had never been born! I wish I were thoughtless and careless, like so many other girls of my age, who seem to get along very well, and to enjoy themselves far more than I do.

Feb. 21.-Dr. Cabot came to see me today. I told him all about it. He could not help smiling as he said:

"When I see a little infant caressing its mother, would you have me say to it, 'You selfish child, how dare you pretend to caress your mother in that way? You are quite unable to appreciate her character you love her merely because she loves you, treats you kindly?'"

It was my turn to smile now, at my own folly.

"You are as yet but a babe in Christ," Dr. Cabot continued. "You love your God and Savior because He first loved you. The time will come when the character of your love will become changed into one which sees and feels the beauty and the perfection of its object, and if you could be assured that He no longer looked on you with favor, you would still cling to Him with devoted affection."

"There is one thing more that troubles me," I said. "Most persons know the exact moment when they begin real Christian lives. But I do not know of any such time in my history. This causes me many uneasy moments."

"You are wrong in thinking that most persons have this advantage over you. I believe that the children of Christian parents, who have been judiciously trained, rarely can 'point to any day or hour when they began to live this new life. The question is not, do you remember, my child, when you entered this world, and how? It is simply this, are you now alive and an inhabitant thereof? And now it is my turn to ask you a question. How happens it that you, who have a mother of rich and varied experience, allow yourself to be tormented with these petty anxieties which she is as capable of dispelling as I am?"

"I do not know," I answered. "But we girls cannot talk to our mothers about any of our sacred feelings, and we hate to have them talk to us."

Dr. Cabot shook his head.

"There is something wrong somewhere," he said, "A young girl's mother is her natural refuge in every perplexity. I hoped that you, who have rather more sense than most girls of your age, could give me some idea what the difficulty is."

After he had gone, I am ashamed to own that I was in a perfect flutter of delight at what he had said about my having more sense than most girls. Meeting poor mother on the stairs while in this exalted state of mind, I gave her a very short answer to a kind question, and made her unhappy, as I have made myself.

It is just a year ago today that I got frightened at my novel-reading propensities, and resolved not to look into one for twelve months. I was getting to dislike all other books, and night after night sat up late, devouring everything exciting I could get hold of. One Saturday night I sat up till the clock struck twelve to finish one, and the next morning I was so sleepy that I had to stay at home from church. Now I hope and believe the back of this taste is broken, and that I shall never be a slave to it again. Indeed, it does not seem to me now that I shall ever care for such books again.

Feb. 24.-Mother spoke to me this morning for the fiftieth time, I really believe, about my disorderly habits. I do not think I am careless because I like confusion, but the trouble is I am always in a hurry and a ferment about something. If I want anything, I want it very much, and right away. So if I am looking for a book, or a piece of music, or a pattern, I tumble everything around, and cannot stop to put them to rights. I wish I were not so-eager and impatient. But I mean to try to keep my room and my drawers in order, to please mother.

She says, too, that I am growing careless about my hair and my dress. But that is because my mind is so full of graver, more important things. I thought I ought to be wholly occupied with my duty to God. But mother says duty to God includes duty to one's neighbor, and that untidy hair, put up in all sorts of rough bunches, rumpled cuffs and collars, and all that sort of thing, make one offensive to all one meets. I am sorry she thinks so, for I find it very convenient to twist up my hair almost any how, and it takes a good deal of time to look after collars and cuffs.

March 14.- Today I feel discouraged and disappointed. I certainly thought that if God really loved me, and I really loved Him, I should find myself growing better day by day. But I am not improved in the least. Most of the time I spend on my knees I am either stupid feeling nothing at all, or else my head is full of what I was doing before I began to pray, or what I am going to do as soon as I get through. I do not believe anybody else in the world is like me in this respect. Then when I feel differently, and can make a nice, glib prayer, with floods of tears running down my cheeks, I get all puffed up, and think how much pleased God must be to see me so fervent in spirit. I go downstairs in this frame, and begin to scold Susan for misplacing my music, till all of a sudden I catch myself doing it, and stop short, crestfallen, and confounded. I have so many such experiences that I feel like a baby just learning to walk, who is so afraid of falling that it has half a mind to sit down once for all.

Then there is another thing. Seeing mother so fond of Thomas A Kempis, I have been reading it, now and then, and am not fond of it at all. From beginning to end, it exhorts to self-denial in every form and shape. Must I then give up all hope of happiness in this world, and modify all my natural tastes and desires? Oh, I do love so to be happy! I do so hate to suffer! The very thought of being sick, or of being forced to nurse sick people, with all their cross ways, and of losing my friends, or of having to live with disagreeable people, makes me shudder. I want to please God, and to be like Him. I certainly do. But I am so young, and it is so natural to want to have a good time! And now I am in for it I may as well tell the whole story. When I read the lives of good men and women who have died and gone to heaven, I find they all liked to sit and think about God and about Christ. Now I do not. I often try, but my mind flies off in a tangent. The truth is I am perfectly discouraged.

March 17.-I went to see Dr. Cabot today, but he was out, so I thought I would ask for Mrs. Cabot, though I was determined not to tell her any of my troubles. But somehow, she got the whole story out of me, and instead of being shocked, as I expected she would be, she actually burst out laughing! She recovered herself immediately, however.

"Do excuse me for laughing at you, you dear child you!" she said. "But I remember so well how I use to flounder through just such needless anxieties, and life looks so different, so very different, to me now from what it did then! What should you think of a man who, having just sowed his field, was astonished not to see it at once ripe for the harvest, because his neighbor's, after long months of waiting, was just being gathered in?"

"Do you mean," I asked, "that by and by I shall naturally come to feel and think as other good people do?"

"Yes, I do. You must make the most of what little Christian life you have be thankful God has given you so much, cherish it, pray over it, and guard it like the apple of your eye. Imperceptibly, but surely, it will grow, and keep on growing, for this is its nature."

"But I do not want to wait," I said, despondently. "I have just been reading a delightful book, full of stories of heroic deeds-not fables, but histories of real events and real people. It has quite stirred me up, and made me wish to possess such beautiful heroism, and that I were a man, that I might have a chance to perform some truly noble, self-sacrificing acts."

"I dare say your chance will come," she replied, "though you are not a man. I fancy we all get, more or less, what we want."

"Do you really think so? Let me see, then, what I want most. But I am staying too long. Were you particularly busy?"

"No," she returned smilingly, "I am learning that the man who wants me is the man I want."

"You are very good to say so. Well, in the first place, I do really and truly want to be good. Not with common goodness, you know, but-"

"But uncommon goodness," she put in.

"I mean that I want to be very, very good. I should like next best to be learned and accomplished. Then I should want to be perfectly well and perfectly happy. And a pleasant home, of course, I must have, with friends to love me, and like me, too. And I cannot get along without some pretty, tasteful things about me. But you are laughing at me! Have I said anything foolish?"

"If I laughed it was not at you, but at poor human nature that would fain grasp everything at once. Allowing that you should possess all you have just described, where is the heroism you so much admire for exercise?"

"That is just what I was saying. That is just what troubles me."

"To be sure, while perfectly well and happy, in a pleasant home with friends to love and admire you—"

"Oh, I did not say admire," I interrupted.

"That was just what you meant, my dear."

I am afraid it was, now I come to think it over.

"Well, with plenty of friends, good in an uncommon way, accomplished, learned, and surrounded with pretty and tasteful objects, your life will certainly be in danger of not proving very sublime."

"It is a great pity," I said, musingly.

"Suppose then you content yourself for the present with doing in a faithful, quiet, persistent way all the little, homely tasks that return with each returning day, each one as unto God, and perhaps by and by you will thus have gained strength for a more heroic life."

"But I do not know how."

"You have some little home duties, I suppose?"

"Yes I have the care of my own room, and mother wants me to have a general oversight of the parlor you know we have but one parlor now."

"Is that all you have to do?"

"Why, my music and drawing take up a good deal of my time, and I read and study more or less, and go out some, and we have a good many visitors."

"I suppose, then, you keep your room in nice lady-like order, and that the parlor is dusted every morning, loose music put out of the way, books restored to their places-"

"Now I know mother has been telling you."

"Your mother has told me nothing at all."

"Well, then," I said, laughing, but a little ashamed, "I do not keep my room in nice order, and mother really sees to the parlor herself, though I pretend to do it."

"And is she never annoyed by this neglect?"

"Oh, yes, very much annoyed."

"Then, dear Katy, suppose your first act of heroism tomorrow should be the gratifying your mother in these little things, little though they are. Surely your first duty, next to pleasing God, is to please your mother, and in every possible way to sweeten and beautify her life. You may depend upon it that a life of real heroism and self-sacrifice must begin and lay its foundation in this little world, wherein it learns its first lesson and takes its first steps."

"And do you really think that God notices such little things?"

"My dear child, what a question! If there is any one truth I would gladly impress on the mind of a you Christian, it is just this, that God notices the most trivial act, accepts the poorest, most threadbare little service, listens to the coldest, feeblest petition, and gathers up with parental fondness all our fragmentary desires and attempts at good works. Oh, if we could only begin to conceive how He loves us, what different creatures we should be!"

I felt inspired by her enthusiasm, though I do not think I quite understand what she means. I did not dare to stay any longer, for, with her great host of children, she must have her hands full.

March 25.-Mother is very much astonished to see how nicely I am keeping things in order. I was flying about this morning, singing, and dusting the furniture, when she came in and began, "He that is faithful in that which is least "-but I ran at her my brush, and would not let her finish. I really, really do not deserve to be praised. For I have been thinking that, if it is true that God notices every little thing we do to please Him, He must also notice every cross word we speak, every shrug of the shoulders, every ungracious look, and that they displease Him. And my list of such offences is as long as my life.

March 29-Yesterday, for the first time since that dreadful blow, I felt some return of my natural gayety and cheerfulness. It seemed to come hand in hand with my first real effort to go so far out of myself as to try to do exactly what would gratify dear mother.

But today I am all down again. I miss Amelia's friendship, for one thing. To be sure, I wonder how I ever came to love such a superficial character so devotedly, but I must have somebody to love, and perhaps I invented a lovely creature, and called it by her name, and bowed down to it and worshiped it. I certainly did so in regard to him whose heart less cruelty has left me so sad, so desolate.

Evening.-Mother has been very patient and forbearing with me all day. To-night, after tea, she said, in her gentlest, tenderest way,

"Dear Katy, I feel very sorry for you. But I see one path that you have not yet tried, which can lead you out of these sore straits. You have tried living for yourself a good many years, and the result is great weariness and heaviness of soul. Try now to live for others. Take a class in the Sunday school. Go with me to visit my poor people. You will be astonished to find how much suffering and sickness there is in this world, and how delightful it is to sympathize with and try to relieve it."

This advice was very repugnant to me. My time is pretty fully occupied with my books, my music, and my drawing. And of all places in the world, I hate a sickroom. But, on the whole, I will take a class in the Sunday school.

Chapter 5

APRIL 6. - I have taken it at last. I would not take one before, because I knew I could not teach little children how to love God, unless I loved Him myself. My class is perfectly delightful. There are twelve dear little things in it, of all ages between eight and nine. Eleven are girls, and the one boy makes me more trouble than all of them put together. When I get them all about me, and their sweet innocent faces look up into mine, I am so happy that I can hardly help stopping every now and then to kiss them. They ask the very strangest questions I mean to spend a great deal of time in preparing the lesson, and in hunting up stories to illustrate it. Oh, I am so glad I was ever born into this beautiful world, where there will always be dear little children to love!

APRIL 13.-Sunday has come again, and with it my darling little class! Dr. Cabot has preached delightfully all day, and I feel that I begin to understand his preaching better, and that it must do me good. I long, I truly long to please God I long to feel as the best Christians feel, and to live as they live.

APRIL 20.-Now that I have these twelve little ones to instruct, I am more than ever in earnest about setting them a good example through the week. It is true they do not, most of them, know how I spend my time, nor how I act. But I know, and whenever I am conscious of not practicing what I preach, I am bitterly ashamed and grieved. How much work, badly done, I am now having to undo. If I had begun in earnest to serve God when I was as young as these children are, how many wrong habits I should have avoided, habits that entangle me now, as in so many nets. I am trying to take each of these little gentle girls by the hand and to lead her to Christ. Poor Johnny Ross is not so docile as they are, and tries my patience to the last degree.

APRIL 27.-This morning I had my little flock about me, and talked to them out of the very bottom of my heart about Jesus. They left their seats and got close to me in a circle, leaning on my lap and drinking in every word. All of a sudden, I was aware, as by a magnetic influence that a great lumbering man in the next seat was looking at me out of two of the blackest eyes I ever saw, and evidently listening to what I was saying. I was disconcerted at first, then angry. What impertinence. What rudeness! I am sure he must have seen my displeasure in my face, for he got up what I suppose he meant for a blush, that is he turned several shades darker than he was before, giving one the idea that he is full of black rather than red blood. I should not have remembered it, however-by it-I mean his impertinence—if he had not shortly after made a really excellent address to the children. Perhaps it was a little above their comprehension, but it showed a good deal of thought and earnestness. I meant to ask who he was, but forgot it.

This has been a delightful Sunday. I have really feasted on .Dr. Cabot's preaching. But I am satisfied that there is something in religion I do not yet comprehend. I do wish I positively knew that God had forgiven and accepted me.

MAY 6.-Last evening Clara Ray had a little party and I was there. She has a great knack at getting the right sort of people together, and of making them enjoy themselves.

I sang several songs, and so did Clara, but they all said my voice was finer and in better training than hers. It is delightful to be with cultivated, agreeable people. I could have stayed all night, but mother sent for me before anyone else had thought of going.

MAY 7.-I have been on a charming excursion today with Clara Ray and all her set. I was rather tired, but had an invitation to a concert this evening that I could not resist.

JULY 21.-So much has been going on that I have not had time to write. There is no end to the picnics, drives, parties, etc., this summer. I am afraid I am not getting on at all. My prayers are dull and short, and full of wandering thoughts. I am brimful of vivacity and good humor in company, and as soon as I get home am stupid and peevish. I suppose this will always be so, as it always has been and I declare I would rather be so than such a vapid, flat creature as Mary Jones, or such a dull, heavy one as big Lucy Merrill.

JULY 24.-Clara Ray says the girls think me reckless and imprudent in speech. I've a good mind not to go with her set any more. I am afraid I have been a good deal dazzled by the attentions I have received of late and now comes this blow at my vanity.

On the whole, I feel greatly out of sorts this evening.

JULY 28.-People talk about happiness to be found in a Christian life. I wonder why I do not find more! On Sundays, I am pretty good, and always seem to start afresh but on weekdays, I am drawn along with those about me. All my pleasures are innocent ones there is surely no harm in going to concerts, driving out, singing, and making little visits! But these things distract me they absorb me they make religious duties irksome. I almost wish I could shut myself up in a cell, and so get out of the reach of temptation.

The truth is, the journey heavenward is all uphill I have to force myself to keep on. The wonder is that anybody gets there with so much to oppose— so little to help one!

JULY 29.-It is high time to stop and think. I have been like one running a race, and am stopping to take breath. I do not like the way in which things have been going on of late. I feel restless and ill at ease. I see that if I would be happy in God, I must give Him all. And there is a wicked reluctance to do that. I want Him-but I want to have my own way, too. I want to walk humbly and softly before Him, and I want to go where I shall be admired and applauded. To whom shall I yield? To God? Or to myself?

JULY 30.-I met Dr. Cabot today, and could not, help asking the question:

"Is it right for me to sing and play in company when all I do it for is to be admired?"

"Are you sure it is all you do it for?" he returned.

"Oh," I said, "I suppose there may be a sprinkling of desire to entertain and please, mixed with the love of display."

"Do you suppose that your love of display, allowing you have it, would be forever slain by your merely refusing to sing in company?"

"I thought that might give it a pretty hard blow," I said, "if not its death-blow."

"Meanwhile, in, punishing yourself you punish your poor innocent friends," he said laughing. "No child, go on singing God has given you this power of entertaining and, gratifying your friends. But ,pray without ceasing, that you may sing from pure benevolence and not from pure self-love."

"Why, do people pray about such things as that?" I cried.

"Of course they do. Why, I would pray about my little finger, if my little finger went astray."

I looked at his little finger, but saw no signs of its becoming schismatic.

AUG. 3.-This morning I took great delight in praying for my little scholars, and went to Sunday school as on wings. But on reaching my seat, what was my horror to find Maria Perry there!

Oh, your seat is changed," said she. "I am to have half your class, and I like this seat better than those higher up. I suppose you do not care?"

"But I do care," I returned, "and you have taken my very best children-the very sweetest and the very prettiest. I shall speak to Mr. Williams about it directly."

"At any rate, I would not fly into such a fury," she said. "It is just as pleasant to me to have pretty children to teach as it is to you. Mr. Williams said he had no doubt you would be glad to divide your class with me, as it is so large and I doubt if you gain anything by speaking to him.

There was no time for further discussion, as school was about to begin. I went to my new seat with great disgust, and found it very inconvenient. The children could not cluster around me as they did before, and I got on with the lesson very badly. I am sure Maria Perry has no gift at teaching little children, and I feel quite vexed and disappointed. This has not been a profitable Sunday, and I and now going to bed, cheerless and uneasy.

AUG. 9.-Mr. Williams called this evening to say that I am to have my old seat and all the children again. All the mothers had been to see him, or had written him notes about it, and requested that I continue to teach them. Mr. Williams said he hoped I would go on teaching for twenty years, and that as fast as his little girls grew old enough to come to Sunday-school he should want me to take charge of them. I should have been greatly elated by these compliments, but for the display, I made of myself to Maria Perry on Sunday. Oh, that I could learn to bridle my unlucky tongue!

JAN.15, 1835.- Today I am twenty. That sounds very old, yet I feel pretty much as I did before. I have begun to visit some of mother's poor folks with her, and am astonished to see how they love her, how plainly they let her talk to them. As a general rule, I do not think poor people are very interesting, and they are always ungrateful.

We went first to see old Jacob Stone. I have been there a good many times with the baskets of nice things mother takes such comfort in sending him, but never would go in. I was shocked to see how worn away he was. He seemed in great distress of mind, and begged mother to pray with him. I do not see how she could. I am perfectly sure that no earthly power could ever induce me to go round praying on bare floors, with people sitting, rocking, and staring all the time, as the two Stone girls stared at mother. How tenderly she prayed for him!

We then went to see Susan Green. She had made a carpet for her room by sewing together little bits of pieces given her, I suppose, by persons for whom she works, for she goes about fitting and making carpets. It looked bright and cheerful. She had a nice bed in the corner, covered with a white quilt, and some little ornaments were arranged about the room. Mother complimented her on her neatness, and said a queen might sleep in such a bed as that, and hoped she found it as comfortable as it looked.

"Mercy on us!" she cried out, "it ain't to sleep in! I sleep up in the loft, which I climb to by a ladder every night."

Mother looked a little amused, and then she sat and listened, patiently, to a long account of how the poor old thing had invested her money how Mr. Jones did not pay the interest regularly, and how Mr. Stevens haggled about the percentage. After we came away, I asked mother how she could listen to such rigmarole in patience, and what good she supposed she had done by her visit.

"Why the poor creature likes to show off her bright carpet and nice bed, her chairs, her vases and her knick-knacks, and she likes to talk about her beloved money, and her bank stock. I may not have done her any good but I have given her a pleasure, and so have you."

"Why, I hardly spoke a word."

"Yes, but your mere presence gratified her. And if she ever gets into trouble, she will feel kindly towards us for the sake of our sympathy with her pleasures, and will let us sympathize with her sorrows."

I confess this did not seem a privilege to be coveted. She is not nice at all, and takes snuff.

We went next to see Bridget Shannon. Mother had lost sight of her for some years, and had just heard that she was sick and in great want. We found her in bed there was no furniture in the room, and three little half-naked children sat with their bare feet in some ashes where there had been a little fire. Three such disconsolate faces I never saw. Mother sent me to the nearest baker's for bread I ran nearly all the way, and I hardly know which I enjoyed most, mother's eagerness in distributing, or the children's in clutching at and devouring it. I am going to cut up one or two old dresses to make the poor things something to cover them. One of them has lovely hair that would curl beautifully if it were only brushed out. I told her to come to see me tomorrow, she is so very pretty. Those few visits used up the very time I usually spend in drawing. But on the whole, I am glad I went with mother, because it has gratified her. Besides, one must either stop reading the Bible altogether, or else leave off spending one's whole time in just doing easy pleasant things one likes to do.

JAN. 20.-The little Shannon girl came, and I washed her face and. hands, brushed out her hair and made it curl in lovely golden ringlets all round her sweet face, and carried her in great triumph to mother.

"Look at the dear little thing, mother!" I cried "doesn't she look like a line of poetry?"

"You foolish, romantic child!" quoth mother. "She looks, to me, like a very ordinary line of prose. A slice of bread and butter and a piece of gingerbread mean more to her than these elaborate ringlets possibly can. They get in her eyes, and make her neck cold see, they are dripping with water, and the child is all in a shiver."

So saying, mother folded a towel round its neck, to catch the falling drops, and went for bread and butter, of which the child consumed a quantity that, was absolutely appalling. To crown all, the ungrateful little thing would not so much as look at me from that moment, but clung to mother, turning its back upon me in supreme contempt.

Moral.-Mothers occasionally know more than their daughters do.

Chapter 6

JANUARY 24. A Message came yesterday morning from Susan Green to the effect that she had had a dreadful fall, and was half killed. Mother wanted to set off at once to see her, but I would not let her go, as she has one of her worst colds. She then asked me to go in her place. I turned up my nose at the bare thought, though I dare say it turns up enough on its own account.

"Oh, mother!" I said, reproachfully that dirty old woman!"

Mother made no answer, and I sat down at the piano, and played a little. But I only played discords.

"Do you think it is my duty to run after such horrid old women ?" I asked mother, at last.

"I think, dear, you must make your own duties, she said kindly. "I dare say that at your age I should have made a great deal out of my personal repugnance to such a woman as Susan, and very little out of her sufferings."

I believe I am the most fastidious creature in the world. Sickrooms with their intolerable smells of camphor, and vinegar and mustard, their gloom and their whines and their groans, actually make me shudder. But was it not just such fastidiousness that made Cha-no, I won't utter his name——that made somebody weary of my possibilities? And has that terrible lesson really done me no good?

JAN. 26.-No sooner had I written the above than I scrambled into my cloak and bonnet, and flew, on the wings of holy indignation, to Susan Green. Such wings fly fast, and got me a little out of breath. I found her lying on that nice white bed of hers, in a frilled cap and nightgown. It seems she fell from her ladder in climbing to the dismal den where she sleeps, and lay all night in great distress with some serious internal injury. I found her groaning and complaining in a fearful way.

"Are you in such pain ?" I asked, as kindly as I could.

"It isn't the pain," she said, "It isn't the pain. It's the way my nice bed is going to wreck and ruin, and the starch all getting out of my frills that I fluted with my own hands. And the doctor's bill, and the medicines oh, dear, dear, dear!"

Just then, the doctor came in. After examining her, he said to a woman who seemed to have charge of her:

"Are you the nurse?"

"Oh, no, I only stepped in to see what I could do for her."

"Who is to be with her to-night, then?"

Nobody knew.

"I will send a nurse, then," he said. "But someone else will be needed also,' he added, looking at me.

"I will stay," I said. But my heart died within me.

The doctor took me aside.

"Her injuries are very serious," he said." If she has any friends, they ought to be sent for."

"You do not mean that she is going to die?" I asked.

"I fear she is. But not immediately." He took leave, and I went back to the bedside. I saw there no longer a stuffy, repulsive old woman, but a human being about to make that mysterious journey a far country whence there is no return. Oh, how I wished mother was there!

"Susan," I said, "have you any relatives?"

"No, I haven't," she answered sharply. "And if I had they needn't come prowling around me. I do not want no relations about my body."

"Would you like to see Dr. Cabot?"

"What should I want of Dr. Cabot? Do not tease, child."

Considering the deference with which she had heretofore treated me, this was quite a new order of things.

I sat down and tried to pray for her, silently, in my heart. Who was to go with her on that long journey, and where was it to end?

The woman who had been caring for her now went away, and it was growing dark. I sat still listening to my own heart, which beat till it half choked me.

"What were you and the doctor whispering about?" she suddenly burst out.

"He asked me, for one thing, if you had any friends that could be sent for."

"I've been my own best friend," she returned. "Who'd have raked and scraped and hoarded and counted for Susan Green if I hadn't ha' done it? I have got enough to make me comfortable as long as I live, and when I lie on my dying bed."

"But you cannot carry it with you," I said. This highly original remark was all I had courage to utter.

"I wish I could," she cried. "I suppose you think I talk awful. They say you are getting most to be as much of a saint as your ma. It's born in some, and in some, it ain't. Do get a light. It's lonesome here in the dark, and cold."

I was thankful enough to enliven the dark room with light and fire. But I saw now that the thin, yellow, hard face had changed sadly. She fixed her two little black eyes on me, evidently startled by the expression of my face.

"Look here, child, I ain't hurt to speak of, am I?"

"The doctor says you are hurt seriously."

My tone must have said more than my words did for she caught me by the wrist and held me fast.

"He didn't say nothing about my-about it being dangerous? I ain't dangerous, am I?"

I felt ready to sink.

"Oh Susan!" I gasped out "you haven't any time to lose. You're going, you're going!" "Going!" she cried, "going where? You do not mean to say I'm a-dying? Why, it beats all my calculations. I was going to live ever so years, and save up ever so much money, and when my time come, I was going to put on my best fluted night-gown and night-cap, and lay my head on my handsome pillow, and draw the clothes up over me, neat and tidy, and die decent. But here's my bed all in a toss, and my frills all in a crumple and my room all upside down, and bottles of medicine setting around alongside of my vases, and nobody here but you, just a girl, and nothing else!"

All this came out by jerks, as it were, and at intervals.

"Do not talk so!" I fairly screamed. "Pray, pray to God to have mercy on you!"

She looked at me, bewildered, but yet as if the truth had reached her at last.

"Pray yourself!" she said, eagerly. "I do not' know how. I cannot think. Oh, my time's come my time's come! And I ain't ready! I ain't ready! Get down on your knees and pray with all your, might and main."

And I did, she holding my wrist tightly in hard hand. All at once, I felt her hold relax. After that, the next thing I knew I was lying on the floor somebody was dashing water in my face.

It was the nurse. She had come at last, and found me by the side of the bed, where I had fallen, ,and had been trying to revive me ever since. I started up and looked about me. The nurse was closing Susan's eyes in a professional way, and performing other little services of the sort. The room wore an air of perfect desolation. The clothes Susan had on when she fell lay in a forlorn heap on a chair her shoes and stockings were thrown hither and thither the mahogany bureau, in which she had taken so much pride, was covered with vials, to make room for which some pretty trifles had been hastily thrust aside. I remembered what I had once said to Mrs. Cabot about having tasteful things about me, with a sort of shudder. What a mockery they are in the awful presence of death!

Mother met me with open arms when I reached home. She was much shocked at what I had to tell, and at my having encountered such a scene alone I should have felt myself quite a heroine under her caresses if I had not been overcome with bitter regret that I had not, with firmness and dignity turned poor Susan's last thoughts to her Savior. Oh, how could I, through miserable cowardice, let those precious moments slip by!

Feb 27.-I have learned one thing by yesterday's experience that is worth knowing. It is this: duty looks more repelling at a distance than when fairly faced and met. Of course, I have read the lines,

"Nor know we anything so fair, as is the smile upon thy face."

But I seem to be one of the stupid sort, who never apprehends a thing till they experience it. Now, however, I have seen the smile, and find it so "fair," that I shall gladly plod through many a hardship and trial to meet it again.

Poor Susan! Perhaps God heard my prayer for her soul, and revealed Himself to her at the very last moment.

March 2.-Such a strange thing has happened! Susan Green left a will, bequeathing her precious savings to whoever offered the last prayer in her hearing! I do not want, I never could touch a penny of that hardly-earned store and if I did, no earthly motive would tempt me to tell a human being, that it was offered by me, an inexperienced, trembling girl, driven to it by mere desperation! So it has gone to Dr. Cabot, who will not use it for himself, I am sure, but will be delighted to have it to give to poor people, who really besiege him. The last time he called to see her he talked and prayed with her, and says she seemed pleased and grateful, and promised to be more regular at church, which she had been, ever since.

March 28.-I feel all out of sorts. Mother says it is owing to the strain I went through at Susan's dying bed. She wants me to go to visit my aunt Mary, who is always urging me to come. But I do not like to leave my little Sunday scholars, nor to give mother the occasion to deny herself in order to meet the expense of such a long journey. Besides, I should have to have some new dresses, a new bonnet, and lots of things.

Today Dr. Cabot has sent me some directions for which I have been begging him a long time. Lest I should wear out this precious letter by reading it over, I will copy it here. After alluding to my complaint that I still "saw men as trees walking," he says:

"Yet he who first uttered this complaint had had his eyes opened by the Son of God, and so have you. Now He never leaves His work incomplete, and He will gradually lead you into clear and open vision, if you will allow Him to do it. I say gradually, because I believe this to be His usual method, while I do not deny that there are cases where light suddenly bursts in like a flood. To return to the blind man When Jesus found that his cure was not complete, He put His hands again upon his eyes, and made him look up and he was restored, and saw every man clearly. Now this must be done for you and in order to have it done you must go to Christ Himself, not to one of His servants. Make your complaint, tell Him how obscure everything still looks to you, and beg Him to complete your cure He may see fit to try your faith and patience by delaying this completion but meanwhile you are safe in His presence, and while led by His hand He will excuse the mistakes you make, and pity your falls. But you will imagine that it is best that He should at once enable you to see clearly. If it is, you may be sure He will do it. He never makes mistakes. But He often deals far differently with His disciples. He lets them grope their way in the dark until they fully learn how blind they are, how helpless, how absolutely in need of Him.

"What His methods will be with you I cannot foretell. But you may be sure that He never works in an arbitrary way. He has a reason for everything He does. You may not understand why He leads you now in this way and now in that, but you may, nay, you must believe that perfection is stamped on His every act.

"I am afraid that you are in danger of falling into an error only too common among young Christians. You acknowledge that there has been enmity to towards God in your secret soul, and that one of the first steps towards peace is to become reconciled to Him and to have your sins forgiven for Christ's sake. This done, you settle down with the feeling that the great work of life is done, and that your salvation is sure. Or, if not sure, that your whole business is to study your own case to see whether you are really in a state of grace. Many persons never get beyond this point. They spend their whole time in asking the question:

"'Do I love the Lord or no? Am I His or am I not?'

"I beg you, my dear child, if you are doing this aimless, useless work, to stop short at once. Life is too precious to spend in a treadmill.. Having been pardoned by your God and Savior, the next thing you have to do is to show your gratitude for this infinite favor by consecrating yourself entirely to Him, body, soul, and spirit. This is the least you can do. He has bought you with a price, and you are no longer, your own. 'But,' you may reply, this is contrary to my nature. I love my own way. I desire ease and pleasure I desire to go to heaven, to be carried thither on a bed of flowers. Can I not give myself so far to God as to feel a sweet sense of peace with Him, and be sure of final salvation, and yet, to a certain extent, indulge and gratify myself? If I give myself entirely away in Him and lose all ownership in myself, He may deny me many things I greatly desire. He may make my life hard and wearisome, depriving me of all that now makes it agreeable.' But, I reply, this is no matter of parley and discussion it is not optional with God's children whether they will pay Him a part of the price they owe Him, and keep back the rest. He asks, and He has a right to ask, for all you have and all you are. And if you shrink from what is involved in such a surrender, you should fly to Him at once and never rest till He has conquered this secret disinclination to give to Him as freely and as fully as He has given to you It is true that such an act of consecration on your part may involve no little future discipline and correction. As soon as you become the Lord's by your own deliberate and conscious act, He will begin that process of sanctification, which is to make you holy, as He is holy, perfect as He is perfect. He becomes at once ,your physician as well as your dearest and best Friend, but He will use no painful remedy that can be avoided. Remember that it is His will that you should be sanctified, and that the work of making you holy is His, not yours. At the same time, you are not to sit with folded hands, waiting for this blessing. You are to avoid laying hindrances in His way, and you are to exercise faith in Him as just as able and just as willing to give you sanctification, as He was to give you redemption. And now if you ask how you may know that you have truly consecrated yourself to Him, I reply, observe every in indication of His will concerning you, no matter how trivial, and see whether you at once close in with that will. Lay down this principle as a law- God does nothing arbitrary. If He takes away your health, for instance, it is because He has some reason for doing so and this is true of everything you value and if you have real faith in Him you will not insist on knowing this reason. If you find, in the course of daily events, that your self-consecration was not perfect-that is, that your will revolts at His will-do not be discouraged, but fly to your Savior and stay in His presence till you obtain the spirit in which He cried in His hour of anguish, 'Father, if Thou be willing, remove this cup from me: nevertheless, not my will but Thine be done.' Every time you do this it will be easier to do it every such consent to suffer will bring you nearer and nearer to Him and in this nearness to Him you will find such peace, such blessed, sweet peace, as will make your life infinitely happy, no matter what may be its mere outside conditions. Just think, my dear Katy, of the honor and the joy of having your will one with the Divine will, and so becoming changed into Christ's image from glory to glory!

"But I cannot say, in a letter, the tithe of what I want to say. Listen to my sermons from week to week and glean from them all the instruction you can, remembering that they are preached to you.

"In reading the Bible I advise you to choose detached passages, or even one verse a day, rather whole chapters. Study every word, ponder and pray over it till you have got out of it all the truth it contains.

"As to the other devotional reading, it is better to settle down on a few favorite authors, and read their works over and over and over until you have digested their thoughts and made them your own.

"It has been said 'that a fixed, inflexible will is a great assistance in a holy life.'

"You can will to choose for your associates those who are most devout and holy.

"You can will to read books that will stimulate you in your Christian life, rather than those that merely amuse.

"You can will to use every means of grace appointed by God.

"You can' will to spend much time in prayer, without regard to your frame at the moment.

"You can will to prefer a religion of principle to one of mere feeling in other, words, to obey the will of God when no comfortable glow of emotion accompanies your obedience.

"You cannot will to possess the spirit of Christ that must come as His gift but you can choose to study His life, and to imitate it. This will infallibly lead to such self-denying work as visiting the poor, nursing the sick, giving of your time and money to the needy, and the like.

"If the thought of such self-denial is repugnant to you, remember that it is enough for the disciple to be as his Lord. And let me assure you that as you penetrate the labyrinth of life in pursuit of Christian duty, you will often be surprised and charmed by meeting your Master Himself amid its windings and turnings, and receive His soul-inspiring smile. Or, I should rather say, you will always meet Him wherever you go."

I have read this letter again and again. It has taken such hold of me that I can think of nothing else. The idea of seeking holiness had never so much as crossed my mind. And even now, it seems like presumption for such a one as I to utter so sacred a word. And I shrink from committing myself to such a pursuit, lest after a time I should fall back into the old routine. And I have an undefined, wicked dread of being singular, as well as a certain terror of self-denial and loss of all liberty. But no choice seems left to me. Now that my duty has been clearly pointed out to me, I do not stand where I did before. And I feel, mingled with my indolence and love of ease and pleasure, some drawings towards a higher and better life. There is one thing I can do, and that is to pray that Jesus would do for me what He did for the blind man-put His hands yet again upon my eyes and make me to see clearly. And I will.

MARCH, 30.-Yes, I have prayed, and He has heard me. I see that I have no right to live for myself, and that I must live for. Him. I have given myself to Him, as I never did before, and have entered, as it were, a new world. I was very happy when I began to believe in His love for me, and that He had redeemed me. But this new happiness is deeper it involves something higher than getting to heaven at last, which has, hitherto, been my great aim.

March 31.-The more I pray, and the more I read the Bible, the more I feel my ignorance. And the more earnestly I desire holiness, the more utterly unholy I see myself to be. But I have pledged myself to the Lord, and I must pay my vows, cost what it may.

I have begun to read Taylor's "Holy Living and Dying." A month ago, I should have found it a tedious, dry book. But I am reading it with a sort of avidity, like one seeking after hid treasure. Mother, observing what I was doing, advised me to read it straight through, but to mingle a passage now and then with chapters from other books. She suggested my beginning on Baxter's "Saints' Rest," and of that I have read every word. I shall read it over, as Dr. Cabot advised, till I have fully caught its spirit. Even this one reading has taken away my lingering fear of death, and made heaven awfully attractive. I never mean to read worldly books again, and my music and drawing I have given up forever.

Chapter 7

Mother asked me last evening to sing and play to her. I was embarrassed to know how to excuse myself without telling her my real reason for declining. But somehow, she got it out of me.

"One need not be fanatical in order to be religious," she said.

"Is it fanatical to give up all for God?" I asked.

"What is it to give up all?" she asked, in reply.

"Why, to deny one's self every gratification and indulgence in order to mortify one's natural inclinations, and to live entirely for Him."

"God is then a hard Master, who allows his children no liberty," she replied. "Now let us see where this theory will lead you. In. the first place you must shut your eyes to all the beautiful things He has made. You must shut your eyes to all the harmonies He has ordained. You must shut your heart against all sweet human affections. You have a body, it is true, and it may revolt at such bondage—"

We are told to keep under the body," I interrupted.

"Oh, mother, do not hinder me! You know my love for music is. A passion and that it is my snare and temptation. And how can I spend my whole time in reading the Bible and praying, if I go on with my drawing? It may do for other people to serve both God and Mammon, but not for me. I must belong wholly to the world or wholly to Christ."

Mother said no more, and I went on with my reading. But somehow, my book seemed to have lost its flavor. Besides, it was time to retire for my evening devotions which I never put off now till the last thing at night, as I used to do. When I came down, Mother was lying on the sofa, by which I knew she was not well. I felt troubled that I had refused to sing to her. Think of the money she had spent on that part of my education! I went to her and kissed her with a pang of terror. What if she were going to be very sick, and to die?

"It is nothing, darling," she said, "nothing at all. I am tired, and felt a little faint."

I looked at her anxiously, and the bare thought that she might die and leave me alone was so terrible that I could hardly help crying out. And I saw, as by a flash of lightning, that if God took her from me, I could not, should not say: Thy will be done.

But she was better after taking a few drops of lavender, and what color she has came back to her dear sweet face.

APRIL 12.-Dr. Cabot's letter has lost all its power over me. A stone has more feeling than I. I do not love to pray. I am sick and tired of this dreadful struggle after holiness good books are all alike, flat and meaningless. But I must have something to absorb and carry me away, and I have come back to my music and my drawing with new zest. Mother was right in warning me against giving them up. Maria Kelley is teaching me to paint in oil colors, and says I have a natural gift for it.

APRIL 13. Mother asked me to go to church with her last evening, and I said I did not want to go. She looked surprised and troubled.

"Are you not well, dear?" she asked.

"I do not know. Yes. I suppose I am. But I could not be still at church five minutes. I am nervous that I feel as if I should fly."

"I see how it is," she said "you have forgotten that body of yours, of which I reminded you, and have been trying to live as if you were all soul and spirit. You have been straining every nerve to acquire perfection, whereas this is God's gift, and one that He is willing to give you, fully and freely."

"I have done seeking for that or anything else that is good," I said, despondently. "And so I have gone back to my music and everything else."

"'Here is just the rock upon which you split," she returned. "You speak of going back to your music as if that implied going away from God. You rush from one extreme to another. The only true way to live in this world, constituted just as we are, is to make all our employments subserve the one great end and aim of existence, namely, to glorify God and to enjoy Him forever. But in order to do this we must be wise taskmasters, and not require of ourselves what we cannot possibly perform. Recreation we must have. Otherwise the strings of our soul, wound up to an unnatural tension, will break."

"Oh, I do wish," I cried, "that God had given us plain rules, about which we could make no mistake!"

"I think His rules are plain," she replied. "And some liberty of action He must leave us, or we should become mere machines. I think that those who love Him, and wait upon Him day by day, learn His will almost imperceptibly, and need not go astray.

"But, mother, music and drawing are sharp-edged tools in such hands as mine. I cannot be moderate in my use of them. And the more I delight in them, the less I delight in God."

"Yes, this is human nature. But God's divine nature will supplant it, if we only consent to let Him work in us of His own good pleasure."

New York, April 16.-After all, mother has come off conqueror, and here I am at Auntie's. After our quiet, plain little home, in our quiet little town, this seems like a new world. The house is large, but is as full as it can hold. Auntie has six children her own, and has adopted two. She says she was meant to imitate the old woman who lived in a shoe. She reminds me of mother, and yet she is very different full of fun and energy flying about the house as on wings, with a kind, bright word for everybody. All her household affairs go on like clockwork the children are always nicely dressed nobody ever seems out of humor nobody is ever sick. Auntie is the central object round which everybody revolves you cannot forget her a moment, she is always doing something for you, and then her unflagging good humor and cheerfulness keep you good-humored and cheerful. I do not wonder Uncle Alfred loves her so.

I hope I shall have just such a home. I mean this is the sort of home I should like if I ever married, which I never mean to do. I should like to be just such a bright, loving wife as Auntie is to have my husband lean on me as Uncle leans on her to have just as many children, and to train them as wisely and kindly us she does hers. Then, I should feel that I had not been born in vain, but had a high and sacred mission on earth. But as it is, I must just pick up what scraps of usefulness I can, and let the rest go.

APRIL 18.-Auntie says I sit writing and reading and thinking too much, and wants me to go out more. I tell her I do not feel strong enough to go out much. She says that is all nonsense, and drags me out. I get tired, and hungry, and sleep like a baby a month old. I see now mother's wisdom and kindness in making me leave home when I did. I had veered about from point to point till I was nearly ill. Now Auntie keeps me well by making me go out, and dear Dr. Cabot's precious letter can work a true and not a morbid work in my soul. I am very happy. I have delightful talks with Auntie, who sets me right at this point and at that and it is beautiful to watch her home-life and to see with what sweet unconsciousness she carries her religion into every detail. I am sure it must do me good to be here and yet, if I am growing better how slowly, how slowly, it is! Somebody has said that 'our course heavenward is like the plan of the zealous pilgrims of old, who for every three steps forward, took one backward."

APRIL 30. Auntie's baby, my dear father's namesake, and hitherto the merriest little fellow I ever saw, was taken sick last night, very suddenly. She sent for the doctor at once, who would not say positively what was the matter, but this morning pronounced it scarlet fever. The three youngest have all come down with it today. If they were my children, I should be in a perfect worry and flurry. Indeed, I am as it is. But Auntie is as bright and cheerful as ever. She flies from one to another, and .keeps up their spirits with her own gayety. I am mortified to find that at such a time as this I can think of myself, and that I find it irksome to be shut up in sickrooms, instead of walking, driving, visiting, and the like. But, as Dr. Cabot says, I can now choose to imitate my Master, who spent His whole life in doing good, and I do hope, too, to be of some little use to Auntie, after her kindness to me.

MAY 1.- The doctor says the children are doing as well as, could be expected. He made a short visit this .morning, as it is Sunday. If I had ever seen him before I should say, I had some unpleasant association with him. I wonder Auntie employs such a great clumsy man. But she says he is good, and very skillful. I wish I did not take such violent likes and dislikes to people. I want my religion to change me in every respect.

MAY 2.-Oh, I know now! This is the very one who was so rude at Sunday school, and afterwards made such a nice address to the children. Well he may know how to speak in public, but I am sure he doesn't in private. I never knew such a shut-up man.

MAY 4.-I have my hands as full as they can hold. The children have got so fond of me, and one or the other is in my lap nearly all the time. I sing to them, tell them stories, build blockhouses, and relieve Auntie all I can. Dull and poky as the doctor is, I am not afraid of him, for he never notices anything I say or do, so while he is holding solemn consultations with Auntie in one corner, I can sing and .talk all sorts of nonsense to my little pets in mine. What fearful black eyes he has, and what masses of black hair!

This busy life quite suits me, now I have got used to it. And it sweetens every bit of work to think that I am doing it in humble, far-off, yet real imitation of Jesus. I am indeed really and truly happy.

MAY 14-It is now two weeks since little Raymond was taken sick, and I have lived in the nursery all the time, though Auntie has tried to make me go out. Little Emma was taken down today, though she has been kept on the third floor all the time I feel dreadfully myself. But this hard, cold doctor of Auntie's is so taken up with the children that he never so much as looks at me. I have been in a perfect shiver all day, but these merciless little folks call for stories as eagerly as ever. Well, let me be a comfort to them if I can! I hate selfishness more and more, and am shocked to see how selfish I have been.

MAY 15.-I was in a burning fever all night, and my head ached, and my throat was and is very sore. If knew I was going to die I would burn up this journal first. I would not have any one see it for the world.

MAY 24.-Dr. Elliott asked me on Sunday morning a week ago if I still felt well. For answer, I behaved like a goose, and burst out crying. Auntie looked more anxious than I have seen her look yet, and reproached herself for having allowed me to be with the children. She took me by one elbow, and the doctor by the other, and they marched me off to my own room, where I was put through the usual routine on such occasions, and then ordered to bed. I fell asleep immediately and slept all day. The doctor came to see me in the evening, and made a short, stiff little visit, gave me a powder, and said thought I should soon be better.

I had two such visits from him the next day, when I began to feel quite like myself again, and in spite of his grave staid deportment, could not help letting my good spirits run away with me in a style that evidently shocked him. He says persons nursing 'scarlet fever often have such little attacks as mine indeed every one of the servants have had a sore throat and headache.

MAY 25.-This morning, just as the doctor shuffled in on his big feet, it came over me how ridiculously I must have looked the day I was taken sick, being walked off between Auntie and himself, crying like a baby. I burst out laughing, and no consideration I could make to myself would stop me. I pinched myself, asked myself how I should feel if one of the children should die, and used other kindred devices all to no purpose. At last the doctor, gravity personified as he is, joined in, though not knowing in the least what he was laughing at. Then he said,

"After this, I suppose, I shall have to pronounce you convalescent."

"Oh, no!" I cried. "I am very-sick indeed."

"This looks like it, to be sure!" said Auntie.

"I suppose this will be your last visit, Dr. Elliott," I went on, "and I am glad of it. After the way I behaved the day I was taken sick, I have been ashamed to look you in the face. But I really felt dreadfully."

He made no answer whatever. I do not suppose he would speak a little flattering word by way of putting one in good humor with one's self for the whole world!

JUNE 1.-We are all as well as ever, but the doctor keeps some of the children still confined to the house for fear of bad consequences following the fever. He visits them twice a day for the same reason, or at least under that pretense, but I really believe he comes because he has got the habit of coming, and because he admires Auntie so much. She has a real affection for him, and is continually asking me if I do not like this and that quality in him, which I cannot see at all. We begin to drive out again. The weather is, very warm, but I feel perfectly well.

JUNE 2.-After the children's dinner today I took care of them while their nurse got hers and Auntie went to lie down, as she is all tired out. We were all full of life and fun, and some of the little ones wanted me to play a play of their own invention, which was to lie down on the floor, cover my face with a handkerchief, and make believe I was dead. They were to gather about me, and I was suddenly to come to life and jump up and try to catch them as they all ran scampering and screaming about. We had played in this interesting way for some time, and my hair, which I keep in nice order nowadays, was pulled down and flying every way when in marched the doctor. I started up and came to life quickly enough when I heard his step, looking red and angry, no doubt.

I should think you might have knocked, Dr. Elliott," I said, with much displeasure.

"I ask your pardon I knocked several times," he returned. "I need hardly ask how my little patients are."

"No," I replied, still ruffled, arid making desperate efforts to get my hair into some sort of order. "They are as well as possible."

"I came a little earlier than usual today," he went on, "because I am called to visit my uncle, Dr. Cabot, who is in a very critical state of health."

"Dr. Cabot!" I repeated, bursting into tears.

"Compose yourself, I entreat," he said, "I hope that I may be able to relieve him. At all events—"

"At all events, if you let him die it will break my heart," I cried passionately. "Do not wait another moment go this instant."

"I cannot go this instant," he replied. "The boat does not leave until four o'clock. And if I may be allowed, as a physician, to say one word, that my brief acquaintance hardly justifies, I do wish to warn you that unless you acquire more self-control-"

"Oh, I know that I have a quick temper, and that I spoke very rudely to you just now," I interrupted, not a little startled by the seriousness of his manner.

"I did not refer to your temper," he said. "I meant your whole passionate nature. Your vehement loves and hates, your ecstasies and your despondencies your disposition to throw yourself headlong into whatever interests you."

"I would rather have too little self-control," I retorted, resentfully, "than to be as cold as a stone, and as hard as a rock, and as silent as the grave, like some people I know."

His countenance fell he looked disappointed, even pained.

"I shall probably see your mother," he said, turning to go "your aunt wishes me to call on her have you any message?"

"No," I said.

Another pained, disappointed look made me begin to recollect myself. I was sorry, oh! so sorry, for my anger and rudeness. I ran after him, into the hall, my eyes full of tears, holding out both hands, which he took in both his.

"Do not go until you have forgiven me for being so angry!" I cried. "Indeed, Dr. Elliott, though you not be able to believe it, I am trying to do right all the time!"

"I do believe it," he said earnestly.

"Then tell me that you forgive me!"

"If I once begin, I shall be tempted to tell something else," he said, looking me through and through with those great dusky eyes. "And I will tell it," he went on, his grasp on my hands growing firmer-"It is easy to forgive when one loves." I pulled my hands away, and burst out crying again.

"Oh, Dr. Elliott this is dreadful!" I said. "You do not, you cannot love me! You are so much older than I am! So grave and silent! You are not in earnest?"

"I am only too much so," he said, and went quietly out.

I went back to the nursery. The children rushed upon me, and insisted that I should "play die." I let them pull me about as they pleased. I only wished I could play it in earnest.

Chapter 8

JUNE 28. - MOTHER writes me that Dr. Cabot is out of danger, Dr. Elliott having thrown new light on his case, and performed some sort of an operation that relieved him at once. I am going home. Nothing would tempt me to encounter those black eyes again. Besides, the weather is growing warm, and Auntie is getting ready to go out of town with the children.

JUNE 29.-Auntie insisted on knowing why I was hurrying home so suddenly, and at last got it out of me inch by inch. On the whole, it was a relief to have someone to speak to.

"Well!" she said, and leaned back in her chair in a fit of musing.

"Is that all you are going to say, Auntie?" I ventured to ask at last.

"No, I have one more remark to add," she said, "and it is this: I do not know which of you has behaved most ridiculously. It would relieve me to give you each a good shaking."

"I think Dr. Elliot has behaved ridiculously," I said, "and he has made me most unhappy."

"Unhappy!" she repeated. "I do not wonder you are unhappy. You have pained and wounded one of the noblest men that walks the earth."

"It is not my fault. I never tried to make him like me."

"Yes, you did. You were perfectly bewitching whenever he came here. No mortal man could help being fascinated."

I knew this was not true, and bitterly resented Auntie's injustice.

"If I wanted to 'fascinate' or 'bewitch' a man," I cried, "I should not choose one old enough to be my father, nor one who was as uninteresting, awkward and stiff as Dr. Elliott. Besides, how should I know he was not married? If I thought anything about it at all, I certainly thought of him as a middle-aged man, settled down with a wife, long ago."

"In the first place he is not old, or even middle aged. He is not more than twenty-seven or eight. As to his being uninteresting, perhaps he is to you, who do not know him. And if he were a married man, what business had he to come here to see as he has done?"

"I did not know he came to see me he never spoke to me. And I always said I would never marry a doctor."

"We all say scores of things we live to repent," she replied. "But I must own that the doctor acted quite out of character when he expected you to take a fancy to him on such short notice, you romantic little thing. Of course knowing him as little as you do, and only seeing him in sick-rooms, you could not have done otherwise than as you did."

"Thank you, Auntie," I said, running and throwing my arms around her "thank you with all my heart. And now won't you take back what you said about my trying to fascinate him?"

"I suppose I must, you dear child," she said. "I was not half in earnest. The truth is I am so fond of you both that the idea of your misunderstanding each other annoys me extremely. Why, you were made for each other. He would tone you down and keep you straight, and you would stimulate him and keep him awake."

"I do not want to be toned down or kept straight," I remonstrated. "I hate prigs who keep their wives in leading-strings. I do not mean to marry any one, but if I should be left to such a piece of folly, it must be to one who will take me for better or worse just as I am, and not as a wild plant for him to prune till he has got it into a shape to suit him. Now, Auntie, promise me one thing. Never mention Dr. Elliott's name to me again."

"I shall make no such promise," she replied, laughing. "I like him, and I like to talk about him and the more you hate and despise him the more I shall love and admire him. I only wish my Lucy were old enough to be his wife, and that he could fancy her but he never could!"

"On the contrary I should think that little model of propriety would just suit him," I exclaimed.

"Do not make fun of Lucy," Auntie said, shaking her head. "She is a dear good child, after all."

"After all" means this (for what with my own observation, and what Auntie has told me, Lucy's portrait is easy to paint) the child is the daughter of a man who died from a lingering illness caused by an accident. She entered the family at a most inauspicious moment, two days after this accident. From the outset, she comprehended the situation and took the ground that a character of irreproachable dignity and propriety became an infant coming at such a time. She never cried, never put improper objects into her mouth, never bumped her head, or scratched herself. Once put to bed at night, you knew nothing more of her till such time next day as you found it convenient to attend to her. If you forgot her existence, as was not seldom the case under the circumstances, she vegetated on, unmoved. It is possible that pangs of hunger sometimes assailed her, and it is a fact that she teethed, had the measles and the whooping cough. But these minute ripples on her infant life only showed the more clearly what a waveless, placid little sea it was. She got her teeth in the order laid down in "Dewees on Children" her measles came out on the appointed day like well-behaved measles as they were and retired decently and in order, as measles should. Her whooping cough had a well-bred, methodical air, and left her conqueror of the field. As the child passed out of her babyhood, she remained still her mother's appendage and glory a monument of pure white marble, displaying to the human race one instance at least of perfect parental training. Those smooth, round hands were always magically clean the dress immaculate and uncrumpled the hair dutifully shining and tidy. She was a model child, as she had been a model baby. No slamming of doors, no litter of carpets, no pattering of noisy feet on the stairs, no headless dolls, and no soiled or torn books indicated her presence. Her dolls were subject to a methodical training, not unlike her own. They rose, they were dressed, they took the air, and they retired for the night, with clock-like regularity. At the advanced age of eight, she ceased occupying herself with such trifles, and began a course of instructive reading. Her lessons were received in mute submission, like medicine so many doses, so many times a day. An agreeable interlude of needlework was afforded, and Dorcas-like, many were the garments that resulted for the poor. Give her the very eyes out of your head, cut off your right hand for her if you choose, but do not expect a gush of enthusiasm that would crumple you collar she would as soon strangle herself as run headlong to embrace you. If she has any passions or emotions, they are kept under but who asks for passion in blanc-mange, or seeks emotion in a comfortable apple-pudding?

When her father had been dead a year, her mother married a man with a large family of children and a very small purse. Lucy had a hard time of it, especially as her stepfather, a quick, impulsive man, took a dislike to her. Auntie had no difficulty persuading them to give the child to her. She took from the purest motives, and it does seem as if she ought to have more reward than she gets. She declares, however, that she has all the reward she could ask in the conviction that God accepts this attempt to please Him.

Lucy is now nearly fourteen very large of her age, with a dead white skin, pale blue eyes, and a little light hair. To hear her talk is most edifying. Her babies are all "babes" she never begins anything but "commences" it she never cries, she "weeps" never gets up in the morning, but "rises." But what am I writing all this for? Why, to escape my own thoughts, which are anything but agreeable companions, and to put off answering the question that must be answered, "Have I really made a mistake in refusing Dr. Elliott? Could I not, in time, have come to love a man who has so honored me?"

JULY 5.-Here I am again, safely at home, and very pleasant it seems to be with dear mother again. I have told her about Dr. E. She says very little about it one way or the other.

JULY 10.-Mother sees that I am restless and out of sorts. "What is it, dear?" she asked, this morning. "Has Dr. Elliott anything to do with the unsettled state you are in?"

"Why, no, mother," I answered. "My going away has broken up all my habits that's all. Still if I knew Dr. Elliott did not care much, and was beginning to forget it, I dare say I should feel better."

If you were perfectly sure that you could never return his affection," she said, "you were quite right in telling him so at once. But if you had any misgivings on the subject, it would have been better to wait, and to ask God to direct you."

Yes, it would. But at the moment, I had no misgivings. In my usual headlong style I settled one of the most weighty questions of my life, without reflection, without so much as one silent appeal to God, to tell me how to act. And now I have forever repelled, and thrown away a heart that truly loved me. He will go his way and I shall go mine. He never will know, what I am only just beginning to know myself, that I yearn after his love with unutterable yearning.

I am not going to sit down in sentimental despondency to weep over this irreparable past. No human being could forgive such folly as mine but God can. In my sorrowfulness and loneliness I fly to Him, and find, what is better than earthly felicity, the sweetest peace. He allowed me to bring upon myself, in one hasty moment, a shadow out of which I shall not soon pass, but He pities and He forgives me, and I have had many precious moments when I could say sincerely and joyfully, "Whom have I in heaven but Thee, and there is none upon earth that I desire besides Thee."

With a character still so undisciplined as mine, I seriously doubt whether I could have made him who has honored me with his unmerited affection. Sometimes I think I am as impetuous and as quick-tempered as ever I get angry with dear mother, and with James even, if they oppose me how unfit, then, I am to become the mistress of a household and the wife of a good a man!

How came he to love me? I cannot, cannot imagine!

August 31.-The last day of the very happiest summer I ever spent. If I had only been willing to believe the testimony of others, I might have been just as happy long ago. But I wanted to have all there was in God and all there was in the world, at once, and there was a constant, painful struggle between the two. I hope that struggle is now over. I deliberately choose and prefer God. I have found a sweet peace in trying to please Him such as I never conceived of. I would not change it for all the best things this world can give.

But I have a great deal to learn. I am like a little child who cannot run to get what he wants, but approaches it step by step, slowly, timidly-and yet approaches it. I am amazed at the patience of my blessed Master and Teacher, but how I love His school!

September.-This, too, has been a delightful month in a certain sense. Amelia's marriage, at which I had to be present, upset me a little, but it was but a little ruffle on a deep sea of peace.

I saw Dr. Cabot today. He is quite well again, ,and speaks of Dr. Elliott's skill with rapture. He asked about my Sunday scholars and my poor folks, etc., and I could not help letting out a little of the new joy that has taken possession of me.

"This is as it should be," he said. I should be sorry to see a person of your temperament enthusiastic in everything save religion. Do not be discouraged if you still have some ups and downs. 'He that is down need fear no fall' but you are away up on the heights, and may have one, now and then."

This made me a little uncomfortable. I do not want any falls. I want to go on to perfection.

OCT. 1.-Laura Cabot came to see me today, and seemed very affectionate.

"I hope we may see more of each other than we have done," she began. "My father wishes it, and so do I."

Katy, mentally.-"Ah! He sees how unworldly, how devoted I am, and so wants Laura under my influence."

Katy, aloud.-" I am sure that is very kind."

Laura.-" Not at all. He knows it will be profitable to me to be with you. I get a good deal discouraged at times, and want a friend to strengthen and help me."

Katy, to herself.-" Yes, yes, he thinks me quite experienced and trustworthy."

Katy, aloud.-" I shall never dare to try to help you.

Laura.-" Oh, yes, you must. I am so far behind you in Christian experience."

But I am ashamed to write down any more. After she had gone, I felt delightfully puffed up for a while. But when I came up to my room this evening, and knelt down to pray, everything looked dark and chaotic. God seemed far away, and I took no pleasure in speaking to Him. I felt sure that I had done something or felt something wrong, and asked Him to show me what it was. There then flashed into my mind the remembrance of the vain, conceited thoughts I had had during Laura's visit and ever since.

How perfectly contemptible! I have had a fall indeed!

I think now my first mistake was in telling Dr. Cabot my secret, sacred joys, as if some merit of mine had earned them for me. That gave Satan a fine chance to triumph over me! After this, I am determined to maintain the utmost reserve in respect to my religious experiences. Nothing is gained by running to tell them, and much is lost.

I feel depressed and comfortless.

Chapter 9

OCT. 10. - WE have very sad news from Auntie. She says my Uncle is quite broken down with some obscure disease that has been creeping stealthily along for months. All his physicians agree that he must give up his business and try the effect of a year's rest. Dr. Elliott proposes his going to Europe, which seems to me about as formidable as going to the next world. Auntie makes the best she can of it, but she says the thought of being separated from Uncle a whole year is dreadful I pray for her day and night, that this wild project may be given up. Why, he would be on the ocean ever so many weeks, exposed to all the discomforts of narrow quarters and poor food, and that just as winter is drawing nigh!

OCT. 12.~ Auntie writes that the voyage to Europe has been decided on, and that Dr. Elliott is to accompany Uncle, travel with him, amuse him, and bring him home a well man. I hope Dr. E.'s power to amuse may exist somewhere, but must own it was in a most latent form when I had the pleasure of knowing him. Poor Auntie! How much better it would be for her to go with Uncle! There are the children, to be sure. Well, I hope Uncle may be the better for this great undertaking, but I do not like the idea of it.

OCT. 15.-Another letter from Auntie, and new plans! The Dr. is to stay at home, Auntie is to go with Uncle, and we-mother and myself-are to take possession of the house and children during their absence! In other words, all this is to be if we say amen. Could anything be more frightful? To refuse would be selfish and cruel. If we consent, I thrust myself under Dr. Elliott's very nose.

OCT. 16.-Mother is surprised that I can hesitate one instant. She seems to have forgotten all about Dr. E. She says we can easily find a family to take this house for a year, and that she is delighted to do anything for Auntie that can be done.

Nov. 4.-Here we are, the whole thing settled. Uncle and Auntie started a week ago, and we are monarchs of all we survey, and this is a great deal. I am determined that mother shall not be worn out with these children, although of course I could not them without her advice and help. It is to be hoped they won't all have the measles in a body, or anything of that sort I am sure it would be annoying to Dr. E. to come here now.

Nov. 25.-Of course the baby must go on teething if only to have the doctor sent for to lance his gums. I told mother I was sure I could not be present when this was being done, so, though she looked surprised, and said people should accustom themselves to such things, she volunteered to hold baby herself.

Nov. 26.-The baby was afraid of mother, not being used to her, so she sent for me. As I entered the room, she gave him to me with an apology for doing so, since I shrank from witnessing the operation. What must Dr. E. think I am made of if I cannot bear to see a child's gums lanced? However, it is my own fault that he thinks me such a coward, for I made mother think me one. It was very embarrassing to hold baby and have the doctor's face so close to mine. I really wonder mother should not see how awkwardly I am situated here.

Nov. 27.-We have a good many visitors, friends of Uncle and Auntie. How uninteresting most people are! They all say the same thing, namely, how strange that Auntie had courage to undertake such a voyage, and to leave her children, etc., etc., etc., and what was Dr. Elliott thinking of to let them go, etc, etc., etc.

Dr. Embury called today, with a pretty little fresh creature, his new wife, who hangs on his arm like a workbag. He is Dr. Elliott's intimate friend, and spoke of him very warmly, and so did his wife, who says she has known him always, as they were born and brought up in the same village. I wonder he did not marry her himself, instead of leaving her for Dr. Embury!

She says he, Dr. Elliott, I mean, was the most devoted son she ever saw, and that he deserves his present success because he has made such sacrifices for his parents. I never met anyone whom I liked so well on so short acquaintance-I mean Mrs. Embury, though you might fancy, you poor deluded journal you, that I meant somebody else.

Nov. 30.-I have so much to do that I have little time for writing. The way the children wear out their shoes and stockings, the speed with which their hair grows, the way they bump their heads and pinch their fingers, and the insatiable demand for stories, is something next to miraculous. Not a day passes that somebody doesn't need something bought that somebody else doesn't choke itself, and that I do not have to tell stories till I feel my intellect reduced to the size of a pea. If ever I was alive and wide awake, however, it is just now, and in spite of some vague shadows of, I do not know what, I am very happy indeed. So is dear mother. She and the doctor have become bosom friends. He keeps her making beef tea, scraping lint, and boiling calves feet for jelly, till the house smells like a hospital.

I suppose he thinks me a poor, selfish, frivolous girl, whom nothing would tempt to raise a finger for his invalids. But, of course, I do not care what he thinks.

Dec. 4.-Dr. Elliott came this morning to ask mother to go with him to see a child who had met with a horrible accident. She turned pale, and pressed her lips together, but went at once to get ready. Then my long-suppressed wrath burst out.

"How can you ask poor mother to go and see such sights?" I cried. "You must think her nothing but a stone, if you suppose that after the way in which my father died-"

"It was indeed most thoughtless in me," he interrupted "but your mother is such a rare woman, so decided and self-controlled, yet so gentle, so full of tender sympathy, that I hardly know where to look for just the help I need today. If you could see this poor child, even you would justify me."

"Even you!" you monster of selfishness, heart of stone, floating bubble, "even you would justify it!"

How cruel, how unjust, how unforgiving he is!

I rushed out of the room, and cried until I was tired.

DEC. 6.-Mother says she feels really grateful to Dr. E. for taking her to see that child, and to help soothe and comfort it while he went through with a severe, painful operation, which she would not describe, because she fancied I looked pale. I said I should think the child's mother the most proper person to soothe it on such an occasion.

"The poor thing has no mother," she said, reproachfully. "What has got into you, Kate? You do not seem at all like yourself."

"I should think you had enough to do with this great house to keep in order, so many mouths to fill, and so many servants to oversee, without wearing yourself out with nursing all Dr. Elliott's poor folks," I said, gloomily.

"The more I have to do the happier I am," she replied. "Dear Katy, the old wound isn't healed yet, and I like to be with those who have wounds and bruises of their own. And Dr. Elliott seems to have divined this by instinct."

I ran and kissed her dear, pale face, which grows more beautiful every day. No wonder she misses father so! He loved and honored her beyond description, and never forgot one of those little courtesies that must have a great deal to do with a wife's happiness. People said of him that he was a gentleman of the old school, and that race is dying out.

I feel a good deal out of sorts myself. Oh, I do so wish to get above myself and all my childish, petty ways, and to live in a region where there is no temptation and no sin!

DEC. 22.-I have been to see Mrs. Embury today. She did not receive me as cordially as usual, and I very soon resolved to come away. She detained me, however.

"Would you mind my speaking to you on a certain subject?" she asked, with some embarrassment.

I felt myself flush up.

"I do not want to meddle with affairs that do not concern me," she went on, "but Dr. Elliott and I have been intimate friends all our lives. And his disappointment has really distressed me."

One of my moods came on, and I couldn't speak a word.

"You are not at all the sort of a girl I supposed he would fancy," she continued. "He always has said he was waiting to find someone just like his mother, and she is one of the gentlest, meekest, sweetest, and fairest among women."

"You ought to rejoice then that he has escaped the snare," I said, in a husky voice, "and is free to marry his ideal, when he finds her."

"But that is just what troubles me. He is not free. He does not attach himself readily, and I am afraid that it will be a long, long time before he gets over this unlucky passion for you."

"Passion!" I cried, contemptuously.

She looked at me with some surprise, and then went on.

"Most girls would jump at the chance of getting such a husband."

"I do not know that I particularly care to be classed with 'most girls,'" I replied, loftily.

"But if you only knew him as well as I do. He is so noble, so disinterested, and is so beloved by his patients. I could tell you scores of anecdotes about him that would show just what he is."

"Thank you," I said, "I think we have discussed Dr. Elliott quite enough already. I cannot say that he has elevated himself in my opinion by making you take up the cudgels in his defense."

"You do him injustice, when you say that," she cried. "His sister, the only person to whom he confided the state of things, begged me to find out, if I could, whether you had any other attachment, and if her brother's case was quite hopeless. But I am sorry I undertook the task as it has annoyed you so much."

I came away a good deal ruffled. When I got home mother said she was glad I had been out at last for a little recreation, and that she wished I did not confine myself so to the children. I said that I did not confine myself more than Auntie did.

"But that is different," mother objected. "She is their own mother, and love helps her to bear her burden."

"So it does me," I returned. "I love the children exactly as if they were my own."

That," she said, "is impossible."

"I certainly do," I persisted.

Mother would not dispute with me, though I wished she would.

A mother," she went on, "receives her children one at a time, and gradually adjusts herself to gradually increasing burdens. But you take a whole houseful upon you at once, and I am sure it is too much for you. You do not look or act like yourself."

"It isn't the children," I said.

"What is it, then?"

"Why, it's nothing," I said, pettishly.

"'I must say, dear," said mother, not noticing my manner, "that your wonderful devotion to the children, aside from its effect on your health and temper, has given me great delight."

"I do not see why," I said.

"Very few girls of your age would give up their whole time as you do to such work."

"That is because very few girls are as fond of children as I am. There is no virtue in doing exactly what one likes best to do."

"There, go away, you contrary child," said mother, laughing. "If you won't be praised, you won't."

So I came up here and moped a little. I do not see what ails me.

But there is an under-current of peace that is not entirely disturbed by any outside event. In spite of my follies and my shortcomings, I do believe that God loves and pities me, and will yet perfect that which concerns me. It is a great mystery. But so is everything.

Dr. Elliott to Mrs. Crofton:

And now, my dear friend, having issued my usual bulletin of health, you may feel quite at ease about your dear children, and I come to a point in your letter which I would gladly pass over in silence. But this would be but a poor return for the interest you express in my affairs.

Both ladies are devoted to your little flock, and Miss Mortimer seems not to have a thought but for them. The high opinion I formed of her at the outset is more than justified by all I see of her daily, household life. I know what her faults are, for she seems to take delight in revealing them. But I also know her rare virtues, and what a wealth of affection she has to bestow on the man who is so happy as to win her heart. But I shall never be that man. Her growing aversion to me makes me dread a summons to your house, and I have hardly manliness enough to conceal the pain this gives me. I entreat you, therefore, never again to press this subject upon me. After all, I would not, if I could, dispense with the ministry of disappointment and unrest.

Mrs. Crofton, in reply:

. . . . So she hates you, does she? I am charmed to hear it. Indifference would be an alarming symptom, but good, cordial hatred, or what looks like it, is a most hopeful sign. The next chance you get to see her alone, assure her that you never shall repeat your first offence. If nothing comes of it, I am not a woman, and never was one nor is she.

MARCH 25, 1836.-The New Year and my birthday have come and gone, and this is the first moment I could find for writing down all that has happened.

The day after my last date, I was full of serious, earnest thoughts, of new desires to live, without one reserve, for God. I was smarting under the remembrance of my folly at Mrs. Embury's, and with a sense of vague disappointment and discomfort, and had to fly closer than ever to Him. In the evening, I thought I would go to the usual weekly service. It is true I do not like prayer meetings, and that is a bad sign, I am afraid. But I am determined to go where good people go, and see if I cannot learn to like what they like.

Mother went with me, of course.

What was my surprise to find that Dr. E. was to preside! I had no idea that he was that sort of a man.

The hymns they sang were beautiful, and did me good. So was his prayer. If all prayers were like that, I am sure I should like evening meetings as much as I now dislike them. He so evidently spoke to God in it, and as if he were used to such speaking.

He then made a little address on the ministry of disappointments, as he called it. He spoke so cheerfully and hopefully that I began to see almost for the first time God's reason for the petty trials and crosses that help to make up every day of one's life. He said there were few who were not constantly disappointed with themselves, with their slow progress, their childishness and weakness disappointed with their friends who, strangely enough, were never quite perfect enough, and disappointed with the world, which was always promising so much and giving so little. Then he urged to a wise and patient consent to this discipline, which, if rightly used, would help to temper and strengthen the soul against the day of sorrow and bereavement. But I am not doing him justice in this meager report there was something almost heavenly in his expression that words cannot describe.

Coming out I heard someone ask, "Who was that young clergyman?" and the answer, "Oh, that is only a doctor!"

Well! The next week I went again, with mother. We had hardly taken our seats when Dr. E. marched in with the sweetest looking little creature I ever saw. He was so taken up with her that he did not observe either mother or myself. As she sat by my side I could not see her full face, but her profile was nearly perfect. Her eyes were of that lovely blue one sees in violets and the skies, with long, soft eyelashes, and her complexion was as pure as a baby's. Yet she was not one of your doll beauties her face expressed both feeling and character. They sang together from the same book, though I offered her a share of mine. Of course, when people do that it can mean but one thing.

So it seems he has forgotten me, and consoled himself with this pretty little thing. No doubt, she is like his mother, that "gentlest, meekest, sweetest, and fairest among women!"

Now if anybody should be sick, and he should come here, I thought, what would become of me? I certainly could not help showing that a love that can so soon take up with a new object could not have been a sentiment of much depth.

It is not pleasant to lose even a portion of one's respect and esteem for another.

The next day mother went to visit an old friend of hers, who has a beautiful place outside of the city. The baby's nurse had ironing to do, so I promised to sit in the nursery till it was finished. Lucy came, with her books, to sit with me. She always follows like my shadow. After a while, Mrs. Embury called. I hesitated a little about trusting the child to Lucy's care, for though her prim ways have given her the reputation of being wise beyond her years, I observe that she is apt to get into trouble, which a quick-witted child would either avoid or jump out of in a twinkling. However, children are often left to much younger girls, so, with many cautions, I went down, resolving to stay only a few moments.

But I wanted so much to know all about that pretty little friend of Dr. E.'s that I let Mrs. Embury stay on and on, though not a ray of light did I get for my pains At last I heard Lucy's step coming downstairs.

"Cousin Katy," she said, entering the room with her usual propriety, "I was seated by the window, engaged with my studies. and the children were playing about, as usual, when suddenly I heard a shriek, and one of them ran past me, all in a blaze and-"

I believe I pushed her out of my way as I rushed upstairs, for I took it for granted I should meet the little figure all in a blaze, coming to meet me. But I found it wrapped in a blanket, the flames extinguished. Meanwhile, Mrs. Embury had roused the whole house, and everybody came running upstairs.

"Get the doctor, some of you," I cried, clasping the poor little writhing form in my arms.

And then I looked to see which of them it was, and found it was Auntie's pet lamb, everybody's pet lamb, our little loving, gentle Emma.

Dr. Elliott must have come on wings, for I had not time to be impatient for his arrival. He was as tender as a woman with Emma we cut off and tore off her clothes wherever the fire had touched her, and he dressed the burns with his own hands. He did not speak a word to me, or I to him. This time he did not find it necessary to advise me to control my-self. I was as cold and hard as a stone.

But when poor little Emma's piercing shrieks began to subside, and she came a little under the influence of some soothing drops he had given her at the outset, I began to feel that sensation in the back of my neck that leads to conquest over the most stubborn and the most heroic. I had just time to get Emma into the doctor's arms, and then down I went. I got over it in a minute, and was up again before anyone had time to come to the rescue. But Dr. E. gave Emma to Mrs. Embury, who had taken off her things and been crying all the time, and said in a low voice,

"I beg you will now leave the room, and lie down. And do not feel obliged to see me when I visit the child. That annoyance, at least, you should spare yourself."

"No consideration shall make me neglect little Emma," I replied, defiantly.

By this time, Mrs. Embury had rocked her to sleep, and she lay, pale and with an air of complete exhaustion, in her arms.

"You must lie down now, Miss Mortimer," Dr. Elliott said, as he rose to go. "I will return in a few hours to see how you both do."

He stood looking at, Emma, but did not go. Then Mrs. Embury asked the question I had not dared to ask.

"Is the poor child in danger?"

"I cannot say I trust not. Miss Mortimer's presence of mind in extinguishing the flames at once, has, I hope, saved its life."

"It was not my presence of mind, it was Lucy's!" I cried, eagerly. Oh, how I envied her for being the heroine, and for the surprised, delighted smile with which he went and took her hand, saying, "I congratulate you, Lucy! How your mother will rejoice at this!"

I tried to think of nothing but poor little Emma, and of the reward Auntie had had for her kindness to Lucy. But I thought of myself, and how likely it was that under the same circumstances I should have been beside myself, and done nothing. This, and many other emotions, made me burst out crying.

"Yes, cry, cry, with all your heart," said Mrs. Embury, laying Emma gently down, and coming to get me into her arms. "It will do you good, poor child!"

She cried with me, till at last I could lie down and try to sleep.

Well, the days and the weeks were very long after that.

Dear mother had a hard time, what with her anxiety about Emma, and my crossness and unreasonableness.

Dr. Elliott came and went, came and went. At last, he said all danger was over, and that our patient little darling would get well. But his visits did not diminish he came twice and three times every day. Sometimes I hoped he would tell us about his new flame, and sometimes I felt that I could not hear her mentioned. One day mother was so unwell that I had to help him dress Emma's burns, and I could not help saying:

"Even a mother's gentlest touch, full of love as it is, is almost rough compared with that of one trained to such careful handling as you are."

He looked gratified, but said:

"I am glad you begin to find that even stones feel, sometimes."

Another time something was said about the fickleness of women. Mrs. Embury began it. I fired up, of course.

He seemed astonished at my attack.

"I said nothing," he declared.

"No, but you looked a good many things. Now the fact is, women are not fickle. When they lose what they value most, they find it impossible to re place it. But men console themselves with the first good thing that comes along."

I dare say I spoke bitterly, for I was thinking how soon Ch———, I mean somebody, replaced me in his shallow heart, and how, with equal speed, Dr. Elliott had helped himself to a new love.

"I do not like these sweeping assertions," said Dr. Elliott, looking a good deal annoyed.

"I have to say what I think," I persisted.

"It is well to think rightly, then," he said, gravely.

"By the bye, have you heard from Helen?" Mrs. Embury most irreverently asked.

"Yes, I, heard yesterday."

"I suppose you will be writing her, then? Will you enclose a little note from me? Or rather let me have the least corner of your sheet?"

I was shocked at her want of delicacy. Of course, this Helen must be the new love, and how could a woman with two grains of sense imagine he would want to spare her a part of his sheet!

I felt tired and irritated. As soon as Dr. Elliott had gone, I began to give her a good setting down.

"I could hardly believe my ears," I said, "when I heard you ask leave to write on Dr. Elliott's sheet."

"No wonder," she said, laughing. "I suppose you never knew what it was to have to count every shilling, and to deny yourself the pleasure of writing to a friend because of what it would cost. I'm sure I never did till I was married."

"But to ask him to let you help write his love-letters," I objected.

"Ah! Is that the way the wind blows?" she cried, nodding her pretty little head. "Well, then, let me relieve your mind, my dear, by informing you that this 'love-letter' is to his sister, my dearest friend, and the sweetest little thing you ever saw."

"Oh!" I said, and immediately felt quite rested, and quite like myself.

Like myself! And who is she, pray!

Two souls dwell in my poor little body, and which of them is me, and which of them isn't, it would be hard to tell. This is the way they behave:

SCENE FIRST.

Katy, to the other creature, whom I will call Kate.-Your mother looks tired, and you have been very cross. Run and put your arms around her, and tell her how you love her.

Kate. -Oh, I cannot it would look queer. I do not like palaver. Besides, who would not be cross who felt as I do?

SCENE SECOND.

Katy.-Little Emma has nothing to do, and ought to be amused. Tell her a story, do.

Kate.-I am tired, and need to be amused myself.

Katy.-But the dear little thing is so patient and has suffered so much.

Kate.-Well, I have suffered, too. If she had not climbed up on the fender she would not have got burned.

SCENE THIRD.

Kate.-You are very irritable today. You had better go upstairs to your room and pray for patience.

Katy.-One cannot be always praying. I do not feel like it.

SCENE FOURTH.

Katy.-You treat Dr. Elliott shamefully. I should think he would really avoid you as you avoid him.

Kate-Do not let me hear his name. I do not avoid him.

Katy.-You do not deserve his good opinion.

Kate.-Yes, I do.

SCENE FIFTH

Just awake in the morning.

Katy.-Oh, dear! How hateful I am! I am cross and selfish, and domineering, and vain. I think of myself the whole time I behave like a heroine when Dr. Elliott is present, and like a naughty, spoiled child when he is not. Poor mother! How can she endure me? As to my piety, it is worse than none.

Kate, a few hours later.-Well, nobody can deny that I have a real gift in managing children! And I am very lovable, or mother would not be so fond of me. I am always pleasant unless I am sick, or worried, and my temper is not half so hasty as it used to be. I never think of myself, but am all the time doing something for others. As to Dr. E., I am thankful to say that I have never stooped to attract him by putting on airs and graces. He sees me just as I am. And I am very devout. I love to read good books and to be with good people. I pray a great deal. The bare thought of doing wrong makes me shudder. Mother is proud of me, and I do not wonder. Very few girls would have behaved as I did when Emma was burned. Perhaps I am not as sweet as some people. I am glad of it. I hate sweet people. I have great strength of character, which is much better, and am certainly very high-toned.

But, my poor journal, you cannot stand any more such stuff, can you? But tell me one thing, am I Katy or am I Kate?

Chapter 10

APRIL 20. - YESTERDAY I felt better than I have done since the accident. I ran about the house quite cheerily, for me. I wanted to see mother for something, and flew singing into the parlor, where I had left her shortly before. But she was not there, and Dr. Elliott was. I started back, and was about to leave the room, but he detained me.

"Come in, I beg of you," he said, his voice growing hoarser and hoarser. "Let us put a stop to this."

"To what?" I asked, going nearer and nearer, and looking up into his face, which was quite pale.

"To your evident terror of being alone with me, of hearing me speak. Let me assure you, once for all, that nothing would tempt me to annoy you by urging myself upon you, as you seem to fear I may be tempted to do. I cannot force you to love me, nor would I if I could. If you ever want a friend, you will find one in me. But do not think of me as your lover, or treat me as if I were always lying in wait for a chance to remind you of it. That I shall never do, never."

"Oh, no, of course not!" I broke forth, my face all in a glow, and tears of mortification raining down my cheeks. "I knew you did not care for me I knew you had got over it!"

I do not know which of us began it, I do not think he did, and I am sure I did not, but the next moment I was folded all up in his great long arms, and a new life had begun!

Mother opened the door not long after, and seeing what was going on, trotted away on her dear feet as fast as she could.

APRIL 21.-I am too happy to write journals. To think how we love each other.

Mother behaves beautifully.

APRIL 25.-One does not feel like saying much about it, when one is as happy as I am. I walk the streets as one treading on air. I fly about the house as on wings. I kiss everybody I see.

Now that I look at Ernest (for he makes me call him so) with unprejudiced eyes, I wonder I ever thought him clumsy. And how ridiculous it was in me to confound his dignity and manliness with age!

It is very odd, however, that such a cautious, well-balanced man should have fallen in love with me that day at Sunday school. And still stranger that with my headlong, impulsive nature, I deliberately walked into love with him!

I believe we shall never get through with what we have to say to each other. I am afraid we are rather selfish to leave mother to herself every evening.

SEPT. 5.-This has been a delightful summer. To be sure, we had to take the children to the country for a couple of months, but Ernest's letters are almost better than Ernest himself. I have written enough to him to fill a dozen books. We are going back to the city now. In his last letter, Ernest says he has been home, and that his mother is delighted to hear of his engagement. He says, too, that he went to see an old lady, one of the friends of his boyhood, to tell the news to her.

"When I told her," he goes on, "that I had found the most beautiful, the noblest, the most loving of human beings, she only said, 'Of course, of course!'

"Now you know, dear, that it is not at all of course, but the very strangest, most wonderful event in the history of the world."

And then he described a scene he had just witnessed at the deathbed of a young girl of my own age, who left this world and every possible earthly joy, with a delight in the going to be with Christ, which made him really eloquent. Oh, how glad I am that God has cast in my lot with a man whose whole business is to minister to others! I am sure this will, of itself, keep him unworldly and unselfish. How delicious it is to love such a character, and how happy I shall be to go with him to sickrooms and to dying-beds! He has already taught me that lessons learned in such scenes far outweigh in value what books and sermons, even, can teach.

And now, my dear old journal, let me tell you a secret that has to do with life, and not with death.

I am going to be married!

To think that I am always to be with Ernest! To sit at the table with him every day, to pray with him, to go to church with him, to have him all mine! I am sure that there is not another man on earth whom I could love as I love him. The thought of marrying Ch——, I mean of having that silly, schoolgirl engagement end in marriage, was always repugnant to me. But I give myself to Ernest joyfully and with all my heart.

How good God has been to me! I do hope and pray that this new, this absorbing love, has not detached my soul from Him, will not detach it. If I knew it would, could I, should I have courage to cut it off and cast it from me?

JAN.16, 1837.-Yesterday was my birthday, and today is my wedding-day. We meant to celebrate the one with the other, but Sunday would come this year on the fifteenth.

I am dressed, and have turned everybody out of this room, where I have suffered so much mortification, and experienced so much joy, that before I give myself to Ernest, and before I leave home forever, I may once more give myself away to God. I have been too much absorbed in my earthly love, and am shocked to find how it fills my thoughts. But I will belong to God. I will begin my married life in His fear, depending on Him to make me an unselfish, devoted wife.

JAN. 25.-We had a delightful trip after the wedding was over. Ernest proposed to take me to his own home that I might see his mother and sister. He never has said that he wanted them to see me. But his mother is not well. I am heartily glad of it.

I mean I was glad to escape going there to be examined and criticized. Every one of them would pick at me, I am sure, and I do not like to be picked at.

We have a home of our own, and I am trying to take kindly to housekeeping. Ernest is away a great deal more than I expected he would be. I am fearfully lonely. Auntie comes to see me as often as she can, and I go there almost every day, but that doesn't amount to much. As soon as I can venture to it, I shall ask Ernest to let me invite mother to come and live with us. It is not right for her to be left all alone so I hoped he would do that himself. But men are not like women. We think of everything.

FEB. 15.-Our honeymoon ends today. There hasn't been quite as much honey in it as I expected. I supposed that Ernest would be at home every evening, at least, and that he would read aloud, and have me play and sing, and that we should have delightful times together. But now he has got me he seems satisfied, and goes about his business as if he had been married a hundred years. In the morning, he goes off to see his list of patients he is going in and out all day after dinner we sit down to have a nice talk together the doorbell invariably rings, and he is called away. Then in the evening, he goes and sits in his office and studies I do not mean every minute, but he certainly spends hours there. Today he brought me such a precious letter from dear mother! I could not help crying when I read it, it was so kind and so loving. Ernest looked amazed he threw down his paper, came and took me in his arms and asked, "What is the matter, darling?" Then it all came out. I said I was lonely, and hadn't been used to spending my evenings all by myself.

"You must get some of your friends to come and see you, poor child," he said.

"I do not want friends," I sobbed out. "I want you."

"Yes, darling why didn't you tell me so sooner? Of course I will stay with you if you wish it."

"If that is your only reason, I am sure I do not want you," I pouted.

He looked puzzled.

"I really do not know what to do," he said, with a most comical look of perplexity. But he went to his office, and brought up a pile of fusty old books.

"Now, dear," he said, "we understand each other I think. I can read here just as well as down stairs. Get your book and we shall be as cozy as possible."

My heartfelt sore and dissatisfied. Am I unreasonable and childish? What is married life? An occasional meeting, a kiss here and a caress there? Or is it the sacred union of the twain who 'walk together side by side, knowing each other's joys and sorrows, and going heavenward hand in hand?

FEB. 17.-Mrs. Embury has been here today. I longed to compare notes with her, and find out whether it really is my fault that I am not quite happy. But I could not bear to open my heart to her on so sacred a subject. We had some general conversation, however, which did me good for the time, at least.

She said she thought one of the first lessons a wife should learn is self-forgetfulness. I wondered if she had seen anything in me to call forth this remark. We meet pretty often partly because our husbands are such good friends, partly because she is as fond of music as I am, and we like to sing and play together, and I never see her that she does not do or say something elevating something that strengthens my own best purposes and desires. But she knows nothing of my conflict and dismay, and never will. Her gentle nature responds at once to holy influences. I feel truly grateful to her for loving me, for she really does love me, and yet she must see my faults.

I should like to know if there is any reason on earth why a woman should learn self-forgetfulness that does not apply to a man.

FEB. 18. -Uncle says he has no doubt he owes his life to Ernest, who, in the face of opposition to other physicians, insisted on his giving up his business and going off to Europe at just the right moment. For his partner, whose symptoms were very like his own, has been stricken down with paralysis, and will not recover.

It is very pleasant to hear Ernest praised, and it is a pleasure I have very often, for his friends come to see me, and speak of him with rapture. A lady told me that through the long illness of a sweet young daughter of hers, he prayed with her every day, ministering so skillfully to her soul, that all fear of death was taken away, and she just longed to go, and did go at last, with perfect delight. I think he spoke of her to me once but he did not tell me that her preparation for death was his work. I could not conceive of him as doing that.

FEB. 24.-Ernest has been gone a week. His mother is worse and he had to go. I wanted to go too, but he said it was not worthwhile, as he should have to return directly. Dr. Embury takes charge of his patients during his absence, and Mrs. E. and Auntie and the children come to see me very often. I like Mrs. Embury more and more. She is not so audacious as I am, but I believe she agrees with me more than she will own.

FEB. 25.-Ernest writes that his mother is dangerously ill, and seems in great distress. I am mean enough to want all his love myself, while I should hate him if he gave none to her. Poor Ernest! If she should die, he would be sadly afflicted!

FEB. 27.-She died the very day he wrote. How I long to fly to him and to comfort him! I can think of nothing else. I pray day and night that God would make me a better wife.

A letter came from mother at the same time with Ernest's. She evidently misses me more than she will own. Just as soon as Ernest returns home, I will ask him to let her come and live with us. I am sure he will he loves her already, and now that his mother has gone, he will find her a real comfort. I am sure she will only make our home the happier.

FEB. 28 - Such a dreadful thing is going to happen! I have cried and called myself names by turns all day. Ernest writes that it has been decided to give up the old homestead, and scatter the family about among the married sons and daughters. Our share is to be his father and his sister Martha, and he desires me to have two rooms got ready for them at once.

So all the glory and the beauty is snatched out of my married life at one swoop! And it is done by the hand I love best, and that I would not have believed could be so unkind.

I am rent in pieces by conflicting emotions and passions. One moment I am all tenderness and sympathy for poor Ernest, and ready to sacrifice everything for his pleasure. The next I am bitterly angry with him for disposing of all my happiness in this arbitrary way. If he had let me make common cause with him and share his interests with him, I know I am not so abominably selfish as to feel as I do now. But he forces two perfect strangers upon me and forever shuts our doors against my darling mother. For, of course, she cannot live with us if they do.

And who knows what sort of people they are? It is not everybody I can get along with, nor is it everybody can get along with me. Now, if Helen were coming instead of Martha, that would be some relief. I could love her, I am sure, and she would put up with my ways. But your Martha's I am afraid of. Oh, dear, dear, what a nest of scorpions this affair has stirred up within me! Who would believe I could be thinking of my own misery while Ernest's mother, whom he loved so dearly, is hardly in her grave! But I have no heart, I am stony and cold. It is well to have found out just what I am!

Since I wrote that, I have been trying to tell God all about it. But I could not speak for crying. And I have been getting the rooms ready. How many little things I had planned to put in the best one, which I intended for mother I have made myself arrange them just the same for Ernest's father. The stuffed chair I have had in my room, and enjoyed so much, has been rolled in, and the Bible with large print placed on the little table near which I had pictured mother with her sweet, pale face, as sitting year after year. The only thing I have taken away is the copy of father's portrait. He won't want that!

When I had finished this business, I went and shook my fist at the creature I saw in the glass.

"You're beaten," I cried. "You didn't want to give up the chair, nor your writing-table, nor the Bible in which you expect to record the names of your ten children I But you've had to do it, so there!"

MARCH 3.-They all got here at 7 o'clock last night, just in time for tea. I was so glad to get hold of Ernest once more that I was gracious to my guests, too. The very first thing, however, Ernest annoyed me by calling me Katherine, though he knows I hate that name, and want to be called Katy as if I were a lovable person, as I certainly am (sometimes). Of course, his father and Martha called me Katherine, too.

His father is even taller, darker, blacker eyed, blacker haired than he.

Martha is a spinster.

I had got up a nice little supper for them, thinking they would need something substantial after their journey. And perhaps there was some vanity in the display of dainties that needed the mortification I felt at seeing my guests both push away their plates in apparent disgust. Ernest, too, looked annoyed, and expressed some regret that they could find nothing to tempt their appetites.

Martha said something about not expecting much from young housekeepers, which I inwardly resented, for the light, delicious bread had been sent by Auntie, together with other luxuries from her own table, and I knew they were not the handiwork of a young housekeeper, but of old Chloe, who had lived in her own and her mother's family twenty years.

Ernest went out as soon as this unlucky repast was over to hear Dr. Embury's report of his patients, and we passed a dreary evening, as my mind was preoccupied with longing for his return. The more I tried to think of something to say the more I couldn't.

At last, Martha asked at what time we breakfasted.

"At half-past seven, precisely," I answered. "Ernest is very punctual about breakfast. The other meals are more irregular."

"That is very late," she returned. "Father rises early and needs his breakfast at once."

I said I would see that he had it as early as he liked, while I foresaw that this would cost me a battle with the divinity who reigned in the kitchen.

"You need not trouble yourself. I will speak to my brother about it," she said.

"Ernest has nothing to do with it," I said, quickly.

She looked at me in a speechless way, and then there was a long silence, during which she shook her head a number of times. At last, she inquired: "Did you make the bread we had on the table to-night?"

"No, I do not know how to make bread," I said, smiling at her look of horror.

"Not know how to make bread?" she cried. The very spirit of mischief got into me, and made me ask:

"Why, can you?"

Now I know there is but one other question I could have asked her, less insulting than this, and that is:

"Do you know the Ten Commandments?"

A spinster fresh from a farm not know how make bread, to be sure!

But in a moment I was ashamed and sorry that I had yielded to myself so far as to forget the courtesy due to her as my guest, and one just home from a scene of sorrow, so I rushed across the room, seized her hand, and said, eagerly:

"Do forgive me! It slipped out before I thought!"

She looked at me in blank amazement, unconscious that there was anything to forgive.

'How you startled me!" she said. "I thought you had suddenly gone crazy."

I went back to my seat crestfallen enough. All this time Ernest's father had sat grim and grave in his corner, without a word. But now he spoke.

"At what hour does my son have family worship? I should like to retire. I feel very weary."

Now family worship at night consists in our kneeling down together hand in hand, the last thing before going to bed, and in our own room. The awful thought of changing this sweet, informal habit into a formal one made me reply quickly:

"Oh, Ernest is very irregular about it. He is often out in the evening, and sometimes we are quite late. I hope you never will feel obliged to wait for him."

I trust I shall do my duty, whatever it costs," was the answer.

Oh, how I wished they would go to bed!

It was now ten o'clock, and I felt tired and restless. When Ernest is out late, I usually lie on the sofa and wait for him, and so am bright and fresh when he comes in. But now I had to sit up, and there was no knowing for how long. I poked at the fire and knocked down the shovel and tongs, now I leaned back in my chair, and now I leaned forward, and then I listened for his step. At last he came.

"What, are you not all gone to bed?" he asked.

As if I could go to bed when I had scarcely seen him a moment since his return!

I explained why we waited, and then we had prayer and escorted our guests to their rooms. When we got back to the parlor, I was thankful to rest my tired soul in Ernest's arms, and to hear what little he had to tell about his mother's last hours.

"You must love me more than ever, now," he said, "for I have lost my best friend."

"Yes," I said, "I will." As if that were possible! All the time we were talking, I heard the greatest racket overhead, but he did not seem to notice it. I found, this morning, that Martha, or her father, or both together, had changed the positions of article of furniture in the room making it look a fright.

Chapter 11

MARCH 10. - THINGS are even worse than I expected. Ernest evidently looked at me with his father's eyes (and this father has got the jaundice, or something), and certainly is cooler towards me than he was before he went home. Martha still declines eating more than enough to keep body and soul together, and sits at the table with the air of a martyr. Her father lives on crackers and stewed prunes, and when he has eaten them, fixes his melancholy eyes on me, watching every mouthful with an air of plaintive regret that I will consume so much unwholesome food.

Then Ernest positively spends less time with me than ever, and sits in his office reading and writing nearly every evening.

Yesterday I came home from an exhilarating walk, and a charming call at Auntie's, and at the dinner table gave a lively account of some of the children's exploits. Nobody laughed, and nobody made any response, and after dinner Ernest took me aside, and said, kindly enough, but still said it,

"My little wife must be careful how she runs on in my father's presence. He has a great deal of everything that might be thought levity."

Then all the vials of my wrath exploded and went off.

"Yes, I see how it is," I cried, passionately. "You and your father and your sister have got a box about a foot square that you want to squeeze me into. I have seen it ever since they came. And I can tell you it will take more than three of you to do it. There was no harm in what I said-none, whatever. If you only married me for the sake of screwing me down and freezing me up, why didn't you tell me so before it was too late?"

Ernest stood looking at me like one staring at a problem he had got to solve, and didn't know where to begin.

"I am very sorry," he said. "I thought you would be glad to have me give you this little hint. Of course I want you to appear your very best before my father and sister."

"My very best is my real self," I cried. "To talk like a woman of forty is unnatural to a girl of my age. If your father doesn't like me I wish he would go away, and not come here putting notions into your head, and making you as cold and hard as a stone. Mother liked to have me 'run on,' as you call it, and I wish I had stayed with her all my life."

"Do you mean," he asked, very gravely," that you really wish that?"

"No," I said, "I do not mean it," for his husky, troubled voice brought me to my senses. "All I mean is, that I love you so dearly, and you keep my heart feeling so hungry and restless and then you went and brought your father and sister here and never asked me if I should like it and you crowded mother out, and she lives all alone, and it isn't right! I always said that whoever married me had got to marry mother, and I never dreamed that you would disappoint me so!"

"Will you stop crying, and listen to me?" he said.

But I could not stop. The floods of the great deep were broken up at last, and I had to cry. If I could have told my troubles to someone I could thus have found vent for them, but there was no one to whom I had a right to speak of my husband.

Ernest walked up and down in silence. Oh, if I could have cried on his breast, and felt that he loved and pitied me!

At last, as I grew quieter, he came and sat by me.

"This has come upon me like a thunderclap," he said. "I did not know I kept your heart hungry. I did not know you wished your mother to live with us. And I took it for granted that my wife, with her high-toned, heroic character, would sustain me in every duty, and welcome my father and sister to our home. I do not know what I can do now. Shall I send them away?"

No, no!" I cried. "Only be good to me, Ernest, only love me, only look at me with your own eyes, and not with other people's. You knew I had faults when you married me I never tried to conceal them."

And did you fancy I had none myself?" he asked.

"No," I replied. "I saw no faults in you. Everybody said you were such a noble, good man and you spoke so beautifully one night at an evening meeting."

"Speaking beautifully is little to the purpose less one lives beautifully," he said, sadly. "And now is it possible that you and I, a Christian man and a Christian woman, are going on and on with scenes as this? Are you to wear your very life out because I have not your frantic way of loving, and am I to be made weary of mine because I cannot satisfy you?"

"But, Ernest," I said, "you used to satisfy me. Oh, how happy I was in those first days when we were always together and you seemed so fond me!" I was down on the floor by this time, and looking up into his pale, anxious face.

"Dear child," he said, "I do love you, and that more than you know. But you would not have me leave my work and spend my whole time telling you so?"

"You know I am not so silly," I cried.. "It is not fair, it is not right to talk as if I were. I ask for nothing unreasonable. I only want those little daily assurances of your affection which I should suppose would be spontaneous if you felt at all towards me as I do to you."

"The fact is," he returned, "I am absorbed in my work. It brings many grave cares and anxieties. I spend most of my time amid scenes of suffering and at dying beds. This makes me seem abstracted and cold, but it does not make you less dear. On the contrary, the sense it gives me of the brevity and sorrowfulness of life makes you doubly precious, since it constantly reminds me that sick beds and dying beds must sooner or later come to our home as to those of others."

I clung to him as he uttered these terrible words in an agony of terror.

"Oh, Ernest, promise me, promise me that you will not die first," I pleaded.

Foolish little thing!" he said, and was as silly, for a while, as the silliest heart could ask. Then he became serious again.

"Katy," he said, "if you can once make up your mind to the fact that I am an undemonstrative man, not all fire and fury and ecstasy as you are, yet loving you with all my heart, however it may seem, I think you will spare yourself much needless pain—and spare me, also."

"But I want, you to be demonstrative," I persisted.

"Then you must teach me. And about my father and sister, perhaps, we may find some way of relieving you by and by. Meanwhile, try to bear with the trouble they make, for my sake."

"But I do not mind the trouble! Oh, Ernest, how you do misunderstand me! What I mind is their coming between you and me and making you love me less."

"By this time there was a call for Ernest-it is a wonder there had not been forty-and he went.

"I feel as heart-sore as ever. What has been gained by this tempest ? Nothing at all! Poor Ernest! How can I worry him so when he is already full of care?

MARCH 20.-I have had such a truly beautiful letter today from dear mother! She gives up the hope of coming to spend her last years with us with a sweet patience that makes me cry whenever I think of it. What is the secret of this instant and cheerful consent to whatever God wills! Oh, that I had it, too! She begs me to be considerate and kind to Ernest's father and sister, and constantly to remind myself that my Heavenly Father has chosen to give me this care and trial on the very threshold of my married life. I am afraid I have quite lost sight of that in my indignation with Ernest for bringing them here.

APRIL 3.-Martha is closeted with Ernest in his office day and night. They never give me the least hint of what is going on in these secret meetings. Then this morning Sarah, my good, faithful cook, bounced into my room to give warning. She said she could not live where there were, two mistresses giving contrary directions.

"But, really, there is but one mistress," I urged. Then it came out that Martha went down every morning to look after the soap-fat, and to scrimp in the housekeeping, and see that there was no food wasted. I remembered then that she had inquired whether I attended to these details, evidently ranking such duties with saying one's prayers and reading one's Bible.

I flew to Ernest the moment he was at leisure and poured my grievances into his ear.

"Well, dear," he said, "suppose you give up the house-keeping to Martha! She will be far happier and you will be freed from much annoying, petty care."

I bit my tongue lest it should say something, and went back to Sarah.

"Suppose Miss Elliott takes charge of the housekeeping, and I have nothing to do with it, will you stay?"

"Indeed, and I won't then. I cannot bear her, and I won't put up with her nasty, scrimping, pinching ways!"

"Very well. Then you will have to go," I said, with great dignity, though just ready to cry. Ernest, on being applied to for wages, undertook to argue the question himself.

"My sister will take the whole charge," he began.

"And may and welcome for all me!" quoth Sarah. "I do not like her and never shall."

"Your liking or disliking her is of no consequence whatever," said Ernest. "You may dislike her as much as you please. But you must not leave us."

"Indeed, and I'm not going to stay and be put upon by her," persisted Sarah. So she has gone. We had to get dinner ourselves that is to say, Martha did, for she said I got in her way, and put her out with my awkwardness. I have been running hither and thither to find some angel who will consent to live in this ill-assorted household. Oh, how different everything is from what I had planned! I wanted a cheerful home, where I should be the centre of every joy a home like Auntie's, without a cloud. But Ernest's father sits, the personification of silent gloom, like a nightmare on my spirits Martha holds me in disfavor and contempt Ernest is absorbed in his profession, and I hardly see him. If he wants advice he asks it of Martha, while I sit, humbled, degraded, and ashamed, wondering why he ever married me at all. And then come interludes of wild joy when he appears just as he did in the happy days of our bridal trip, and I forget every grievance and hang on his words and looks like one intoxicated with bliss.

OCT. 2.-There has been another explosion. I held in as long as I could, and then flew into ten thousand pieces. Ernest had got into the habit of helping his father and sister at the table, and apparently forgetting me. It seems a little thing, but it chafed and fretted my already irritated soul till at last I was almost beside myself.

Yesterday they all three sat eating their breakfast and I, with empty plate, sat boiling over and, looking on, when Ernest brought things to a crisis by saying to Martha,

"If you can find time today I wish you would go out with me for half an hour or so. I want to consult you about-"

"Oh!" I said, rising, with my face all in a flame, do not trouble yourself to go out in order to escape me. I can leave the room and you can have your secrets to yourselves as you do your breakfast!"

I do not know which struck me, most, Ernest's appalled, grieved look or the glance exchanged between Martha and her father.

He did not hinder my leaving the room, and I went upstairs, as pitiable an object as could be seen. I heard him go to his office, then take his hat and set forth on his rounds. What wretched hours I passed, thus left alone! One moment I reproached myself, the next I was indignant at the long series of offences that had led to this disgraceful scene.

At last Ernest came.

He looked concerned, and a little pale.

"Oh, Ernest!" I cried, running to him, "I am so sorry I spoke to you as I did! But, indeed, I cannot stand the way things are going on I am wearing all out. Everybody speaks of my growing thin. Feel of my hands. They burn like fire."

"I knew you would be sorry, dear," he said. "Yes, your hands are hot, poor child."

There was a long, dreadful silence. And yet I was speaking, and perhaps he was. I was begging and beseeching God not to let us drift apart, not to let us lose one jot or tittle of our love to each other, to enable me to understand my dear, dear husband and make him understand me.

Then Ernest began.

"What was it vexed you, dear? What is it you cannot stand? Tell me. I am your husband, I love you, and I want to make you happy."

"Why, you are having so many secrets that you keep from me and you treat me as if I were only a child, consulting Martha about everything. And of late you seem to have forgotten that I am at the table and never help me to anything!"

"Secrets!" he re-echoed. "What possible secrets can I have?"

"I do not know," I said, sinking wearily back on the sofa. "Indeed, Ernest, I do not want to be selfish or exacting, but I am very unhappy."

"Yes, I see it, poor child. And if I have neglected you at the table, I do not wonder you are out of patience. I know how it has happened. While you were pouring out the coffee, I busied myself in caring for my father and Martha, and so forgot you. I do not give this as an excuse, but as a reason. I have really no excuse, and am ashamed of myself."

"Do not say that, darling," I cried, "it is I who ought to be ashamed for making such ado about a trifle."

"It is not a trifle," he said "and now to the other points. I dare say I have been careless about consulting Martha. But she has always been a sort of oracle in our family, and we all look up to her, and she is so much older than you. Then as to the secrets. Martha comes to my office to help me look over my books. I have been careless about my accounts, and she has kindly undertaken to attend to them for me."

"Could not I have done that?"

"No why your little head should be troubled about money matters? But to go on. I see that it was thoughtless in me not to tell you what we were about. But I am greatly perplexed and harassed in many ways. Perhaps you would feel better to know all about it. I have only kept it from you to spare you all the anxiety I could."

"Oh, Ernest," I said, "ought not a wife to share in all her husband's cares?"

"'No," he returned "but I will tell you all that is annoying me now. My father was in business in our native town, and went on prosperously for many years. Then the tide turned-he met with loss after loss, till nothing remained but the old homestead, and on that there was a mortgage. We concealed the state of things from my mother her health was delicate, and we never let her know a trouble we could spare her. Now she has gone, and we have found it necessary to sell our old home and to divide and scatter the family my father's mental distress when he found others suffering from his own losses threw him into the state in which you see him now. I have therefore assumed his debts, and with God's help hope in time to pay them to the uttermost farthing. It will be necessary for us to live economically until this is done. There are two pressing cases that I am trying to meet at once. This has given me a preoccupied air, I have no doubt, and made you suspect and misunderstand me. But now you know the whole, my darling."

I felt my injustice and childish folly very keenly, and told him so.

"But I think, dear Ernest," I added, "if you will not be hurt at my saying so, that you have led me to it by not letting me share at once in your cares. If you had at the outset just told me the whole story, you would have enlisted my sympathies in your father's behalf, and in your own. I should have seen the reasonableness of your breaking up the old home and bringing him here, and it would have taken the edge of my bitter, bitter disappointment about my mother."

"I feel very sorry about that," he said. "It would be a real pleasure to have her here. But as things are now, she could not be happy with us."

"There is no room," I put in.

"I am truly sorry. And now my dear little wife must have patience with her stupid blundering old husband, and we'll start together once more fair and square. Do not wait, next time, till you are so full that you boil over the moment I annoy you by my inconsiderate ways, come right and tell me."

I called myself all the horrid names I could think of.

"May I ask one thing more, now we are upon the subject?" I said at last. "Why couldn't your sister Helen have come here instead of Martha?"

He smiled a little.

"In the first place, Helen would be perfectly if she had the care of father in his present she is too young to have such responsibility. In the second place, my brother John, with whom she has gone to live, has a wife who would be quite crushed by my father and Martha. She is one of those little tender, soft souls one could crush fingers. Now, you are not of that sort you have force of character enough to enable you to live with them, while maintaining your own dignity and remaining yourself in spite of circum stances."

"I thought you admired Martha above all things and wanted me to be exactly like her."

"I do admire her, but I do not want you to be like anybody but yourself."

"But you nearly killed me by suggesting that I should take heed how I talked in your father's presence."

"Yes, dear it was very stupid of me, but my father has a standard of excellence in his mind by which he tests every woman this standard is my mother. She had none of your life and fun in her, and perhaps would not have appreciated your droll way of putting things any better than he and Martha do."

I could not help sighing a little when I thought what sort of people were watching my every word.

"There is nothing amiss to my mind," Ernest continued, "in your gay talk but my father has his own views as to what constitutes a religious character and cannot understand that real earnestness and real, genuine mirthfulness are consistent with each other."

He had to go now, and we parted as if for a week's separation, this one talk had brought us so near to each other. I understand him now as I never have done, and feel that he has given me as real a proof of his affection by unlocking the door of his heart and letting me see its cares, as I give him in my wild pranks and caresses and foolish speeches. How truly noble it is in him to take up his father's burden in this way! I must contrive to help to lighten it.

Chapter 12

NOVEMBER 6. - AUNTIE has put me in the way of doing that. I could not tell her the whole story, of course, but I made her understand that Ernest needed money for a generous purpose, and that I wanted to help him in it. She said the children needed both music and drawing lessons, and that she should be delighted if I would take them in hand. Auntie does not care a fig for accomplishments, but I think I am right in accepting her offer, as the children ought to learn to sing and to play and to draw. Of course, I cannot have them come here, as Ernest's father could not bear the noise they would make besides, I want to take him by surprise, and keep the whole thing a secret.

Nov. 14.-I have seen by the way Martha draws down the corners of her mouth of late, that I am unusually out of favor with her. This evening, Ernest, coming home quite late, found me lolling back in my chair, idling, after a hard day's work with my little cousins, and Martha sewing nervously away at the rate of ten knots an hour, which is the first pun I ever made.

"Why will you sit up and sew at such a rate, Martha?" he asked.

She twitched at her thread, broke it, and began with a new one before she replied.

"I suppose you find it convenient to have a whole shirt to your back."

I saw then that she was making his shirts! It made me both hot and cold at once. What must Ernest think of me?

It is plain enough what he thinks of her, for he said, quite warmly, for him—

"This is really too kind."

What right has she to prowl round among Ernest's things and pry into the state of his wardrobe? If I had not had my time so broken up with giving lessons, I should have found out that he needed new shirts and set to work on them. Though I must own I hate shirt making. I could not help showing that I felt aggrieved. Martha defended herself by saying that she knew young people would be young people, and would gad about, shirts or no shirts. Now it is not her fault that she thinks I waste my time gadding about, but I am just as angry with her as if she did. Oh, why couldn't I have had Helen, to be a pleasant companion and friend to me, instead of this old-well I won't say what.

And really, with so much to make me happy, what would become of me if I had no trials?

Nov. 15.-Today Martha has a house-cleaning mania, and has dragged me into it by representing the sin and misery of those deluded mortals who think servants know how to sweep and to scrub. In spite of my resolution not to get under her thumb, I have somehow let her rule and reign over me to such an extent that I can hardly sit up long enough to write this. Does the whole duty of woman consist in keeping her house distressingly clean and prim in making and baking and preserving and pickling in climbing to the top shelves of closets lest haply a little dust should lodge there, and getting down on her hands and knees to inspect the carpet? The truth is there is not one point of sympathy between Martha and myself, not one. One would think that our love to Ernest would furnish it. But her love aims at the abasement of his character and mine at its elevation. She thinks I should bow down to and worship him, jump up and offer him my chair when he comes in, feed him with every unwholesome dainty he fancies, and feel myself honored by his acceptance of these services. I think it is for him to rise and offer me a seat, because I am a woman and his wife and that a silly subservience on my part is degrading to him and to myself. And I am afraid I make known these sentiments to her in a most unpalatable way.

Nov. 18.-Oh, I am so happy that I sing for joy! Dear Ernest has given me such a delightful surprise! He says he has persuaded James to come and spend his college days here, and finally study medicine with him. Dear, darling old James! He is to be here tomorrow. He is to have the little hall bedroom fitted up for him, and he will be here several years. Next to having mother, this is the nicest thing that could happen. We love each other so dearly, and get along so beautifully together I wonder how he'll like Martha with her grim ways, and Ernest's father with his melancholy ones.

Nov. 30.-James has come, and the house already seems lighter and cheerier. He is not in the least annoyed by Martha or her father, and though he is as jovial as the day is long, they actually seem to like him. True to her theory on the subject, Martha invariably rises at his entrance, and offers him her seat! He pretends not to see it, and runs to get one for her! Then she takes comfort in seeing him consume her good things, since his gobbling them down is a sort of tacit tribute to their merits.

Mrs. Embury was here today. She says there is not much the matter with Ernest's father, that he has only got the hypo. I do not know exactly what this is, but I believe it is thinking something is the matter with you when there isn't. At any rate, I put it to you, my dear old journal, whether it is pleasant to live with people who behave in this way?

In the first place, all he talks about is his fancied disease. He gets book after book from the office and studies and ponders his case till he grows quite yellow. One day he says he has found out the seat of his disease to be the liver, and changes his diet to meet that view of the case. Martha has to do him up in mustard, and he takes kindly to blue pills. In a day or two, he finds his liver is all right, but that his brain is all wrong. The mustard goes now to the back of his neck, and he takes solemn leave of us all, with the assurance that his last hour has come. Finding that he survives the night, however, he transfers the seat of his disease to the heart, spends hours in counting his pulse, refuses to take exercise lest he should bring on palpitations, and warns us all to prepare to follow him. Everybody who comes in has to hear the whole story, every one prescribes something, and he tries each remedy in turn. These all failing to reach his case, he is s plunged into ten-fold gloom. He complains that God has cast him off forever, and that his sins are like the sands of the sea for number. I am such a goose that I listen to all these varying moods and symptoms with the solemn conviction that he is going to die immediately I bathe his head, and count his pulse, and fan him, and take down his dying depositions for Ernest's solace after he has gone. And I talk theology to him by the hour, while Martha bakes and brews in the kitchen, or makes mince pies, after eating which one might give him the whole Bible at one dose, without the smallest effect.

Today I stood by his chair, holding his head and whispering such consoling passages as I thought might comfort him, when James burst in, singing and tossing his cap in the air.

"Come here, young man, and hear my last testimony. I am about to die. The end draws near," were the sepulchral words that made him bring his song to an abrupt close.

"I shall take it very ill of you, sir," quoth James, "if you go and die before giving me that cane you promised me."

Who could die decently under such circumstances? The poor old man revived immediately, but looked a good deal injured. After James had gone out, he said:

"It is very painful to one who stands on the very verge of the eternal world to see the young so thoughtless."

"But James is not thoughtless," I said. "It is only his merry way."

"Daughter Katherine," he went on, "you are very kind to the old man, and you will have your reward. But I wish I could feel sure of your state before God. I greatly fear you deceive yourself, and that the ground of your hope is delusive."

I felt the blood rush to my face. At first, I was staggered a good deal. But is a mortal man who cannot judge of his own state to decide mine? It is true he sees my faults anybody can, who looks. But he does not see my prayers, or my tears of shame and sorrow he does not know how many hasty words I repress how earnestly I am aiming, all the day long, to do right in all the little details of life. He does not know that it costs my fastidious nature an appeal to God every time I kiss his poor old face, and that what would be an act of worship in him is an act of self-denial in me. How should he? The Christian life is a hidden known only by the eye that sees in secret. And I do believe this life is mine.

Up to this time, I have contrived to get along without calling Ernest's father by any name. I mean now to make myself turn over a new leaf.

DECEMBER 7.-James is my perpetual joy and pride. We read and sing together, just as we used to do in our old school days. Martha sits by, with her work, grimly approving for is he not a man? And, as if my cup of felicity were not full enough, I am to have my dear old pastor come here to settle over this church, and I shall once more hear his beloved voice in the pulpit. Ernest has managed the whole thing. He says the state of Dr. C.'s health makes the change quite necessary, and that he can avail himself of the best surgical advice this city affords, in case his old difficulties recur. I rejoice for myself and for this church, but mother will miss him sadly.

I am leading a very busy, happy life, only I am, perhaps, working a little too hard. What with my scholars, the extra amount of housework Martha contrives to get out of me, the practicing I must keep up if I am to teach, and the many steps I have to take, I have not only no idle moments, but none too many for recreation. Ernest is so busy himself that he fortunately does not see what a race I am running.

JANUARY 16, 1838.-The first anniversary of our wedding-day, and like all days, has had its lights and its shades. I thought I would celebrate it in such a way as to give pleasure to everybody, and spent a good deal of time in getting up a little gift for each, from Ernest and myself. And I took special pains to have a good dinner, particularly for father. Yes, I had made up my mind to call him by that sacred name for the first time today, cost what it may. But he shut himself up in his room directly after breakfast, and when dinner was ready refused to come down. This cast a gloom over us all Then Martha was nearly distracted because a valuable dish had been broken in the kitchen, and could not recover her equanimity at all. Worst of all Ernest, who is not in the least sentimental, never said a word about our wedding-day, and. didn't give me a thing! I have kept hoping all day that he would make me some little present, no matter how small, but now it is too late he has gone out to be gone all night, probably, and thus ends the day, an utter failure.

I feel a good deal disappointed. Besides, when I look back over this my first year of married life, I do not feel satisfied with myself at all. I cannot help feeling that I have been selfish and unreasonable towards Ernest in a great many ways, and as contrary towards Martha as if I enjoyed a state of warfare between us. And I have felt a good deal of secret contempt for her father, with his moods and tenses, his pillboxes and his plasters, his feastings and his fastings. I do not understand how a Christian can make such slow progress as I do, and how old faults can hang on so.

If I had made any real progress, should I not be sensible of it?

I have been reading over the early part of this journal, and when I came to the conversation I had with Mrs. Cabot, in which I made a list of my wants, I was astonished that I could ever have had such contemptible ones. Let me think what I really and truly most want now.

First of all, then, if God should speak to me at this moment and offer to give just one thing, and that alone, I should say without hesitation,

Love to Thee, O my Master!

Next to that, if I could have one thing more, I would choose to be a thoroughly unselfish, devoted wife. Down in my secret heart I know there lurks another wish, which I am ashamed of. It is that in some way or other, some right way, I could be delivered from Martha and her father. I shall never be any better while they are here to tempt me!

FEBRUARY 1.-Ernest spoke today of one of his patients, a Mrs. Campbell, who is a great sufferer, but whom he describes as the happiest, most cheerful person he ever met. He rarely speaks of his patients. Indeed, he rarely speaks of anything. I felt strangely attracted by what he said of her, and asked so many questions that at last he proposed to take me to see her. I caught at the idea very eagerly, and have just come home from the visit greatly moved and touched. She is confined to her bed, and is quite helpless, and at times her sufferings are terrible. She received me with a sweet smile, however, and led me on to talk more of myself than I ought to have done. I wish Ernest had not left me alone with her, so that I should have had the restraint of his presence.

FEB. 14.-I am so fascinated with Mrs. Campbell that I cannot help going to see her again and again. She seems to me like one whose conflict and dismay are all over, and who looks on other human beings with an almost divine love and pity. To look at life as she does, to feel as she does, to have such a personal love to Christ as she has, I would willingly go through every trial and sorrow. When I told her so, she smiled, a little sadly.

"Much as you envy me," she said, "my faith is not yet so strong that I do not shudder at the thought of a young enthusiastic girl like you, going through all I have done in order to learn a few simple lessons which God was willing to teach me sooner and without the use of a rod, if I had been ready for them."

"But you are so happy now," I said.

"Yes, I am happy," she replied, "and such happiness is worth all it costs. If my flesh shudders at the remembrance of what I have endured, my faith sustains God through the whole. But tell me a little more about yourself, my dear. I should so love to give you a helping hand, if I might."

"You know," I began, "dear Mrs. Campbell, that there are some trials that cannot do us any good. They only call out all there is in us that is unlovely and severe."

"I do not know of any such trials," she replied.

"Suppose you had to live with people who were perfectly uncongenial who misunderstood you, and who were always getting into your way as stumbling-blocks?"

"If I were living with them and they made me unhappy, I would ask God to relieve me of this trial if He thought it best. If He did not think it best, I would then try to find out the reason. He might have two reasons. One would be the good they might do me. The other the good I might do them."

"But in the case I was supposing, neither party can be of the least use to the other."

"You forget perhaps the indirect good one may in by living with uncongenial, tempting persons. First, such people do good by the very self-denial and self-control their mere presence demands. Then, their making one's home less home-like and perfect than it would be in their absence, may help to render our real home in heaven more attractive."

"But suppose one cannot exercise self-control, and is always flying out and flaring up?" I objected.

"I should say that a Christian who was always doing that," she replied, gravely, "was in pressing need of just the trial God sent when He shut him up to such a life of hourly temptation. We only know ourselves and what we really are, when the force of circumstances bring us out."

"It is very mortifying and painful to find how weak one is."

"That is true. But our mortifications are some of God's best physicians, and do much toward healing our pride and self-conceit."

"Do you really think, then, that God deliberately appoints to some of His children a lot where their worst passions are excited, with a desire to bring good out of this seeming evil? Why I have always supposed the best thing that could happen to me, instance, would be to have a home exactly to my mind a home where all were forbearing, loving and good-tempered, a sort of little heaven below."

"If you have not such a home, my dear, are you sure it is not partly your own fault?"

"Of course it is my own fault. Because I am very quick-tempered I want to live with good-tempered people."

"That is very benevolent in you," she said, archly.

I colored, but went on.

"Oh, I know I am selfish. And therefore I want live with those who are not so. I want to live with persons to whom I can look for an example, and who will constantly stimulate me to something higher."

"But if God chooses quite another lot for you, you may be sure that He sees that you need something totally different from what you want. You just now that you would gladly go through any trial in order to attain a personal love to Christ that should become the ruling principle of your life. Now as soon as God sees this desire in you, is He not kind, is He not wise, in appointing such trials as He knows will lead to this end?"

I meditated long before I answered. Was God really asking me not merely to let Martha and her father live with me on sufferance, but to rejoice that He had seen fit to let them harass and embitter my domestic life?"

"I thank you for the suggestion," I said, at last.

"1 want to say one thing more," Mrs. Campbell resumed, after another pause. "We look at our fellow-men too much from the standpoint of our own prejudices. They may be wrong, they may have their faults and foibles, and they may call out all that is meanest and most hateful in us. But they are not all wrong they have their virtues, and when they excite our bad passions by their own, they may be as ashamed and sorry as we are irritated. And I think some of the best, most contrite, most useful of men and women, whose prayers prevail with God, and bring down blessings into the homes in which they dwell often possess unlovely traits that furnish them with their best discipline. The very fact that they are ashamed of themselves drives them to God they feel safe in His presence, and while they lie in the very dust of self-confusion at His feet they are dear to Him and have power with Him."

"That is a comforting word, and I thank you for it," I said. My heart was full, and I longed to stay and hear her talk on. But I had already exhausted her strength. On the way home, I felt as I suppose people do when they have caught a basketful of fish. I always am delighted to catch a new idea I thought I would get all the benefit out of Martha and her father, and as I went down to tea, after taking off my things, felt like a holy martyr who had as good as won a crown.

I found, however, that the butter was horrible. Martha had insisted that she alone was capable of selecting that article, and had ordered a quantity from her own village, which I could not eat myself and was ashamed to have on my table. I pushed back my plate in disgust.

"I hope, Martha, that you have not ordered much of this odious stuff!" I cried.

Martha replied that it was of the very first quality, and appealed to her father and Ernest, who both agreed with her, which I thought very unkind and unjust. I rushed into a hot debate on the subject, during which Ernest maintained that ominous silence that indicates his not being pleased, and it irritated and led me on. I would far rather he should say, "Katy, you are behaving like a child and I wish you would stop talking."

"Martha," I said, "you will persist that the butter is good, because you ordered it. If you will only own that, I won't say another word."

"I cannot say it," she returned. "Mrs. Jones' butter is invariably good. I never heard it found fault with before. The trouble is you are so hard to please."

"No, I am not. And you cannot convince me that if the buttermilk is not perfectly worked out, the butter could be fit to eat."

This speech I felt to be a masterpiece. It was time to let her know how learned I was on the subject of butter, though I wasn't brought up to make it or see it made.

But here Ernest put in a little oil.

"I think you are both right," he said. "Mrs. Jones makes good butter, but just this once she failed. I dare say it won't happen again, and mean while this can be used for making seed-cakes, and we can get a new supply."

This was his masterpiece. A whole firkin of butter made up into seed cakes!

Martha turned to encounter him on that head, and I slipped off to my room to look, with a miserable sense of disappointment, at my folly and weakness in making so much ado about nothing. I find it hard to believe that it can do me good to have people live with me who like rancid butter, and who disagree with me in everything else.

Chapter 13

MARCH 1. - AUNTIE sent for us all to dine with her today to celebrate Lucy's fifteenth birthday. Ever since Lucy behaved so heroically in regard to little Emma, really saving her life, Ernest says Auntie seems to feel that she cannot do enough for her. The child has taken the most unaccountable fancy to me, strangely enough, and when we got there, she came to meet me with something like cordiality.

"Mamma permits me to be the bearer of agreeable news," she said, "because this is my birthday. A friend, of whom you are very fond, has just arrived, and is impatient to embrace you.

"To embrace me?" I cried. "You foolish child!" And the next moment I found myself in my mother's arms!

The despised Lucy had been the means of giving me this pleasure. It seems that Auntie had told her she should choose her own birthday treat, and that, after solemn meditation, she had decided that to see dear mother again would be the most agreeable thing she could think of. I have never told you, dear journal, why I did not go home last summer, and never shall. If you choose to fancy that I couldn't afford it, you can!

Well! Wasn't it nice to see mother, and to read in her dear, loving face that she was satisfied with her poor, wayward Katy, and fond of her as ever! I only longed for Ernest's coming, that she might see us together, and see how he loved me.

He came I rushed out to meet him and dragged him in. But it seemed as if he had grown stupid and awkward. All through the dinner, I watched for one of those loving glances, which should proclaim to mother the good understanding between us, but watched in vain.

"It will come by and by," I thought. "When we get by ourselves mother will see how fond of me he is." But "by and by" it was just the same. I was preoccupied, and mother asked me if I were well. It was all very foolish I dare say, and yet I did want to have her know that with all my faults he still loves me. Then, besides this disappointment, I have to reproach myself for misunderstanding poor Lucy as I have done. Because she was not all fire and fury like myself, I need not have assumed that she had no heart. It is just like me I hope I shall never be so severe in my judgment again.

APRIL 30.-Mother has just gone. Her visit has done me a world of good. She found out something to like in father at once, and then something good in Martha. She says father's sufferings are real, not fancied that his error is not knowing where to locate his disease, and is starving one week and over-eating the next. She charged me not to lay up future misery for myself by misjudging him now, and to treat him as a daughter ought without the smallest regard to his appreciation of it. Then as to Martha, she declares that I have no idea how much she does to reduce our expenses, to keep the house in order and to relieve us from care. "But, mother," I said, "did you notice what horrid butter we have? And it is all her doing."

"But the butter won't last forever," she replied. "Do not make yourself miserable about such a trifle. For my part, it is a great relief to me to know that with your delicate health you have this tower of strength to lean on."

"But my health is not delicate, mother."

"You certainly look pale and thin."

"Oh, well," I said, whereupon she fell to giving me all sorts of advice about getting up on stepladders, and climbing on chairs, and sewing too much and all that.

JUNE 15.-The weather, or something, makes me rather languid and stupid. I begin to think that Martha is not an entire nuisance in the house. I have just been to see Mrs. Campbell. In answer to my routine of lamentations, she took up a book and read me what was called, as nearly as I can remember, "Four steps that lead to peace."

"Be desirous of doing the will of another rather than thine own."

"Choose always to have less, rather than more."

"Seek always the lowest place, and to be inferior to everyone."

"Wish always, and pray, that the will of God may be wholly fulfilled in thee."

I was much struck with these directions but I said, despondently:

"If peace can only be found at the end of such hard roads, I am sure I shall always be miserable."

"Are you miserable now?" she asked.

"Yes, just now I am. I do not mean that I have no happiness I mean that I am in a disheartened mood, weary of going round and round in circles, committing the same sins, uttering the same confessions, and making no advance."

"My dear," she said, after a time, "have you a perfectly distinct, settled view of what Christ is to the human soul?"

"I do not know. I understand, of course, more or less perfectly, that my salvation depends on. Him alone it is His gift."

"But do you see, with equal clearness, which your sanctification must be as fully His gift, as your salvation is?"

"No," I said, after a little thought. "I have had a feeling that He has done His part, and now I must do mine."

"My dear," she said, with much tenderness and feeling, "then the first thing you have to do is to learn Christ."

"But how?"

"On your knees, my child, on your knees!" She was tired, and I came away and I have indeed been on my knees.

JULY 1.-I think that I do begin, dimly it is true, but really, to understand that this terrible work which I was trying to do myself, is Christ's work, and must be done and will be done by Him. I take some pleasure in the thought, and wonder why it has all this time been hidden from me, especially after what Dr. C. said in his letter. But I get hold of this idea in a misty, unsatisfactory way. If Christ is to do all, what am I to do? And have I not been told, over and over again, that the Christian life is one of conflict, and that I am to fight like a good soldier?

AUGUST 5.-Dr. Cabot has come just as I need him most. I long for one of those good talks with him, which always used to strengthen me so. I feel a perfect weight of depression that makes me a burden to myself and to poor Ernest, who, after visiting sick people all day, needs to come home to a cheerful wife. But he comforts me with the assurance that this is merely physical despondency, and that I shall get over it by and by. How kind, how even tender he is! My heart is getting all it wants from him, only I am too stupid to enjoy him as I ought. Father, too, talks far less about his own bad feelings, and seems greatly concerned at mine. As to Martha, I have done trying to get sympathy or love from her. She cannot help it, I suppose, but she is very hard and dry towards me, and I feel such a longing to throw myself on her mercy, and to have one little smile to assure me that she has forgiven me for being Ernest's wife, and so different from what she would have chosen for him.

Dr. Elliott to Mrs. Mortimer:

OCTOBER 4, 1838. - My dear Katy's Mother-You will rejoice with us when I tell you that we are the happy parents of a very fine little boy. My dearest wife sends "an ocean of love" to you, and says she will write herself tomorrow. That I shall not be very likely to allow, as you will imagine. She is doing extremely well, and we have everything to be grateful for. Your affectionate Son, J. E. ELLIOTT.

Mrs. Crofton to Mrs. Mortimer:

I am sure, my dear sister, that the doctor has riot written you more than five lines about the great event that has made such a stir in our domestic circle. So I must try to supply the details you will want to hear…1 need not add that our darling Katy behaved nobly. Her self-forgetfulness and consideration for others were really beautiful throughout the whole scene. The doctor may well be proud of her, and I took care to tell him so ill presence of that dreadful sister of his. I never met so angular, so uncompromising a person as she is in all my life. She does not understand Katy, and never can, and I find it hard to realize that living with such a person can furnish a wholesome discipline, which is even more desirable than the most delightful home. And yet I not only know that is true in the abstract, but I see that it is so in the fact. Katy is acquiring both self-control and patience and her Christian character is developing in a way that amazes me. I cannot but hope that God will, in time, deliver her from this trial indeed, feel sure that when it has done its beneficent work He will do so. Martha Elliott is a good woman, but her goodness is without grace or beauty. She takes excellent care of Katy, keeps her looking as if she had just come out of a bandbox, as the saying and always has her room in perfect order. But one misses the loving word, the re-assuring smile, the delicate, thoughtful little forbearance, that ought to adorn every sickroom, and light it up with genuine sunshine. There is one comfort about it, however, and that is that I can spoil dear Katy to my heart's content.

As to the baby, he is a fine little fellow, and his mother is so happy in him that she can afford to do without some other pleasures. I shall write again in a few days. Meanwhile, you may rest assured that I love your Katy almost as well as you do, and shall be with her most of the time till she is quite herself again.

James

To his mother:

Of course, there never was such a baby before on the face of the earth. Katy is so nearly wild with joy, that you cannot get her to eat or sleep or do any of the proper things that her charming sister-in-law thinks becoming under the circumstances. You never saw anything so pretty in your life, as she is now. I hope the doctor is as much in love with her as I am. He is the best fellow in the world, and Katy is just the wife for him.

Nov. 4.-My darling baby is a month old today. I never saw such a splendid child. I love him so that I lie awake nights to watch him. Martha says, in her dry way, that I had better show my love by sleeping and eating for him, and Ernest says I shall, as soon as I get stronger. But I do not get strong, and that discourages me.

Nov. 26.-I begin to feel rather more like myself, and as if I could write with less labor. I have had in these few past weeks such a revelation of suffering, and such a revelation of joy, as mortal mind can hardly conceive of. The world I live in now is a new world a world full of suffering that leads to unutterable felicity. Oh, this precious, precious baby! How can I thank God enough for giving him to me!

I see now why He has put some thorns into my domestic life but for them I should be too happy to live. It does not seem just the moment to com plain, and yet, as I can speak to no one, it is a relief, a great relief, to write about my trials. During my whole sickness, Martha has been so hard, so cold, so unsympathizing that sometimes it has seemed as if my cup of trial could not hold another drop. She routed me out of bed when I was so languid that everything seemed a burden, and when sitting up made me faint away. I heard her say to herself, that I had no constitution and had no business to get married. The worst of all is that during that dreadful night before baby came, she kept asking Ernest to lie down and rest, and was sure he would kill himself, and all that, while she had not one word of pity for me. But, oh, why need I let this rankle in my heart! Why cannot I turn my thoughts entirely to my darling baby, my dear husband, and all the other sources of joy that make my home a happy one in spite of this one discomfort! I hope I am learning some useful lessons from my joys and from my trials, and that both will serve to make me in earnest, and to keep me so.

DEC. 4.-We have had a great time about poor baby's name. I expected to call him Raymond, for my own dear father, as a matter of course. It seemed a small gratification for mother in her loneliness. Dear mother! How little I have known all these years what I cost her! But it seems there has been a Jotham in the family ever since the memory of man, each eldest son handing down his father's name to the next in descent, and Ernest's real name is Jotham Ernest—of all the extraordinary combinations! His mother would add the latter name in spite of everything. Ernest behaved very well through the whole affair, and said he had no feeling about it all. But he was so gratified when I decided to keep up the family custom that I feel rewarded for the sacrifice.

Father is in one of his gloomiest moods. As I sat caressing baby today, he said to me:

"Daughter Katherine, I trust you make it a subject of prayer to God that you may be kept from idolatry."

"No, father," I returned, "I never do. An idol is something one puts in God's place, and I do not put baby there."

He shook his head and said the heart is deceitful above all things, and desperately wicked.

"I have heard mother say that we might love an earthly object as much as we pleased, if we only love God better." I might have added, but of course, I didn't that I prayed every day that I might love Ernest and baby better and better. Poor father seemed puzzled and troubled by what I did say, and after musing a while, went on thus:

'The Almighty is a great and terrible Being. He cannot bear a rival He will have the whole heart or none of it. When I see a young woman so absorbed in a created being as you are in that infant, and in your other friends, I tremble for you, and I tremble for you!"

'But, father," I persisted, "God gave me this child, and He gave me my heart, just as it is."

'Yes and that heart needs renewing."

"I hope it is renewed," I replied. "But I know there is a great work still to be done in it. And the more effectually it is done the more loving I shall grow. Do not you see, father? Do not you see that the more Christ-like I become the more I shall be filled with love for every living thing?"

He shook his head, but pondered long, as he always does, on whatever he considers audacious. As for me, I am vexed with my presumption in disputing with him, and am sure, too, that I was trying to show off what little wisdom I have picked up. Besides, my mountain does not stand so strong as it did. Perhaps I am making idols out of Ernest and the baby.

JANUARY 16, 1839.-This is our second wedding day. I did not expect much from it, after last year's failure. Father was very gloomy at breakfast, and retired to his room directly after it. No one could get in to make his bed, and he would not come down to dinner. I wonder Ernest lets him go on so. But his rule seems to be to let everybody have their own way. He certainly lets me have mine. After dinner he gave me a book I have been wanting for some time, and had asked him for-"The Imitation of Christ." Ever since that day at Mrs. Campbell's I have felt that, I should like it, though I did think, in old times, that it preached too hard a doctrine. I read aloud to him the "Four Steps to Peace" he said they were admirable, and then took it from me and began reading to himself, here and there. I felt the precious moments when I had got him all to myself were passing away, and was becoming quite out of patience with him when the words "Constantly seek to have less, rather than more," flashed into my mind. I suppose this direction had reference to worldly good, but I despise money, and despise people who love it, the riches I crave are not silver and gold, but my husband's love and esteem. And of these must I desire to have less rather than more? I puzzled myself over this question in vain, but when I silently prayed to be satisfied with just what God chose to give me of the wealth I crave, yes, hunger and thirst for, I certainly felt a sweet content, for the time, at least, that was quite resting and quieting. And just as I had reached that acquiescent mood, Ernest threw down his book, and came and caught me in his arms.

"I thank God," he said, "my precious wife, that I married you this day. The wisest thing I ever did was when I fell in love with you and made a fool of myself!"

What a speech for my silent old darling to make! Whenever he says and does a thing out of character, and takes me all by surprise, how delightful he is! Now the world is a beautiful world, and so is everybody in it. I met Martha on the stairs after Ernest had gone, and caught her and kissed her. She looked perfectly astonished.

"What spirits the child has!" I heard her whisper to herself "no sooner down than up again."

And she sighed. Can it be that under that stern and hard crust there lie hidden affections and perhaps hidden sorrows?

I ran back and asked, as kindly as I could, "What makes you sigh, Martha? Is anything troubling you? Have I done anything to annoy you?"

"You do the best you can," she said, and pushed past me to her own room.

Chapter 14

JAN.30. - WHO would have thought I would have anything more to do with poor old Susan Green? Dr. Cabot came to see me today, and told me the strangest thing! It seems that the nurse who performed the last offices for her was taken sick about six months ago, and that Dr. Cabot visited her from time to time. Her physician said she needed nothing but rest and good, nourishing food to restore her strength, yet she did not improve at all, and at last it came out that she was not taking the food the doctor ordered, because she could not afford to do so, having lost what little money she had contrived to save. Dr. Cabot, on learning this, gave her enough out of Susan's legacy to meet her case, and in doing so told her about that extraordinary will. The nurse then assured him that when she reached Susan's room and found the state that she was in, and that I was praying with her, she had remained waiting in silence, fearing to interrupt me. She saw me faint, and sprang forward just in time to catch me and keep me from falling.

"I take great pleasure, therefore," Dr. Cabot continued, "in making over Susan's little property to you, to whom it belongs and I cannot help congratulating you that you have had the honor and the privilege of perhaps leading that poor, benighted soul to Christ, even at the eleventh hour."

"Oh, Dr. Cabot '." I cried, "What a relief it is to hear you say that! For I have always reproached myself for the cowardice that made me afraid to speak to her of her Savior. It takes less courage to speak to God than to man."

"It is my belief," replied Dr. Cabot, "that every prayer offered in the name of Jesus is sure to have its answer. Every such prayer is dictated by the Holy Spirit, and therefore finds acceptance with God and if your cry for mercy on poor Susan's soul did not prevail with Him in her behalf, as we may hope it did, then He has answered it in some other way."

These words impressed me very much. To think that every one of my poor prayers is answered! Every one!

Dr. Cabot then returned to the subject of Susan's will, and in spite of all I could say to the contrary, insisted that he had no legal right to this money, and that I had. He said he hoped that it would help to relieve us from some of the petty economies now rendered necessary by Ernest's struggle to meet his father's liabilities. Instantly my idol was rudely thrown down from his pedestal. How could he reveal to Dr. Cabot a secret he had pretended it cost him so much to confide to me, his wife? I could hardly restrain tears of shame and vexation, but did control myself so far as to say that I would sooner die than appropriate Susan's hard earnings to such a purpose, and that I should use it for the poor, as I was sure he would have done. He then advised me to invest the principal, and use the interest from year to year, as occasions presented themselves. So, I shall have more than a hundred dollars to give away each year, as long as I live! How perfectly delightful! I can hardly conceive of anything that give me so much pleasure! Poor old Susan! How many hearts she shall cause to sing for joy!

Feb. 25.-Things have not gone on well of late. Dearly as I love Ernest, he has lowered himself in my eye by telling that to Dr. Cabot. It would have been far nobler to be silent concerning his sacrifices and he certainly grows harder, graver, sterner every day. He is all shut up within himself, and I am growing afraid of him. It must be that he is bitterly disappointed in me, and takes refuge in this awful silence. Oh, if I could only please him, and know that I pleased him, how different my life would be!

Baby does not .seem well. I have often plumed myself on the thought that having a doctor for his father would be such an advantage to him, as he would be ready 'to attack the first symptoms of disease. But Ernest hardly listens to me when I express anxiety. About this or that, and if I ask a question he replies, "Oh, you know better than I do. Mothers know' by instinct how to manage babies." But I do not know by instinct, or in any other way, and I often wish that the time I spent over my music had been spent learning how to meet all the little emergencies that are constantly arising since baby came. How I used to laugh in my sleeve at those anxious mothers who lived near us and always seemed to be in hot water. Martha will take baby when I have other things to attend to, and she keeps him every Sunday afternoon that I may go to church, but she knows no more about his physical training than I do. If my dear mother were only here! I feel a good deal worn out. What with the care of baby, who is restless at night, and with whom I walk about lest he should keep Ernest awake, the depressing influence of father's presence, Martha's disdain, and Ernest keeping so aloof from me, life seems to me little better than a burden that I have not strength to carry and would gladly lay down.

MARCH 3.-If it were not for James I believe I should sink. He is so kind and affectionate, so ready to fill up the gaps Ernest leaves empty, and is so sunshiny and gay that I cannot be entirely sad. Baby, too, is a precious treasure it would be wicked to cloud his little life with my depression. I try to look at him always with a smiling face, for he already distinguishes between a cheerful and a sad countenance.

I am sure that there is something in Christ's gospel that would soothe and sustain me amid these varied trials, if I only knew what it is, and how to put forth my hand and take it. But as it is, I feel very desolate. Ernest often congratulates me on having had such a good night's rest, when I have been up and down every hour with baby, half asleep frozen and exhausted. But he shall sleep at any rate.

April 5.-The first rays of spring make me more languid than ever Martha cannot be made to understand that nursing such a large, voracious baby, losing sleep, and confinement within doors, are enough to account for this. She is constantly speaking in terms of praise of those who keep up even when they do feel a little out of sorts, and says she always does. In the evening, after baby gets to sleep, I feel fit for nothing but to lie on the sofa, dozing but she sees in this only a lazy habit, which ought not to be tolerated, and is constantly devising ways to rouse and set me at work. If I had more leisure for reading, meditation, and prayer, I might still be happy. But all the morning, I must have baby till he takes his nap, and as soon as he gets to sleep I must put my room in order, and by that time all the best part of the day is gone. And at night, I am so tired that I can hardly feel anything but my weariness. That, too, is .my only chance of seeing Ernest and if I lock my door and fall upon my knees, I keep listening for his step, ready to spring to welcome should he come. This is wrong, I know, but how can I live without one loving word from him, and every day I am hoping it will come.

MAY 2-Auntie was here today. I had not seen her for some weeks. She exclaimed at my looks in a tone that seemed to upbraid Ernest and Martha though of course she did not mean to do that.

"You are not fit to have the whole care of that great boy at night," said she, "and you ought to begin to feed him, both for his sake and your own.

"I am willing to take the child at night," Martha said, a little stiffly. "But I supposed his mother preferred to keep him herself."

"And so I do," I cried. "I should be perfectly miserable if I had to give him up just as he is getting teeth, and so wakeful."

"What are you taking to keep up your strength, dear?" asked Auntie.

"Nothing in particular," I said.

"Very well, it is time the doctor looked after that," she cried. "It really never will do to let you run down in this way. Let me look at baby. Why, my child, his gums need lancing."

"So I have told Ernest half a dozen times," I declared. "But he is always in a hurry, and says another time will do."

"I hope baby won't have convulsions while he is waiting for that other time," said Auntie, looking almost savagely at Martha. I never saw Auntie so nearly out of humor.

At dinner, Martha began.

"I think, brother, the baby needs attention. Mrs. Crofton has been here and says so. And she seems to find Katherine run down. I am sure if I had known it I should have taken her in hand and built her up. But she did not complain."

"She never complains," father here put in, calling all the blood I had into my face, my heart so leaped for joy at his kind word.

Ernest looked at me and caught the illumination of my face.

"You look well, dear," he said. "But if you do not feel so you ought to tell us. As to baby, I will attend to him directly."

So Martha's one word prevailed where my twenty fell to the ground.

Baby is much relieved, and has fallen into a sweet sleep. And I have had time to carry my tired, oppressed heart to my compassionate Savior, and to tell Him what I cannot utter to any human ear. How strange it is that when, through many years of leisure and strength, prayer was only a task, it is now my chief solace if I can only snatch time for it.

Mrs. Embury has a little daughter. How glad I am for her! She is going to give it my name. That is a real pleasure.

JULY 4.-Baby is ten months old today, and in spite of everything is bright and well. I have come home to mother. Ernest waked up at last to see that something must be done, and when he is awake, he is very wide awake. So he brought me home. Dear mother is perfectly delighted, only she will make an ado about my health. But I feel a good deal better, and think I shall get nicely rested here. How pleasant it is to feel myself watched by friendly eyes, my faults excused and forgiven, and what is best in me called out. I have been writing to Ernest, and have told him honestly how annoyed and pained I was at learning that he had told his secret to Dr. Cabot.

JULY 12.-Ernest writes that he has had no communication with Dr. Cabot or anyone else on subject that, touching his father's honor as it does, he regards as a sacred one.

"You say, dear," he said, "You often say, that I do not understand you. Are you sure that you understand me?"

Of course, I do not. How can I? How can I reconcile his marrying me and professing to do it with delight, with his indifference to my society, his reserve, his carelessness about my health?

But his letters are very kind, and really warmer than he is. I can hardly wait for them, and then, though my pride bids me to be reticent as he is, my heart runs away with me, and I pour out upon him such floods of affection that I am sure he is half drowned.

Mother says baby is splendid.

AUGUST 1.-When I took leave of Ernest I was glad to get away. I thought he would perhaps find after I was gone that he missed something out of his life and would welcome me home with a little of the old love. But I did not dream that he would not find it easy to do without me till summer was over, and when, this morning, he came suddenly upon us, carpet-bag in hand, I could do nothing but cry in his arms like a tired child.

And now I had the silly triumph of having mother see that he loved me!

"How could you get away?" I asked at last. "And what made you come? And how long can you stay?"

"I could get away because I would," he replied. "And I came because I wanted to come. And I can stay three days."

Three days of Ernest all to myself!

AUGUST 5.-He has gone, but he has left behind him a happy wife and the memory of three happy days.

After the first joy of our meeting was over, we had time for just such nice long talks as I delight in. Ernest began by upbraiding me a little for my injustice in fancying he had betrayed his father to Dr. Cabot.

"That is not all," I interrupted, "I even thought you had made a boast of the sacrifices you were making."

"That explains your coldness," he returned.

"My coldness! Of all the ridiculous things in the world!" I cried.

"You were cold, for you and I felt it. Do not you know that we undemonstrative men prefer loving winsome little women like you, just because you are our own opposites? And when the pet kitten turns into a cat with claws-"

"Now, Ernest, that is really too bad! To compare me to a cat!"

"You certainly did say some sharp things to me about that time."

"Did I, really? Oh, Ernest, how could I?"

"And it was at a moment when I particularly needed your help. But do not let us dwell upon it. We love each other we are both trying to do right in all the details of life. I do not think we shall ever get very far apart."

"But, Ernest-tell me-are you very, very much disappointed in me?"

"Disappointed? Why, Katy!"

"Then what did make you seem so indifferent? What made you so slow to observe how miserably I was, as to health?"

"Did I seem indifferent? I am sure I never loved you better. As to your health, I am ashamed of myself. I ought to have seen how feeble you were. But the truth is, I was deceived by your bright ways with baby. For him you were all smiles and gayety."

"That was from principle," I said, and felt a good deal elated as I made the announcement.

"He fell into a fit of musing, and none of my usual devices for arousing him had any effect. I pulled his hair and his ears, and shook him, but he remained unmoved.

At last, he began again.

"Perhaps I owe it to you, dear, to tell you that when I brought my father and sister home to live with us, I did not dream how trying a thing it would be to you. I did not know that he was a confirmed invalid, or that she would prove to possess a nature so entirely antagonistic to yours. I thought my father would interest himself in reading, visiting, etc, as he used to do. And I thought Martha's judgment would be of service to you, while her household skill would relieve you of some care. But the whole thing has proved a failure. I am harassed by the sight of my father, sitting there in his corner so penetrated with gloom, I reproach myself for it, but I almost dread coming home. When a man has been all day encompassed with sounds and sights of suffering, he naturally longs for cheerful faces and cheerful voices in his own house. Then Martha's pertinacious-I won't say hostility to my little wife-what shall I call it?"

"It is only want of sympathy. She is too really good to be hostile to anyone."

"Thank you, my darling," he said, "I believe you do her justice."

"I am afraid I have not been as forbearing with her as I ought," I said. "But, oh, Ernest, it is because I have been jealous of her all along!"

"That is really too absurd."

"You certainly have treated her with more deference than you have me. You looked up to her and looked down upon me. At least it seemed so."

"My dear child, you have misunderstood the whole thing. I gave Martha just what she wanted most she likes to be looked up to. And I gave you what I thought you wanted most, my tenderest love. And I expected that I should have your sympathy amid the trials with which I am burdened, and that with your strong nature I might look to you to help me bear them. I know you have the worst of it, dear child, but then you have twice my strength. I believe women almost always have more than men."

"I have, indeed, misunderstood you. I thought you liked to have them here, and that Martha's not fancying me influenced you against me. But now I know just what you want of me, and I can give it, darling."

After this all, our cloud melted away. I only long to go home and show Ernest that he shall have one cheerful face about him, and have one cheerful voice.

AUGUST 12.-I have had a long letter from Ernest today. He says he hopes he has not been selfish and unkind in speaking of his father and sister as he has done, because he truly loves and honors them both, and wants me to do so, if I can. His father had called them up twice to see him die and to receive his last messages. This always happens when Ernest has been up all the previous night there seems a fatality about it.

Chapter 15

OCTOBER 4 - HOME again, and with my dear Ernest delighted to see me. Baby is a year old today, and, as usual, father, who seems to abhor anything like a merry-making, took himself off to his room. Tomorrow he will be all the worse for it, and will be sure to have a theological battle with somebody.

OCTOBER 5.-The somebody was his daughter Katherine, as usual. Baby was asleep in my lap and I reached out for a book which proved to be a volume of Shakespeare which had done long service as an ornament to the table, but which nobody ever read on account of the small print. The battle then began thus:

Father.-" I regret to see that worldly author in your hands, my daughter."

Daughter-a little mischievously.-"Why, were you wanting to talk, father?

"No, I am too feeble to talk today. My pulse is very weak."

"Let me read aloud to you, then."

"Not from that profane book."

"It would do you good. You never take any recreation. Do let me read a little."

Father gets nervous.

"Recreation is a snare. I must keep my soul ever fixed on divine things."

"But can you?"

"No, alas, no. It is my grief and shame that I do not."

"But if you would indulge yourself in a little harmless mirth now and then, your mind would get rested and you would return to divine things with fresh zeal. Why should not the mind have its seasons of rest as well as the body?"

"We shall have time to rest in heaven. Our business here on earth is to be sober and vigilant because of our adversary not to be reading plays."

"I do not make reading plays my business, dear father. I make it my rest and amusement."

"Christians do not need amusement they find rest, refreshment, all they want, in God."

"Do you, father?"

"'Alas, no. He seems a great way off."

"To me He seems very near. So near that He can see every thought of my heart Dear father, it is your disease that makes everything so unreal to you. God is really so near, really loves us so is so sorry for us! And it seems hard, when you are so good, and so intent on pleasing Him, that you get no comfort out of Him."

"I am not good, my daughter I am a vile worm of the dust."

"Well, God is good, at any rate, and He would never have sent His Son to die for you if He did not love you." So then, I began to sing. Father likes to hear me sing, and the sweet sense I had that all I had been saying was true and more than true, made me sing with joyful heart.

I hope it is not a mere miserable presumption that makes me dare to talk so to poor father. Of course, he is ten times better than I am, and knows ten times as much, but his disease, whatever it is, keeps his mind befogged. I mean to begin now to pray that light may shine into his soul. It would be delightful to see the peace of God shining in that pale, stern face.

MARCH 28.-It is almost six months since I wrote that. About the middle of October father had one of his ill turns one night, and we were all called up. He asked for me particularly, and Ernest came for me at last. He was a good deal agitated, and would not stop to half dress myself, and as I had a slight cold already, I suppose I added to it then. At any rate I was taken very sick, and the worst cough ever had has racked my poor frame almost to pieces. Nearly six months confinement to my room six months of uselessness during which I have been a mere cumberer of the ground. Poor Ernest! What a hard time he has had! Instead of the cheerful welcome home I was to give him whenever he entered the house, here I have lain exhausted, woe- begone and good for nothing. It is the bitterest disappointment I ever had. My ambition is to be the sweetest, brightest, best of wives and what with my childish follies, and my sickness, what a weary life my dear husband has had! But how often I have prayed that God would do His will in defiance, if need be, of mine! I have tried to remind myself of that every day. But I am too tired to write any more now.

MARCH 30.-This experience of suffering has filled my mind with new thoughts. At one time, I was so sick that Ernest sent for mother. Poor mother, she had to sleep with Martha. It was a great comfort to have her here, but I knew by her coming how sick I was, and then I began to ponder the question whether I was ready to die. Death looked to me as a most solemn, momentous event-but there was something very pleasant in the thought of being no longer a sinner, but a redeemed saint, and of dwelling forever in Christ's presence. Father came to see me when I had just reached this point.

"My dear daughter," he asked, "are you prepared to face the Judge of all the earth?"

"No, dear father," I said, "Christ will do that for me."

"Have you no misgivings?"

I could only smile I had no strength to talk.

Then I heard Ernest—my dear, calm, self-controlled Ernest—burst out crying and rush out of the room. I looked after him, and how I loved him! But I felt that I loved my Savior infinitely more, and that if He now let me come home to be with Him I could trust Him to be a thousand-fold more to Ernest than I could ever be, and to take care of my darling baby and my precious mother far better than I could. The very gates of heaven seemed open to let me in. And then they were suddenly shut in my face, and I found myself a poor, weak, tempted creature here upon earth. I, who fancied myself an heir of glory, was nothing but a peevish, human creature-very human indeed, overcome if Martha shook the bed, as she always did, irritated if my food did not come at the right moment, or was not of the right sort, hurt and offended if Ernest put on at one less anxious and tender than he had used when I was very ill, and-in short, my own poor faulty self once more. Oh, what fearful battles I fought for patience, forbearance, and unselfishness! What sorrowful tears of shame I shed over hasty, impatient words and fretful tones! No wonder I longed to be gone where weakness should be swallowed up in strength, and sin give place to eternal perfection!

But here I am, and suffering and work lie before me, for which I feel little physical or mental courage. But "blessed be the will of God."

APRIL 5.-I was alone with father last evening, Ernest and Martha both being out, and soon saw by the way he fidgeted in his chair that he had something on his mind. So I laid down the book I was reading, and asked him what it was.

"My daughter," he began, "can you bear a plain word from an old man?"

I felt frightened, for I knew I had been impatient to Martha of late, in spite of all my efforts to the contrary. I am still so miserably unwell.

"I have seen many death-beds," he went on "but I never saw one where there was not some dread of the King of Terrors exhibited nor one where there was such absolute certainty of having found favor with God to make the hour of departure entirely free from such doubts and such humility as becomes a guilty sinner about to face his Judge."

"I never saw such a one, either," I replied "but ere have been many such deaths, and I hardly know of any scene that so honors and magnifies the Lord."

"Yes," he said, slowly "but they were old, mature, ripened Christians."

"Not always old, dear father. Let me describe to you a scene Ernest described to me only yesterday."

He waved his hand in token that this would delay his coming to the point he was aiming at.

"To speak plainly," he said, "I feel uneasy about you, my daughter. You are young and in the bloom of life, but when death seemed staring you in the face, you expressed no anxiety, asked for no counsel, showed no alarm. It must be pleasant to possess so comfortable a persuasion of our acceptance with God but is it safe to rest on such an assurance while we know that the human heart is deceitful above all things and desperately wicked?"

I thank you for the suggestion," I said "and, dear father, do not be afraid to speak still more plainly. You live in the house with me, see all my shortcomings and my faults, and I cannot wonder that you think me a poor, weak Christian. But do you really fear that I am deceived in believing that notwithstanding this I do really love my God and Savior and am His Child?"

"No," he said, hesitating a little, "I cannot say that, exactly—I cannot say that."

This hesitation distressed me. At first, it seemed to me that my life must have uttered a very uncertain sound if those who saw it could misunderstand its language. But then I reflected that it was, at best, a very faulty life, and that its springs of action were not necessarily seen by lookers-on.

Father saw my distress and perplexity, and seemed touched by them.

Just then, Ernest came in with Martha, but seeing that something was amiss, the latter took herself off to her room, which I thought really kind of her.

"What is it, father? What is it, Katy?" asked Ernest looking from one troubled face to the other.

I tried to explain.

"I think, father, you may safely trust my wife's spiritual interests to me," Ernest said, with warmth. "You do not understand her. I do. Because there is nothing morbid about her, because she has a sweet, cheerful confidence in Christ you doubt and misjudge her. You may depend upon it that people are individual in their piety as in other things, and cannot all be run in one mould. Katy has a playful way of speaking, I know, and often expresses her strongest feelings with what seems like levity, and is, perhaps, a little reckless about being misunderstood in consequence."

He smiled on me, as he thus took up the cudgels in my defense, and I never felt so grateful to him in my life. The truth is, I hate sentimentalism so cordially, and have besides such an instinct to conceal my deepest, most sacred emotions, that I do not wonder people misunderstand and misjudge me.

"I did not refer to her playfulness," father returned. "Old people must make allowances for the young they must make allowances. What pains me is that this child, full of life and gayety as she is, sees death approach without that becoming awe and terror which befits mortal man."

Ernest was going to reply, but I broke in eagerly upon his answer:

"It is true that I expressed no anxiety when I believed death to be at hand. I felt none. I had given myself away to Christ, and He had received me and why should I be afraid to take His hand and go where He led me? And it is true that I asked for no counsel. I was too weak to ask questions or to like to have questions asked, but my mind was bright and wide awake while my body was so feeble, and I took counsel of God. Oh, let me read to you two passages from the life of Caroline Fry, which will make you, understand how a poor sinner looks upon death. The first is an extract from a letter written after learning that her days on earth were numbered.

"'As many will hear and will not understand, why I want no time of, preparation, often desired by far holier ones than I, I tell you why, and shall tell others, and so shall you. It is not because I am so holy but because I am so sinful. The peculiar character of my religious experience has always been a deep, an agonizing sense of sin the sin of yesterday, of today, confessed with anguish hard to be endured, and cried for pardon that could not be unheard each day cleansed anew in Jesus' blood, and each day more and more hateful in my own sight what can I do in death I have not done in life? What, do in this week, when I am told I cannot live, other than I did last week, when knew it not?

Alas, there is but one thing undone, to serve Him better and the deathbed is no place for that. Therefore, I say, if I am not ready now, I shall not be by delay, so far as I have to do with it. If He has, more to do in me that is His part. I need not ask Him not to spoil His work by too much haste.'

"And these were her dying words, a few days later:

"'This is my bridal-day, the beginning of my life. I wish there should be no mistake about the reason of my desire to depart and to be with Christ. I confess myself the vilest, chiefest of sinners, and I desire to go to Him that I may be rid of the burden of sin-the sin of my nature-not the past, repented of every day, but the present, hourly, momentary sin, which I do commit, or may commit -the sense of which at times drives me half mad with grief!'"

I shall never forget the expression of father's face, as I finished reading these remarkable words. He rose slowly from his seat, and came and kissed me on the forehead. Then he left the room, but returned with a large volume, and pointing to a blank page, requested me to copy them there. He complains that I do not write legibly, so I printed them as plainly as I could, with my pen.

JUNE 20.-On the first of May, there came to us, with other spring flowers, our little fair-haired, blue-eyed daughter. How rich I felt when I heard Ernest's voice, as he replied to a question asked at the door, proclaim, "Mother and children all well." To think that we, who thought ourselves rich before are made so much richer now!

But she is not large and vigorous, as little Ernest was, and we cannot rejoice in her without some misgiving. Yet her very frailty makes her precious to us. Little Ernest hangs over her with an almost lover-like pride and devotion, and should she live I can imagine what a protector he will be for her. I have had to give up the care of him to Martha. During my illness I do not know what would have become of him but for her. One of the pleasant events of every day at that time, was her bringing him to me in such exquisite order, his face shining with health and happiness, his hair and dress so beautifully neat and clean. Now that she has the care of him, she has become very fond of him, and he certainly forms one bond of union between us, for we both agree that he is the handsomest, best, most remarkable child that ever lived, or ever will live.

JULY 6.-I have come home to dear mother with both my children. Ernest says our only hope for baby is to keep her out of the city during the summer months.

What a petite wee maiden she is! Where does all the love come from? If I had had her always, I do not see how I could be more fond of her. And do people call it living who never had any children?

JULY 10.-If this darling baby lives, I shall always believe it is owing to my mother's prayers.

I find little Ernest has a passionate temper, and a good deal of self-will. But he has fine qualities. I wish he had a better mother. I am so impatient with him when he is wayward and perverse! What he needs is a firm, gentle hand, moved by no caprice, and controlled by the constant fear of God. He never ought to hear an irritable word, or a sharp tone but he does hear them, I must own with grief and shame. The truth is, it is so long since I really felt strong and well that I am not myself, and cannot do him justice, poor child. Next to being a perfect wife, I want to be a perfect mother. How mortifying, how dreadful in all things to come short of even one's own standard. What approach, then, does one make to God's standard?

Mother seems very happy to have us here, though we make so much trouble. She encourages me in all my attempts to control myself and to control my dear little boy, and the chapters she gives me out of her own experience are as interesting as a novel, and a good deal more instructive.

AUGUST.-Dear Ernest has come to spend a week with us. He is all tired out, as there has been a great deal of sickness in the city, and father has had quite a serious attack. He brought with him a nurse for baby, as one more desperate effort to strengthen her constitution.

I reproached him for doing it without consulting me, but he said mother bad written to tell him that I was all worn out and not in a state to have the care of the children. It has been a terrible blow to me One by one I am giving up the sweetest maternal duties. God means that I shall be nothing and do nothing a mere useless sufferer. But when I tell Ernest so, he says I am everything to him, and that God's children please him just as well when they sit patiently with folded hands, if that is His will, as when they are hard at work. But to be at work, to be useful, to be necessary to my husband and children, is just what I want, and I. do find it hard to be set against the wall, as it were, like an old piece of furniture no longer of any service I see now that my first desire has not been to please God, but to please myself, for I am restless under His restraining hand, and find my prison a very narrow one. I would be willing to bear any other trial, if I could only have health and strength for my beloved ones. I pray for patience with bitter tears.

Chapter 16

OCTOBER.- WE are all at home together once more. The parting with mother was very painful. Every year that she lives now increases her loneliness, and makes me long to give her the shelter of my home. But in the midst of these anxieties, how much I have to make me happy! Little Ernest is the life and soul of the house the sound of his feet pattering about, and all his prattle, are the sweetest music to my ear and his heart is brimful of love and joy, so that he shines on us all like a sunbeam. Baby is improving every day, and is one of those tender, clinging little things that appeal to everybody's love and sympathy. I never saw a more angelic face than hers. Father sits by the hour looking at her. Today he said:

"Daughter Katherine, this lovely little one is not meant for this sinful world."

"This world needs to be adorned with lovely little ones," I said. "And baby was never so well as she is now."

"Do not set your heart too fondly upon her," he returned. "I feel that she is far too dear to me."

"But, father, we could give her to God if He should ask for her. Surely, we love Him better than we love her."

But as I spoke a sharp pang shot through and through my soul, and I held my little fair daughter closely in my arms, as if I could always keep her there It may be my conceit, but it really does seem as if poor father was getting a little fond of me. Ever since my own sickness I have felt great sympathy for him, and he feels, no doubt, that I give him something that neither Ernest nor Martha can do, since they were never sick one day in their lives. I do wish he could look more at Christ and at what He has done and is doing for us. The way of salvation is to me a wide path, absolutely radiant with the glory of Him who shines upon it I see my shortcomings I see my sins, but I feel myself bathed, as it were, in the effulgent glow that proceeds directly from the throne of God and the Lamb. It seems as if I ought to have some misgivings about my salvation, but I can hardly say that I have one. How strange, how mysterious that is! And here is father, so much older, so much better than I am, creeping along in the dark! I spoke to Ernest about it. He says I owe it to my training, in a great measure, and that my mother is fifty years in advance of her age. But it cannot be all that. It was only after years of struggle and prayer that God gave me this joy.

NOVEMBER 24.-Ernest asked me yesterday if I knew that Amelia and her husband had come here to live, and that she was very ill.

"I wish you would go to see her, dear," he added. "She is a stranger here, and in great need of a friend." I felt extremely disturbed. I have lost my old affection for her, and the idea of meeting her husband was unpleasant.

"Is she very sick?" I asked.

"Yes. She is completely broken down. I promised her that you should go to see her."

"Are you attending her?"

"Yes her husband came for me himself."

"I do not want to go," I said. "It will be very disagreeable."

"Yes, dear, I know it. But she needs a friend, as I said before."

I put on my things very reluctantly, and went. I found Amelia in a richly furnished house, but looking untidy and ill-cared-for. She was lying on a couch in her bedroom three delicate-looking children were playing about, and their nurse sat sewing at the window.

A terrible fit of coughing made it impossible for her to speak for some moments. At last, she recovered herself sufficiently to welcome me, by throwing her arms around me and bursting into tears.

"Oh, Katy!" she cried, "should you have known me if we had met in the street? Do not you find me sadly altered?"

"You are changed," I said, "but so am I."

"Yes, you do not look strong. But then you never did. And you are as pretty as ever, while I— oh, Kate! Do you remember what round, white arms I used to have? Look at them now!"

And she drew up her sleeve, poor child. Just then, I heard a step in the passage, and her husband sauntered into the room, smoking.

"Do go away, Charles," she said impatiently. "You know how your cigar sets me coughing."

He held out his hand to me with the easy, nonchalant air of one who is accustomed to success and popularity.

I looked at him with an aversion I could not conceal. The few years since we met has changed him so completely that I almost shuddered at the sight of his already bloated face, and at the air that told of a life worse than wasted.

"Do go away, Charles," Amelia repeated.

He threw himself into a chair without paying the least attention to her, and still addressing himself to me again, said:

"Upon my word, you are prettier than ever,

and—

"I will come to see you at another time, Amelia," I said, putting on all the dignity I could condense in my small frame, and rising to take leave.

"Do not go, Katy!" he cried, starting up, "do not go. I want to have a good talk about old times."

Katy, indeed! How dared he? I came away burning with anger and mortification. Is it possible that I ever loved such a man? That to gratify that love I defied and grieved my dear mother through a whole year! Oh, from what hopeless misery God saved me, when He snatched me out of the depth of my folly!

DECEMBER 1.-Ernest says I can go to see Amelia with safety now, as her husband has sprained his ankle, and keeps to his own room. So I am going. But, I am sure,. I shall say something imprudent or unwise, and wish I could think it right to stay away. I hope God will go with me and teach me what words to speak.

DEC. 2.-I found Amelia more unwell than on my first visit, and she received me again with tears.

"How good you are to come so soon," she began. "I did not blame you for running off the other day Charley's impertinence was shameful. He said, after you left, that he perceived you had not yet lost your quickness to take offence, but I know he felt that you showed a just displeasure, and nothing more."

"No, I was really angry," I replied. "I find the road to perfection lies up-hill, and I slip back so often that sometimes I despair of ever reaching the top."

"What does the doctor say about me?" she asked. "Does he think me very sick?"

"I dare say he will tell you exactly what he thinks," I returned, "if you ask him. This is his rule with all his patients."

"If I could get rid of this cough I should soon be myself again," she said. "Some days I feel quite bright and well. But if it were not for my poor little children, I should not care much how the thing ended. With the life Charley leads me, I haven't much to look forward to."

"You forget that the children's nurse is in the room," I whispered.

"Oh, I do not mind Charlotte. Charlotte knows he neglects me, do not you, Charlotte ?"

Charlotte was discreet enough to pretend not to hear this question, and Amelia went on:

"It began very soon after we were married. He would go round with other girls exactly as he did before then when I spoke about it he would just laugh in his easy, good-natured way, but pay no attention to my wishes. Then when I grew more in earnest he would say, that as long as he let me alone I ought to let him alone. I thought that when our first baby came that would sober him a little, but he wanted a boy and it turned out to be a girl. And my being unhappy and crying so much, made the poor thing fretful it kept him awake at night, so he took another room. After that, I saw him less than ever, though now and then he would have a little love-fit, when he would promise to be at home more and treat me with more consideration. We had two more little girls-twins and then a boy. Charley seemed quite fond of him, and did certainly seem improved, though he was still out a great deal with a set of idle young men, smoking, drinking wine, and, I do not know what else. His uncle gave him too much money, and he had nothing to do but to spend it."

"You must not tell me any more now," I said. "Wait until you are stronger."

The nurse rose and gave her something that seemed to refresh her. I went to look at the little girls, who were all pretty, pale-faced creatures, very quiet and mature in their ways.

"I am rested now," said Amelia, "and it does me good to talk to you, because I can see that you are sorry for me."

"I am, indeed!" I cried.

"When our little boy was three months old I took this terrible cold and began to cough. Charley at first remonstrated with me for coughing so much he said it was a habit I had got, and that I ought to cure myself of it. Then the baby began to pine and pine, and the more it wasted the more I wasted. And at last it died."

Here the poor child burst out again, and I wiped away her tears as fast as they fell, thankful that she could cry.

"After that," she went on, after awhile, "Charley seemed to lose his last particle of affection for me he kept away more than ever, and once when I besought him not to neglect me and my children so, he said he was well paid for not keeping up his engagement with you, that you had some strength of character, and-"

"Amelia," I interrupted, "do not repeat such things. They only pain and mortify me."

"Well," she sighed, wearily, "this is what he has at last brought me to. I am sick and broken-hearted, and care very little what becomes of me."

There was a long silence. I wanted to ask her if, when earthly refuge failed her, she could not find shelter in the love of Christ. But I have what is, I fear, a morbid terror of seeking the confidence of others. I knelt down at last, and kissed the poor faded face.

"Yes, I knew you would feel for me," she said. "The only pleasant thought I had when Charley insisted on coming here to live was, that I should see you."

"Does your uncle live here, too?" I asked.

"Yes, he came first, and it was that that put it into Charley's head to come. He is very kind to me."

"Yes," I said, "and God is kind, too, isn't He ?"

"Kind to let me get sick and disgust Charley? Now, Katy, how can you talk so?" I replied by repeating two lines from a hymn of which I am very fond:

O Savior, whose mercy severe in its kindness,   Hath chastened my wanderings, and guided my way."

"I do not much care for hymns," she said. "When one is well, and everything goes quite to one's mind, it is nice to go to church and sing with the rest of them. But, sick as I am, it isn't so easy to be religious."

"But isn't this the very time to look to Christ for comfort?"

"What's the use of looking anywhere for comfort?" she said, peevishly. "Wait till you are sick and heart-broken yourself, and you'll see that you won't feel much like doing anything but just groan and cry your life out."

"I have been sick, and I know what sorrow means, I said. "And I am glad that I do. For I have learned Christ in that school, and I know that He can comfort when no one else can."

"You always were an odd creature," she replied. "I never pretended to understand half you said."

I saw that she was tired, and came away. Oh, how I wished that I had been able to make Christ look to her as He did to me all the way home.

DEC. 24.-Father says he does not like Dr. Cabot's preaching. He thinks that it is not doctrinal enough, and that he does not preach enough to sinners. But I can see that it has influenced him already, and that he is beginning to think of God, as manifested in Christ, far more than he used to do. With me, he has endless discussions on his and my favorite subjects, and though I can never tell along what path I walked to reach a certain conclusion, the earnestness of my convictions does impress him strangely. I am sure there is a great deal of conceit mixed up with all I say, and then when I compare my life with my own standard of duty, I wonder I ever dare to open my mouth and undertake to help others.

Baby is not at all well. To see a little frail, tender thing really suffering, tears my soul to pieces. I think it would distress me less to give her to God just as she is now, a vital part of my very heart, than to see her live a mere invalid life. But I try to feel, as I know I say, Thy will be done! Little Ernest is the very picture of health and beauty. He has vitality enough for two children He and his little sister will make very interesting contrasts as they grow older. His ardor and vivacity will rouse her, and her gentleness will soften him.

JAN. 1, 1841.-Every day brings its own duty and its own discipline. How is it that I make such slow progress while this is the case? It is a marvel to me why God allows characters like mine to defile His church. I can only account for it with the thought that if I ever am perfected, I shall be a great honor to His name, for surely worse material for building up a temple of the Holy Ghost was never gathered together before. The time may come when those who know me now, crude, childish, incomplete, will look upon me with amazement, saying, "What hath God wrought!" If I knew such a time would never come, I should want to flee into the holes and caves of the earth.

I have everything to inspire me to devotion. My dear mother's influence is always upon me. To her I owe the habit of flying to God in every emergency, and of believing in prayer. Then I am in close fellowship with a true man and a true Christian. Ernest has none of my fluctuations he is always calm and self-possessed. This is partly his natural character but he has studied the Bible more than any other book, his convictions of duty are fixed because they are drawn thence, and his constant contact with the sick and the suffering has revealed life to him just as it is. How he has helped me on! God bless him for it!

Then I have James. To be with him one half hour is an inspiration. He lives in such blessed communion with Christ that he is in perpetual sunshine, and his happiness fertilizes even this disordered household there is not a soul in it that does not catch somewhat of his joyousness.

And there are my children! My darling, precious children! For their sakes I am continually constrained to seek after an amended, a sanctified life what I want them to become I must become myself.

So I enter on a new year, not knowing what it will bring forth, but surely with a thousand reasons for thanksgiving, for joy, and for hope.

JAN. 16.-One more desperate effort to make harmony out of the discords of my house, and one more failure. Ernest forgot that it was our wedding-day, which mortified and pained me, especially as he had made an engagement to dine out. I am always expecting something from life that I never get. Is it so with everybody? I am very uneasy, too, about James. He seems to be growing fond of Lucy's society. I am perfectly sure that she could not make him happy. Is it possible that he does not know what a brilliant young man he is, and that he can have whom he pleases? It is easy, in theory, to let God plan our own destiny, and that of our friends. But when it comes to a specific case, we fancy we can help His judgments with our poor reason. Well, I must go to Him with this new anxiety, and trust my darling brother's future to Him, if I can.

I shall try to win James' confidence. If it is not Lucy, who or what is it that is making him so thoughtful and serious, yet so wondrously happy?

JAN. 17.-I have been trying to find out whether this is a mere notion of mine about Lucy. James laughs, and evades my questions. But he owns that a very serious matter is occupying his thoughts, of which he does not wish to speak at present. May God bless him in it, whatever it is.

MAY 1.-My delicate little Una's first birthday. Thank God for sparing her to us a year. If He should take her away, I should still rejoice that this life was mingled with ours, and has influenced them. Yes, even an unconscious infant is an ever-felt influence in the household what an amazing thought!

I have given this precious little one away to her Savior and to mine living or dying, she is His.

DEC. 13.-Writing journals does not seem to be my mission on earth of late. My busy hands find so much else to do And sometimes when I have been particularly exasperated and tried by the jarring elements that form my home, I have not dared to indulge myself with recording things that ought to be forgotten.

How I long to live in peace with all men, and how I resent interference in the management of my children! If the time ever comes that I live, a spinster of a certain age, in the family of an elder brother, what a model of forbearance, charity, and sisterly loving-kindness I shall be!

Chapter 17

JANUARY 1, 1842 - I MEAN to resume my journal, and be more faithful to it this year. How many precious things, said by dear Mrs. Campbell and others, are lost forever, because I did not record them at the time!

I have seen her today. At Ernest's suggestion, I have let Susan Green provide her with a comfortable chair, which enables her to sit up during a part of each day. I found her in it, full of gratitude, her sweet, tranquil face shining, as it always is, with a light reflected from heaven itself. She looks like one who has had her struggle with life and conquered it. During last year, I visited her often and gradually learned much of her past history, though she does not love to talk of herself. She has outlived her husband, a houseful of girls and her ill health is chiefly the result of years of watching by their sickbeds, and grief at their loss.

For she does not pretend not to grieve, but always says, "It is repining that dishonors God, not grief."

I said to her today:

"Doesn't it seem hard when you think of the many happy homes there are in the world, that you should be singled out for such bereavement and loneliness?"

She replied, with a smile:

"I am not singled out, dear. There are thousands of God's own dear children, scattered over the world, suffering far more than I do. And I do not think there are many persons in it who are happier than I am. I was bound to my God and Savior before I knew a sorrow, it is true. But it was by a chain of many links and every link that dropped away, brought me to Him, till at last, having nothing left, I was shut up to Him, and learned fully, what I had only learned partially, how soul-satisfying He is."

"You think, then," I said, while my heart died within me, "that husband and children are obstacles in our way, and hinder our getting near to Christ."

"Oh, no!" she cried. "God never gives us hindrances. On the contrary, He means, in making us wives and mothers, to put us into the very conditions of holy living. But if we abuse His gifts by letting them take His place in our hearts, it is an act of love on His part to take them away, or to destroy our pleasure in them. It is delightful," she added, after a pause, "to know that there are some generous souls on earth, who love their dear ones with all their hearts, yet give those hearts unreservedly to Christ. Mine was not one of them."

I had some little service to render her, which interrupted our conversation. The offices I have had to have rendered me in my own long days of sickness have taught me to be less fastidious about waiting upon others. I am thankful that God has at last made me willing to do anything in a sickroom that must be done. She thanked me, as she always does, and then I said:

"I have a great many little trials, but they do not do me a bit of good. Or, at least, I do not see that they do."

"No, we never see plants growing," she said.

"And do you really think then, that perhaps I am growing, though unconsciously ?"

"I know you are, dear child. There cannot be life without growth."

This comforted me. I came home, praying all the way, and striving to commit myself entirely to Him in whose school I sit as learner. Oh, that I were a better scholar but I do not half learn my lessons, I am heedless and inattentive, and I forget what is taught. Perhaps this is the reason that weighty truths float before my mind's eye at times, but do not fix themselves there.

MARCH 20.-I have been much impressed by Dr. Cabot's sermons today. While I am listening to his voice and hear him speak of the beauty and desirableness of the Christian life, I feel as he feels, that I am waiting to count all things but dross that I may win Christ. But when I come home to my worldly cares, I get completely absorbed in them, it is only by a painful wrench that I force my soul back to God. Sometimes I almost envy Lucy her calm nature, which gives her so little trouble. Why need I throw my whole soul into whatever I do? Why cannot I make so much as an apron for little Ernest without the ardor and eagerness of a soldier marching to battle? I wonder if people of my temperament ever get toned down, and learn to take life coolly?

JUNE 10.-My dear little Una has had a long and very severe illness. It seems wonderful that she could survive such sufferings. And it is almost as wonderful that I could look upon them, week after week, without losing my senses.

At first, Ernest paid little attention to my repeated entreaties that he would prescribe for her, and some precious time was thus lost. But the moment he was fully aroused to see her danger, there was something beautiful in his devotion. He often walked the room with her by the hour together, and it was touching to see her lying like a pale crushed lily in his strong arms. One morning she seemed almost gone, and we knelt around her with bursting hearts, to commend her parting soul to Him in whose arms we were about to place her. But it seemed as if all He asked of us was to come to that point, for then He gave her back to us, and she is still ours, only seven-fold dearer. I was so thankful to see dear Ernest's faith triumphing over his heart, and making him so ready to give up even this little lamb without a word. Yes, we will give our children to Him if he asks for them. He shall never have to snatch them from us by force.

OCT. 4.-We have had a quiet summer in the country, that is, I have with my darling little ones. This is the fourth birthday of our son and heir, and he has been full of health and vivacity, enjoying everything with all his heart. How he lights up our somber household! Father has been fasting today, and is so worn out and so nervous in consequence, that he could not bear the sound of the children's voices. I wish, if he must fast, he would do it moderately, and do it all the time. Now he goes without food until he is ready to sink, and now he eats quantities of improper food. If Martha could only see how mischievous all this is for him. After the children had been hustled out of the way, and I~ had got them both off to bed, he said in his most doleful manner, "I hope, my daughter, that you are faithful to your son. He has now reached the age of four years, and is a remarkably intelligent child. I hope you teach him that he is a sinner, and that he is in a state of condemnation."

"Now, father, do not," I said. "You are all tired out, and do not know what you are saying. I would not have little Ernest hear you for the world."

Poor father! He fairly groaned.

"You are responsible for that child's soul" he said, "You have more influence over him than all the world beside."

"I know it," I said, "and sometimes I feel ready to sink when I think of the great work God has entrusted to me. But my poor child will learn that he is a sinner only too soon, and before that dreadful day arrives, I want to fortify his soul with the only antidote against the misery that knowledge will give him. I want him to see his Redeemer in all His love, and all His beauty, and to love Him with all his heart and soul, and mind and strength. Dear father, pray for him, and pray for me, too."

"I do, I will," he said, solemnly. And then followed the inevitable long fit of silent musing, when I often wonder what is passing in that suffering soul. For a sufferer he certainly is who sees a great and good and terrible God who cannot look upon iniquity, and does not see His risen Son, who has paid the debt we owe, and lives to intercede for us before the throne of the Father.

JAN. I, 1842.-James came to me yesterday with a letter he had been writing to mother.

"I want you to read this before it goes," he said, "for you ought to know my plans as soon as mother does."

I did not get time to read it till after tea. Then I came up here to my room, and sat down curious to know what was coming.

Well, I thought I loved him as much as one human being could love another, already, but now my heart embraced him with a fervor and delight that made me so happy that I could not speak a word when I knelt down to tell my Savior all about it.

He said that he had been led, within a few months, to make a new consecration of himself to Christ and to Christ's cause on earth, and that this had resulted in his choosing the life of a missionary, instead of settling down, as he had intended to do, as a city physician. Such expressions of personal love to Christ, and delight in the thought of serving Him, I never read. I could only marvel at what God had wrought in his soul. For me to live to Christ seems natural enough, for I have been driven to Him not only by sorrow but by sin. Every outbreak of my hasty temper sends me weeping and penitent to the foot of the cross, and I love much because I have been forgiven much. But James, as far as I know, has never had a sorrow, except my father's death, and that had no apparent religious effect and his natural character is perfectly beautiful. He is as warm-hearted and loving and simple and guileless as a child, and has nothing of my intemperance, hastiness, and quick temper. I have often thought that she would be a rare woman who could win and wear such a heart as his. Life has done little but smile upon him he is handsome and talented and attractive everybody is fascinated by him, everybody caresses him and yet he has turned his back on the world that has dealt so kindly with him, and given himself, as Edwards says, "clean away to Christ!" Oh, how thankful I am! And yet to let him go! My only brother-mother's Son! But I know what she will say she will him God-speed!

Ernest came upstairs, looking tired and jaded. I read the letter to him. It impressed him strangely: but he only said

"This is what we m might expect, who knew James, dear fellow!"

But when we knelt down to pray together, I saw how he was touched, and how his soul kindled within him in harmony with that consecrated, devoted spirit. Dear James! It must be mother's prayers that have done for him this wondrous work that is usually the slow growth of years and this is the mother who prays for you, Katy! So take courage!

JAN. 2.~James means to study theology as well as medicine, it seems. That will keep him with us for some years. Oh, is it selfish to take this view of it? Alas, the spirit is willing to have him go, but the flesh is weak, and cries out.

OCT. 22.-Amelia came to see me today. She has been traveling, for her health, and certainly looks much improved.

"Charley and I are quite good friends again," she began. "We have jaunted about everywhere, and have a delightful time. What a snug little box of a house you have!"

It is inconveniently small," I said, "for our family is large and the doctor needs more office room."

"Does he receive patients here? How horrid! Do not you hate to have people with all sorts of ills and aches in the house? It must depress your spirits."

"I dare say it would if I saw them but I never do."

"I should like to see your children. Your husband says you are perfectly devoted to them."

"As I suppose all mothers are," I replied, laughing.

"As to that," she returned, "people differ."

The children were brought down. She admired little Ernest, as everybody does, but only glanced at the baby.

"What a sickly-looking little thing!" she said. "But this boy is a splendid fellow! Ah, if mine had lived he would have been just such a child! But some people have all the trouble and others all the comfort. I am, sure I do not know what I have done that I should have to lose my only boy, and have nothing left but girls. To be sure, I can afford to dress them elegantly, and as soon as they get old enough I mean to have them taught all sorts of accomplishments. You cannot imagine what a relief it is to have plenty of money!"

"Indeed I cannot!" I said, "It is quite beyond the reach of my imagination."

"My uncle—that is to say Charley's uncle-has just given me a carriage and horses for my own use. In fact, he heaps everything upon me. Where do you go to church?"

I told her, reminding her that Dr. Cabot was its pastor.

"Oh, I forgot! Poor Dr. Cabot! Is he as old-fashioned as ever?"

"I do not know what you mean," I cried. "He is as good as ever, if not better. His health is very delicate, and that one thing seems to be a blessing to him."

"A blessing! Why, Kate Mortimer! Kate Elliott, I mean. It is a blessing I, for one, am very willing to dispense with. But you always did say queer things. Well, I dare say Dr. Cabot is very good and all that, but his church is not a fashionable one, and Charley and I go to Dr. Bellamy's. That is, I go once a day, pretty regularly, and Charley goes when he feels like it. Good-by. I must go now I have all my fall shopping to do. Have you done yours? Suppose you jump into the carriage and go with me? You cannot imagine how it passes away the morning to drive from shop to shop looking over the new goods."

"There seem to be a number of things I cannot imagine," I replied, dryly. "You must excuse me this morning."

She took her leave.. I looked at her rich dress as she gathered it about her and swept away, and recalled all her empty, frivolous talk with contempt.

She and Ch—-, her husband, I mean, are well matched. They need their money, and their palaces and their fine clothes and handsome equipages, for they have nothing else. How thankful I am that I am as unlike them as ex—

OCTOBER 30.-I'm sure I do not know what I was going to say when I was interrupted just then. Something in the way of self-glorification, most likely. I remember the contempt with which I looked after Amelia as she left our house, and the pinnacle on which I sat perched for some days, when I compared my life with hers. Alas, it was my view of life of which I was lost in admiration, for I am sure that if I ever come under the complete dominion of Christ's gospel I shall not know the Sentiment of disdain. I feel truly ashamed and sorry that I am still so far from being penetrated with that spirit.

My pride has had a terrible fall. As I sat on my throne, looking down on all the Amelia's in the world, I felt a profound pity at their delight in petty trifles, their love of position, of mere worldly show and passing vanities.

"They are all alike," I said to myself. "They are incapable of understanding a character like mine, or the exalted, ennobling principles that govern me. They crave the applause of this world, they are satisfied with fine clothes, fine houses, and fine equipages. They think and talk of nothing else I have not one idea in common with them. I see the emptiness and hollowness of these things. I am absolutely unworldly my ambition is to attain whatever they, in their blind folly and ignorance, absolutely despise."

Thus communing with myself, I was not a little pleased to hear Dr. Cabot and his wife announced. I hastened to meet them and to display to them the virtues I so admired in myself. They had hardly a chance to utter a word. I spoke eloquently of my contempt for worldly vanities, and of my enthusiastic longings for a higher life. I even went into particulars about the foibles of some of my acquaintances, though faint misgivings as to the propriety of such remarks on the absent made me half repent the words I still kept uttering. When they took leave, I rushed to my room with my heart beating, my cheeks all in a glow, and caught up and caressed the children in a way that seemed to astonish them. Then I took my work and sat down to sew. What a horrible reaction now took place! I saw my refined, subtle, disgusting pride, just as I suppose Dr. and Mrs. Cabot saw it! I sat covered with confusion, shocked at myself, shocked at the weakness of human nature. Oh, to get back the good opinion of my friends! To recover my own self-respect! But this was impossible. I threw down my work and walked about my room. There was a terrible struggle in my soul. I saw that instead of brooding over the display I had made of myself to Dr. Cabot I ought to be thinking solely of my appearance in the sight of God, who could see far more plainly than any earthly eye could all my miserable pride and self-conceit. But I could not do that, and chafed about till I was worn out, body and soul. At last, I sent the children away, and knelt down and told the whole story to Him who knew what I was when He had compassion on me, called me by my name, and made me His own child. And here, I found a certain peace. Christian, on his way to the celestial city, met and fought his Apollyons and his giants, too but he got there at last!

Chapter 18

NOVEMBER. - THIS morning Ernest received an early summons to Amelia. I got out of all manner of patience with him because he would take his bath and eat his breakfast before he went, and should have driven anyone else distracted by my hurry and flurry.

"She has had a hemorrhage!" I cried. "Do, Ernest, make haste."

"Of course," he returned, "that would come, sooner or later."

"You do not mean," I said, "that she has been in danger of this all along?"

"I certainly do."

"Then it was very unkind in you not to tell me so."

"I told you at the outset that her lungs were diseased."

"No, you told me no such thing. Oh, Ernest, is she going to die?"

"I did not know you were so fond of her," he said, apologetically.

It is not that," I cried. "I am distressed at the thought of the worldly life she has been living-at my never trying to influence her for her good. If she is in danger, you will tell her so? Promise me that."

"I must see her before I make such a promise," he said, and went out.

I flew up to my room and threw myself on my knees, sorrowful, self-condemned. I had thrown away my last opportunity of speaking a word to her in season, though I had seen how much she needed one, and now she was going to die! Oh, I hope God will forgive me, and hear the prayers I have offered her!

EVENING.-Ernest says he had a most distressing scene at Amelia's this morning. She insisted on knowing what he thought of her, and then burst out bitter complaints and lamentations, charging it to husband that she had this disease, declaring that she could not, and would not die, and insisting that he must prevent it. Her uncle urged for a consultation of physicians, to which Ernest consented, of course, though he says no mortal power can save her now. I asked him how her husband appeared, to which he made the evasive answer that he appeared just as one would expect him to do.

DECEMBER.-Amelia was so determined to see me that Ernest thought it best for me to go. I found her looking very feeble.

"Oh, Katy," she began at once," do make the doctor say that I shall get well!"

"I wish he could say so with truth," I answered. "Dear Amelia, try to think how happy God's own children are when they are with Him."

"I cannot think," she replied. "I do not want to think. I want to forget all about it. If it were not for this terrible cough I could forget it, for I am really a great deal better than I was a month ago."

I did not know what to say or what to do.

"May I read a hymn or a few verses from the Bible?" I asked, at last.

"Just as you like," she said, indifferently.

I read a verse now and then, but she looked tired, and I prepared to go.

"Do not go," she cried. "I do not dare to be alone. Oh, what a terrible, terrible thing it is to die! To leave this bright, beautiful world, and be nailed in a coffin and buried up in a cold, dark grave.

"Nay," I said, "to leave this poor sick body there, and to fly to a world ten thousand times brighter, more beautiful than this."

"I had just got to feeling nearly well," she said, "and I had everything I wanted, and Charley was quite good to me, and I kept my little girls looking like fairies, just from fairy-land. Everybody said they wore the most picturesque costumes when they were dressed according to my taste. And I have got to go and leave them, and Charley will be marrying somebody else, and saying to her all the nice things, he has said to me.

"I really must go now," I said. "You are wearing yourself all out."

"I declare you are crying," she exclaimed. "You do pity me after all."

"Indeed I do," I said, and came away, heartsick.

Ernest says there is nothing I can do for her now but to pray for her, since she does not really believe herself in danger, and has a vague feeling that if she can once convince him how much she wants to live, he will use some vigorous measures to restore her Martha is to watch with her to-night. Ernest will not let me.

JAN. 18, 1843.-Our wedding-day has passed unobserved. Amelia's suffering condition absorbs us all. Martha spends much time with her, and prepares almost all the food she eats.

JAN. 20.-I have seen poor Amelia once more, and perhaps for the last time. She has failed rapidly of late, and Ernest says may drop away at almost any time.

When I went in, she took me by the hand, and with great difficulty, and at intervals said something like this:

"I have made up my mind to it, and I know it must come. I want to see Dr. Cabot. Do you think he would be willing to visit me after my neglecting him so?"

"I am sure he would," I cried.

"I want to ask him if he thinks I was a Christian at that time-you know when. If I was, then I need not be so afraid to die."

"But, dear Amelia, what he thinks is very little to the purpose. The question is not whether you ever gave yourself to God, but whether you are His now. But I ought not to talk to you. Dr. Cabot will know just what to say."

"No, but I want to know what you thought about it."

I felt distressed, as I looked at her wasted dying figure, to be called on to help decide such a question. But I knew what I ought to say, and said it:

"Do not look back to the past it is useless. Give yourself to Christ now."

She shook her head.

"I do not know how," she said. "Oh, Katy, pray to God to let me live long enough to get ready to die. I have led a worldly life. I shudder at the bare thought of dying I must have time."

"Do not wait for time," I said, with tears, "get ready now, this minute. A thousand years would not make you more fit to die."

So I came away, weary and heavy- laden, and on the way home stopped to tell Dr. Cabot all about it, and by this time he is with her.

"MARCH 1.-Poor Amelia's short race on earth is over. Dr. Cabot saw her every few days and says he hopes she did depart in Christian faith, though without Christian joy. I have not seen her since that last interview. That excited me so that Ernest would not let me go again.

Martha has been there nearly the whole time for three or four weeks, and I really think it has done her good. She seems less absorbed in mere outside things, and more lenient toward me and my failings.

I do not know what is to become of those mother little girls. I wish I could take them into my own home, but, of course, that is not even to be thought at this juncture. Ernest says their father seemed nearly distracted when Amelia died, and that his uncle is going to send him off to Europe immediately.

I have been talking with Ernest about Amelia.

"What do you think," I asked, "about her last days on earth? Was there really any preparation for death?

"These scenes are very painful," he returned. "Of course there is but one real preparation for Christian dying, and that is Christian living."

"But the sick-room often does what a prosperous life never did!"

"Not often. Sick persons delude themselves, or are deluded by their friends they do not believe they are really about to die. Besides, they are bewildered and exhausted by disease, and what mental strength they have is occupied with studying symptoms, watching for the doctor, and the like. I do not now recall a single instance where a worldly Christian died a happy, joyful death, in all my practice."

"Well, in one sense it makes no difference whether they die happily or not. The question is do they die in the Lord?"

"It may make no vital difference to them, but we must not forget that God is honored or dishonored by the way a Christian dies, as well as by the way in which he lives. There is great significance in the description given in the Bible of the death by which John should 'Glorify God' to my mind it that to die well is to live well."

"But how many thousands die suddenly, or of such exhausting disease that they cannot honor God by even one feeble word."

"Of course, I do not, refer to such cases. All I ask is that those whose minds are clear, who are able to attend to all other final details, should let it be seen what the gospel of Christ can do for poor sinners in the great exigency of life, giving Him the glory. I can tell you, my darling, that standing, as I so often do, by dying beds, this whole subject has become one of great magnitude to my mind And it gives me positive personal pain to see heirs of the eternal kingdom, made such by the ignominious death of their Lord, go shrinking and weeping to the full possession of their inheritance."

Ernest is right, I am sure, but how shall the world, even the Christian world, be convinced that it may have blessed foretastes of heaven while yet plodding upon earth, and faith to go thither joyfully, for the simple asking?

Poor Amelia! But she understands it all now. It is a blessed thing to have this great faith, and it is a blessed thing to have a Savior who accepts it when it is but a mere grain of mustard-seed!

MAY 24.-I celebrated my little Una's third birthday by presenting her with a new brother. Both the children welcomed him with delight that was itself compensation enough for all it cost me to get up such a celebration. Martha takes a most prosaic view of this proceeding, in which she detects malice pretense on my part. She says I shall now have one mouth the more to fill, and two feet the more to shoe more disturbed nights, more laborious days, and less leisure for visiting, reading, music, and drawing.

Well! This is one side of the story, to be sure, but I look at the other. Here is a sweet, fragrant mouth to kiss here are two more feet to make music with their pattering about my nursery. Here is a soul to train for God, and the body in which it dwells is worthy all it will cost, since it is the abode of a kingly tenant. I may see less of friends, but I have gained one dearer than them all, to whom, while I minister in Christ's name, I make a willing sacrifice of what little leisure for my own recreation my other darlings had left me. Yes, my precious baby, you are welcome to your mother's heart, welcome to her time, her strength, her health, her tenderest cares, to her life- long prayers! Oh, how rich I am, how truly, how wondrously blest!

JUNE 5.-We begin to be woefully crowded. We need a larger house, or a smaller household. I am afraid I secretly, down at the bottom of my heart, wish Martha and her father could give place to my little ones. May God forgive me if this is so! It is a poor time for such emotions when He has just given me another darling child, for whom I have as rich and ample a love as if I had spent no affection on the other twain. I have made myself especially kind to poor father and to Martha lest they should perceive how inconvenient it is to have them here, and be pained by it. I would not for the world despoil them of what little satisfaction they may derive from living with us. But, oh! I am so selfish, and it is so hard to practice the very law of love I preach to my children! Yet I want this law to rule and reign in my home, that it may be a little heaven below, and I will not, no, I will not, cease praying that it may be such, no matter what it costs me. Poor father! Poor old man! I will try to make your home so sweet and home-like to you that when you change it for heaven it shall be but a transition from one bliss to a higher!

EVENING.-Soon after writing that I went down to see father, whom I have had to neglect of late, baby has so used up both time and strength.. I found him and Martha engaged in what seemed to be an exciting debate, as Martha had a fiery little red spot on each cheek, and was knitting furiously. I was about to retreat, when she got up in a flurried way and went off, saying, as she went:

"You tell her, father I cannot."

I went up to him tenderly and took his hand. Ah, how gentle and loving we are when we have just been speaking to God!

"What is it, dear father?" I asked, "Is anything troubling you?"

"She is going to be married," he replied.

"Oh, father!" I cried, "How n-" nice, I was going to say, but stopped just in time.

All my abominable selfishness that I thought I had left at my Master's feet ten minutes before now came trooping back in full force.

"She's going to be married she'll go away, and will take her father to live with her! I can have room for my children, and room for mother! Every element of discord will now leave my home, and Ernest will see what I really am!"

These were the thoughts that rushed through my mind, and that illuminated my face.

"Does Ernest know?" I asked.

"Yes, Ernest has known it for some weeks."

Then I felt injured and inwardly accused Ernest of unkindness in keeping so important a fact a secret. But when I went back to my children, vexation with him took flight at once. The coming of each new child strengthens and deepens my desire to be what I would have it become makes my faults more odious in my eyes, and elevates my whole character. What a blessed discipline of joy and of pain my married life has been how thankful I am to reap its fruits even while pricked by its thorns!

JUNE 21.-It seems that the happy man who has wooed Martha and won her is no less a personage than old Mr. Underhill. His ideal of a woman is one who has no nerves, no sentiment, no backaches, no headaches, who will see that the wheels of her household machinery are kept well oiled, so that he need never hear them creak, and who, in addition to her other accomplishments, believes in him and will be kind enough to live forever for his private accommodation. This expose of his sentiments he has made to me in a loud, cheerful, pompous way, and he has also favored me with a description of his first wife, who lacked all these qualifications, and was obliging enough to depart in peace at an early stage of their married life, meekly preferring thus to make way for a worthier successor. Mr. Underhill with all his foibles, however, is on the whole a good man. He intends to take Amelia's little girls into his own home, and be a father, as Martha will be a mother, to them. For this reason, he hurries on the marriage, after which they will all go at once to his countryseat, which is easy of access, and which he says he is sure father will enjoy. Poor old father I hope he will, but when the subject is alluded to he maintains a somber silence, and it seems to me he never spent so many days alone in his room, brooding over his misery, as he has of late. Oh, that I could comfort him.

JULY 12.-The marriage was appointed for the first of the month, as old Mr. Underhill wanted to get out of town before the Fourth. As the time drew near, Martha began to pack father's trunk as well as her own, and brush in and out of his room till he had no rest for the sole of his foot, and seemed as forlorn as a pelican in the wilderness.

I know no more striking picture of desolation than that presented by one of these quaint birds, standing upon a single leg, feeling as the story has it, "den Jammer und das Elend der Welt."

On the last evening in June, we all sat together on the piazza, enjoying, each in our own way, a refreshing breeze that had sprung up after a sultry day. Father was quieter than usual, and seemed very languid. Ernest who, out of regard to Martha's last evening at home, had joined our little circle, ob served this, and said, cheerfully:

"You will feel better as soon as you are once more out of the city, father."

Father made no reply for some minutes, and when he did speak, we were all startled to find that his voice trembled as if he were shedding tears. We could not understand what he said. I went to him and made him lean his head upon me as he often did when it ached. He took my hand in both his.

"You do love the old man a little?" he asked, in the same tremulous voice.

"Indeed, I do!" I cried, greatly touched by his helpless appeal, "I love you dearly, father. And I shall miss you sadly."

"Must I go away then?" he whispered. "Cannot I stay here till my summons hence? It will not be long, it will not be long, my child."

With the cry of a hurt animal, Martha sprang up and rushed past us into the house. Ernest followed her, and we heard them talking together a long time. At last, Ernest joined us.

"Father," he said, "Martha is a good deal wounded and disappointed, at your reluctance to, go with her. She threatened to break off her engagement rather than to be separated from you. I really think you would be better off with her than with us. You would enjoy country life, because it is what you have been accustomed to you could spend hours of every day in driving about just what your health requires."

Father did not reply. He took Ernest's arm and tottered into the house. Then we had a most painful scene. Martha reminded him with bitter tears that her mother had committed him to her with her last breath and set before him all the advantages he would have in her house over ours. Father sat pale and inflexible tear after tear rolling down his cheeks. Ernest looked distressed and ready to sink. As for me, I cried with Martha, and with her father by turns, and clung to Ernest with a feeling that all the foundations of the earth were giving way. It came time for evening prayers, and Ernest prayed as he rarely does, for he is rarely so moved. He quieted us all by a few simple words of appeal to Him who loved us, and father then consented to spend the summer with Martha if he might call our home his home, and be with us through the winter. But this was not till long after the rest of us went to bed, and a hard battle with Ernest. He says Ernest is his favorite child, and that I am his favorite daughter, and our children inexpressibly dear to him. I am ashamed to write down what he said of me. Besides, I am sure there is a wicked, wicked triumph over Martha in my secret heart. I am too elated with his extraordinary preference for us, to sympathize with her mortification and grief as ought. Something whispered that she who has never pitied me deserves no pity now. But I do not like this mean and narrow spirit in myself any more, I hate and abhor it.

The marriage took place and they all went off together, father's rigid, white face, whiter, more rigid than ever. I am to go to mothers with the children at once. I feel that a great stone has been rolled away from before the door of my heart the one human being who refused me a kindly smile, a sympathizing word, has gone, never to return. May God go with her and give her a happy home, and make her true and loving to those motherless little ones!

Chapter 19

OCTOBER 1. - I have had a charming summer with dear mother and now I have the great joy, so long deferred, of having her in my own home. Ernest has been very cordial about it, and James has settled up all her worldly affairs, so that she has nothing to do now but to love us and let us love her. It is a pleasant picture to see her with my little darlings about her, telling the old sweet story she told me so often, and making God and Heaven and Christ such blissful realities. As I listen, I realize that it is to her I owe that early, deeply seated longing to please the Lord Jesus, which I never remember as having a beginning, or an ending, though it did have its fluctuations. And it is another pleasant picture to see her sit in her own old chair, which Ernest was thoughtful enough to have brought for her, pondering cheerfully over her Bible and her Thomas a Kempis just as I have seen her do ever since I can remember. And there is still a third pleasant picture, only that it is a new one it is as she sits at my right hand at the table, the living personification of the blessed gospel of good tidings, with father, opposite, the fading image of the law given by Moses. For father has come back father and all his ailments, his pillboxes, his fits of despair and his fits of dying. But he is quiet and gentle, and even loving, and as he sits in his corner, his Bible on his knees, I see how much more he reads the New Testament than he used to do, and that the fourteenth chapter of St. John almost opens to him of itself.

I must do Martha the justice to say that her absence, while it increases my domestic peace and happiness, increases my cares also. What with the children, the housekeeping, the thought for mother's little comforts and the concern for father's, I am like a bit of chaff driven before the wind, and always in a hurry. There are so many stitches to be taken, so many things to pass through one's brain ! Mother says no mortal woman ought to undertake so much, but what can I do? While Ernest is straining every nerve to pay off those debts, I must do all the needlework, and we must get along with servants whose want of skill makes them willing to put up with low wages. Of course, I cannot tell mother this, and I really believe she thinks I scrimp and pinch and overdo out of mere stinginess.

DECEMBER 30.-Ernest came to me today with our accounts for the last three months. He looked quite worried, for him, and asked me if there were any expenses we could cut down.

My heart jumped up into my mouth, and I said in an irritated way:

"I am killing myself with over-work now. Mother says so. I sew every night till twelve o'clock, and I feel all jaded out,"

"I did not mean that I wanted you to do anymore than you are doing now, dear," he said, kindly. "I know you are all jaded out, and I look on this state of feverish activity with great anxiety. Are all these stitches absolutely necessary?"

"You men know nothing about such things," I said, while my conscience pricked me as I went on hurrying to finish the fifth tuck in one of Una's little dresses. "Of course I want my children to look decent."

Ernest sighed.

"I really do not know what to do," he said, in a hopeless way. "Father's persisting in living with us is throwing a burden on you, that with all your other cares is quite too much for you. I see and feel it every day. Do not you think I had better explain this to him and let him go to Martha's?"

"No, indeed!" I said. "He shall stay here if it kills me, poor old man!"

Ernest began once more to look over the bills.

"I do not know how it is," he said, "but since Martha left us our expenses have increased a good deal."

Now the truth is that when Auntie paid me most generously for teaching her children, I did not dare to offer my earnings to Ernest, lest he should be annoyed. So I had quietly used it for household expenses, and it had held out till about the time of Martha's marriage. Ernest's injustice was just as painful, just as insufferable as if he had known this, and I now burst out with whatever my rasped, over-taxed nerves impelled me to say, like one possessed.

Ernest was annoyed and surprised.

"I thought we had done with these things," he said, and gathering up the papers, he went off.

I rose and locked my door and threw myself down upon the floor in an agony of shame, anger, and physical exhaustion. I did not know how large a part of what seemed mere childish ill-temper was really the cry of exasperated nerves, that had been on too strained a tension, and silent too long, and Ernest did not know it either. How could he? His profession kept him for hours every day in the open air there were times when his work was done and he could take entire rest and his health is absolutely perfect. But I did not make any excuse for myself at the moment. I was overwhelmed with the sense of my utter unfitness to be a wife and a mother.

Then I heard Ernest try to open the door and finding it locked, he knocked, calling pleasantly:

"It is I, darling let me in."

I opened it reluctantly enough.

"Come," he said, "put on your things and drive about with me on my rounds. I have no long visits to make, and while I am seeing my patients you will be getting the air, which you need."

"I do not want to go," I said. "I do not feel well enough. Besides, there's my work." "You cannot see to sew with these red eyes," he declared. "Come! I prescribe a drive, as your physician."

"Oh, Ernest, how kind, how forgiving you are?", I cried, running into the arms he held out to me, "If you knew how ashamed, how sorry, I am!"

"And if you only knew how ashamed and sorry I am!" he returned. "I ought to have seen how you taxing and over-taxing yourself, doing your work and Martha's too. It must not go on so."

By this time, with a veil over my face, he had got me downstairs and out into the air, which fanned my fiery cheeks and cooled my heated brain. It seemed to me that I have had all this tempest about nothing at all, and that with a character still so undisciplined, I was utterly unworthy to be either a wife or a mother. But when I tried to say so in broken words, Ernest comforted me with the gentleness and tenderness of a woman.

"Your character is not undisciplined, my darling," he said. "Your nervous organization is very peculiar, and you have had unusual cares and trials from the beginning of our married life. I ought not to have confronted you with my father's debts at a moment when you had every reason to look forward to freedom from most petty economies and cares."

"Do not say so," I interrupted. "If you had not told me you had this draft on your resources I should have always suspected you of meanness. For you know, dear, you have kept me-that is to say-you 'could not help it, but I suppose men cannot understand how many demands are made upon a mother for money almost every day. I got along very well till the children came, but since then it has been very hard."

"Yes," he said, "I am sure it has. But let me finish what I was going to say. I want you to make a distinction for yourself, which I make for you, between mere ill temper, and the irritability that is the result of a goaded state of the nerves. Until you do that, nothing can be done to relieve you from what I am sure, distresses and grieves you exceedingly. Now, I suppose that whenever you speak to me or the children in this irritated way you lose your own self-respect, for the time, at least, and feel degraded in the sight of God also."

"Oh, Ernest! There are no words in any language that mean enough to express the anguish I feel when I speak quick, impatient words to you, the one human being in the universe whom I love with all my heart and soul, and to my darling little children who are almost as dear! I pray and mourn over it day and night. God only knows how I hate myself on account of this one horrible sin!"

"It is a sin only as you deliberately and willfully fulfill the conditions that lead to such results. Now I am sure if you could once make up your mind in the fear of God, never to undertake more work of any sort than you can carry on calmly, quietly, without hurry or flurry, and the instant you find yourself growing nervous and like one out of breath, would stop and take breath, you would find this simple, common-sense rule doing for you what no prayers or tears could ever accomplish. Will you try it for one month, my darling?"

"But we cannot afford it," I cried, with almost a groan. "Why, you have told me this very day that our expenses must be cut down, and now you want me to add to them by doing less work. But the work must be done. The children must be clothed, there is no end to the stitches to be taken for them, and your stockings must be mended-you make enormous holes in them! And you do not like it if you ever find a button wanting to a shirt or your supply of shirts getting low."

"All you say may be very true," he returned, "but I am determined that you shall not be driven to desperation as you have been of late."

By this time we had reached the house where his visit was to be made, and I had nothing to do but lean back and revolve all he had been saying, over and over again, and to see its reasonableness while I could not see what was so be done for my relief. Ah, I have often felt in moments of bitter grief at my impatience with my children, that perhaps God pitied more than He blamed me for it! And now my dear husband was doing the same!

When Ernest had finished his visit, we drove on again in silence.

At last, I asked:

"Do tell me, Ernest, if you worked out this problem all by yourself?"

He smiled a little.

"No, I did not. But I have had a patient for two or three years whose case has interested me a good deal, and for whom I finally prescribed just as I have done for you. The thing worked like a charm, and she is now physically and morally quite well.

"I dare say her husband is a rich man," I said.

"He is not as poor as your husband, at any rate," Ernest replied. "But rich or poor I am determined not to sit looking on while you exert yourself so far beyond your strength. Just think, dear, suppose for fifty or a hundred or two hundred dollars a year you could buy a sweet, cheerful, quiet tone of mind, would you hesitate one moment to do so? And you can do it if you will. You are not ill-tempered but quick-tempered the irritability which annoys you so is a physical infirmity which will disappear the moment you cease to be goaded into it by that exacting mistress you have hitherto been to yourself."

All this sounded very plausible while Ernest was talking, but the moment I got home, I snatched up my work from mere force of habit.

"I may as well finish this as it is begun," I said to myself, arid the stitches flew from my needle like sparks of fire. Little Ernest came and begged for a story, but I put him off. Then Una wanted to sit in my lap, but I told her I was too busy. In the course of an hour the influence of the fresh air and Ernest's talk had nearly lost their power over me my thread kept breaking, the children leaned on and tired me, the baby woke up and cried, and I got all out of patience.

"Do go away, Ernest," I said, "and let mamma have a little peace. Do not you see how busy I am? Go and play with Una like a good boy." But he would not go, and kept teasing Una till she too, began to cry, and she and baby made a regular concert of it.

"Oh dear!" I sighed, "This work will never be done!" and threw it down impatiently, and took the baby impatiently, and began to walk up and down with him impatiently. I was not willing that this little darling, whom I love so dearly, should get through with his nap and interrupt my work yet I was displeased with myself, and tried by kissing him to make some amends for the hasty, un pleasant tones with which I had grieved him and frightened the other children. This evening Ernest came to me with a larger sum of money than he had ever given me at one time.

"Now every cent of this is to be spent," he said, "in having work done. I know any number of poor women who will be thankful to have all you can give them."

Dear me I it is easy to talk, and I do feel grateful to Ernest for his thoughtfulness and kindness. But I am almost in rags, and need every cent of this money to make myself decent. I am positively ashamed to go anywhere, my clothes are so shabby. Besides, supposing I leave off sewing and all sorts of over-doing of a kindred nature, I must nurse baby, I suppose, and be up with him nights and others will have their cross days and their sick and father will have his. Alas, there can be for no royal road to a "sweet, cheerful, quiet tone of mind!"

JANUARY I, 1844.-Mother says Ernest is entirely right in forbidding my working so hard. I own that I already feel better. I have all the time I need to read my Bible and to pray now, and the children do not irritate and annoy me as they did. Who knows but I shall yet become quite amiable?

Ernest made his father very happy today by telling him that ,the last of those wretched debts is paid. I think that he might have told me that this deliverance was at hand. I did not know but we had years of these struggles with poverty before us. What with the relief from this anxiety, my improved state of health, and father's pleasure, I am in splendid spirits today. Ernest, too, seems wonderfully cheerful, and we both feel that we may now look forward to a quiet happiness we have never known. With such a husband and such children as mine, I ought to be the most grateful creature on earth. And I have dear mother and James besides. I do not quite know what to think about James' relation to Lucy. He is so brimful running over with happiness that he is also full of fun and of love, and after all, he may only like her as a cousin.

FEB. 14.-Father has not been so well of late. It seems as if he kept up until he was relieved about those debts, and then sunk down. I read to him a good deal, and so does mother, but his mind is still dark, and he looks forward to the hour of death with painful misgivings. He is getting a little childish about my leaving him, and clings to me exactly as if I were his own child. Martha spends a good deal of time with him, and fusses over him in a way that I wonder she does not see is annoying to him. He wants to be read to, to hear a hymn sung or a verse repeated, and to be left otherwise in perfect quiet. But she is continually pulling out and shaking up his pillows, bathing his head in hot vinegar and soaking his feet. It looks so odd to see her in one of the elegant silk dresses old .Mr. Underhill makes her wear, with her sleeves rolled up, the skirt hid away under a large apron, rubbing away at poor father till it seems as if his tired soul would fly out of him.

FEB. 20.-Father grows weaker every day. Ernest has sent for his other children, John and Helen. Martha is no longer able to come here her husband is very sick with a fever, and cannot be left alone. No doubt, he enjoys her bustling way of nursing, and likes to have his pillows pushed from under him every five minutes. I am afraid I feel glad that she is kept away, and that I have father all to myself. Ernest never was so fond of me as he is now. I do not know what to make of it.

FEB 22.-John and his wife and Helen have come. They stay at Martha's, where there is plenty of room. John's wife is a little soft dumpling thing, and looks up to him as a mouse would up at a steeple. He strikes me as a very selfish man. He steers straight for the best seat, leaving her standing, if need be, accepts her humble attentions with the air of one collecting his just debt, and is continually snubbing and setting her right. Yet in some things he is very like Ernest, and perhaps a wife destitute of self-assertion and without much individuality would have spoiled him as Harriet has spoiled John. For I think it must be partly her fault that he dares to be so egotistical. Helen, is the dearest, prettiest creature I ever saw. Oh, why would James take a fancy to Lucy! I feel the new delight of having a sister to love and to admire. And she will love me in time I feel sure of it.

MARCH 1.-Father is very feeble and in great mental distress. He gropes about in the dark, and shudders at the approach of death. We can do nothing but pray for him. And the cloud will be lifted when he leaves this world, if not before. For I know he is a good, yes, a saintly man, dear to and dear to Christ.

MARCH 4.-Dear father has gone. We were all kneeling and praying and weeping around him, when suddenly he called me to come to him. I went and let him lean his head on my breast, as he loved to do. Sometimes I have stood so by the hour together ready to sink with fatigue, and only kept up with the thought that if this were my own precious father's bruised head I could stand and hold it forever.

"Daughter Katherine," he said, in his faint, tremulous way, "you have come with me to the very brink of the river. I thank God for all your cheering words and ways. I thank God for giving you to be a helpmeet to my son. Farewell, now," he added, in a low, firm voice, "I feel the bottom, and it is good!"

He lay back on his pillow looking upward with an expression of seraphic peace and joy on his worn, meager face, and so his life passed gently away.

Oh, the affluence of God's payments! What a recompense for the poor love I had given my husband's father, and the poor little services I had rendered him! Oh, that I had never been impatient with him, never smiled at his peculiarities, never in my secret heartfelt him unwelcome to my home! And how wholly I overlooked, in my blind selfishness, what he must have suffered in feeling himself, homeless, and dwelling with us on sufferance, but master and head nowhere on earth! May God carry the lessons home to my heart of hearts, and make the cloud of mingled remorse and shame which now envelops me to descend in showers of love and benediction on every human soul that mine can bless!

Chapter 20

APRIL. - I HAVE had a new lesson, which has almost broken my heart. In looking over his father's papers, Ernest found a little journal, brief in its records indeed, but we learn from it that on all those wedding and birthdays, when I fancied his austere religion made him hold aloof from our merry-making, he was spending the time in fasting and praying for us and for our children! Oh, shall I ever learn the sweet charity that thinks no evil, and believes all things? What blessings may not have descended upon us and our children through those prayers! What evils may they not have warded off! Dear old father! Oh, that I could once more put my loving arms about him and bid him welcome to our home! And how gladly would I now confess to him all my unjust judgments concerning him and entreat his forgiveness! Must life always go on thus? Must I always be erring, ignorant and blind? How I hate this arrogant sweeping past my brother man this utter ignoring of his hidden life?

I see now that it is well for mother that she did not come to live with me at the beginning of my married life. I should not have borne with her little peculiarities, nor have made her half so happy as I can now. I thank God that my varied disappointments and discomforts, my feeble health, my poverty, my mortifications have done me some little good, and driven me to Him a thousand times because I could not get along without His help. But I am not satisfied with my state in His sight. I am sure something is lacking, though I know not what it is.

MAY Helen is going to stay here and live with Martha How glad how enchanted I am! Old Mr. Underhill is getting well. I saw him today. He can talk of nothing but his illness, of Martha's wonderful skill in nursing him declaring that he owes his life to her. I felt a little piqued at this speech, because Ernest was very attentive to him, and no doubt did his share towards the cure. We have fitted up father's room for a nursery. Hitherto all the children have had to sleep in our room, which has been bad for them and bad for us. I have been so afraid they would keep Ernest awake if they were unwell and restless. I have secured an excellent nurse, who is as fresh and blooming as the flower whose name she bears. The children are already attached to her, and I feel that the worst of my life is now over.

JUNE.-Little Ernest was taken sick on the day I wrote that. The attack was fearfully sudden and violent. He is still very, very ill. I have not forgotten that I said once that I would give my children to God should He ask for them. But oh, this agony of suspense! It eats into my soul and eats it away. Oh, my little Ernest! My first-born son! My pride, my joy, my hope! And I thought the worst of my life was over!

AUGUST.-We have come into the country with what God has left us, our two youngest children. Yes, I have tasted the bitter cup of bereavement, and drunk it down to its dregs. I gave my darling to God, I gave him, I gave him! But, oh, with what anguish I saw those round, dimpled limbs wither and waste away, the glad smile fade forever from that beautiful face! What a fearful thing it is to be a mother! But I have given my child to God. I would not recall him if I could. I am thankful He has counted me worthy to present Him so costly a gift.

I cannot shed a tear, and I must find relief in writing, or I shall lose my senses. My noble, beautiful boy! My first-born son! And to think that my delicate little Una still lives, and that death has claimed that bright, glad creature who was the sunshine of our home!

But let me not forget my mercies. Let me not forget that I have a precious husband and two darling children, and my kind, sympathizing mother left to me. Let me not forget how many kind friends gathered about us in our sorrow. Above all, let me remember God's loving-kindness and tender mercy. He has not left us to the bitterness of a grief that refuses and disdains to be comforted. We believe in Him, we love Him, we worship as we never did before. My dear Ernest has felt this sorrow to his heart's core. But he has not for one moment questioned the goodness or the love of our Father in thus taking from us the child who promised to be our greatest earthly joy Our consent to God's will has drawn us together very closely, together we bear the yoke in our youth, together we pray and sing praises in the very midst of our tears "I was dumb with silence because Thou didst it."

SEPT. The old pain and cough have come back with the first cool nights of this month Perhaps I am going to my darling- I do not know I am certainly very feeble Consenting to suffer does not annul the suffering Such a child could not go hence without rending and tearing its way out of the heart that loved it. This world is wholly changed to me and I walk in it like one in a dream. And dear Ernest is changed, too. He says little, and is all kindness and goodness to me, but I can see here is a wound that will never be healed. I am confined to my room now with nothing do but to think, think, think. I do not believe God has taken our child in mere displeasure, but cannot but feel that this affliction might not have been necessary if I had not so chafed and writhed and secretly repined at the way in which my home was invaded, and at our galling poverty. God has exchanged the one discipline for the other and oh, how far more bitter is this cup!

Oct. 4.- My darling boy would have been six years old today. Ernest still keeps me shut up, but he rather urges my seeing a friend now and. People say very strange things in the way of consolation. I begin to think that a tender clasp of the hand is about all one can give to the afflicted. One says I must not grieve, because my child is better off in heaven. Yes, he is better off I know it, I .feel it but I miss him nonetheless. Others say he might have grown up to be a bad man and broken my heart. Perhaps he might, but I cannot make myself believe that likely. One lady asked me if this affliction was not a rebuke of my idolatry of my darling and another, if I had not been in a cold, worldly state, needing this severe blow on that account.

But I find no consolation or support in the remarks. My comfort is in my perfect faith in the goodness and love of my Father, my certainty that He had a reason in thus afflicting me that I should admire and adore if I knew what it was. And in the midst of my sorrow, I have had and do have a delight in Him hitherto unknown, so that sometimes this room in which I am a prisoner seems like the very gate of heaven.

MAY.-A long winter in my room, and all sorts of painful remedies and appliances and deprivations. And now I am getting well, and drive out every day. Martha sends her carriage, and mother goes with me. Dear mother! How nearly perfect she is! I never saw a sweeter face, nor ever heard sweeter expressions of faith in God, and love to all about her than hers. She has been my tower strength all through these weary months and she has shared my sorrow and made it her own.

I can see that dear Ernest's affliction and this prolonged anxiety about me have been a heavenly benediction to him I am sure that every mother whose sick child he visits will have a sympathy he could not have given while all our own little ones were alive and well. I thank God that He has thus increased my dear husband's usefulness as I think that He has mine also How tenderly I already feel towards all suffering children, and how easy it will be now to be patient with them!

KEENE N H JULY 12 It is a year ago this day that the brightest sunshine faded out of our lives, and our beautiful boy was taken from us. I have been tempted to spend this anniversary in bitter tears and lamentations for oh, this sorrow is not healed by time! I feel it more and more but I begged God when I first awoke this morning not to let me so dishonor and grieve Him. I may suffer, I must suffer, He means it, He wills it, but let it be without repining, without gloomy despondency. The world is full of sorrow it is not I alone who taste its bitter draughts, nor have I the only right to a sad countenance. Oh, for patience to bear on, cost what it may!

"Cheerfully and gratefully I lay myself and all that I am or own at the feet of Him who redeemed me with His precious blood, engaging to follow Him, bearing the cross He lays upon me." This is the least I can do, and I do it while my heart lies broken and bleeding at His feet.

My dear little Una has improved somewhat in health, but I am never free from anxiety about her. She is my milk-white lamb, my dove, my fragrant flower. One cannot look in her pure face without a sense of peace and rest. She is the sentinel who voluntarily guards my door when I am engaged at my devotions she is my little comforter when I am sad, my companion, and friend at all times. I talk to her of Christ, and always have done, just as I think of Him, and as if I expected sympathy from her in my love to Him. It was the same with my darling Ernest. If I required a little self-denial, I said cheerfully, "This is hard, but doing it for our best Friend sweetens it," and their alacrity was pleasant to see. Ernest threw his whole soul into whatever he did, and sometimes when engaged in play would hesitate a little when directed to do something else, such as carrying a message for me, and the like. But if I said, "If you do this cheerfully and pleasantly, my darling, you do it for Jesus, and that will make Him smile upon you," he would invariably yield at once.

Is not this the true, the natural way of linking every little daily act of a child's life with that Divine Love, that Divine Life which gives meaning to all things?

But what do I mean by the vain boast that I have always trained my children thus? Alas! I have done it only at times for while my theory was sound, my temper of mind was but too often unsound. I was often and often impatient with my dear little boy often my tone was a worldly one I often full of eager interest in mere outside things, and forgot that I was living or that my children were living save for the present moment.

It seems now that I have a child in heaven, and am bound to the invisible world by such a tie that I can never again be entirely absorbed by this.

I fancy my ardent, eager little boy as having some such employments in his new and happy home as he had here. I see him loving Him who took children in His arms and blessed them, with all the warmth of which his nature is capable, and as perhaps employed as one of those messengers whom God sends forth as His ministers. For I cannot think of those active feet, those busy hands as always quiet. Ah, my darling, that I could look in upon you for a moment, a single moment, and catch one of your radiant smiles just one!

AUGUST 4.-How full are David's Psalms of the cry of the sufferer! He must have experienced every kind of bodily and mental torture. He gives most vivid illustrations of the wasting, wearing process of disease-for instance, what a contrast is the picture we have of him when he was "ruddy, and withal of a beautiful countenance, and goodly to look to," and the one he paints of himself in after years, when he says, "I may tell all my bones. They look and stare upon me my days are like a, shadow that declines, and I am withered like grass. I am weary with groaning all the night make I my bed to swim I water my couch with my tears. For my soul is full of troubles and my life draws near unto the grave,"

And then what wails of anguish are these!

"I am afflicted, and ready to die from my youth up, while I suffer thy terrors I am distracted. Thy wrath lies hard upon me and thou hast afflicted me with all thy waves. All thy waves and thy billows have gone over me. Lover and friend hast thou put far from me, and mine acquaintance into utter darkness."

Yet through it all what grateful joy in God, what expressions of living faith and devotion! During my long illness and confinement to my room, the Bible has been almost a new book to me, and I see that God has always dealt with His children as He deals with them now, and that no new thing has befallen me. All these weary days so full of languor, these nights so full of unrest, have had their appointed mission to my soul. And perhaps I have had no discipline so salutary as this forced inaction and uselessness, at a time when youth and natural energy continually cried out for room and work.

AUGUST 15.-I dragged out my drawing materials in a listless way this morning, and began to sketch the beautiful scene from my window. At first, I could not feel interested. It seemed as if my hand was crippled and lost its cunning when it unloosed its grasp of little Ernest, and let him go. But I prayed, as I worked, that I might not yield to the inclination to despise and throw away the gift with which God has Himself endowed me. Mother was gratified, and said it rested her to see me act like myself once more. Ah, I have been very selfish, and have been far too much absorbed with my sorrow and my illness and my own petty struggles.

AUGUST 19.-I met today an old friend, Maria Kelly, who is married, it seems, and settled down in this pretty village. She asked so many questions about my little Ernest that I had to tell her the whole story of his precious life, sickness, and death. I forced myself to do this quietly, and without any great demand on her sympathies. My reward for the constraint I thus put upon myself was the abrupt question:

"Haven't you grown stoical?"

I felt the angry blood rush' through my veins as it has not done in a long time. My pride was wounded to the quick, and those cruel, unjust words still rankle in my heart. This is not as it should be. I am constantly praying that my pride may be humbled, and then when it is attacked, I shrink from the pain the blow causes, and am angry with the hand that inflicts it. It is just so with two or three unkind things Martha has said to me. I cannot help brooding over them and feeling stung with their injustice, even while making the most desperate struggle to rise above and forget them. It is well for our fellow-creatures that God forgives and excuses them, when we fail to do it, and I can easily fancy that poor Maria Kelly is at this moment dearer in His sight than I am who have taken fire at a chance word And I can see now, what I wonder I did not see at the time, that God was dealing very kindly and wisely with me when He made Martha overlook my good qualities, of which I suppose I have some, as everybody else has, and call out all my bad ones, since the axe was thus laid at the root of self-love. And it is plain that self-love cannot die without a fearful struggle.

MAY 26, 1846.-How long it is since I have written in my journal! We have had a winter full of cares, perplexities, and sicknesses. Mother began it by such a severe attack of inflammatory rheumatism as I could not have supposed she could live through. Her sufferings were dreadful, and I might almost say her patience was, for I often thought it would be less painful to hear her groan and complain, than to witness such heroic fortitude, such sweet docility under God's hand. I hope I shall never forget the lessons I have learned in her sick-room. Ernest says he never shall cease to rejoice that she lives with us, and that he can watch over her health. He, has indeed been like a son to her, and this has been a great solace amid all her sufferings. Before she was able to leave the room, poor little Una was prostrated by one of her ill turns, and is still very feeble. The only way in which she can be diverted is by reading to her, and I have done little else these two months but hold her in my arms, singing little songs and hymns, telling stories and reading what few books I can find that are unexciting, simple, yet entertaining. My precious little darling! She bears the yoke in her youth without a frown, but it is agonizing to see her suffer so. How much easier it would be to bear all her physical infirmities myself! I suppose to those who look on from the outside, we must appear like a most unhappy family, since we hardly get free from one trouble before another steps in. But I see more and more that happiness is not dependent on health or any other outside prosperity. We are at peace with each other and at peace with God His dealings with us do not perplex or puzzle us, though we do not pretend to understand them. On the other hand, Martha with absolutely perfect health, with a husband entirely devoted to her, and with every wish gratified, yet seems always careworn and dissatisfied. Her servants worry her very life out she misses the homely household duties to which she has been accustomed and her conscience stumbles at little things, and overlooks greater ones. It is very interesting, I think, to study different homes, as well as the different characters that form them.

Amelia's little girls are quiet, good children, to whom their father writes what Mr. Underhill and Martha pronounce "beautiful" letters, wherein he always styles himself their "broken-hearted but devoted father." "Devotion," to my mind, involves self-sacrifice, and I cannot reconcile its use, in this case, with the life of ease he leads, while all the care of his children is thrown upon others. But some people, by means of a few such phrases, not only impose upon themselves but upon their friends, and pass for persons of great sensibility.

As I have been confined to the house nearly the whole winter, I have had to derive my spiritual support from books, and as mother gradually recovered, she enjoyed Leighton with me, as I knew she would. Dr. Cabot comes to see us very often, but, I do not now find it possible to get the instruction from him I used to do. I see that the Christian life must be individual, as the natural character is-and that I cannot be exactly like Dr. Cabot, or exactly like Mrs. Campbell, or exactly like mother, though they all three stimulate and re an inspiration to me. But I see, too, that the great points of similarity in Christ's disciples have always been the same. This is the testimony of all the good books, sermons, hymns, and, memoirs I read-that God's ways are infinitely perfect that we are to love Him for what He is, and therefore equally as much when He afflicts as when He prospers us that there is no real happiness but in doing and suffering His will, and that this life is but a scene of probation through which we pass to the real life above.

Chapter 21

MAY 30. - ERNEST asked me to go with him to see one of his patients, as he often does when there is a lull in the tempest at home. We both feel that as we have so little money of our own to give away, it is a privilege to give what services and what cheering words we can. As I took it for granted that we were going to see some poor old woman, I put up several little packages of tea and sugar, with which Susan Green always keeps me supplied, and added a bottle of my own raspberry vinegar, which never comes amiss, I find, to old people. Ernest drove to the door of an aristocratic-looking house, and helped me to alight in his usual silence.

"It is probably one of the servants we are going to visit," I thought, within myself "but I am surprised at his bringing me. The family may not approve it."

The next thing I knew I found myself being introduced to a beautiful, brilliant young lady, who sat in a wheel chair like a queen on a throne in a room full of tasteful ornaments, flowers, and birds. Now, I had come away just as I was, when Ernest called me, and that "was" means a very plain gingham dress wherein I had been darning stockings all the morning. I suppose a saint would not have cared for that, but I did, and for a moment stood the picture of confusion, my hands full of oddly shaped parcels, and my face all in a flame.

My wife, Miss Clifford," I heard Ernest say, and then I caught the curious, puzzled look in her eyes, which said as plainly as words could do:

"What has the creature brought me?"

I ask your pardon, Miss Clifford," I said, thinking it best to speak out just the honest truth, "but I supposed the doctor was taking me to see some of his old women, and so I have brought you a little tea, and a little sugar, and a bottle of raspberry vinegar!"

"How delicious!". cried she. "It really rests me to meet with a genuine human being at last! Why didn't you make some stiff, prim speech, instead of telling the truth out and out? I declare I mean to keep all you have brought me, just for the fun of the thing."

This put me at ease, and I forgot all about my dress in a moment.

"I see you are just what the doctor boasted you were," she went on. "But he never would bring you to see me before. I suppose he has told you why I could not go to see you?"

"To tell the truth, he never speaks to me of his patients unless he thinks I can be of use to them."

"I dare say I do not look much like an invalid," said she "but here I am, tied to this chair. It is six months since I could bear my own weight upon my feet."

I saw then that though her face was so bright and full of color, her hand was thin and transparent. But what a picture she made as she sat there in magnificent beauty, relieved by such a background of foliage, flowers, and artistic objects!

"I told the doctor the other day that life was nothing but a humbug, and he said he should bring me a remedy against that false notion the next time he came, and you, I suppose, are that remedy," she continued. "Come, begin I am ready to take any number of doses."

I could only laugh and try to look daggers at Ernest, who sat looking over a magazine, apparently absorbed in its contents.

"Ah!" she cried, nodding her head sagaciously, "I knew you would agree with me."

"Agree with you in calling life a humbug!" I cried, now fairly aroused. "Death itself is not more a reality!"

"I have not tried death yet," she said, more seriously "but I have tried life twenty-five years and I know all about it. It is eat, drink, sleep yawn and be bored. It is what shall I wear, where shall I go, how shall I get rid of the time it says, 'How do you do? How is your husband? How are your children? '-it means, 'Now I have asked all the conventional questions, and I do not care a fig what their answer may be.'"

"This may be its meaning to some persons," I replied, "for instance, to mere pleasure-seekers. But of course, it is interpreted quite differently by others. To some it means nothing but a dull, hopeless struggle with poverty and hardship- and its whole aspect might be changed to them, should those who do not know what to do to get rid of the time, spend their surplus leisure in making this struggle less brutalizing."

"Yes, I have heard such doctrine, and at one time I tried charity myself. I picked up a dozen or so of dirty little wretches out of the streets, and undertook to clothe and teach them. I might as well have tried to instruct the chairs in my room. Besides the whole house had to be aired after they had gone, and mamma missed two teaspoons and a fork and was perfectly disgusted with the whole thing. Then I fell to knitting socks for babies, but they only occupied my hands, and my head felt as empty as ever. Mamma took me off on a journey, as she always did when I took to moping, and that diverted me for a while. But after that, everything went on in the old way. I got rid of part of the day by changing my dress, and putting on my pretty things-it is a great thing to have a habit of wearing one's ornaments, for instance and then in the evening one could go to the opera or the theater, or some other place of amusement, after which one could sleep all through the next morning, and so get rid of that. But I had been used to such things all my life, and they had got to be about as flat as flat can be. If I had been born a little earlier in the history of the world, I would have gone into a convent but that sort of thing is out of fashion now."

"The best convent," I said, "for a woman is the seclusion of her own home. There she may find vocation and fight her battles, and there she may learn the reality and the earnestness of life."

"Pshaw!" cried she. "Excuse me, however, saying that but some of the most brilliant girls I know have settled down into mere married women and spend their whole time in nursing babies! Think how belittling!"

"Is it more so than spending it in dressing, driving, dancing, and the like?"

"Of course it is. I had a friend once who shone like a star in society. She married, and children as fast as she could. Well! What consequence? She lost her beauty, lost her spirit and animation, lost her youth, and lost her health. The only earthly things she can talk about are teething, dieting, and the measles!"

I laughed at this exaggeration, and looked round to see what Ernest thought of such talk. But he had disappeared.

"As you have spoken plainly to me, knowing, me, to be a wife and a mother, you must allow me to 'speak plainly in return," I began.

"Oh, speak plainly, by all means! I am quite sick and tired of having truth served up in pink cotton, and scented with lavender."

"Then you will permit me to say that when you speak contemptuously of the vocation of maternity, you dishonor, not only the mother who bore you, but the Lord Jesus Himself, who chose to be born of woman, and to be ministered unto by her through a helpless infancy."

Miss Clifford was a little startled.

'How terribly in earnest you are! she said. It is plain that to you, at any rate, life is indeed no humbug."

I thought of my dear ones, of Ernest, of my children, of mother, and of James, and I thought of my love to them and of theirs to me. And I thought of Him who alone gives reality to even such joys as these. My face must have been illuminated by the thought, for she dropped the bantering tone, she had used hitherto, and asked, with real earnestness:

"What is it you know, and that I do not know, that makes you so satisfied, while I am so dissatisfied?"

I hesitated before I answered, feeling as I never felt before how ignorant, how unfit to lead others, I really am. Then I said:

"Perhaps you need to know God, to know Christ?"

She looked disappointed and tired. So I came away, first promising, at her request, to go to see her again. I found Ernest just driving up, and told him what had passed. He listened in his usual silence, and I longed to have him say whether I had spoken wisely and well.

JUNE 1.-I have been to see Miss Clifford again and made mother go with me. Miss Clifford took a fancy to her at once.

"Ah!" she said, after one glance at the dear, loving face, "nobody need tell me that you are good and kind. But I am a little afraid of good people. I fancy they are always criticizing me and expecting me to imitate their perfection."

"Perfection does not exact perfection," was mother's answer. "I would rather be judged by an angel than by a man." And then mother led her on, little by little, and most adroitly, to talk of herself and of her state of health. She is an orphan and lives in this great, stately house alone with her servants. Until she was laid aside by the state of her health, she lived in the world and of it. Now she is a prisoner, and prisoners have time to think.

"Here I sit," she said, "all day .long. I never was fond of staying at home, or of reading, and needlework I absolutely hate. In fact, I do not know how to sew."

"Some such pretty, feminine work might beguile you of a few of the long hours of these long days," said mother. "One cannot be always reading."

"But a lady came to see me, a Mrs. Goodhue, one of your good sorts, I suppose, and she preached me quite a sermon on the employment of time. She said I had a solemn admonition of Providence, and ought to devote myself entirely to religion. I had just begun to be interested in a bit of embroidery, but she frightened me out of it. But I cannot bear such dreadfully good people, with faces a mile long."

Mother made her produce the collar, or whatever it was, showed her how to hold her needle and arrange her pattern, and they both got so absorbed in it that I had leisure to look at some of the beautiful things with which the room was full.

"Make the object of your life right," I heard mother say, at last, "and these little details will take care of themselves."

"But I haven't any object," Miss Clifford objected, "unless it is to get through these tedious days somehow. Before I was taken ill my chief object was to make myself attractive to the people I met and the easiest way to do that was to dress becomingly and make myself look as well as I could."

"I suppose," said mother, "that most girls could say the same. They have an instinctive desire to please, and they take what they conceive to be the shortest and easiest road to that end. It requires no talent, no education, no thought to dress tastefully the most empty-hearted frivolous young person can do it, provided she has money enough. Those who cannot get the money make up for it by fearful expenditure of precious time. They plan, they cut, they fit, they rip, and they trim till they can appear in society looking exactly like everybody else. They think of nothing, talk of nothing but how this shall be fashioned and that be trimmed and as to their hair, Satan uses it as his favorite net, and catches them in it every day of their lives."

"But I never cut or trimmed," said Miss Clifford.

"No, because you could afford to have it done for you. But you acknowledge that you spent a great deal of time in dressing because you thought that the easiest way of making yourself attractive. But it does not follow that the easiest way is the best way, and sometimes the longest way round is the shortest way home."

"For instance?"

"Well, let us imagine a young lady, living in the world as you say you lived. She has never seriously reflected on any subject one half hour in her life. She has been borne on by the current and let it take her where it would. But at last, some influence is brought to bear upon her, which leads her to stop to look about her and to think. She finds herself in a world of serious, momentous events. She see she cannot live in it, was not meant to live in it forever, and that her whole unknown future depends on what she is, not on how she looks. She begins to cast about for some plan of life, and this leads——"

"A plan of life?" Miss Clifford interrupted. "I never heard of such a thing."

"Yet you would smile at an architect, who having a noble structure to build, should begin to work on it in a haphazard way, putting in a brick here and a stone there, weaving in straws and sticks if they come to hand, and when asked on what work he was engaged, and what manner of building he intended to erect, should reply he had no plan, but thought something would come of it."

Miss Clifford made no reply. She sat with her head resting on her band, looking dreamily before her, a truly beautiful, but unconscious picture.. I too, began to reflect, that while I had really aimed to make the most out of life, I had not done it methodically or intelligently.

We are going to try to stay in town this summer. Hitherto Ernest would not listen to my suggestion of what an economy this would be. He always said this would turn out anything but an economy in the end. But now we have no teething baby little Raymond is a strong, healthy child, and Una remarkably well for her, and money is so slow to come in and so fast to go out. What discomforts we suffer in the country it would take a book to write down, and here we shall have our own home, as usual. I shall not have to be separated from Ernest, and shall have leisure to devote to two very interesting people who must stay in town all the year round, no matter who goes out of it. I mean dear Mrs. Campbell and Miss Clifford, who both attract me, though in such different ways.

Chapter 22

OCTOBER. - WELL, I had my own way, and I am afraid it has been an unwise one, for though I have enjoyed the leisure afforded by everybody being out of town, and the opportunity it has given me to devote myself to the very sweetest work on earth, the care of my darling little ones, the heat and the stifling atmosphere have been trying for me and for them. My pretty Rose went last May, to bloom in a home of her own, so I thought I would not look for a nurse, but take the whole care of them myself. This would not be much of a task to a strong person, but I am not strong, and a great deal of the time just dressing them and taking them out to walk has exhausted me. Then all the mending and other sewing must be done, and with the over-exertion creeps in the fretful tone, the impatient word. Yet I never can be as impatient with little children as I should be but for the remembrance that I should count it only a joy to minister once more to my darling boy, cost what weariness it might.

But now new cares are at hand, and I have been searching for a person to whom I can safely trust my children when I am laid aside. Thus far, I have had, in this capacity, three different Temptations in human form.

The first, a smart, tidy-looking woman, informed me at the outset that she was perfectly competent to take the whole charge of the children, and should prefer my attending to my own affairs while she attended to hers.

I replied that my affairs lay chiefly in caring for and being with my children to which she returned that she feared I should not suit her, as she had her own views concerning the training of children. She added, with condescension that at all events she should expect in any case of difference (of judgment) between us that I, being the younger and least experienced of the two should always yield to her. She then went on to give me her views on the subject of nursery management.

"In the first place," she said, "I never pet or fondle children. It makes them babyish and sickly."

"Oh, I see you will not suit me," I cried. "You need go no farther. I consider love the best educator for a little child."

"Indeed, I think I shall suit you perfectly," she replied, nothing daunted. "I have been in the business twenty years, and have always suited wherever I lived. You will be surprised to see how much sewing I shall accomplish, and how quiet I shall keep the children."

"But I do not want them kept quiet," I persisted. "I want them to be as merry and cheerful as crickets, and I care a great deal more to have them amused than to have the sewing done, though that is important, I confess."

"Very well, ma'am, I will sit and rock them by the hour if you wish it."

"But I do not wish it," I cried, exasperated at the coolness which gave her such an advantage over me. "Let us say no more about it you do not suit me, and the sooner we part the better. I must be mistress of my own house, and I want no advice in relation to my children."

"I shall hardly leave you before you will regret parting with me," she returned, in a placid, pitying, way.

I was afraid I had not been quite dignified in my interview with this person, with whom I ought to have had no discussion, and my equanimity was not restored by her shaking hands with me a patronizing way at parting, and expressing the hope that I should one day "be a green tree in the Paradise of God." Nor was it any too great a consolation to find that she had suggested to my cook that my intellect was not quite sound.

Temptation the second confessed that she knew nothing, but was willing to be taught. Yes, she might be willing, but she could not be taught. She could not see why Herbert should not have everything he chose to cry for, nor why she should not take the children to the kitchens where her friends abode, instead of keeping them out in the air. She could not understand why she must not tell Una every half hour that she was as fair as a lily, and that the little angels in heaven cried for such hair as hers. And there was no rhyme or reason, to her mind, why she could not have her friends visit in her nursery, since, as she declared, the cook would hear all her secrets if she received them in the kitchen. Her assurance that she thought me a very nice lady, and that there never were two such children as mine, failed to move my hard heart, and I was thankful when I got her out of the house.

Temptation the third appeared, for a time, the perfection of a nurse. She kept herself and the nursery and the children in most refreshing order she amused Una when she was more than usually unwell with a perfect fund of innocent stories the work flew from her nimble fingers as if by magic. I boasted everywhere of my good luck, and sang her praises in Ernest's ears till he believed in her with all his heart. But one night we were out late we had been spending the evening at Auntie's, and came in with Ernest's night-key as quietly as possible, in order not to arouse the children. I stole softly to the nursery to see if all was going on well there. Bridget, it seems, had taken the opportunity to wash her clothes in the nursery, and they hung all about the room drying, a hot fire raging for the purpose. In the midst of them, with a candle and prayer book on a chair, Bridget knelt fast asleep, the candle within an inch of her sleeve. Her assurance when I aroused her that she was not asleep, but merely rapt in devotion, did not soften my hard heart, nor was I moved by the representation that she was a saint, and always wore black on that account. I packed her off in anything but a saintly frame, and felt that a fourth Temptation would scatter what little grace I possessed to the four winds. These changes upstairs made discord too, below. My cook was displeased at so much coming and going, and made the kitchen a sort of a purgatory that I dreaded to enter. At last, when her temper fairly ran away with her, and she became impertinent to the last degree, I said, coolly:

"If any lady should speak to me in this way I should resent it. But no lady would so far forget herself. And I overlook your rudeness on the ground that you do not know better than to use of such expressions."

This capped the climax! She declared that she had never been told before that she was no and did not know how to behave, and gave warning at once.

I wish I could help running to tell Ernest all -these annoyances. It does no good, and only worries him. But how much of a woman's life is made up of such trials and provocations! And how easy is when on one's knees to bear them aright, and how far easier to bear them wrong when one finds the coal going too fast, the butter out just as sitting down to breakfast, the potatoes watery, and the bread sour or heavy! And then when one is well nigh desperate, does one's husband fail to say, in bland tones:

"My dear, if you would just speak to Bridget, I am sure she would improve."

Oh, that there were indeed magic in a spoken word!

And do what I can, the money Ernest gives me will not hold out. He knows absolutely nothing about that hydra-headed monster, a household. I, have had to go back to sewing as furiously as ever. And with the sewing the old pain in the side has come back, and the sharp, quick speech that I hate, and, that Ernest hates, and that everybody hates. I groan, being burdened, and am almost weary of my life. And my prayers are all mixed up with worldly thoughts and cares. I am appalled at all the things that have got to be done before winter, and am tempted to cut short my devotions in order to have more time to accomplish what I must accomplish.

How have I got into this slough? When was it that I came down from the Mount where I had seen the Lord, and came back to make these miserable, petty things as much my business as ever? Oh, these fluctuations in my religious life amaze me! I cannot, doubt that I am really God's child it would be dishonor to Him to doubt it. I cannot doubt that I have held as real communion with Him as with any earthly friend-and oh, it has been far sweeter!

OCT. 20.-I made a parting visit to Mrs. Campbell today, and, as usual, have come away strengthened and refreshed. She said all sorts of kind things to cheer and encourage me, and stimulated me to take up the burden of life cheerfully and patiently, just as it comes. She assures me that these fluctuations of feeling will by degrees give place to a calmer life, especially if I avoid, so far as I can do it, all unnecessary work, distraction, and hurry. And a few quiet, resting words from her have given me courage to press on toward perfection, no matter how much imperfection I see in myself and others. And now I am waiting for my Father's next gift, and the new cares and labors it will bring with it. I am glad it is not left for me to decide my own lot. I am afraid I should never see precisely the right moment for welcoming a new bird into my nest, dearly as I love the rustle of their wings and the sound of their voices when they do come. And surely, He knows the right moments who knows all my struggles with a certain sort of poverty, poor health, and domestic care. If I could feel that all the time, as I do at this moment, how happy I should always be!

JANUARY 16, 1847.-This is the tenth anniversary of our wedding day, and it has been a delightful one. If I were called upon to declare what has been the chief element of my happiness, I should say it was not Ernest's love to me or mine to him, or that I am once more the mother of three children, or that my own dear mother still lives, though I revel in each and all of these. But underneath them all, deeper, stronger than all, lies a peace with God that I can compare to no other joy, which I guard as I would guard hid treasure, and which must abide if all things else pass away.

My baby is two months old, and her name is Ethel. The three children together form a beautiful picture that I am never tired of admiring. But they will not give me much time for writing. This little new comer takes all there, is of me. Mother brings me pleasant reports of Miss Clifford, who under her gentle, wise influence is becoming an earnest Christian, already rejoicing in the Providence that arrested her where it did, and forced her to reflection. Mother says we ought to study God's providence more than we do since He has a meaning and a purpose in everything He does. Sometimes I can do this and find it a source of great happiness. Then worldly cares seem mere worldly cares, and I forget that His wise, kind hand is in every one of them.

FEBRUARY.-Helen has been spending the whole day with me, as she often does, helping me with her skillful needle, and with the children, in a very sweet way. I am almost ashamed to indulge in writing down how dearly she seems to love me, and how disposed she is to sit at my feet as a learner at the very moment I am longing to possess her sweet, gentle temper. But one thing puzzles me, in her, and that is the difficulty she finds in getting hold of these simple truths her father used to grope after but never found till just as he was passing out of the world. It seems as if God had compensated such turbulent, fiery natures as mine, by revealing Himself to them, for the terrible hours of shame and sorrow through which their sins and follies cause them to pass. I suffer far more than Helen does, suffer bitterly, painfully, but I enjoy tenfold more. For I know whom I have believed, and I cannot doubt that I am truly united to Him. Helen is naturally very reserved, but by degrees she has come talk with me quite frankly. Today as we sat together in the nursery, little Raymond snatched a toy from Una, who, as usual, yielded to him without a frown. I called him to me he came reluctantly.

"Raymond, dear," I said, "Did you ever see papa snatch anything from me?"

He smiled, and shook his head.

"Well then, until you see him do it to me, never do it to your sister. Men are gentle and polite to women, and little boys should be gentle and polite to little girls."

The children ran off to their play, and Helen said,

"Now how different that is from my mother's management with us! She always made us girls yield to the boys. They would not have thought they could go up to bed unless one of us got a candle for them."

"That, I suppose, is the reason then that Ernest expected me to wait upon him after we were married," I replied. "I was a little stiff about yielding 'to him, for besides mother's precepts, I was influenced by my father's example. He was so courteous, treating her with as much respect as if she were a queen, and yet with as much love as if were always a girl. I naturally expected the like from my husband."

"You must have been disappointed then," she said.

"Yes, I was. It cost me a good many pouts and tears of which I am now ashamed. And Ernest seldom annoys me now with the little neglects that I used to make so much of."

"Sometimes I think there are no 'little' neglects," said Helen. "It takes less than nothing to annoy us."

"And it takes more than everything to please us!" I cried. "But Ernest and I had one stronghold to which we always fled in our troublous times, and that was our love for each other. No matter how he provoked me by his little heedless ways, I had to forgive him because I loved him so. And he had to forgive me my faults for the same reason."

"I had no idea husbands and wives loved each other so," said Helen. "I thought they got over it as soon as their cares and troubles came on, and just jogged on together, somehow."

We both laughed and she went on.

"If I thought I should be as happy as you are, I should be tempted to be married myself."

"Ah, I thought your time would come!" I cried.

"Do not ask me any questions," she said, her pretty face growing prettier with a bright warm glow. "Give me advice instead for instance, tell me how I can be sure that if I love a man I shall go on loving him through all the wear and tear of married life and how can I be sure he can and will go on loving me?"

"Well, then, setting aside the fact that you are both lovable and loving, I will say this: Happiness, in other words love, in married life is not a mere accident. When the union has been formed, as most Christian unions are, by God Himself, it is His intention and His will that it shall prove the unspeakable joy of both husband and wife, and become more and more so from year to year. But we are imperfect creatures, wayward and foolish as little children, horribly unreasonable, selfish, and willful. We are not capable of enduring the shock of finding at every turn that our idol is made of clay, and that it is prone to tumble off its pedestal and lie in the dust, till we pick it up and set it in its place again. I was struck with Ernest's asking in the very first prayer he offered in my presence, after our marriage, that God would help us love each other. I felt that love was the very foundation on which I was built, and that there was no danger that I should ever fall short in giving to my husband all he wanted, in full measure. But as he went on day after day repeating this prayer, and I naturally made it with him, I came to see that this most precious of earthly blessings had been and must be God's gift, and that while we both looked at it in that light, and felt our dependence on Him for it, we might safely encounter together all the assaults made upon us by the world, the flesh, and the devil. I believe we owe it to this constant prayer that we have loved each other so uniformly and with such growing comfort in each other so that our little discords always have ended in fresh accord, and our love has felt conscious of resting on a rock and that that rock was the will of God."

"It is plain, then," said Helen, "that you and Ernest are sure of one source of happiness as long as you live, whatever vicissitudes you may meet with. I thank you so much for what you have said. The fact is you have been brought up to carry religion into everything. But I was not. ~ My mother was as good as she was lovely, but I think she felt and taught us to feel, that we were to put it on as we did our Sunday clothes, and to wear it, as we did them, carefully and reverently, but with pretty long, grave faces. But you mix everything up so, that when I am with you I never know whether you are most like or most unlike other people. And your mother is just so."

"But you forget that it is to Ernest I owe my best ideas about married life I do not remember ever talking with my mother or anyone else on the subject. And as to carrying religion into everything, how can one help it if one's religion is a vital part of one's self, not a cloak put on to go to church in and hang up out of the way against next Sunday?"

Helen laughed. She has the merriest, yet gentlest little laugh one can imagine. I long to know who it is that has been so fortunate as to touch her heart!

MARCH.-I know now, and glad I am! The sly little puss is purring at this moment in James' arms at least I suppose she is, as I have discreetly come up to my room and left them to themselves So it seems I have had all these worries about Lucy for naught. What made her so fond of James was simply the fact that a friend of his had looked on her with a favorable eye, regarding her as a very proper mother for four or five children who are in need of a shepherd. Yes, Lucy is going to marry a man so much older than herself, that on a pinch he might have been her father. She does it from a sense of duty, she says, and to a nature like hers, duty may perhaps suffice, and no cry of the heart have to be stifled in its performance. We are all so happy in the happiness of James and Helen that we are not in the mood to criticize Lucy's decision. I have a strange and most absurd envy when I think what a good time they are having at this moment downstairs, while I sit here alone, vainly wishing I could see more of Ernest. Just as if my happiness were not a deeper, more blessed one than theirs, which must be purged of much dross before it will prove itself to be like fine gold. Yes, I suppose I am as happy in my dear, precious husband and children as a wife and mother can be in a world, which must not be a real heaven lest we should love the land we journey through so well as to want to pitch our tents in it forever, and cease to look and long for the home whither we are bound.

James will be married almost immediately, I suppose, as he sails for Syria early in April. How much a missionary and his wife must be to each other, when, severing themselves from all they ever loved before, they go forth, hand in hand, not merely to be foreigners in heathen lands, but to be henceforth strangers in their own should they ever return to it!

Helen says, playfully, that she has not a missionary spirit, and is not at all sure that she shall go with James. But I do not think that he feels very anxious on that point!

MARCH.-It does one's heart good to see how happy they are! And it does one's heart good to have one's husband set up an opposition to the goings on by behaving like a lover himself.

Chapter 23

JANUARY 1, 1851 - IT is a great while since I wrote that. "God has been just as good as ever" I want to say that before I say another word. But He has indeed smitten me very sorely.

While we were in the midst of our rejoicings about James and Helen, and the bright future that seemed opening before them, he came home one day very ill. Ernest happened to be in and attended to him at once. But the disease was, at the very outset, so violent, and raged with such absolute fury, that no remedies had any effect. Everything, even now, seems confused in my mind. It seems as if there was a sudden transition from the most brilliant, joyous health, to a brief but fearful struggle for life, speedily followed by the awful mystery and stillness of death. Is it possible, I still ask myself, that four short days wrought an event whose consequences must run through endless years ?— Poor mother! Poor Helen!-When it was all over, I do not know what to say of mother but that she behaved and quieted herself like a weaned child. Her sweet composure awed me I dared not give way to my own vehement, terrible sorrow in the presence of this Christ-like patience, all noisy demonstrations seemed profane. I thought no human being was less selfish, more loving than she had been for many years, but the spirit that now took possession of her flowed into her heart and life directly from that great Heart of love, whose depth I had never even begun to sound. There was, therefore, something absolutely divine in her aspect, in the tones of her voice, in the very smile on her face. We could compare its expression to nothing but Stephen, when he, being full of the Holy Ghost, looked up steadfastly to heaven and saw the glory of God, and Jesus standing on the right hand of God. As soon as James was gone Helen came to our home there was never any discussion about it, she came naturally to be one of us. Mother's health, already very frail, gradually failed, and encompassed as I was with cares, I could not be with her constantly. Helen took the place to her of a daughter, and found herself welcomed like one. The atmosphere in which we all lived was one which cannot be described the love for all of us and for every living thing that flowed in mother's words and tones passed all knowledge. The children's little joys and sorrows interested her exactly as if she was one of themselves they ran to her with every petty grievance, and every new pleasure. During the time she lived with us she had won many warm friends, particularly among the poor and the suffering. As her strength would no longer allow her to go to them, those who could do so came to her, and I was struck to see she had ceased entirely from giving counsel, and now gave nothing but the most beautiful, tender compassion and sympathy. I saw that she was failing, but flattered myself that her own serenity and our care would prolong her life still for many years. I longed to have my children become old enough to appreciate fully her sanctified character and I thought she would gradually fade away and be set free, as light winds wandering through groves of bloom, Detach the delicate blossoms from the tree.

But God's thoughts are not as our thoughts not His ways as our ways. Her feeble body began to suffer from the rudest assaults of pain day and night, night and day. She lived through a martyrdom in which what might have been a lifetime of suffering was concentrated into a few months. To witness these sufferings was like the sundering of joints and marrow, and once, only once, thank God! My faith in Him staggered and reeled to and fro. "How can He look down on such agonies?" I cried in my secret soul "is this the work of a God of love, of mercy?" Mother seemed to divine my thoughts, for she took my hand tenderly in hers and said, with great difficulty:

"Though He slay me, yet will I trust in Him. He is just as good as ever." And she smiled. I ran away to Ernest, crying, "Oh, is there nothing you can do for her?"

"What should a poor mortal do where Christ has done so much, my darling?" he said, taking me in his arms. "Let us stand aside and see the glory of God, with our shoes from off our feet." But he went to her with one more desperate effort to relieve her, yet in vain.

Mrs. Embury, of whom mother was fond, and who is always very kind when we are in trouble, came in just then, and after looking on a moment in tears she said to me: "God knows whom He can trust! He would not lay His hand thus on all His children."

Those few words quieted me. Yes, God knows. And now it is all over. My precious, precious mother has been a saint in heaven more than two years, and has forgotten all the battles she fought on earth, and all her sorrows and all her sufferings in the presence of her Redeemer. She knew that she was going, and the last words she uttered-and they were spoken with somewhat of the playful, quaint manner in which she had spoken all her life, and with her own bright smile-still sound in my ears:

"I have given God a great deal of trouble, but He is driving me into pasture now!"

And then, with her cheek on her hand, she fell asleep, and slept on, until just at sundown she awoke to find herself in the green pasture, the driving all over forever and ever.

Who by searching can find out God? My dear father entered heaven after a prosperous life path wherein he was unconscious of a pang, and beloved James went bright, fresh, and untarnished by conflict straight to the Master's feast. But what a long lifetime of bereavement, sorrow, and suffering was my darling mother's pathway to glory!

Surely, her felicity must be greater than theirs, and the crown she has won by such a struggle must be brighter than the stars! And this crown she is even now, while I sit here choked with tears, casting joyfully at the feet of her Savior!

My sweet sister, my precious little Helen, still nestles in our hearts and in our home. Martha made one passionate appeal to her to return to her, but Ernest interfered:

"Let her stay with Katy," he said. "James would have chosen to have her with the one human being like himself."

Does he then think me, with all my faults, the languor of frail health, and the cares and burdens of life weighing upon me, enough like that sparkling, brave boy to be of use and comfort to dear Helen? I take courage at the thought and rouse myself afresh, to bear on with fidelity and patience. My steadfast aim now is to follow in my mother's footsteps, to imitate her cheerfulness, her benevolence, her bright, inspiring ways, and never to rest until in place of my selfish nature I become as full of Christ's love as she became. I am glad she is at last relieved from the knowledge of all my cares, and though I often and often yearn to throw myself into her arms and pour out my cares and trials into her sympathizing ears, I would not have her back for the entire world. She has got away from all the turmoil and suffering of life let her stay!

The scenes of sorrow through which we have been passing have brought Ernest nearer to me than ever, and I can see that this varied discipline has softened and sweetened his character. Besides, we have modified each other. Ernest is more demonstrative, more attentive to those little things that make the happiness of married life, and I am less childish, less vehement-I wish I could say less selfish, but here I seem to have come to a standstill. But I do understand Ernest's trials in his profession far better than I did, and can feel and show some sympathy in them. Of course, the life of a physician is necessarily one of self-denial, spent as it is amid scenes of suffering and sorrow, which he is often powerless to alleviate. But there is besides the wear and tear of years of poverty his bills are disputed or allowed to run on year after year unnoticed he is often dismissed because he cannot put himself in the place of Providence and save life, and a truly grateful, generous patient is almost an unknown rarity. I do not speak of these things to complain of them. I suppose they are a necessary part of that whole providential plan by which God moulds and fashions and tempers the human soul, just as my petty, but incessant household cares are. If I had nothing to do but love my husband and children and perform for them, without let or hindrance, the sweet ideal duties of wife and mother, how content I should be to live always in this world! But what would become of me if I were not called, in the pursuit of these duties and in contact with real life, to bear restless nights, ill-health, unwelcome news, the faults of servants, contempt, ingratitude of friends, my own failings, lowness of spirits, the struggle in overcoming my corruption, and a score of kindred trials!"

Bishop Wilson charges us to bear all these things "as unto God," and "with the greatest privacy." How seldom I have met them save as lions in my way, that I would avoid if I could, and how I have tormented my friends by tedious complaints about them! Yet when compared with the great tragedies of suffering I have both witnessed and suffered, how petty they seem!

Our household, bereft of mother's and James' bright presence, now numbers just as many members as it did before they left us. Another angel has flown into it, though not on wings, and I have four darling children, the baby, who can hardly be called a baby now, being nearly two years old. My hands and my heart are full, but two of the children go to school, and that certainly makes my day's work easier.

The little things are happier for having regular employment, and we are so glad to meet each other again after the brief separation! I try to be at home when it is time to expect them, for I love to hear the eager voices ask, in chorus, the moment the door opens, "Is mamma at home?" Helen has taken Daisy to sleep with her, which after so many years of ups and downs at night, now with restless babies, now to answer the bell when Ernest is out, is a great relief to me. Poor Helen! She has never recovered her cheerfulness since James' death. It has crushed her energies and left her very sorrowful. This is partly owing to a soft and tender nature, easily borne down and overwhelmed, partly to what seems an almost constitutional inability to find rest in God's will. She assents to all we say to her about submission, in a sweet, gentle way, and then comes the invariable, mournful wail, "But it was so unexpected! It came so suddenly!" But I love the little thing, and her affection for us all is one of our greatest comforts.

Martha is greatly absorbed in her own household, its cares, and its pleasures. She brings her little Underhills to see us occasionally, when they put my children quite out of countenance by their consciousness of the fine clothes they wear, and their knowledge of the world. Even I find it hard not to feel abashed in the presence of so much of the sort of wisdom in which I am lacking. As to Lucy, she is exactly in her sphere: the calm dignity with which she reigns in her husband's house, and the moderation and self-control with which she guides his children, are really instructive. She has a baby of her own, and though it acts just like other babies and kicks, scratches, pulls. And cries when it is washed and dressed, she goes through that process with a serenity and deliberation that I envy with all my might. Her predecessor in the nursery was all nerve and brain, and has left four children made of the same material behind her. But their wild spirits on one day, and their depression and languor on the next, have no visible effect upon her. Her influence is always quieting she tones down their vehemence with her own calm decision and practical good sense. It is amusing to see her seated among those four little furies, who love each other in such a distracted way that somebody's feelings are always getting hurt, and somebody always crying. By a sort of magnetic influence, she heals these wounds immediately, and finds some prosaic occupation as an antidote to these poetical moods. I confess that I am instructed and reproved whenever I go to see her, and wish I were more like her.

But there is no use in trying to engraft an opposite nature on one's own. What I am, that I must be, except as God changes me into His own image. And everything brings me back to that, as my supreme desire. I see more and more that I must be myself what I want my children to be, and that I cannot make myself over even for their sakes. This must be His work, and I wonder that it goes on so slowly that all the disappointments, sorrows, sicknesses I have passed through, have left me still selfish, still full of imperfections.

MARCH 5, 1852.-This is the sixth anniversary of James' death. Thinking it all over after I went to bed last night, his sickness, his death, and the weary months that followed for mother, I could not get to sleep till long past midnight. Then Una woke, crying with the earache, and I was up till nearly daybreak with her, poor child. I got up jaded and depressed, almost ready to faint under the burden of life, and dreading to meet Helen, who is doubly sad on these anniversaries. She came down to breakfast dressed as usual in deep mourning, and looking as spiritless as I felt. The prattle of the children relieved the somber silence maintained by the rest of us, each of whom acted depressingly on the others. How things do flash into one's mind. These words suddenly came to mine, as we sat so gloomily at the table God had spread for us, and which He had enlivened by the four young faces around it—

"Why should the children of a King,   Go mourning all their days?"

Why, indeed? Children of a King? I felt grieved that I was so intent on my own sorrows as to lose sight of my relationship to Him. And then I asked myself what I could do to make the day less wearisome and sorrowful to Helen. She came, after a time, with her work to my room. The children took their goodbye kisses and went off to school Ernest took his, too, and set forth on his day's work, while Daisy played quietly about the room.

"Helen, dear," I ventured at last to begin "I want you to do me a favor today."

"Yes," she said, languidly.

"I want you to go to see Mrs. Campbell. This is the day for her beef tea, and she will be looking out for one of us."

"You must not ask me to go today," Helen answered.

"I think I must, dear. When other springs of comfort dry up, there is one always left to us. And that as mother often said, is usefulness."

"I do try to be useful," she said.

"Yes, you are very kind to me and to the children. If you were my own sister, you could not do more. But these little duties do not relieve that aching void in your heart which yearns so for relief."

"No," she said, quickly, "I have no such yearning. I just want to settle down as I am now."

"Yes, I suppose that is the natural tendency of sorrow. But there is great significance in the prayer for 'a heart at leisure from itself, to soothe and sympathize.'"

"Oh, Katy!" she said, "you do not know, you cannot know, how I feel. Until James began to love me so I did not know there was such a love as that in the world. You know our family is different from yours. And it is so delightful to be loved. Or rather it was!"

"Do not say was," I said. "You know we all love you dearly, dearly"

"Yes, but not as James did!"

"That is true. It was foolish in me to expect to console you by such suggestions. But to go back to Mrs. Campbell. She will sympathize with you, if you will let her, as very few can, for she has lost both husband and children."

"Ah, but she had a husband for a time, at least. It is not as if he were snatched away before they had lived together."

If anybody else had said this, I should have felt that it was out of mere perverseness. But dear little Helen is not perverse she is simply overburdened.

"I grant that your disappointment was greater than hers," I went on. "But the affliction was not. Every day that a husband and wife walk hand in hand together upon earth makes of the twain more and more one flesh. The selfish element, which at first formed so large a part of their attraction to each other, disappears, and the union becomes as pure and beautiful as to form a fitting type of the union of Christ and His church. There is nothing else on earth like it."

Helen sighed.

"I find it hard to believe," she said, "there can be anything more delicious than the months in which James and I were so happy together."

"Suffering together would have brought you even nearer," I replied. "Dear Helen, I am very sorry for you I hope you feel that, even when, according to my want, I fall into arguments, as if one could argue a sorrow away!"

"You are so happy," she answered. "Ernest loves you so dearly, and is so proud of you, and you have such lovely children! I ought not to expect you to sympathize perfectly with my loneliness.

"Yes, I am happy," I said, after a pause "but you must own, dear, that I have had my sorrows, too. Until you become a mother yourself, you cannot comprehend what a mother can suffer, riot merely for herself, in losing her children, but in seeing their sufferings. I think I may say of my happiness that it rests on something higher and deeper than even Ernest and my children."

"And what is that?"

The will of God, the sweet will of God. If He should take them all away, I might still possess a peace that would flow on forever. I know this partly from my own experience and partly from that of others. Mrs. Campbell says that the three months that followed the death of her first child were the happiest she had ever known. Mrs. Wentworth, whose husband was snatched from her almost without warning, and while using expressions of affection for her such as a lover addresses to his bride, said to me, with tears rolling down her cheeks, yet with a smile, I thank my God and

Savior that He has not forgotten and passed me by, but has counted me worthy to bear this sorrow for His sake.' And hear this passage from the life of Wesley, which I lighted on this morning:

"He visited one of his disciples, who was ill in bed and after having buried seven of her family in six months, had just heard that the eighth, her husband, whom she dearly loved, had been cast away at sea. 'I asked her,' he says, 'do you not fret at any of those things?' She says, with a lovely smile, 'Oh, no! How can I fret at anything that is the will of God? Let Him take all beside, He has given me Himself. I love, I praise Him every moment.'"

"Yes," Helen objected, "I can imagine people as saying such things in moments of excitement but afterwards, they have hours of terrible agony."

"They have 'hours of terrible agony,' of course. God's grace does not harden our hearts, and make them proof against suffering, like coats of mail. They can all say, 'Out of the depths have I cried unto Thee,' and it is they alone who have been down into the depths, and had rich experience of what God could be to His children there, who can utter such testimonials to His honor, as those I have just repeated."

"Katy,' Helen suddenly asked, "do you always submit to God's will thus?"

"In great things I do," I said. "What grieves me is that I am constantly forgetting to recognize God's hand in the little every-day trials of life, and instead of receiving them as from Him, find fault with the instruments by which He sends them. I can give up my child, my only brother, my darling mother without a word but to receive every tire some visitor as sent expressly and directly to weary me by the Master Himself to meet every negligence on the part of the servants as His choice for me at the moment to be satisfied and patient when Ernest gets particularly absorbed in his books because my Father sees that little discipline suitable for me at the time all this I have not fully learned."

"All you say discourages me," said Helen, in a tone of deep dejection. "Such perfection was only meant for a few favored ones, and I do not dare so much as to aim at it. I am perfectly sure that I must be satisfied with the low state of grace I am in now and always have been."

She was about to leave me, but I caught her hand as she would have passed me, and made one more attempt to reach her poor, weary soul.

"But are you satisfied, dear Helen?" I asked, as tenderly as I would speak to a little sick child. "Surely you crave happiness, as every human soul does!"

"Yes, I crave it," she replied, "but God has taken it from me."

"He has taken away your earthly happiness, I know, but only to convince you what better things He has in store for you. Let me read you a letter which Dr. Cabot wrote me many years ago, but which has been an almost constant inspiration to me ever since."

She sat down, resumed her work again, and listened to the letter in silence. As I came to its last sentence the three children rushed in from school, at least the boys did, and threw themselves upon me like men assaulting a fort. I have formed the habit of giving myself entirely to them at the proper moment, and now entered into their frolicsome mood as joyously as if I had never known a sorrow or lost an hour's sleep. At last, they went off to their play-room, and Una settled down by my side to amuse Daisy, when Helen began again.

"I should like to read that letter myself," she said. "Meanwhile I want to ask you one question. What are you made of that you can turn from one thing to another like lightning? Talking one moment as if life depended on your every word, and then frisking about with those wild boys as if you were a child yourself?"

I saw Una look up curiously, to hear my answer, as I replied,

"I have always aimed at this flexibility. I think a mother, especially, ought to learn to enter into the gayer moods of her children at the very moment when her own heart is sad. And it may be as religious an act for her to romp with them at the time as to pray with them at another."

Helen now went away to her room with Dr Cabot's letter, which I silently prayed might bless her as it had blessed me. And then a jaded, disheartened mood came over me that made me feel that all I had been saying to her was but as sounding brass and a tinkling cymbal, since my life and my professions did not correspond. Hitherto my consciousness of imperfection has made me hesitate to say much to Helen. Why are we so afraid of those who live under the same roof with us? It must be the conviction that those who daily see us acting in a petty, selfish, trifling way, must find it hard to conceive that our prayers and our desires take a wider and higher aim. Dear little Helen! May the ice once broken remain broken forever?

Chapter 24

MARCH 20. - HELEN returned Dr. Cabot's letter in silence this morning, but, directly after breakfast, set forth to visit Mrs. Campbell, with the little bottle of beef-tea in her hands, which ought to have gone yesterday. I had a busy day before me. The usual Saturday baking and Sunday dinner to oversee, the children's lessons for tomorrow to superintend and hear them repeat, their clean clothes to lay out, and a basket of stockings to mend. My mind was somewhat distracted with these cares, and I found it a little difficult to keep on with my morning devotions in spite of them. But I have learned, at least, to face and fight such distractions, instead of running away from them as I used to do. My faith in prayer, my resort to it, becomes more and more the foundation of my life, and I believe, with one wiser and better than myself, that nothing but prayer stands between my soul and the best gifts of God in other words, that I can and shall get what I ask for.

I went down into the kitchen, put on my large baking apron, and began my labors of course the doorbell rang, and a poor woman was announced. It is very sweet to follow Fenelon's counsel and give oneself to Christ in all these interruptions but this time I said, "oh, dear!" before I thought. Then I wished I had not, and went up, with a cheerful face at any rate, to my unwelcome visitor, who proved to be one of my aggravating poor folks-a great giant of a woman, in perfect health, and with a husband to support her if he will. I told her that I could do no more for her she answered me rudely, and kept urging her claims. I felt ruffled why my time should be thus frittered away, I asked myself. At last, she went off, abusing me in a way that chilled my heart. I could only beg God to forgive her, and return to my work, which I had hardly resumed when Mrs. Embury sent for a pattern I had promised to lend her. Off came my apron, and up two pairs of stairs I ran after a long search it came to light. Work resumed doorbell again. Auntie wanted the children to come to an early dinner. Going to Auntie's is next to going to Paradise to them. Everything was now hurry and flurry I tried to be patient and not to fret their temper by undue attention to nails, ears, and other susceptible parts of the human frame, but after it was all over, and I had kissed all the sweet, dear faces good-by, and returned to the kitchen, I felt sure that I had not been the perfect mother I want to be in all these little emergencies- yes, far from it. Bridget had let the milk I was going to use boil over, and finally burn up. I was annoyed and irritated, and already tired, and did not see how I was to get more, as Mary was cleaning the silver (to be sure, there is not much of it), and had other extra Saturday work to do. I thought Bridget might offer to run to the corner for it, though it is not her business, hut she is not obliging, and seemed as sulky as if I had burned the milk, not she. "After all," I said to myself, "what does it signify, if Ernest gets no dessert? It isn't good for him, and how much precious time is wasted over just this one thing?" However, I reflected, that arbitrarily refusing to indulge him in this respect is not exactly my mission as his wife he is perfectly well, and likes his little luxuries as well as other people do. So I humbled my pride and asked Bridget to go for the milk, which she did, in a lofty way of her own. While she was gone the marketing came home, and I had everything to dispose of. Ernest had sent home some apples, which plainly said, "I want some apple pie, Katy." I looked nervously at the clock, and undertook to gratify him. Mary came down, crying, to say that her mother, who lived in Brooklyn, was very sick could she go to see her? I looked at the clock once more told her she should go, of course, as soon as lunch was over this involved my doing all her absence left undone.

At last, I got through with the kitchen, the Sunday dinner being well under way, and ran upstairs to put away the host of little garments the children had left when they took their flight, and to make myself presentable at lunch. Then I began to be uneasy lest Ernest should not be punctual, and Mary be delayed but he came just as the clock struck one. I ran joyfully to meet him, very glad now that I had something good to give him. We bad just got through lunch, and I was opening my mouth to tell Mary she might go, when the doorbell rang once more, and Mrs. Fry, of Jersey City, was announced. I told Mary to wait till I found whether she had lunched or not no, she had not had come to town to see friends off, was half famished, and would I do her the favor, etc., etc. She had a fashionable young lady with her, a stranger to me, as well as a Miss Somebody else, from Albany, whose name I did not catch. I apologized for having finished lunch. Mrs. Fry said all they wanted was a cup of tea and a bit of bread and butter, nothing else, dear now do not put yourself out.

"Now be bright and animated, and like yourself," she whispered, "for I have brought these girls here on purpose to hear you talk, and they are prepared to fall in love with you on the spot"

This speech sufficed to shut my mouth.

Mary had to get ready for these unexpected guests, whose appetites proved equal to a raid on a good many things besides bread and butter. Mrs. Fry said, after she had devoured nearly half a loaf of cake, that she would really try to eat a morsel more, which Ernest remarked, dryly, was a great triumph of mind over matter. As they talked and 'laughed and ate leisurely on, Mary stood looking the picture of despair. At last I gave her a glance that said she might go, when a new visitor was announced-Mrs. Winthrop, from Brooklyn, one of Ernest's patients a few years ago, when she lived here. She professed herself greatly indebted to him, and said she had come at this hour because she should make sure of seeing him. I tried to excuse him, as I knew he would be thankful to have me do, but no, see him she must he was her "pet doctor," he had such "sweet, bedside manners," and "I am such a favorite with him, you know!"

Ernest did not receive his "favorite" with any special warmth but invited her out to lunch and gallanted her to the table we had just left. Just like a man! Poor Mary! She had to fly round and get up what she could Mrs. Winthrop devoted herself to Ernest with a persistent ignoring of me that I thought rude and unwomanly. She asked if he had read a certain book he had not she then said, "I need not ask, then, if Mrs. Elliott has done so? These charming dishes, which she gets up so nicely, must absorb all her time." "Of course," replied Ernest. "But she contrives to read the reports of all the murders, of which the newspapers are full."

Mrs. Winthrop took this speech literally, drew away her skirts from me, looked at me through her eyeglass, and said, "Yes?" At last, she departed. Helen came home, and Mary went. I gave Helen an account of my morning she laughed heartily, and it did me good to hear that musical sound once more.

"It is nearly five o'clock," I said, as we at last had restored everything to order, "and this whole day has been frittered away in the veriest trifles. It is not living to live so. Who is the better for my being in the world since six o'clock this morning?"

"I am for one," she said, kissing my hot cheeks "and you have given a great deal of pleasure to several persons. Your and Ernest's hospitality is always graceful. I admire it in you both and this is one of the little ways, not to be despised, of giving enjoyment." It was nice in her to say that, it quite rested me.

At the dinner table, Ernest complimented me on my good housekeeping.

"I was proud of my little wife at lunch," he said.

"And yet you said that outrageous thing about my reading about nothing but murders!" I said.

"Oh, well, you understood it," he said, laughingly.

"But that dreadful Mrs. Winthrop took it literally."

"What do we care for Mrs. Winthrop?" he returned. "If you could have seen the contrast between you two in my eyes!"

After all, one must take life as it comes, its homely details are so mixed up with its sweet charities, and loves, and friendships that one is forced to believe that God has joined them together and does not will that they should be put asunder. It is something that my husband has been satisfied with his wife and his home today that does me good.

MARCH 30.-A stormy day and the children home from school, and no little frolicking and laughing going on. It must, be delightful to feel well and strong while one's children are young; there is so much to do for them. I do it but no one can tell the effort, it costs me. What a contrast there is between their vitality and the languor under which I suffer! When their noise became intolerable, I proposed to read to them of course they made ten times as much clamor of pleasure and of course, they leaned on me, ground their elbows into my lap, and tired me all out. As I sat with this precious little group about me, Ernest opened the door, looked in, gravely and without a word, and instantly disappeared. I felt uneasy and asked him, this evening, why he looked so. Was I indulging the children too much, or what was it? He took me into his arms and said:

"My precious wife, why will you torment yourself with such fancies? My very heart was yearning over you at that moment, as it did the first time I saw you surrounded by your little class at Sunday-school, years ago, and I was asking myself why God had given me such a wife, and my children such a mother."

Oh, I am glad I have got this written down! I will read it over when the sense of my deficiencies overwhelms me, while I ask God why He has given me such a patient, forbearing husband.

APRIL 1.-This has been a sad day to our church. Our dear Dr. Cabot has gone to his eternal home, and left us as sheep without a shepherd.

His death was sudden at the last and found us all unprepared for it. But my tears of sorrow are mingled with tears of joy. His heart had long been in heaven, he was ready to go at a moment's warning never was a soul so constantly and joyously on the wing as his. Poor Mrs. Cabot! She is left very desolate, for all their children are married and settled at a distance. But she bears this sorrow like one who has long felt herself a pilgrim and a stranger on earth. How strange that we ever forget that we are all such!

APRIL 16.-The desolate pilgrimage was not long. Dear Mrs. Cabot was this day laid away by the side of her beloved husband, and it is delightful to think of them as not divided by death, but united by it in a complete and eternal union.

I never saw a husband and wife more tenderly attached to each other, and this is a beautiful close to their long and happy married life. I find it hard not to wish and pray that I may as speedily follow my precious husband, should God call him away first. But it is not for me to choose.

How I shall miss these faithful friends, who, from my youth up, have been my stay and my staff in the house of my pilgrimage! Almost all the disappointments and sorrows of my life have had their Christian sympathy, particularly the daily, wasting solicitude concerning my darling Una, for they too watched for years over as delicate a flower, and saw it fade and die. Only those who have suffered thus can appreciate the heart-soreness through which, no matter how outwardly cheerful I may be, I am always passing. But what then! Have I not ten thousand times made this my prayer, that in the words of Leighton, my will might become, identical with God's will?"

And shall He not take me at my word?" Just as I was writing these words, my canary burst forth with a song so joyous that a song was put also into my mouth. Something seemed to say, this captive sings in his cage because it has never known liberty, and cannot regret a lost freedom. So the soul of my child, limited by the restrictions of a feeble body, never having known the gladness of exuberant health, may sing songs that will enliven and cheer. Yes, and does sing them! What should we do without her gentle, loving presence, whose frailty calls forth our tenderest affections and whose sweet face makes sunshine in the shadiest places! I am sure that the boys are truly blessed by having a sister always at home to welcome them, and that their best manliness is appealed to by her helplessness.

What this child is to me I cannot tell and yet, if the skillful and kind Gardener should house this delicate plant before frosts come, should I dare to complain?

Chapter 25

MAY 4 - Miss CLIFFORD came to lunch with us on Wednesday. Her remarkable restoration to health has attracted a good deal of attention, and has given Ernest a certain reputation, which does not come amiss to him. Not that he is ambitious a more unworldly man does not live but his extreme reserve and modesty have obscured the light that is now beginning to shine. We all enjoyed Miss Clifford's visit. She is one of the freshest, most original creatures I ever met with, and kept us all laughing with her quaint speeches, long after every particle of lunch had disappeared from the table. But this mobile nature turns to the serious side of life with marvelous ease and celerity, as perhaps all sound ones ought to do. I took her up to my room where my workbasket was, and Helen followed, with hers.

"I have brought something to read to you, dear Mrs. Elliott," Miss Clifford began, the moment, we had seated ourselves, "which I have just lighted on, and I am sure you will like. A nobleman writes to Fenelon asking certain questions, and a part of these questions, with the replies, I want to enjoy with you, as they cover a good deal of the ground we have often discussed together":

"I.-How shall I offer my purely indifferent actions to God walks, visits made and received, dress, little proprieties, such as washing the hands, etc.', the reading of books of history, business with which I am charged for my friends, other amusements, such -as shopping, having clothes made, and equipages. I want to have some sort of prayer, or method of offering each of these things to God.

"REPLY.-The most indifferent actions cease to be such, and become good as soon as one performs them with the intention of conforming one's self in them to the will of God. They are often better and purer than certain actions which appear more virtuous: 1st, because they are less of our own choice and more in the order of Providence when one is obliged to perform them 2nd, because they are simpler and less exposed to vain complaisance 3rd, because if one yields to them with moderation, one finds in them more of death to one's inclinations than in certain acts of fervor in which self-love mingles finally, because these little occasions occur more frequently, and furnish a secret occasion for continually making every moment profitable.

"It is not necessary to make neither great efforts nor acts of great reflection, in order to offer what are called indifferent actions. It is enough to lift the soul one instant to God, to make a simple offering of it. Everything which God wishes us to do, and which enters into the course of occupation suitable to our position, can and ought to be offered to God nothing is unworthy of Him but sin. When you feel that an action cannot be offered to God, conclude that it does not become a Christian it is at least necessary to suspect it, and seek light concerning it. I would not have a special prayer for each of these the elevation of the heart at the moment suffices.

"As for visits, commissions and the like, as there is danger of following one's own taste too much, I would add to this elevating of the heart a prayer to moderate myself and use precaution.

"II-In prayer I cannot fix my mind, or I have intervals of time when it is elsewhere and it is often distracted for a long time before I perceive it. I want to find some means of becoming its master.

"REPLY.-Fidelity in following the rules that have been given you, and in recalling your mind every time you perceive its distraction, will gradually give you the grace of being more recollected. Meanwhile bear your involuntary distractions with patience and humility you deserve nothing better. Is it surprising that recollection is difficult to a man so long dissipated and far from God?

"III.-I wish to know if it is best to record, on my tablets, the faults and the sins I have committed, in order not to run the risk of forgetting them. I excite in myself to repentance for my faults as much as I can but I have never felt any real grief on account of them. When I examine myself at night, I see persons far more perfect than I complain of more sin: as for me, I seek, I find nothing and yet it is impossible there should not be many points on which to implore pardon every day of my life.

"REPLY.-You should examine yourself every night, but simply and briefly. In the disposition to which God has brought you, you will not voluntarily commit any considerable fault without remembering and reproaching yourself for it. As to little faults, scarcely perceived, even if you sometimes forget them, this need not make you uneasy.

"As to lively grief on account of your sins, it is not necessary. God gives it when it pleases Him. True and essential conversion of the heart consists in a full will to sacrifice all to God. What I call full will is a fixed immovable disposition of the will to resume none of the voluntary affections, which may alter the purity of the love to God, and to abandon itself to all the crosses, which it will -perhaps -be necessary to bear, in order to accomplish the will of God always and in all things. As to sorrow for sin, when one has it, one ought to return thanks for it when one perceives it to be wanting, one should humble one's self peacefully before God without trying to excite it by vain efforts.

"You find in your self-examination fewer faults than persons more advanced and more perfect do it is because your interior light is still feeble. It will increase, and the view of your infidelities will increase in proportion. It suffices, without making yourself uneasy, to try to be faithful to the degree of light you possess, and to instruct yourself by reading and meditation. It will not do to try to forestall the grace that belongs to a more advanced period. It would only serve to trouble and discourage you, and even to exhaust you by continual anxiety the time that should be spent in loving God would be given to forced returns upon yourself, which secretly nourish self-love.

"IV.——In my prayers my mind has difficulty in finding anything to say to God. My heart is not in it, or it is inaccessible to the thoughts of my mind.

"REPLY.-It is not necessary to say much to God. Oftentimes one does not speak much to a friend whom one is delighted to see one looks at him with pleasure one speaks certain short words to him, which are mere expressions of feeling. The mind has no part in them, or next to none, one keeps repeating the same words. It is not so much a variety of thoughts that one seeks in intercourse with a friend, as a certain repose and correspondence of heart. It is thus we are with God, who does not disdain to be our tenderest, most cordial,-most familiar, most intimate friend. A word, a sigh, a sentiment, says all to God it is not always necessary to have transports of sensible tenderness a will all naked and dry, without life, without vivacity, without pleasure, is often purest in the sight of God. In fine, it is necessary to content one's self with giving to Him what He gives it to give, a fervent heart when it is fervent, and a heart firm and faithful in its aridity, when He deprives it of sensible fervor. It does not always depend on you to feel but it is necessary to wish to feel. Leave it to God to choose to make you feel sometimes, in order to sustain your weakness and infancy in Christian life sometimes weaning you from that sweet and consoling sentiment which is the milk of babes, in order to humble you, to make you grow, and to make you robust in the violent exercise of faith, by causing you to sweat the bread of the strong in the sweat of your brow. Would you only love God according as He will make you take pleasure in loving Him? You would be loving your own tenderness and feeling, fancying that you were loving God. Even while receiving sensible gifts, prepare yourself by pure faith for the time when you might be deprived of them and you will suddenly succumb if you had only relied on such support.

"O forgot to speak of some practices which may, at the beginning, facilitate the remembrance of the offering one ought to make to God, of all the ordinary acts of the day.

"1. Form the resolution to do so, every morning, and call yourself to account in your self-examination at night.

"2. Make no resolutions but for good reasons, either from propriety or the necessity of relaxing the mind, etc. Thus, in accustoming one's self to retrench the useless little by little, one accustoms one's self to offer what is not proper to curtail.

"3. Renew one's self in this disposition whenever one is alone, in order to be better prepared to recollect it when in company.

"4. Whenever one surprises one's self in too great dissipation, or in speaking too freely of his neighbor, let him collect himself and offer to God all the rest of the conversation.

"5. To flee, with confidence, to God, to act according to His will, when one enters company, or engages in some occupation which may cause one to fall into temptation. The sight of danger ought to warn of the need there is to lift the heart toward Him by one who may be preserved from it."

We both thanked her as she finished reading, and I begged her to lend me the volume that I might make the above copy.

I hope I have gained some valuable hints from this letter, and that I shall see more plainly than ever that it is a religion of principle that God wants from us, not one of mere feeling.

Helen remarked that she was most struck by the assertion that one cannot forestall the graces that belong to a more advanced period. She said she had assumed that she ought to experience all that the most mature Christian did, and that it rested her to think of God as doing this work for her, making repentance, for instance, a free gift, not a conquest to be won for one's self.

Miss Clifford said that the whole idea of giving one's self to God in such little daily acts as visiting, shopping, and the like, was entirely new to her.

"But fancy," she went on, her beautiful face lighted up with enthusiasm, "what a blessed life that must be, when the base things of this world and things that are despised, are so many links to the invisible world and to the things God has chosen!"

"In other words," I said, "the top of the ladder that rests on earth reaches to heaven, and we may ascend it as the angels did in Jacob's dream."

"And descend too, as they did," Helen put in, despondently.

"Now you shall not speak in that tone," cried Miss Clifford. "Let us look at the bright side of life, and believe that God means us to be always ascending, always getting nearer to Him, always learning something new about Him, and always loving Him better and better. To be sure, our souls are sick, and of themselves cannot keep 'ever on the wing,' but I have had some delightful thoughts of late from just hearing the title of a book, 'God's method with the maladies of the soul.' It gives one such a conception of the seeming ills of life to think of Him as our Physician, the ills all remedies, the deprivations only a wholesome regimen, the losses all gains. Why, as I study this individual case and that, see how patiently and persistently He tries now this remedy, now that, and how infallibly He cures the souls that submit to His remedies, I love Him so! I love Him so! And I am so astonished that we are restive under His unerring hand! Think how He dealt with me. My soul was sick unto death, sick with worldliness, and self-pleasing and folly. There was only one way of making me listen to reason, and that was just the way He took. He snatched me right out of the world and shut me up in one room, crippled, helpless, and alone, and set me to thinking, thinking, thinking, till I saw the emptiness and shallowness of all in which I had hitherto been involved. And then He sent you and your mother to show me the reality of life, and to reveal to me my invisible, unknown Physician. Can I love Him with half my heart? Can I be asking questions as to how much I am to pay towards the debt I owe Him?"

By this time, Helen's work had fallen from her hands and tears were in her eyes.

"How I thank you," she said softly, "for what you have said. You have interpreted life to me! You have given me a new conception of my God and Savior!"

Miss Clifford seemed quenched and humbled by these words her enthusiasm faded away and she looked at Helen with a deprecatory air as she replied:

"Do not say that! I never felt so unfit for anything but to sit at the feet of Christ's disciples and learn of them."

Yet I, so many years one of those disciples, been sitting at her feet, and had learned of her. Never had I so realized the magnitude of the work to be done in this world, nor the power and goodness of Him who has undertaken to do it all. I was glad to be alone, to walk my room singing praises to Him for every instance in which, as my Physician, He had "disappointed my hope and defeated my joys" and given me to drink of the cup of sorrow and bereavement.

MAY 24.-I read to Ernest the extract from Fenelon, which has made such an impression on me.

"Every business man, in short every man leading an active life, ought to read that," he said. "We should have a new order of things as the result Instead of fancying that our ordinary daily work was one thing and our religion quite another thing, we should transmute our drudgery into acts of worship. Instead of going to prayer-meetings to get into a 'good frame' we should live in a good frame from morning till night, from night till morning, and prayer and praise would be only another form for expressing the love and faith and obedience we had been exercising amid the pressure of business."

"I only wish I had understood this years ago," I said." I have made prayer too much of a luxury, and have often inwardly chafed and fretted when the care of children, at times, made it utterly impossible to leave them for private devotion-when they have been sick, for instance, or in other like emergencies. I reasoned this way: 'Here is a special demand on my patience, and I am naturally impatient I must have time to go away and entreat the Lord to equip me for this conflict.' But I see now that the simple act of cheerful acceptance of the duty imposed and the solace and support withdrawn would have united me more fully to Christ than the highest enjoyment of His presence in prayer could."

"Yes, every act of obedience is an act of worship," he said.

"But why do not we learn that sooner? Why do we waste our lives before we learn how to live?"

"I am not sure," he returned, "that we do not learn as fast as we are willing to learn. God does not force instruction upon us, but when we say, as Luther did, 'More light, Lord, more light,'- the light comes."

I questioned myself after he had gone as to whether this could be true of me. Is there not in my heart some secret reluctance to know the truth, lest that knowledge should call to a higher and holier life than I have yet lived?

JUNE 2.-I went to see Mrs. Campbell a few days ago, and found, to my great joy, that Helen had just been there, and that they had had an earnest conversation together. Mrs. Campbell failed a good deal of late, and it is not probable we shall have her with us much longer. Her every look and word is precious to me when I think of her as one who is so soon to enter the unseen world and see our Savior, and be welcomed home by Him. If it is so delightful to be with those who are on the way to heaven, what would it be to have fellowship with one who had come thence, and could tell us what it is!

She spoke freely about death, and said Ernest had promised to take charge of her funeral, and to see that she was buried by the side of her husband.

"You see, my dear,' she added, with a smile, "though I am expecting to be so soon a saint in heaven, I am a human being still, with human weaknesses. What can it really matter where this weary old body is laid away, when I have done with it, and gone and left it forever? And yet I am leaving directions about its disposal!"

I said I was glad that she was still human but that I did not think it a weakness to take thought for the abode in which her soul had dwelt so long. I saw that she was tired and was coming away, but she held me and would not let me go.

"Yes, I am tired," she said, "but what of that? It is only a question of days now, and all my tired feelings will be over. Then I shall be as young and fresh as ever, and shall have strength to praise and to love God, as I cannot do now. But before I go I want once more to tell you how good He is, how blessed it is to suffer with Him, how infinitely happy He has made me in the very hottest heat of the furnace. It will strengthen you in your trials to recall this my dying testimony. There is no wilderness so dreary but that His love can illuminate it, no desolation so desolate but that He can sweeten it. I know what I am saying. It is no delusion. I believe that the highest, purest happiness is known only to those who have learned Christ in sick-rooms, in poverty, in racking suspense and anxiety, amid hardships, and at the open grave."

Yes, the radiant face, worn by sickness and suffering, but radiant still, said in language yet more unspeakably impressive,—

"To learn Christ, this is life!"

I came into the busy and noisy streets as one descending from the mount, and on reaching home found my darling Una very ill in Ernest's arms. She had fallen, and injured her head. How I had prayed that God would temper the wind to this shorn lamb, and now she had had such a fall! We watched over her till far into the night, scarcely speaking to each other, but I know by the way in which Ernest held my hand clasped in his that, her precious life was in danger. He consented at last to lie down, but Helen stayed with me. What a night it was! God only knows what the human heart can experience in a space of time that men call hours. I went over all the past history of the child, recalling all her sweet looks and words, and my own secret repining at the delicate health that cut her off from so many of the pleasures that belong to her age. And the more I thought, the more I clung to her, on whom, frail as she is, I was beginning to lean, and whose influence in our home I could not think of losing without a shudder. Alas, my faith seemed, for a time, to flee, and I see just what a poor, weak human being is without it. But before daylight crept into my room light from on high streamed into my heart, and I gave even this, my ewe-lamb, away, as my free-will offering to God. Could I refuse Him my child because she was the very apple of my eye? Nay then, but let me give to Him, not what, I value least, but what I prize and delight in most. Could I not endure heart-sickness for Him who had given His only Son for me! And just as I got to that sweet consent to suffer, He who had only lifted the rod to try my faith laid it down. My darling opened her eyes and looked at us intelligently, and with her own loving smile. But I dared not snatch her and press her to my heart for her sake I must be outwardly calm at least.

JUNE 6.-I am at home with my precious Una, all the rest having gone to church. She lies peacefully on the bed, sadly disfigured, for the time, but Ernest says he apprehends no danger now, and we are a most happy, a most thankful household. The children have all been greatly moved by the events of the last few days, and hover about their sister with great sympathy and tenderness. Where she fell from, or how she fell, no one knows she remembers nothing about it herself, and it will always remain a mystery.

This is the second time that this beloved child has been returned to us after we had given her away to God.

And as the giving cost us ten-fold more now than it did when she was a feeble baby, so we receive her as a fresh gift from our loving Father's hand, with ten-fold delight. Ah, we have no excuse for not giving ourselves entirely to Him. He has revealed Himself to us in so many sorrows and in so many joys revealed Himself, as He does not unto the world!

Chapter 26

MAY 13.-THIS has been a Sunday to be held in long remembrance. We were summoned early this morning to Mrs. Campbell, and have seen her joyful release from the fetters that have bound her long. Her loss to me is irreparable. But I truly thank God that one more tired traveler had a sweet "welcome home." I can minister no longer to her bodily wants, and listen to her counsels no more, but she has entered as an inspiration into my life, and through all eternity I shall bless God that He gave me that faithful, praying friend. How little they know who languish in what seem useless sickrooms, or amid the restrictions of frail health, what work they do for Christ by the power of saintly living, and by even fragmentary prayers.

Before her words fade out of my memory I want to write down, from hasty notes made at the time, her answer to some of the last questions I asked her on earth. She had always enjoyed intervals of comparative ease, and it was in one of these that I asked her what she conceived to be the characteristics of an advanced state of grace. She replied, "I think that the mature Christian is always, at all times, and in all circumstances, what he was in his best moments in the progressive stages of his life. There were seasons, all along his course, when he loved God supremely when he embraced the cross joyfully and penitently when he held intimate communion with Christ, and loved his neighbor as himself But he was always in terror, lest under the force of temptation, all this should give place to deadness and dullness, when he should chafe and rebel in the hour of trial, and judge his fellow-man with a harsh and bitter judgment, and give way to angry, passionate emotions. But these fluctuations cease, after a time, to disturb his peace. Love to Christ becomes the abiding, inmost principle of his life he loves Him rather for what He is, than for what He has done or will do for him individually, and God's honor becomes so dear to him that he feels personally wounded when that is called in question. And the will of God becomes so dear to him that he loves it best when it 'triumphs at his cost.'

"Once he only prayed at set times and seasons, and idolized good frames and fervent emotions. Now he prays without ceasing, and whether on the mount or down in the depths depends wholly upon His Savior.

"His old self-confidence has now given place to child-like humility that will not let him take a step alone, and the sweet peace that is now habitual to him combined with the sense of his own imperfections, fills him with love to his fellow-man. He hears and believes and hopes and endures all things and thinks no evil. The tones of his voice, the very expression of his countenance, become changed, love now controlling where human passions held sway. In short, he is not only a new creature in Jesus Christ, but also the habitual and blessed consciousness that this is so.

These words were spoken deliberately and with reflection.

"You have described my mother, just as she was from the moment her only son, the last of six, was taken from her," I said, at last. "I never quite understood how that final sorrow weaned her, so to say, from herself, and made her life all love to God and all love to man. But I see it now. Dear Mrs. Campbell, pray for me that I may yet wear her mantle!"

She smiled with a significance that said she had already done so, and then we parted-parted that she might end her pilgrimage and go to her rest-parted that I might pursue mine, I know not how long, nor amid how many cares, and sorrows, nor with what weariness and heart-sickness-parted to meet again in the presence of Him we love, with those who have come out of great tribulation, whose robes have been made white in the blood of the Lamb, and who are before the throne of God, and serve Him day and night in His temple, to hunger no more, neither thirst any more, for the Lamb which is in the midst of the .throne shall lead them into living fountains of waters and God shall wipe away all tears from their eyes.

MAY 25.-We were talking of Mrs. Campbell, and of her blessed life and blessed death. Helen said it discouraged and troubled her to see and hear such things.

"The last time I saw her when she was able to converse," said she, "I told her that when I reflected on my want of submission to God's will, I doubted whether I really could be His child. She said, in her gentle, sweet way-:

"Would you venture to resist His will, if you could? Would you really have your dear James back again in this world, if could?'

"I would, I certainly would," I said.

"She returned, 'I sometimes find it a help, when dull and cramped in my devotions, to say to myself: Suppose Christ should now appear before you, and you could see Him as He appeared to His disciples on earth, what would you say to Him? This brings Him near, and I say what I would say if He were visibly present. I do the same when a new sorrow threatens me. I imagine my Redeemer as coming personally to say to me, "For your sake I am a man of sorrows and acquainted with grief now for My sake give me this child, bear this burden, submit to this loss." Can I refuse Him? Now, dear, he has really come thus to you, and asked you to show your love to Him, your faith in Him, by giving Him the most precious of your treasures. If He were here at this moment, and offered to restore it to you, would you dare to say, "Yea, Lord, I know, far better than Thou dost, what is good for him and good for me I will have him return to me, cost what it may in this world of uncertainties and disappointments I shall be sure of happiness in his society, and he will enjoy more here on earth with me than he could enjoy in the companionship of saints and angels and of the Lord Himself in heaven." Could you dare to say this?' Oh, Katy, what straits she drove me into! No, I could not dare to say that!'"

"Then, my darling little sister" I cried, "you will give up—this struggle? You will let God do what He will with His own?"

"I have to let Him," she replied "but I submit because I must."

I looked at her gentle, pure face as she uttered these words, and could only marvel at the will that had no expression there.

"Tell me," she said, "do you think a real Christian can feel as I do? For my part, I doubt it. I doubt everything."

"Doubt everything, but believe in Christ," I said. "Suppose, for argument's sake, you are not a Christian. You can become one now." The color rose in her lovely face she clasped her hands in a sort of ecstasy.

"Yes," she said, "I can."

At last, God had sent her the word she wanted.

MAY 28.-Helen came to breakfast this morning in a simple white dress. I had not time to tell the children not to allude to it, so they began in chorus:

"Why, Aunt Helen! You have put on a white dress!"

"Why, Auntie, how queer you look!"

"Hurrah! If she does not look like other folks!"

She bore it all with her usual gentleness or rather with a positive sweetness that captivated them, as her negative patience had never done. I said nothing to her, nor did she to me till late in the day, when she came to me, and said:

"Katy, God taught you what to say. All these years I have been tormenting myself with doubts, as to whether I could be His child while so unable to say, Thy will be done. If you had said,' 'Why, yes, you must be His child, for you professed yourself one a long time ago, and ever since have lived like one,' I should have remained as wretched as ever As it is, a mountain has been rolled off, my heart. Yes, if I was not His child yesterday, I can become one today if I did not love Him then, I can begin now"

I do not doubt that, she was His child, yesterday and last year, and years ago. But let her think, what she pleases. A new life is opening before her I believe it is to be a life of entire devotion to God, and that out of her sorrow there shall spring up a wondrous joy.

SEPT. 2, Sweet Briar Farm.-Ernest spent Sunday with us, and I have just driven him to the station and seen him safely off. Things have prospered with us to such a degree that he has been extravagant enough to give me the use, for the summer, of a bonnie little nag and an antiquated vehicle, and I have learned to drive. To be sure, I broke one of the shafts of the poor old thing the first time I ventured forth alone, and the other day -nearly upset my cargo of children in a pond where I was silly enough to undertake to water my horse. But Ernest, as usual, had patience with me and begged me to spend as much time as possible in driving about with the children. It is a new experience, and I enjoy it quite as much as he hoped I should. Helen is not with us she has spent the whole summer with Martha for Martha, poor thing, is suffering terribly from rheumatism, and is almost entirely helpless. I am so sorry for her, after so many years of vigorous health, how hard it must be to endure this pain. With this drawback, we have had a delightful summer not one sick day or one sick night. With no baby to keep me awake, I sleep straight through, as Raymond says, and wake in the morning refreshed and cheerful. We shall have to go home soon how cruel it seems to bring up children in a great city! Yet what can be done about it? Wherever there are men and women there must be children what a howling wilderness either city or country would be without them!

The only drawback on my felicity is the separation, from Ernest, which becomes more painful every year to us both. God has blessed our married life it has had its waves and its billows, but, thanks unto Him, it has at last settled down into a calm sea of untroubled peace. While I was secretly braiding my dear husband for giving so attention to his profession as to neglect my children, and me he was becoming, every day, more the ideal of a physician, cool, calm, thoughtful, studious, ready to sacrifice his life at any moment in the interests of humanity. How often I have mistaken his preoccupied air for indifference how many times I have inwardly accused him of coldness, when his whole heart and soul were filled with the grave problem of life, aye, and of death likewise.

But we understand each other now, and I am sure that God dealt wisely and kindly with us when He brought together two such opposite natures. No man of my vehement nature could have borne with me as Ernest has done, and if he had married a woman as calm, as undemonstrative as him what a strange home his would have been for the nurture of little children? But the heart was in him, and only wanted to be waked up, and my life has called forth music from his. Ah, there are no partings and meetings now that leave discords in the remembrance, no neglected birthdays, no forgotten courtesies. It is beautiful to see the thoughtful brow relax in presence of wife and children, and to know that ours is, at last, the happy home I so long sighed for. Is the change all in Ernest? Is it not possible that I have grown more reasonable, less childish, and aggravating?

We are at a farmhouse. Everything is plain, but neat and nice. I asked Mrs. Brown, our hostess the other day, if she did not envy me my four little pets she smiled, said they were the best children she ever saw, and that it was well to have a family if you have means to start them in the world for her part, she lived from, hand to mouth as it was, and was sure she could never stand the worry and care of a house full of young ones.

"But the worry and care is only half the story," I said. "The other half is pure joy and delight."

"Perhaps so, to people that are well-to-do," she replied "but to poor folks, driven to death as we are, it's another thing. I was telling him yesterday what a mercy it was there wasn't any young ones round under my feet, and I could take city boarders, and help work off the mortgage on the farm."

"And what did your husband say to that?"

"Well, he said we were young and hearty, and there was no such tearing hurry about the mortgage and that he'd give his right hand to have a couple of boys like yours."

"Well?" - "Why, I said, supposing we had a couple, of boys, they wouldn't be like yours, dressed to look genteel and to have their genteel ways but a pair of wild colts, into everything, tearing their clothes off their backs, and wasting faster than we could earn. He said 'twasn't the clothes, 'twas the flesh and blood he wanted, and 'twasn't no use to argufy about it a man that hadn't got any children wasn't mor'n half a man. 'Well,' says I, supposing you had a pack of, 'em, what have you got to give 'em?' 'Jest exactly what my father and mother gave me,' says he 'two hands to earn their bread with, and a welcome you could have heard from Dan to Beersheba.'"

"I like to hear that!" I said. "And I hope many such welcomes will resound in this house. Suppose money does come in while little goes-out suppose you get possession of the whole farm what then? Who will enjoy it with you? Who will you leave it to when you die? And in your old age who will care for you?"

"You seem awful earnest," she said.

"Yes, I am in earnest. I want to see little children adorning every home, as flowers adorn every meadow and every wayside. I want to see them welcomed to the homes they enter, to see their parents grow less and less selfish, and more and more loving, because they have come. I want to see God's precious gifts accepted, not frowned upon, and refused."

Mr. Brown came in, so I could say no more. But my heart warmed towards him, as I looked at his frank good-humored face, and I should have been glad to give him the right hand of fellowship, as it was I could only say a word or two about the beauty of his farm, and the scenery of this whole region.

"Yes," he said, gratified that I appreciated his fields and groves, "it is a tormented pretty-laying farm. Part of it was her father's, and part of it was my father's there ain't another like it in the country. As to the scenery, I do not know as I ever looked at it city folks talk a good deal about it, but they've nothing to do but look round." Walter came trotting in on two bare, white feet, and with his shoes in his hand. He had had his nap, felt, as bright and fresh as he looked rosy, and I did not wonder at Mr. Brown's catching him up and clasping his sunburnt arms about the little fellow, and pressing him against the warm heart that yearned for nestlings of its own.

Sept. 23-Home again, and the full of the thousand cares that follow the summer and precede the winter. But let mothers and wives fret, as they will, they enjoy these labors of love, and would feel lost without them. For what amount of leisure, ease, and comfort would I exchange husband and children and this busy home?

Martha is better, and Helen has come back to us. I do not know how we have lived without her so long. Her life seems necessary to the completion of every one of ours. Some others have fancied it necessary to the completion of theirs, but she has not agreed with them. We are glad enough to keep her and yet I hope the day will come when she, so worthy of it, will taste the sweet joys of wifehood and motherhood.

JANUARY 1, 1853.-It is not always so easy to practice, as it is to preach. I can see in my wisdom forty reasons for having four children and no more. The comfort of sleeping in peace, of having a little time to read, and to keep on with my music strength with which to look after Ernest's poor people when they are sick and, to tell the truth, strength to be bright and fresh and lovable to him—all these little joys have been growing very precious to me, and now-I must give them up. I want to do it cheerfully and without a frown. But I find I love to have my own way, and that at the very moment I was asking God to appoint my work for me, I was secretly marking it out for myself. It is mortifying to find my will less in harmony with His than I thought it was and that I want to prescribe to Him how I shall spend the time and the health and the strength which are His, not mine. But I will not rest until till this struggle is over till I can say with a smile, "Not my will! Not my will! But Thine!"

We have been, this winter, one of the happiest families on earth. Our love to each other, Ernest's and mine, though not perfect-nothing on earth is-has grown less selfish, more Christ like it has been sanctified by prayer and by the sorrows we have borne together. Then the children have been well and happy, and the source of almost unmitigated joy and comfort. And Helen's presence in this home, her sisterly affection, her patience with the children and her influence over them, is a benediction for which I cannot be thankful enough. How delightful it is to have a sister! I think it is not often the case that one's sisters have such perfect Christian sympathy with each other as we have. Ever since the day she ceased to torment herself with the fear that she was not a child of God, and laid aside the somber garments she had worn so long, she has had a peace that has hardly known a cloud. She says, in a note written me about the time:

I want you to know, my darling sister, which the despondency that made my affliction so hard to bear fled before those words of yours, which, as I have already told you, God taught you to speak. I do not know whether I was really His child, at the time, or not. I had certainly had an experience very different from yours prayer had never been much more to me than a duty and I had never felt the sweetness of that harmony between God and I the human soul that I now know can take away all the bitterness from the cup of sorrow. I knew-who can help knowing it that reads God's word?-that he required submission from His children and that His children gave it, no matter what it cost. The Bible is full of beautiful expressions of it so are our hymns so are the written lives of all good men and good women and I have seen it in you, my dear Katy, at the very moment you were accusing yourself of the want of it. Entire oneness of the will with the Divine Will seem to me to be the law and the gospel of the Christian life and this evidence of a renewed nature, I found wanting in myself. At any moment during the three years following James' death I would have snatched away from God, if I could I was miserably lonely and desolate without him, not merely because he had been so much, to me, but because his loss revealed to me the distance between Christ and my soul. All I could do was to go on praying, year after year, in a dreary, hopeless way, that I might learn to say, as David did, 'I opened not my mouth because Thou didst it.' When you suggested that instead of trying to figure out whether I had loved God, I should begin to love Him now, light broke in upon my soul I gave myself to Him that instant and as soon as I could get away by myself I fell upon my knees and gave myself up to the sense of His sovereignty for the first time in my life. Then, too, I looked at my 'light affliction,' and at the 'weight of glory 'side by side, and thanked Him that through the one He had revealed to me the other. Katy, I know the human heart is deceitful above all things, but I think it would be a dishonor to God to doubt that He then revealed Himself to me as He doth not to the world, and that the sweet peace I then found in yielding to Him will be more or less mine so long as I live. Oh, if all sufferers could learn what I have learned! That every broken heart could be healed as mine has been healed! My precious sister, cannot we make this one part of our mission on earth, to pray for every sorrow-stricken soul, and whenever we have influence over such, to lead it to honor God by instant obedience to His will, whatever that may be? I have dishonored Him by years of rebellious, carefully-nursed sorrow I want to honor Him now by years of resignation and grateful joy."

Reading this letter over in my present mood has done me good. More beautiful faith in God than Helen's I have never seen let me have it, too. May this prayer, which, under the inspiration of the moment, I can offer without a misgiving, become the habitual, deep-seated desire of my soul?

"Bring into captivity every thought to the obedience of Christ. Take what I cannot give—my heart, body, thoughts, time, abilities, money, health, strength, nights, days, youth, age, and spend them in Thy service, O my crucified Master, Redeemer, God. Oh, let these not be mere words! Whom have I in heaven but Thee? And there is none upon earth that I desire in comparison of Thee. My heart is thirsty for God, for the living God. When shall I come and appear before God?"

Chapter 27

AUGUST 1 - I HAVE just written to Mrs. Brown to know whether she will take us for the rest of the summer. A certain little man, not a very old little man either, has kept us in town till now. Since he has come, we are all very glad of him, though he came on his own invitation, brought no wardrobe with him, does not pay for his board, never speaks a word, takes no notice of us, and wants more waiting on than anyone else in the house. The children are full of delicious curiosity about him, and overwhelm him with presents of the most heterogeneous character.

Sweet Briar Farm, AUG. 9.-We got there this afternoon, bag and baggage. I had not said a word to Mrs. Brown about the addition to our family circle, knowing she had plenty of room, and as we alighted from the carriage, I snatched my baby from his nurse's arms and ran gaily up the walk with him in mine. "If this splendid fellow doesn't convert her nothing will," I said to myself. At that instant what should I see but Mrs. Brown, running to meet me with a boy in her arms exactly like Mr. Brown, only not quite six feet long, and not sunburnt.

"There!" I cried, holding up my little old man.

"There!" said she, holding up hers.

We laughed till we cried she took my baby and I took hers after looking at him I liked mine better than ever after looking at mine she was perfectly satisfied with hers.

We got into the house at last that is to say, we mothers did the children darted through it and out of the door that led to the fields and woods, and vanished in the twinkling of an eye.

Mrs. Brown had always been a pretty woman, with bright eyes, shining, well-kept hair, and a color in her cheeks like the rose that had given its name to her farm. But there was now a new beauty in her face the mysterious and sacred sufferings and joys of maternity had given it thought and feeling.

"I had no idea I should be so fond of a baby," she said, kissing it, whenever she stopped to put in a comma "but I do not know how I ever got along without one. He's off at work nearly the whole day, and when I had got through with mine, and had put on my afternoon dress, and was ready to sit down, you cannot think how lonesome it was. But now by the time I am dressed, baby is ready to go out to get the air he knows the minute he sees me bring out his little hat that he is going to see his father and he's awful fond of his father. Though that isn't so strange, either, for his father's awful fond of him. All his little ways are so pretty, and he never cries unless he's hungry or tired. Tell mother a pretty story now yes, mother hears, bless his little heart!"

Then when Mr. Brown came home to his supper, his face was a sight to see, as he caught sight of me at my open window, and came to it with the child's white arms clinging to his neck, looking as happy and as bashful as a girl.

"You see she must needs go to quartering this bouncing young one on to me," he said, "as if I didn't have to work hard enough before. Well, maybe he'll get his feed off the farm we'll see what we can do."

"Mamma," Una whispered, as he went off his facsimile, to kiss it rapturously, behind a woodpile, "do you think Mrs. Brown's baby very pretty?

Which was so mild a way of suggesting the fact of the case, that I kissed her without trying to hide my amusement?

AUG. 10.-After being cooped up in town so large a part of the summer; the children are nearly wild with delight at being in the country once more. Even our demure Una skips about with buoyancy I have never seen in her she never has her ill turns when out of the city, and I wish, for her sake, we could always live here. As to Raymond and Walter, I never pretend to see them except at their meals and their bedtime they just live outdoors, following the men at their work, asking all sorts of absurd questions, which Mr. Brown reports to me every night, with shouts of delighted laughter. Two gay and gladsome boys they are really good without being priggish I do not think I could stand that. People ask me how it happens that my children are all so promptly obedient and so happy. As if it chanced that some parents have such children, or chanced that some have not! I am afraid it is only too true, as someone has remarked, "this is the age of obedient parents!" What then will be the future of their children? How can they yield to God who has never been taught to yield to human authority? And how well fitted will they be to rule their own households who have never learned to rule themselves?

AUG. 31.-This has been one of those cold, dismal, rainy days which are not infrequent during the month of August. So the children have been obliged to give up the open air, of which. They are so fond, and fall back upon what entertainment could be found within the house. I have read to them the little journal I kept during the whole life of the brother I am not willing they should forget. His quaint and sagacious sayings were delicious to them the history of his first steps, his first words sounded to them like a fairy tale. And the story of his last steps, his last words on earth, had for them such a tender charm, that there was a cry of disappointment from them all, when I closed the little book and told them we should have to wait till we got to heaven before we could know anything more about his precious life.

How thankful I am that I kept this journal, and that I have almost as charming ones about most of my other children! What I speedily forgot amid the pressure of cares and of new events is safely written down, and. will be the source of endless pleasure to them long after the hand that wrote has ceased from its .labors, and lies inactive and at rest.

Ah, it is a blessed thing to be a mother!

SEPTEMBER 1-This baby of mine, is certainly the sweetest and best I ever had I feel an inexpressible tenderness for it, which I cannot quite explain to myself, for I have loved them all dearly, most dearly. Perhaps it is so with all mothers, perhaps they all grow more loving, more forbearing, and more patient as they grow older, and yearn over these helpless little ones with an ever-increasing, yet chastened delight. One cannot help sheltering their tender infancy, which will so soon pass forth to fight the battle of life, each one waging an invisible warfare against invisible foes. How thankfully we would fight it for them, if we might!

SEPTEMBER 20.-. The mornings and evenings are very cool now, while in the middle of the day it is quite hot. Ernest comes to see us very often, under the pretense that he cannot trust me with so young a baby! He is so tender and thoughtful, and spoils me so, that this world is very bright to me I am a little jealous of it I do not want to be so happy in Ernest, or in my children, as to forget for one instant that I am a pilgrim and a stranger on earth.

EVENING.-There is no danger that I shall. Ernest suddenly made his appearance tonight, and in a great burst of distress quite unlike anything I ever saw in him, revealed to me that he had been feeling the greatest anxiety about me ever since the baby came. It is all nonsense. I cough, to be sure but that it is owing to the varying temperature we always have at this season. I shall get over, it as soon as we get home, I dare say.

But suppose I should not what then? Could I leave this precious little flock, uncared for, untended? Have I faith to believe that if God calls me away from them, it will be in love to them? I do not know. The thought of getting away from the sin that still so easily besets me is very delightful, and I have enjoyed so many, many such foretastes of the bliss of heaven that I know I should be happy there, but then my children, all of them under twelve years old! I will not choose, I dare not.

My married life has been a beautiful one. It is true that sin and folly, and sickness and sorrow, have marred its perfection, but it has been adorned by a love that has never faltered. My faults have never alienated Ernest. His faults, for like other human beings he has them, have never overcome my love to him. This has been the gift of God in answer to our constant prayer, that whatever other bereavement we might have to suffer, we might never be bereft of this benediction. It has been the glad secret of a happy marriage, and I wish I could teach it to every human being who enters upon a state that must bring with it the depth of misery, or life's most sacred and mysterious joy.

OCTOBER 6. - Ernest has let me stay here to see the autumnal foliage in its ravishing beauty for the first, perhaps for the last, time. The woods and fields and groves are lighting up my very soul! It seems as if autumn had caught the inspiration and the glow of summer, had hidden its floral beauty, it's gorgeous sunsets and its bow of promise in its heart of hearts, and was now flashing it forth upon 'the world with a lavish and opulent hand. I can hardly tear myself away, and return to the prose of city life. But Ernest has come for us, and is eager to get us home before colder weather. I laugh at his anxiety about his old wife. Why need he fancy that this trifling cough is not to give way as it often has done before? Dear Ernest! I never knew that he loved me so.

OCTOBER 31.-Ernest's fear that he had let me stay too long in the country does not seem to be justified. We went so late that I wanted to indulge the children by staying late. So we have only just got home. I feel about as well as usual it is true I have a little soreness about the chest, but it does not signify anything.

I never was so happy, in my husband and children, in other words in my home, as I am now. Life looks very attractive. I am glad that I am going to get well.

But Ernest watches me carefully, and wants me, as a precautionary measure, to give up music, writing, sewing, and painting-the very things that occupy me! And lead an idle, useless life, for a time. I cannot refuse what he asks so tenderly, and as a personal favor to himself. Yet I should like to fill the remaining pages of my journal I never like to leave things incomplete.

JUNE 1, 1858.-I wrote that seven years ago, little dreaming how long it, would be before I should use a pen. Seven happy years ago!

I suppose that some who have known what my outward life has been during' this period would think of me as a mere object of pity. There has certainly been suffering and deprivation enough to justify the sympathy of my dear husband and children and the large circle of friends who have rallied about us. How little we knew we had so many!

God has dealt very tenderly with me. I was not stricken down by sudden disease, nor were the things I delighted in all taken away at once There was a gradual loss of strength and gradual increase of suffering, and it was only by degrees that I was asked to give up the employments in which I'd delighted, my household duties, my visits to the sick and suffering, the society of beloved friends. Perhaps Ernest perceived and felt my deprivations sooner than I did his sympathy always seemed to out-run my disappointments. When I compare him, as he is now, with what he was when I first knew him I bless God for all the precious lessons He has taught him at my cost. There, is a tenacity and persistence about his love for me that has made these years almost as wearisome to him as they have been to me. As to myself, if I had been told what I was to learn through these protracted sufferings I am afraid I should have shrunk back in terror and so have lost all the sweet lessons God proposed to teach me. As it is He has led me on, step by step, answering my prayers in His own way and I cannot bear to have a single human being doubt that it has been a perfect way. I love and adore it just as it is.

Perhaps the suspense has been one of the most trying features of my case. Just as I have unclasped my hand from my dear Ernest's just as I have let go my almost frantic hold of my darling children just as heaven opened before me and I fancied my weariness over and my wanderings done just then almost every alarming symptom would disappear and life recall me from the threshold of heaven itself. Thus, I have been emptied from vessel to vessel, til I have learned that he only is truly happy who has no longer a choice of his own, and lies passive in God's hand.

Even now, no one can foretell the issue of this sickness. We live a day at a time not knowing what shall be on the morrow. But whether I live or die my happiness is secure and so I believe is of my beloved ones. This is a true picture of our home:

A sickroom full of the suffering ravages the body but cannot touch the soul. A worn, wasting mother ministered unto by a devoted husband and by unselfish Christian children. Some of the peace of God if not all of it, shines in every face, is heard in every tone. It is a home that typifies and foreshadows the home that is perfect and eternal.

Our dear Helen has been given us for this emergency. Is it not strange that seeing our domestic life should have awakened in her some yearnings for a home and a heart and children of her own? She has said that there was a weary point in her life when she made up her mind that she was never to know these joys. But she accepted her lot gracefully. I do not know any other word that describes so well the beautiful offering she made of her life to God and then to us. He accepted it, and as given her all the cares and responsibilities of domestic life without the transcendent joys that sustain the wife and the mother. She has been all in all to our children and God has been all in all to her. And she is happy in His service and in our love.

JUNE 20-It took me nearly two weeks to write the above at intervals as my strength allowed. Ernest has consented to my finishing this volume, of which so few pages yet remain. And he let me see a dear old friend who came all the way from my native town to see me-Dr. Eaton, our family physician as long as I could remember. He is and with a healthful glow on his cheek. But he says he is waiting and longing for his summons home. About that home, we had a delightful talk together that did my very heart good. Then he made me tell him about this long sickness and the years of frail health and some of the sorrows through which I had toiled.

"Ah, these lovely children are explained now," he said.

"Do you really think," I asked, "that it has been good for my children to have a feeble, afflicted mother?"

"Yes, I really think so. A disciplined mother—disciplined children."

This comforting thought is one of the last drops in a cup of felicity already full.

JUNE 2-Another Sunday, and all at church except my darling Una who keeps watch over her mother. These Sundays when I have had them each alone in turn have been blessed days to them and to me. Surely, this is some compensation for what they lose in me of health and vigor. I know the state of each soul as far as it can be known, and have every reason to believe that my children all love my Savior and are trying to live for Him. I have learned at last not to despise the day of small things, to cherish the tenderest blossom, and to expect my dear ones to be imperfect before they become perfect Christians.

Una is a sweet composed young girl now eighteen years old and what can I say more of the love her brothers bear her than this: they never tease her. She has long ceased asking why she must have delicate health when so many others of her age are full of animal life and vigor but stands in her lot and place doing what she can, suffering what she must, with a meekness that makes her lovely in my eyes, and that I am sure unites her closely to Christ.

JUNE 27.-It was Raymond's turn to stay with me today. He opened his heart to me more freely than he had ever done before.

"Mamma," he began, "if papa is willing, I have made up my mind-that is to say if I get decently good-to go on a mission."

I said playfully:

"And mamma's consent is not to be asked?"

"No," he said, "getting hold of what there is left of my hand. "I know you would not say a word. Do not you remember telling me once when I was a little boy that I might go and welcome?"

"And do not you remember," I returned, "that you cried for joy, and then relieved your mind still farther by walking on your hands with your feet in the air?"

We both laughed heartily at this remembrance, and then I said:

"My dear boy, you know your fathers plan for you?"

"Yes, I know he expects me to study with him, and take his place in the world."

"And it is a very important place."

His countenance fell as he fancied I was not entering heartily into his wishes.

"Dear Raymond," I went on, "I gave you to God long before you gave yourself to Him. If He can make you useful in your own, or in other lands, I bless His name. Whether I live to see you a man, or not, I hope you will work in the Lord's vineyard, wherever He calls. I never asked anything but usefulness, in all my prayers for you never once. His eyes filled with tears he kissed me and walked away to the window to compose himself. My poor, dear, lovable, loving boy! He has all his mother's trials and struggles to contend with but what matter it if they bring him the same peace?

JUNE 30.—Everybody wonders to see me once more interested in my long-closed Journal, and becoming able to see the dear friends from whom I have been, in a measure cut off. We cannot ask the meaning of this remarkable increase of strength.

I have no wish to choose. But I have come to the last page of my Journal, and living or dying, shall write in this volume no more. It closes upon a life of much childishness and great sinfulness, whose record makes me blush with shame but I no longer need to relieve my heart with seeking sympathy in its unconscious pages nor do I believe it well to go on analyzing it as I have done. I have had large experience of both joy and sorrow I have the nakedness and the emptiness and I have seen the beauty and sweetness of life. What I say now, let me say to Jesus what time and strength

I used to spend in writing here, let me spend in praying for all men, for all sufferers who are out of the way, for all whom I love. And their name is Legion for I love everybody.

Yes, I love everybody! That crowning joy has come to me at last. Christ is in my soul He is mine I am as conscious of it as that my husband and children are mine and His Spirit flows from mine in the calm peace of a river whose banks are green with grass and glad with flowers. If I die, it will be to leave a wearied and worn body, and a sinful soul to go joyfully to be with Christ, to weary and to sin no more. If I live, I shall find much blessed work to do for Him. So living or dying I shall be the Lord's.

But I wish, oh how earnestly, that whether I go or stay, I could inspire some lives with the joy that is now mine. For many years I have been rich in faith, rich in an unfaltering confidence that I was beloved of my God and Savior. But something was wanting. I was ever groping for a mysterious grace the want of which made me often sorrowful in the very midst of my most sacred joy, imperfect when I most longed for perfection. It was that personal love to Christ of which my precious mother so often spoke to me that she often urged me to seek upon my knees. If I had known then, as I know now what this priceless treasure could be to a sinful human soul, I would have sold all that I had to buy the field wherein it lay hidden. But not till I was shut up to prayer and to the study of God's word by the loss of earthly joys, sickness destroying the flavor of them all, did I begin to penetrate the mystery that is learned under the cross. And wondrous as it is, how simple is this mystery! To love Christ and to know that I love Him-this is all!

And when I entered upon the sacred yet oft-times homely duties of married life, if this love had been mine, how would that life have been transfigured! The petty faults of my husband under which I chafed would not have moved me I should have welcomed Martha and her father to my home and made them happy there I should have had no conflicts with my servants, shown no petulance to my children. For it would not have been I who spoke and acted but Christ who lived in me.

Alas! I have had less than seven years in which to atone for a sinful, wasted past and to live a new and a Christ-like life. If I am to have yet more, thanks be to Him who has given me the victory, that Life will be Love. Not the love that rests in the contemplation and adoration of its object but the love that gladdens, sweetens, solaces other lives.

O gifts of gifts! O grace of faith
My God! How can it be
That Thou who hast discerning love,
Should give that gift to me?
How many hearts thou might have had
More innocent than mine!
How many souls more worthy far
Of that sweet touch of Thine?
Oh grace! Into unlikeliest hearts,
It is thy boast to come
The glory of Thy light to find
In darkest spots a home.
Oh happy. Happy that I am!
If thou canst be, O faith
The treasure that thou art in life
What wilt thou be in death?

STEPPING WESTWARD. - WHILE my fellow-traveler and I were walking by the side of Loch Katrine one fine evening after sunset in our road to a hut where in the course of our tour we had been hospitably entertained some weeks before, we met, in one of the loneliest parts of that solitary region two well-dressed women, one of whom said to us by way of greeting, "What, you are stepping westward?"

"What, you are stepping westward?" "Yea." —'Twould be a wildish destiny if we who thus together roam in a strange land and far from home Were in this place the guests of chance: Yet who would stop, or fear to advance, though home or shelter he had none, with such a sky to lead him on? The dewy ground was dark and cold Behind, all gloomy to behold and stepping westward seemed to be A kind of heavenly destiny: I liked the greeting 'twas a sound Of something without place and bound, And seemed to give me spiritual right To travel through that region bright. The voice was soft and she who spoke Was walking by her native lake: The salutation had to me The very sound of courtesy: Its power was felt and while my eye Was fixed upon the glowing sky, The echo of the voice wrought A human sweetness with the thought Of traveling through the world that lay Before me in my endless way. — WORDSWORTH.

The End

THE LIFE AND LETTERS OF ELIZABETH PRENTISS

BY GEORGE L. PRENTISS

This memoir was undertaken at the request of many of Mrs. Prentiss' old and most trusted friends, who felt that the story of her life should be given to the public. Much of it is in the nature of an autobiography. Her letters, which with extracts from her journals form the larger portion of its contents, begin when she was in her twentieth year, and continue almost to her last hour. They are full of details respecting herself, her home, her friends, and the books she wrote. A simple narrative, interspersed with personal reminiscences, and varied by a sketch of her father, and passing notices of others, who exerted a molding influence upon her character, completes the story. A picture is thus presented of the life she lived and its changing scenes, both on the natural and the spiritual side. While the work may fail to interest some readers, the hope is cherished that, like STEPPING HEAVENWARD, it will be welcomed into Christian homes and prove a blessing to many hearts thus realizing the desire expressed in one of her last letters: *Much of my experience of life has cost me a great price and I wish to use it for strengthening and comforting other souls.*

G. L. P.
KAUINFELS, September 11, 1882.

CHAPTER 1 - THE CHILD AND THE GIRL - 1818-1839.

> I. Birth-place and Ancestry. Seth Payson. Edward Payson. His Mother. A Sketch of his Life and Character. The Fervor of his Piety. Despondent Moods and their Cause. Bright, natural Traits. How he prayed and preached. Conversational Gift. Love to Christ. Triumphant Death.

Mrs. Prentiss was fortunate in the place of her birth. She first saw the light at Portland, Maine. Maine was then a district of Massachusetts, and Portland was its chief town and seaport, distinguished for beauty of situation, enterprise, intelligence, social refinement and all the best qualities of New England character. Not a few of the early settlers had come from Cape Cod and other parts of the old Bay State, and the blood of the Pilgrim Fathers ran in their veins. Among its leading citizens at that time were such men as Stephen Longfellow, Simon Greenleaf, Prentiss Mellen, Samuel Fessenden, Ichabod Nichols, Edward Payson, and Asa Cummings men eminent for private and public virtue, and some of whom were destined to become still more widely known, by their own growing influence, or by the genius of their children.

But while favored in the place of her birth, Mrs. Prentiss was more highly favored still in her parentage. For more than half a century the name of her father has been a household word among the churches not of New England only, but throughout the land and even beyond the sea. It is among the most beloved and honored in the annals of American piety. [1] He belonged to a very old Puritan stock, and to a family noted during two centuries for the number of ministers of the Gospel who have sprung from it. The first in the line of his ancestry in this country was Edward, who came over in the brig Hopewell, William Burdeck, Master, in 1635-6, and settled in the town of Roxbury. He was a native of Nasing, Essex Co., England. Among his fellow-passengers in the Hopewell was Mary Eliot, then a young girl, sister of John Eliot, the illustrious "Apostle to the Indians." Some years later, she became his wife. Their youngest son, Samuel, was father of the Rev. Phillips Payson, who was born at Dorchester, Massachusetts, 1705, and settled at Walpole, in the same State, in 1730. He had four sons in the ministry, all, like himself, graduates of Harvard College. The youngest of these, the Rev. Seth Payson, D.D., Mrs. Prentiss' grandfather, was born September 30, 1758, was ordained and settled at Rindge, New Hampshire, December 4, 1782, and died there, after a pastorate of thirty-seven years, February 26, 1820. His wife was Grata Payson, of Pomfret, Conn. He was a man widely known in his day and of much weight in the community, not only in his own profession but in civil life, also, having several times filled the office of State senator. When in 1819, a plan was formed to remove Williams College to a more central location, and several towns competed for the honor, Dr. Payson was associated with Chancellor Kent of New York, and Governor John Cotton Smith of Connecticut, as a committee to decide upon the rival claims. He is described as possessing a sharp, vigorous intellect, a lively imagination, a very retentive memory, and was universally esteemed as an able and faithful minister of Christ. [2]

Edward, the eldest son of Seth and Grata Payson, was born at Rindge, July 25, 1783. His mother was noted for her piety, her womanly discretion, and her personal and mental graces. Edward was her first-born, and from his infancy to the last year of his life, she lavished upon him her love and her prayers. The relation between them was very beautiful.

His letters to her are models of filial devotion, and her letters to him are full of tenderness, good sense, and pious wisdom. He inherited some of her most striking traits, and through him, they passed on to his youngest daughter, who often said that she owed her passion for the use of the pen and her fondness for rhyming to her grandmother Grata. [3]

Edward Payson was in all respects a highly gifted man. His genius was as marked as his piety. There is a charm about his name and the story of his life, which is not likely soon to pass away. He belonged to a class of men who seem to be chosen of Heaven to illustrate the sublime possibilities of Christian attainment—men of seraphic fervor of devotion, and whose one overmastering passion is to win souls for Christ and to become wholly like Him themselves. Into this goodly fellowship he was early initiated. There is something startling in the depth and intensity of his religious emotions, as recorded in his journal and letters. Nor is it to be denied that they are often marred by a very morbid element. Like David Brainerd, the missionary saint of New England, to whom in certain features of his character he bore no little resemblance, Edward Payson was of a melancholy temperament and subject, therefore, to sudden and sharp alternations of feeling. While he had great capacity for enjoyment, his capacity for suffering was equally great. Nor were these native traits suppressed, or always overruled, by his religious faith on the contrary, they affected and modified his whole Christian life. In its earlier stages, he was apt to lay too much stress by far upon fugitive "frames," and to mistake mere weariness, torpor, and even diseased action of body or mind, for coldness toward his Savior. And almost to the end of his days he was, occasionally, visited by seasons of spiritual gloom and depression, which, no doubt, were chiefly, if not solely, the result of physical causes. It was an error that grew readily out of the brooding introspection and self-anatomy which marked the religious habit of the times. The close connection between physical causes and morbid or abnormal conditions of the spiritual life, was not as well understood then as it is now. Many things were ascribed to Satanic influence that should have been ascribed rather to unstrung nerves and loss of sleep, or to a violation of the laws of health. [4] The disturbing influence of nervous and other bodily or mental disorders upon religious experience deserves a fuller discussion than it has yet received. It is a subject that both modern science and modern thought, if guided by Christian wisdom, might help greatly to elucidate.

The morbid and melancholy element, however, was only a painful incident of his character. It tinged his life with a vein of deep sadness and led to undue severity of self-discipline but it did not seriously impair the strength and beauty of his Christian manhood. It rather served to bring them into fuller relief, and even to render more striking those bright natural traits—the sportive humor, the ready mother wit, the facetious pleasantry, the keen sense of the ridiculous, and the wondrous story-telling gift—which made him a most delightful companion to young and old, to the wise and the unlettered alike. It served, moreover, to impart peculiar tenderness to his pastoral intercourse, especially with members of his flock tried and tempted like as he was. He had learned how to counsel and comfort them by the things that he also had suffered. He may have been too exacting and harsh in dealing with himself but in dealing with other souls, nothing could exceed the gentleness, wisdom, and soothing influence of his ministrations.

As a preacher, he was the impersonation of simple, earnest, and impassioned utterance. Although not an orator in the ordinary sense of the term, he touched the hearts of his hearers with a power beyond the reach of any oratory. Some of his printed sermons are models in their kind that *e.g.* on "Sins estimated by the Light of Heaven," and that addressed to Seamen. His theology was a mild type of the old New England Calvinism, modified, on the one hand, by the influence of his favorite authors—such as Thomas à Kempis, and Fenelon, the Puritan divines of the seventeenth century, John Newton and Richard Cecil—and on the other, by his own profound experience and seraphic love. Of his theology, his preaching, and his piety alike, Christ was the living centre. His expressions of personal love to the Savior are surpassed by nothing in the writings of the old mystics. Here is a passage from a letter to his mother, written while he was still a young pastor:

I have sometimes heard of spells and charms to excite love, and have wished for them, when a boy, that I might cause others to love me. But how much do I now wish for some charm, which should lead men to love the Savior! Could I paint a true likeness of Him, methinks I should rejoice to hold it up to the view and admiration of all creation, and be hid behind it forever. It would be heaven enough to hear Him praised and adored. But I cannot paint Him I cannot describe Him I cannot make others love Him nay, I cannot love Him a thousandth part so much as I ought myself. O, for an angel's tongue! O, for the tongues of ten thousand angels, to sound His praises.

He had a remarkable familiarity with the word of God and his mind seemed surcharged with its power. "You could not, in conversation, mention a passage of Scripture to him but you found his soul in harmony with it—the most apt illustrations would flow from his lips, the fire of devotion would beam from his eye, and you saw at once that not only could he deliver a sermon from it, but that the ordinary time allotted to a sermon would be exhausted before he could pour out the fullness of meaning which a sentence from the word of God presented to his mind." [5]

He was wonderfully gifted in prayer. Here all his intellectual, imaginative, and spiritual powers were fused into one and poured themselves forth in an unbroken stream of penitential and adoring affection. When he said, "Let us pray," a divine influence seemed to rest upon all present. His prayers were not mere pious mental exercises, they were devout inspirations.

No one can form an adequate conception of what Dr. Payson was from any of the productions of his pen. Admirable as his written sermons are, his extempore prayers and the gushings of his heart in familiar talk were altogether higher and more touching than anything he wrote. It was my custom to close my eyes when he began to pray, and it was always a letting down, a sort of rude fall, to open them again, when he had concluded, and find myself still on the earth. His prayers always took my spirit into the immediate presence of Christ, amid the glories of the spiritual world and to look round again on this familiar and comparatively misty earth was almost painful. At every prayer I heard him offer, during the seven years in which he was my spiritual guide, I never ceased to feel new astonishment, at the wonderful variety and depth and richness and even novelty of feeling and expression that were poured forth. This was a feeling with which every hearer sympathized, and it is a fact well known, that Christians trained under his influence were generally remarkable for their devotional habits. [6]

Dr. Payson possessed rare conversational powers and loved to wield them in the service of his Master. When in a genial mood—and the mild excitement of social intercourse generally put him in such a mood—his familiar talk was equally delightful and instructive. He was, in truth, an improvisator. Quick perception, an almost intuitive insight into character, an inexhaustible fund of fresh, original thought and incident, the happiest illustrations, and a memory that never faltered in recalling what he had once read or seen, easy self-control, and ardent sympathies, all conspired to give him this preeminence. Without effort or any appearance of incongruity, he could in turn be grave and gay, playful and serious. This came of the utter sincerity and genuineness of his character. There was nothing artificial about him nature and grace had full play and, so to say, constantly ran into each other. A keen observer, who knew him well, both in private and in public, testifies: "His facetiousness indeed was ever a near neighbor to his piety, if it was not a part of it and his most cheerful conversations, so far from putting his mind out of tune for acts of religious worship, seemed but a happy preparation for the exercise of devotional feelings." [7] This coexistence of serious with playful elements is often found in natures of unusual depth and richness, just as tragic and comic powers sometimes co-exist in a great poet.

The same qualities that rendered him such a master of conversation, lent a potent charm to his familiar religious talks in the prayer meeting, at the fireside, or in the social circle. Always eager to speak for his Master, he knew how to do it with a wise skill and a tenderness of feeling that disarmed prejudice and sometimes won the most determined foe. Even in administering reproof or rebuke there was the happiest union of tact and gentleness. "What makes you blush so?" said a reckless fellow in the stage, to a plain country girl, who was receiving the mailbag at a post office from the hand of the driver. "What makes you blush so, my dear?" "Perhaps," said Dr. Payson, who sat near him and was unobserved till now, "Perhaps it is because someone spoke rudely to her when the stage was along here the last time."

Edward Payson was graduated at Harvard College in the class of 1803. In the autumn of that year, he took charge of an academy then recently established in Portland. Resigning this position in 1806, he returned home and devoted himself to the study of divinity under his father's care. He was licensed to preach in May, 1807, and a few months later received a unanimous call to Portland, where he was ordained in December of the same year. On the 8th of May, 1811, he was married to Ann Louisa Shipman, of New Haven, Conn. An extract from a manly letter to Miss Shipman, written a few weeks after their engagement, will show the spirit that inspired him as both a lover and a husband:

When I wrote my first letter after my late visit, I felt almost angry with you and quite so with myself. And why angry with you? Because I began to fear, you would prove a dangerous rival to my Lord and Master, and draw away my heart from His service. My Louisa, should this be the case, I should certainly hate you. I am Christ's I must be Christ's He has purchased me dearly, and I should hate the mother who bore me, if she proved even the *innocent* occasion of drawing me from Him. I feared that you would do this. For a little time the conflict of my feelings was dreadful beyond description. For a few moments, I wished I had never seen you. Had you been a right hand, or a right eye, had you been the life-blood in my veins (and you are dear to me as either) I must have given you up, had I continued to feel as I did. But blessed be God, He has shown me my weakness only to strengthen me. I now feel very differently. I still love you dearly as ever, but my love leads me *to* Christ and not *from* Him.

Dr. Payson received repeated invitations to important churches in Boston and New York, but declining them all, continued in the Portland pastorate until his death, which occurred October 22, 1827, in the forty-fifth year of his age. The closing months of his life were rendered memorable by an extraordinary triumph of Christian faith and patience, as well as of the power of mind over matter. His bodily suffering and agonies were indescribable, but, like one of the old martyrs in the midst of the flames, he seemed to forget them all in the greatness of his spiritual joy. In a letter written shortly after his death, Mrs. Payson gives a touching account of the tender and thoughtful concern for her happiness, which marked his last illness. Knowing, for example, that she would be compelled to part with her house, he was anxious to have a smaller one purchased and occupied at once, so that his presence in it for a little while might make it seem more home like to her and to her children after he was gone. "To tell you (she adds) what he was the last six memorable weeks would be altogether beyond my skill. All who beheld him called his countenance angelic." She then repeats some of his farewell words to her. Begging that, she would "not dwell upon his poor, shattered frame, but follow his blessed spirit to the realms of glory," he burst forth into an exultant song of delight, as if already he saw the King in His beauty! The well-known letter to his sister Eliza, dated a few weeks before his departure, breathes the same spirit. Here is an extract from it:

Were I to adopt the figurative language of Bunyan, I might date this letter from the land of Beulah, of which I have been for some weeks a happy inhabitant. The celestial city is full in my view. Its glories beam upon me, its breezes fan me, its odors are wafted to me, its sounds strike upon my ear, and its spirit is breathed into my heart. Nothing separates me from it but the river of death, which now appears but as an insignificant rill, which may be crossed at a single step, whenever God shall give permission. The Sun of Righteousness has been gradually drawing nearer and nearer, appearing larger and brighter as He approached, and now He fills the whole hemisphere, pouring forth a flood of glory, in which I seem to float like an insect in the beams of the sun, exulting yet almost trembling while I gaze on this excessive brightness, and wondering, with unutterable wonder, why God should deign thus to shine upon a sinful worm. A single heart and a single tongue seem altogether inadequate to my wants I want a whole heart for every separate emotion, and a whole tongue to express that emotion. But why do I speak thus of my feelings and myself? Why not speak only of our God and Redeemer? It is because I know not what to say—when I would speak of them my words are all swallowed up.

And thus, gazing already upon the Beatific Vision, he passed on into glory. What is written concerning his Lord and Master might with almost literal truth have been inscribed over his grave: *The zeal of Thy house hath eaten me up.*

* * * * *

II.

Birth and Childhood of Elizabeth Payson. Early Traits. Devotion to her Father. His Influence upon her. Letters to her Sister. Removal to New York. Reminiscences of the Payson Family.

Elizabeth Payson was born "about three o'clock"—so her father records it—on Tuesday afternoon, October 26, 1818. She was the fifth of eight children, two of whom died in infancy. All good influences seem to have encircled her natal hour. In a letter to his mother, dated October 27, Dr Payson enumerates six special mercies, by which the happy event had been crowned. One of them was the gratification of the mother's "wish for a daughter rather than a son." Another was God's goodness to him in sparing both the mother and the child in spite of his fear that he should lose them. This fear, strangely enough, was occasioned by the unusual religious peace and comfort, which he had been enjoying. He had a presentiment that in this way God was forearming him for some extraordinary trial and the loss of his wife seemed to him most likely to be that trial. "God has been so gracious to me in spiritual things, that I thought He was preparing me for Louisa's death. Indeed, it may be so still, and if so His will be done. Let Him take all—and if He leaves us Himself we still have all and abound." The next day he writes:

Still God is kind to us. Louisa and the babe continue as well as we could desire. Truly, my cup runs over with blessings. I can still scarcely help thinking that God is preparing me for some severe trial but if He will grant me, His presence as He does now, no trial can seem severe. Oh, could I now drop the body, I would stand and cry to all eternity without being weary: God is holy, God is just, God is good God is wise and faithful and true. Either of His perfections alone is sufficient to furnish matter for an eternal, unwearied song. Could I sing upon paper I should break forth into singing, for day and night I can do nothing but sing "Let the saints be joyful," etc., etc. But I must close. I cannot send so much love and thankfulness to my parents as they deserve. My present happiness, all my happiness I ascribe under God to them and their prayers.

Surely, a home inspired and ruled by such a spirit was a sweet home to be born into!

The notices of Elizabeth's childhood depict her as a dark-eyed, delicate little creature, of sylph-like form, reserved and shy in the presence of strangers, of a sweet disposition, and very intense in her sympathies. "Until I was three years old mother says I was a little angel," she once wrote to a friend. Her constitution was feeble, and she inherited from her father his high-strung nervous temperament. "I never knew what it was to feel well," she wrote in 1840. Severe pain in the side, fainting turns, the sick headache, and other ailments troubled her, more or less, from infancy. She had an eye wide open to the world about her, and quick to catch its varying aspects of light and beauty, whether on land or sea. The ships and wharves not far from her father's house, the observatory and fort on the hill overlooking Casco Bay, the White Mountains far away in the distance, Deering's oaks, the rope-walk, and the ancient burying-ground—these and other familiar objects of "the dear old town," commemorated by Longfellow in his poem entitled "My Lost Youth," were indelibly fixed in her memory and followed her wherever she went, to the end of her days. In her movements, she was light-footed, venturesome to rashness, and at times wild with fun and frolic. Her whole being was so impressionable that things pleasant and things painful stamped themselves upon it as with the point of a diamond. Whatever she did, whatever she felt, she felt and did as for her life. Allusion has been made to the intensity of her sympathies. The sight or tale of suffering would set her in a tremor of excitement and in her eagerness to give relief she seemed ready for any sacrifice, however great. This trait arrested the observant eye of her father, and he expressed to Mrs. Payson his fear lest it might someday prove a real misfortune to the child. "She will be in danger of marrying a blind man, or a helpless cripple, out of pure sympathy," he once said.

But by far the strongest of all the impressions of her childhood related to her father. His presence was to her the happiest spot on earth, and any special expression of his affection would throw her into an ecstasy of delight. When he was away, she pined for his return. "The children all send a great deal of love, and Elizabeth says, do tell Papa to come home," wrote her mother to him, when she was six years old. Her recollections of her father were singularly vivid. She could describe minutely his domestic habits, how he looked and talked as he sat by the fireside or at the table, his delight in and skillful use of carpenters' tools, his ingenious devices for amusing her and diverting his own weariness as he lay sick in bed, *e.g.*, tearing up sheets of white paper into tiny bits, and then letting her pour them out of the window to "make believe it snowed," or counting all the bristles in a clothes-brush, and then as she came in from school, holding it up and bidding her guess their number—his coolness and efficiency in the wild excitements of a conflagration, the calm deliberation with which he walked past the horror-stricken lookers on and cut the rope by which a suicide was suspended these and other incidents she would recall a third of a century after his death, as if she had just heard of or just witnessed them. To her child's imagination, his memory seemed to be invested with the triple halo of father, hero, and saint. A little picture of him was always near her. She never mentioned his name without tender affection and reverence. Nor is this at all strange. She was almost nine years old when he died and his influence, during these years, penetrated to her inmost being. She once said that of her father's virtues one only—punctuality—had descended to her. But here she was surely wrong. Not only did she owe to him some of the most striking peculiarities of her physical and mental constitution, but also her piety itself, if not inherited, was largely inspired and shaped by his. In the whole tone and expression of her earlier religious life, at least, one sees him clearly reflected. His devotional habits, in particular, left upon her an indelible impression. Once, when four or five years old, rushing by mistake into his room, she found him prostrate upon his face—completely lost in prayer. A short time before her death, speaking of this scene to a friend, she remarked that the remembrance of it had influenced her ever since. What somebody said of Sara Coleridge might indeed have been said with no less truth of Elizabeth Payson: "Her father had looked down into her eyes and left in them the light of his own."

The only records of her childhood from her own pen consist of the following letters, written to her sister, while the latter was passing a year in Boston. She was then nine years old.

PORTLAND, *May 18, 1828.*

My dear sister:—I thank you for writing to such a little girl as I am, when you have so little time. I was going to study a little catechism, which Miss Martin has got, but she said I could not learn it. I want to learn it. I do not like to stay so long at school. We have to write composition by dictation, as Miss Martin calls it. She reads to us out of a book a sentence at a time. We write it and then we write it again on our slates, because we do not always get the whole then we write it on a piece of paper. Miss Martin says I may say my Sunday school [lesson] there. Mr. Mitchell has had a great many new books. I have been sick. Doctor Cummings has been here and says E. is better and he thinks he will not have a fever.... G. goes to school to Miss Libby, and H. goes to Master Jackson. H. sends his love. Goodbye.

Your affectionate sister, E. PAYSON,

September 29, 1828.

My dear sister:—I think you were very kind to write to me, when you have so little time. I began to go to Mrs. Petrie's school a week ago yesterday. I stay at home Mondays in the morning to assist in taking care of Charles or such little things as I can do. G. goes with me. When mother put Charles and him to bed, as soon as she had done praying with them, G. said, Mother, will this world be all burnt up when we are dead? She said, Yes, my dear, it will. What, and all the dishes too? Will they melt like lead? And will the ground be burnt up too? O what a nasty fire it will make. I saw the Northern lights last night. I sleep in a very large pleasant room in the bed with mother.... I have a very pleasant room for my baby-house over the porch, which has two windows and a fireplace in it, and a little cupboard too. E. Wood and I are as intimate as ever. I suppose you know that Mr. Wood is building him a brick house. Mrs. Merril's little baby is dead. It was buried yesterday afternoon. Mr. Mussey lives across the street from us. He has a great many elm trees in his front yard. His house is three stories high and the trees reach to the top. We have heard two or three times from E. since he went away. Yesterday all the Sabbath-schools walked in a procession and then went to our meetinghouse and Mr. William Cutter addressed them.

I am your affectionate sister, E. Payson.

Her feeble constitution exposed her to severe attacks of disease, and in May, 1830, she was brought to the verge of the grave by a violent fever. Her mother was deeply moved by this event, and while recording in her journal God's goodness in sparing Elizabeth, wonders whether it is to the end that she may one day devote herself to her Savior and do something for the "honor of religion." In the latter part of 1830, Mrs. Payson removed to New York, where her eldest daughter opened a school for girls. It was during this residence in New York that Elizabeth, at the age of twelve years, made a public confession of Christ and came to the Lord's Table for the first time. She was received into the Bleecker street—now the Fourth avenue—Presbyterian Church, then under the pastoral care of the Rev. Erskine Mason, D.D., May 1, 1831. Toward the close of the same year, the family returned to Portland.

In a letter addressed to her husband, one of Mrs. Prentiss' oldest friends now living, Miss Julia D. Willis, has furnished the following reminiscences of her early years. While they confirm what has been said about her childhood, they are especially valuable for the glimpses they give of her father and mother and sister. The Willis and Payson families were very intimate and warmly attached to each other. Mr. Nathaniel Willis, the father of N. P. Willis the poet, was well known in connection with "The Boston Recorder," of which he was for many years the conductor and proprietor. Both Mr. and Mrs. Willis cherished the most affectionate veneration for the memory of Dr. Payson. So long as she lived, their house was a home to Mrs. Payson and her daughters, whenever they visited Boston.

As a preacher, Dr. Payson could not fail to make a strong impression even on a child. Years ago in New York I once told Mrs. Prentiss, who was too young, at her father's death, to remember him well in the pulpit, that the only public speaker who ever reminded me of him, was Edwin Booth in Hamlet. I surprised, and, I am afraid, a little shocked her, but it was quite true. The slender figure, the dark, brilliant eyes, the deep earnestness of tone, the rapid utterance combined with perfect distinctness of enunciation, in spite of surroundings the best calculated to repel such an association, recalled him vividly to my memory.

My father's connection with the religious press after his removal from Portland to Boston, brought many clergymen to our house, who often, in the kindness of their hearts, requited hospitality by religious conversation with the children, not church members, and presumably, therefore, impenitent. I did not always appreciate this kindness as it deserved, and often exercised considerable ingenuity to avoid being alone with them. In Dr. Payson's case, I soon learned, on the contrary, to seek such occasions. I was sure that before long he would look up from his book, or his manuscript, and have something pleasant or playful to say to me. His general conversation, however, was oftener on religious than on any other subjects, but it was so evidently from the fullness of his heart, and his vivid imagination afforded him such a wealth of illustration, that it was delightful even to an "impenitent" child. Years afterward when I read in his Memoir of his desponding temperament, of his seasons of gloom, of the sense of sin under which he was bowed down, it seemed impossible to me that it could be *my* Dr. Payson.

I visited Portland and was an inmate of his family, at the commencement of the illness that finally proved fatal. He was not confined to his bed, or to his room, but he was forbidden, indeed unable, to preach, unable to write or study he could only read and think. Still he did not shut himself up in his study with his sad thoughts. I remember him as usually seated with his book by the side of the fire, surrounded by his family, as if he would enjoy their society as long as possible, and the children's play was never hushed on his account. Nor did he forget the young visitor. When the elder daughter, to whom my visit was made, was at school, he would care for my entertainment by telling a story, or propounding a riddle, or providing an entertaining book to beguile the time till Louisa's return.

Among the group in that cheerful room, I remember Lizzy well, a beautiful child, slender, dark-eyed, light-footed, very quiet, evidently observant, but saying little, affectionate, yet not demonstrative.

One evening during my visit, Mrs. Payson not being quite well, the elders had retired early, leaving Louisa and I by the side of the fire, she preparing her school lesson and I occupied in reading. The lesson finished, Louisa proposed retiring, but I was too much interested in my book to leave it and promised to follow soon. She left me rather reluctantly, and I read on, too much absorbed in my book to notice the time, till near midnight, when I was startled by hearing Dr. Payson's step upon the stairs. I expected the reproof which I certainly deserved, but though evidently surprised at seeing me, he merely said, "You here? You must be cold. Why did you let the fire go out?" Bringing in some wood, he soon rekindled it, and began to talk to me of the book I was reading, which was one of Walter Scott's poems. He then spoke of a poem that he had been reading that day, Southey's "Curse of Kehama." He related to me with perfect clearness the long and rather involved story, with that wonderful memory of his, never once forgetting or confusing the strange Oriental names, and repeating word for word the curse:

> I charm thy life, from the weapons of strife,
> From stone and from wood, from fire and from flood,
> From the serpent's tooth, and the beasts of blood,
> From sickness I charm thee, and time shall not harm thee, etc., etc.

I listened, intent, fascinated, forgot to ask why he was there instead of in his bed, and forgot that it was midnight instead of mid-day. It was not till on bidding me good night he added, "I hope you will have a better night than I shall," that it occurred to me that he must be suffering. The next day I learned from his wife that when unable to sleep on account of his racking cough, he often left his bed at night, the cough being more endurable when in a sitting posture. I never saw Dr. Payson after that visit, nor for several years any of the family, except Louisa, who spent a year with us while attending school in Boston to fit herself as a teacher to aid in the support of her younger brothers and sister. When I was next with them, Louisa was already at the head of a school in which her young sister was the brightest pupil, and to the profits of which she laid no personal claim, all going untouched into the family purse. Several young girls, Louisa's pupils, had been received as boarders in the family, and occasionally a clergyman was added to the number. It was during this visit that I first learned to appreciate Mrs. Payson. Now that she stood alone at the head of the household, either her fine qualities were in bolder relief, or I being older, was better able to estimate them. The singular vivacity of her intellect made her a delightful companion. Then her youth had been passed in the literary circles of New Haven and Andover, and she had much to tell of distinguished people known to me only by reputation. I admired her firm yet gentle rule, so skillfully adapted to the varying natures under her charge her conscientious study of that homely virtue economy, so distasteful to one of her naturally lavish temper, always ready to give to those in need to an extent which called forth constant remonstrances from more prudent friends her alacrity also in all household labors, which the more excited my wonder, knowing the little opportunity she could have had to practice them amid the wealth of her father's house before the Embargo, which later wrecked his fortune with those of so many other New England merchants. She was, indeed, of a most noble nature, hating all meanness and injustice, and full of helpful kindness and sympathy. No woman ever had warmer or more devoted friends.

Both at this time and in subsequent visits, as she advanced from childhood to girlhood, I remember Lizzy well although my attention was chiefly absorbed by the elder sister of my own age, my principal companion when present, and correspondent when absent. The two sisters were strongly contrasted. Louisa, as a child, was afflicted with a sensitive, almost morbid shyness and reserve, and an incapacity for enjoying the society of other children whose tastes were uncongenial with her own. The shyness passed with her childhood, but the sensitiveness and exclusiveness never quite left her. Her love of books was a passion, and she would resent an unfair criticism of a favorite author as warmly as if it were an attack on a personal friend. To Lizzy, on the contrary, a friend was a book that she loved to read. Human nature was her favorite study. There seemed to be no one in whom she could not find something to interest her, none with whom there was not some point of sympathy. Combined with this wide and genial sympathy was another quality, which helped to endear her to her companions, viz., an entire absence of all attempts to show her best side, or put the best face on anything that concerned her. An ingenuous frankness about herself and her affairs—even about her little weaknesses—was one of her most striking traits. No one, indeed, could know her without learning to love her dearly. Yet if I should say that in my visits to Portland, Lizzy always appeared to me pre-eminently the life and charm of the household, it would not be exactly true, though she would have been so of almost any other household. The Payson family was a delightful one to visit, all were so bright, and in the contest of wits that took place often between Lizzy and her merry brothers, it was sometimes hard to tell which bore off the palm.

I do not know that I ever thought of her at that time as an author. If anybody had predicted to me that one of that group would be the writer of books, which would not only have a wide circulation at home, but be translated into foreign languages, I should certainly have selected Louisa, and I think most persons who knew them would have done the same. The elder sister's passion for books, her great powers of acquisition, the range of her attainments—embracing not only modern languages and their literature, but Latin, Greek and Hebrew—her ability to maintain discussions on German metaphysics and theology with learned Professors, all seemed to point her out as the one likely to achieve distinction in the literary world.

I do not remember whether it was Lizzy's early contributions to "The Youth's Companion," showing already the germ of the creative power in her, or her letters to her sister, which first suggested to me that the pleasure her friends found in her conversation, might yet be enjoyed by those who would never see her. Louisa had given up her school for the more congenial employment of contributing to magazines and reviews and of writing children's books. And as the greater literary resources of Boston drew her thither, she was often for months a welcome guest at our house, where she first met Professor Hopkins of Williamstown, and whom she afterward married. The letters that Lizzy wrote to her at those times were never allowed to be the monopoly of one person we all claimed a right to read them. The ease with which in these she seemed to talk with her pen, the mingled pathos and humor with which she would relate all the little joys and sorrows of daily life, leaving her readers between a smile and a tear, showed the same characteristics which afterward made her published writings so much more generally attractive than the graver ones of her elder sister. But Louisa's failing health soon after her marriage, and the long years of suffering that followed, prevented her ever doing justice to the expectations her friends had formed for her.

The occasion of my next visit to Portland was a letter from Mrs. Payson to my mother, who was her constant correspondent, in which she spoke sadly of an indisposition she feared was the precursor of serious illness, but which chiefly troubled her on account of Lizzy's distress that her school prevented her being constantly with her mother. An offer on my part to come and take her place, in her hours of necessary absence, was at once accepted. Mrs. Payson's illness proved less serious than had been feared, and once more I passed several pleasant weeks in that house but the pleasantest hours of the day were those in which Lizzy, returning from school, sat down at her mother's bedside and amused her with her talk about her pupils, their various characters and the progress they had made in their studies, or related little incidents of the school-room—with her usual frankness not omitting those which revealed some fault, or what she considered such, on her part, especially her impulsiveness that led her often to say things she afterward regretted. As an example, one of her pupils was reading French to her and coming to the expression Mon Dieu! So common in French narratives, had pronounced it so badly that Lizzy exclaimed, "Mon Doo? He would not know himself what you meant!" The laugh, which it was impossible to repress, did not diminish her compunction at what she feared her pupils would regard as irreverence on her part. I believe I always cherished sufficient affection for my teachers, and yet I was not a little astonished on accompanying Lizzy to school one day, to see as we turned the corner of a street a rush of girls with unbonneted heads, to greet their young teacher for whom they had been watching, and escort her to her throne in the school-room, and evidently in their hearts. For a year or two after this visit, I have no recollection of her, or indeed of any of the Payson family. Death, meanwhile, had been busy in my own home, and my memory is a blank for anything beyond that sad circle.

Since that date, you have known her better than I have. I wish that these recollections of a time when I knew her better than you, were not so meager. If we were not thousands of miles apart, and I could talk with you, instead of writing to you, perhaps they would not appear quite so unsatisfying. Yet, trivial as they are, I send them, in the persuasion that any trifle that concerned her or hers is of interest to you.

GENEVA, Switzerland, *Feb. 1, 1879.*

* * * * *

III.

Recollections of Elizabeth's Girlhood by an early Friend and Schoolmate.
Her own Picture of Herself before her Father's Death. Favorite Resorts.
Why God permits so much Suffering. Literary Tastes. Letters. "What are
Little Babies For?" Opens a School. Religious Interest.

It is to be regretted that the letters referred to by Miss Willis, and indeed nearly all of Elizabeth's family letters, written before she left her mother's roof, have disappeared. But the following recollections by Mrs. M. C. H. Clark, of Portland, will in part supply their place and serve to fill up the outline, already given, of the first twenty years of her life.

In the volume of sketches entitled, "Only a Dandelion," you will find, in the story of Anna and Emily, some very pleasing incidents relating to the early life of dear Elizabeth. Anna was Lizzy Wood, her earliest playmate and friend. Miss Wood was a sweet girl, the only sister of Dr. William Wood, of Portland. She died at an early age. Emily was Mrs. Prentiss herself. I remember her once telling me about the visit at "Aunt W.'s," and believe that nearly all the details of the story are founded in fact. It is her own picture of herself as a little girl, drawn to the life. Several traits of the character of Emily, as given in the sketch, are on this account worthy of special note. One is her very intense desire not only to be loved, but also to be loved *alone*, or much more than anyone else is and to be assured of it "over and over again." When Anna returned from her journey, she brought the same presents to Susan Morton as to Emily. On discovering this fact, Emily was greatly distressed.

"I thought you would be so glad to get all these things!" said Anna.

"And so I am," said Emily, "I only want you to love me better than any other little girl, because I love you better."

"Well, and so I do," returned Anna "I love you ten times as well as I love Susan Morton."

This satisfied Emily, and "for many days her restless little heart was as quiet and happy as a lamb's."

Another trait is brought out in the incident that occurred on her returning home from Anna's. She had written, or rather scratched, the word "Anna," over one whole side of her room, while odd lines of what purported to be poetry filled the other.

But this was not all. Her sister produced the beautiful Bible which had been given Emily by her Aunt Lucy, on her seventh birthday, and showed her father how all its blank leaves were covered with Annas. Her father took the book with reverence, and Emily understood and felt the seriousness with which he examined her idle scrawls. It was a look that would have risen up before her and made her stay her hand, should she ever again in her life-long have been tempted thus to misuse the word of God just as the angel stood before Balaam in the narrow path he was struggling to push through. But Emily never again was thus tempted and ever after, her Bible was sacredly kept free from "blot, or wrinkle, or any such thing."

Her father now took her with him to his study, and gave her a great many pieces of paper, some large and some small, on which he told her with a smile, she could write Anna's name to her heart's content. Emily felt very grateful this little kindness on her father's part did her more good than a month's lecture could have done, and made her resolve never to do anything that could possibly grieve him again. She went away to her own little baby-house and wrote on one of the bits of paper, some verses, in which she said she had the best father in the world. When they were done, she read them over once or twice, and admired them exceedingly after which, with a very mysterious air, she went and threw them into the kitchen fire.

This incident, so prettily related, illustrates the intensity of her friendships, shows that she had begun to write verses when a mere child, and gives a very pleasant glimpse of her father and of her devotion to him.

My intimate acquaintance with her commenced in 1832, when we were members of Miss Tyler's Sabbath-school class. Miss Tyler was a daughter of Rev. Dr. Bennett Tyler, her father's successor. She was greatly pleased when I told her I was going to attend her sister's school, which was opened in the spring of 1833, on the corner of Middle and Lime streets. My seat was next to hers and we were placed in the same classes. Our homes were near each other on Franklin Street, and we always walked back and forth together. She was at this time a prolific writer of notes. Sometimes she would meet me on Monday morning with not less than four, written since we had parted on Saturday afternoon. She used to complain now and then, that I wrote her only one to four or five of hers to me. In the pleasant summer afternoons, we loved to take long walks together. One was down by the shore behind the eastern promenade. Here we would find a sheltered nook, and with our backs to the world and our faces toward the islands and the ocean, would sit in "rapt enjoyment" of the scene, speaking scarcely a word, until one or the other exclaimed with a long-drawn sigh: "Well, it is time for us to go home."

Another of our places of resort was the old cemetery on Congress Street, which in those days was very retired. Our favorite spot here was the summit of a tomb, which stood on the highest point in the grounds. It was the old style of tomb—a broad marble slab, supported by six small stone pillars on a stone foundation, and surrounded by two steps raised above the soil. It was a very quiet retreat. We could hear the distant hum of the city and at the same time enjoy a view of the water and shipping, as the land sloped down toward the harbor. I remember well that one dark spring day, as we sat there cuddled up under the broad slab, Lizzy gave me an account of a book she had just been reading. It was the Memoir of Miss Susanna Anthony, by old Dr. Hopkins, of Newport. She told me what a good and holy woman Miss Anthony was, how much she suffered and how beautifully she bore her sufferings. My sympathy was strongly excited and I exclaimed, "I do not see how it is *right* for God, who can control all things, to permit such suffering!" Lizzy replied very sweetly, "Well, Carrie, we cannot understand it, but I have been thinking that this *might* be God's way of preparing His children for very high degrees of service on earth, or happiness in heaven." I was deeply impressed with this remark somehow it seemed to *stand by me*, and I think it was a corner stone of her faith.

This summer—that of 1833—her mother fitted up for her exclusive use a small room called the "Blue Room," where she had all her books and treasures—among them a writing desk which had been her father's. Here all her leisure hours were spent. It was my privilege to be admitted to this sanctuary, and many pleasant hours we passed together there. I think Elizabeth was always religious. She knew a great deal then about the Bible and often talked with me of divine things. She seemed to feel a deep interest in my spiritual welfare. She loved to share with me her favorite books. To her I was indebted for my acquaintance with George Herbert, and with Wordsworth. She induced me to read "Owen on the 133rd Psalm," and Flavel's "Fountain of Life." In 1834, we both began to attend the Free street Seminary, of which the Rev. Solomon Adams was then principal. Her sister had become assistant teacher with him. Our desks adjoined each other and we were together a great deal. She was an admirable scholar, very studious, prompt, and ready at recitation. Her influence and example, added to her friendship and sympathy, were invaluable to me at this period. One day, about this time, she told me of her engagement with Mr. Willis, to become a contributor to "The Youth's Companion." This paper was one of the first, if not the first, of its class published in this country, and had a wide circulation among the children throughout New England. Most of the pieces in "Only a Dandelion," first appeared, I think, in the "Youth's Companion," among the rest several in verse. They are written in a sprightly style, are full of bright fancies as well as sound feeling and excellent sense, and foretoken plainly the author of the 'Susy' books.

In 1835, Lizzy went to Ipswich and spent the summer in the school there. It was then under the care of Miss Grant, and was the most noted institution of its kind in New England. A year or two later, Mr. N. P. Willis returned from Europe, and with his English bride made a short visit at Mrs. Payson's. Miss Payson talked with him of Elizabeth's taste for writing poetry and showed him some of her pieces. He praised and encouraged her warmly, and this was, I think, one of the influences that strengthened her in the purpose to become an author. Upon my telling her one day how much I liked a certain Sunday-school book I had just read, she smilingly asked, "What would you think if some day I should write a book as good as that?"

I saw a good deal of her home life at this time. It was full of filial and sisterly love and devotion. Amidst the household cares by which her mother was often weighed down and worried, she was an ever-near friend and sympathizer. To her brothers, too, she endeared herself exceedingly by her helpful, cheery ways and the strong vein of fun and mirthfulness that ran through her daily life.

In the spring of 1837, Mrs. Payson sold her house on Franklin Street and rented one in the upper part of the city. Lizzy used to call it "the pumpkin house," because it was old and ugly but its situation and the opportunity to indulge her rural tastes made amends for all its defects. In a letter to her friend Miss E. T. of Brooklyn, N. Y., dated May 21, 1837, she thus refers to it:

Since your last letter arrived, we have left our pleasant home for an old yellow one above John Neal's. Now do not imagine it to be a delicate straw-color, neither the smiling hue of the early dandelion. No, it once shone forth in all the glories of a deep pumpkin but time's "effacing fingers" have sadly marred its beauty. Mr. Neal's Aunt Ruth, a quiet old Quakeress, occupies a part of it and we Paysons bestow ourselves in the remainder. This comes to you from its great garret. Here I sit every night till after dark as merry as a grig. "The mind is its own place." With all the inconveniences of the house, I would not exchange it at present for any other in the city. The situation is perfectly delightful. Casco Bay and part of Deering's Oaks lie in full view. [8] The Oaks are within a few minutes' walk. Back-Cove is seen beyond, and rising far above the *blue* White Mountains. The Arsenal stares us in the face, if we look out the end windows and the Westbrook meetinghouse is nearer than Mr. Vail's by a quarter of a mile. I never believed there was anything half so fine in this region. I think nothing of walking anywhere now. One day, after various domestic duties, I worked in my tiny garden four hours, and in the afternoon a party of girls came up for me to go with them to Bramhall's hill. We walked from three till half past six, came back, and ate a hasty, with some of us a *furious* supper, and then all paraded down to second parish to singing-school. I expect to live out in the air most of the summer. I mean to have as pleasant a one as possible, because we shall never live so near the Oaks and other pretty places another summer. If you were not so timid I should wish you were here to run about with me, but who ever heard of E. T. *running*? Now, Ellen, I never was *meant* to be dignified and sometimes—yea, often—I run, skip, hop, and *once* I did climb over a fence! Very unladylike, I know, but I am not a lady.

In the fall of 1837, Mrs. Payson moved again. The incident deserves mention, as it brought Lizzy into daily intercourse with the Rev. Mr. French and his wife. Mr. French was rector of the Episcopal Church in Portland, and afterward Professor and Chaplain at West Point. He was a man of fine literary culture and Mrs. French was a very attractive woman. In a letter dated "Night before Thanksgiving," and addressed to the early friend already mentioned, Lizzy refers to this removal and also gives a glimpse of her active home life:

I have been busy all day and am so tired I can scarcely hold a pen. Amidst the beating of eggs, the pounding of spices, the furious rolling of pastry of all degrees of shortness, the filling of pies with pumpkins, mince-meat, apples, and the like, the stoning of raisins and washing of currants, the beating and baking of cake, and all the other *ings*, (in all of which I have had my share) thoughts of your ladyship have somehow squeezed themselves in. We have really bidden adieu to "Pumpkin Place," as Mrs. Willis calls it, and established ourselves in a house formerly occupied by old Parson Smith—and very snug and comfortable we are, I assure you.

In the midst of our "moving," after I had packed and stowed and lifted, and been elbowed by all the sharp corners in the house, and had my hands all torn and scratched, I spied the new "Knickerbocker" 'mid a heap of rubbish and was tempted to peep into it. Lo and behold, the first thing that met my eye was the Lament of the Last Peach. [9] I didn't care to read more and forthwith returned to fitting of carpets and arranging tables and chairs and bureaus—but all the while meditating how I should be revenged upon you. As to ——'s request I am sorry to answer nay for I feel it would be the greatest presumption in me to think of writing for a magazine like that. I do not wish to publish anything, anywhere, though it would be quite as wise as to entrust my scraps to *your* care. My mother often urges me to send little things that she happens to fancy, to this and that periodical. Without her interference, nothing of mine would ever have found its way into print. But mammas look with rose-colored spectacles on the actions and performances of their offspring. Have you laughed over the Pickwick Papers? We have almost laughed ourselves to death over them. I have not seen Lizzy D. for a long time, but hear she is getting along rapidly. If I could go to school two years more, I should be glad, but of course, that is out of the question.... It is easier for you to write often than it is for me. You have not three tearing, growing brothers to mend and make for. I am become quite expert in the arts of patching and darning. I am going to get some pies and cake and raisins and other goodies to send to our girl's sick brother. If I had not so dear and happy a home, I should envy you yours. You say you do not remember whether I love music or not. I love it extravagantly *sometimes*—but have not the knowledge to enjoy scientific performances. The simple melody of a single voice is my delight. Mrs. French, the Episcopal minister's wife, who is a great friend of ours and lives next door (so near that she and sister talk together out of their windows), has a baby two days old with black curly hair and black eyes, and I shall have a nice time with it this winter. Do you love babies?

The question with which this letter closes, suggests one of Lizzy's most striking and loveliest traits. She had a perfect passion for babies, and reveled in tending, kissing, and playing with them. Here are some pretty lines in one of her girlish contributions to "The Youth's Companion," which express her feeling about them:

> *What are little babies for?*
> *Say! say! say!*
> *Are they good-for-nothing things?*
> *Nay! nay! nay!*
> *Can they speak a single word?*
> *Say! say! say!*
> *Can they help their mothers sew?*
> *Nay! nay! nay!*
> *Can they walk upon their feet?*
> *Say! say! say!*
> *Can they even hold themselves?*
> *Nay! nay! nay!*
> *What are little babies for?*
> *Say! say! say!*
> *Are they made for us to love?*
> *Yea! YEA!! YEA!!!*

In the fall of 1838, Mrs. Payson purchased a house in Cumberland Street, which continued to be her residence until the family was broken up. You remember the charming little room Lizzy had fitted up over the hall in this house, how nicely she kept it, and how happy she was in it. One of the windows looked out on a little flower garden and at the close of the long summer days; the sunset could be enjoyed from the west window. She had had some fine books given her, which, added to the previous store, made a somewhat rare collection for a young girl in those days.

About this time, having been relieved of her part of domestic service by the coming into the family of a young relative—whose devotion to her was unbounded—she opened in the house a school for little girls. It consisted at first of perhaps eight or ten, but their number increased until the house could scarcely hold them. She was a born teacher and her young pupils fairly idolized her. [10] In this year, too, she took a class in the Sabbath-school composed of nearly the same group who surrounded her on the weekdays, and they remained under her care as long as she lived in Portland.

The Rev. Mr. Vail having retired from the pastorate of the second parish in the autumn of 1837, Cyrus Hamlin, just from the Theological Seminary at Bangor, became the stated supply for some months. His preaching attracted the young people and during the winter and spring, there was much interest in all the Congregational churches. Following the example of the other pastors, Mr. Hamlin invited persons seriously disposed to meet him for religious conversation. Elizabeth besought me, with all possible earnestness and affection, to "go to Mr. Hamlin's meeting." One day she came to see me a short time before the hour, saying that I was ever on her mind and in her prayers, which she had talked with Mr. Hamlin about me, nor would she leave me until I had promised to attend the meeting. I did so and from that time we were united in the strong bonds of Christian love and sympathy. What a spiritual helper she was to me in those days! What precious notes I was all the time receiving from her! The memory of her tender, faithful friendship is still fresh and delightful, after the lapse of more than forty years. [11]

In the summer of 1838, the Rev. Jonathan B. Condit, D.D., was called from his chair in Amherst College and installed pastor of our church. He was a man of very graceful and winning manners and wonderfully magnetic. He at once became almost an object of worship with the enthusiastic young people. The services of the Sabbath and the weekly meetings were delightful. The young ladies had a praying circle, which met every Saturday afternoon, full of life and sunshine. Indeed, the exclusive interest of the season was religious our reading and conversation were religious well-nigh the sole subject of thought was learning something new of our Savior and His blessed service. All Lizzy's friends and several of her own family were rejoicing in hope. And she herself was radiant with joy. For a little while, it seemed almost as if the shadows in the Christian path had fled away, and the crosses vanished out of sight. The winter and spring of 1840 witnessed another period of general religious interest in Portland. Large numbers were gathered into the churches. Lizzy was greatly impressed by the work, her own Christian life was deepened and widened, she was blessed in guiding several members of her beloved Sunday-school class to the Savior, and was thus prepared, also, for the sharp trial awaiting her in the autumn of the same year, when she left her home and mother for a long absence in Richmond.

From her earliest years, she was in the habit of keeping a journal, and she must have filled several volumes. I wonder that she did not preserve them as mementos of her childhood and youth. Perhaps because her afterlife was so happy that she never needed to refer to such reminiscences of days gone by.

I have thus given you, in a very informal manner, some recollections of her earlier years. I have been astonished to find how vividly I recalled scenes, events, and conversations so long past. I was startled and shocked when the news came of her sudden death. But I cannot feel that she was called to her rest too soon. She seemed to me singularly happy in all the relations of life and then as an author, hers was an exceptional case of full appreciation and success. I have ever regarded her as "favored among women"—blessed in doing her Master's will and testifying for Him, blessed in her home, in her friends, and in her work, and blessed in her death.

PORTLAND, *December 31, 1878.*

* * * * *

IV.

The Dominant Type of Religious Life and Thought in New England in the
First Half of this Century. Literary Influences. Letter of Cyrus Hamlin.
A Strange Coincidence.

A brief notice of the general type of religious life and thought, which prevailed at this time in New England, will throw light upon both the preceding and following pages. Elizabeth's early Christian character, although largely shaped by that of her father, was also, like his, vitally affected by the religious spirit and methods then dominant. Several distinct elements entered into the piety of New England at that period, (1.) There was, first of all, the old Puritan element which the Pilgrim Fathers and their immediate successors brought with them from the mother-country, and which had been nourished by the writings of the great Puritan divines of the seventeenth century—such as Baxter, Howe, Bunyan, Owen, Matthew Henry, and Flavel—by the "Imitation of Christ," and Bishop Taylor's "Holy Living and Dying," and by such writers as Doddridge, Watts, and Jonathan Edwards of the last century. This lay at the foundation of the whole structure, giving it strength, solidity, earnestness, and power. (2.) But it was modified by the so-called Evangelical element, which marked large sections of the Church of England and most of the Dissenting bodies in Great Britain during the last half of the eighteenth and the early part of the nineteenth century. The writings of John Newton, Richard Cecil, Hannah More, Thomas Scott, Cowper, Wilberforce, Leigh Richmond, John Foster, Andrew Fuller, and Robert Hall—not to mention others—were widely circulated in New England and had great influence in its pulpits and its Christian homes. Their admirable spirit infused itself into thousands of lives, and helped in many ways to improve the general tone both of theological and devotional sentiment. (3.) But another element still was the new Evangelistic spirit, which inaugurated and still informs those great movements of Christian benevolence, both at home and abroad, that are the glory of the age. Dr. Payson's ministry began just before the formation of the American Board of Commissioners for Foreign Missions, and before his death, mission-work had come to be regarded as quite essential to the piety and prosperity of the Church. The Lives of David Brainerd, Henry Martyn, Harriet Newell, and others like them, were household books. (4.) Nor should the "revival" element be omitted in enumerating the forces that then shaped the piety and religious thought of New England. The growth of the Church and the advancement of the cause of Christ were regarded as inseparable from this influence. A revival was the constant object of prayer and effort on the part of earnest pastors and of the more devout among the people. Far more stress was laid upon special seasons and measures of spiritual interest and activity than now—less upon Christian nurture as a means of grace, and upon the steady, normal development of church life. Many of the most eminent, devoted, and useful servants of Christ, whose names, during the last half century, have adorned the annals of American faith and zeal, owed their conversion, or, if not their conversion, some of their noblest and strongest Christian impulses, to "revivals of religion." (5.) To all these should perhaps, be added another element—namely, that of the new spirit of reform and the new ethical tone, which, during the third and fourth decades of this century especially, wrought with such power in New England. Of this influence and of the philanthropic idea that inspired it, Dr. Channing may be regarded as the most eminent representative. It brought to the front the humanity and moral teaching of Christ, as at once the pattern and rule of all true progress, whether individual or social and it was widely felt, even where it was not distinctly recognized or understood. Whatever errors or imperfections may have belonged to it, this influence did much to soften the dogmatism of opinion, to arouse a more generous, catholic type of sentiment, to show that the piety of the New Testament is a principle of universal love to man, as well as of love to God, and to emphasise the sovereign claims of personal virtue and social justice. These truths, to be sure, were not new but in the great moral-reform movements and conflicts—to a certain extent even in theological discussions—that marked the times, they were asserted and applied with extraordinary clearness and energy of conviction and, as the event has proved, they were harbingers of a new era of Christian thought, culture and conduct, both in private and public life.

Such were some of the religious influences which surrounded Mrs. Prentiss during the first twenty years of her life, and which helped to form her character. She was also strongly affected, especially while passing from girlhood into early womanhood, by the literary influences of the day. Poetry and fiction were her delight. She was very fond of Wordsworth, Tennyson, and Longfellow while the successive volumes of Dickens were read by her with the utmost avidity. Mrs. Payson's house was a good deal visited by scholars and men of culture. Her eldest daughter had already become somewhat widely known by her writings. In the extent, variety, and character of her attainments she was, in truth, a marvel. Indeed, she quite overshadowed the younger sister by her learning and her highly intellectual conversation. And yet Elizabeth also attracted no little attention from some who had been first drawn to the house by their friendship for Louisa. [12] Among her warmest admirers was Mr. John Neal, then well known as a man of letters he predicted for her a bright career as an author. Still, it was her personal character that most interested the visitors at her mother's house. This may be illustrated by an extract from a letter of Mr. Hamlin to a friend of the family in New York, written in April, 1838, while he was their temporary pastor. Mr. Hamlin has since become known throughout the Christian world by his remarkable career as a missionary in Turkey, and as organizer of Robert College. A few months after the letter was written he set sail for Constantinople, accompanied by his wife, whose early death was the cause of so much grief among all who knew her. [13] I should like to write a long letter about dear Elizabeth. I have seen her more since Louisa left and I love her more. She has a peculiar charm for me. I think she has a quick and excellent judgment, refined sensibilities, and an *instinctive* perception of what is fit and proper.... It seems to me there is a great deal of purity—of the *spirituelle*—about her feelings. But I cannot tell you exactly what it is that makes me think so highly of her. It is a nameless something resulting from her whole self, from her sweet face and mouth, her eye full of love and soul, her form and motion. I do not think she likes me much. I have paid so much attention to Louisa and so little to herself. Yet she is not one of those who *claim* attention, but rather shrinks from it. She may have faults of which I have no knowledge. But I am charmed with everything I have seen of her.

How strange are the chance coincidences of human life! In another letter to the same friend in New York, in which Mr. Hamlin refers in a similar manner to Elizabeth, occur these words:

In a few weeks, I hope to be in Dorset, among the Green Mountains, where my thoughts and feelings have their centre above all places on this earth. I wish you could be present at my wedding there on the third of September.

How little did he dream, when penning these words, or did his friend dream while reading them, that, after the lapse of more than forty years, the "dear Elizabeth" would find her grave near by the old parsonage in which that wedding was to be celebrated, while the dust of the lovely daughter of Dorset would be sleeping on the distant shores of the Bosporus!

[1] For many years after the publication of his Memoir, it was so often given to children at their baptism that at one time those who bore it, in and out of New England, were to be numbered by hundreds, if not thousands. "I once saw the deaths of *three* little Edward Paysons in one paper," wrote Mrs. Prentiss in 1832.

[2] He was the author of a curious work entitled, "Proofs of the real Existence, and dangerous Tendency, of Illuminism." Charlestown, 1802. By "Illuminism," he means an organized attempt, or conspiracy, to undermine the foundations of Christian society and establish upon its ruins the system of atheism.

[3] "I spent part of last evening reading over some old letters of my grandmother's and never realized before what a remarkable woman she was both as to piety and talent."—*From a letter of Mrs. Prentiss, written in 1864.*

[4] In a letter to his mother,—written when Elizabeth was three years old, he says: "E. has a terrible abscess, which we feared would prove too much for her slender constitution. We were almost worn out with watching and, just as she began to mend, I was seized with a violent ague in my face, which gave me incessant anguish for six days and nights together, and deprived me almost entirely of sleep. Three nights I did not close my eyes. When well nigh distracted with pain and loss of sleep, Satan was let loose upon me, to buffet me, and I verily thought would have driven me to desperation and madness."

[5] The late President Wayland.

[6] Prof. Calvin E. Stowe, D.D.

[7] The late Rev. Absalom Peters, D.D.

[8]I can see the breezy dome of groves,
The shadows of Deering's Woods
And the friendships old and the early loves
Come back with a Sabbath sound, as of doves
In quiet neighborhoods.
And the verse of that sweet old song,

> It flutters and murmurs still:
> "A boy's will is the wind's will,
> And the thoughts of youth are long, long thoughts."
> —LONGFELLOW'S *My Lost Youth*.

[9] "The Lament of the Last Peach" had been written by her a year before when in Brooklyn, and her friend's brother had sent it to "The Knickerbocker," the popular Magazine of that day. Here it is:

LAMENT OF THE LAST PEACH.

> In solemn silence here I live,
> A lone, deserted peach
> So high that none but birds and winds
> My quiet bough can reach.
> And mournfully, and hopelessly,
> I think upon the past
> Upon my dear departed friends,
> And I, the last—the last.
> My friends! oh, daily one by one
> I've seen them drop away
> Unheeding all the tears and prayers
> That vainly bade them stay.
> And here I hang alone, alone—
> While life is fleeing fast
> And sadly sigh that I am left
> The last, the last, the last.
> Farewell, then, thou my little world
> My home upon the tree,
> A sweet retreat, a quiet home
> Thou may no longer be
> The willow trees stand weeping nigh,
> The sky is overcast,
> The autumn winds moan sadly by,
> And say, the last—the last!

[10] "Dear Lizzy is in her little school. Her pupils love her dearly. She will have about thirty in the summer."—*Letter of Mrs. Payson, March 28, 1839.*

[11] Three years later Elizabeth thus referred to this period in the life of her friend:—"During the time in which she was seeking the Savior with all her heart, I was much with her and had an opportunity to see every variety of feeling as she daily set the whole before me. The affection thus acquired is, I believe, never lost. If I live forever, I shall not lose the impressions which I then received—the deep anxiety I felt lest she should finally come short of salvation, and then the happiness of having her lost in contemplation of the character of Him whom she had so often declared it impossible to love."

[12] Old friends of her father also became much interested in her. Among them was Simon Greenleaf, the eminent writer on the law of evidence, and Judge Story's successor at Harvard. On removing to Cambridge, in 1833, he gave her with his autograph a little volume entitled, "Hours for Heaven a small but choice selection of prayers, from eminent Divines of the Church of England," which long continued to be one of her books of devotion.

[13] See the touching memorial of her, "Light on the Dark River," prepared by her early friend, Mrs. Lawrence.

CHAPTER 2 - THE NEW LIFE IN CHRIST - 1840-1841.

I.

> A Memorable Experience. Letters to her Cousin. Goes to Richmond as a
> Teacher. Mr. Persico's School. Letters.

Miss Payson was now in her twenty-first year, a period that she always looked back to as a turning point in her spiritual history. The domestic influences that encompassed her childhood, her early associations, and the books of devotion which she read, all conspired to imbue her with an earnest sense of divine things, and while yet a young girl, as we have seen, she publicly devoted herself to the service of her God and Savior. For several years her piety, if marked by no special features, was still regarded by her young friends, and by all who knew her, as of a decided character. But during the general religious interest in the winter of 1837-8, even while absorbed in solicitude for others, she began herself to question its reality. "For some months I had no hope that I was a Christian, and *pride* made me go on just as if I felt myself perfectly safe. Nothing could at that time have made me willing to have any eye a witness to my daily struggles." And yet she "often longed for the sympathy and assistance of Christian friends," and to her unwillingness to confide in them, she afterwards attributed much of the suffering that followed. "I do not know exactly how I passed out of that season, but my school commenced in April, and I became so interested in it that I had less time to think of and to watch myself. The next winter most of my scholars were deeply impressed by divine things, and, of course, I could not look on without having my own heart touched. It was my privilege to spend many delightful weeks in watching the progress of minds earnestly seeking the way of life and early consecrating themselves to their Savior." [1] But after a while, a severe reaction set in and in the course of the summer, she became careless in her religious habits, shrank from the Lord's Table as a "place of absolute torture," and while spending a fortnight in Boston in the fall, entirely omitted all exercises of private devotion.

She had now reached a crisis that was to decide her course for life. During the winter of 1839-40, she passed through very deep and harrowing exercises of soul. Her spiritual nature was shaken to its foundation, and she could say with the Psalmist, *Out of the depths have I cried unto Thee, O Lord.* For several months she was in a state similar to that which the old divines depict so vividly as being "under conviction." Her sense of sin, and of her own unworthiness in the sight of God, grew more and more intense and oppressive. At times, she abandoned all hope, accused herself of having played the hypocrite, and fancied she was given over to hardness of heart. At length she sought counsel of her pastor and confided to him her trouble, but he "did not know exactly what to do with me." In the midst of her distress, and as its effect, no doubt, she was taken ill and confined to her room, where in solitude she passed several weeks seeking rest and finding none. "Sometimes I tried to pray, but this only increased my distress and made me cry out for annihilation to free me from the agony which seemed insupportable." With a single interval of comparative indifference, this state of mind continued for nearly four months. She thus describes it:

It was in vain that I sought the Lord in any of the lofty pathways through which my heart wished to go. At last, I found it impossible to carry on the struggle any longer alone. I would gladly have put myself at the feet of a little child, if by so doing I could have found peace. I felt so guilty and the character of God appeared so perfect in its purity and holiness, that I knew not which way to turn. The sin which distressed me most of all was the rejection of the Savior. This haunted me constantly and made me fly first to one thing and then another, in the hope of finding somewhere the peace which I would not accept from Him. It was at this time that I kept reading over the first twelve chapters of Doddridge's "Rise and Progress,"—the rest of the book I abhorred. So great was my agony that I can only wonder at the goodness of Him who held my life in His hands, and would not permit me in the height of my despair to throw myself away.

It was in this height of despair that thoughts of the infinite grace and love of Christ, which she says she had hitherto repelled, began to irradiate her soul. A sermon on His ability to save "unto the uttermost" deeply affected her. [2] "While listening to it my weary spirit *rested* itself, and I thought, 'surely it cannot be wrong to think of the Savior, although He is not mine.' With this conclusion I gave myself up to admire, to love and to praise Him, to wonder why I had never done so before, and to hope that all the great congregation around me were joining with me in acknowledging Him to be chief among ten thousand and the One altogether lovely." On going home, she could at first scarcely believe in her own identity, the feeling of peace and love to God and to all the world was so unlike the turbulent emotions that had long agitated her soul. "From this time my mind went slowly onward, examining the way step by step, trembling and afraid, yet filled with a calm contentment which made all the dealings of God with me appear just right. I know myself to be perfectly helpless. I cannot promise to do or to be anything but I do want to put everything else aside, and to devote myself entirely to the service of Christ."

Her account of this memorable experience is dated August 28, 1840. "While writing it," she adds, "I have often laid aside my pen, to sit and think over in silent wonder the way in which the Lord has led me."

How in later years she regarded certain features of this experience, is not fully known. The record passed at once out of her hands, and until after her death was never seen by anyone, excepting the friend for whose eye it was written. Many of its details had, probably, faded entirely from her memory. It cannot be doubted, however, that she would have judged her previous state much less severely, would hardly have charged it with hypocrisy, or denied that the Savior had been graciously leading her, and that she had some real love to Him, before as well as after this crisis. So much may be inferred from the record itself and from the narrative in the preceding chapter. Her tender interest in the spiritual welfare of her friends and pupils, the high tone of religious sentiment that marks her early writings, the books she delighted in, her filial devotion, the absolute sincerity of her character, all forbid any other conclusion. [3] The indications, too, are very plain that her morbidly sensitive, melancholy temperament had much to do with this experience. Her account of it shows, also, that her mind was unhappily affected by certain false notions of the Christian life and ordinances then, and still, more or less prevalent—notions based upon a too narrow and legal conception of the Gospel. Hence, her shrinking from the Lord's Table as a place of "torture," instead of regarding it in its true character, as instituted on purpose to feed hungry souls, like her own, with bread from heaven. But for all that, the experience was a blessed reality and, as these pages will attest, wrought a lasting change in her religious life. No doubt, the Spirit of God was leading her through all its dark and terrible mazes. It virtually ended a conflict, which the intensely proud elements of her nature rendered inevitable, if she was to become a true heroine of faith — the conflict between her Master's will, and her own. Her Master conquered, and henceforth to her dying hour His will was the sovereign law of her existence, and its sweetest joy also.

The following extracts from letters to her cousin, George E. Shipman, of New York, now widely known as the founder of a Foundling Home at Chicago, will throw additional light upon her state of mind at this period. Mr. Shipman was the friend to whom the account of her experience already mentioned was addressed. He had just spent several weeks in Portland, and to his Christian sympathy, kindness, and counsels while there and during the two following years, she felt herself very deeply indebted. [4]

PORTLAND, *August 22, 1840.*

I am always wondering if anybody in the world is the better off for my being in it. And so if I was of any comfort to you, I am very glad of it. I do want, I confess, the privilege of offering you sometimes the wine and oil of consolation, and if I do it in such a way as to cause pain with my unskillful hand, why, you must forgive me…. Mr. —— talked to me as if he imagined me a bluestocking. Just because my sister wears spectacles, folks take it for granted that I also am literary.

Aug. 25th.—You ask if I find it easy to engage in religious meditation, referring in particular to that on our final rest. This is another of my trials. I cannot meditate upon anything, except indeed it be something quite the opposite of what I wish to occupy my mind. You know that some Christians are able in their solitary walks and rides to hold, all the time, communion with God. I can very seldom do this. Yesterday I was obliged to take a long walk alone, and it was made very delightful in this way so that I quite forgot that I was alone…. I am beginning to feel, that I have enough to do without looking out for a great, wide place in which to work, and to appreciate the simple lines:

> "The trivial round, the common task,
> Would furnish all we ought to ask
> Room to deny ourselves a road
> To bring us daily nearer God."

Those words "daily nearer God" have an inexpressible charm for me. I long for such nearness to Him that all other objects shall fade into comparative insignificance,—so that to have a thought, a wish, and a pleasure apart from Him shall be impossible.

Sept. 12th.—At Sabbath-school this morning, while talking with my scholars about the Lord Jesus, my heart, which is often so cold and so stupid, seemed completely melted within me, with such a view of His wonderful, wonderful love for sinners, that I almost believed I had never felt it till then. Such a blessing is worth toiling and wrestling for a whole life. If a glimpse of our Savior here upon earth can be so refreshing, so delightful, what will it be in heaven!

Sept. 17th.—I have been reading today some passages from Nevins' "Practical Thoughts." [5] Perhaps you have seen them if so, do you remember two articles headed, "I must pray more," and "I must pray differently"? They interested me much because in some measure they express my own feelings. I have less and less confidence in *frames*, as they are called. I am glad that you think it better to have a few books and to read them over and over, for my own inclination leads me to that. One gets attached to them as to Christian friends. Do not hesitate to direct me over and over again, to go with difficulties and temptations, and sin to the Savior. I love to be led there and *left* there. Sometimes when the exceeding "sinfulness of sin" becomes painfully apparent, there is nothing else for the soul to do but to lie in the dust before God, without a word of excuse, and that feeling of abasement in His sight is worth more than all the pleasures in the world…. You will believe me if I own myself tired, when I tell you that I made fourteen calls this afternoon. But even the unpleasant business of call making has had one comfort. Some of the friends of whom I took leave, spoke so tenderly of Him whose name is so precious to His children that my heart warmed towards them instantly, and I thought it worthwhile to have parting hours, sad though they may be, if with them came so naturally thoughts of the Savior. Besides, I have been thinking since I came home, that if I did not love Him, it could not be so refreshing to hear unexpectedly of Him…. I did not know that mother had anything to do with your father's conversion, and when I mentioned it to her, she seemed much surprised and said she did not know it herself. Pray tell me more of it, will you? I have felt that if, in the course of my life, I should be the means of leading one soul to the Savior, and it would be worth staying in this world for no matter how many years.

Did you ever read Miss Taylor's "Display"? Sister says the character of Emily there is like mine. I think so myself save in the best point.

We come now to an important change in her outward life. She had accepted an invitation to become a teacher in Mr. Persico's school at Richmond, Virginia. Mr. Persico was an Italian, a brother of the sculptor of that name, a number of whose works are seen at Washington. He early became interested in our institutions, and as soon as he was able, came to this country and settled in Philadelphia as an artist. He married a lady of that city, and afterward on account of her health went to Richmond, where he opened a boarding and day school for girls. There were four separate departments, one of which was under the sole care of Miss Payson. Her letters to her family, written at this time, have all been lost, but a full record of the larger portion of her Richmond life is preserved in letters to her cousin, Mr. Shipman. The following extracts from these letters show with what zeal she devoted herself to her new calling and how absorbed her heart was still in the things of God. They also throw light upon some marked features of her character.

BOSTON, *September 23*.

I had, after leaving home, an attack of that terrible pain, of which I have told you, and believed myself very near death. It became a serious question whether, if God should so please, I could feel willing to die there alone, for I was among entire strangers. I never enjoyed more of His presence than that night when, sick and sad and full of pain, I felt it sweet to put myself in His hands to be disposed of in His own way.

The attack referred to in this letter resembled *angina pectoris*, a disease to which for many years she was led to consider herself liable. Whatever it may have been, its effect was excruciating. "Mother was telling me the other day," she wrote to a friend, "that in her long life she had never seen an individual suffer more severe bodily pain than she had often tried to relieve in me. I remember scores of such hours of real agony." In the present instance, the attack was doubtless brought on, in part at least, by mental agitation. "No words," she wrote a few months later, "can describe the anguish of my mind the night I left home it seemed to me that all the agony I had ever passed through was condensed into a small space, and I certainly believe that I should die, if left to a higher degree of such pain."

RICHMOND, *September 30, 1840*.

About twelve o'clock, when it was as dark as pitch, we were all ordered to prepare for a short walk. In single file then out we went. It seems that a bridge had been burned lately, and so we were all to go round on foot to another train of cars. There were dozens of bright, crackling bonfires lighted at short intervals all along, and as we wound down narrow, steep and rocky pathways, then up steps which had been rudely cut out in the side of the elevated ground, and as far as we could see before us could watch the long line of moving figures in all varieties of form and color, my spirits rose to the very tiptop of enjoyment. I wished you could have a picture of the whole scene, which, though one of real life, was to me at least exceedingly beautiful. We reached Richmond at one o'clock. Mr. Persico was waiting for us and received us cordially…. When I awoke at eight o'clock, I felt forlorn enough. Imagine, if you can, the room in which I opened my eyes. It is in the attic, is very low, and has two windows. My first thought was, "I never can be happy in this miserable hole" but in a second this wicked feeling took flight, and I reproached myself for my ingratitude to Him who had preserved me through all my journey, had made much of it so delightful and profitable, and who still promised to be with me.

Oct. 2.—I will try to give you some account of our doings, although we are not fully settled. We have risen at six so far, but intend to be up by five if we can wake. As soon as we are dressed, I take my Bible out into the entry, where is a window and a quiet corner, and read and think until Louisa [6] is ready to give me our room and take my place. At nine, we go into school, where Miss Lord [7] reads a prayer, and from that hour until twelve, we are engaged with our respective classes. At twelve, we have a recess of thirty minutes. This over, we return again to school, where we stay until three, when we are to dine. All day Saturday, we are free. This time we are to have Monday, too, as a special holiday, because of a great Whig convention, which is turning the city upside-down. There is one pleasant thing, pleasant to me at least, of which I want to tell you. As Mr. Persico is not a religious man, I supposed we should have no blessing at the table, and was afraid I should get into the habit of failing to acknowledge God there. But I was much affected when, on going to dine the first day I came, he stood leaning silently and reverentially over his chair, as if to allow all of us time for that quiet lifting up of the heart, which is, ever acceptable in the sight of God. It is very impressive. Miss Lord reads prayers at night, and when Mrs. Persico comes home, we are to have singing….

That passage in the 119th Psalm, of which you speak, is indeed delightful. I will tell you what were some of my meditations on it. I thought to myself that if God continued His faithfulness toward me, I shall have afflictions such as I now know nothing more of than the name, for I need them constantly. I have trembled ever since I came here at the host of new difficulties to which I am exposed. Surely I did again and again ask God to decide the question for me as to whether I should leave home or not, and believed that He *had* chosen for me. It certainly was against my own inclinations....

Oct. 12th.—This morning I had a new scholar, a pale, thin little girl who stammers, and when I spoke to her, and she was obliged to answer, the color spread over her face and neck as if she suffered the utmost mortification. I was glad when recess came, to draw her close to my side and to tell her that I had a friend afflicted in the same way, and that consequently, I should know how to understand and pity her. She held my hand fast in hers and the tears came stealing down one after another, as she leaned confidingly upon my shoulder, and I could not help crying too, with mingled feelings of gratitude and sorrow. Certainly, it will be delightful to soothe and to console this poor little thing.... You do not like poetry and I have spent the best part of my life in reading or trying to write it. N. P. Willis told me some years ago, that if my husband had a soul, he would love me for the poetical in me, and advised me to save it for him.

Oct. 27th.—Sometimes when I feel almost sure that the Savior has accepted and forgiven me and that I *belong to Him*, I can only walk my room repeating over and over again, *How wonderful!* And then when my mind strives to take in this love of Christ, it seems to struggle in vain with its own littleness and falls back weary and exhausted, to *wonder* again at the heights and depths which surpass its comprehension.... If there is a spark of love in my heart for anybody, it is for this dear brother of mine, and the desire to have his education thorough and complete has grown with my growth. You, who are not a sister, cannot understand the feelings with which I regard him, but they are such as to call forth unbounded love and gratitude toward those who show kindness to him.

Nov. 3rd.—I have always felt a peculiar love for the passage that describes the walk to Emmaus. I have tried to analyze the feeling of pleasure which it invariably sheds over my heart when dwelling upon it, especially upon the words, "Jesus Himself drew near and went with them," and these, "He made as though He would go further," but yielded to their urgent, "Abide with us." ... This is one of the comforts of the Christian God understands him fully whether he can explain his troubles or not. Sometimes I think all of a sudden that I do not love the Savior at all, and am ready to believe that all my pretended anxiety to serve Him has been but a matter of feeling and not of principle but of late I have been less disturbed by this imagination, as I find it extends to earthly friends who are dear to me as my own soul. I thought once yesterday that I didn't love anybody in the world and was perfectly wretched in consequence.

Nov. 12th.—The more I try to understand myself, the more I am puzzled. That I am a mixture of contradictions is the opinion I have long had of myself. I call it a compound of sincerity and reserve. Unless you see just what I mean in your own consciousness, I doubt whether I can explain it in words. With me it is both an open and a shut heart—open when and where and as far as I please, and shut as tight as a vise in the same way. I was probably born with this same mixture of frankness and reserve, having inherited the one from my mother and the other from my father.... I have often thought that, humanly speaking, it would be a strange, and surely a very sad thing if we none of us inherit any of our father's piety for when he prayed for his children it was, undoubtedly, that we might be very peculiarly the Lord's. H. was to be the missionary but if he cannot go himself, and is prospered in business, I hope he will be able to help send others. I have been frightened, of late, in thinking how little good I am doing in the world. And yet I believe that those who love to do good always find opportunities enough, wherever they are. Whether I shall do any here, I dare not try to guess.

Dec. 3rd.—How I thank you for the interest you take in my Bible class. They are so attentive to every word I say that it makes me deeply feel the importance of seeking each of those words from the Holy Spirit. Many of them had not even a Bible of their own until now, nor were they in the habit of reading it at all. Among others, there are two granddaughters of Patrick Henry. I wish I could give you a picture of them, as they sit on Sabbath evening around the table with their eyes fixed so eagerly on my face, that if I did not feel that the Lord Jesus was present, I should be overwhelmed with confusion at my unworthiness.... Mr. Persico is a queer man. Last Sabbath Miss L. asked him if he had been to church. "Oui, Mlle.," said he "*vous étiez à l'église de l'homme—moi, j'étais à l'église de Dieu—dans les bois.*" There is the bell for prayers it is an hour since I began to write, but I have spent a great part of it with my eyes shut because I happened to feel more like meditating than writing, if you know what sort of a feeling that is. Oh, that we might be enabled to go onward day by day—and *upward too*.

I have been making violent efforts for years to become meek and lowly in heart. At present, I do hope that I am less irritable than I used to be. It was no small comfort to me when sister was home last summer, to learn from her that I had succeeded somewhat in my efforts. But though I have not often the last year been guilty of "harsh speeches," I have felt my pride tugging with all its might to kindle a great fire when some unexpected trial has caught me off my guard. I am persuaded that real meekness dwells deep within the heart and that it is only to be gained by communion with our blessed Savior, who when He was reviled, reviled not again.

Sabbath Evening, 8th.—I wanted to write last evening but had a worse pain in my side and left arm than I have had since I came here. While it lasted, which was an hour and a half, I had such pleasant thoughts for companions as would make any pain endurable. I was asking myself if, supposing God should please suddenly to take me away in the midst of life, whether I should feel willing and glad to go, and oh, it did seem *delightful* to think of it, and to feel sure that, sooner or later, the summons will come. Those pieces that you marked in the "Observer," I have read and like them exceedingly, especially those about growth in grace…. You speak of the goodness of God to me in granting me so much of His presence, while I am here away from all earthly friends. Indeed, I want to be able to praise Him as I never yet have done, and I do not know where to begin. I have felt more pain in this separation from home on mother's account than any other, as I feel that she needs me at home to comfort and to love her. Since she lost her best earthly friend, I have been her constant companion. I once had a secret desire for a missionary life, if God should see fit to prepare me for it, but when I spoke of it to mother she was so utterly overcome at its bare mention that I instantly promised I would *never* for any inducement leave or forsake her. I want you to pray for me that if poor mother's right hand is made forever useless, [8] I may after this year be a right hand for her, and be enabled to make up somewhat to her for the loss of it by affection and tenderness and sympathy…. I do not remember feeling any way in particular, when I first began to "write for the press," as you call it. I never could realize that more than half a dozen people would read my pieces. Besides, I have no desire of the sort you express, for fame. I care a great deal too much for the approbation of those I love and respect, but not a fig for that of those I do not like or do not know.

* * * * *

II.

Her Character as a Teacher. Letters. Incidents of School-Life. Religious Struggles, Aims, and Hopes. Oppressive Heat and Weariness.

Miss Payson had been in Richmond but a short time before she became greatly endeared to Mr. and Mrs. Persico, and to the whole school. She had a rare natural gift for teaching. Fond of study herself, she knew how to inspire her pupils with the same feeling. Her method was excellent. It aimed not merely to impart knowledge but to elicit latent powers, and to remove difficulties out of the way. While decided and thorough, it was also very gentle, helpful, and sympathetic. She had a quick perception of mental diversities, saw as by intuition the weak and the strong points of individual character, and was skillful in adapting her influence, as well as her instructions, to the peculiarities of every one under her care. The girls in her own special department almost idolized her. The parents also of some of them, who belonged to Richmond and its vicinity, seeing what she was doing for their daughters, sought her acquaintance, and showed her the most grateful affection.

Although her school labors were exacting, she carried on a large correspondence, spent a good deal of time in her favorite religious reading, and together with Miss Susan Lord, the senior teacher and an old Portland friend, pursued a course of study in French and Italian. At the table, Mr. Persico spoke French, and in this way, she was enabled to perfect herself in the practice of that language. Of her spiritual history and of incidents of her school life during the New Year, some extracts from letters to her cousin will give her own account.

RICHMOND, *January 3, 1841.*

If I tell you that I am going to take under my especial care and protection one of the family—a little girl of eleven years whom nobody can manage at all, you may wonder why. I found on my plate at dinner a note from Mrs. Persico saying that if I wanted an opportunity of doing good, here was one that if Nanny could sleep in my room, etc., it might be of great benefit to her. The only reason why I hesitated was the fear that she might be in the way of our best hours. But I have thought all along that I was living too much at my ease, and wanted a place in which to deny myself for the sake of the One who yielded up every comfort for my sake. Nanny has a fine character but has been mismanaged at home, and since coming here. She often comes and puts her arms around me and says, "There is *one* in this house who loves me, I do *know.*" I receive her as a trust from God, with earnest prayer to Him that we may be enabled to be of use to her. From morning to night, she is found fault with, and this is spoiling her temper and teaching her to be deceitful…. I have been reading lately the Memoir of Martyn. I have, of course, read it more than once before, but everything appears to me now in such a different light. I rejoice that I have been led to read the book just now. It has put within me new and peculiar desires to live wholly for the glory of God.

Jan. 13th.—I understand the feeling about wishing one's self a dog, or an animal without a soul. I have sat and watched a little kitten frisking about in the sunshine till I could hardly help killing it in my envy—but oh, how different it is now! I have felt lately that perhaps God has something for me to do in the world. I am satisfied, indeed, that in calling me nearer to Himself He has intended to prepare me for His service. Where that is to be is no concern of mine as yet. I only wish to belong to Him and wait for His will, whatever it may be.

Jan. 14th.—I used to go through with prayer merely as a duty, but now I look forward to the regular time for it, and hail opportunities for special seasons with such delight as I once knew nothing of. Sometimes my heart feels ready to break for the longing it hath for a nearer approach to the Lord Jesus than I can obtain without the use of words, and there is not a corner of the house, which I can have to myself. I think sometimes that I should be thankful for the meanest place in the universe. You ask if I ever dream of seeing the Lord. No—I never did, neither should I think it desirable, but a few days ago, when I woke, I had fresh in my remembrance some precious words, which, as I had been dreaming, He had spoken to me. It left an indescribable feeling of love and peace on my mind. I seemed in my dream to be very near Him, and that He was encouraging me to ask of Him all the things of which I felt the need.

Jan. 17th.—I did not mean to write so much about myself, for when I took out my letter I was thinking of things and beings far above this world. I was thinking of the hour when the Christian first enters into the joy of his Lord, when the first note of the "new song" is borne to his ear, and the first view of the Lamb of God is granted to his eye. It seems to me as if the bliss of that one minute would fully compensate for all the toils and struggles he must go through here and then to remember the ages of happiness that begin at that point! Oh, if the unseen presence of Jesus can make the heart to sing for joy in the midst of its sorrow and sin here, what will it be to dwell with Him forever!

My Bible class, which now consists of eighteen, is every week more dear to me. I am glad that you think poor Nanny well off. She has an inquiring mind, and though before coming here she had received no religious instruction and had not even a Bible, she is now constantly asking me questions that prove her to be a first-rate thinker and reasoner. She went to the theatre last night and came home quite disgusted, saying to herself, "I shouldn't like to die in the midst of such gayeties as these." She urged me to tell her if I thought it wrong for her to go, but I would not, because I did not want her to stay away for my sake. I want her to settle the question fairly in her own mind and to be guided by her own conscience rather than mine. She is so grateful and happy that, if the sacrifice had been greater, we should be glad that we had made it. And then if we can do her any good, how much reason we shall have to thank God for having placed her here!

Feb. 11th.—My thoughts of serious things should, perhaps, be called prayers, rather than anything else. I have constant need of looking up to God for help, so utterly weak and ignorant am I and so dependent upon Him. Sometimes in my walks, especially those of the early morning, I take a verse from the "Daily Food" to think upon at others, if my mind is where I want it should be, everything seems to speak and suggest thoughts of my Heavenly Father, and when it is otherwise, I feel as if that time had been wasted. This is not "keeping the mind on the stretch," and is delightfully refreshing. All I wish is that I were always thus favored. As to a hasty temper, I know that anybody who ever lived with me, until within the last two or three years, could tell you of many instances of outbreaking passion. I am ashamed to say how recently the last real tempest occurred, but I will not spare myself. It was in the spring of 1838, and I did not eat anything for so long that I was ill in bed and barely escaped a fever. Mother nursed me so tenderly that, though she forgave me, I *never* shall forgive myself. Since then I should not wish you to suppose that I have been perfectly amiable, but for the last year I think I have been enabled in a measure to control my temper, but of that you know more than I do, as you had a fair specimen of what I am when with us last summer. It has often been a source of encouragement to me that everybody said I was gentle and amiable till my father's death, when I was nine years old…. While reading tonight that chapter in Mark, where it speaks of Jesus as walking on the sea, I was interested in thinking how frequently such scenes occur in our spiritual passage over the sea, which is finally to land us on the shores of the home for which we long. "While they were toiling in rowing," Jesus went to them upon the water and "would have passed by" till He heard their cries, and then He manifested Himself unto them saying, *"It is I."* And when He came to them, the wind ceased and they "wondered." Surely we have often found in our toiling that Jesus was passing by and ready at the first trembling fear to speak the word of love and of consolation and to give us the needed help, and then to leave us *wondering* indeed at the infinite tenderness and kindness so unexpectedly vouchsafed for our relief.

Feb. 13th.—I do not think we should make our enjoyment of religion the greatest end of our struggle against sin. I never once had such an idea. I think we should fight against sin simply because it is something hateful to God, because it is something so utterly unlike the spirit of Christ, whom it is our privilege to strive to imitate in all things. On all points connected with the love I wish to give my Savior, and the service I am to render Him, I feel that I want teaching and am glad to obtain assistance from any source. I hardly know how to answer your question. I do not have that constant sense of the Savior's presence, which I had here for a long time, neither do I feel that I love Him as I thought I did, but it is not always best to judge of ourselves by our feelings, but by the general principle and guiding desire of the mind. I do think that my prevailing aim is to do the will of God and to glorify Him in everything. Of this, I have thought a great deal of late. I have not a very extensive sphere of action, but I want my conduct, my every word and look and motion, to be fully under the influence of this desire for the honor of God. You can have no idea of the constant observation to which I am exposed here.

Feb. 21st.—I spent three hours this afternoon in taking care of a little black child (belonging to the house), who is very ill, and as I am not much used to such things, it excited and worried me into a violent nervous headache. I finished Brainerd's Life this afternoon, amid many doubts as to whether I ever loved the Lord at all, so different is my piety from that of this blessed and holy man. The book has been a favorite with me for years, but I never felt the influence of his life as I have while reading it of late.

She alludes repeatedly in her correspondence to the delight, which she found on the Sabbath in listening to that eminent preacher and divine, the Rev. Dr. Wm. S. Plumer, who was then settled in Richmond. In a letter to her cousin, she writes:

I have become much attached to him he seems more than half in heaven, and every word is full of solemnity and feeling, as if he had just held near intercourse with God. I wish that you could have listened with me to his sermons today. They have been, I think, blessed messages from God to my soul.

All her letters at this time glow with religious fervor. "How wonderful is our divine Master!" she seemed to be always saying to herself. "It has become so delightful to me to speak of His love, of His holiness, of His purity, that when I try to write to those who know Him not, I hardly know what is worthy of even a mention, if He is to be forgotten." And several years afterwards, she refers to this period as a time when she "shrank from everything that in the slightest degree interrupted her consciousness of God."

The following letter to a friend, whose name will often recur in these pages, well illustrates her state of mind during the entire winter.

To Miss Anna S. Prentiss. Richmond, Feb 26, 1841.

Your very welcome letter, my dear Anna, arrived this afternoon, and, as my labors for the week are over, I am glad of a quiet hour in which to thank you for it. I do not thank you simply because you have so soon answered my letter, but because you have told me what no one else could do so well about your own very dear self. When I wrote you, I doubted very much whether I might even allude to the subject of religion, although I wished to do so, since that almost exclusively has occupied my mind during the last year. I saw you in the midst of temptations to which I have ever been a stranger, but which I conceived to be decidedly unfavorable to growth in any of the graces, which make up Christian character. It was not without hesitation that I ventured to yield to the promptings of my heart, and to refer to the only things, which have at present much interest for it. I cannot tell you how I do rejoice that you have been led to come out thus upon the Lord's side, and to consecrate yourself to His service. My own views and feelings have within the last year undergone such an entire change, that I have wished I could take now some such stand in the presence of all who have known me in days past, as this which you have taken. My first and only wish is henceforth to live but for Him, who has graciously drawn my wandering affections to Himself.... You speak of the faintness of your heart—but "they who wait upon the Lord shall renew their strength," and I do believe the truth of these precious words not only because they are those of God, but also because my own experience adds happy witness to them. I have lived many years with only just enough of hope to keep me from actual despair. The least breath was sufficient to scatter it all and to leave me, fearful and afraid, to go over and over again the same ground thus allowing neither time nor strength for progress in the Christian course. I trust that you will not go through years of such unnecessary darkness and despondency. There is certainly enough in our Savior, if we only open our eyes that we may see it, to solve every doubt and satisfy every longing of the heart and He is willing to give it in full measure. When I contemplate the character of the Lord Jesus, I am filled with wonder which I cannot express, and with unutterable desires to yield myself and my all to His hand, to be dealt with in His own way and His way is a blessed one, so that it is delightful to resign body and soul and spirit to Him, without a will opposed to His, without a care but to love Him more, without a sorrow which His love cannot sanctify or remove. In following after Him faithfully and steadfastly, the feeblest hopes may be strengthened and I trust that you will find in your own happy experience that "joy and peace" go hand in hand with love—so that in proportion to your devotion to the Savior will be the blessedness of your life. When I begin I hardly know where to stop, and now I find myself almost at the end of my sheet before I have begun to say what I wish. This will only assure you that I love you a thousand times better than I did when I did not know that your heart was filled with hopes and affections like my own, and that I earnestly desire, if Providence permits us to enjoy intercourse in this or in any other way, we may never lose sight of the one great truth that we are *not our own*. I pray you sometimes remember me at the throne of grace. The more I see of the Savior, the more I feel my own weakness and helplessness and my need of His constant presence, and I cannot help asking assistance from all those who love Him.... Oh, how sorry I am that I have come to the end! I wish I had any faculty for expressing affection, so that I might tell you how much I love and how often I think of you.

Her cousin having gone abroad, a break in the correspondence with him occurred about this time and continued for several months. In a letter to her friend, Miss Thurston, dated April 21st, she thus refers to her school:

There are six of us teachers, five of them born in Maine—which is rather funny, as that is considered by most of the folks here as the place where the world comes to an end. Although the South lifts up its wings and crows over the North, it is glad enough to get its teachers there, and ministers too, and treats them very well when it gets them, into the bargain. We have in the school about one hundred and twenty-five pupils of all ages. I never knew till I came here the influence which early religious education exerts upon the whole future age. There is such a wonderful difference between most of these young people and those in the North, that you might almost believe them another race of beings. Mrs. Persico is beautiful, intelligent, interesting, and pious. Mr. Persico is just as much like John Neal as difference of education and of circumstances can permit. Mr. N.'s strong sense of justice, his enthusiasm, his fun and wit, his independence and self-esteem, his tastes, too, as far as I know them, all exist in like degree in Mr. Persico.

The early spring, with its profusion of flowers of every hue, so far in advance of the spring in her native State, gave her the utmost pleasure but as the summer approached, her health began to suffer. The heat was very intense, and hot weather always affected her unhappily. "I feel," she wrote, "as if I were in an oven with hot melted lead poured over my brain." Her old trouble, too—"organic disease of the heart" it was now suspected to be—caused her much discomfort. "While writing," she says in one of her letters, "I am suffering excruciating pain I cannot call it anything else." Her physical condition naturally affected more or less her religious feelings. Under date of July 12th, she writes:

The word *conflict* expresses better than any other my general state from day to day. I have seemed of late like a straw floating upon the surface of a great ocean, blown hither and thither by every wind, and tossed from wave to wave without the rest of a moment. It was a mistake of mine to imagine that God ever intended man to rest in this world. I see that it is right and wise in Him to appoint it otherwise…. While suffering from my Savior's absence, nothing interests me. But I was somewhat encouraged by reading in my father's memoir, and in reflecting that he passed through far greater spiritual conflicts than will probably ever be mine…. I see now that it is not always best for us to have the light of God's countenance. Do not spend your time and strength in asking for me that blessing, but this—that I may be transformed into the image of Christ in His own time, in His own way.

Early in August, she left Richmond and flew homeward like a bird to its nest.

* * * * *

III.

Extracts from her Richmond Journal.

Were her letters to her cousin the only record of Miss Payson's Richmond life, one might infer that they give a complete picture of it for they were written in the freedom and confidence of Christian friendship, with no thought that a third eye would ever see them. But it had another and hidden side, of which her letters contain only a partial record. Her early habit of keeping a journal has been already referred to. She kept one at Richmond, and was prevented several years later from destroying it, as she had destroyed others, by the entreaty of the only person who ever saw it. This journal depicts many of her most secret thoughts and feelings, both earthward and heavenward. Some passages in it are of too personal a nature for publication, but the following extracts seem fairly entitled to a place here, as they bring out several features of her character with sun like clearness, and so will help to a better understanding of the ensuing narrative:

RICHMOND, *October 3, 1840.*

How funny it seems here! Everything is so different from home! I foresee that I shan't live nearly a year under these new influences without changing my old self into something else. Heaven forbid that I should grow old because people treat me as if I were grown up! I hate old young folks. Well! Whoever should see me and my scholars would be at a loss to know wherein consists the difference between them and me. I am only a little girl after all, and yet folks do treat me as if I were as old and as wise as Methuselah. And Mr. Persico says, "Oui, Madame." Oh! Oh! Oh! It makes me feel so ashamed when these tall girls, these damsels whose hearts are developed as mine won't be these half dozen years (to say nothing of their minds), ask me if they may go to bed, if they may walk, if they may go to Mr. So-and-so's, and Miss Such-a-one's to buy—a stick of candy for aught I know. Oh, oh, oh! I shall have to take airs upon myself. I shall have to leave off little words and use big ones. I shall have to leave off sitting curled up on my feet, turkey-fashion. I shall have to make wise speeches (But a word in your ear, Miss—I *won't*).

Oct. 27th—This Richmond is a queer sort of a place and I should be as miserable in it as a fish out of water, only there is sunshine enough in my heart to make any old hole bright. In the first place, this dowdy chamber is in one view a perfect den—no carpet, whitewashed walls, loose windows that have the shaking palsy, fire-red hearth, blue paint instead of white, or rather a suspicion that there was once some blue paint here. But what do I care? I'm as merry as a grig from morning till night. The little witches down-stairs love me dearly, everybody is kind, and—and—and—when everybody is locked out and I am locked into this same room, this low attic, there's not a king on the earth so rich, as happy as I! Here is my little pet desk. Here are my books, my papers. I can write and read and study and moralize, I do not pretend to say *think*—and then besides, every morning and every night, within these four walls, heaven itself refuses not to enter in and dwell—and I may grow better and better and happier and happier in blessedness with which nothing may intermeddle.

Mr. Persico is a man by himself, and quite interesting to me in one way, that is, in giving me something to puzzle out. I like him for his exquisite taste in the picture line and for having adorned his rooms with such fine ones—at least they're fine to my inexperienced eye for when I'm in the mood, I can go and sit and dream as it seemeth me good over them, and as I dream, won't good thoughts come into my heart? As to Mrs. P., I hereby return my thanks to Nature for making her so beautiful. She has a face and figure to fall in love with. K. has also a fine face and a delicate little figure. Miss —— I shall avoid as far as I can do so. I do not think her opinions and feelings would do me any good. She has a fine mind and likes to cultivate it, and for that I respect her, but she has nothing natural and girlish in her, and I am persuaded, never had. She hates little children says she hates to hear them laugh, thinks them little fools. Why, how odd all this is to me! I could as soon hate the angels in heaven and hate to hear them sing. That, to be sure, is my way, and the other way is hers—but somehow it doesn't seem good-hearted to be so very, very superior to children as to shun the little loving beautiful creatures. I do not believe I ever shall grow up! But, Miss ——, I do not want to do you injustice, and I'm much obliged to you for all the flattering things you've said about me, and if you like my eyes and think there is congeniality of feeling between us, why, I thank you. But oh, do not teach me that the wisdom of the world consistent in forswearing the simple beauties with which life is full. Do not make me fear my own happy girlhood by talking to me about love—oh, do not!

Dec. 1.—I wonder if all the girls in the world are just alike? Seems to me they might be so sweet and lovable if they'd leave off chattering forever and ever about lovers…. If mothers would keep their little unfledged birds under their own wings, would not they make better mother- birds? Now some girls down-stairs, who ought to be thinking about all the beautiful things in life but just lovers, are reading novels, love-stories and poetry, till they cannot care for anything else…. Now, Lizzy Payson, where's the use of fretting so? Go right to work reading Leighton and you'll forget that all the world isn't as wise as you think you are, you little vain thing, you! Alas and alas, but this is such a nice world, and the girls do not know it!

Dec. 2.—What a pleasant walk I had this morning on Ambler's Hill. The sun rose while I was there and I was so happy! The little valley, clothed with white houses and completely encircled by hills, reminded me of the verse about the mountains round about Jerusalem. Nobody was awake so early and I had all the great hill to myself, and it was so beautiful that I could have thrown myself down and kissed the earth itself. Oh, sweet and good and loving Mother Nature! I choose you for my own. I will be your little ladylove. I will hunt you out whenever you hide, and you shall comfort me when I am sad, and laugh with me when I'm merry, and take me by the hand and lead me onward and upward till the image of the heavenly force out that of the earthly from my whole heart and soul. Oh, how I prayed for a holy heart on that hillside and how sure I am that I shall grow better! And what companionable thoughts I've had all day for that blessed walk!

8th.—My life is a nice little life just now, as regular as clockwork. We walk and we keep school, and our scholars kiss and love us, and we kiss and love them, and we read Lamartine and I worship Leighton, good, wise, holy Leighton, and we discourse about everything together and dispute and argue and argue and dispute, and I'm quite happy, so I am! As to Lamartine, he's no great things, as I know of, but I want to keep up my knowledge of French and so we read twenty pages a day. And as to our discourses, my fidgety, moralizing sort of mind wants to compare its doctrines with those of other people, though it's as stiff as a poker in its own opinions. You're a very consistent little girl! You call yourself a child, are afraid to open your mouth before folks, and yet you're as obstinate and proud as a little man, daring to think for yourself and act accordingly at the risk of being called odd and incomprehensible. I do not care, though! Run on and break your neck if you will. You're nothing especial after all.

9th.—To-night, in unrolling a bundle of work I found a little note therein from mother. Whew, how I kissed it! I thought I should fly out of my senses, I was so glad. But I cannot fly now-a-days, I'm growing so unethereal. Why, I take up a lot of room in the world and my frocks won't hold me. That's because my heart is so quiet, lying as still as a mouse, after all its tossing about and trying to be happy in the things of this life. Oh, I am so happy now in the *other* life! But as for telling other people so—as for talking religion—I do not see how I *can*. It doesn't come natural. Is it because I am proud? But I pray to be so holy, so truly a Christian, that my *life* shall speak and gently persuade all who see me to look for the hidden spring of my perpetual happiness and quietness. The only question is: Do I live so? I'm afraid I make religion seem too grave a thing to my watching maiden's down-stairs but, oh, I'm afraid to rush into *their* pleasures.

25th. — … I've been "our Lizzy" all my life and have not had to display my own private feelings and opinions before folks, but have sat still and listened and mused and lived within myself, and shut myself up in my corner of the house and speculated on life and the things thereof till I've got a set of notions of my own which do not *fit into* the notions of anybody I know. I do not open myself to anybody on earth I cannot there is a world of something in me which is not known to those about me and perhaps never will be but sometimes I think it would be *delicious* to love a mind like mine in some things, only better, wiser, nobler. I do not quite understand life. People do not live as they were made to live, I'm sure ... I want *soul*. I want the gracious, glad spirit that finds the good and the beautiful in everything, joined to the manly, exalted intellect—rare unions, I am sure, yet possible ones. Little girl! Do you suppose such a soul would find anything in yours to satisfy it? No—no—no—I do not. I know I am a poor little goose that ought to be content with some equally poor little gander, but I *won't*. I'll never give up one inch of these the demands of my reason and of my heart for all the truths, you tell me about myself—never! But descend from your elevation, oh speculating child of mortality, and go down to school. Oh, no, no school for a week, and I guess I'll spend the week in fancies and follies. It won't hurt me. I've done it before and got back to the world as satisfied as ever, indeed I have.

Jan. 1, 1841.—We've been busy all the week getting our presents ready for the servants, and a nice time I've had this morning, seeing them show their ivory threat. James made a little speech, the amount of which was, he hoped I would not get married till I'd "done been" here two or three years, because my face was so pleasant it was good to look at it! I was as proud as Lucifer at this compliment, and shall certainly look pleasant all day today, if I never did before. Monsieur and the rest wished me, I won't say how many, good wishes, rushing at me as I went in to breakfast—and Milly privately informed Lucy that she liked Miss Payson "a heap" better than she did anybody else, and then came and begged me to buy her! I buy her! Heaven bless the poor little girl. I had some presents and affectionate notes from different members of the family and from my scholars—also letters from sister and Ned, which delighted me infinitely more than I'm going to tell *you*, old journal. Took tea at Mr. P.'s and Mrs. P. laughed at her husband because he had once an idea of going to New England to get my little ladyship to wife (for the sake of my father, of course). Mr. P. blushed like a boy and fidgeted terribly, but I didn't care a snap—I am not old enough to be wife to anybody, and I'm not going to mind if people do joke with me about it. I've had better things to think of on this New Year's day—good, heavenward thoughts and prayers and hopes, and if I do not become more and more transformed into the Divine, then are prayers and hopes things of naught. Oh, how dissatisfied I am with myself. How I long to be like unto Him into whose image I shall one day be changed when I see Him as He is!

I believe nobody understands me on religious points, for I cannot, and, it seems to me, *need* not parade my private feelings before the world. Cousin G., God bless him! Knows enough, and yet my letters to him do not tell the hundredth part of that which these four walls might tell, if they would. I do not know that I am not wrong, but I do dislike the present style of talking on religious subjects. Let people pray—earnestly, fervently, not simply morning and night, but the *whole day long*, making their lives one continued prayer but, oh, do not let them tell others of, or let others know *half* how much of communion with Heaven is known to their own hearts. Is it not true that those who talk most, go most to meetings, run hither and thither to all sorts of societies and all sorts of readings—is it not true that such people would not find peace and contentment—yes, blessedness of blessedness—in solitary hours when to the Searcher of hearts alone are known their aspirations and their love? I do not know, I am puzzled but I may say here, where nobody will ever see it, what I *do* think, and I say it to my own heart as well as over the hearts of others—there is not enough of real, true communion with God, not enough nearness to Him, not enough heart-searching before Him and too much parade and bustle and noise in doing His work on earth. Oh, I do not know exactly what I mean—but since I have heard so many apparently Christian people own that of this sense of nearness to God they know absolutely nothing—that they pray because it is their habit without the least expectation of meeting the great yet loving Father in their closets—since I have heard this I am troubled and perplexed. Why, is it not indeed true that the Christian believer, God's own adopted, chosen, beloved child, may speak face to face with his Father, humbly, reverently, yet as a man talks with his friend? Is it not true? Do not I *know* that it is so? Oh, I sometimes want the wisdom of an angel that I may not be thus disturbed and wearied.

14th.—Now either Miss ——'s religion is wrong and mine right, or else it's just the other way. I wrote some verses, funny ones, and sent her today, and she returned for answer that verse in Proverbs about vinegar on the teeth, and seemed distressed that I ever had such worldly and funny thoughts. I told her I should like her better if she ever had any but solemn ones, whence we rushed into a discussion about proprieties and I maintained that a mind was not in a state of religious health, if it could not *safely* indulge in thoughts funny as funny could be. She shook her head and looked as glum as she could, and I'm really sorry that I vexed her righteous soul, though I'm sure I feel funny ever so much of the time, cannot help saying funny things and cutting up capers now and then. I'll take care not to marry a glum man, anyhow not that I want my future lord and master to be a teller of stories, a wit, or a particularly funny man—but he shan't wear a long face and make me wear a long one, though he may be as pious as the day is long and *must* be, what's more. Oh, my! I do not think I was so very naughty. I saw Miss —— laughing privately at these same verses and she rushed in to Mrs. P. and read them to her, and then copied them for her aunt and paid twenty-five cents postage on the letter. I should like to know how she dared waste so much time in unholy employments! As I was saying, and am always thinking, it's rather queer that people are so oddly different in their ideas of religion. Heaven forbid I should trifle with serious and holy thoughts of my head and heart—but if my religion is worth a straw, such verse writing will not disturb it.

January 16th.—I wonder what's got into me today—I feel cross, without the least bit of reason for so feeling. I guess I'm not well, for I'm sure I've felt like one great long sunbeam, I do not know how many months, and it doesn't come natural to be fretful.

17th.—I knew I wasn't well yesterday and today am half-sick. We got through breakfast at twenty minutes to eleven, and as I was up at seven, I got kind o' hungry and out of sorts. This afternoon went to church and heard one of Dr. E.'s argumentative sermons. But there's something in those Prayer-book prayers, certainly, if men won't or cannot put any grace into their sermons. I wish I had a perfect ideal Sunday in my head or heart, or both. If I'm *very* good I'm tired at night, and if I'm bad my conscience smites me—so any way I'm not very happy just now and I'm sick and mean to go to bed and so!

18th.—Had a talk with Nanny. She has a thoughtful mind and who knows but we may do her some good. I love to have her here, and for once in my life like to feel a little bit—just the least bit—*old* that is, old enough to give a little sage advice to the poor thing, when she asks it. She says she won't read any more novels and will read the Bible and dear knows what else she said about finding an angel for me to marry, which heaven forbid she should do, since I'm too fond of being a little mite naughty, to desire anything of that sort. After she was in bed, she began to say her prayers most vehemently and among other things, prayed for Miss Payson. I had the strangest sensation, and yet an almost heavenly one, if I may say so. May it please Heaven to listen to her prayer for me, and mine for her, dear child? But suppose I do her no good while she lives so under my wing?

19th.—Up early—walked and read Leighton. Mr. P. amused us at dinner by giving a funny account in his funny way, of a mistake of E.——— H.———'s. She asked me the French for *as*. "Aussi" quoth I. Thereupon she tucked a great O. C. into her exercise and took it to him and they jabbered and sputtered over it, and she insisted that Miss Payson said so and he put his face right into hers and said, "Will you try to prove that Miss Payson is a fool, you little goose?" and at last Miss A. understood and explained. Read Leighton after school and thirty-two pages of Lamartine—then Mr. P. called—then Miss ——— teased me to love her and kept me in her paws till the bell rang for tea. Why cannot I like her? I should be so ashamed if I should find out after all that she is as good as she *seems*, but I never did get cheated yet when I trusted my own mother wits, my instinct, or whatever it is by which I know folks—and she is found wanting by this something.

28th.—Mrs. Persico has comforted me today. She says Mr. T. came to Mr. P. with tears in his eyes (could such a man shed tears?) and told him that I should be the salvation of his child—that she was already the happiest and most altered creature, and begged him to tell me so. I was ashamed and happy too—but I think Mr. P. should have told him that if good has been done to Nanny, it is *as* much—to say the least—owing to Louisa as to me. L. always joins me in everything I do and say for her, and I would not have even an accident deprive her of her just reward for anything. Nanny sat on the floor to-night in her nightgown, thinking. At last, she said, "Miss Payson?" "Well, little witch?" "You would not care much if you should die to-night, should you?" "No, I think not." "Nor I," said she. "Why, do you think you should be better off than you are here?" "Yes, in heaven," said she. "Why how do you know you'll go to heaven?" She looked at me seriously and said, "Oh, I do not know—I do not know—I do not think I should like to go to the other place." We had then a long talk with her and it seems she's a regular little believer in Purgatory—but I would not dispute with her. I guess there's a way of getting at her heart better than that…. Why is it that I have such sensitiveness on religious points, such a dream of having my own private aims and emotions known by those about me? Is it right? I should like to be just what the Christian ought to be in these relations. Miss ——— expects me to make speeches to her, but I *cannot*. If I thought I knew ever so much, I could not, and she annoys me so. Oh, I wish it didn't hurt my soul so to touch it! It's just like a butterfly's wing—people cannot help tearing off the very invisible *down* so to speak, for which they take a fancy to it, if they get it between fingers and thumb, and so I have to suffer for their curiosity's sake. Am I bound to reveal my heart-life to everybody who asks? Must I not believe that the heavenly love may, in one sense, be *hidden* from outward eye and outward touch? Or am I wrong?

Feb. 1, 1841.—Rose later than usual—cold, dull, rainy morning. Read in Life of Wilberforce. Defended Nanny with more valor than discretion. This evening the storm departed and the moonlight was more beautiful than ever and I was so sad and so happy, and the life beyond and above seemed so beautiful. Oh, how I have longed today for heaven within my own soul! There has been much unspoken prayer in my heart to-night. I do not know what I should do if I could have my room all to myself—and not have people know it if even a good thought comes into my mind. I shall be happy in heaven, I know I shall—for even here prayer and praise are so infinitely more delightful than anything else is.

3rd.—Woke with headache, got through school as best I could, then came and curled myself up in a ball in the easy-chair and didn't move till nine, when I crept down to say goodbye to poor Mrs. Persico. Miss L. and Miss J. received me in their room so tenderly and affectionately that I was ashamed. What makes them love me? I am sure I should not think they could.

10th.—I wonder who folks think I am, and what they think? Sally R—— sent me up her book of autographs with a request that I would add mine. I looked it over and found very great names, and did not know whether to laugh or cry at her funny request, which I couldn't have made up my mouth to grant. How queer it seems to me that people won't let me be a little girl and will act as if I were an old maid or matron of ninety-nine! Poor Mr. Persico is terribly unhappy and walks up and down perpetually with *such* a step.

12th.— ... I am sure that in these little things God's hand is just as clearly to be seen as in His wonderful works of power, and tried to make Miss —— see this, but she either couldn't or would not. It seems to me that God is my Father, my own Father, and it is so natural to turn right to Him, every minute almost, with either thank-offerings or petitions, that I never once stop to ask if such and such a matter is sufficiently great for His notice. Miss —— seemed quite astonished when I said so.

16th.— ... I've been instituting an inquiry into myself today and have been worthily occupied in comparing myself to an onion, though in view of the fragrance of that highly useful vegetable, I hope the comparison won't go on all fours But I have as many natures as an onion has—what d'ye call 'em—coats? First, the outside skin or nature—kind o' tough and ugly _anybody may see that and welcome. Then comes my next nature—a little softer—a little more removed from curious eyes then my inner one—myself—that 'ere little round ball which nobody ever did or ever will see the whole of—at least, s'pose not. Now most people see only the outer rind—a brown, red, yellow, tough skin and that's all but I *think* there's something inside that's better and more truly an onion than might at first be guessed. And so I'm an onion and that's the end.

17th.—Mrs. P.'s birthday, in honor of which cake and wine. Mr. P. was angry with us because we took no wine. If he had asked me civilly to drink his wife's health, I should probably have done so, but I am not to be *frightened* into anything. I made a funny speech and got him out of his bearish mood, and then we all proceeded to the portico to see if the new President had arrived—by which means we obtained a satisfactory view of two cows, three geese, one big boy in a white apron and one small one in a blue apron, three darkies of feminine gender and one old horse but Harrison himself we saw not. Mr. Persico says it's Tyler's luck to get into office by the death of his superior, and declares Harrison must infallibly die to secure John Tyler's fate. It's to be hoped this won't be the case. [9]

March 6th.—Miss L. read to us today some sprightly and amusing little notes written her years ago by a friend with whom she still corresponds. I was struck with the contrast between these youthful and light-hearted fragments and her present letters, now that she is a wife and mother. I wonder if there is always this difference between the girl and woman? If so, heaven forbid I should ever cease to be a child!

18th.—Headache—Nanny sick held her in my arms two or three hours had a great fuss with her about taking her medicine, but at last out came my word *must*, and the little witch knew it meant all it said and down went the oil in a jiffy, while I stood by laughing at myself for my pretension of dignity. The poor child couldn't go to sleep till she had thanked me over and over for making her mind and for taking care of her, and would not let go my hand, so I had to sit up until very late—and then I was sick and sad and restless, for I couldn't have my room to myself and the day didn't seem finished without it.

It is a perfect mystery to me how folks get along with so little praying. Their hearts must be better than mine, or something. What is it? But if God sees that the desire of my whole heart is tonight—has been all day—towards Himself, will He not know this as prayer, answer it as such? Yes, prayer is certainly something more than bending of the knees and earnest words, and I do believe that goodness and mercy will descend upon me, though with my lips I ask not.

24th.—Had a long talk with Mr. Persico about my style of governing. He seemed interested in what I had to say about appeals to the conscience, but said my *youthful enthusiasm* would get cooled down when I knew more of the world. I told him, very pertly, that I hoped I should never know the world then. He laughed and asked, "You expect to make out of these stupid children such characters, such hearts as yours?" "No—but better ones." He shook his head and said I had put him into good humor. I do not know what he meant. I've been acting like Sancho today—rushing up stairs two at a time, frisking about, catching up Miss J—— in all her maiden dignity and tossing her right into the midst of our bed. Who's going to be "schoolma'am" out of school? Not I! I mean to be just as funny as I please, and what's more I'll make Miss —— funny, too,—that I will! She'd have so much more health—Christian health, I mean—if she would leave off trying to get to heaven in such a dreadful bad "way." I cannot think *religion* makes such a long, gloomy face. It must be that she is wrong, or else I am. I wonder which? Why it's all sunshine to me—and all clouds to her! Poor Miss ——, you might be so happy!

April 9th.—Holiday. We all took a long walk, which I enjoyed highly. I was in a half moralizing mood all the way, wanted to be by myself very much. We talked more than usual about home and I grew so sad. Oh, I wonder if anybody loves me as *I love*! I wonder! I long for mother, and if I could just see her and know that she is happy and that she will be well again! It is really a curious question with me, whether provided I ever fall in love (for I'll *fall* in love, else not go in at all) I shall leave off loving mother best of anybody in the world? I suppose I shall be in love sometime or other, but that's nothing to do with me now nor I with it. I've got my hands full to take care of my naughty little self.

17th.—Mrs. Persico got home to-night [10] and what a meeting we had! What rejoicing! How beautiful she looked as she sat in her low chair, and we stood and knelt in a happy circle about her! A queen—an angel—could not have received love and homage with a sweeter grace. Sue Irvine cried an hour for joy and I wished I were one of the crying sort, for I'm sure I was glad enough to do almost anything. Beautiful woman! We sang to her the Welcome Home, Miss F. singing as much with her eyes as with her voice, and Mr. and Mrs. Persico both cried, he like a little child. Oh, that such evenings as this came oftener in one's life! All that was beautiful and good in each of our hidden natures came dancing out to greet her at her coming, and all petty jealousies were so quieted and—why, what a rhapsody I'm writing! And tomorrow, our good better natures tucked away, dear knows where, we shall descend with business-like airs to breakfast, wish each other good morning, pretend that we haven't any hearts. Oh, is this life! I won't believe it. Our good genius has come back to us now all things will again go on smoothly once more I can be a little girl and frolic up here instead of playing Miss Dignity down-stairs.

May 7th.—This evening I passed unavoidably through Miss ———'s room. She was reading Byron as usual and looked so wretched and restless, that I could not help yielding to a loving impulse and putting my hand on hers and asking why she was so sad. She told me. It was just what I supposed. She is trying to be happy, and cannot find out how reads Byron and gets sickly views of life sits up late dreaming about love and lovers then, too tired to pray or think good thoughts, tosses herself down upon her bed and wishes herself dead. She did not tell me this, to be sure, but I gathered it from her story. I alluded to her religious history and present hopes. She said she did not think continued acts of faith in Christ necessary she had believed on Him once, and now He would save her whatever she did and she was not going to torment herself trying to live so very holy a life, since, after all, she should get to heaven just as well through Him as if she had been particularly good (as she termed it). I do not know whether a good or a bad spirit moved me at that minute, but I forgot that I was a mere child in religious knowledge, and talked about *my* doctrine and made it a very beautiful one to my mind, though I do not think she thought it so. Oh, for what would I give up the happiness of praying for a holy heart—of striving, struggling for it! Yes, it is indeed true that we are to be saved simply, only, apart from our own goodness, through the love of Christ. But who can believe himself thus chosen of God—who can think of and hold communion with Infinite Holiness and not long for the Divine image in his own soul? It is a mystery to me—these strange doctrines. Is not the fruit of love aspiration after the holy? Is not the act of the newborn soul, when it passes from death unto life, that of desire for assimilation to and oneness with Him who is its all in all? How can love and faith be *one act* and then cease? I dare not believe—I would not for a universe believe—that my very sense of safety in the love of Christ is not to be just the sense that shall bind me in grateful self-renunciation wholly to His service. Let me be *sure* of final rest in heaven—sure that at this moment I am really God's own adopted child and I believe my prayers, my repentings, my weariness of sin, would be just what they now are nay, more deep, more abundant. Oh, it is *because* I believe—fully believe that I shall be saved through Christ—that I want to be like Him here upon earth it is because I do not fear final misery that I shrink from sin and defilement here. Oh, that I could put into that poor bewildered heart of hers just the sweet repose upon the ever present Savior, which He has given unto me! The quietness with which my whole soul rests upon Him is such blessed quietness! I shall not soon forget this strange evening.

[1] She refers to this, doubtless, in a note to Mr. Hamlin, dated March 28, 1839. Mr. H. was then in Constantinople. "It seems as if a letter to go so far ought to be a good one, so I am afraid to write to you. But we '*think to you*' every day, and hope you think of us sometimes. I have been so happy all winter that I have some happiness to spare, and if you need any you shall have as much as you want."

[2] The sermon was preached by her pastor, the Rev. Dr. Condit, April 19th.

[3] There is one thing I recall as showing the very early religious tendency of Lizzy's mind. It was a little prayer meeting that she held with a few little friends, as long ago as her sister kept school in the large parlor of the house on Middle Street, before the death of her father. It assembled at odd hours and in odd places. I also remember her interest in the spiritual welfare of her young companions, after the return of the family from their sojourn in New York. She showed this by accompanying some of us, in the way of encouragement, to Dr. Tyler's inquiry meeting. Then during the special religious interest of 1838, she felt still more deeply and entered heartily into the rejoicing of those of us who at that time found "peace in believing." The next year I accompanied my elder sister Susan to Richmond, and during

my absence, she gave up her Christian hope and passed through a season of great darkness and despondency, emerging, however, into the light upon a higher plane of religious experience and enjoyment. She sometimes thought this the very beginning of the life of faith in her soul. But as I used to say to her when the next year we were together at Richmond, it seemed to me quite impossible that anyone who had not already received the grace of God could have felt what she had felt and expressed. I do not doubt in the least that for years she had been a true follower of Christ.—*Letter from Miss Ann Louisa P. Lord, dated Portland, December 30, 1878.*

[4] It may be proper to say here, that while but few of her letters are given entire, it has not been deemed needful specially to indicate all the omissions. In some instances, also, where two letters, or passages of letters, relate to the same subject, they have been combined.

[5] An excellent little work by Rev. William Nevins, D.D. Dr. Nevins was pastor of the first Presbyterian Church in Baltimore, where he died in 1835, at the age of thirty-seven. He was one of the best preachers and most popular religious writers of his day.

[6] Miss Ann Louisa P. Lord.

[7] Miss Susan Lord.

[8] Referring to a serious accident, by which her mother was for some time deprived of the use of her right hand.

[9] But, singularly enough, it was. President Harrison died April 4, 1841, just a month after his inauguration, and Mr. Tyler succeeded him.

[10] From Philadelphia, where she had undergone a surgical operation.

CHAPTER 3 - PASSING FROM GIRLHOOD INTO WOMANHOOD - 1841-1845.

I.

At Home again. Marriage of her Sister. Ill-Health. Letters. Spiritual Aspiration and Conflict. Perfectionism. "Very, very Happy." Work for Christ what makes Life attractive. Passages from Her Journal. A Point of Difficulty.

Not long after Elizabeth's return from Richmond, her sister was married to the Rev. Albert Hopkins, Professor in Williams College. The wedding had been delayed for her coming. "I would rather wait six years than not have you present," her sister wrote. This event brought her into intimate relations with a remarkable man a man much beloved in his day, and whose name will often reappear in these pages.

The next two or three months showed that her Richmond life, although so full of happy experiences, had yet drawn heavily upon her strength. They were marked by severe nervous excitement and fits of depression. This, however, passed away and she settled down again into a busy home life. But it was no longer the home life of the past. The year of absence had left a profound impression upon her character. Her mind and heart had undergone a rapid development. She was only twenty-two on her return, and had still all the fresh, artless simplicity of a young girl, but there was joined to it now the maturity of womanhood. Of the rest of the year, a record is preserved in letters to her cousin. These letters give many little details respecting her daily tasks and the life she led in the family and in the world but they are chiefly interesting for the light they shed upon her progress heavenward. Her whole soul was still absorbed in divine things. At times her delight in them was sweet and undisturbed then again, she found herself tossed to and fro upon the waves of spiritual conflict. Perfectionism was just then much discussed, and the question troubled her not a little, as it did again thirty years later. But whether agitated or at rest, her thoughts all centered in Christ, and her constant prayer was for more love to Him.

PORTLAND, *Sept. 15, 1841.*

The Lord Jesus is indeed dear to me. I cannot doubt it. His name is exceedingly precious. Oh, help me, my dear cousin, to love Him more, to attain His image, to live only for Him! I blush and am ashamed when I consider how inadequate are the returns I am making Him yet I can praise Him for all that is past and trust Him for all that is to come. I cannot tell you how delightful prayer is. I feel that in it, I have communion with God—that He is here—that He is mine and that I am His. I long to make progress every day, each minute seems precious, and I constantly tremble lest I should lose one in returning, instead of pressing forward with all my strength. No, not *my* strength, for I have none, but with all which the Lord gives me. How can I thank you enough that you pray for me!

Sept. 18th.—I am all the time so nervous that life would be insupportable if I had not the comfort of comforts to rejoice in. I often think mother would not trust me to carry the dishes to the closet, if she knew how strong an effort I have to make to avoid dashing them all to pieces. When I am at the head of the stairs I can hardly help throwing myself down, and I believe it a greater degree of just such a state as this which induces the suicide to put an end to his existence. It was never so bad with me before. Do you know anything of such a feeling as this? To-night, for instance, my head began to feel all at once as if it were enlarging till at last it seemed to fill the room, and I thought it large enough to carry away the house. Then every object of which I thought enlarged in proportion. When this goes off the sense of the contraction is equally singular. My head felt about the size of a pin's head our church and everybody in it appeared about the bigness of a cup, etc. These strange sensations terminate invariably with one still more singular and particularly pleasant. I cannot describe it—it is a sense of smoothness and a little of dizziness. If you never had such feelings this will be all nonsense to you, but if you have and can explain them to me, why I shall be indeed thankful. I have been subject to them ever since I can remember. I never met with a physician yet who seemed to know what is the matter with me, or to care a fig whether I got well or not. All they do is to roll up their eyes and shake their heads and say, "Oh!" ... As to the wedding, we had a regular fuss, so that I hardly knew whether I was in the body or out of it. The Professor was here only two days. He is very eminently holy, his friends say, and from what I saw of him, I should think it true. This was the point that interested sister in him. As soon as the wedding was over my spirits departed and fled. It is true enough that "marriage involves one union, but *many separations*."

Oct. 17th.—We had a most precious sermon this afternoon from the Baptist minister on the words, "Christ is all and in all." I longed to have you hear the Savior thus dwelt upon. I did not know how full the Apostles were of His praise—how constantly they dwelt upon Him, till it was spread before me thus in one delightful view. Oh, may He become our all—our beginning and our ending—our first and our last! I do love to hear Him thus honored and adored. Let us, dear cousin, look at our Savior more. Let us never allow ought to come between our hearts and our God. Speak to me as to your own soul, urging me onward, and if you do not see the fruits of your faithfulness here, may you see when sowing is turned to reaping.

Oct. 24th.—I must call upon you to rejoice with me that I have today got back my old Sunday-school class. I wondered at their being so earnest about having me again, yet I trust that God has given me this hold upon their affections for some good purpose.... I do not know exactly how to discriminate between the suggestions of Satan and those of my own heart, but for a week past, even while my inclinations and my will were set upon Christ, something followed me in my down-sittings and my uprisings, urging me to hate the Lord Jesus asking if His strict requirements were not too strait to be endured and it has grieved me deeply that such a thought could find its way into my mind. "I have prayed for thee that thy faith fail not" is my last refuge. How graciously did Jesus provide a separate consolation for each difficulty, which He foresaw, could meet His disciples on their way?

Nov. 8th.—Mother has been sick. The doctor feared inflammation of the brain but she is better now. I have had my first experience as a nurse, and Dr. Mighels says I am a good one.

Whenever I think of God's wonderful, *wonderful* goodness to me and of my own sinfulness, I want to find a place low at the foot of the cross where I may cover my face in the dust, and yet go on praising Him. You do not know how all things have been made new to me within less than two years. Still, I struggle fiercely every hour of my life. For instance, my desire to be much beloved by those dear to me, is a source of constant grief. Some weeks ago, a person, who probably did not know this, told me that I was remarkably lovable and that everybody said so. I was so foolish, so wicked, as to be more pleased by this than I dare to tell—but enough so to give me after-hours of bitter sorrow. Sometimes it seems to me that I grow prouder every day, and I wanted to ask mother if she did not think so but I thought perhaps God is showing me my pride as I had never seen it that I may wage war against this, His enemy and mine. I do not believe anybody else has such an evil nature as I. But let us never rest till we are satisfied with being counted as nothing, that our Savior may be all in all. It seems no small portion of the joy I long for in heaven, to be thus self-forgetful in love to Christ. How strange that we do not now supremely love Him. How I do long to live with those who praise Him. I long to have every Christian with whom I meet speak of Him with love and exalt Him. [1]

Nov. 12th.—I have been very unwell and low-spirited. The cause of this, folks seem to agree, was over-exertion during mother's sickness. To tell the truth, I was so anxious about her that I did not try to save my strength at all, and excitement kept me up, so that I was not conscious of any special fatigue till all was over and the reaction came, when I just went into a dead-and-alive state and had the "blues" outrageously. It seemed as if I could do nothing but fold my hands and cry.

Sister is coming home this winter. I would like you to see this letter of hers. She is as nearly a perfectionist now as your father is. She begs me to read the New Testament and to pray for a knowledge of the truth. And so I have for a year and a half, and this is what I learn thereby: "The heart is deceitful above all things and desperately wicked"—at least such I find mine to be. To be sure, that I am not perfect is no proof that I may not become so however, I feel most sympathy with those who, like Martyn, Brainerd, and my father, had to *fight* their way through. Yet her remarks threw my mind into great confusion at first and I knew not what to do thereupon I went at once with my difficulties to the Lord and tried to *seek the truth*, whatever it might be, from Him. It seems to me that I am safe while in His hands and that if those things are essential, He will not withhold them from me. Truly, if there is a royal road to holiness, and if in one moment of time sin may be crushed and forever slain, I of all others should know it for at present the way is thronged with difficulties. [2] It seems to me that I am made of wants"—I need everything. At the same time, how great is the goodness of God to me! I long to have my heart so filled with the one single image of my Redeemer, that it shall ever flow in spontaneous adoration. Such a Savior! I am pained to the very depths of my soul because I love Him so little.… If I am only purified and made entirely the Lord's, let Him take His own course and make the refining process ever so painful.

> "When the shore is won at last,
> Who will count the billows past?"

Dec. 16th.—Do you remember what father said about losing his will when near the close of his life? That remark has always made the subject of a *lost will* interesting to me. There is another place where he wishes he had known this blessedness twenty years before. [3]

Dec. 18th.—"I am very, very happy and yet it is hardly a happiness which I can describe. You know what it is to rejoice in the sweet consciousness that there is a Savior—a near and a present Savior and thus am I now rejoicing grateful to Him for His holy nature, for His power over me, for His dealings with me, for a thousand things which I can only try to express to Him. Oh, how excellent above all treasures does He now appear! One minute of nearness to the Lord Jesus contains more of delight than years spent in intercourse with any earthly friend. I could not but own to-night that God can make me happy without a right hand or a right eye. Lord, make me Thine, and I will cheerfully give Thee all.

Dec. 22nd.—"As to my Italian and Tasso, I am ashamed to tell you how slow I have been. Between company and housework and sewing, I have my hands about full, and precious little time for reading and study. Still, I feel that I live a life of too much ease. I should love to spend the rest of my existence in the actual service of the Lord, without a question as to its ease and comfort. Reading Brainerd this afternoon made me long for his loose hold on earthly things. I do not know how to attain to such a spirit. Is it by prayer alone and the consequent sense of the worth of Divine things that this deadness to the world is to be gained—or, by giving up, casting away the treasures which withdraw the heart or have a tendency to withdraw it from God? This is quite an interesting question to me now, and I should really like it settled. The thought of living apart from God is more dreadful than any affliction I can think of.

Here are some passages from two leaves of her journal, which escaped the flames. They touch upon another side of her life at this period.

December 1, 1841.—"I went to the sewing-circle this afternoon and had such a stupid time! Enough gossip and nonsense was talked to make one sick, and I'm sure it wasn't the fault of my head that my hair didn't stand on end. Now my mother is a very sensible mother, but when she urges me into company and exhorts me to be more social, she runs the risk of having me become as silly as the rest of 'em. She fears I may be harmed by reading, studying and staying with her, but heaven forbid I should find things in books worse than things out of them. I cannot think the girls are the silly creatures they make themselves appear. They want an aim in life, some worthy *object* give them that, and the good and excellent, which, I am sure, lies hidden in their nature, will develop itself at once. When the young men rushed in and the girls began looking unutterable things, I rushed out and came home. I cannot and won't talk nonsense and flirt with those boys! Oh, what is it I do want? Somebody who feels as I feel and thinks as I think but where shall I find the somebody?

7th.—"Frolicked with G., rushed up stairs with a glass-lamp in my hand, went full tilt against the door, smashed the lamp, got the oil on my dress, on two carpets, besides spattering the wall. First consequence, a horrible smell of lamp-oil Second, great quakings, shakings, and wonderings what my ma would say when she came home Third, ablutions, groanings, ironings Fourth, a story for the Companion long enough to pay for that 'ere old lamp. Letting alone that, I've been a very good girl today studied, made a call, went to see H. R. with books, cakes, apples, and what's more, my precious tongue wherewith I discoursed to her.

14th.—"Busy all day. Carried a basket full of "whittles" to old Ma'am Burns, heard an original account of the deluge from the poor woman, wished I was as near heaven as she seems to be, studied, sewed, taught T. and E., tried to be a good girl and didn't have the blues once.

20th.—"Spent most of the afternoon with Lucy, who is sick. She held my hand in hers and kissed it over and over, and expressed so much love and gratitude and interest in the Sunday school that I felt ashamed.

24th—Helped mother bake all the morning, studied in the afternoon, got into a frolic, and went out after dark with G. to shovel snow, and then paddled down to L——'s with a Christmas-pudding, whereby I got a real backache, leg ache, neck ache, and all-over ache, which is just good enough for me. I was in the funniest state of mind this afternoon! I guess anybody, who had seen me, would have thought so!

25th, Saturday.—Got up early and ran down to Sally Johnson's with a big pudding, consequence whereof a horrible pain in my side. I do not care, though. I do love to carry puddings to good old grannies.

Jan. 1, 1842.—Began the New Year by going to see Lucy, fainting, tumbling down flat on the floor and scaring everybody half out of their wits. I do not think people ought to like me, on the whole, but when they do, ain't I glad? I wonder if perfectly honest-hearted people want to be loved better than they deserve, as in one sense I, with yet a pretty honest heart, do? I wonder how other folks think, feel inside? Wish I knew!

Most of the year 1842 was passed at home in household duties, in study, and in trying to do good. Never had she been busier, or more helpful to her mother and never more interested in the things of God. It was a year of genuine spiritual growth and also of sharp discipline. The true ideal of the Christian life revealed itself to her more and more distinctly, while at the same time she had opportunity both to learn and to practice some of its hardest lessons. A few extracts from letters to her cousin will give an inkling of its character.

March 19, 1842.—Sometimes I have thought my desire to live for my Savior and to labor for Him had increased. It certainly seems wonderful to me now that I could ever have wished to die, as I used to do, *when I had done nothing for God.* The way of life which appears most attractive, is that spent in persevering and unwearyingly toil for Him. There was warmth and fervency to my religious feelings the first year after my true hope, which I do not find now and often sigh for but I think my mind is more seriously determined for God than it was then, and that my principles are more fixed. Still I am less than the least of all.... I have read not quite five cantos of Tasso. You will think me rather indolent, but I have had a great deal to do, which has hindered study and reading.

May 3rd—The Christian life was never dearer to me than it is now, but it throngs with daily increasing difficulties. You, who have become a believer in perfection, may say that this conflict is not essential, and indeed, I have been so weary, of late, of struggling that I am almost ready to fly to the doctrine myself. I have certainly been made more willing to seek knowledge on this point from the Holy Spirit.

Sept. 30th—You speak of indulging unusually, of late, in your natural vivacity and finding it prejudicial. Here is a point on which I am completely bewildered. I find that if for a month or two I steadily set myself to the unwearied pursuit of spirituality of mind and entire weanedness from the world, a sad reaction *will* follow. My efforts slightly relax, I indulge in mirthful or worldly (in the sense of not religious) conversation, delight in it, and find my health and spirits better for it. But then my spiritual appetites at once become less keen, and from conversation I go to reading, from reading to writing, and then comes the question: Am I not going back?—and I turn from all to follow hard after the Lord. Is this a part of our poor humanity, above which we cannot rise? This is a hard world to live in and it will prove a trying one to me or I shall love it dearly. I have had temptations during the last six months on points where I thought I stood so safely that there was no danger of a fall. Perhaps it is good for us to be allowed to go to certain lengths, that we may see what wonderful supplies of grace our Lord gives us every hour of our lives.

October 1st—I have had two or three singular hours of excitement since I left writing to you last evening. If you were here, I should be glad to read you a late passage in my history, which has come to its crisis and is over with—thanks to Him, who so wonderfully guides me by His counsel. If I ever saw the hand of God distinctly held forth for my help, I have seen it here, coming in the right time, in the right way, *all* right.

* * * * *

II.

Returns to Richmond. Trials there. Letters. Illness. School Experiences.
"To the Year 1843." Glimpses of her daily Life. Why her Scholars
love her so. Homesick. A Black Wedding. What a Wife should be. "A
Presentiment." Notes from her Diary.

In November of this year, at the urgent solicitation of Mr. Persico, Miss Payson returned to Richmond, and again became a teacher in his school. But everything was now changed, and that for the worse. Mr. Persico, no longer under the influence of his wife, who had fallen a prey to cruel disease, lost heart, fell heavily in debt, and became at length hopelessly insolvent. Later, he is said to have been lost at sea on his way to Italy. The whole period of Miss Payson's second residence in Richmond was one of sharp trial and disappointment. But it brought out in a very vivid manner her disinterestedness and the generous warmth of her sympathies. At the peril of her health, she remained far into the summer of 1843, faithfully performing her duties, although, as she well knew, it was doubtful if she would receive any compensation for her services. As a matter of fact, only a pittance of her salary was ever paid. Of this second residence in Richmond, no other record is needed than a few extracts from letters written to a beloved friend who was passing the winter at the South, and whose name has already been mentioned.

A sentence in the first of these letters deserves to be noted as affording a key to one side of her character, namely: "the depressing sense of inferiority which was born with me." All her earlier years were shadowed by this morbid feeling nor was she ever quite free from its influence. It was, probably, at once a cause and an effect of the sensitive shyness that clung to her to the last. Perhaps, too, it grew in part out of her irrepressible craving for love, coupled with utter incredulity about herself possessing the qualities that rendered her so lovable. "It is one of the faults of my character," she wrote, "to fancy that nobody cares for me."

When, dear Anna, I had taken my last look at the last familiar face in Portland (I fancy you know whose face it was) I became quite as melancholy as I ever desire to be, even on the principle that "by the sadness of the countenance the heart is made better." I dare say you never had a chance to feel, and therefore will not be able to understand, the depressing sense of inferiority which was born with me, which grew with my growth and strengthened with my strength, and which, though somewhat repressed of late years, gets the mastery very frequently and makes me believe myself the most unlovable of beings. It was with this feeling that I left home and journeyed hither, wondering why I was made, and if anybody on earth will ever be a bit the happier for it, and whether I shall ever learn where to put myself in the scale of being. This is not humility, please take notice—for humility is contented, I think, with such things as it hath.

To Miss Anna S. Prentiss. Richmond, Nov. 26, 1842

When I reached Richmond last night, tired and dusty and stupefied, I felt a good deal like crawling away into some cranny and staying there the rest of my life but this morning, when I had remembered mother's existence and yours and that of some one or two others, I felt more disposed to write than anything else. Your note was a great comfort to me during two and a half hours at Portsmouth, and while on my journey. I thought pages to you in reply. How I should love to have you here in Richmond, even if I could only see you once a month, or *know* only that you were here and never see you! With many most kind friends about me, I still shall feel very keenly the separation from you. There is nobody here to whom I can speak confidingly, and my hidden spirit will have to sit with folded wings for eight months to come. To whom shall I talk about you, pray? On the way hither I fell in love with a little girl who also fell in love with me, and as I sat with her over our lonely fire at Philadelphia and in Washington, I could not help speaking of you now and then, till at last she suddenly looked up and asked me if you hadn't a brother, which question effectually shut my mouth. In a religious point of view, I am sadly off here. There is a different atmosphere in the house from what there used to be, and I look forward with some anxiety to the future.

The "little girl" referred to received soon after a letter from Miss Payson. In enclosing it to a friend, more than thirty-seven years later, she wrote: "I cried bitterly when she left us for Richmond. She was out and out good and true. When my father was taking leave of us, the last night in Washington, she proposed that as we had enjoyed so much together, we should not separate without a prayer of thanks and blessing-seeking, a proposal to which my father most heartily responded." Here is an extract from the letter:

When I look over my schoolroom I am frequently reminded of you, for my thirty-six pupils are, most of them, about your age. I have some very lovable girls under my wing. I should be too happy if there were no "unruly members" among these good and gentle ones but in the little world where I shall spend the greater part of the next eight months, as well as in the great and busy one, which as yet neither you or I know much about, I fancy there are mixtures of "the just and the unjust," of "the evil and the good." We have a very pleasant family this year. The youngest (for I omit the black baby in the kitchen) we call Lily. She is my pet and plaything, and is quite as affectionate as you are. Then comes a damsel named Beatrice, who has taken me upon *trust* just as you did. You may be thankful that your parents are not like hers, for she is to be educated *for the world* music, French and Italian crowds almost everything else out of place, and as for religious influences, she is under them here for the first time. How thankful I feel when I see such cases as this, that God gave me pious parents, who taught me from my very birth, that His fear is the *beginning* of wisdom! My roommate we call Kate. She is pious, intelligent, and very warm-hearted, and I love her dearly. She is an orphan—Mrs. Persico's daughter ...

I am rather affectionate by nature, if not in practice, and though I know that nearness to the Friend, whom I hope I have chosen, could make me happy in any circumstances, I do not pretend to be above the desire for earthly friends, provided He sees fit to give them to me. I believe my father used to say that we could not love them too much, if we only gave Him the first place in our hearts. Let us earnestly seek to make Him our all in all. It is delightful, in the midst of adversities and trials, to be able to say, "There is none upon earth that I desire besides Thee," but it requires more grace, I think, to be able to use such language when the world is bright about us. You have known little of sorrow as yet, but if you have given your whole, undivided heart to God, you will not need affliction, or to have your life made so desolate that "weariness must toss you to His breast." There is a bright side to religion, and I love to see Christians walking in the sunshine. I trust you have found this out for yourself and that your hope in Christ makes you happy in the life that now is, as well as gives you promise of blessedness in that which is to come.

Before she had been long in Richmond, she was seized with an illness, which caused her many painful, wearisome days and nights. Referring to this illness, in a letter to Miss Prentiss, she writes:

It is dull music being sick away from one's mother, but I have a knack at submitting myself to my fate so my spirit was a contented one, and I was not for a moment unhappy, except for the trouble, which I gave those who had to nurse me. I thought of you, at least two-thirds of the time. As my little pet, Lily L., said to me last night, when she had very nearly squeezed the breath out of my body, "I love you a great deal harder than I hug you" so I say to you—I love you harder than I tell, or can tell you. A happy New-Year to you, dear Anna. How much and how little in those few old words! Consider yourself kissed and goodnight.

The "New Year" was destined to be a very eventful one alike to her friend and to herself. She seemed to have a presentiment of it, at least in her own case, as some lines written on a blank leaf of her almanac for that year attest:

> With mingling hope and trust and fear
> I bid thee welcome, untried year
> The paths before me pause to view
> Which shall I shun and which pursue?
> I read my fate with serious eye
> I see dear hopes and treasures fly,
> Behold thee on thy opening wing
> Now grief, now joy, now sorrow bring.
> God grant me grace my course to run
> With one blest prayer—*His* will be done.

A little journal kept by her during the following months gives bright glimpses of her daily life. The entries are very brief, but they show that while devoted to the school, she also spent a good deal of time among her books, kept up a lively correspondence with absent friends, and contributed her full share to the entertainment of the household by "holding soirees" in her room, "reading to the girls," writing stories for them, and helping to "play goose" and other games.

To Miss Anna S. Prentiss, Richmond, Feb. 22, 1843.

Thanks to the Father of his Country for choosing to be born in Virginia! for it gives us a holiday, and I can write to you, dearest of Annas. You do not know how delighted I was to get your long-watched-for letter. You very kindly express the wish that you could bear some of my school drudgery with me. I would not give you that, but you should have love from some of these warm-hearted damsels, which would make you happy even in the midst of toil and vexation. I cannot think what makes my scholars love me so. I'm sure it is a gift for which I should be grateful, as coming from the same source with all the other blessings, which are about me. I believe my way of governing is a more fatiguing one than that of scolding, fretting, and punishing. There is a little bit of a tie between each of these hearts and mine—and the least mistake on my part severs it forever so I have to be exceedingly careful what I do and say. This keeps me in a constant state of excitement and makes my pulse fly rather faster than, as a pulse arrived at years of discretion, it ought to do. I come out of school so happy, though half tired to death, wishing I were better, and hoping I shall become so for the more my scholars love me, the more I am ashamed that I am not the pink of perfection they seem to fancy me.

Evening.—I have just come up here to my lonely room (which, if I hadn't the happiest kind of a heart in the world, would look right gloomy) and have read for the third time your dear, good letter, and all I wish is that I could tell you how I love you, and how angry I am with myself that I did not know and love you sooner. It seems so odd that we should have been born and "raised" so near each other and yet apart. You say you are a believer in destiny. So am I—particularly in affairs of the heart and I hope that we are made friends now for something more than the satisfaction that we find in loving. I am in danger of forgetting that I am to stay in this world only a little while and then *go home*. Will you help me to bear it in mind? How must the "Pilgrim's Progress" interest a mind that has never learned the whole book by rote in childhood. I have often wished I could read it as a first-told tale, and so I wish about the xiv. Of John and some other chapters in the Bible.

Your incidental mention that you have family prayers every evening produced a thousand strange sensations in my mind. I hardly know why. Did I ever tell you how I love and admire the new Bishop Johns? And how if I *am* a "good Presbyterian," as they say here, I go to hear him whenever and wherever he preaches. I do not think him a *great* man, but he has that sincerity and truthfulness of manner, which win your love at once. [4] … What nice times you must have studying German! I dreamed the night I read your account of it that I was with you, and that you said I was as stupid as an owl. I have the queerest mind somehow. It won't work like those of other people, but goes the farthest way round when it wants to go home, and I never could do anything with it but just let it have its own way, and live the longer. They are having a nice time down in the parlor worshipping Miss Ford, the light and sunshine of the house, who leaves tomorrow for Natchez, and I am going down to help them. So, goodnight.

To the same. April 24.

Since I wrote you last we have all had a good deal to put our patience and philosophy and faith to the test, and I must own that I have been for some weeks about as uncomfortable as mortal damsel could be. Everything went wrong with Mr. Persico, and his gloom extended to all of us. I never spent such melancholy weeks in my life, and became so homesick that I could hardly drag myself into school. In the midst of it, however, I made fun for the rest, as I believe I should do in a dungeon and now it is all over, I look back and laugh still.

We had a black wedding—a very black one—in my schoolroom the other night our cook having decided to take to herself a lord and master. It was the funniest affair I ever saw. Such comical dresses! Such heaps of cake, wine, coffee, and candy! Such kissings and huggings! The man who performed the ceremony prayed that they might *obey each other*, wherein I think he showed his originality and good sense, too. Then he held a book upside down and pretended to read, dear knows what! but the Professor—that is to say, Mrs. P.—laughed so loud when he said, "Will you take this woman to be your wedded *husband*" that we all joined in full chorus, whereupon the poor priest (who was only the sexton of St. James') was so confused that he married them over twice. I never saw a couple in their station in life provided with a tenth part of the luxuries with which they abounded. We worked all day Saturday in the kitchen, making and icing cake for them, and a nice frolic we had of it, too. Do you love babies? We have a black one in the lot whom I pet for want of something on which to expend my love.

When I find anything that will interest the whole family, I read it aloud for general edification. The girls persuaded me into writing a story to read to them, and locked me into my room till it was done. It was the first love-story I ever wrote, for hitherto I have not known enough about such things to be able to do it. This reminds me that you asked if I intend forgetting you after I am married. I have no sort of idea what I shall do, provided I ever marry. But if I ever fall in love, I dare say I shall do it so madly and absorbingly as to become, in a measure and for a season, forgetful of everything and everybody else. Still, though I hate professions, I do not see how I can ever cease to love you, whatever else I forget or neglect. There is a restlessness in my affection for you that I do not understand—a half wish to avoid enjoyment now, that I may in some future time share it with you. And yet I have a presentiment that we may have sympathy in trials of which I now know nothing.

I am ashamed of myself, of late, that these subjects of love and matrimony find a place in my thoughts, which I never have been in the habit of giving them, but people here talk of little else and I am borne on with the current. I think that to give happiness in married life a woman should possess oceans of self-sacrificing love and I, for one, haven't half of that self-forgetting spirit which I think essential.

I am glad you like the "Christian Year," and I see you are quite an Episcopalian. Well, if you are like the good old English divines, nobody can find fault with your choice. Mr. Persico was brought up a Catholic but professes to be a *nothingarian* now. For myself, this only I know that I earnestly wish all the tendencies of my heart to be heavenward, and I believe that the sincere inquirer after truth will be guided by the Infinite Mind. And so on, that faith I venture myself and feel safe as a child may feel, who holds his father's hand. Life seems full of mysteries to me of late—and I am tempted to strange thoughtfulness in the midst of its gayest scenes.

How true was the "presentiment" described in this letter, will appear in her correspondence with the same friend more than a quarter of a century later.

To Anna S. Prentiss, Richmond, June 1, 1843

I believe you and I were intended to know each other better I have found a certain something in you that I have been wanting all my life. While I wish you to know me just as I am, faults and all, I can t bear to think of ever seeing anything but the good and the beautiful in your character, dear Anna, and I believe my heart would break outright should I find you to be otherwise than just that which I imagine you are. I do not know why I am saying this but I have learned more of the world during the last year than in any previous half dozen of my life, and the result is dissatisfaction and alarm at the things I see about me. I wish I could always live, as I have hitherto done, under the shelter of my mother's wing.... I ought to ask your pardon for writing in this horrid style, but I was born to do things by steam, I believe, and cannot do them moderately. As I write to, so I love you, dear Anna, with all my interests and energies tending to that one point. I was amused the other day with a young lady who came and sat on my bed when I was sick (for I am just getting well from a quite serious illness), and after some half dozen sighs, wished she were Anna Prentiss that she might be loved as intensely as she desired. This is a roundabout way of saying how very dear you are to me. What chatterboxes girls are! I wonder how many times I've stopped to say "My dear, do not talk so much—for I am writing in school."

June 27th—Mr. —— brought "The Home" to me and I have laughed and cried over it to my heart's content. Out of pure self-love, because they said she was like me, I liked poor Petra with the big nose, best of the bunch—though, to be sure, they liken me to somebody or other in every book we read till I begin to think myself quite a bundle of contradictions. I have a thousand and one things to say to you, but I wonder if as soon as I see you I shall straightway turn into a poker, and play the stiffy, as I always do when I have been separated from my friends. I am writing in a little bit of a den that, by a new arrangement, I have all to myself. What if there's no table here and I have to write upon the bureau, sitting on one foot in a chair and stretching upwards to reach my paper like a monkey? What do I care? I am writing to *you*, and your spirit, invoked when I took possession of the premises, comes here sometimes just between daylight and dark, and talks to me till I am ready to put forth my hand to find yours. Oh! Anna, you must be everything that is pure and good, through to the very depths of your heart, that mine may not ache in finding it has loved only an imaginary being. Not that I expect you to be perfect—for I shouldn't love you if you were immaculate—but pure in aim and intention and desire, which I believe you to be.

29th.—Do you want to know what mischief I've just been at? There lay poor Miss ———, alias "Weaky" as we call her, taking her siesta in the most innocent manner imaginable, with a babe-in-the-wood kind of air, which proved so highly attractive that I could do no less than pick her up in my arms and pop her (I do not know *but* it was *head* first), right into the bathing-tub which happened to be filled with fresh cold water. Poor, good little Weaky! There she sits shaking and shivering and laughing with such perfect sweet humor, that I am positively taking a vow never to do so again. Well, I had something quite sentimental to say to you when I began writing, but as the spirit moved me to the above perpetration of nonsense, I've nothing left in me but fun, and for that you've no relish, have you?

I made out to cry yesterday and thereby have so refreshed my soul as to be in the best possible humor just now. The why and wherefore of my tears, which by the way I do not shed once in an age, was briefly the withdrawal from school of one of my scholars, one who had so attached herself to me as to have become almost a part of myself, and whom I had taught to love you, dear Anna, that I might have the exquisite satisfaction of talking about you every day—a sort of sweet interlude between grammar and arithmetic which made the dull hours of school grow harmonious. She had a presentiment that her life was to close with our school session, from which I couldn't move her even when her health was good, and she says that she prays every day, not that her life may be lengthened, but that she may die before I am gone. I am superstitious enough to feel that the prayer may have its answer, now that I see her drooping and fading away without perceptible disease. The only time I ever witnessed the rite of confirmation was when the hands of the good bishop rested upon her head, and no wonder if I have half taken up arms in defense of this "laying-on of hands," out of the abundance of my heart if not from the wisdom of my head. Well, I've lost my mirthful mood, speaking of her, and do not know when it will come again.

I have taken it into my head that you will visit Niagara on your way home from the South and have half a mind to go there myself. Did your brother bring home the poems of R. M. Milnes? I half hope that he did not, since I want to see you enjoy them for the first time, particularly a certain "Household Brownie" story, with which I fell in love when President Woods sent us the volume.

Here follow a few entries in her diary:

May 1.—Holiday. Into the country all of us, white, black, and gray. Sue Empie devoted herself to me like a lover and so did Sue Lewis, so I was not at a loss for society. My girls made a bower, wherein I was ensconced and obliged to tell stories to about forty listeners till my tongue ached. *July 18th.*—Left Richmond. *Aug. 2nd.*—Left Reading for Philadelphia. *5th.*—Williamstown and saw mother, sister and baby. *16th.*—President Hopkins' splendid address before the Alumni—also that of Dr. Robbins. *18th.*—Left Williamstown and reached Nonantum House at night. Saw Aunt Willis, Julia, Sarah, Ellen, etc. *22nd.*—Came home, oh so very happy! Dear, good home! *23rd.*—Callers all day, the second of whom was Mr. P. There have been nineteen people here and I'm tired! *25th.*—What *didn't* I hear from Anna P. today! *31st.*—Rode with Anna P. to Saccarappa to see Rev. Mr. and Mrs. H. B. Smith—took tea at the P.s and went with them to the Preparatory Lecture. I do nothing but go about from place to place. *Sept. 1st.*—Just as cold as cold could be all day. Spent evening at Mrs. B.'s, talking with Neal Dow. *9th.*—Cold and blowy and disagreeable. Went to see Carrie H. Came home and found Mr. P. here he stayed to tea—read us some interesting things—told us about Mary and William Howitt. *10th.*—Our church was re-opened today. Mr. Dwight preached in the morning and Mr. Chickering in the afternoon.

September 11th she marked with a white stone and kept ever after as one of the chief festal days of her life, but of the reason why there is here no record. The diary for the rest of the year is blank with the exception of a single leaf, which contains these sentences:

"Celle qui a besoin d'admirer ce qu'elle aime, celle, do not le judgment est pénétrant, bien que son imagination exaltée, il n'y a pour elle qu'un objet dans l'univers."

"Celui qu'on aime, est le vengeur des fautes qu'on a commis sur cette terre la Divinité lui prête son pouvoir."

MAD. DE STAEL.

* * * * *

III.

Her Views of Love and Courtship. Visit of her Sister and Child. Letters. Sickness and Death of Friends. Ill-Health. Undergoes a Surgical Operation. Her Fortitude. Study of German. Fenelon.

The records of the next year and a half are very abundant, in the form of notes, letters, verses, and journals but they are mostly of too private a character to furnish materials for this narrative, belonging to what she called "the deep story of my heart." They breathe the sweetness and sparkle with the morning dew of the affections and while some of them are full of fun and playful humor, others glow with all the impassioned earnestness of her nature, and others still with deep religious feeling. She wrote:

My heart seems to me somewhat like a very full church at the close of the services—the great congregation of my affections trying to find their way out and crowding and hindering each other in the general rush for the door. Do not you see them—the young ones scampering first down the aisle, and the old and grave and stately ones coming with proud dignity after them?... I feel now that "dans les mystères de notre nature aimer, *encore aimer,* est ce qui nous est resté de notre heritage céleste," and oh, how I thank God for my blessed portion of this celestial endowment!

Love in a word was to her, after religion, the holiest and most wonderful reality of life and in the presence of its mysteries she was—to use her own comparison—"like a child standing upon the seashore, watching for the onward rush of the waves, venturing himself close to the water's edge, holding his breath and wooing their approach, and then, as they come dashing in, retreating with laughter and mock fear, only to return to tempt them anew." Her only solicitude was lest the new interest should draw her heart away from Him who had been its chief joy. In a letter to her cousin, she touches on this point:

You know how by circumstances my affections have been repressed, and now, having found *liberty to love,* I am tempted to seek my heaven in so loving. But, my dear cousin, there is nothing worth having apart from God I feel this every day more and more and the fear of satisfying myself with something short of Him—this is my only anxiety. This drives me to the throne of His grace and makes me refuse to be left one moment to myself. I believe I desire first of all to love God supremely and to do something for Him, if He spares my life.

Early in December her sister, Mrs. Hopkins, with an infant boy, came to Portland and passed a part of the winter under the maternal roof. The arrival of this boy—her mother's first grandchild—was an event in the family history. Here is her own picture of the scene:

It was a cold evening, and grandmamma, who had been sitting by the fire, knitting, and reading, had at last let her book fall from her lap, and had dropped to sleep in her chair. The four uncles sat around the table, two of them playing chess, and two looking on, while Aunt Fanny, with her cat on her knees, studied German a little, looked at the clock very often, and started at every noise.

"I have said, all along, that they would not come," she cried at last. "The clock has just struck nine, and I am not going to expect them any longer. I *knew* Herbert would not let Laura undertake such a journey in the depth of winter or, at any rate, that Laura's courage would tail at the last moment."

She had hardly uttered these words, when there was a ring at the doorbell, then a stamping of feet on the mat, to shake off the snow, and in they Came, Lou, and Lou's papa, and Lou's mamma, bringing ever so much fresh, cold air with them. Grandmamma woke up, and rose to meet them with steps as lively as if she were a young girl Aunt Fanny tossed the cat from her lap, and seized the bundle that held the baby the four uncles crowded about her, eager to get the first peep at the little wonder. There was such a laughing, and such a tumult, that poor Lou, coming out of the dark night into the bright room, and seeing so many strange faces, did not know what to think. When his auntie's eager hands at last pulled off his cloaks, shawls, and capes, there came into view a serious little face, a pair of bright eyes, and a head as smooth as ivory, on which there was not a single hair. His sleeves were looped up with corals, and showed his plump white arms, and he sat up very straight, and took a good look at everybody.

"What a perfect little beauty!" "What *splendid* eyes!" "What a lovely skin!" "He's the perfect image of his father!" "He's *exactly* like his mother!" "What a dear little nose!" "What fat little hands, full of dimples!" "Let *me* take him!" "Come to his own grandmamma!" "Let his uncle toss him—so he will!" "What does he eat?" "Is he tired?" "Now, Fanny! You've had him ever since he came he wants to come to me I know he does!"

These, and nobody knows how many more exclamations of the sort, greeted the ears of the little stranger, and were received by him with unruffled gravity.

"Aunt Fanny" devoted herself during the following weeks to the care of her little nephew. Her letters written at the time—some of them with him in her arms—are full of his pretty ways and when, more than a score of years later, he had given his young life to his country and was sleeping in a soldier's grave, his "sayings and doings" formed the subject of one of her most attractive juvenile books.

A few extracts from her letters will give glimpses of her state of mind during this winter, and show also how the thoughtful spirit, which from the first tempered the excitements of her new experience, was deepened by the loss of very dear friends.

PORTLAND, *December 9, 1843.*

Last evening I spent at Mrs. H.———'s with Abby and a crowd of other people. John Neal told me I had a great bump of love of approbation, and conscientiousness very large, and self-esteem hardly any and that he hoped whoever had most influence over me would remedy that evil. He then went on to pay me the most extravagant compliments, and said I could become distinguished in any way I pleased. Thinks I to myself, "I should like to be the best little wife in the world, and that's the height of my ambition." Do not imagine now that I believe all he says, for he has been saying just such things to me since I was a dozen years old, and I do not see, as I am any great things yet. Do you?

Jan. 3rd, 1844.—Sister is still here and will stay with us a month or two yet. Her husband has gone home to preach and pray himself into contentment without her. However, he was here only a week, his quiet Christian excellence made us all long to grow better. It is always the case when he comes, though he rather lives than talks his religion. I never saw, as far as piety is concerned, a more perfect specimen of a man in his every-day life.

Do you pray for me every night and every morning? Do not forget how I comfort myself with thinking that you every day ask for me those graces of the Spirit which I so long for. Indeed, I have had lately such heavenward yearnings! Why do you ask *if* I pray for you, as if I could love you and *help* praying for you continually and always? I have no light sense of the holiness a Christian minister should possess. I half wish there were no veil upon my heart on this point, which you might see how, from the very first hour of your return from abroad, my interest in you, went hand-in-hand with this *looking upward.*

Jan. 22nd.—We have all been saddened by the repeated trials with which our friends the Willises are visited this winter. Mrs. Willis is still very ill, and there is no hope of her recovery and Ellen, the pet of the whole household—the always happy, loving, beautiful young thing—who had been full of delight in the hope of becoming a mother, lies now at the point of death having lost her infant, and with it her bright anticipations. For fourteen years, there had not been a physician in their house, and you may imagine how they are all now taken, as it were, by surprise by the first break, death has threatened to make in their peculiarly happy circle. Our love for all the family has grown with our growth and strengthened with our strength and what touches them we all feel.

Feb. 8th.—How is it that people who have no refuge in God live through the loss of those they love? I am very sad this morning, and almost wish I had never loved you or anybody. Last night we heard of the death of Julia Willis' sister, and this morning learn that a dear little girl in whom we all were much interested, and whom I saw on Saturday only slightly unwell, is taken away from her parents, who have no manner of consolation in losing this only child. There is a great cloud throughout our house, and we hardly know what to do with ourselves. When I met mother and sister yesterday on my return from your house, I saw that something was the matter of which they hesitated to tell me and of whom should I naturally think but of you—you in whom my life is bound up and, when mother finally came to put her arms around me, I suffered for the moment that intensity of anguish which I should feel in knowing that something dreadful had befallen you. She told me, however, of poor Ellen's death, and I was so lost in recovering you again that I cared for nothing else all the evening, and until this morning had scarcely thought of the aching, aching hearts she has left behind. Her poor young husband, who loved her so tenderly, is half-distracted.

Oh, I have blessed God today that until He had given me a sure and certain hold upon Himself, He had not suffered me to love as I love now! It is a mystery, which I cannot understand, how the heart can live on through the moment, which rends it asunder from that of which it has become a part, except by hiding itself in God. I have felt Ellen's death the more, because she and her husband were associated in my mind with you. I hardly know how or why but she told me much of the history of her heart when I saw her last summer on my way home from Richmond, at the same time that she spoke much of you. She had seen you at our house before you went abroad, and seemed to have a sort of presentiment that we should love each other.

But I ought to beg you to forgive me for sending you this gloomy page yet I was restless and wanted to tell you the thoughts that have been in my heart towards you today—the serious and saddened love with which I love you, when I think of you as one whom God may take from me at any moment. I do not know that it is unwise to look this truth in the face sometimes—for if ever there was heart tempted to idolatry, to giving itself up fully, utterly, with perfect abandonment of every other hope and interest, to an earthly love, so is mine tempted now.

Feb. 13th.—Mother is going to Boston with sister on Saturday, provided I am well enough (which I mean to be), as Mrs. Willis has expressed a strong wish to see her once more. We heard from them yesterday again. Poor Ellen's coffin was placed just where she stood as a bride, less than eight months ago, and her little infant rested on her breast. There is rarely a death so universally mourned as hers she was the most winning and attractive young creature I ever saw.

Feb. 21st.—Are you in earnest? Are you in earnest? Are you really coming home in March? I am afraid to believe, afraid to doubt it. I am crying, laughing, and writing all at once. You would not tell me so unless you *really were coming*, I know ... And you are coming home! (How madly my heart is beating! lie still, will you?) I almost feel that you are here and that you look over my shoulder and read while I write. Are you sure that you will come? Oh, do not repent and send me another letter to say that you will wait until it is pleasanter weather it is pleasant now. I walked out this morning, and the air was a spring air, and gentlemen go through the streets with their cloaks hanging over their arms, and there is a constant plashing against the windows, of water dripping down from the melting snow yes, I verily believe that it is warm, and that the birds will sing soon—I do, upon my word ... I would not have the doctor come and feel my pulse this afternoon for anything. He would prescribe fever powders or fever drops, or something of the sort, and bleed me and send me to bed, or to the insane hospital, I do not know which. I could cry, sing, dance, and laugh, all at once. Oh, that I knew exactly when you will be here—the day, the hour, the minute, that I might know to just what point to govern my impatient heart—for it would be a pity to punish the poor little thing too severely. I have been reading today something which delighted me very much do you remember a little poem of Goethe's, in which an imprisoned count sings about the flower he loves best, and the rose, the lily, the pink, and the violet, each in turn fancy themselves the objects of his love. [5] You see I put you in the place of the prisoner at the outset, and I was to be the flower of his love, whatever it might be. Well, it was the "Forget-me-not." If there were a flower called the "Always-loving," maybe I might find out to what order and class I belong. Dear me there's the old clock striking twelve, and I verily meant to go to bed at ten, so as to sleep away as much of the time as possible before your coming, but I fell into a fit of loving meditation, and forgot everything else. You should have seen me pour out tea to-night! Why, the first thing I knew, I had poured it all out into my own cup till it ran over, and half filled the waiter, which is the first time I ever did such a ridiculous thing in my life. But, dearest, I bid you good night, praying you may have sweet dreams and an inward prompting to write me a long, long, blessed letter, such as shall make me dance about the house and sing.

Feb. 22nd.—Oh, I am frightened at myself, I am so happy! It seems as if even this whole folio would not in the least convey to you the gladness with which my heart is dancing, singing, and making merry. The doctor seems quite satisfied with my shoulder, and says, "*It's first-rate*" so set your heart at rest on that point. I hope there will be nobody within two miles of our meeting. Suppose you stop in some out of the way place just out of town, and let me trot out there to see you? Oh, are you really coming?

To G, E. S. March 4, 1844.

I must write a few lines to tell you, my dear cousin that I am thinking of and praying for you on your birthday. I have but one request to offer either for you or for myself, and that is for more love to our Redeemer. I bless God that I have no other want.... I do not know why it is, but I never have thought so much of death and of the certainty that I, sooner or later, must die, as within a few months past. I am not exactly superstitious, but this daily and hourly half-presentiment that my life will not be a long one, is singularly subduing, and seems to lay a restraining hand upon future plans. I am not sorry, whatever may be the event, that it is so. I dread clinging to this world and seeking my rest in it. I am not afraid to die, or afraid that anything I love may be taken from me I only have this serious and thoughtful sense of death upon my mind. You know how we have loved the Willis family, and can imagine how we felt the death of their youngest daughter, who was dear to everybody. And Mrs. Willis is, probably, not living. This has added to my previous feeling on the subject, which was, perhaps, first occasioned by the sudden and terrible loss of my poor friend, Mr. Thatcher, a year ago this month. [6] God forbid I should ever forget the lessons He saw I needed, and dare to feel that there is a thing upon earth which death may not touch. Oh, in how many ways He has sought to win my whole heart for His own!

March 22nd.—I was interrupted last night by the arrival of G. L. P., after his four months' absence in Mississippi, improved in health, and in looks, and in spirits, and quite as glad to see me, I believe, as even you, in your goodness of heart, say my lover ought to be. However, I will tell you the truth, my dear cousin, I am *afraid* of love. There is no other medium, save that of the happiness of loving and being loved, which could effectually turn my affections from divine to earthly things. Am I not then on dangerous ground? Yet God mercifully shows me that it is so, and when I think how He has saved me hitherto through sharp temptations, it seems wicked, distrust of Him, not to feel that He will save me through those to come. I know now there are some of the great lessons of life yet to be learned I believe I must *suffer* as long as I have an earthly existence. Will not then God make that suffering but as a blessed reproof to bring me nearer Himself? I hope so.

During the winter, her health had become so much impaired, that great anxiety was felt as to the issue. In a letter to her friend, Miss Ellen Thurston, dated April 20, 1844, she writes:

You remember, perhaps, that on the afternoon you were so good as to come and spend with me, I was making a fuss about a little thing on my shoulder. Well, I had at last to have it removed, and though the operation was not in itself very painful, its effects on my whole nervous system have been most powerful. I have lost all regular habits of sleep—for a week I do not know that I slept two hours—and am ready to fly into a fit at the bare thought of sitting still long enough to write a common letter. I have, however, the consolation of being pitied and consoled with, as there is something in the idea of cutting at the flesh that touches the heart, a thousand times more than some severer sufferings would do. I am getting quite thin and weak upon it, and I believe mother firmly expects me to shrink into nothing, though I am a pretty bouncing girl still.

Owing to some mishap, the healing process was entirely thwarted, and after a very trying summer, the operation had to be repeated. This time it was performed by that eminent surgeon and admirable Christian man, Dr. John C. Warren of Boston, assisted by his son, Dr. J. M. W. Dr. Warren told Miss Payson's friend, who had accompanied an invalid sister to New York, that he thought it would require "about five minutes" but it proved to be much more serious than he had anticipated. Miss Willis, in her letter from Geneva already quoted, thus refers to it:

My next meeting with Lizzy revealed a striking trait of her character, which hitherto I had had no opportunity of observing—her wonderful fortitude under suffering. I was at the seashore with my sister and family when, her little child, being taken suddenly very ill in the night, I went up to Boston by an early train to bring down as soon as possible our family physician. On arriving at his house I was disappointed at being told that he could not come at once, being engaged to perform an operation that morning. While waiting for the return train, I called at my father's office and was surprised to hear that Lizzy was the patient. A painful tumor had developed itself on the back of her neck, and she had come up with her mother to Boston to consult Dr. Warren, who had advised its immediate removal.

I went at once to see her. She greeted me with even more than her usual warmth and after stating in a few words the object of her coming to Boston and that she was expecting the doctors every moment, she added: "You will stay with me, I am sure. Mother insists on being present, but she cannot bear it. She will be sure to faint. If you will promise to stay, I can persuade her to remain in the next room." Seeing the distress in my face at the request, she said, "I will be very good. You will have nothing to do but sit in the room, to satisfy mother." It was impossible to refuse and I remained. There was no chloroform then to give blessed unconsciousness of suffering and every pang had to be endured, but she more than kept her promise to "be good." Not a sound or a movement betrayed suffering. She spoke only once. After the knife was laid aside and the threaded needle was passed through the quivering flesh to draw the gaping edges of the wound together, she asked, after the first stitch had been completed, in a low, almost calm tone, with only a slight tremulousness, how many more were to be taken. When the operation was over, and the surgeons were preparing to depart, she questioned them minutely as to the mark, which would be left after healing. I was surprised that she could think of it at such a moment, knowing how little value she had always set on her personal appearance, but her mother explained it afterward by referring to her betrothal to you, and the fear that you would find the scar disfiguring. [7]

In a letter to Mrs. Stearns, [8] she herself writes, Sept. 6:

I had no idea of the suffering that awaited me. I thought I should get off as I did the first time. But I have a great deal to be thankful for. On Wednesday, to my infinite surprise and gladness, George pounced down upon me from New York, having been quite cut to the heart by the account mother gave him. Everybody is so kind, and I have had so many letters, and seen so many sympathizing faces, and "dear Lizzy" sounds so sweet to my insatiable ears and yet—and yet—I would rather die than live through the forty-eight hours again which began on Monday morning. Somebody must have prayed for me, or I never should have got through.

An extract from another of her letters, dated Portland, September 11th, belongs here:

I must tell you, too, about Dr. Warren (the old one). When mother asked him concerning the amount he was to receive from her for his professional services, he smiled and said, "I shall not charge *you* much, and as for Miss Payson, when she is married and rich, she may pay me and welcome—but not till then." I told him I never expected to be rich, and he replied, with what mother thought an air of contentment that said he knew all about it: "Well, we can be happy without riches," and such a good, happy smile shone all over his face as I have seldom been so fortunate as to see in an old man. As for the young one, he seemed as glad when I was dressed on Sunday with a clean frock and no shawl, as if it were really a matter of consequence to him to see his patients looking comfortable and well. I am getting along finely there is only one spot on my shoulder which is troublesome, and they ordered me on a very strict diet for that—so I am half-starved this blessed minute. We went to Newburyport on Monday, and stayed there with Anna until yesterday afternoon. I think the motion of the cars hurt me somewhat, but by the time you get here, I do hope I shall be quite well.

Evening. — ... I have had such happy thoughts and prayers to-night! You should certainly have knelt with me in my little room, where, for the first time a year ago this evening, I asked God to bless *us* and you too, perhaps, then began first to pray for me. Oh, what a wonderful time it was! I hope you have prayed for me today—I do not mean as you always do, but with new prayers wherewith to begin the New Year. God bless you and love you!

But this period was also one of large mental growth. It was marked especially by two events that had a shaping influence upon both her intellectual and religious character. One was the study of German. She was acquainted already with French and Italian she now devoted her leisure hours to the language and works of Schiller and Goethe. These opened to her a new world of thought and beauty. Her correspondence contains frequent allusions to the progress of her German reading. Here is one in a letter to her cousin:

I have read George Herbert a good deal this winter. I have also read several of Schiller's plays—William Tell and Don Carlos among the rest—and got a great deal more excited over them than I have over anything for a long while. George has a large German library, but I do not suppose I shall be much the wiser for it, unless I turn to studying theology. Did you read in Goethe's Wilhelm Meister, the "Bekenntnisse einer schönen Seele"? I do think it did my soul good when I read it last July. The account she gives of her religious history reminded me of mine in some points very strongly.

The other incident was her introduction to the writings of Fenelon—an author whom, in later years, she came to regard as an oracle of spiritual wisdom. In the letter just quoted, she writes, "I am reading Fenelon's 'Maximes des Saints,' and many of his ideas please me exceedingly. Some of his 'Lettres Spirituelles' are delicious—so heavenly, so child-like in their spirit." [9]

[1] *Jan, 1, 1845.*—I used never to confide my religious feelings to anyone in the world. I went on my toilsome, comfortless way quite by myself. But when at the end of this long, gloomy way, I saw and knew and rejoiced in Christ, then I forgot myself and my pride and my reserve, and was glad if a little child would hear me say "I love Him!"—glad if the most ignorant, the most hitherto despised, would speak of Him.

[2] Later, she writes, "I have had a long talk with sister today about Leighton. She claims him, as all the Perfectionists do, as one of their number though, by the way, in the common acceptation of the word, she is not a Perfectionist herself, but only on the boundary-line of the enchanted ground. I am completely puzzled when I think on such subjects. I doubt if sister is right, yet know not where she is wrong. She does not obtrude her peculiar opinions on any one, and I began the conversation this afternoon myself."

[3] "Oh, what a blessed thing it is to lose one's will! Since I have lost my will, I have found happiness. There can be no such thing as disappointment to me, for I have no desires but that God's will may be accomplished." "Christians might avoid much trouble if they would only believe what they profess, viz.: that God is able to make them happy without anything but Himself. They imagine that if such a dear friend were to die, or such and such blessings to be removed, they should be miserable whereas God can make them a thousand times happier without them. To mention my own case: God has been depriving me of one blessing after another but as everyone was removed, He has come in and filled up its place and now, when I am a cripple and not able to move, I am happier than ever I was in my life before or ever expected to be and if I had believed this twenty years ago, I might have been spared much anxiety."

[4] The Right Rev. John Johns, Bishop of the Protestant Episcopal Church of Virginia, was a man of apostolic simplicity and zeal, and universally beloved. An almost ideal friendship existed between him and Dr. Charles Hodge, of Princeton. *Dear, blessed, old John,* Dr. H. called him when he was seventy-nine years old. See Life of Dr. Hodge, pp. 564-569. Bishop Johns died in 1876.

[5] Das Blümlein Wunderschön. *Lied des gefangenen Grafen*, is the title of the poem. Goethe's Samtliche Werke. Vol. I., p. 151.

[6] See appendix A

[7] The horrible operation is over, Heaven be praised! It was far more horrible than we had anticipated. They were *an hour and a quarter*, before all was done. I was very brave at first and would not leave the room, but I found myself so faint that I feared falling and had to go. Lizzy behaved like a heroine indeed, so that even the doctors admired her fortitude. She never spoke, but was deadly faint, so that they were obliged to lay her down that the dreadful wound might bleed then there was an artery to be taken up and tied then six stitches to be taken with a great big needle. Most providentially dear Julia Willis came in about ten minutes before the doctors and though she was greatly distressed, she never faints, and staid till Lizzy was laid in bed…. She was just like a marble statue, but even more beautiful, while the blood stained her shoulders and bosom. You could not have looked on such suffering without fainting, man that you are.—*From a letter of Mrs. Payson, dated Boston, Sept. 2, 1844.*

[8] Her friend, Miss Prentiss, had been married, in the previous autumn, to the Rev. Jonathan F. Stearns, of Newburyport.

[9] "Explication des Maximes des Saints sur la Vie Intérieure" is the full title of the famous little work first named. It appeared in January, 1697. If measured by the storm it raised in France and at Rome, or by the attention it attracted throughout Europe, its publication may be said to have been one of the most important theological events of that day. The eloquence of Bossuet and the power of Louis XIV were together exerted to the utmost in order to brand its illustrious author as a heretical Quietist and, through their almost frantic efforts, it was at last condemned in a papal

brief. But, for all that, the little work is full of the noblest Christian sentiments. It pushes the doctrine of pure love, perhaps, to a perilous extreme, but still an extreme that leans to the side of the highest virtue. After its condemnation the Pope, Innocent XII., wrote to the French prelates, who had been most prominent in denouncing Fenelon: *Peccavit excessu amoris divini, sed vos peccastis defectu amoris proximi*—i.e., "He has erred by too much love of God, but ye have erred by too little love of your neighbor."

CHAPTER 4 - THE YOUNG WIFE AND MOTHER - 1845-1850.

I.

Marriage and Settlement in New Bedford. Reminiscences. Letters. Birth of her First Child. Death of her Sister-in-Law. Letters.

On the 16th of April, 1845, Miss Payson was married to the Rev. George Lewis Prentiss, then just ordained as pastor of the South Trinitarian church in New Bedford, Mass. Here she passed the next five and a half years rendered memorable by precious friendships formed in them, by the birth of two of her children, by the death of her mother, and by other deep joys and sorrows. New Bedford was then known, the world over, as the most important centre of the whale-fishery. In quest of the leviathans of the deep, its ships traversed all seas, from the tumbling icebergs of the Arctic Ocean to the Southern Pacific. But it was also known nearer home for the fine social qualities of its people. Many of the original settlers of the town were Quakers, and its character had been largely shaped by their friendly influence. Husbands and wives, whether young or old, called each other everywhere by their Christian names, and a charming simplicity marked the daily intercourse of life. Into this attractive society, Mrs. Prentiss was at once welcomed. The Arnold family in particular—a family representing alike the friendly spirit, the refinement and taste, the wealth, and the generous hospitality of the place—here deserve mention. Their kindness was unwearied flowers and fruit came often from their splendid garden and greenhouses and, in various other ways, they contributed from the moment of her coming to render New Bedford a pleasant home to her.

But it was in her husband's parish that she found her chief interest and joy. His people at first welcomed her in the warmest manner on her sainted father's account, but they soon learned to love her for her own sake. She early began to manifest among them that wonderful sympathy, which made her presence like sunshine in sick rooms and in the house of mourning, and, in later years, endeared her through her writings to so many hearts. While her natural shyness and reserve caused her to shrink from everything like publicity, and even from that leadership in the more private activities of the church, which properly belonged to her sex and station, any kind of trouble instantly aroused and called into play all her energies. The sickness and death of little children wrought upon her with singular power and, in ministering aid and comfort to bereaved mothers, she seemed like one specially anointed of the Lord for this gentle office. Now, after the lapse of more than a third of a century, there are those in New Bedford and its vicinity who bless her memory, as they recall scenes of sharp affliction cheered by her presence and her loving sympathy.

The following reminiscences by one of her New Bedford friends, written not long after her death, belong here:

Oh, that I had the pen of a ready writer! How gladly would I depict her just as she came to New Bedford, a youthful bride and our pastor's wife, more than a third of a century ago! My remembrances of her are still fresh and delightful but they have been for so many years' *silent* memories that I feel quite unable fully to express them. And yet I will try to give you a few simple details. Several things strike me as I recall her in those days. Our early experiences in the struggle of life had been somewhat similar and this drew us near to each other. She was naturally very shy and in the presence of strangers, or of uncongenial persons, her reserve was almost painful but with her friends—especially those of her own sex—all this vanished and she was full of animated talk. Her conversation abounded in bright, pointed sayings, in fine little touches of humor, in amusing anecdotes and incidents of her own experience, which she related with astonishing ease and fluency, sometimes also in downright girlish fun and drollery and all was rendered doubly attractive by her low, sweet woman's voice and her merry, fitful laugh. Yet these things were but the sparkle of a very deep and serious nature. Even then, her religious character was to me wonderful. She seemed always to know just what was prompting her, whether, nature, or grace and her perception of the workings of the two principles was like an instinct. While I, though cherishing a Christian hope, was still struggling in bondage under the law, she appeared to enjoy to the full the glorious liberty of the children of God. And when I would say to her that I was constantly doing that which I ought not and leaving undone so much that I ought to do, she would try to comfort me and to encourage me to exercise more faith by responding, "Oh, you do not know what a great sinner I am but Christ's love is greater still." There was a helpful, assuring, sunshiny influence about her piety, which I have rarely seen or felt in any other human being. And almost daily, during all the years of separation, I have been conscious of this influence in my own life.

I remember her as very retiring in company, even among our own people. But if there were children present, she would gather them about her and hold them spellbound by her talk. Oh, she was a marvelous storyteller! How often have I seen her in the midst of a little group, who, all eyes and ears, gazed into her face and eagerly swallowed every word, while she, intent on amusing them, seemed quite unconscious that anybody else was in the room. Mr. H——— used to say, "How I envy those children and wish I were one of them!"

Mrs. Prentiss received much attention from persons outside of our congregation, and who, from their position and wealth, were pretty exclusive in their habits. But they could not resist the attraction of her rare gifts and accomplishments. New Bedford at that time, as you know, had a good deal of intellectual and social culture. This was particularly the case among the Unitarians, whose minister, when you came to us, was that excellent and very superior man, the Rev. Ephraim Peabody, D.D., afterwards of King's Chapel in Boston. One of the leading families of his flock was the "Arnold family," whose garden and grounds were then among the finest in the State and at whose house such men as Richard H. Dana, the poet, the late Professor Agassiz, and others eminent for their literary and scientific attainments, were often to be seen. This whole family were warmly attached to Mrs. Prentiss, and after you left New Bedford, often referred to their acquaintance with her in the most affectionate manner. And I believe Mr. Arnold and his daughter used to visit you in New York. The father, mother, daughter, and aunt are all gone. And what a change have all these vanished years wrought in the South Trinitarian society! I can think of only six families then worshipping there, that are worshipping there now. But so long as a single one remains, the memory of Mrs. Prentiss will still be precious in the old church.

The story of the New Bedford years may be told, with slight additions here and there, by Mrs. Prentiss' own pen. Most of her letters to her own family are lost but the letters to her husband, when occasionally separated from her, and others to old friends, have been preserved and afford an almost continuous narrative of this period. A few extracts from some of those written in 1845, will show in what temper of mind she entered upon her new life. The first is dated Portland, January both, just after Mr. Prentiss received the call to New Bedford:

I have wished all along, beyond anything else, not so much that we might have a pleasant home, pleasant scenery, and circumstances, good society and the like, as that we might have good, holy influences about us, and God's grace and love within us. And for you, dear George, I did not so much desire the intellectual and other attractions, about which we have talked sometimes, as a dwelling-place among those whom you might train heavenward or who would not be a hindrance in your journey thither. Through this whole affair I know I have thought infinitely more of you than of myself. And if you are happy at the North Pole shan't I be happy there too? I shall be heartily thankful to see you a pastor with a people to love you. Only I shall be jealous of them.

To her friend, Miss Thurston, she writes from New Bedford, April 28th:

I thank you with all my heart for your letter and for the very pretty gift, which I suppose to be the work of your own hands. I cannot tell you how inexpressibly dear to me are all the expressions of affection I have received and am receiving from old friends. We have been here ten days, and very happy days they have been to me, notwithstanding I have had to see so many strange faces and to talk to so many new people. And both my sister and Anna tell me that the first months of married life are succeeded by far happier ones still so I shall go on my way rejoicing. As to what your brother says about disappointment, nobody believes his doctrine better than I do but life is as full of blessings as it is of disappointments, I conceive, and if we only know how, we may often, out of mere *will*, get the former instead of the latter. I have had some experience of the "conflict and dismay" of this present evil world but then I have also had some of its smiles. Neither of these ever made me angry with this life, or in love with it. I believe I am pretty cool and philosophical, but it will not do for me at this early day to be boasting of what is in me. I shall have to wait until circumstances bring it out. I can only answer for the past and the present—the one having been blessed and gladdened and the other *being* made happy and cheerful by lover and husband. I will tell you truly, as I promised to do, if my heart sings another tune on the 17th of April, 1848. I only hope I shall enter soberly and thankfully on my new life, expecting sunshine and rain, drought and plenty, heat and cold—and adapting myself to alternations contentedly—but who knows? We are boarding at a hotel, which is not over pleasant. However, we have two good rooms and have home things about us. I like to sit at work while Mr. Prentiss writes his sermons and he likes to have me—so, for the present, a study can be dispensed with. In a few weeks, we hope to get to housekeeping. I like New Bedford very much.

To her husband she writes, June 18:

I cannot help writing you again, though I did send you a letter last night. It is a very pleasant morning, and I think of you all the time and love you with the happiest tears in my eyes. I have just been making some nice crispy gingerbread to send Mrs. H———, as she has no appetite, and I thought anything from home would taste good to her. I hope this will please you. Mother called with me to see her yesterday. She looks very ill. I have no idea she will ever get well. We had a nice time at the garden last night. Mr. and Miss Arnold came out and walked with us nearly an hour, though tea was waiting for them, and Miss A. was very particularly attentive to me (for your dear sake!), and gave me flowers, beautiful ones, and spoke with much interest of your sermons. Oh, I am ready to jump for joy, when I think of seeing you home again. Do please be glad as I am. I suppose your mother wants you too but then she cannot love you as I do—I'm sure she cannot—with all the children among whom she has to divide her heart. Give my best love to her and Abby. How I wish I were in Portland, helping you pack your books. But I cannot write any more as we are going to Mrs. Gibbs' to tea. Mother is reading Hamlet in her room. She is enjoying herself very much.

Mrs. Gibbs, whose name occurs in this letter, was one of those inestimable friends, who fulfill the office of mother, as it were, to the young minister's wife. She was tenderly attached to Mrs. Prentiss and her loving-kindness, which was new every morning and fresh every evening, ceased only with her life. Her husband, the late Capt. Robert Gibbs, was like her in unwearied devotion to both the pastor and the pastor's wife.

The summer was passed in getting settled in her new home, and receiving visits from old friends. Early in the autumn, she spent several weeks in Portland. After her return, Nov. 2, she writes to Miss Thurston:

I was in Portland after you had left, and got quite rested and recruited after my summer's fatigue, so that I came home with health and strength, if not to lay my hand to the plough, to apply it to the broom-handle and other articles of domestic warfare. Just what I expected would befall me has happened. I have got immersed in the whirlpool of petty cares and concerns which swallow up so many other and higher interests, and talk as anxiously about good "help" and bad, as the rest of 'em do. I sometimes feel really ashamed of myself to see how virtuously I fancy I am spending my time, if in the kitchen, and how it seems to be wasted if I venture to take up a book. I take it that wives who have no love and enthusiasm for their husbands are more to be pitied than blamed if they settle down into mere cooks and good managers…. We have had right pleasant times since coming home never pleasanter than when, for a day or two, I was without "help," and my husband ground coffee and drew water for me, and thought everything I made tasted good. One of the deacons of our church—a very old man—prays for me once a week at meeting, especially that my husband and I may be "mutual comforts and enjoyments of each other," which makes us laugh a little in our sleeves, even while we say Amen in our hearts. We have been reading aloud Mary Howitt's "Author's Daughter," which is a very good story indeed—do not ask me if I have read anything else. My mind has become a complete mummy, and therefore incapable of either receiving or originating a new idea. I did wade through a sea of words, and nonsense on my way home in the shape of two works of Prof. Wilson—"The Foresters" and "Margaret Lindsay"—which I fancy he wrote before he was out of his mother's arms or soon after leaving them. The girls in Portland are marrying off like all possessed. It reminds me of a shovel full of popcorn, which the more you watch it the more it won't pop, till at last it all goes racketing off at once, pop, pop, pop without your having time to say Jack Robinson between.

My position as wife of a minister secures for me many affectionate attentions, and opens to me many little channels of happiness, which conspire to make me feel contented and at home here. I do not know how a stranger would find New Bedford people, but I am inclined to think society is hard to get into, though its heart is warm when you once do get in. We are very pleasantly situated, and our married life has been abundantly blessed. I doubt if we could fail to be contented anywhere if we had each other to love and care for.

We went to hear Templeton sing last night. I was perfectly charmed with his hunting song and with some others, and better judges than I were equally delighted. I had a letter from Abby last week. She is in Vicksburg and in fine spirits, and fast returning health.

Her letters during 1846 glow with the sunshine of domestic peace and joy. In its earlier months, her health was unusually good and she depicts her happiness as something "wonderful." All the daylong her heart, she says, was "running over" with a love and delight she could not begin to express. But her letters also show that already she was having foretastes of that baptism of suffering, which was to fit her for doing her Master's work. In January, she revisited Portland, where she had the pleasure of meeting Prof, and Mrs. Hopkins with their little boy, and of passing several weeks in the society of her own and her husband's family. But Portland had now lost for her much of its attraction. "I've seen all the folks," she wrote, "and we've said about all we've got to say to each other, and though I love to be at home, of course, it is not the home it used to be before you had made such another dear, dear home for me. Oh, do you miss me? Do you feel a *little bit* sorry you let me leave you? Do say, yes…. But I cannot write, I am so happy! I am so glad I am going home!" Early in December her first child was born. Writing a few weeks later to Mrs. Stearns, she thus refers to this event:

What a world of new sensations and emotions come with the first child! I was quite unprepared for the rush of strange feelings—still more so for the saddening and chastening effect. Why should the world seem more than ever empty when one has just gained the treasure of a living and darling child?

The saddening effect in her own case was owing in part, no doubt, to anxiety occasioned by the fatal illness of her husband's eldest sister, to whom she was tenderly attached. The following letter was written under the pressure of this anxiety:

To Miss Thurston, New Bedford, Jan. 31, 1847

I dare say the idea of *Lizzy Payson* with a *baby* seems quite funny to you, as it does to many of the Portland girls but I assure you it doesn't seem in the least funny to me, but as natural as life and I may add, as wonderful, almost. She is a nice little plump creature, with a fine head of dark hair, which I take some comfort in brushing round a quill to make it curl, and a pair of intelligent eyes, either black or blue, nobody knows which. I find the care of her very wearing, and have cried ever so many times from fatigue and anxiety, but now I am getting a little better and she pays me for all I do. She is a sweet, good little thing, her chief fault being a tendency to dissipation and sitting up late o' nights. The ladies of our church have made her a beautiful little wardrobe, fortunately for me.

I had a lot of company all summer my sister, her husband, and boy, Mr. Stearns and Anna, Mother Prentiss, Julia Willis, etc. I had also my last visit from Abby, whom I little thought then I should never see again. Our happiness in our little one has been checked by our constant anxiety with regard to Abby's health, and it is very hard now for me to give up one who has become in every sense a sister, and not even to have the privilege of bidding her farewell. George went down about a week since and will remain until all is over. I do not even know that while I write she is yet living. She had only one wish remaining and that was to see George, and she was quite herself the day of his arrival, as also the day following, and able to say all she desired. Since then she has been rather unconscious of what was passing, and I fervently trust that by this time her sufferings are over and that she is where she longed and prayed to be. [1] You can have no idea how alike are the emotions occasioned by a birth and a death in the family. They seem equally solemn to me and I am full of wonder at the mysterious new world into which I have been thrown. I used to think that the change I saw in young, giddy girls when they became mothers, was owing to suffering and care wearing upon the spirits, but I see now that its true source lies far deeper. My brother H. has been married a couple of months, so I have one sister more. I shall be glad when they are all married. Some sisters seem to feel that their brothers are lost to them on their marriage, but if I may judge by my husband, there is fully as much gain as loss. I am sure no son or brother could be more devoted to mother and sisters than he is. Of course, the baby is his perfect comfort and delight but I need not enlarge on this point, as I suppose you have seen papas with their first babies. A great sucking of a very small thumb admonishes me that the little lady in the crib meditates crying for supper, so I must hurry off my letter.

Abby Lewis Prentiss died on Saturday, January 30, 1847, at the age of thirty-two. Long and wearisome sufferings, such as usually attend pulmonary disease, preceded the final struggle. It was toward the close of a stormy winter's day, that she gently fell asleep. A little while before she had imagined herself in a "very beautiful region" which her tongue in vain attempted to describe, surrounded by those she loved. Among her last half-conscious utterances was the name of her brother Sergeant. The next morning witnessed a scene of such wondrous splendor and loveliness as made the presence of Death seem almost incredible. The snowfall, mist, and gloom had ceased and as the sun rose, clear and resplendent, every visible object—the earth, trees, houses—shone as if enameled with gold, pearls, and precious stones. It was the Lord's Day and well did the aspect of nature symbolize the glory of Him, who is the Resurrection and the Life.

On receiving the news of his sister's death, her brother Sergeant, writing to his mother, thus depicted her character:

My heart bleeds to the core, as I sit down to mingle my tears with yours, my dear, beloved mother. I cannot realize that it is all over that I shall never again, in this world, see our dear, dear Abby. Gladly would I have given my own life to preserve hers. But we have consolation, even in our extreme grief for she was so good that we know she is now in heaven, and freed from all care, unless it be that her affectionate heart is still troubled for us, whom she loved so well. We can dwell with satisfaction, after we have overcome the first sharpness of our grief, upon her angel-like qualities, which made her, long before she died, fit for the heaven where she now is.... You have lost the purest, noblest, and best of daughters I, a sister, who never to my knowledge did a selfish act or uttered a selfish thought. With the exception of yourself, dear mother, she was, of all our family circle, the best prepared to enter her Father's house.

Some extracts from letters written at this time, will show the tenderness of Mrs. Prentiss' sisterly love and sympathy, and give a glimpse also of her thoughts and occupations as a young mother.

To Mrs. Stearns, New Bedford, Feb. 17, 1847

If I loved you less, my dear Anna, I could write you twenty letters where I now can hardly get courage to undertake one. How very dearly I do love you I never knew, until it rushed upon my mind that we might sometime lose you as we have lost dear Abby. How mysteriously your and Mary's and my baby are given us just at this very time, when our hearts are so sore that we are almost afraid to expose them to new sufferings by taking in new objects of affection! But it does seem to me a great mercy that, trying as it is in many respects, these births and this death come almost hand in hand. Surely, we three young mothers have learned lessons of life that must influence us forever in relation to these little ones!

I have been like one in the midst of a great cloud, since the birth of our baby, entirely unconscious how much I love her but I am just beginning to take comfort in and feel sensible affection for her. I long to show the dear little good creature to you. But I can hardly give up my long-cherished plans and hopes in regard to Abby's seeing and loving our first child. Almost as much as I depended on the sympathy and affection of my own mother in relation to this baby, I was depending on Abby's. But I rejoice that she is where she is, and would not have her back again in this world of sin and conflict and labor, for a thousand times the comfort her presence could give. But you do not know how I dread going home next summer and not finding her there! It was a great mercy that you could go down again, dear Anna. And indeed there are manifold mercies in this affliction—how many we may never know, till we get home to heaven ourselves and find, perhaps, that this was one of the invisible powers that helped us on our way thither. I had a sweet little note from your mother today. I would give anything if I could go right home, and make her adopt me as her daughter by a new adoption, and be a real blessing and comfort to her in this lonely, dark time. Eddy Hopkins calls my baby *his*. How children want to use the possessive case in regard to every object of interest!

I find the blanket that Mrs. Gibbs knit for me so infinitely preferable, from its elasticity, to common flannel, that I could not help knitting one for you. If I say that I have thought as many affectionate thoughts to you, while knitting it, as it contains stitches, I fancy I speak nothing but truth and soberness—for I love you now with the love I have returned on my heart from Abby, who no longer is in want of earthly friends. Dear little baby thought I was knitting for her special pleasure, for her bright eyes would always follow the needles as she lay upon my lap, and she would smile now and then as if thanking me for my trouble. The ladies have given her an elegant cloak, and Miss Arnold has just sent her a little white satin bonnet that was made in England, and is quite unlike anything I ever saw. Only to think, I walked down to church last Sunday and heard George preach once more!

March 3rd.—We could with difficulty, and by taking turns, get through reading your letter—not only because you so accurately describe our own feelings in regard to dear Abby, but because we feel so keenly for you. I often detect myself thinking, "Now I will sit down, and write Abby a nice long letter" or imagining how she will act when we go home with our baby and as you say, I dream about her almost every night. I used always to dream of her as suffering and dying, but now I see her just as she was when well, and hear her advising this and suggesting that, just as I did when she was here last summer. Life seems so different now from what it did! It seems to me that my *youth* has been touched by Abby's death, and that I can never be as cheerful and light-hearted as I have been. But, dear Anna, though I doubt not this is still more the case with you, and that you see far deeper into the realities of life than I do, we have both the consolations that are to be found in Christ—and these will remain to us when the buoyancy and the youthful spirit have gone from our hearts.

March 12th. ... I had been reading a marriage sermon to George from "Martyria," and we were having a nice *conjugal* talk just as your little stranger was coming into the world. G. is so hurried and driven that he cannot get a moment in which to write. He has a funeral this afternoon, that of Mrs. H., a lady whom he has visited for two years, and a part, if not all, of that time once a week. I have made several calls since I wrote you last—two of them to see babies, one of whom took the shine quite off of mine with his great blue-black eyes and eyelashes that lay halfway down his cheeks.

The latter part of April she visited Portland while there she wrote to her husband, April 27:

Just as I had the baby to sleep and this letter dated, I was called down to see Dr. and Mrs. Dwight and their little Willie. The baby woke before they had finished their call, and behaved as prettily and looked as bright and lovely as heart could wish. Dr. Dwight held her a long time and kissed her heartily. [2] I got your letter soon after dinner, and from the haste and the *je ne sais quoi* with which it was written, I feared you were not well. Alas, I am full of love and fear. How came you to *walk* to Dartmouth to preach? Wasn't it by far too long a walk to take in one day? I heard Dr. Carruthers on Sunday afternoon. He made the finest allusion to my father I ever heard and mother thought of it as I did. Today I have had a good many callers—among the rest Deacon Lincoln. [3] When he saw the baby he said, "Oh, what a homely creature. Do tell if the New Bedford babies are so ugly?" Mrs. S., thinking him in earnest, rose up in high dudgeon and said, "Why, we think her beautiful, Deacon Lincoln." "Well, I do not wonder," said he. I expect she will get measles and everything else, for *lots* of children come to see her and eat her up. Mother, baby, and I spend tomorrow at your mother's. Do up a lot of sleeping and grow fat, pray do! And oh, love me and think I am a darling little wife, and write me loving words in your next letter. *Wednesday.*—We have a fine day for going up to your mother's. And the baby is bright as a button and full of fun. Aren't you glad?

To Mrs. Stearns, Portland, May 22, 1847

We have just been having a little quiet Saturday evening talk about dear Abby, as we sat here before the lighting of the lamps, and I dare say I was not the only one who wished you here too. I came up here from my mother's on

Monday morning and have had a delightful week. I cannot begin to tell you how glad I am that we are going to make you a little visit on our way home. I do so want to see you and your children, and show you our darling little baby that I can hardly wait until the time comes. I suppose you have got your little folks off to bed, and so if you will take a peep into the parlor here you will see how we are all occupied—mother in her rocking-chair, with her "specs" on, studying my Dewees on Children George toe to toe with her, reading some old German book, and Lina [4] curled upon the sofa, asleep I fancy, while I sit in the corner and write you from dear Abby's desk with her pen. Mercy and Sophia watch over the cradle in the dining room, where mother's fifteenth grandchild reposes, and unconscious of the honor of sleeping where honorables, reverends, and reverendesses have slumbered before her. How strange it seems that *my* baby is one of this family—bone of their bone, and flesh of their flesh! I need not say how I miss dear Abby, for you will see at once that that which was months ago a reality to you, has just become such to me. It pains me to my heart's core to hear how she suffered. Dear, dear Abby! How I did love her, and how thankful I am for her example to imitate and her excellencies to rejoice in! Your uncle James Lewis [5] spent last night here, and this morning he prayed a delightful prayer, which really softened my whole soul. I do not know when I have had my own wants so fervently expressed, or been more edified at family worship, and his allusion to Abby was very touching.

The following extracts from letters written to her husband, while he was absent in Maine, may be thought by some to go a little too much into the trifling details of daily life and feeling, but do not such details after all form no small part of the moral warp and woof of human experience?

To her husband New Bedford, August 27th.

I heard this morning that old Mrs. Kendrick was threatened with typhus fever, and went down soon after breakfast to see how she did, and, as I found Mrs. Henrietta had watched with her and was looking all worn out, I begged her to let me have her baby this afternoon, that she might have a chance to rest so, after dinner, Sophia went down and got her. At first, she set up a lamentable scream, but we huddled on her cloak and put her with our baby into the carriage and gave them a ride. She is a *proper* heavy baby, and my legs ache well with trotting round the streets after the carriage. Think of me as often as you can and pray for me, and I will think of you and pray for you all the time.

Tuesday Evening.—You see I am writing you a sort of little journal, as you say you like to know all I do while you are away. Our sweet baby makes your absence far less intolerable than it used to be before she came to comfort me.... I have felt all soul and as if I had no body, ever since your precious letter came this morning. I have so pleased myself with imagining how funny and nice it would be if I could creep in unperceived by you, and hear your oration! I long to know how you got through, and what Mr. Stearns and Mr. Smith thought of it. I always pray for you more when you are away than I do when you are at home, because I know you are interrupted and hindered about your devotions more or less when journeying. I have had callers a great part of today, among them Mrs. Leonard, Mrs. Gen. Thompson, Mrs. Randall, and Capt. Clark. [6] Capt. C. asked for nobody but the baby. The little creature almost sprang into his arms. He was much gratified and held her a long while, kissing and caressing her. I think it was pretty work for you to go to reading your oration to your mother and old Mrs. Coe, when you had not read it to me. I felt a terrible pang of jealousy when I came to that in your letter. I am going now to call on Miss Arnold.

Friday, Sept, 3rd.—Yesterday forenoon I was *perfectly wretched*. It came over me, as things will in spite of us, "Suppose he didn't get safely to Brunswick!" and for several hours I could not shake it off. It had all the power of reality, and made me so faint that I could do nothing and fairly had to go to bed. I suppose it was very silly, and if I had not tried in every way to rise above it might have been even wicked, but it frightened me to find how much I am under the power of mere feeling and fancy. But do not laugh at me. Sometimes I say to myself, "What MADNESS to love any human being so intensely! What would become of you if he were snatched from you?" and then I think that though God justly denies us comfort and support for the future, and bids us lean upon Him *now* and trust Him for the rest, He can give us strength for the endurance of His most terrible chastisements when their hour comes.

Saturday.—I am a mere baby when I think of your getting sick in this time of almost universal sickness and sorrow and death.... Yesterday Mrs. Gibbs and Mrs. Leonard took me, with Sophia and baby, to the cemetery, and on a long ride of three hours—all of which was delightful. In the afternoon baby had an ill-turn that alarmed me excessively, because so many children are sick, but I gave her medicine and think she will soon be well again. Mrs. Gibbs and Mrs. Randall and others sent me yesterday a dozen large peaches, two melons, a lot of shell-beans and tomatoes, a dish of blackberries and some fried corn-cakes—not an atom of the whole of which shall I touch, taste, handle, or smell so you need not fear my killing myself. Mrs. Capt. Delano, where the Rev. Mr. Brock from England stayed, has just lost two children after a few days' illness. They were buried in one coffin. Old Gideon Howland, the richest man here, is also dead. The papers are full of deaths. Our dear baby is nine months old today, and may God, if He *sees best*, spare her to us as many more and if He does not, I feel as if I could give her up to Him—but we do not know what we can do till the time comes. I hear her sweet little voice down stairs and it sounds happy, so I guess she feels pretty comfortable.

Sabbath Evening.—The baby is better, and I dare say it is my imagination that says she looks pale and puny. She is now asleep in your study, where too I am sitting in your chair. I came down as soon as I could this morning, and have stayed here all day. It is so quiet and pleasant among your books and papers, and it was so dull up-stairs! I thought before your letter came, while standing over the green, grassy graves of Lizzie Read, Mary Rodman, and Mrs. Cadwell, [7] how I should love to have dear Abby in such a green, sweet spot, where we could sometimes go together to talk of her. I must own I should like to be buried under grass and trees, rather than cold stone and heavy marble. Should not you?

* * * * *

II.

Birth of a Son. Death of her Mother. Her Grief. Letters. Eddy's Illness and her own Cares. A Family Gathering at Newburyport. Extracts from Eddy's Journal.

Passing over another year, which was marked by no incidents requiring special mention, we come again to a birth and a death in close conjunction. On the 22nd of October, 1848, her second child, Edward Payson, was born. On the 17th of November, her mother died. Of the life of this child she herself has left a minute record, portions of which will be given later. In a letter to his sister, dated New Bedford, November 21st, her husband thus refers to her mother's departure:

We have just received the sad intelligence of Mother Payson's death. She passed away very peacefully, as if going to sleep, at half-past five on Friday afternoon. Dear Lizzy was at first quite overwhelmed, as I knew she would be—for her attachment to her mother was uncommonly tender and devoted but she is now perfectly tranquil and will soon, I trust, be able to think of her irreparable loss with a melancholy pleasure even. There is much in the case that is peculiarly fitted to produce a cheerful resignation. Mrs. Payson has been a severe sufferer and since the breaking up of her home in Portland, she has felt, I think, an increasing detachment from the world. I was exceedingly struck with this during her visit here last winter. She seemed to me to be fast ripening for heaven. It is such a comfort to us that she was able to *name* our little boy! [8]

Mrs. Payson died in the 65th year of her age. She was a woman of most attractive and admirable qualities, full of cheerful life and energy, and a whole-hearted disciple of Jesus. A few extracts from Mrs. Prentiss' letters will show how deeply she felt her loss. To her youngest brother she writes:

How gladly I would go, if I could, to see you all, and talk over with you the thousand things that are filling our minds and hearts! We cannot drain this bitter cup at one draught and then go on our way as though it had never been. The loss of a mother is never made up or atoned for and ours was such a mother so peculiar in her devotion and tenderness and sympathy! I cannot mourn that her sorrowful pilgrimage is over, cannot think for a moment of wishing she were still on earth, weeping and praying and suffering—but for myself and for you and for all I mourn with hourly tears. She has sacrificed herself for us.

To her friend, Miss Lord, she writes, Jan. 31:

It seems to me that every day and hour I miss my dear mother more and more, and I feel more and more painfully how much she suffered during her last years and months. Dear Louise, I thought I knew that she could not live long, but I never realized it, and even now, I keep trying to hope that she has not really gone. Just in this very spot where I now sit writing, my dear mother's great easy chair used to sit, and here, only a year ago, she was praying for and loving me. O, if I had only *known* she was dying then, and could have talked with her about heaven until it had grown to seeming like a home to which she was going, and whither I should follow her sooner or later! But it is all over and I would not have her here again, if the shadow of a wish could restore her to us. I only earnestly long to be fitting, day by day, to meet her again in heaven. God has mingled many great mercies with this affliction, and I do not know that I ever in my life so felt the delight of praying to and thanking Him. When I begin to pray, I have so much to thank Him for, which I hardly know how to stop. I have always thought I would not for the universe is left unchastised—and now I feel the smart, I still can say so. Lotty's visit was a great comfort and service to me, but I was very selfish in talking to her so much about my own loss, while she was so great a sufferer under hers. Since she left, my little boy has been worse than ever and pined away last week very rapidly. You can form no idea, by any description of his sufferings, of what the dear little creature has undergone since his birth. I feel a perfect longing to see Portland and mother's many dear friends there, especially your mother and a few like her. I am very tired as I have written a great part of this with baby in my lap—so I can write no more.

To Mrs. Stearns, Feb. 17, 1849.

Dear little Eddy has found life altogether unkind thus far, and I have had many hours of heartache on his account but I hope he may weather the storm and come out safely yet. The doctor examined him all over yesterday, particularly his head, and said he could not make him out a *sick* child, but that he thought his want of flesh owing partly to his

~ 143 ~

sufferings but more to the great loss of sleep occasioned by his sufferings. Instead of sleeping twelve hours out of the twenty-four, he sleeps but about seven and that by means of laudanum. Isn't it a mercy that I have been able to bear so well the fatigue and care and anxiety of these four hard months? I feel that I have nothing to complain of, and a *great deal* to be thankful for. On the whole, notwithstanding my grief about my dear mother's loss, and my perplexity and distress about baby, I have had as much real happiness this winter as it is possible for one to glean in such unfavorable circumstances. *By far* the greatest trial I have to contend with, is that of losing all power to control my time. A little room all of my own, and a regular hour, morning and night, all of my own would enable me, I think, to say, "*Now* let life do its worst!"

I am no stranger, I assure you, to the misgivings you describe in your last letter I think them the result of the *wish* without the *will* to be holy. We pray for sanctification and then are afraid God will sanctify us by stripping us of our idols and feel distressed lest we cannot have them and Him too. Reading the life of Madame Guyon gave me great pain and anxiety, I remember. I thought that if such spiritual darkness and trial as she was in for many years, was a necessary attendant on eminent piety, I could not summon courage to try to live such a life. Of all the anguish in the world there is nothing like this—the sense of God, without the sense of nearness to Him. I wish you would always "think aloud" when you write to me. I long to see you and the children and Mr. S., and so does George. Poor G. has had a very hard time of it ever since little Eddy's birth—so much care and worry and sleeplessness and labor, and how he is ever to get any rest I do not see. These are the times that try our souls. Let nobody condole with me about our *bodies*. It is the struggle to be patient and gentle and cheerful, when pressed down and worn upon and distracted, that costs us so much. I think when I have had all my children, if there is anything left of me, I shall write about the "Battle of Life" more eloquently than Dickens has done. I had a pleasant dream about mother and Abby the other night. They came together to see me and both seemed so well and so happy! I feel *perfectly happy* now, that my dear mother has gone home.

To the Same, May 7, 1849.

I used to think it hard to be sick when I had dear mother hanging over me, doing all she could for my relief, but it is harder to be denied the poor comfort of being let alone and to have to drag one's self out of bed to take care of a baby. Mr. Stearns must know how to pity me, for my real sick headaches are very like his, and when racked with pain, dizzy, faint and exhausted with suffering, starvation, and sleeplessness, it is terrible to have to walk the room with a crying child! I thought as I lay, worn out even to childishness, obliged for the baby's sake to have a bright sunlight streaming into the chamber, and to keep my eyes and ears on the alert for the same cause, how still we used to think the house must be left when my father had these headaches and how mother busied herself all day long about him, and how nice his little plate of hot steak used to look, as he sat up to eat it when the sickness had gone—and how I am suffering here all alone with nobody to give me even a look of encouragement. George was out of town on my sickest day. When he was at home he did everything in the world he could do to keep the children still, but here they must be and I must direct about every trifle and have them on the bed with me. I am getting desperate and feel disposed to run furiously in the traces until I drop dead on the way. Do not think me very wicked for saying so. I am jaded in soul and body and hardly know what I do want. If T. comes, George, at all events, will get relief and that will take a burden from my mind.... I want Lina to come this summer. There is a splendid swing on iron hooks under a tree, at the house we are going to move into. Won't that be nice for Jeanie and Mary's other children, if they come? I wish I had a little fortune, not for myself but to gather my "folks" together with. I shall not write you, my dear, another complaining letter do excuse this.

This letter shows the extremity of her trouble but it is a picture, merely. The reality was something beyond description only young mothers, who know it by experience, could understand its full meaning. Now, however, the storm for a while abated. The young relative, whose loving devotion had ministered to the comfort of her dying mother, came to her own relief and passed the next six months at New Bedford, helping take care of Eddy. In the course of the spring, too, his worst symptoms disappeared and hope took the place of fear and despondency. Referring to this period, his mother writes in Eddy's journal:

On the Saturday succeeding his birth, we heard of my dear mother's serious illness, and, when he was about three weeks old, of her death. We were not surprised that his health suffered from the shock it thus received. He began at once to be affected with distressing colic, which gave him no rest day or night. His father used to call him a "little martyr," and such indeed he was for many long, tedious months. On the 16th of February, the doctor came and spent two hours in carefully investigating his case. He said it was a most trying condition of things, and he would gladly do something to relieve me, as he thought I had been through "enough to *kill ten men*." ... When Eddy was about eight months old, the doctor determined to discontinue the use of opiates. He was now a fine, healthy baby, bright-eyed and beautiful, and his colic was reducing itself to certain seasons on each day, instead of occupying the whole day and night as heretofore. We went through fire and water almost in trying to procure for him natural sleep. We swung him in blankets, wheeled him in little carts, walked the room with him by the hour, etc., etc., but it was wonderful how little sleep he obtained after all. He always looked wide-awake and as if, he did not *need* sleep. His eyes had gradually become black, and when, after a day of fatigue and care with him he would at last close them, and we would flatter ourselves that now we too should snatch a little rest, we would see them shining upon us in the most amusing manner with an expression of content and even merriment. About this time, he was baptized. I well remember how in his father's study, and before taking him to church, we gave him to God. He was very good while his papa was performing the ceremony, and looked so bright and so well, that many who had never seen him in his state of feebleness, found it hard to believe he had been aught save a vigorous and healthy child. My own health was now so broken down by long sleeplessness and fatigue, which it became necessary for me to leave home for a season. Dr. Mayhew promised to run in *every day* to see that all went well with Eddy. His auntie was more than willing to take this care upon herself, and many of our neighbors offered to go often to see him, promising to do everything for his safety and comfort if I would only go. Not aware how miserable a state I was in, I resolved to be absent only one week, but was away for a whole month.

A part of the month, with her husband and little daughter, she passed at Newburyport. His brother, S. S. Prentiss—whose name was then renowned all over the land as an orator and patriot—had come North for the last time, bringing his wife and children with him. It was a never-to-be-forgotten family gathering under the aged mother's roof.

On my return, (she continues in Eddy's journal), I found him looking finely. He had had an ill turn owing to teething which they had kept from me, but had recovered from it and looked really beautiful. His father and uncle S. S. had been to see him once during our vacation, and we were now expecting them again with his Aunt Mary and her three children and his grandmother. We depended a great deal on seeing Eddy and Una together, as she was his *twin* cousin and only a few hours older than he. But on the very evening of their arrival he was taken sick, and, although they all saw him that night looking like himself, by the next morning he had changed sadly. He grew ill and lost flesh and strength very fast, and no remedies seemed to have the least effect on his disorder, which was one induced by teething.... For myself I did not believe anything could now save my precious baby, and had given him to God so unreservedly, that I was not conscious of even a wish for his life.... When at last we saw evident tokens of returning health and strength, we felt that we received him a second time as from the grave. To me he never seemed the same child. My darling Eddy was lost to me and another—*and yet the same*—filled his place. I often said afterward that a little stranger was running about my nursery, not mine, but God's. Indeed, I cannot describe the peculiar feelings with which I always regarded him after this sickness, nor how the thought constantly met me, "He is not mine he is God's." Every night I used to thank Him for sparing him to me one day longer thus truly enjoying him *a day at a time*.

An extract from a letter to Miss Lord, written on the anniversary of her mother's death, will close the account of this year.

If I were in Portland now, I should go right down to see you. I feel just like having a dear, old-fashioned talk with you. I was thinking how many times death had entered that old Richmond circle of which you and I once formed a part Mrs. Persico, Susan, Charlotte Ford, Kate Kennedy, and now our own dearest Lotty, all gone. I cannot tell you how much I miss and grieve for Lotty. [9] I cannot be thankful enough that I went to Portland in the summer and had that last week with her, nor for her most precious visit here last winter. Whenever you think of any little thing she said, I want you to write it down for me, no matter whether it seems worth writing or not. I know by experience how precious such things are. This is a sad day to me. Indeed, all of this month has been so, recalling as it has done, all I was suffering at this time last year, and all my dear mother was then suffering. I can hardly realize that she has been in heaven a whole year, and that I feel her loss as vividly as if it were but yesterday—indeed, more so. I do not feel that this affliction has done me the good that it ought to have done and that I hoped it would. As far as I have any excuse, it lies in my miserable health. I want so much to be more of a Christian to live a life of constant devotion. Do tell me, when you write, if you have such troubled thoughts, and such difficulty in being steadfast and unmovable? Oh, how I sigh for the sort of life I led in Richmond, and which was more or less the life of the succeeding years at home! My husband tries to persuade me that the difference is more in my way of life, and that then being my time for contemplation, now is my time for action. However, I know, myself, that I have lost ground. You must bear me in mind when you pray, my dear Louise, for I never had so much need of praying nor so little time or strength for it.

* * * * *

III.
Further Extracts from Eddy's Journal. Ill health. Visit to Newark. Death of her Brother-in-law, S. S. Prentiss. His Character. Removal to Newark. Letters.

The record of the New Year opens with this entry in Eddy's journal:

~ 145 ~

January, 1850.—Eddy is now fourteen months old, has six teeth, and walks well, but with timidity. He is, at times, really beautiful. He is very affectionate, and will run to meet me, throw his little arms round my neck, and keep pat-pat-patting me, with delight. Miss Arnold sent him, at New Year's, a pretty ball, with which he is highly pleased. He rolls it about by knocking it with a stick, and will shout for joy when he sees it moving. He is *crazy* to give everybody something, and when he is brought down to prayers, hurries to get the Bible for his father, his little face all smiles and exultation, and his body in a quiver with emotion. He is like lightning in all his movements, and is never still for an instant. It is worth a good deal to see his face, it is so *brimful* of life and sunshine and gladness.

Her letters, written during the winter and spring, show how in the midst of bodily suffering, depression, and sorrow her views of life were changing and her faith in God growing stronger. Three of her brothers were now in California, seeking their fortunes in the newly discovered gold mines. To one of them she writes, March 10th:

I was delighted yesterday by the reception of your letter. I do not wonder that Lotty's death affected you as it did—but however sharp the instruments by which these lessons come to us, they are full of good when they do come. As I look back to the time when I did not know what death was doing and could do, I seem to myself like a child who has not yet been to school. The deaths of our dear mother and of Lotty have taken fast hold of me. Life is *entirely changed*. I do not say this in a melancholy or repining temper, for I would not have life appear otherwise than in its true light. All my sickly, wicked disgust with it has been put to the blush and driven away. I see now that to live for God, whether one is allowed ability to be actively useful or not, is a great thing, and that it is a wonderful mercy to be allowed to live and suffer even, if thereby one can glorify Him. I desire to live if it is God's will, though I confess heaven looks most attractive when either sin, sorrow, or sickness weary me. But I must not go on at this rate, for I could not in writing begin to tell you how different everything looks as I advance into a knowledge of life and see its awful sorrows and sufferings and changes and know that I am subject to all its laws, soon to take my turn in its mysterious close. My dear brother, let us learn by heart the lessons we are learning, and go in their strength and wisdom all our days.... Our children are well. Eddy has gone to be weighed (he weighed twenty-four pounds). He is a fine little fellow. I have his nurse still, and ought to be in excellent health, but am a nervous old thing, as skinny and bony as I can be. I can think of nothing but birds' claws when I look at my hands. But I have so much to be thankful for in my dear husband and my sweet little children, and love all of you so dearly, that I believe I am as rich as if I had the flesh and strength of a giant. I am going this week to hear Miss Arnold read a manuscript novel. This will give spice to my life. Warmest love to you all.

Again, May 10th, she writes:

It would be a great pleasure to me to keep a journal for you if I were well enough, but I am not. I have my sick headache now once a week, and it makes me really ill for about three days. Towards night of the third day, I begin to brighten up and to eat a morsel, but hardly recover my strength before I have another pull-down, just as I had got to this point the doorbell rang, and lo! A beautiful May-basket hanging on the latch for "Annie," full of pretty and good things. I can hardly wait until morning to see how her eyes will shine and her little feet fly when she sees it. George has been greatly distressed about S. S., and has, I think, very little, if any, hope that he will recover. Dr. Tappan [10] spent Tuesday night here. We had a really delightful visit from him. He spoke highly of your classmate, Craig, who is just going to be married. He told us a number of pleasant anecdotes about father. Eddy has got big enough to walk in the street. He looks like a little picture, with his great forehead and bright eyes. He is in every way as large as most children are at two years. His supreme delight is to tease A. by making believe strike her or in some other real boy's hateful way. She and he play together on the grass-plat, and I feel quite matronly as I sit watching them with their balls and wheelbarrows and whatnots. This little scamp has, I fear, broken my constitution to pieces. It makes me crawl all over when I think of you three fagging all day at such dull and unprofitable labor. But I am sure Providence will do what is really best for you all. We think and talk of and pray for you every day and more than once a day, and, in all my ill health and sufferings, the remembrance of you is pleasant and in great measure refreshing. I depend more upon hearing from you all than I can describe. What an unconquerable thing family affection is!

She thus writes, May 30th, to her old Portland friend, Miss Lord:

I have written very few letters and not a line of anything else the past winter, owing to the confusion my mind is in most of the time from distress in my head. Three days out of every seven, I am as sick as I well can be—the rest of the time languid, feeble, and exhausted by frequent faint turns, so that I cannot do the smallest thing in my family. I hardly know what it is so much as to put a clean apron on to one of my children. To me this is a constant pain and weariness for our expense in the way of servants is greater than we can afford and everything is going to destruction under my face and eyes, while I dare not lift a finger to remedy it. I live in constant alternations of hope and despondency about my health. Whenever I feel a little better, as I do today, I am sanguine and cheerful, but the next ill turn depresses me exceedingly. I do not think there is any special danger of my dying, but there is a good deal of my getting run down beyond the power of recovery, and of dragging out that useless existence of which I have a perfect horror. But I would not have you think I am not happy for I can truly say that I *am*, most of the time, as happy as I believe one can be in this world. All my trials and sufferings shut me up to the one great Source of peace, and I know there has been need of every one of them.

I have not yet made my plans for the summer. Our doctor urges me to go away from the children and from the salt water, but I do not believe it would do me a bit of good. I want you to see my dear little boy. He is now nineteen months old and as fat and well as can be. He is a beautiful little fellow, we think, and very interesting. He is as gallant to A. as you please, and runs to get a cushion for her when their supper is carried in, and will not eat a morsel himself until he sees her nicely fixed. George has gone to Boston, and I am lonely enough. I would write another sheet if I dared, but I do not dare.

What she here says of her happiness, amidst the trials of the previous winter, is repeated a little later in a letter to her husband:

I can truly say I have not spent a happier winter since our marriage, in spite of all my sickness. It seems to me I can never recover my spirits and be as I have been in my best days, but what I lose in one way perhaps I shall gain in another. Just think how my ambition has been crushed at every point by my ill health, and even the ambition to be useful and a comfort to those about me trampled underfoot, to teach me what I could not have learned in any other school!

In the month of June she went on a visit to Newark, New Jersey, where her husband's mother and sister now resided Dr. Stearns having in the fall of 1849 accepted a call to the First Presbyterian church in that city. While she was in Newark news came of the dangerous illness, and, soon after, of the death at Natchez of her brother-in-law, Mr. S. S. Prentiss. The event was a great shock to her, and she knew that it would be a crushing blow to her husband. Her letters to him, written at this time, are full of the tender love and sympathy that infuse solace into sorrow-stricken hearts. Here is an extract from one of them, dated July 11th:

I cannot tell you how it grieves and distresses me to have had this long-dreaded affliction come upon you when you were alone. Though I could do so little to comfort you, it seems as if I *must* be near you…. But I know I am doing right in staying here—doing as you would tell me to do, if I could have your direct wish, and you do not know how thankful I am that it has pleased God to let me be with dear mother at a time when she so needed constant affection and sympathy. Yes, there are wonderful mercies with this heavy affliction, and we all see and feel them. Poor mother has borne all the dreadful suspense and then the second blow of today far better than any of us dared to hope, but she weeps incessantly. Anna is with her all she can possibly be, and Mr. Stearns is an angel of mercy. I have prayed for you a great deal this week, and I know God is with you, comforts you, and will enable you to bear this great sorrow. And yet I cannot help feeling that I want to comfort you myself. Oh, may we all reap its blessed fruits as long as we live! Let us withdraw a while from everything else, that we may press nearer to God.

We were in a state of terrible suspense all day Tuesday, all day Wednesday, and until noon today starting at every footfall, expecting telegraphic intelligence either from you or from the South, and deplorably ignorant of Sergeant's alarming condition, notwithstanding all the warning we had had. With one consent, we had put far off the evil day…. And now I must bid you goodnight, my dearest husband, praying that you may be the beloved of the Lord and rest in safety by Him.

The early years of Mrs. Prentiss' married life were in various ways closely connected with that of this lamented brother so much so that he may be said to have formed one of the most potent, as well as one of the sunniest, influences in her own domestic history. Not only was he very highly gifted, intellectually, and widely known as a great orator, but he was also a man of extraordinary personal attractions, endeared to all his friends by the sweetness of his disposition, by his winning ways, his wit, his playful humor, his courage, his boundless generosity, his fraternal and filial devotion, and by the charm of his conversation. His death at the early age of forty-one called forth expressions of profound sorrow and regret from the first men of the nation. After the lapse of nearly a third of a century, his memory is still fresh and bright in the hearts of all, who once knew and loved him. [11]

Notwithstanding the shock of this great affliction, Mrs. Prentiss returned to New Bedford much refreshed in body and mind. In a letter to her friend Miss Lord, dated September 14th, she writes:

I spent six most profitable weeks at Newark went out very little, saw very few people, and had the quiet and retirement I had long hungered and thirsted for. Since I have had children my life has been so distracted with care and sickness that I have sometimes felt like giving up in despair, but this six weeks' rest gave me fresh courage to start anew. I have got some delightful books—Manning's Sermons. [12] They are (letting the High-churchism go) most delightful I think Susan would have feasted on them. But she is feasting on angels' food and has need of none of these things.

In October of this year, Mrs. Prentiss bade adieu to New Bedford, never to revisit it, and removed to Newark her husband having become associate pastor of the Second Presbyterian church in that place. In the spring of the following year, he accepted a call to the Mercer street Presbyterian Church in New York, and that city became her home the rest of her days. Although she tarried so short a time in Newark, she received much kindness and formed warm friendships while there. She continued to suffer much, however, from ill health and almost entirely suspended her correspondence. A few letters to New Bedford friends are all that relate to this period. In one to Mrs. J. P. Allen, dated November 2nd, she thus refers to an accident, which came near proving fatal:

Yesterday we went down to New York to hear Jenny Lind a pleasure to remember for the rest of one's life. If anything, she surpassed our expectations. In coming home, a slight accident to the cars obliged us to walk about a mile, and I must needs fall into a hole in the bridge, which we were crossing, and bruise and scrape one knee quite badly. The wonder is that I did not go into the river, as it was a large hole, and pitch dark. I think if I had been walking with Mr. Prentiss I should not only have gone in myself, but pulled him in too but I had the arm of a stronger man, who held me up until I could extricate myself. You cannot think how I miss you, nor how often I wish you could run in and sit with me, as you used to do. I have always loved you, and shall remember you and yours with the utmost interest. We had a pleasant call the other day from Captain Gibbs. Seeing him made me homesick enough. I could hardly keep from crying all the time he stayed. It seems to us both as if we had been gone from New Bedford more months than we have days. Mr. Prentiss said yesterday that he should expect if he went back directly, to see the boys and girls grown up and married.

To Mrs. Reuben Nye, Newark, Feb 12, 1851.

Mr. Prentiss and Mr. Poor have just taken Annie and Eddy out to walk, and I have been moping over the fire and thinking of New Bedford friends, and wishing one or more would "happen in." I am just now getting over a severe attack of rheumatism, which on leaving my back entrenched itself in Mr. P.'s shoulder. I dislike this climate and am very suspicious of it. Everybody has a horrible cold, or the rheumatism, or fever and ague. Mr. Prentiss says if I get the latter, he shall be off for New England in a twinkling. I think he is as well as can be expected while the death of his brother continues so fresh in his remembrance. All the old cheerfulness, which used to sustain me amid sickness and trouble, has gone from him. But God has ordered the iron to enter his soul, and it is not for me to resist that will. Our children are well. We have had much comfort in them both this winter. Mother Prentiss is renewing her youth, it is so pleasant to her to have us all near her. (Eddy and A. are hovering about me, making such a noise that I can hardly write. Eddy says, "When I was tired, *Poor* tarried me.") Mr. Poor carries all before him. [13] He is *very* popular throughout the city, and I believe Mrs. P. is much admired by their people. Mr. Prentiss is preaching every Sabbath evening, as Dr. Condit is able to preach every morning now. I feel as much at home as I possibly could anywhere in the same time, but instead of mourning less for my New Bedford friends, I mourn more and more every day.

To Mrs. Allen she writes, Feb. 21:

I know all about those depressed moods when it costs one as much to smile, or to give a pleasant answer, as it would at other times to make a world. What a change it will be to us poor sickly, feeble, discouraged ones, when we find ourselves where there is neither pain or lassitude or fatigue of the body, or sorrow or care or despondency of the mind!

I miss you more and more. People here are kind, excellent, and friendly, but I cannot make them, as yet, fill the places of the familiar faces I have left in New Bedford. I am all the time walking through our neighborhood, dropping into Deacon Barker's or your house, or welcoming some of you into our old house on the corner. Eddy is pretty well. He is a sweet little boy, gentle and docile. He learns to talk very fast, and is crazy to learn hymns. He says, "Tinkle, tinkle *leetleeverybody*, and give 'tatoes to beggar boys." Mother Prentiss seems to *thrive* on having us all about her. She lives so far off that I see her seldom, but Mr. P. goes every day, except Sundays, when he cannot go—rain or shine, tired or not tired, convenient or not convenient. Since my mother's death, he has felt that he must do quickly whatever he has to do for his own.

[1] "I found dear Abby still alive and rejoiced beyond expression to see me. She had had a very feeble night, but brightened up towards noon and when I arrived seemed entirely like her old self, smiling sweetly and exclaiming, "This is the last blessing I desired! Oh, how good the Lord is, isn't He?" It was very delightful. The doctor has just been in and he says she may go any instant, and yet may live a day or two. Mother is wonderfully calm and happy, and the house seems like the very gate of heaven…. I so wish you could have seen Abby's smile when I entered her room. And then she inquired so affectionately for you and baby: "Now tell me everything about them." She longs and prays to be gone. There is something perfectly childlike about her expressions and feelings, especially toward mother. She cannot bear to have her leave the room and holds her hand a good deal of the time. She sends ever so much love."— *Extract from a letter, dated Portland, January 27, 1847.*

[2] The late Rev. William T. Dwight, D.D., pastor of the Third Church in Portland. He was a son of President Dwight, an accomplished man, a noble Christian citizen, and one of the ablest preachers of his day. For many years, his house almost adjoined Mrs. Payson's, and both he and Mrs. Dwight were among her most cherished friends.

[3] A devoted friend of her father's, one of his deacons, and a genial, warm-hearted, good man.

[4] A niece of her husband, a lovely child, who died a few years later in Georgia.

[5] Rev. James Lewis, a venerated elder and local preacher of the Methodist Episcopal Church, then nearly eighty years of age. He died in 1855, universally beloved and lamented. He entered upon his work in 1800. During most of those fifty-five years he was wont to preach every Sabbath, often three times, rarely losing an appointment by sickness, and still more rarely by storms in summer or winter. He lived in Gorham, Maine, and his labors were pretty equally divided among all the towns within fifteen miles round. His rides out and back, often over the roughest roads or through heavy snows, averaged, probably, from fifteen to twenty miles. It was estimated that he had officiated at not less than 1,500 funerals, sometimes riding for the purpose forty miles. His funeral and camp meeting sermons included, he could not have preached less than from 8,000 to 9,000 times. He never received a dollar of compensation for his ministerial services. Though a hard-working farmer, his hospitality to his itinerant brethren was unbounded. In several towns of Cumberland and adjoining counties, he was the revered patriarch, as half a century earlier he had been the youthful pioneer of Methodism. When he departed to be with Christ, there was no better man in all the State to follow after him.

[6] One of a number of old whaling captains in her husband's congregation, in whom she was interested greatly. They belonged to a class of men *sui generis*—men who had traversed all oceans, had visited many lands, and were as remarkable for their jovial large-hearted, social qualities, when at home, as for their indomitable energy, Yankee push, and adventurous seamanship, when hunting the monsters of the deep on the other side of the globe.

[7] Two bright girls and a young mother, who had died not long before.

[8] Her sickness lasted six weeks, dating from the day of her being entirely confined to bed. Her life was prolonged much beyond what her physicians or anyone else, who saw her, had believed possible. During the last week, her sufferings were less, and she laid quiet part of the time. Friday morning she had an attack of faintness, in the course of which she remarked, "I am dying." She recovered and before noon sank into a somnolent state, from which she never awoke. Her breathing became softer and fainter until it ceased at half-past five in the afternoon. Oh, what a transition was that! From pain and weariness and woe to the world of light! To the presence of the Savior! To unclouded bliss! I felt, and so I believe did all assembled round her bed, that it was time for exultation rather than grief. We could not think of ourselves, so absorbed were we in contemplation of her happiness. She was able to say scarcely anything during her sickness, and left not a single message for the absent children, or directions to those who were present. Her extreme weakness, and the distressing effect of every attempt to speak, made her abandon all such attempts except in answer to questions. But the tenor of her replies to all inquiries was uniform, expressing entire acquiescence in the will of God, confidence in Him through Christ, and a desire to depart as soon as He should permit. Tranquility and peace, unclouded by a single doubt or fear, seem to have filled her mind. There were several reasons that led us to decide that the interment should take place here but on the following Saturday a gentleman arrived from Portland, sent by the Second Parish to remove the remains to that place, if we made no objection. As we made none, the body was disinterred and taken to P., my brother G. accompanying it. So that her mortal remains now rest with those of my dear father.—*Letter from Mrs. Hopkins to her aunt in New Haven, dated Williamstown, Dec. 1, 1848.*

[9] The wife of her brother, Mr. Henry M. Payson.

[10] The Rev. Benjamin Tappan, D.D., an old friend of her father's and one of the patriarchs of the Maine churches.

[11] See appendix B, for a brief sketch of his life.

[12] Sermons by Henry Edward Manning, Archdeacon of Chichester (now Cardinal Manning), 1st, 2nd, and 3rd Series.

[13] The Rev. D. W. Poor, D.D., now of Philadelphia. He had been settled at Fair Haven, near New Bedford, and was then a pastor in Newark.

CHAPTER 5 - IN THE SCHOOL OF SUFFERING - 1851-1858.

I.

Removal to New York and first summer there. Letters. Loss of Sleep and Anxiety about Eddy. Extracts from Eddy's Journal, describing his last Illness and Death. Lines entitled "To my Dying Eddy."

Mrs. Prentiss' removal to New York was an important link in the chain of outward events, which prepared her for her special life work. It introduced her at once into a circle unsurpassed, perhaps, by any other in the country, for its intelligence, its domestic and social virtues, and its earnest Christian spirit. The Mercer street Presbyterian Church contained at that time many members whose names were known and honored the world over, in the spheres of business, professional life, literature, philanthropy, and religion and among its homes were some that seemed to have attained almost the perfection of beauty. In these homes, the new pastor's wife soon became an object of tender love and devotion. Here she found herself surrounded by all congenial influences. Her mind and heart alike were refreshed and stimulated in the healthiest manner. And to add to her joy, several dear old friends lived near her and sat in adjoining pews on the Sabbath.

But happy as were the auspices that welcomed her to New York, the experience of the past two years had taught her not to expect too much from any outward conditions. She entered, therefore, upon this new period of her life in a very sober mood. Nor had many months elapsed before she began to hear premonitory murmurs of an incoming sea of trouble. Most of the summer of 1851 she remained in town with the children. An extract from a letter to her youngest brother, dated August 1, will show how she whiled away many a weary hour:

It has been very hot this summer our house is large and cool, and above all, I have a nice bathing-room opening out of my chamber, with hot and cold water and a shower bath, which is a world of comfort. We spent part of last week at Rockaway, L. I., visiting a friend. [1] I nearly froze to death, but George and the children were much benefited. I have improved fast in health since we came here. Yesterday I walked two and a half miles with George, and a year ago at this time, I could not walk a quarter of a mile without being sick after it for some days. When I feel miserably, I just put on my bonnet, get into an omnibus, and go rattlety-bang down town the air, the shaking, the jolting, and the sightseeing make me feel better and so I get along. If I could safely leave my children, I should go with George. He hates to go alone and surely I hate to be left alone in fact instead of liking each other's society less and less, we every day get more and more dependent on each other, and take separation harder and harder. Our children are well.

To her husband, who had gone to visit an old friend, at Harpswell, on the coast of Maine, she writes a few days later:

On Saturday very early, Professor Smith called with the House of Seven Gables. I read about half of it in the evening. One sees the hand of the *artist* as clearly in such a work as in painting, and the hand of a skilful one, too. I have read many books with more interest, but never one in which I was so diverted from the story to a study of the author himself. So far, there is nothing exciting in it. I do not know who supplied the pulpit on Sunday morning. The sermon was to young men, which was not as appropriate as it might have been, considering there were no young men present, unless I except our Eddy and other sprigs of humanity of his age. I suppose you will wonder what in the world I let Eddy go for. Well, I took a fancy to let Margaret try him, as nobody would know him in the gallery and he coaxed so prettily to go. He was highly excited at the permission, and as I was putting on his sacque, I directed Margaret to take it off if he fell asleep. "Ho! I shan't go to sleep," quoth he "Christ doesn't have rocking-chairs in His house." He set off in high spirits, and during the long prayer I heard him laugh loud soon after I heard a rattling as of a parasol and Eddy saying, "There it is!" by which time Margaret, finding he was going to begin a regular frolic, sagely took him out.

August 7th—The five girls from Brooklyn all spent yesterday here. They had a regular frolic towards night, bathing and shower bathing. Afterwards we all went on top of the house. It was very pleasant up there. I took the children to Barnum's Museum, as I proposed doing. They were delighted, particularly with the "Happy Family," which consisted of cats, rats, birds, dogs, rabbits, monkeys, etc., etc., dwelling together in unity. I observed that though the cats forbore to lay a paw upon the rats and mice about them, they yet took a melancholy pleasure in *looking* at these dainty morsels, from which nothing could persuade them to turn off their eyes. I am glad that you got away from New Bedford alive and that you did not stay longer, but hearing about our friends there made me quite long to see them myself. Do have just the best time in the world at Harpswell, and do not let the Rev. Elijah drown you for the sake of catching your mantle as you go down. I dare not tell you how much I miss you, lest you should think I do not rejoice in your having this vacation. May God bless and keep you.

During the autumn she suffered much again from feeble health and incessant loss of sleep. "I have often thought," she wrote to a friend, "that while so stupefied by sickness I should not be glad to see my own mother if I had to speak to her." But neither sick days nor sleepless nights could quench the Brightness of her spirit or wholly spoil her enjoyment of life. A little diary which she kept contains many gleams of sunshine, recording pleasant visits from old friends, happy hours and walks with the children, excursions to Newark, and how "amazingly" she "enjoyed the boys" (her brothers) on their return from the pursuit of golden dreams in California. In the month of November, the diary shows that her watchful eye observed in Eddy signs of disease, which filled her with anxiety. Before the close of the year, her worst fears began to be realized. She wrote, Dec. 31, "I am under a constant pressure of anxiety about Eddy. How little we know what the New Year will bring forth." Early in January, 1852, his symptoms assumed a fatal type, and on the 16th of the same month, the beautiful boy was released from his sufferings, and found rest in the kingdom of heaven, that sweet home of the little children. A few extracts from Eddy's journal will tell the story of his last days:

On the 19th of December, the Rev. Mr. Poor was here. On hearing of it, Eddy said he wanted to see him. As he took now so little interest in anything that would cost him an effort, I was surprised, but told Annie to lead him down to the parlor on reaching it they found Mr. Poor not there, and they then went up to the study. I heard their father's joyous greeting as he opened his door for them, and how he welcomed Eddy, in particular, with a perfect shower of kisses and caresses. This was the last time the dear child's own feet ever took him there but his father afterwards frequently carried him up in his arms and amused him with pictures, especially with what Eddy called the "bear books." [2] One morning Ellen told him she was going to make a little pie for his dinner, but on his next appearance in the kitchen told him she had let it burn all up in the oven, and that she felt *dreadfully* about it. "Never mind, Ellie," said he, "mamma does not like to have me eat pie, but when I *get well* I shall have as many as I want."

On the 24th of December, Mr. Stearns and Anna were here. I was out with the latter most of the day on my return Eddy came to me with a little flag which his uncle had given him, and after they had left us he ran up and down with it, and as my eye followed him, I thought he looked happier and brighter and more like himself than I had seen him for a long time. He kept saying, "Mr. Stearns gave me this flag!" and then would correct himself and say, "I mean my *Uncle* Stearns." On this night, he hung up his bag for his presents, and after going to bed, surveyed it with a chuckle of pleasure peculiar to him, and finally fell asleep in this happy mood. I took great delight in arranging his and A.'s presents, and getting them safely into their bags. He enjoyed Christmas as much as I had reason to expect he would, in his state of health, and was busy among his new playthings all day. He had taken a fancy within a few weeks to kneel at family prayers with me at my chair, and would throw one little arm round my neck, while with the other hand he so prettily and seriously covered his eyes. As their heads touched my face as they knelt, I observed that Eddy's felt hot when compared with A.'s just enough so to increase my uneasiness. On entering the nursery on New Year's morning, I was struck with his appearance as he lay in bed his face being spotted all over. On asking Margaret about it, she said he had been crying, and that this occasioned the spots. This did not seem probable to me, for I had never seen anything of this kind on his face before. How little I knew that these were the last tears my darling would ever shed.

On Sunday morning, January 4, not being able to come himself, Dr. Buck sent Dr. Watson in his place. I told Dr. W. that I thought Eddy had water on the brain he said it was not so, and ordered nothing but a warm bath. On Thursday, January 8, while Margaret was at dinner, I knelt by the side of the cradle, rocking it very gently, and he asked me to tell him a story. I asked what about, and he said, "A little boy," on which I said something like this: Mamma knows a dear little boy who was very sick. His head ached and he felt sick all over. God said, I must let that little lamb come into my fold then his head will never ache again, and he will be a very happy little lamb. I used the words little lamb because he was so fond of them. Often he would run to his nurse with his face full of animation and say, "Marget! Mamma says I am her little lamb!" While I was telling him this story, his eyes were fixed intelligently on my face. I then said, "Would you like to know the name of this boy?" With eagerness he said, "Yes, yes, mamma!" Taking his dear little hand in mine, and kissing it, I said, "It was Eddy." Just then, his nurse came in and his attention was diverted, so I said no more.

On Sunday, January 11, at noon, while they were all at dinner, I was left alone with my darling for a few moments, and could not help kissing his unconscious lips. To my utter amazement, he looked up and plainly recognized me and warmly returned my kiss. Then he said feebly, but distinctly twice, "I want some meat and potato." I do not think I should have been more delighted if he had risen from the dead, once more to recognize me. Oh, it was *such* a comfort to have one more kiss, and to be able to gratify one more wish!

On Friday, January 16th, his little weary sighs became more profound, and, as the day advanced, more like groans but appeared to indicate extreme fatigue, rather than severe pain. Towards night, his breathing became quick and laborious, and between seven and eight slight spasms agitated his little feeble frame. He uttered cries of distress for a few minutes, when they ceased, and his loving and gentle spirit ascended to that world where thousands of holy children and the blessed company of angels and our blessed Lord Jesus, I doubt not, joyfully welcomed him. Now we were able to say, *it is well with the child!*

"Oh," said the gardener, as he passed down the garden-walk, "who plucked that flower? Who gathered that plant?" His fellow servants answered, "The MASTER!" And the gardener held his peace.

The feelings of the mother's heart on Friday found vent in some lines entitled *To My Dying Eddy January 16th*. Here are two stanzas:

>Blest child! dear child! For thee is Jesus calling
>And of our household thee—and only thee!
>Oh, hasten hence! to His embraces hasten!
>Sweet shall thy rest and safe thy shelter be.
>Thou who unguarded ne'er hast left our threshold,
> Alone must venture now an unknown way

<blockquote>
Yet, fear not! Footprints of an Infant Holy
Lie on thy path. Thou canst not go astray.
</blockquote>

In a letter to her friend, Mrs. Allen, of New Bedford, dated January 28, she writes:

During our dear little Eddy's illness we were surrounded with kind friends and many prayers were offered for us and for him. Nothing that could alleviate our affliction was left undone or unthought of, and we feel that it would be most unchristian and ungrateful in us to even wonder at that Divine will which has bereaved us of our only boy—the light and sunshine of our household. We miss him *sadly*. I need not explain to you, who know all about it, *how* sadly but we rejoice that he has got away from this troublous life, and that we have had the privilege of giving so dear a child to God. When he was well he was one of the happiest creatures I ever saw, and I am sure he is well now, and that he is as happy as his joyous nature makes him susceptible of becoming. God has been most merciful to us in this affliction, and, if a bereaved, we are still a *happy* household and full of thanksgiving. Give my love to both the children and tell them they must not forget us, and when they think and talk of their dear brother and sisters in heaven, they must sometimes think of the little Eddy who is there too.

* * * * *

II.
Birth of her Third Child. Reminiscence of a Sabbath-Evening Talk. Story of the Baby's Sudden Illness and Death. Summer of 1852. Lines entitled "My Nursery."

The shock of Eddy's death proved almost too much for Mrs. Prentiss' enfeebled frame. She bore it, however, with sweet submission, and on the 17th of the following April her sorrow was changed to joy, and Eddy's empty place filled, as she thought, by the birth of Elizabeth, her third child, a picture of infantine health and beauty. But, although the child seemed perfectly well, the mother herself was brought to the verge of the grave. For a week or two, her life wavered in the balance, and she was quite in the mood to follow Eddy to the better country. Her husband, recording a "long and most interesting conversation" with her on Sabbath evening, May 2nd, speaks of the "depth and tenderness of her religious feelings, of her sense of sin and of the grace and glory of the Savior," and then adds, "Her old Richmond exercises seem of late to have returned with their former strength and beauty increased many-fold." On the 14th of May, she was able to write in pencil these lines to her sister, Mrs. Hopkins:

I little thought that I should ever write to you again, but I have been brought through a great deal, and now have reason to expect to get well. I never knew how much I loved you until I gave up all hope of ever seeing you again, and I have not strength yet to tell you all about it. Poor George has suffered much. I hope all will be blessed to him and to me. I am still confined to bed. The doctor thinks there may be an abscess near the hip joint, and, until that is cured, I can neither lie straight in bed or stand on my feet or ride out. Everybody is kind. Our cup has run over. It is a sore trial not to be allowed to nurse baby. She is kept in another room. I only see her once a day. She begins to smile, and is very bright-eyed. I hope your journey will do you good. If you can, do write a few lines—not more. But, goodbye.

Hardly had she penned these lines, when, like a thunderbolt from a clear sky, another stunning blow fell upon her. On the 19th of May, after an illness of a few hours, Bessie, too, was folded forever in the arms of the Good Shepherd. Here is the mother's own story of her loss:

Our darling Eddy died on the 16th of January. The baby he had so often spoken of was born on the 17th of April. I was too feeble to have any care of her. Never had her in my arms but twice once the day before she died and once while she was dying. I never saw her little feet. She was a beautiful little creature, with a great quantity of dark hair and very dark blue eyes. The nurse had to keep her in another room on account of my illness. When she was a month old, she brought her to me one afternoon. "This child is perfectly beautiful," said she "tomorrow I mean to dress her up and have her likeness taken." I asked her to get me up in bed and let me take her a minute. She objected, and I urged her a good deal, until at last she consented. The moment I took her I was struck by her unearthly, absolutely angelic expression and, not having strength enough to help it, burst out crying bitterly, and cried all the afternoon while I was struggling to give her up.

Her father was at Newark. When he came home at dark, I told him I was sure that baby was going to die. He laughed at me, said my weak health made me fancy it, and asked the nurse if the child was not well. She said she was—perfectly well. My presentiment remained, however, in full force, and the first thing next morning I asked Margaret to go and see how baby was. She came back, saying, "She is very well. She lies there on the bed scolding to herself." I cried out to have her instantly brought to me. M. refused, saying the nurse would be displeased. But my anxieties were excited by the use of the word "scolding," as I knew no baby a month old did anything of that sort, and insisted on its being brought to me. The instant I touched it I felt its head to be of a burning heat, and sent for the nurse at once. When she came, I said, "This child is *very sick*." "Yes," she said, "but I wanted you to have your breakfast first. At one o'clock in the night, I found a little swelling. I do not know what it is, but the child is certainly very sick." On examination, I knew it was erysipelas. "Do not say that," said the nurse, and burst into tears. I made them get me up and partly dress me, as I was so excited I could not stay in bed.

Dr. Buck came at ten o'clock he expressed no anxiety, but prescribed for her and George went out to get what he ordered. The nurse brought her to me at eleven o'clock and begged me to observe that the spot had turned black. I knew at once that this was fearful, fatal disease, and entreated George to go and tell the doctor. He went to please me, though he saw no need of it, and gave the wrong message to the doctor, to the effect that the swelling was increasing, to which the doctor replied that it naturally would do so. The little creature, whose moans Margaret had termed scolding, now was heard all over that floor every breath a moan that tore my heart in pieces. I begged to have her brought to me but the nurse sent word she was too sick to be moved. I then begged the nurse to come and tell me exactly what she thought of her, but she said she could not leave her. I then crawled on my hands and knees into the room, being unable then and for a long time after to bear my own weight.

What a scene our nursery presented! Everything upset and tossed about, medicines here and there on the floor, a fire like a fiery furnace, and Miss H. sitting hopelessly and with falling tears with the baby on a pillow in her lap—all its boasted beauty gone forever. The sight was appalling and its moans heart-rending. George came and got me back to my sofa and said he felt as if he should jump out of the window every time he heard that dreadful sound. He had to go out and made me promise not to try to go to the nursery until his return. I foolishly promised. Mrs. White [3] called, and I told her I was going to lose my baby she was very kind and went in to see it but I believe expressed no opinion as to its state. But she repeated an expression which I repeated to myself many times that day, and have repeated thousands of times since—*"God never makes a mistake."*

Margaret went soon after she left to see how the poor little creature was, and did not come back. Hour after hour passed and no one came. I lay racked with cruel torture, bitterly regretting my promise to George, listening to those moans until I was nearly wild. Then in a frenzy of despair, I pulled myself over to my bureau, where I had arranged the dainty little garments my darling was to wear, and which I had promised myself so much pleasure in seeing her wear. I took out everything she would need for her burial, with a sort of wild pleasure in doing for her one little service, where I had hoped before to render so many. She it was whom we expected to fill our lost Eddy's vacant place we thought we had *had* our sorrow and that now our joy had come. As I lay back exhausted, with these garments on my breast, Louisa Shipman [4] opened the door. One glance at my piteous face, for oh, how glad I was to see her! Made her burst into tears before she knew what she was crying for.

"Oh, go bring me news from my poor dying baby!" I almost screamed, as she approached me. "And see, here are her grave-clothes." "Oh, Lizzy, have you gone crazy?" cried she, with a fresh burst of tears. I besought her to go, told her how my promise bound me, made her listen to those terrible sounds that two doors could not shut out. As she left the room, she met Dr. B. and they went to the nursery together. She soon came back, quiet and composed, but very sorrowful. "Yes, she is dying," said she, "the doctor says so she will not live an hour." … At last, we heard the sound of George's key. Louise ran to call him. I crawled once more to the nursery, and snatched my baby in fierce triumph from the nurse. At least once, I would hold my child, and nobody should prevent me. George, pale as death, baptized her as I held her in my trembling arms there were a few more of those terrible, never-to-be-forgotten sounds, and at seven o'clock, we were once more left with only one child. A short, sharp conflict and our baby were gone.

Dr. B. came in later and said the whole thing was to him like a thunderclap—as it was to her poor father. To me it followed closely on the presentiment that in some measure prepared me for it. Here I sit with empty hands. I have had the little coffin in my arms, but my baby's face could not be seen, so rudely had death marred it. Empty hands, empty hands, a worn-out, exhausted body, and unutterable longings to flee from a world that has had for me so many sharp experiences. God help me, my baby, my baby! God help me, my little lost Eddy!

But although the death of these two children tore with anguish the mother's heart, she made no show of grief, and to the eye of the world, her life soon appeared to move on as aforetime. Never again, however, was it exactly the same life. She had entered into the fellowship of Christ's sufferings, and the new experience wrought a great change in her whole being.

A part of the summer and the early autumn of 1852 were passed among kind friends at Newport, in Portland, and at the Ocean House on Cape Elizabeth. She returned much refreshed, and gave herself up cheerfully to her accustomed duties. But a cloud rested still upon her home, and at times, the old grief came back again with renewed poignancy. Here are a few lines expressive of her feelings. They were written in pencil on a little scrap of paper:

MY NURSERY. 1852.

> I thought that prattling boys and girls
> Would fill this empty room

> That my rich heart would gather flowers
> From childhood's opening bloom.
> One child and two green graves are mine,
> This is God's gift to me
> A bleeding, fainting, broken heart—
> This is my gift to Thee.

* * * * *

III.

> Summer at White Lake. Sudden Death of her Cousin, Miss Shipman.
> Quarantined. *Little Suzy's Six Birthdays*. How she wrote it. *The
> Flower of the Family*. Her Motive in writing it. Letter of Sympathy to a
> bereaved Mother. A Summer at the Seaside. *Henry and Bessie*.

The year 1853 was passed quietly and in better health. In the early summer, she made a delightful visit at The Island, near West Point, the home of the author of "The Wide, Wide World." She was warmly attached to Miss Warner and her sister, and hardly less so, to their father and aunt, whose presence then adorned that pleasant home with so much light and sweetness.

> Early in August she went with her husband and child to White Lake,
> Sullivan Co., N. Y., where, in company with several families from the
> Mercer street church, she spent six weeks in breathing the pure country
> air, and in healthful outdoor exercise. [5]

About the middle of October she was greatly distressed by the sudden death of the young cousin, already mentioned, who was staying with her during her husband's absence on a visit to New Bedford. Miss Shipman was a bright, attractive girl, and enthusiastic in her devotion to Mrs. Prentiss. The latter, in a letter to her husband, dated Saturday morning, October 15th, 1853, writes:

I imagine you enjoying this fine morning, and cannot rejoice enough, that you are having such weather. A. is bright and well and is playing in her baby-house and singing. Louise is still quite sick, and I see no prospect of her not remaining so for some time. The morning after you left, I thought to be sure she had the smallpox. The doctor, however, calls it a rash. It makes her look dreadfully and feel dreadfully. She gets hardly a moment of sleep and takes next to no nourishment. Arrowroot is all the doctor allows. He comes twice a day and seems *very* kind and full of compassion. She crawled down this morning to the nursery, and seems to be asleep now. Mrs. Bull very kindly offered to come and do anything if Louise should need it, but I do not think she will be sick enough for that. I feel well and able to do all that is necessary. The last proof sheets came last night, so that job is off my hands. [6] And now, darling, I cannot tell you how I miss you. I never missed you more in my life, if as much. I hope you are having a nice visit. Give my love to Capt. and Mrs. Gibbs and all our friends. Your most loving little wife.

On the following Wednesday, October 19th, she writes to her husband's mother:

You will be shocked to hear that Louisa Shipman died on Sunday night and was buried yesterday. Her disease was spotted fever of the most malignant character, and raged with great fury. She dropped away most unexpectedly to us, before I had known five minutes that she was in danger, and I came near being entirely alone with her. Dr. M. happened to be here and also her mother-in-law but I had been alone in the house with her all day. It is a dreadful shock to us all, and I feel perfectly stupefied. George got home in time for the funeral, but Dr. Skinner performed the services. Anna will go home tomorrow and tell you all about it. She and Mr. S. slept away, as the upper part of the house is airing and tonight they will sleep at Prof. Smith's.

The case was even more fearful than she supposed while writing this letter. Upon her describing it to Dr. Buck, who called a few hours later, he exclaimed, "Why, it was malignant small-pox! You must all be vaccinated instantly and have the bedding and house disinfected." This was done but it was too late. Her little daughter had the disease, though in a mild form and one of her brothers, who was passing the autumn with her, had it so severely as barely to escape with his life. She herself became a nurse to them both, and passed the next two months quarantined within her own walls. To her husband's mother she wrote:

I am not allowed to see *anyone*—am very lonesome, and hope Anna will write and tell me every little thing about you all. The scenes I have lately passed through make me tremble when I think what a fatal malady lurks in every corner of our house. And speaking after the manner of men, does it not seem almost incredible that this child, watched from her birth like *the apple of our eyes*, should yet fall into the jaws of this loathsome disease? I see more and more that parents *must* leave their children to Providence.

In the early part of this year, Mrs. Prentiss wrote *Little Suzy's Six Birthdays*, the book that has given so much delight to tens of thousands of little children, wherever the English tongue is spoken. Like most of her books, it was an inspiration and was composed with the utmost rapidity. She read the different chapters, as they were written, to her husband, child, and brother, who all with one voice expressed their admiration. In about ten days, the work was finished. The manuscript was in a clear, delicate hand and without an erasure. Upon its publication, it was at once recognized as a production of real genius, inimitable in its kind, and neither the popular verdict nor the verdict of the children as to its merits has ever changed.

Mrs. Prentiss, as has been stated already, began to write for the press at an early age. But from the time of her going to Richmond till 1853—a period of thirteen years—her pen was well nigh idle, except in the way of correspondence. When, therefore, she gave herself again to literary labor, it was with a largely increased fund of knowledge and experience upon which to draw. These thirteen years had taught her rich lessons, both in literature and in life. They had been especially fruitful in revealing to her the heart of childhood and quickening her sympathy with its joys and sorrows. And all these lessons prepared her to write Little Suzy's Six Birthdays and the other Susy books.

The year 1854 was marked by the birth of her fourth child, and by the publication of *The Flower of the Family*. This work was received with great favor both at home and abroad. It was soon translated into French under the title, *La Fleur de la Famille*, and later into German under the title, *Die Perle der Familie*. In both languages, it received the warmest praise.

In a letter to her friend Mrs. Clark, of Portland, she thus refers to this book:

I long to have it doing good. I never had such desires about anything in my life and I never sat down to write without first praying that I might not be suffered to write anything that would do harm, and that, on the contrary, I might be taught to say what would do good. And it has been a great comfort to me that every word of praise I ever have received from others concerning it has been "it will do good," and this I have had from so many sources that amid much trial and sickness ever since its publication, I have had rays of sunshine creeping in now and then to cheer and sustain me.

To the same friend, just bereft of her two children, she writes a few months later:

Is it possible, is it possible that you are made childless? I feel distressed for you, my dear friend I long to fly to you and weep with you it seems as if I *must* say or do something to comfort you. But God only can help you now, and how thankful I am for a throne of grace and power where I can commend you, again and again, to Him who doeth all things well.

I never realize my own affliction in the loss of my children as I do when death enters the house of a friend. Then I feel that *I cannot have it so*. But why should I think I know better than my Divine Master what is good for me, or good for those I love! Dear Carrie,' trust that in this hour of sorrow you have with you that Presence, before which alone sorrow and sighing flee away. *God* is left *Christ* is left sickness, accident, death cannot touch you here. Is not this a blissful thought? As I sit at my desk my eye is attracted by the row of books before me, and what a comment on life are their very titles: "Songs in the Night," "Light on Little Graves," "The Night of Weeping," "The Death of Little Children," "The Folded Lamb," "The Broken Bud," these have strayed one by one into my small enclosure, to speak peradventure a word in season unto my weariness. And yet, dear Carrie, this is not all of life. You and I have tasted some of its highest joys, as well as its deepest sorrows, and it has in reserve for us only just what is best for us. May sorrow bring us both nearer to Christ! I can almost fancy my little Eddy has taken your little Maymee by the hand and led her to the bosom of Jesus. How strange our children, our own little infants, have seen Him in His glory, which we are only yet longing for and struggling towards!

If it will not frighten you to own a Unitarian book, there is one called "Christian Consolation" by Rev. A. P. Peabody, that I think you would find very profitable. I see nothing, or next to nothing, Unitarian in it, while it is *full* of rich, holy experience. One sermon on "Contingent Events and Providence" touches your case exactly.

No event of special importance marked the year 1855. She spent the month of July among her friends in Portland, and the next six weeks at the Ocean House on Cape Elizabeth. This was one of her favorite places of rest. She never tired of watching the waves and their "multitudinous laughter," of listening to the roar of the breakers, or climbing the rocks and wandering along the shore in quest of shells and sea-grasses. In gathering and pressing the latter, she passed many a happy hour. In August of this year appeared one of her best children's books, *Henry and Bessie or, What they Did in the Country*.

* * * *

IV.

A Memorable Year. Lines on the Anniversary of Eddy's Death. Extracts from her Journal. *Little Suzy's Six Teachers*. The Teachers' Meeting. A New York Waif. Summer in the Country. Letters. *Little Suzy's Little Servants*. Extracts from her Journal. "Alone with God."

The records of the year 1856 are singularly full and interesting. It was a year of poignant suffering, of sharp conflicts of soul, and of great peace and joy. Its earlier months, especially, were shadowed by a dark cloud of anxiety and distress. And her feeble bodily state caused by care-worn days and sleepless nights, added to the trouble. Old sorrows, too, came back again. On the 16th of January, the anniversary of Eddy's death, she gave vent to her feelings in some pathetic verses, of which the following lines form a part:

>Four years, four weary years, my child,
>Four years ago to-night,
>With parting cry of anguish wild
>Thy spirit took its flight ah me!
>Took its eternal flight.
>And in that hour of mortal strife
>I thought I felt the throe,
>The birth-pang of a grief, whose life
>Must soothe my tearless woe, must soothe
>And ease me of my woe.
>Yet folded far through all these years,
>Folded from mortal eyes,
>Lying alas "too deep for tears,"
>Unborn, unborn it lies, within
>My heart of heart it lies.
>My sinless child! upon thy knees
>Before the Master pray
>Methinks thy infant hands might seize
>And shed upon my way sweet peace
>Sweet peace upon my way.

Here follow some extracts from her journal.

Jan 3rd. 1856.—Had no time to write on New Year's Day, as we had a host of callers. It was a very hard day, as I was quite unwell, and had at last to give up and go to bed.

15th—Am quite uneasy about baby, as it seems almost impossible she should long endure such severe pain and want of sleep. My life is a very anxious one. I feel every day more and more longing for my home in heaven. Sometimes I fear it amounts almost to a sinful longing—for surely I ought to be willing to live or die, just as God pleases.

Feb. 1st.—I have had no heart to make a record of what has befallen us since I last wrote. And yet I may, sometime, want to recall this experience, painful as it is. Dear little baby had been improving in health, and on Wednesday we went to dine at Mrs. Wainright's. We went at four. About eight, word came that she was ill. When I got home, I found her insensible, with her eyes wide open, her breathing terrific, and her condition in every respect very alarming. Just as Dr. Buck was coming in, she roused a little, but soon relapsed into the same state. He told us she was dying. I felt like a stone, *In a moment* I seemed to give up my hold on her. She appeared no longer mine but God's. It is always so in such great emergencies. *Then,* my will that struggles so about trifles, makes no effort. But as we sat hour after hour watching the alternations of color in her purple face and listening to that terrible gasping, rattling sound, I said to myself "A few more nights like this, and I do believe my body and soul would yield to such anguish." Oh, why should I try to tell myself what a night it was? God knows, God only! How He has smitten me by means of this child, He well knows. She remained thus about twelve hours. Twelve hours of martyrdom to me such as I never had known. Then to our unspeakable amazement she roused up, nursed, and then fell into a sweet sleep of some hours.

Sunday, Feb. 3rd.—The stupor, or whatever it is, in which that dreadful night has left me, is on me still. I have no more sense or feeling than a stone. I kneel down before God and do not say a word. I take up a book and read, but get hold of nothing. At church, I felt afraid I should fall upon the people and tear them. I could wish no one to pity me or even know that I am smitten. It does seem to me that those who can sit down and cry, know nothing of misery.

Feb. 4th.—At last the ice melts and I can get near my God—my only comfort, my only joy, my All in all! This morning I was able to open my heart to Him and to cast some of this burden on Him, who alone *knows* what it is.... I see that it is sweet to be a pilgrim and a stranger, and that it matters *very little* what befalls me on the way to my blessed home. If God pleases to spare my child a little longer, I will be very thankful. May He take this season, when earthly comfort fails me, to turn me more than ever to Himself. For some months, I have enjoyed a *great deal* in Him. Prayer has been very sweet and I have had some glimpses of joys indescribable.

6th.—She still lives. I know not what to think. One moment I think one thing and the next another. It is harder to submit to this suspense than to a real, decided blow. But I desire to leave it to my God. He knows all her history and all mine. He orders all these aggravating circumstances and I would not change them. My darling has not lived in vain. For eighteen months, she has been the little rod used by my Father for my chastisement and not, I think, quite in vain. Oh my God! Stay not Thy hand until Thou hast perfected that which concerneth me. Send anything rather than unsanctified prosperity.

Feb. 10th.—To help divert my mind from such incessant brooding over my sorrows, I am writing a new book. I had just begun it when baby's ill turn arrested me. I trust it may do some little good at least I would not dare to write it, if it *could* do none. May God bless it!

Feb. 14th.—Wanted to go to the prayer meeting but concluded to take A. to hear Gough at the Tabernacle. Seeing such a crowd always makes me long to be in that happy crowd of saints and angels in heaven, and hearing children sing so sweetly made me pray for an entrance into the singing, praising multitude there. Oh, when shall I be one of that blessed company who *sin* not! My book is done may God bless it to *one* child at least—then it will not have been wasted time.

The book referred to was *Little Suzy's Six Teachers*. It was published in the spring, and at once took its place beside the *Six Birthdays* in the hearts of the children a place it still continues to hold. The six teachers are Mrs. Love, Mr. Pain, Aunt Patience, Mr. Ought, Miss Joy, and the angel Faith. At the end of six years, they hold a meeting and report to little Suzy's parents what they have been doing. The closing chapter, herewith quoted, gives an account of this meeting, and may serve as a specimen of the style and spirit of all the Little Susy books.

"If Mr. Pain is to be at the meeting, I cannot go," said Miss Joy.

She stood on tiptoe before the glass, dressing herself in holiday clothes.

"Perhaps he would be willing to leave his rod behind him," said Mrs. Love. "I will ask him at all events."

Mr. Pain thought he should not feel at home without his rod. He said he always liked to have it in his hands, whether he was to use it or not.

Miss Joy was full of fun and mischief about this time, so she slipped up slyly behind Mr. Pain while he was talking and snatched away the rod before he could turn round. Mrs. Love smiled on seeing this little trick, and they all went down to the parlor and seated themselves with much gravity. Little Susy sat in the midst in her own low chair looking wide awake, you may depend. Her papa and mamma sat on each side like two judges. Mrs. Love rocked herself in the rocking chair in a contented, easy way and Aunt Patience, who liked to do such things, helped Miss Joy to find the leaves of her report—which might have been roseleaves, they were so small.

Mr. Ought looked very good indeed, and the angel Faith shone across the room like a sunbeam.

"Susy will be six years old tomorrow," said her papa. "You have all been teaching her ever since she was born. We will now listen to your reports and hear what you have taught her, and whether you have done her any good."

They were all silent, but everybody looked at Mrs. Love as much as to say she should begin. Mrs. Love took out a little book with a sky-blue cover and began to read:

"I have not done much for Susy, but love her dearly and I have not taught her much, but to love everybody. When she was a baby I tried to teach her to smile, but I do not think I could have taught her if Miss Joy had not helped me. And when she was sick, I was always sorry for her, and tried to comfort her."

"You have done her a great deal of good," said Suzy's papa, "we will engage you to stay six years longer, should God spare her life."

Then Mr. Pain took up his book. It had a black cover, but the leaves were gilt-edged and the cover was spangled with stars.

"I have punished Susy a good many times," said Mr. Pain. "Sometimes I slapped her with my hand sometimes I struck her with my rod sometimes I made her sick but I never did any of these things because I was angry with her or liked to hurt her. I only came when Mrs. Love called me."

"You have taught her excellent lessons," said Suzy's papa, "if it had not been for you she would be growing up disobedient and selfish. You may stay six years longer."

Then Mr. Pain made a low bow and said he was thinking of going away and sending his brother, Mr. Sorrow, and his sister, Mrs. Disappointment, to take his place."

"Oh, no!" cried Suzy's mamma, "not yet, not yet! Susy is still so little!"

Then Mr. Pain said he would stay without a rod, as Susy was now too old to be whipped.

Then Miss Joy took up her book with its rainbow cover and tried to read. But she laughed so heartily all the time, and her leaves kept flying out of her hands at such a rate, that it was not possible to understand what she was saying. It was all about clapping hands and running races, and picking flowers and having a good time. Everybody laughed just because she laughed, and Suzy's papa could hardly keep his face grave long enough to say:

"You have done more good than tongue can tell. You have made her just such a merry, happy, laughing little creature as I wanted her to be. You must certainly stay six years longer."

Then Mr. Ought drew forth his book. It had silver covers and its leaves were of the most delicate tissue.

"I have taught little Susy to be good," said he. "Never to touch what is not hers never to speak a word that is not true never to have a thought she would not like the great and holy God to see. If I stay six years longer, I can teach her a great deal more, for she begins now to understand my faintest whisper. She is such a little girl as I love to live with."

Then Susy turned rosy-red with pleasure and her papa and mamma got up and shook hands with Mr. Ought and begged him never, never to leave their darling child as long as she lived.

It was now the turn of Aunt Patience. Her book had covers wrought by her own hands in grave and gay colors well mingled together.

"When I first came here," she said, "Susy used to cry a great deal whenever she was hurt or punished. When she was sick, she was very hard to please. When she sat down to learn to sew and to read and to write, she would break her thread in anger, or throw her book on the floor, or declare she never could learn. But now she has left off crying when she is hurt, and tries to bear the pain quietly. When she is sick she does not fret or complain, but takes her medicine without a word. When she is sewing, she does not twitch her thread into knots, and when she is writing she writes slowly and carefully. I have rocked her to sleep a thousand times. I have been shut up in a closet with her again and again, and I hope I have done her some good and taught her some useful lessons."

"Indeed you have, Aunt Patience," said Suzy's papa, "but Susy is not yet perfect. We shall need you six years longer."

And now the little angel Faith opened his golden book and began to read:

"I have taught Susy that there is another world besides this, and have told her that it is her real home, and what a beautiful and happy one it is. I have told her a great deal about Jesus and the holy angels. I do not know much myself. I am not very old, but if I stay here six years longer I shall grow wiser and I will teach Susy all I learn, and we will pray together every morning and every night, till at last she loves the Lord Jesus with all her heart and soul and mind and strength."

Then Suzy's papa and mamma looked at each other and smiled, and they both said:

"Oh, beautiful angel, never leave her!"

And the angel answered:

"I will stay with her as long as she lives, and will never leave her till I leave her at the very door of heaven."

Then the teachers began to put up their books, and Suzy's papa and mamma kissed her, and said:

"We have had a great deal of comfort in our little daughter and, with God's blessing, we shall see her grow up a loving, patient, and obedient child—full of joy and peace and rich in faith and good works."

So they all bade each other goodnight and went thankfully to bed.

The next entry in the journal notes a trait of character, or rather of temperament, which often excited the wonder and also the anxiety of her friends. It caused her no little discomfort, but she could never withstand its power.

March 21st.—I have been busy with a sewing fit and find the least interesting piece of work I can get hold of, as great a temptation as the most charming. For if its *charm* does not absorb my time and thoughts, the eager haste to finish and get it out of the way, does. This is my life. I either am stupefied by ill health or sorrow, so as to feel no interest in anything, or am *absorbed* in whatever business, work, or pleasure I have on hand.

But neither anxiety about her child, household cares, or any work she had so absorbed her thoughts as to render her insensible to the sorrows and trials of others. On the contrary, they served rather to call forth and intensify her kindly sympathies. A single case will illustrate this. A poor little girl—one of those waifs of humanity in which a great city abounds—had been commended to her by a friend. In a letter to this friend, dated March 17, 1856, she writes:

That little girl came, petticoat and all we gave her some breakfast, and I then went down with her to Avenue A. On the way, she told me that you gave her some money. To my great sorrow we found, on reaching the school, that they could not take another one, as they were already overflowing. As we came out, I saw that the poor little soul was just ready to burst into tears, and said to her "Now you're disappointed, I know!" whereupon she actually looked up into my face and *smiled*. You know I was afraid I never should make her smile, she looked so forlorn. I brought her home to get some books, as she said she could read, and she is to come again tomorrow. A lady to whom I told the whole story, sent me some stockings that would about go on to her big toe however, they will be nice for her little sister. The weather has been so mild that I thought it would not be worthwhile to make her a cloak or anything of that sort but next fall I shall see that she is comfortably clad, if she behaves as well as she did the day she was here. Oh, dear! What a drop in the great bucket of New York misery, one such child is! Yet somebody must look out for the drops, and I am only too thankful to seize on this one.

In June she went, with the children, to Westport, Conn., where in rural quiet and seclusion she passed the next three months. Here are some extracts from her letters, written from that place:

Westport, *June 25, 1856.*

We had a most comfortable time getting here both the children enjoyed the ride, and baby seemed unusually bright. Judge Betts was very attentive and kind to us. Mrs. G. grows more and more pleasant every day. We have plenty of good food, but she worries because I do not eat more. You know I never was famous for eating meat, and country dinners are not tempting. You cannot think how we enjoy seeing the poultry fed. There are a hundred and eighty hens and chickens, and you should see baby throw her little hand full of corn to them. We went strawberrying yesterday, all of us, and the way she was poked through bars and lifted over stonewalls would have amused you. She is already quite sunburnt but I think she is looking sweetly. I find myself all the time peeping out of the window, thinking every step is yours, or that every wagon holds a letter for me.

To Miss A. H. Woolsey, Westport, June 27.

Mr. P. enclosed your kind note in one of his own, after first reading it himself, if you ever heard of such a man. I had to laugh all alone while reading it, which was not a little provoking. We are having very nice times here indeed. Breakfast at eight, dinner at half-past twelve, and tea at half-past six, giving us an afternoon of unprecedented length for such lounging, strawberrying or egg-hunting as happens to be on the carpet. The air is perfectly loaded with the fragrance of clover blossoms and fresh hay. I never saw such clover in my life roses are nothing in comparison. I only want an old nag and a wagon, so as to drive a load of children about these lovely regions, and that I hope every moment to attain. To be sure, it would be amazingly convenient if I had a table, and did not have to sit on the floor to write upon a trunk but then one cannot have everything, and I am almost too comfortable with what I have. A. is busy reading Southey to her "children" baby is off searching for eggs, and her felicity reached its height when she found an ambitious hen had laid two in her carriage, which little thought what it was coming to the country for. I think the dear child already looks better she lives in the open air and enjoys everything.

Mrs. Buck lives about half a mile below us, and we run back and forth many times a day. I have already caught the country fashion of rushing to the windows the moment a wheel or an opening gate is heard. I fancy everybody is bringing me a letter or else want to send one to the office, and the only way to do that is to scream at passers-by and ask them if they are going that way. If you hear that I am often seen driving a flock of geese down the road, or climbing stone walls, or creeping through bar fences, you need not believe a word of it, for I am a pattern of propriety, and pride myself on my dignity. I hope, now you have begun so charmingly, that you will write again. You know what letters are in the country.

To her Husband, Westport, June 27.

I wonder where you are this lovely morning? Having a nice time somewhere, I do hope, for it is too fine a day to be lost. If you want to know where I am, why I am sitting at the window writing on a trunk that I have just lifted into a chair, in order to make a table. For table there, is none in this room, and how am I to write a book without one? If ever I get down to the village, I hope to buy, beg, borrow, or steal one, and until that time am putting off beginning my new Little Susy. [7] That note from Miss Warner, by the by, spoke so enthusiastically of the Six Teachers that I felt compensated for the mortification of hearing ———— call it a "nice" book. You will be sorry to hear that I have no prospect of getting a horse. I am quite disappointed, as besides the pleasure of driving our children, I hoped to give Mrs. Buck and the boys a share in it. Only to think of her bringing up from the city a beefsteak for baby, and proposing that the doctor should send a small piece for her every day! Thank you, darling, for your proposal about the Ocean House. I trust no such change will be needful. We are all comfortable now, the weather is delicious, and there are so many pretty walks about here, which I am only afraid I shall be too well off. Everything about the country is charming to me, and I never get tired of it. The first few days nurse seemed a good deal out of sorts but I must expect some such little vexations of course, I cannot have perfection, and for dear baby's sake, I shall try to exercise all the prudence and forbearance I can.

Sunday.—We went to church this morning and heard a most instructive and, I thought, superior sermon from Mr. Burr of Weston, on progress in religious knowledge. He used the very illustration about the cavern and the point of light that you did.

July 7th.—We all drove to the beach on Saturday. It was just the very day for such a trip, and baby was enchanted. She sat right down and began to gather stones and shells, as if she had the week before her. We were gone three hours and came home by way of the village, quite in the mood for supper. Yesterday we had a pleasant service Mr. Atkinson appears to be a truly devout, heavenly man to whom I felt my heart knit at the outset on this account, I am taking great delight in reading the Memoir of Miss Allibone. [8] How I wish I had a friend of so heavenly a temper! I fear my new Little Susy will come out at the little end of the horn. I am sure it will not be as good as the others. It is more than one quarter done.

July 21st.—What do you think I did this forenoon? Why, I finished Little Susy and shall lay it aside for some days, when I shall read it over, correct, and pack it off out of the way. Yes, I wish you would bring my German Hymn Book. I am so glad you liked the hymns I had marked! [9] And do get well so as not to have to leave off preaching the Gospel. My heart dies within me whenever I think of your leaving the ministry. Every day I live, it appears to me that the office of a Christian pastor and teacher is the best in the world. I shall not be able to write you a word tomorrow, as we are to go to Greenfield Hill to Miss Murray's, and you must take tomorrow's love to-night—if you think you can stand so much at once. God be with you and bless you.

July 30th.—Baby and I have just been having a great frolic. She was so pleased with your message that she caught up your letter and kissed it, which I think very remarkable in a child who, I am sure, never saw such a thing done. A. seems well and happy, and is as good as I think we ought to expect. I see more and more every day, that if there ever *was* such a thing as human perfection, it was as long ago as David's time when, as he says, he saw the "end" of it. How very kind the W.'s have been!

August 3rd.—I got hold of Dr. Boardman's "Bible in the Family," at the Bucks yesterday, and brought it home to read. I like it very much. There is a vein of humor running through it which, subdued as it is, must have awakened a good many smiles. He quotes some lines of Coleridge, which I wonder I did not have as a motto for Suzy's Teachers:

Love, Hope and Patience, these must be thy graces,   and in thine own heart let them first *keep school.*

To Miss Mary B. Shipman, Westport, August 11.

Dr. Buck, who has seen her twice since we came here, thinks baby wonderfully improved, and says every day she lives increases her chance of life. I have been exceedingly encouraged by all he has said, and feel a great load off my heart. Last Friday, on fifteen minutes' notice, I packed up and went *home,* taking nurse and biddies, of course. I was so restless and so perfectly *possessed* to go to meet George, that I could not help it. We went in the six o'clock train, as it was after five when I was "taken" with the fit that started me off got home in a soft rain, and to our great surprise and delight found G. there, he having got homesick at Saratoga, and just rushed to New York on his way here. We had a great rejoicing together, you may depend, and I had a charming visit of nearly three days. We got back on Monday night, rather tired, but none of us at all the worse for the expedition. Mr. P. sits here reading the Tribune, and A. is reading "Fremont's Life." She is as brown as an Indian and about as wild.

A few passages from her journal will also throw light upon this period:

June 30th.—I am finding this solitude and leisure very sweet and precious God grant it may bear the rich and abundant fruit it ought to do! Communion with Him is such a blessing, here at home in my own room, and out in the silent woods and on the wayside. Saturday, especially, I had a long walk full of blissful thoughts of Him whom I do believe I love—oh, that I loved Him better!—and in the evening Mrs. Buck came and we had some very sweet beginnings of what will, I trust, ripen into most profitable Christian communion. My heart delights in the society of those who love Him. Yesterday I had a more near access to God in prayer than usual, so that during the whole service at church I could hardly repress tears of joy and gratitude.

July 7th.—I do trust God's blessed, blessed Spirit is dealing faithfully with my soul—searching and sifting it, revealing it somewhat to itself and preparing it for the indwelling of Christ. This I do heartily desire. Oh, God! Search me and know me, and show me my own guilty, poor, meager soul, that I may turn from it, humbled and ashamed and penitent, to my blessed Savior. How very, very thankful I feel for this seclusion and leisure this quiet room where I can seek my God and pray and praise, unseen by any human eye—and which sometimes seems like the very gate of heaven.

July 23rd.—This is my dear little baby's birthday. I was not able to sleep last night at all, but at last got up and prayed specially for her. God has spared her two years I can hardly believe it! Precious years of discipline they have been, for which I do thank Him. I have prayed much for her today, and with some faith, that if her life is spared it will be for His glory. How far rather would I let her go this moment, than grow up without loving Him! Precious little creature!

27th.—This has been one of the most oppressive days I ever knew. I went to church, however, and enjoyed all the services unusually. As we rode along and I saw the grain ripe for the harvest, I said to myself, "God gathers in *His* harvest as soon as it is ripe, and if I devote myself to Him and pray much and turn entirely from the world I shall ripen, and so the sooner get where I am *all the time* yearning and longing to go!" I fear this was a merely selfish thought, but I do not know. This world seems less and less homelike every day I live. The more I pray and meditate on heaven and my Savior and saints who have crossed the flood, the stronger grows my desire to be bidden to depart hence and go up to that sinless, blessed abode. Not that I forget my comforts, my mercies here they are *manifold* I know they are. But Christ appears so precious sin so dreadful! So dreadful! Today I gave way to pride and irritation, and my agony on account of it outweighs weeks of merely earthly felicity. The idea of a Christian as he should be, and the reality of most Christians—particularly myself—why, it almost makes me shudder my only comfort is, in heaven, I *can*not sin! In heaven, I shall see Christ, and see Him as He is, and praise and honor Him as I never do and never shall do here. And yet I know my dear little ones need me, poor, and imperfect a mother as I am and I pray every hour to be made willing to wait for their sakes. For at the longest it will not be long. Oh, I do believe it is the *sin* I dread and not the suffering of life—but I know not I may be deluded. My love to my Master seems to me very shallow and contemptible. I am astonished that I love anything else. Oh, that He would this moment come down into this room and tell me I never, never, shall grieve Him again!

Some verses entitled "Alone with God," belong here:

> Into my closet fleeing, as the dove
> Doth homeward flee,
> I haste away to ponder o'er Thy love
> Alone with Thee!
> In the dim wood, by human ear unheard,
> Joyous and free,
> Lord! I adore Thee, feasting on Thy word,
> Alone with Thee!
> Amid the busy city, thronged and gay,
> But One I see,
> Tasting sweet peace, as unobserved I pray
> Alone with Thee!
> Oh, sweetest life! Life hid with Christ in God!
> So making me
> At home, and by the wayside, and abroad,
> Alone with Thee!

WESTPORT, *August 22, 1856*.

* * * * *

V.

Ready for new Trials. Dangerous Illness. Extracts from her Journal.
Visit to Greenwood. Sabbath Meditations. Birth of another Son. Her
Husband resigns his pastoral Charge. Voyage to Europe.

The summer at Westport was so beneficial to the baby and so full both of bodily and spiritual refreshment to herself, that on returning to town, she resumed her home tasks with unwonted ease and comfort. The next entry in her journal alludes to this:

November 27th.—Two months, and not a word in my journal! I have done far more with my needle and my feet than with my pen. One comes home from the country to a good many cares, and they are worldly cares, too, about eating and about wearing. I hope the worst of mine are over now and that I shall have more leisure. But no, I forget that now comes the dreaded, dreaded experience of weaning baby. But what then? I have had a good rest this fall. Have slept unusually well why, only think, some nights not waking once—and some nights only a few times and then we have had no sickness baby better—all better. Now I ought to be willing to have the trials I need so much, seeing I have had such a rest. And heaven! Heaven! Let me rest on that precious word. Heaven is at the end and God is there.

Early in March, 1857, she was taken very ill and continued so until May. For some weeks, her recovery seemed hardly possible. She felt assured her hour had come and was eager to go. All the yearnings of her heart, during many years, seemed on the point of being gratified. The next entry in her journal refers to this illness:

Sunday, May 24th, 1857.—Just reading over the last record how ashamed I felt of my faithlessness! To see dear baby so improved by the very change I dreaded, and to hear her pretty, cheerful prattle, and to find in her such a source of joy and comfort—what undeserved, what unlooked-for mercies! But like a physician who changes his remedies as he sees occasion, and who forbears using all his severe ones at once, my Father first relieved me from my wearing care and pain about this dear child, and then put me under new discipline. It is now nearly six months since I have been in usual health, and eight weeks of great prostration and suffering have been teaching me many needed lessons. Now, contrary to my hopes and expectations, I find myself almost well again. At first, having got my heart *set* toward heaven and after fancying myself almost there, I felt disappointed to find its gates still shut against me. [10]

But God was very good to me and taught me to yield in this point to His wiser and better will He made me, as far as I know, as peaceful in the prospect of living as joyful in the prospect of dying. Heaven did, indeed, look very attractive when I thought myself so near it I pictured myself as no longer a sinner but a blood-washed saint I thought I shall soon see Him whom my soul loveth, and see Him as He is I shall never wound, never grieve Him again, and all my companions will be they who worship Him and adore Him. But not yet am I there! Alas, not yet a saint! My soul is oppressed, now that health is returning, to find old habits of sin returning too, and this monster Self usurping God's place, as of old, and pride and love of ease and all the infirmities of the flesh thick upon me. After being encompassed with mercies for two months, having every comfort this world could offer for my alleviation, I wonder at myself that I can be anything but a meek, docile child, profiting by the Master's discipline, sensible of the tenderness that went hand-in-hand with every stroke, and walking softly before God and man! But I am indeed a wayward child and in need of many more stripes. May I be made willing and thankful to bear them?

Indeed, I do thank my dear Master that He does not let me alone, and that He has let me suffer so much it has been a rich experience, this long illness, and I do trust He will so sanctify it that I shall have cause to rejoice over it all the rest of my life. Now may I return patiently to all the duties that lie in my sphere? May I not forget how momentous a thing death appeared when seen face to face, but be ever making ready for its approach. And may the glory of God be, as it never yet has been, my chief end. My love to Him seems to me so very feeble and fluctuating. Satan and self keep up a continual struggle to get the victory. But God is stronger than either. He must and will prevail, and at last, and in a time far better than any I can suggest, He will open those closed gates and let me enter in to go no more out, and then "I shall never, never sin."

As might be inferred from this record, she was at this time in the sweetest mood, full of tenderness and love. The time of the singing of birds had now come, and all nature was clothed with that wondrous beauty and verdure which mark the transition from spring to summer. The drives, which she was now able to take into the country, on either side of the river, gave her the utmost delight. On the 30th of May—the day that has since become consecrated to the memory of the Nation's heroic dead—she went, with her husband and eldest daughter, to visit and place flowers upon the graves of Eddy and Bessie. Never is Greenwood more lovely and impressive than at the moment when May is just passing into June. It is as if Nature were in a transfiguration and the glory of the Lord shone upon the graves of our beloved! Mrs. Prentiss made no record of this visit, but on the following day thus wrote in her journal:

May 31st.—Another peaceful, pleasant Sunday, whose only drawback has been the want of strength to get down on my knees and praise and pray to my Savior, as I long to do. For well as I am and astonishingly improved in every way, a very few minutes' use of my voice, even in a whisper, in prayer, exhausts me to such a degree that I am ready to faint. This seems so strange when I can go on talking to any extent—but then it is talking without emotion and in a desultory way. Ah well! God knows best in what manner to let me live, and I desire to ask for nothing but a docile, acquiescent temper, whose only petition shall be, "What wilt Thou have me to do?" not how can I get most enjoyment along the way. I cannot believe if I am His child, that He will let anything hinder my progress in the divine life. It seems dreadful that I have gone on so slowly, and backward so many times—but then I have been thinking this is "to humble and to prove me, and to do me good in the latter end." ... I thank my God and Savior for every faint desire He gives me to see Him as He is, and to be changed into His image, and for every struggle against sin He enables me to make. It is all of Him. I do wish I loved Him better! I do wish He were never out of my thoughts and that the aim to do His will swallowed up all other desires and strivings. Satan whispers that will never be. But it shall be! One day—oh, longed-for, blessed, blissful day!—Christ will become my All in all! Yes, even mine!

This is the last entry in her journal for more than a year her letters, too, during the same period are very few. In August of 1857, she was made glad by the birth of another son, her fifth child. Her own health was now much better than it had been for a long time but that of her husband had become so enfeebled that in April, 1858, he resigned his pastoral charge and by the advice of his physician determined to go abroad, with his family, for a couple years the munificent kindness of his people having furnished him with the means of doing so. The tender sympathy and support, which she gave him in this hour of extreme weakness and trial, more than everything else, after the blessing of Heaven, upheld his fainting spirits and helped to restore him at length to his chosen work. They set sail for the old world in the steamship Arago, Capt. Lines, June 26th, amidst a cloud of friendly wishes and benedictions.

[1] The friend was Mr. Wm. G. Bull, who had a summer cottage at Rockaway. He was a leading member of the Mercer street church and one of the best of men. The poor and unfortunate blessed him all the year round. To Mrs. Prentiss and her husband he was indefatigable in kindness. He died at an advanced age in 1859.

[2] Godman's "American Natural History."

[3] Mrs. Norman White, mother of the Rev. Erskine N. White, D.D., of New York.

[4] Her cousin, whose sudden death occurred under the same roof in October of the next year.

[5] "We were all weighed soon after coming here," she wrote, "and my ladyship weighed 96, which makes me out by far the leanest of the ladies here. When thirteen years old I weighed but 50 pounds."

[6] Referring to "Little Suzy's Six Birthdays."

[7] *Little Suzy's Little Servants.*

[8] A Life hid with Christ in God, being a memoir of Susan Allibone. By Alfred Lee, Bishop of the Protestant Episcopal Church in Delaware.

[9] See appendix C.

[10] Many years afterward, speaking to a friend of this illness, she related the following incident. One day she lay, as was supposed, entirely unconscious and *in articulo mortis*. Repeated but vain attempts had been made to administer a medicine ordered by the doctor to be used in case of extremity. Her husband urged one more attempt still it might possibly succeed. She heard distinctly every word that was spoken and instantly reasoned within herself, whether she should consent or refuse to swallow the medicine. Fancying herself just entering the eternal city, she longed to refuse but decided it would be wrong and so consented to come back again to earth.

CHAPTER 6 - IN RETREAT AMONG THE ALPS - 1858-1860.

I.

Life abroad. Letters about the Voyage and the Journey from Havre to Switzerland. Chateau d'Oex. Letters from there. The Châlet Rosat. The Free Church of the Canton de Vaud. Pastor Panchaud.

Mrs. Prentiss passed more than two years abroad, mostly in Switzerland. They were years burdened with heavy cares, with ill health and keen solicitude concerning her husband. But they were also years hallowed by signal mercies of Providence, bright every now and then with floods of real sunshine, and sweetened by many domestic joys. Although quite secluded from the world a large portion of the time, her solitude was cheered by the constant arrival of letters from home. During these years, also, she was first initiated into full communion with Nature and what exquisite pleasure she tasted in this new experience, her own pen will tell. Indeed, this period affords little of interest except that which blossomed out of her domestic life, her friendships, and her love of nature. She travelled scarcely at all and caught only fugitive glimpses of society or of the treasures of European art.

A few simple records, therefore, of her retired home-life and of the impressions made upon her by Alpine scenery, as contained in her letters, must form the principal part of this chapter. Her correspondence, while abroad, would make a large volume by itself in selecting from it what follows, the aim has been to present, as far as possible, a continuous picture of her European sojourn, drawn by herself. Were a faithful picture of its quiet yet varied scenes to be drawn by another hand, it would include features wholly omitted by her features radiant with a light and beauty not of earth. It would reflect a sweet patience, a heroic fortitude, a tender sympathy, a faith in God and an upholding, comforting influence, which in sharp exigencies the Christian wife and mother knows so well how to exercise, and which are inspired only by the Lord Jesus Himself.

The friend to whom the following letter was addressed years ago passed away from earth. But her name is still enshrined in many hearts. The story of her generous and affectionate kindness, as also that of her children, would fill a whole chapter. "You will never know how we have loved and honored you all, *straight through*," wrote Mrs. Prentiss to one of them, many years later.

To Mrs. Charles W. Woolsey, Havre, July 11, 1858.

How many times during our voyage we had occasion to think of and thank you and yours, a dozen sheets like this would fail to tell you. Of all your kind arrangements for our comfort, not one failed of its object. Whether the chair or my sacque had most admirers I do not know, but I cannot imagine how people ever get across the ocean without such consolations on the way. As to the grapes they kept perfectly to the last day and proved delicious, the box then became a convenient receptacle for the children's toys while the cake-box has turned into a medicine chest. We had not so pleasant a voyage as is usual at this season, it being cold, and rainy and foggy much of the time. However, none of us suffered much from seasickness—Mr. Prentiss not in the least his chief discomfort was from want of sleep. On the whole, we had a less dreary time than we anticipated, and perhaps the stupidity in which we were engulfed for two weeks was a wholesome refuge from the excitement of the month previous to our departure. We landed in a deluge of rain, and the only article in our possession that alarmed the officers of the Custom House was *not* the sewing-machine, which was hardly vouchsafed a look, but your cake-box. We were thankful to tumble pell-mell into a carriage, and soon to find ourselves in a comfortable room, before a blazing fire. We go round with a phrase book and talk out of it, so if anybody ever asks you what sort of people the Prentiss family are and what are our conversational powers, you may safely and veraciously answer, "They talk like a book." M. already asks the French names of almost everything and is very glad to know that "we have got at Europe," and when asked how she likes France, declares, "Me likes *that*." We go off to Paris in the morning. I will let Mr. Prentiss tell his own story. Meanwhile we send you everyone our warmest love and thanks.

After a few days in Paris, the family hastened to Chateau d'Oex, where New York friends awaited them. Chateau d'Oex is a mountain valley in the canton of Vaud, on the right bank of the Sarine, twenty-two miles east of Lausanne, and is one of the loveliest spots in Switzerland. Aside from its natural beauties, it has some historical interest. It was once the home of the Counts of Gruyere, and the ruins of their ancient chateau are still seen there. The Free Church of the village was at this time under the care of Pastor Panchaud, a favorite pupil and friend of Vinet. He was a man of great simplicity and sweetness of character, an excellent preacher, and wholly devoted to his little flock. Mrs. Prentiss and her husband counted his society and ministrations a smile of Heaven upon their sojourn in Chateau d'Oex.

To Mrs. Henry B. Smith, Chateau D'Oex July 25, 1858.

Our ride from Havre to Paris was charming. We had one of those luxurious cars, to us unknown, which is intended to hold only eight persons, but which has room for ten the weather was perfect, and the scenery all the way very lovely and quite novel. A. and I kept mourning for you and M. to enjoy it with us, and both agreed that we would gladly see only half there was to see, and go half the distance we were going, if we could only share with you our pleasures of every kind. On reaching Paris and the hotel, we found we could not get pleasant rooms below the fifth story. They were directly opposite the garden of the Tuileries, where birds were flying and singing, and it was hard to realize that we were in the midst of that great city. We went sightseeing very little. A. and I strolled about here and there, did a little shopping, stared in at the shop windows, wished M. had this and you had that, and then strolled home and panted and toiled and groaned up our five flights, and wrote in our journals, or rested, or made believe study French. We went to the Jardin des Plantes in order to let the children see the Zoological Garden. We also drove through the Bois de Boulogne, and spent part of an evening in the garden of the Palais Royal, and watched the people drinking their tea and coffee, and having all sorts of good times. We found Paris far more beautiful than we expected, and certainly as to cleanliness it puts New York ages behind. We were four days in coming from Paris to this place. We went up the lake of Geneva on one of the finest days that could be asked for, and then the real joy of our journey began Paris and all its splendors faded away at once and forever before these mountains, and as George had never visited Geneva, or seen any of this scenery, my pleasure was doubled by his. Imagine, if you can, how we felt when Mt. Blanc appeared in sight! We reached Vevay just after sunset, and were soon established in neat rooms of quite novel fashion. The floors were of unpainted white wood, checked off with black walnut the stairs were all of stone, the stove was of porcelain, and every article of furniture was odd. But we had not much time to spend in looking at things within doors, for the lake was in full view, and the mountain tops were roseate with the last rays of the setting sun, and the moon soon rose and added to the whole scene all it wanted to make us half believe ourselves in a pleasant dream. I often asked myself, "Can this be I!" "And *if* it be I, as I hope it be"—

Early next morning, which was dear little M.'s birthday, we set off in grand style for Chateau d'Oex. We hired a monstrous voiture which had seats inside for four, and on top, with squeezing, seats for three, besides the driver's seat had five black horses, and dashed forth in all our splendor, ten precious souls and all agog. I made a sandwich between Mr. S. and George on top, and the "bonnes" and children were packed inside. This was our great day. The weather was indescribably beautiful we felt ourselves approaching a place of rest and a welcome home the scenery was magnificent, and already the mountain air was beginning to revive our exhausted souls and bodies. We sat all day hand in hand, literally "lost in wonder." With all I had heard ever since I was born about these mountains, I had not the faintest idea of their real grandeur and beauty. We arrived here just after sunset, and soon found ourselves among our friends. Mrs. Buck brought us up to our new home, which we reached on foot (as our voiture could not ascend so high) by a little winding path, by the side of which a little brook kept running along to make music for us. It is a regular Swiss châlet, much like the little models you have seen, only of a darker brown, and on either side the mountains stand ranged, so that look where we will we are feasted to our utmost capacity.

We have four small, but very neat, pretty rooms. Our floors are of unpainted pine, as white and clean as possible. The room in which we spend our time, and where I am now writing, I must fully set before you.... Our centre table has had a nice new red cover put on it today, with a vase of flowers it holds all our books, and is the ornament of the room. In front of the sofa is a red rug on which we say our prayers. Over it is a picture, and over G.'s table is another. Out of the window, you see first a pretty little flower garden, then the valley dotted with brown châlets, then the background of mountains. Behind the house you go up a little winding path—and can go on forever without stopping if you choose—along the sides of which flowers such as we cultivate at home grow in profusion you cannot help picking them and throwing them away to snatch a new handful. The brook takes its rise on this side, and runs musically along as you ascend. Yesterday we all went to church at nine and a half o'clock, and had our first experience of French preaching, and I was relieved to find myself understanding whole sentences here and there. And now I need not, I suppose, wind up by saying we are in a charming spot. All we want, as far as this world goes, is health and strength with which to enjoy all this beauty and all this sweet retirement, and these, I trust, it will give us in time. Isabella "wears like gold." She is everything I hoped for, and from her there has not been even a *tone* of discomfort since we left. But my back aches and my paper is full. We all send heaps of love to you all and long to hear.

August 10th.—We breakfast at eight on bread and honey, which is the universal Swiss breakfast, dine at one, and have tea at seven. I usually sew and read and study all the forenoon. After dinner we take our Alpine-stocks and go up behind the house—a bit of mountain climbing, which makes me realize that I am no longer a young girl. I get only so high, and then have to come back and lie down. George and Annie beat me all to pieces with their exploits. I do not believe we could have found anywhere in the world a spot better adapted to our needs. How *you* would enjoy it! I perfectly yearn to show you these mountains and this entire green valley. The views I send will give you a very good idea of it, however. The smaller châlet in the print is ours. In a little summer house opposite Isabella now sits at work on the sewing machine. My best love to all three of your dear "chicks," and to your husband if "he's willin'."

To Mrs. H.B. Washburn, Chateau d'Oex, August 21, 1858.

… We slipped off without any leave-taking, which I was not sorry for. I did not want to bid you goodbye. We had to say it far too often as it was, and, when we fairly set sail we had not an emotion left, but sank at once into a state of entire exhaustion and stupidity…. We thought Paris very beautiful until we came in view of the Lake of Geneva, Mt. Blanc, and other handiworks of God, when straightway all its palaces and monuments and fountains faded into insignificance. I began to feel that it was wicked for a few of my friends, who were born to enjoy the land of lakes and mountains, not to be here enjoying it, and you were one of them, you may depend. However, whenever I have had any such pangs of regret in relation to you, I have consoled myself with the reflection that with your enthusiastic temperament, artist eye, and love of nature, you never would survive even a glimpse of Switzerland the land of William Tell would be the death of you. When you are about eighty years old, have cooled down about ten degrees below zero, have got a little dim about the eyes, and a little stiff about the knees, it may possibly be safe for you to come and break yourself in gradually. I have not forgotten how you felt and what you did at the White Mountains, you see.

Well, joking apart, we are in a spot that would just suit you in every respect. We are not in a street or a road or any of those abominations you like to shun, but our little châlet, hardly accessible save on foot, is just tucked down on the side of the gentle slope leading up the mountain. It is remote from all sights but those magnificent ones afforded by the range of mountains, the green rich valley, and the ever-varying sky and cloudland, and all sounds save that of a brook, which runs hurrying down its rocky little channel, and keeps us company when we want it. I ought, however, to add that my view of this particular valley is that of a novice. People say the scenery here is tame in comparison with what may be seen elsewhere but look which way I will, from front windows or back windows, at home or abroad, I am as one at a continual feast and what more can one ask? Mr. Prentiss feels that this secluded spot is just the place for him, and as it is a good point from which to make excursions on foot or otherwise, he and Mr. Stearns have already made several trips and seen splendid sights. How much we have to be grateful for! For my part, I would rather—far rather—have come here and stayed here blindfold, than not to have come with my dear husband. So all I have seen and am experiencing I regard as beauty and felicity *thrown in*.

To Mrs. Abigail Prentiss, Chateau d'Oex, Sept. 5, 1858.

I wish we had you, my dear mother, here among these mountains, for the cool, bracing air would help to build you up. Both Mr. Stearns and George have come back from Germany looking better than when they started on their trip two weeks ago. It has been very cold the thermometer some mornings at eight o'clock standing at 46°, and the mountains being all covered with snow. We slept with a couple of bottles of hot water at our feet, and two blankets and a comforter of eiderdown over us, after going to bed early to get warm. My sewing machine is a great comfort, and the peasants enjoy coming down from the mountains to see it. Besides, I find something to do on it every day.

I often wish I could set you down in the midst of the church to which we go every Sunday, if only to show you how the people dress. A bonnet is hardly seen there, everybody wearing a black silk cap or a bloomer. *I* wear a bloomer a brown one trimmed with brown ribbon. An old lady sits in front of me who wears a white cap much after the fashion of yours, and on top of that is perked a monstrous bloomer trimmed with black gauze ribbon. Her dress is linsey-woolsey, and for outside garment she wears a black silk half-handkerchief, as do all the rest. No light dress or ribbon is seen. I must tell you now, something that amused A. and me very much yesterday at dinner. A French gentleman, who married a Spanish lady four years ago, sits opposite us at the table, and he and his wife are quite fascinated with M., watch all her motions, and whisper together about all she does. Yesterday they got to telling us that the lady had been married when only twelve years old to a gentleman of thirty-two, had two children, and was a grandmother, though not yet thirty-six years old. She said she carried her doll with her to her husband's house, and he made her learn a geography lesson every day until she was fourteen, when she had a baby of her own. I asked her if she loved her husband, and she said "Oh, yes," only he was very grave and scolded her and shut her up when she would not learn her lessons. She said that her own mother when thirty-six years old had fourteen children, all of whom are now living, twelve of them boys, and that the laws of Spain allow the father of six sons to ask a favor for them of the King, but the father of twelve may ask a favor for each one so every one of her brothers had an office under the Government or was an officer in the army. I do not know when I have been more amused, for she, like all foreigners, was full of life and gesture, and showed us how she tore her hair and threw down her books when angry with her husband.

The children are all bright and well. The first time we took the cars after landing, M. was greatly delighted. "Now we're going to see grandma," she cried. Mrs. Buck got up a picnic for her, and had a treat of raspberries and sponge cake—frosted. The cake had "M." on the top in red letters. Baby is full of life and mischief. The day we landed, he said "Papa," and now he says "Mamma." Isabella [1] is everything we could ask. She is trying to learn French, and A. hears her recite every night. George found some furnished rooms at Montreux, which he has taken for six months from October, and we shall thus be keeping house. A. has just rushed in and snatched her French Bible, as she is going to the evening service with some of the English family. You will soon hear all about us from Mr. Stearns.

The following letter will show how little power either her own cares, or the charms of nature around her, had to quench her sympathy for friends in sorrow:

To Miss A. H. Woolsey, Chateau D'Oex, Sept. 11, 1858.

We received your kind letter this morning. We had already had our sympathies excited in behalf of you all, by seeing a notice of the death of the dear little child in a paper lent to us by Mrs. Buck, and were most anxious to hear all the particulars you have been so good as to give us. This day, which fifteen years ago we marked with a white stone, and which we were to celebrate with all our hearts, has passed quite wearily and drearily. There is something indescribably sad in the details of the first bereavement which has fallen within the circle of those we love perhaps, too, old sorrows of our own clamored for a hearing and then, too, there was the conviction, "This is not all death will do while the ocean severs you from kindred and friends." We longed to speak to you many words of affectionate sympathy and Christian cheer but long before we can make them reach you, I trust you will have felt sure that you were at least remembered and prayed for. It is a comfort that no ocean separates us from Him who has afflicted you. The loss to you each and all is very great, but to the mother of such a child it is beyond description. Faith alone can bear her through it, but faith *can*. What a wonderful little creature the sweet Ellie must have been! We were greatly touched by your account of her singing that beautiful hymn. It must have been divinely ordered that she should leave such a precious legacy behind her. And though her loveliness makes her loss the greater, the loss of an unlovely wayward child would surely be a heavier grief.

I never know where to stop when I begin to talk about the death of a little one but before I stop I want to ask you to tell Mrs. H. one word from me, which will not surprise and will perhaps comfort her. It is this. Neither his father nor I would be willing to have God now bereave us of the rich experience of seven years ago, when our noble little boy was taken away. We have often said this to each other, and oftener said it to Him, who if He took, also gave much. But after all, we cannot *say* much to comfort either Mrs. H. or you. We can only truly, heartily, and always sympathize with you…. Mr. Prentiss and Mr. Stearns have spent a fortnight in jaunting about beginning at Thun and ending at Munich. They both came home looking fresher and better than when they left, but Mr. P. is not at all well now, and will have his ups and downs, I suppose, for a long time to come…. We can step out at any moment into a beautiful path, and, turn which way we will, meet something charming. Yesterday he came back for me, having found a new walk, and we took our sticks, and went to enjoy it together until we got, as it were, fairly locked in by the mountains, and could go no further. Only to think of having such things as gorges and waterfalls and roaring brooks, right at your back door! The seclusion of this whole region is, however, its great charm to us, and to tell the truth, the primitive simplicity of style of dress, etc., is quite as charming to me as its natural beauty. We took tea one night last week with the pastor of the Free church he lives in a house for which he pays thirty dollars a year, and we were quite touched and pleased with his style of living white pine walls and floors, unpainted, and everything else to match. We took our tea at a pine table, and the drawing room to which we retired from it, was a corner of the same room, where was a little mite of a sofa and a few books, and a cheerful lamp burning.

All this time I have not answered your question about the Fourth of July. We had great doings, I assure you. Mr. P. made a speech, and ran up and down the saloon like a warhorse. He was so excited and pale that I did not enjoy it much, thinking any instant he would faint and fall. Mr. Cleaveland was the orator of the day and acquitted himself very well, they all said. I was in my berth at the time of its delivery, saving myself for the dinner and toasts, and so did not hear it. The whole affair is to be printed. There was a great cry of "Prentiss! Prentiss!" after the "Captain's dinner," and at last the poor man had to respond in a short speech to a toast to the ladies. I suppose you know that he considers all women as angels. Mr. Stearns left us on Thursday to set his face homewards.

* * * * *

II.

Montreux. The Swiss Autumn. Castle of Chillon. Death and Sorrow of
Friends at Home. Twilight Talks. Spring Flowers.

Early in October, the family removed to Montreux, at the upper end of the lake of Geneva, where the next six months were passed in what was then known as the Maison des Bains. Montreux was at this time the centre of a group of pleasant villages, scattered along the shore of the lake, or lying back of it among the hills. One of these villages, Clarens, was rendered famous in the last century by the pen of Rousseau and early in this by the pen of Byron. The grave of Vinet, the noble leader, and theologian of the Free Church of the canton of Vaud, now renders the spot sacred to the Christian scholar. Montreux was then a favorite resort of invalids in quest of a milder climate. At many points, it commands fine views of the lake, and the whole region abounds in picturesque scenery. The Maison des Bains is said to have long since disappeared but in 1858, it seemed to hang upon the side of the Montreux hill and was one of the most noticeable features of the landscape, as seen from the passing steamer.

To Mrs. Henry B. Smith, Montreux, October 31, 1858.

Your letter was a real comfort and I am so thankful to the man that invented letter writing that I do not know what to do. We feast on everything we hear from home, however sick, or weak it is a sort of sea-air appetite. Your letters are not a thousandth part long enough, but if you wrote all the time, I suppose they would not be.... You see I am experimenting with two kinds of ink, hoping my letters may be easier to read. George tried it the other day by writing me a little note, telling me first how he loved me in black ink and then how he loved me in blue, after which he tore it up was not that a shame? Anna writes that you seemed miserable the day she was at your house. The fact is people of such restless mental activity as you and I, my dear, never need expect to be well long at a time—for, as soon as we get a little health we consume it just as children do candy. George and I are both able, however, to take long walks, and the other day we went to see the castle of Chillon. I was much impressed with all I saw. Under Byron's name, which I saw on one of the columns, there were the initials "H. B. S."—"H. B. Smith," says I. "You do not say so!" cries George, "where? Let me see—oh, I do not think it can be his, for here are some more letters," which I knew all the time, but for all that H. B. S. *does* stand for H. B. Smith. There are ever so many charming walks about here and from some points the scenery is wonderfully picturesque. I never was in the country so late as to see the trees after a frost, and although the foliage here is less brilliant, it is said, than that of American forests, I find it hard to believe that there can be anything more beautiful than the wooded mountains covered with the softest tints of every shade and coloring interspersed with snowcapped peaks and bare, gray rocks. The glory has departed somewhat within two days, as we have had a little snowstorm, and the leaves have fallen sadly. We began to have a fire yesterday and to put on some of our winter clothing yet roses bloom just outside our door, and mignonette, nasturtiums, and a variety of other flowers adorn every house. The Swiss love for flowers is really beautiful. I wish you would let the children go to the hot-house which they pass on the way from school and get me some flower-seeds, as it will be pleasant to me to have the means of giving pleasure. I presume the gardener would be able to select a dozen or so of American varieties which would be a treasure here. I amuse myself with making flower-pictures, with which to enliven our parlor, and assure you that these works of art are remarkable specimens of genius. I do not know where the time goes, but I do not have half enough of it, or else do not understand the art of making the most of it. We have just subscribed to a library at a franc a month, and hope to read a little French.... I suppose Z. will be a regular young lady by the time we come home, and that I shall be afraid of her, as I am of all young ladies. How nicely she and M. would look in the Auntie, little hats they all wear here. I wonder if the fashion will stretch across the ocean? I dare say it will. Never was there anything so becoming in the world.

To Mrs. Stearns, Montreux, Nov. 21, 1858.

We were glad to hear from your last letter that you are all so well, and especially to hear such good accounts of Mr. Stearns. It is a real comfort to us to find that his little trip has done him so much good. I was sorry to hear of the loss of that friend of the Thurstons in the Austria, for I heard Ellen speak of her in the most rapturous manner. This world is full of mysteries. Only to think of the shock George received when expecting to meet Mr. Butler in Paris and perhaps spend several weeks with him there, he heard at Geneva the news of his sudden death! [2] He loved and honored Mr. B. most warmly and truly. You will remember that the latter came abroad on account of the health of his daughter her younger sister accompanied them, and they were all full of the brightest anticipations. But the same steamer that brought them over, carried home his remains on the next trip, and those two poor young girls are left in a strange land, afflicted and disappointed and alone. Mr. Butler died a most peaceful and happy death, and George was very glad to be in Paris in time to comfort the young ladies, who were perfectly delighted to see him. He got back yesterday very much exhausted and has spent most of the day on the sofa. A. has a teacher who comes three times a week from Vevay, and spends most of the day. She is a young lady of about twenty-five, well educated and accustomed to teaching, and has taken hold of A. with no little energy. She cannot speak a word of English. Tell your A. we cannot get over it that the horses, dogs, and cats here all understand French. I have been ever so busy fixing and fussing for winter, which has come upon us all in a rush. Isabella has been bewitched for about a week, having got at last a letter from her beau, and every speck of work she has done on the sewing machine was either wrong side out or upside down. While George was gone I made up a lot of flower-pictures to adorn the walls of our parlor he is walking about admiring them, and I wish you would drop in and help him. He had a real homesick fit to see you all today, feeling so tired after his journey but seems brighter to-night, and promises faithfully to get well now, right off.

Dec. 5th.—The death of Sarah P. must have excited all your sympathies. The loss of a little child—and I shudder when I recall the pangs of such a loss!—can be nothing in comparison with such an affliction as this. I well remember what a bright young thing she was. Her poor mother's grief and amazement must be all the greater for the fact of the perfect vigor and sound health which had, as it were, assured her of long life and happiness and usefulness. I had an inexpressible sadness upon me as soon as I heard that she was dangerously ill often in such moments one bitterly realizes that all this world's idols are likewise perishable.

A.'s teacher gives lessons also in a family half an hour from Vevay, who are going to Germany to spend a year, and she gave such an account of the place, that George let her persuade him into going to see it, as the owner desired to rent it during his absence. He took A. with him, as I could not go. They came back in ecstasies, and have both set their hearts so on taking it that I should not at all wonder if that should be the end. We left some of our things at Chateau d'Oex, fully expecting to return there, but this Vevay countryseat with its cherry, apple and pear trees, its seclusion, its vicinity to reading-room and library, has quite disgusted George with the idea of spending another summer "en pension." The family entertained G. and A. very hospitably, gave them a lunch of bologna sausage, bread and butter, cake, wine, and grapes, and above all, the little girls gave A. two little Guinea pigs, which you may imagine filled her with delight. The whole affair was very agreeable to her, as she had not spoken to a child (save M.) since we came to Montreux.

January 3rd, 1859.—We read your letter, written at Bedford, with no little interest and sympathy. While we could not but rejoice that one more saint had got safely and without a struggle home, we felt the exceeding disappointment you must have had in losing the last smile you came so near receiving. [3] I think you had a sort of presentiment last winter what this one might bring forth, for I remember your saying it would probably be the last visit to you, and that you wanted to make it as pleasant as possible. And pleasant I do not doubt you and the whole household made it to her. Still there always will be regrets and vain wishes after the death of one we love. What a pity that we cannot be to our friends while they live all we wish we had been after they have gone! George and I feel an almost childish clinging to mother, while we hope and believe she will live to bless us if we ever return home.

Jan. 23rd.—We have been afflicted in the sudden death of our dear friend, Mrs. Wainwright. The news came upon us without preparation—for she was ill only a few days—and was a great shock to us. You and mother know what she was to us during the whole time of our acquaintance with her I loved her most heartily. I cannot get over the saddening impression which such deaths cause, by receiving new ones our lives here are so quiet and uneventful, that we have full leisure to meditate on the breaches already made in our circle of friends at home, and to forebode many more such sorrowful tidings. Mrs. Wainwright was like a *mother* to me, and I am too old to take up a new friend in her place. [4]

I do not know whether I mentioned the afflictions of my cousin H. They have been very great, and have excited my sympathies keenly. Her first child died when eighteen months old, after a feeble, suffering life. Then the second child, an amiable, loving creature—I almost see her now sitting up so straight with her morsel of knitting in her hands!—she was taken sick and died in five days. Her sister, about eight years old, came near dying of grief she neither played, ate nor slept, and they wrote me that her wails of anguish were beyond description. Just as she was getting a little over the first shock, the little boy, then about three years old, died suddenly of croup. Poor H. is almost broken-hearted. I have felt dreadfully at being away when she was so afflicted they had not been long enough in New York to have a minister of their own, and they all said, oh, if George and I had only been there!

Her letters during the rest of the winter are tinged with the sadness caused by these and other distressing afflictions among friends at home. Her sympathies were kept under a constant strain. But her letters contain also many gleams of sunshine. Although very quiet and secluded, and often troubled by torturing neuralgic pains, as well as by sudden shocks of grief, her life at Montreux was not without its own peculiar joys. One of the greatest of these was to while away the twilight or evening hours in long talks with her husband about home and former days. Distance, together with the strange Alpine scenes about her, seemed to have the effect of a score of years in separating her from the past, and throwing over it a mystic veil of tenderness and grace. Old times and old friends, when thus viewed from the beautiful shores of Lake Leman, appeared to the memory in a softened light and invested with something of that ideal loveliness which the grave itself imparts to the objects of our affections. Many of these old friends, indeed, had passed through the Grave—some, long before, some recently—and to talk of *them* was sweet talk about the blessed home above, as well as the home beyond the ocean.

Another joy that helped to relieve the monotony and weariness of the Montreux life was in her children especially as, on the approach of spring, she wandered with them over the hillsides in quest of flowers then her delight knew no bounds. In a letter to Mrs. Washburn, dated March 19, she writes:

M. and G. catch A.'s and my enthusiasm, and come with their little hands full of dandelions, buttercups and daisies, and their hats full of primroses. Even Mr. Prentiss conies in with his hands full of crocuses, purple and white, and lots of an extremely pretty flower, "la fille avant la mère," which he gathers on the mountains where I cannot climb…. I often think of you and Mrs. B——, when I revel among the beautiful profusion of flowers with which this country is adorned. As early as it is, the hills and fields are *covered* with primroses, daisies, cowslips, violets, lilies, and I do not know what not in five minutes we can gather a basketful.

* * * * *

III.

The Campagne Genevrier. Vevay. Beauty of the Region. Letters. Birth of a Son. Visit from Professor Smith. Excursion to Chamouni. Whooping-cough and Scarlet-fever among the Children. Doctor Curchod. Letters.

At the end of March the family removed to the campagne Genevrier, about two miles back of Vevay, in the direction of St. Leger. At one point, it overlooked the town and the lake, and commanded a fine view of the mountains of Savoy and of the distant Jura range. On the opposite shore of the lake is the village where Lord Byron passed some time in 1816, and where he is said to have written the wonderful description of a thunderstorm, in the third canto of Childe Harold. At all events, the very scene, so vividly depicted by him, was witnessed from Genevrier. [5]

To Mrs. Stearns, Genevrier, April 5, 1859

Your letter describing how nicely your party went off followed us from Montreux, to enliven us here in our new home. We only wish we could have been there. You need not have apologized for giving so many details, for it is just such little events of your daily life that we want to hear about. My mouth quite waters for a bit of the cake they sent you I remember Mrs. Dr. J. and others used to send us big loaves, which were delicious, and such as I never tasted out of Newark. We came here last Thursday in a great snowstorm, which was cheerless and cold enough after the warm weather we had had for so many weeks. I do not suppose more snow fell on any day through the winter, and we all shivered and lamented and huddled over the fire at a great rate. Yet I have just been driven indoors by the heat of the sun, having begun to write at a little table just outside the house, and fires and snow have disappeared. George has gone to town with Jules in the wagon to buy sugar, oil, oats, buttons, and I do not know what not, and is no doubt thinking of you all for we do nothing but cry out how we wish you were here with us to enjoy this beautiful spot. We are entirely surrounded by mountains in the distance, and with green fields, vineyards, and cultivated grounds nearer home. How your children would delight in the flowers, the white doves, the seven little tiny guinea pigs, no bigger than your Annie's hand shut up, and the ample, neat play-places all about us. I cannot tell you how George and I enjoy seeing M. trotting about, so eager and so happy, and gathering up, as we hope, health and strength every hour! We find the house, on the whole, very convenient, and it is certainly as pleasant as can be every room cheerful and every window commanding a view, which is ravishing.

To Mrs. Smith, Genevrier, April 7, 1859.

You will be surprised, I dare say, to hear that I am writing out of doors I can hardly, myself, believe that it is possible to do so with comfort and safety at this season, but it is perfectly charming weather, neither cold or hot, and with a small shawl and my bloomer on, I am out a large part of the day. You would fly here in a balloon if you knew what a beautiful spot we are in. We are surrounded with magnificent views of both the lake and the mountains, and cannot turn in any direction without being ravished. The house is pretty, and in most respects well and even handsomely furnished damask curtains, a Titian, a Rembrandt, and a Murillo in the parlor the floors are waxed and carpetless, to be sure, but Mrs. Buck has given us lots of large pieces of carpeting such as are used in this country to cover the middle of the rooms, and these will make us comfortable next winter. But the winters here are so short that one hardly gets fixed to meet them, when they are over.

We have quite a nice garden, from which we have already eaten lettuce, spinach, and parsley our potatoes were planted a day or two ago, and our peas are just up. One corner of the house, unconnected with our part, is occupied by a farmer who rents part of the land he is obliged to do our marketing, etc., and we get milk and cream from him. I wish the latter was as easy to digest as it is palatable and cheap. They beat it up here until it looks like pure white lather and eat it with sugar. The grounds about our house are very neat and we shall have oceans of flowers of all sorts several kinds are in full bloom now. The wild flowers are so profuse, so beautiful and so various that A. and I are almost demented on the subject. From the windows I see first the wide, graveled walk which runs round the house then a little bit of a green lawn in which there is a little bit of a pond and a tiny *jet d'eau* which falls agreeably on the ear beyond this the land slopes gently upward till it is not land but bare, rugged mountain, here and there sprinkled with snow and interspersed with pine-trees. The sloping land is ploughed up and men and women are busy sowing and planting too far off to disturb us with noise, but looking, the women at least, rather picturesque in their short blue dresses and straw hats. On the right hand the Dent du Midi is seen to great advantage, it is now covered with snow. The little village of St. Leger lies off in the distance you can just see its roofs and the quaint spire of a very old church otherwise you see next to no houses, and the stillness is very sweet. *Now* won't you come? The children seem to enjoy their liberty greatly, and are running about all the time. They have each a little garden and I hope will live out of doors all summer.

The state of her health during the next three months was a source of constant and severe suffering, but could not quench her joy in the wonders of nature around her. "My drives about this lovely place," she wrote in June, "have begun to give me an *immense* amount of pleasure indeed, my faculty for enjoyment is so great, that I sometimes think one day's felicity pays for weeks of misery, and that if it hadn't been for my poor health, I should have been *too* happy here." Nor did her suffering weaken in the least her sympathy with the troubles of her friends at home. While for the most part silent as to her own peculiar trials, her letters were full of cheering words about theirs. To one of these she wrote at this time:

God has taken care that we should not enjoy so much of this world's comfort since we left home as to *rest* in it. Your letters are so sad, that I have fancied you perhaps overestimated our situation, feeling that you and your feeble husband were bearing the burden and heat of the day while we were standing idle. My dear ——, there are trials everywhere and in every sphere, and every heart knows its own bitterness, or else physical burdens are sent to take the place of mental depression. After all, it will not need more than *an hour* in heaven to make us ashamed of our want of faith and courage here on earth. Do cheer up, dear child, and "look aloft!" Poor Mr. ——! I know his work is hard and up the hill, but it will not be *lost* work and cannot last forever. It seems to me God might accept with special favor the services of those who "*toil* in rowing." After all, it is not the *amount* of work He regards, but the spirit with which it is done.

Early in July she was made glad by the birth of her sixth child—her "Swiss boy," as she liked to call him. Her gladness was not a little increased by a visit soon after from Professor Henry B. Smith, of the Union Theological Seminary. This visit was one of the memorable events of her life abroad. Professor Smith was not merely a great theologian and scholar he was also a man of most attractive personal qualities. And, when unbending among friends from his exacting literary labors, the charm of his presence and conversation was perfect. His spirits ran high, and he entered with equal zest into the amusements of young or old. His laugh was as merry as that of the merriest girl no boy took part more eagerly in any innocent sports nobody could beat him in climbing a mountain. He was a keen observer, and his humor—sometimes very dry, sometimes fresh and bright as the early dew—rendered his companionship at once delightful and instructive. His learning and culture were so much a part of himself that his most familiar talk abounded in the happiest touches about books and art and life. All his finest traits were in full play while he was at Genevrier, and, when he left, his visit seemed like a pleasant dream.

To Mrs. Smith, Genevrier, July 25th.

I am only too glad of the chance your husband gives me to write you another bit of a note. We are enjoying his visit amazingly. There are only two drawbacks to its felicity one is that he will not stay all summer, and the other that you are not here. The children were enchanted with the presents he brought them. When I shall be on my feet and well and strong again, time only can tell. A. has *devoted* herself to me in the sweetest way. What she has been to me all winter and up to this time, tongue could not tell. My doctor is as kind as a brother. He was a perfect stranger to me, and was brought to my bedside when I was writhing in agony but in ten minutes his tenderness and sympathy made me forget that he was a stranger, and, through that long night of distress and the long day that followed, he did *every*thing that mortal could do to relieve and comfort me. He brought his wife up to see me the other day, and I begged her to tell him how grateful I felt. "He *is* kind," she answered, "but then he *loves you so!*" (They both speak English.) I am so puffed up by his praises! I am sure I thought I groaned, but he says "pas une gemissement."

August 14th.—Our two husbands have gone to Lausanne for the day, taking A. with them. They seem to be having real nice times together, and if, as your husband says, "his old wife were here," his felicity and ours would be too great. They lounge about, talk, drink soda water, and view the prospect. Dr. Buck came up from Geneva on Thursday and spent the night and part of Friday with us, and it would have done you good to hear him and your husband laugh. He was quite enchanted with the place, and says we never shall want to go home. *August 23rd.*—Your husband has given me leave to write you a little bit of a note out of my little bit of a heart on this little bit of paper. He and A. have just gone off to get some pretty grass for you. He will tell you when he gets home how he baptized his namesake on Sunday. We have enjoyed his visit more than tongue can tell. George says *he* has enjoyed it as much as he thought he should, and I am sure I have enjoyed it a great deal more, as I have been so much better in health than I expected. But how you must miss him!

On the 12th of September—a faultless autumn day—she set out with her husband and eldest daughter for Chamouni. It was her first excursion for pleasure since coming to Switzerland. A visit to this great and marvelous handiwork of God is an event in the dullest life. In her case, the experience was so full of delight that it seemed almost to compensate for the cares and disappointments of the whole previous year. The plan was to return to Genevrier and then pass on to the Bernese Oberland, but the visit to Chamouni proved to be her last as well as her first pleasure excursion in Switzerland.

To Mrs. Stearns, Genevrier, October 2, 1859.

I have, been so absorbed with anxiety about the children since we got back from our journey that I have not felt like writing you a description of it. George told you, I suppose, that the news awaiting us when we reached Vevay was of the baby's having whooping cough. It was a great shock to us, for the weather was dismally cold, and it did not seem as if the little thing could get safely through the disease at so unfavorable a time of year. Then there were the other two to have it also. On Friday, last baby's cry had become a sad sort of wail, and he was so pale and weak, that I did not see how he was going to rally but he is better today, so that I begin to take breath…. To go back to Chamouni, it seems a mercy that we went when we did. We enjoyed the whole trip. We made the excursion to the Mer de Glace in a pouring rain, without injury to any of us, and were well repaid for our trouble by the novelty of the whole expedition and the extraordinary sights we saw. George intended taking us to the Oberland if we found the children well on our return, but all hope of accomplishing another journey was destroyed when we found what different business was before us. It is a real disappointment, for the weather is now mild and very fine, just adapted to journeying, and so many things have conspired to confine me to this spot, that I have found it quite hard to be as patient and cheerful as I am sure I ought to be. Alas and alas! What an insatiable thing human nature is! How it craves *every*thing the world can offer, instead of contenting itself with what ought to content it. However, I shall soon get over my fidgets, and as to George, of course, he is only disappointed for A., and me as he has visited the Oberland, and was only going to give us pleasure. In addition, if I must choose between the two, I would rather have the littlest baby in the world than see all the biggest mountains in it. We are thankful to hear that mother continues to be so well. We long to see her, and I think a look at her or a smile from her would do George good like a medicine.

October 17th.—I went to church yesterday for the first time in ten months we came out at half-past ten, so you see we have a tolerably long day before us when church is done. It is not at all like going to church at home you not only find it painful to listen with such strict attention as the foreign tongue requires, but you miss the neat, well-ordered sanctuary, the picture of family life (for there are no little children present!) and the agreeable array of dress. The flapping, monstrous bloomers tire your eyes, and so do the grotesque, coarse clothes and the tokens of extreme poverty. I grow more and more patriotic every day, and am astonished at what I see and hear of life in Europe.

I snatched one afternoon when the baby was better than usual to go to Villeneuve with George to call on Mr. and Mrs. H. and the sister of Mrs. H., who is one of our Mercer street young ladies. They were at the Hotel Byron, where you stayed. What a beautiful spot it is! Mr. H. afterwards came and dined with us, and was so charmed with the place that he was tempted to take it when we leave his wife, however, had set her heart on going home at that time, as she had left one child there. The vintage is going on here at Genevrier today, and we are all invited to go and eat our fill.

To Mrs. Henry B. Smith, Genevrier, Oct. 20, 1859.

You ask how I find time to make flower-pictures. Why, I have been confined to the house a good deal by the baby's sickness, and could hardly set myself about anything else when I was not watching and worrying about him. When we got home from Chamouni, we found him with what proved to be a very serious disease in the case of so young a child. It has shaken his little frame nearly to pieces, leaving him after weeks of suffering not much bigger than a doll, and all eyes and bones. It was a pretty hard struggle for life, and I hardly know how he has weathered the storm.

The idea of leaving our dear little Swiss baby in a little Swiss grave, instead of taking him home with us, was very distressing to me, and I cannot help earnestly desiring that death may not assail us in this foreign land.

Our trip to Chamouni was very pleasant and did me a deal of good. If I could have kept on the mule riding and mountain viewing a few weeks I should have been quite built up, but the children's coughs made it impossible to take any more journeys. Mr. de Palèzieux, our landlord, called Monday to see if I would sell him my sewing machine, as his wife was crazy to have one, and did not feel as if she could wait to get one from New York. I told him I would, and all night could not sleep for teaching him how to use it—for his wife is in Germany, and he had to learn for her. I invited him to come to dinner on Wednesday and take his lessons. On Tuesday, George said he wanted me to make a pair of sleeves for Mrs. Tholuck before the machine went off, so I went to town to get the stuff, at three o'clock began the sleeves, and worked like a lion for a little over two hours, when they were done, beautifully. This morning I made four collars, which I shall want for Christmas presents, and a shirt for Jules (our old hired man), who never had one made of linen, and will go off the handle when he gets it. So, I am tolerably used up, and shall be almost glad to send away the tempter tomorrow, though I dare say I shall miss it. I wish you could look out of my window this minute, and see how beautiful the autumnal foliage is already beginning to look. But my poor old head, what I shall do with it! You ask about my health I am as well as I can be without sleep. I have had only one really good night since the baby came, to say nothing of those before some worse than others, to be sure but all wakeful to a degree that tries my faith not a little. I do not see what is to hinder my going crazy one of these days. However, I will not if I can help it. George goes to Germany this week. Well, my dear, goodbye.

To Mrs. Stearns, Dec. 12th.

George got home a fortnight ago, after his three weeks' absence looking nicely, and more like himself than I have seen him in a long time. He had a most refreshing time in Germany among his old friends. It does my heart good to see him so cheery and hopeful. I have just seen the three babies safely in bed, after no little scampering and carrying-on, and now am ready for a little chat with you and dear mother. George sits by me, piously reading "Adam Bede." I was disappointed in the "Minister's Wooing," which he brought from Germany, and cannot think Mrs. Stowe came up to herself this time, whatever the newspapers may say about it and as for the plot, I do not see why she couldn't have let Mary marry good old Dr. Hopkins, who was vastly more of a man than that harum-scarum James. As to "Adam Bede," I think it a wonderful book, beyond praise. I hope these literary observations will be blessed to you, my dear. Mrs. Tholuck sent me a very pretty worsted cape to wear about house, or under a cloak. We went to Lausanne last Wednesday (George, A. and I) to do a little shopping for Christmas, and had quite a good time, only as life is always mingled in sweet and bitter, bitter and sweet, we had the melancholy experience of finding, when we got ready to come home, that Jules had taken a drop too much, and was in a state of ineffable silliness, which made George prefer to drive himself.

We begin now to think and talk about Paris. We have been buying this afternoon some Swiss châlets and other things, brought to the door by two women, and I had hard work to keep George from taking a bushel or two. He got leaf-cutters enough to stab all his friends to the heart. Most of our lady friends will receive a salad-spoon and fork from one or the other of us. In fact, I have no doubt we shall be seized at the Customhouse as merchants in disguise. Well, I must bid you good night.

The latter part of December her husband was requested to go to Paris and take the temporary charge of the American chapel there. He decided to do so, with the understanding that she and the children should soon follow him. But scarcely had he left Geneva, when first one and then another of the children was seized with scarlet fever. Here are a few extracts from her letters on the subject:

Dec. 31st.—Jules had hardly gone to the office, when I became satisfied that G. had scarlet fever beyond a doubt, and therefore sent Jeanette instantly to town to tell the doctor so, and to ask him to come up. He came, and said at once that I was quite right.... As to our leaving here, he said decidedly that it *could* not be under less than forty days. I cannot tell you, my darling, how grieved I am for you to hear this news. Now I know your first impulse will be to come home, and perhaps to renounce the chaplaincy, but I beg you to think twice—thrice before you decide to do so.... How one thing hurries on after another! But it is the universal cry, everywhere everybody is groaning and travailing in pain together and we shall doubtless learn, in eternity, that our lot was not peculiar, but that we had millions of unknown fellow-sufferers on the way. Do not be too disappointed, but let us rather be thankful, that if our poor children must be sick, it was here and not in Paris, and now, good night. Betake yourself to your knees, when you have read this, and pray for us with all your might.

Jan. 5, 1860.—The doctor has been here and says the other children must not meet G. until the end of this month, unless they are taken sick meantime. Poor M. melted like a snowflake in the fire, when she heard that she begins to miss her little playmate, and keeps running to say things to him through the keyhole, and to serenade him with singing, accompanied with a rattling of knives. I see but one thing to be done for you to stay and preach and me to stay and nurse, each in the place God has assigned us.... You must pray for me, that I may be patient and willing to have my coming to Europe turn out a failure as far as my special enjoyment of it is concerned. There are better things than going to Paris, being with you and hearing you preach pray that I may have them in full measure. I cannot bear to stop writing—goodbye, my dearest love!

Jan. 15th—If you could look in upon us this evening, you would be not a little surprised to see me writing in the corner of my room, close to the wash-stand where my lamp is placed but you would see at a glance that the curtain of the bed is let down to shade our darling little M.'s eyes, as she lies close at my side. How sorry I am, as you cannot see all this, to have to tell it to you! I have let her decide for me, and she wants dear papa to know that she is sick. Oh, why need I add another care to those you already suffer on our account! As to baby, we are disposed to think that *he has had the fever*. Of course, we do not know, but it is pleasant to hope the best.... Now, my precious darling, you see there is more praying work to do, as I hinted in my Saturday's note when my heart was pretty heavy within me. I need not tell you what to ask for the dear child but for me do pray that I may have no will of my own. All these trials and disappointments are so purely Providential that it frightens me to think I may have much secret discontent about them, or may like to plan for myself in ways different from God's plans. Yet in the midst of so much care and fatigue, I hardly know how I do feel I am like a feather blown here and there by an unexpected whirlwind and I suppose I ought not to expect much of myself. "Though He slay me yet will I trust in Him," I keep saying over and over to myself, and if you are going to write a new sermon this week, suppose you take that for your text. I have not had one regret that you went to Paris, and as to your coming on, I do hope you will not think of it, unless you are sent for. You could do nothing and would be very lonely and uncomfortable. The doctor told me to tell you to stay where you were, and that you ought to rejoice that the children are not sick in Paris. I do trust that in the end we shall come forth from this troublous time like gold from the furnace. So far, I have been able to do all that was necessary and I trust I shall continue so. God bless you, and bring us to a happy meeting in His own good time!

To Mrs. Stearns, Genevrier, Jan. 21, 1860.

... Boiling over does one good of itself, and I am sure you feel the better for having done so. I do not know why *men* seem to get along without such reliefs as women almost always seek in this way whether there is less water in their kettles or whether their kettles are bigger than ours and boil with more safety. It is a comfort to believe that, whatever our troubles, in the end all will work together for our good. The New Year has opened upon us here at Genevrier pretty gloomily, as George has told you. You will not be surprised, therefore, to hear that M. is also quite sick, much sicker than G. She is one of those meek, precious little darlings whom it is painful to see suffer, and I have hardly known what I was about, or where I was, since she was taken down. My baby is deserted by us all I have only seen him in *moments* for three weeks. You cannot think how lonely poor A. is half the time she eats alone in the big solitary dining-room nobody has any time to walk out with her, what few children she knew are afraid to come here or to have her come nigh them, and I feel as if I should fly, when I think of it—for she is not strong or well and her life here in Switzerland has been a series of disappointments and anxieties. The only leisure moments I can snatch in the course of the twenty-four hours I have to spend in writing to George but the last few evenings M. has slept, so that I could play a game of chess with her and try to cheer and brace her up against next day's dreariness. All her splendid dreams of getting off from this solitude to the life and stir of Paris have been dissipated, but she has never uttered one word of complaint I have not heard her say as much as "Isn't it too bad!" And indeed we ought none of us to say so or to feel so, for the doctor assures me that for three such delicate children as he considers ours, to pass safely through whooping-dough and scarlet-fever, is a perfect wonder and that he is sure it is owing to the pure country air. And when I think how different a scene our house might present if our three little ones had been snatched away, as three or four even have been from other families, I am ashamed of myself that I dare to sigh, that I am lonely and friendless here, or that I have anything to complain of. It has been no small trial, however, to pass through such anxieties in so remote a place, with George gone while on the other hand I have been most thankful that he has been spared all the details of the children's ailments, and permitted once more to feel himself about his Master's business. Providence most plainly called him to Paris, and I trust he will stay there and get good until we can join him. But I feel uneasy about him, too, lest his anxiety about the children should hang as a dead weight on his not quite rested head and heart. At any rate, I shall be tolerably glad to see him again at the end of our two months' separation. How I should love to drop in on you tonight! Doesn't it seem as if one *could* if one tried hard enough! Well, good night to you.

To Mrs. Smith, Genevrier, Jan. 29, 1860.

I believe George has written you about our private hospital. He had not been gone to Paris forty-eight hours when G. was taken sick that was a month ago, and I have only tasted the air twice in all that time. G. had the disease lightly. M., poor little darling, was much sicker than he was. It is a fortnight since she was taken and she hardly sits up at all an older child would be in bed, but little ones never will give up if they can help it I suppose it is because they can be held in the arms and rocked, and carried about. I have passed through some most anxious hours on account of M., and it seems little less than a miracle that she is still alive. The baby is well, and he is a nice little rosy fellow. It was a dreadful disappointment to us to be detained here instead of going to Paris. I felt that I could not live longer in such entire solitude and just then, lo and behold, George was whisked off and I was shut up closer than ever. It is a great comfort to me that he got off just when he did, and has had grace to stay away on the other hand, I need not say how his absence has aggravated my cares, how solitary the season of anxiety has been, and how, at times, my faith and courage have been put to their utmost stretch. The whole thing has been so evidently ordered and planned by God that I have not dared to complain but, my dear child, if you had come in now and then with a little of your strengthening talk, I cannot deny I should have been most thankful. It has been pretty trying for George to hear such doleful accounts from home, but I hope the worst is over, and that we shall be the wiser and the better for this new lesson of life. Dr. Curchod's rule is the same as Dr. Buck's—forty days confinement to one room so we have a month more to spend here. I am afraid I am writing a gloomy letter. If I am, you must try to excuse me and say, "Poor child, she isn't well, and she hasn't had any good sleep lately, and she's tired, and I do not believe she *means* to grumble." Do so much for me, and I will do as much for you sometime. I hear your husband has taken up a Bible-class. It is perfectly shocking. Does he *want* to kill himself, or what ails him? The pleasantest remembrance we shall have of this place is his visit.... Our doctor and his family stand out as bright lights in this picture he has been like a brother in sympathy and kindness. We shall never forget it. God has been so good to you and to me in sparing our children when assailed by so fearful a disease, which we ought to love Him better than we ever did. I do so want my weary solitude to bear that fruit.

* * * * *

IV.

Paris. Sight-seeing. A sick Friend. London and its Environs. The Queen and Prince Albert. The Isle of Wight. Homeward.

On the 20th of February the family gladly bade adieu to Switzerland and set out for Paris, arriving there on the morning of the 22nd. Mrs. Prentiss was overjoyed to find herself once more in the world. On the 23rd, she wrote to Mrs. Smith:

We have got here safe and sound with our little batch of invalids. They bore the journey very well and are heartily glad to get into the world again. I am chock-full of worldliness. All I think of is dress and fashion, and, on the whole, I do not know that you are worth writing to, as you were never in Paris and do not know the modes, and have perhaps foolishly left off hoops and open sleeves. I long, however, to hear from you and your new baby, and will try to keep a small spot swept clear of finery in my heart of hearts, where you can sit down when you have a mind. Our little fellow is getting to be a sweet-looking baby, with what his nurse calls a most "gracieuse" smile—if you can guess what kind of a smile that is. But he is getting teeth and is looking delicate and soft, and your Hercules will knock him down, I know.

But Paris was far from fulfilling to her or to the children the bright anticipations with which it had been looked forward to from lonely Genevrier. The weather could hardly have been worse the house soon became another hospital and sightseeing was a task. Friends, however, soon gathered about her, and by their hospitality and little kindnesses, relieved the tedium of the weary days.

To Mrs. Stearns, Paris, March 27, 1860.

We pass many lonely hours in this big city, and often long for you and Mr. Stearns to drop in, or for a chance to run in to see dear mother. Getting nearer home makes it attractive. It works in the natural life just as it does in the spiritual in that respect. The weather is *dreadful* and has been for five months—scarcely one cheery day in that whole time. What with this and the children's ill health, I should not wonder if we left Paris as ignorant of its beauties as when we came. But I hope we shall not let that worry us too much, but rather be thankful that, bad as things are, they are not as bad as they might be. Our sympathies are greatly excited now for the Rev. Mr. Little, formerly of Bangor, who is in Paris—alone, friendless, and sick. If we could by any miraculous power stretch our scanty accommodations, we should certainly take him home and nurse him until his wife could be got here. You know, perhaps, that Mrs. Little is a daughter of Dr. Cornelius and, when I recall the love and honor I was taught to feel towards him when I was a little girl, my heart quite yearns towards her, especially in this time of fearful anxiety about her husband. How insignificant my own trials look to me, when I think of the sorrow that is probably before her.

April 26th.—Our patience is still tried by the cold, damp, and most unwholesome weather, which prevents the children from going to see anything. But we do not care so much for ourselves or for them as for poor Mr. Little, who is exceedingly feeble, chiefly confined to his room, and so forlorn in this strange, homeless land. While George was with him last evening, he had a bad fit of coughing, which resulted in the raising of a gill or so of blood. I know you will feel interested to hear about him, and will not wonder that our hearts are so full of sympathy for him and for his poor wife, that we can hardly talk of anything else. He expects her in about a week. What a coming to Europe for her! How little those who stand on the shore to watch the departure of a foreign steamer, know what they do when they envy its passengers! We buckled on our armor and began sightseeing the other day, going to see the Sainte Chapelle and the galleries and museum of the Louvre among the rest. The Sainte Chapelle is quite unlike anything I ever saw and delighted us extremely. As to the Louvre, one needs several entire days to do justice to it, besides an amount of youthful enthusiasm and bodily strength which we do not possess for, amid midnight watchings over our sick children and the like, the oil of gladness has about burnt out, and we find sight-seeing a weary task.

May 25th.—It does seem as if George's preaching was listened to with more and more serious attention, and it may be seen long after he has rested from his labors on earth, that he has done a good work here. We both are much interested in Professor [6] Huntington's sermons, [7] sent us by Miss W. This is a great deal for me to say, because I do not like to read sermons. During the last three weeks, before Mr. and Mrs. Little left, we accomplished very little. It was not that we did or could do so very much for them, but they had nobody to depend on but us, and George was constantly going back and forth trying to make them comfortable, arranging all their affairs, etc. She had a weary, anxious two weeks here, and now has set her face homewards, not knowing but Mr. L. may sink before reaching America. It is a great comfort to us to have been able to soothe them somewhat as long as they stayed in Paris. George says it was worth coming here for that alone. I say *we*, but I *mean* George, for what was done, he did. The most I could do was to feel dreadfully for them. [8]

We are now to begin sightseeing again, and do all we can as speedily as possible, for only two weeks remain. The children are now pretty well. The baby is at that dangerous age when they are forever getting upon their feet and tumbling over backward on their heads. M. is the oddest little soul. Belle says she would rather go to a funeral than see all the shops in Paris, and, when they are out, she can hardly keep her from following every such procession they meet. I asked her the last time they went out if she had had a nice walk. She said not very nice, as she had only seen *one* pretty thing, and that was a police officer taking a man to jail. The idea of going to England is very pleasant, and, if we only keep tolerably well, I think it will do us all good. What is dear mother doing about these times? I always think of her as sitting by the little worktable in her room, knitting and watching the children. Give lots of love and kisses to her, and tell her we long to see her face to face. Kiss all the children for us—I suppose they will let *you*! Boys and all—and you may do as much for Mr. S. if you want to. Goodbye.

On the 7th of June, the family left Paris for London. A first visit to England—

That precious stone set in the silver sea—

Is always an event full of interest to children of the New England Puritans. The "sceptered isle" is still in a sense their mother country, and a thousand ancestral ties attract them to its shores. There is no other spot on earth where so many lines of their history, domestic and public, meet. And in London, what familiar memories are for them associated with almost every old street and lane and building!

The winter and spring of 1860 had been cold, wet, and cheerless well nigh beyond endurance and the summer proved hardly less dreary. It rained nearly every day, sometimes all day and all night the sun came out only at long intervals, and then often but for a moment the atmosphere, much of the time, was like lead the moon and stars seemed to have left the sky even the English landscape, in spite of its matchless verdure and beauty, put on a forbidding aspect. All nature, indeed, was under a cloud. This, added to her frail health, made the summer a very trying one to Mrs. Prentiss, and yet it afforded her not a little real delight. Some of her pleasantest days in Europe were spent in England. The following extracts are from a little journal kept by her in London:

June 10th.—We went this morning to hear Dr. Hamilton, and were greatly edified by the sermon, which was on the text: "Hitherto hath the Lord helped us." In the afternoon, we decided to go to Westminster Abbey. It began to rain soon after we got out, and we had a two miles' walk through the mud. The old abbey looked as much like its picture as it could, but pictures cannot give a true idea of the grandeur of such a building. We were a little late, and every seat was full and many were standing, as we had to do through the whole service. The sermon struck me as a very ordinary affair, though it was delivered by a lord. But the music was so sweet, performed for aught I know by angel—for the choir was invisible—and we stood surrounded by such monuments and covered by such a roof, that we were not quite throwing away our time. Albert B—— dined with us, and in the evening, with one accord, we went to hear Dr. Hamilton again. We had good seats and heard a most beautiful as well as edifying discourse on the first verses of the 103rd Psalm. Some of the images were very fine, and the whole tone of the sermon was moderate, sensible, and serious. I use these words advisedly, for I had an impression that he was a flowery, popular man whom I should not relish. At the close of the service a little prayer-meeting of half an hour was held, and we came home satisfied with our first English Sunday, feeling some of our restless cravings already quieted as only contact with God's own people could quiet them.

11th.—Went to see the Crystal Palace. It proved a fine day, and we took M. with us. None of us felt quite well, but we enjoyed this new and beautiful scene for all that. It is a little fairyland.

14th.—Went to Westminster Abbey, and spent some time there. On coming out we made a rapid, but quite amusing passage through several courts where we saw numerous great personages in stiff little gray wigs. To my untrained, irreverent eyes, they all looked perfectly funny. George was greatly interested and edified. It has been raining and shining by turns all day, and is this evening very cold.

15th.—Another of those days which the English so euphoniously term "*nasty*." Not knowing what else to do with it, we set off in search of No. 5 Sermon Lane, a house connected with a stereoscopic establishment in Paris, which we reached after many evolutions and convolutions, and found it to be a wholesale concern only. Pitying us for the trouble we had been at in seeking them, they let us have what views we wanted, but at higher prices than they sell them at Paris. We then went to the Tract House, and while selecting French and other tracts, a gentleman came and asked for a quantity of the "Last Hours of Dr. Payson."

16th.—Went to the Tower, and had a most interesting visit there. We were particularly struck by some spots shown us by one of the wardens, after the regular round had been gone through with, and the other visitors dispersed—namely, the cell where prisoners were confined with thumbscrews attached to elicit confession, and the floor where Lady Jane Grey was imprisoned. We looked from the window where she saw her husband carried to execution, and A. was locked up in the room so as to be able to say she had been a prisoner in the Tower.

17th.—Heard Dr. Hamilton again. Met Dr. and Mrs. Adams of New York there, and had a most kind and cordial greeting from them. Dr. A. introduced us to Dr. Hamilton. In the evening, we went to hear Dr. Adams at Dr. H.'s church, and came home quite proud of our countryman, who gave us a most excellent sermon. At the close of the service Dr. H. invited us to take tea with him next week, and introduced us to his wife a young, quiet little lady, looking as unlike most of us American parsonesses as possible, her parochial cares being, perhaps, less weighty than ours.

18th.—Two things made this day open pleasantly. One was a decided attempt on the part of the sun to come out and shine. The second was Dr. Adams' dropping in and taking breakfast with us. We also got letters from home, and the news that Mr. Little had reached New York in safety. After lunch, George went off in glory to the House of Commons, hinting that he might stay there until tomorrow morning, and begging for a night-key to let himself in. The rest of us went to the Zoological Garden, which is much more ample and interesting than the Jardin des Plantes.

20th.—Yesterday it poured in torrents all day, so that going out was not possible. Today we went out in the drops and between the drops, to do a little shopping in the way of razors, scissors, knives, needles, and such like sharp and pointed things. We stepped into Nesbit's and took a view of Little Susy, who looked as usual, bought a few books, subscribed to a library, coveted our neighbor's property, and came home covered with mud and mire.

22nd.—Went out to Barnet to call on Miss Bird. On reaching the station, we found Miss B. awaiting us with phaeton and pony. We were driven over a pretty three miles route to "Hurst Cottage," where we were introduced to Mrs. Bird and a younger daughter, and I had a nice little lunch, together with pleasant chat about America in general and E. L. S. in particular. Miss Bird said she showed her likeness to a gentleman, who is a great physiognomic, and asked his opinion of her. He replied, "She is a genius, a poetess, a Christian, and a true wife and mother." We then went up-stairs, and looked at Miss B.'s little study, after which she took us to see the church in Hadley, a very old building dating back to 1494. It has been repaired and restored and is a beautiful little church. On leaving it, Miss Bird came with us a part of the way to the station and we got home in good season for dinner. The weather, true to its rule, could not last fine, and so this evening it is raining again. [9]

24th.—No rain all day! Can it be true? George went in the morning to hear Mr. Binney, and A. and I to Dr. Hamilton's, who preached a very good sermon on a favorite text of mine, "I beseech Thee show me Thy glory." In the evening, Dr. Patton, of New York, induced us to go with himself and wife to a meeting at a theatre three miles off. The Rev. Mr. Graham preached. It was an interesting, but touching and saddening sight to look upon the congregation to wonder why they came, and whether they would come again, and whether under those stolid and hardened faces there yet lay humanity. Many came with babies in their arms, who made themselves very much at home some were in dirty weekday clothes "some in rags and some in jags." Coming home, we passed the spot where John Rogers was burned, and that where in time of the plague dead bodies were thrown in frightful heaps into one grave.

25th.—We took tea at Dr. Hamilton's, where we had a very pleasant evening, meeting Dr. and Mrs. Adams, as well as all Dr. H.'s session. Dr. H. strikes one most agreeably, and seems as genial and as full of life as a boy.

26th.—Visited Windsor Castle with Dr. Adams and his party, ten of us in all. We drove afterward to see the country churchyard, where Grey wrote his elegy and where he now lies buried. This was a most charming little trip and we all enjoyed it exceedingly. The young folks gathered leaves and flowers for their books.

29th.—Last evening we had a nice time and a cup of tea with the Adamses. Today—another nasty day—they lunched with us, which broke up its gloom and we went with them to see Sloan's museum, a most interesting collection. We all enjoyed its novelty as well as its beauty.

She also records the pleasure with which she visited the National Gallery, Madame Tussaud's Collection, the British Museum, Richmond, the Kew Gardens, and Bunhill Fields Burying-Ground, and, in particular, the grave of "Mr. John Bunyan."

Not long before leaving London, she attended a Sunday evening service for the people in Westminster Abbey, which interested her deeply. It suggested—or rather was the original of—the scene in The Story Lizzie Told:

When we first got into that grand place, I was scared, and thought they would drive us poor folks out. But when I looked round, most everybody was poor too. At last, I saw some of them get down on their knees, and some shut their eyes, and some took off their hats and held them over their faces. Father could not, because he had me in his arms and so I took it off, and held it for him.

"What's it for?" says I.

"Hush," says father, "the parson's praying."

When I showed IT to God, the room seemed full of Him. But that is a small room. The church is a million and a billion times as big, isn't it, ma'am? But when the minister prayed, that big church seemed just as full as it could hold. Then, all of a sudden, they burst out a-singing. Father showed me the card with large letters on it, and says he, "Sing, Lizzie, Sing!"

And so I did. It was the first time in my life. The hymn said,

> Jesus, lover of my soul,
> Let me to Thy bosom fly,

And I whispered to father, "Is Jesus God?" "Yes, yes," said he, "Sing, Lizzie, sing!"

After the praying and the singing, came the preaching, I heard every word. It was a beautiful story. It told how sorry Jesus was for us when we did wrong, bad things, and how glad He was when we were good and happy. It said we must tell Him all our troubles and all our joys, and feel sure that He knew just how to pity us, because He had been a poor man three and thirty years, on purpose to see how it seemed.

The most stirring sight by far which she witnessed while in London, was a review of 20,000 volunteers by the Queen in Hyde Park, on the 23rd of June. She waited for it several hours, standing much of the time upon a campstool. As her Majesty appeared, accompanied by Prince Albert, the curiosity of the immense crowd "rose to such a pitch that every conceivable method was resorted to, to catch a glimpse of the field. Men climbed on each other's shoulders, gave 'fabulous prices' for chairs, boxes, and baskets, raised their wives and sweethearts high in the air, and so by degrees our view was quite obstructed." [10] The scene did not, perhaps, in numbers or in the brilliant array of fashion, rank, and beauty surpass, nor in military pomp and circumstance did it equal, a grand review she had witnessed not long before in the Champ de Mars but in other respects it was far more impressive. Among the volunteers were thousands of young men in whose veins ran the best and most precious blood in England. And then to an American wife and mother, Queen Victoria was a million times more interesting than Louis Napoleon. She stood then, as happily she still stands, at the head of the Christian womanhood of the world and that in virtue not solely of her exalted position and influence, but of her rare personal and domestic virtues as well. She was then also at the very height of her felicity. How little she or anyone else in that thronging multitude dreamed, that before the close of the coming year the form of the noble Prince, who rode by her side wearing an aspect of such manly beauty and content, and who was so worthy to be her husband, would lie moldering in the grave! [11]

About the middle of July Mrs. Prentiss with her husband and children left London for Ventnor on the Isle of Wight, where, in spite of cold and rainy weather, she passed two happy months. With the exception of Chateau d'Oex, no place in Europe had proved to her such a haven of rest. Miss Scott, the hostess, was kindness itself. The Isle of Wight in summer is a little paradise and in the vicinity of Ventnor are some of its loveliest scenes. Her enjoyment was enhanced by the society of Mr. and Mrs. Jacob Abbott, who were then sojourning there. An excursion taken with Mr. Abbott was doubly attractive for, as might be inferred from his books, he was one of the most genial and instructive of companions, whether for young or old. A pilgrimage to the home and grave of the Dairyman's Daughter and to the grave of "Little Jane," and a day and night at Alum Bay, were among the pleasantest incidents of the summer at Ventnor.

Of the visit to "Little Jane's" grave, she gives the following account in her journal:

Aug. 10th.—Today being unusually fine, we undertook our long-talked-of expedition to Brading. On reaching the churchyard, we asked a little boy who followed us in if he could point out "Little Jane's" grave he said he could and led us at once to the spot. How little she dreamed that pilgrimages would be made to her grave! Our pigmy guide next conducted us to the gravestones, where her task was learned. "How old are you, little fellow?" I asked. "*Getting an to five*," he replied. "And does everybody who comes here give you something?" "*Some* do not." "That's very naughty of them," I continued "after all your trouble they ought to give you something." A shrewd smile was his answer, and George then gave him some pennies. "What do you do with your pennies?" I asked. "I puts them in my pocket." "And then what do you do?" "I saves them up." "And what then?" "My mother buys shoes when I get enough. She is going to buy me some soon with *nails* in them! These are dropping to pieces" (no such thing). "If that is the case," quoth George, "I think I must give you some more pennies." "Thank you," said the boy. "Do you see my sword?" George then asked him if he went to church and to Sunday school. "Oh, yes, and there was an organ, and they learned to sing psalms." "And to love God?" asked George. "Yes, yes," he answered, but not with much unction, and so we turned about and came home.

To Mrs. Stearns, Ventnor, Aug. 24, 1860.

As this is to be our last letter home, it ought to be a very brilliant one, but I am sure it will not and when I look back over the past two years and think how many stupid ones I have written you, I feel almost ashamed of myself. But on the other hand, I wonder I have written no duller ones, for our staying so long at a time in one place has given small chance for variety and description. It is raining and blowing at a rate that you, who are roasting at home, can hardly conceive we agreed yesterday that if you were blindfolded and suddenly set down here and told to guess what season of the year it was, you would judge by your feelings and the wind roaring down the chimney, that it was December. However disagreeable this may be it is more invigorating than hot weather, and George and the children have all improved very much. George enjoys bathing and climbing the "downs" and the children are out nearly all day when it does not rain. You may remember that the twilight is late in England, and even the baby is often out until half-past eight or nine.... I just keep my head above water by having no cares or fatigue at night. I feel *dreadfully* that I am so helpless a creature, but I believe God keeps me so for my mortification and improvement, and that I ought to be willing to lead this good-for-nothing life if He chooses. We have had the pleasure of meeting Mr. and Mrs. Abbott here. They have gone now to spend the winter in Paris. Mrs. A. sent her love to you again and again, and I was very glad to meet her for your sake as well as her own, and to know Mr. A. better than I did before, and it was very pleasant to George to chat with him. We walked together to see Shanklin Chine. A. went with us, and Mr. Abbott amused her so on the way that she came home quite dissatisfied with her stupid papa and mamma.

We are talking of little else now but getting home, and it is a pity you could not take down the walls of our hidden souls and see the various wishes and feelings we have on the subject. I forgot to say how glad we were that you found George Prentiss such a nice boy. [12] I always loved him for Abby's sake and he certainly was worthy of the affection she felt for him as the most engaging child I ever knew he is a thorough Prentiss still, it seems. What is he going to be? You must feel queer to have a boy in college it is like a strange dream. Our boys are two spunky little toads who need, or will need, all our energies to bring up. I have quite got my hand out; M. is so good—and hates to begin. But goodbye, with love to mother, Mr. S. and the children.

The family embarked at Cowes on the magnificent steamship "Adriatic," September 13th, and, after a rough voyage, reached New York on the 24th of the same month. Old friends awaited their coming and welcomed them home again with open arms. It was a happy day for Mrs. Prentiss, and in the abundance of its joy, she forgot the anxious and solitary months through which she had just been passing. She came back with four children instead of three her husband was, partially at least, restored to health and she breathed once more her native air.

[1] A most faithful servant, to whom Mrs. P. was greatly attached.

[2] The Hon. Benjamin F. Butler, of New York, was one of the most honored members of the Mercer street church. He was known throughout the country as an eminent lawyer and patriotic citizen. In the circle of his friends, he was admired and beloved for his singular purity of character, his scholarly tastes, the kindness of his heart, and all the other fine qualities that go to form the Christian gentleman. During a portion of President Jackson's administration Mr. Butler was Attorney-General of the United States. He died in the sixty-third year of his age.

[3] Referring to the death of Dr. Stearns' mother, Mrs. Abigail Stearns, of Bedford, Mass.

[4] Mrs. Wainwright and her husband, the late Eli Wainwright, were members of the old Mercer street Presbyterian Church, and both of them unwearied in their kindness to Mrs. Prentiss and her husband.

[5]

"Far along,
From peak to peak, the rattling crags among,
Leaps the live thunder! Not from one lone cloud,
But every mountain now hath found a tongue,
And Jura answers, through her misty shroud,
Back to the joyous Alps, which call to her aloud!"

[6] Now Bishop of the P. E. Church of Central New York.

[7] "Christian Believing and Living."

[8] The Rev. George B. Little was born in Castine, Maine, December 21, 1821. He was graduated at Bowdoin College in 1843. Having studied theology at Andover, he was ordained in 1849 pastor of the First Congregational church in Bangor, Me. In 1850, he married Sarah Edwards, daughter of that admirable and whole-souled servant of Christ, the Rev. Elias Cornelius, D.D. In November, 1857, Mr. Little was installed as pastor of the Congregational church in West Newton, Mass. Early in March, 1860, he went abroad for his health, but returned home again in May, and died among his own people, July 20, 1860. The last words he littered were, "I shall soon be with Christ." Mr. Little was a man of superior gifts, full of scholarly enthusiasm, and devoted to his Master's work.

[9] Miss Bird is known to the world by her remarkable books of travel in Japan and elsewhere.

[10] An account of the Volunteer Review in Hyde Park is given in Sir Theodore Martin's admirable Life of the Prince Consort, Vol. V., pp. 105-6, Am. Ed. The Prince himself, in responding to a toast the same evening, speaks of it as "a scene which will never fade from the memory of those who had the good fortune to be present."

[11] It is hardly possible to allude to the great affliction of this illustrious lady without thinking also of the persistent acts of womanly sympathy by which, during the anguish and suspense of the past two months, she has tried to minister comfort to the stricken wife of our suffering and now sainted President. Certainly, the whole case is unique in the history of the world. By this most tender and Christ-like sympathy, she has endeared herself in a wonderful manner to the heart of the American people. God bless Queen Victoria! They say with one voice.—*New York, September* 24, 1881.

[12] The eldest son of her brother-in-law, Mr. S. S. Prentiss, a youth of rare promise, and who had especially endeared himself to his Aunt Abby. He died of fever at Tallahoma, Tennessee, during the war.

CHAPTER 7 - THE STRUGGLE WITH ILL-HEALTH - 1861-1865.

I.

At Home again in New York. The Church of the Covenant. Increasing Ill-health. The Summer of 1861. Death of Louisa Payson Hopkins. Extracts from her Journal. Summer of 1862. Letters. Despondency.

We come now to a new phase of Mrs. Prentiss' experience as a pastor's wife. Before her husband resigned his New York charge, during the winter of 1857-8, the question of holding a service in the upper part of the city, with the view to another congregation, was earnestly discussed in the session and among the leading members of the church, but nothing then came of it. Soon after his return from Europe, however, the project was revived, and resulted at length in the formation of the Church of the Covenant. In consequence of the great civil war, which was then raging, the undertaking encountered difficulties so formidable, that nothing but extraordinary zeal, liberality, and wise counsel on the part of his friends and the friends of the movement could overcome them. For two or three years the new congregation held service in what was then called Dodworth's Studio Building at the corner of Fifth avenue and Twenty-sixth street, but in 1864 it entered the chapel on Thirty-fifth street, and in 1865 occupied the stately edifice on Park avenue. In the manifold labors, trials, and discouragements connected with this work, Mrs. Prentiss shared with her husband and, when finally crowned with the happiest success, it owed perhaps as much to her as to him. This brief statement seems needful in order to define and render clear her position, as a pastor's wife, during the next twelve years.

After spending some weeks in Newark and Portland, she found herself once more in New York in a home of her own and surrounded by friends, both old and new. The records of the following four or five years are somewhat meager and furnish few incidents of special significance. The war, with its terrible excitement and anxieties, absorbed all minds and left little spare time for thought or feeling about anything else. Domestic and personal interests were entirely overshadowed by the one supreme interest of the hour—that of the imperiled National life. It was for Mrs. Prentiss a period also of almost continuous ill health. The sleeplessness from which she had already suffered so much assumed more and more a chronic character, and, aggravated by other ailments and by the frequent illness of her younger children, so undermined her strength, that life became at times a heavy burden. She felt often that her days of usefulness were past. But the Master had yet a great work for her to do, and—

In ways various, Or, might I say, contraries—

He was training her for it during these years of bodily infirmity and suffering.

The summer of 1861 was passed at Newport. In a letter to Mrs. Smith, dated July 28th, she writes:

We find the Cliff House delightful, within a few minutes' walk of the sea, which we have in full view from one of our windows. And we have no lack of society, for the Bancroft's, Miss Aspinwall and her sister, as well as the Skinners, are very friendly. But I am so careworn and out of sorts, that this beautiful ocean gives me little comfort. I seem to be all the time toting one child or another about, or giving somebody paregoric or rhubarb, or putting somebody to sleep, or scolding somebody for waking up papa, who is miserable, and his oration untouched. There, do not mind me it is at the end of a churchless Sunday, and I dare say I am "only peevis'," as the little boy said.

But in a few weeks the children were well again and her own health so much improved, that she was able to indulge in surf bathing, which she "enjoyed tremendously," and early in the fall the whole family returned to town greatly refreshed by the summer's rest.

On the 24th of January, 1862, her sister, Mrs. Hopkins, died. This event touched her deeply. She hurried off to Williamstown, whence she wrote to her husband, who was unable to accompany her:

If you had known that I should not get here until half-past nine last night, and that in an open sleigh from North Adams, you would not have let me come. But so far I am none the worse for it and, when I came in and found the Professor and T. and Eddy sitting here all alone and so forlorn in their unaccustomed leisure, I could not be thankful enough that a kind Providence had allowed me to come. It is a very great gratification to them all, especially to the Professor, and even more so than I had anticipated. In view of the danger of being blocked up by another snowstorm, I shall probably think it best to return by another route, which they all say is the best. I hope you and my precious children keep well.

No picture of Mrs. Prentiss' life would be complete, in which her sister's influence was not distinctly visible. To this influence, she owed the best part of her earlier intellectual training and it did much to mould her whole character. Mrs. Hopkins was one of the most learned, as well as most gifted, women of her day and had not ill health early disabled her for literary labors, she might, perhaps, have won for herself an enduring name in the literature of the country. There were striking points of resemblance between her and Sara Coleridge the same early intellectual bloom the same rare union of feminine delicacy and sensibility with masculine strength and breadth of understanding the same taste for the beautiful in poetry, in art, and in nature, joined to similar fondness for metaphysical studies the same delight in books of devotion and in books of theology and the same varied erudition. Only one of them seems to have been an accomplished Hebraist, but both were good Latin and Greek scholars and both were familiar with Italian, Spanish, French, and German. Even in Sara Coleridge's admiration and reverence for her father, Mrs. Hopkins was in full sympathy with her. She lacked, indeed, that poetic fancy which belonged to the author of "Phantasmion" nor did she possess her mental self-poise and firmness of will but in other respects, even in physical organization and certain features of countenance, they were singularly alike. And they both died in the fiftieth year of their age.

Louisa Payson was born at Portland, February 24, 1812. Even as a child, she was the object of tender interest to her father on account of her remarkable intellectual promise. He took the utmost pains to aid and encourage her in learning to study and to think. The impression he made upon her may be seen in the popular little volume entitled "The Pastor's Daughter," which consists largely of conversations with him, written out from memory after his death. She was then in her sixteenth year. The records of the next eight years, which were mostly spent in teaching, are very meager but a sort of literary journal, kept by her between 1835 and 1840, shows something of her mental quality and character, as also of her course of reading. She was twenty-three years old when the journal opens. Here are a few extracts from it:

BOSTON, Nov. 18, 1835.

Last evening I passed in company with Mr. Dana. [1] I conversed with him only for a few moments about Mr. Alcott's school, and had not time to ask one of the ten thousand questions I wished to ask. I have been trying to analyze the feeling I have for men of genius, Coleridge, Wordsworth and Dana, for example. I can understand why I feel for them unbounded admiration, reverence and affection, but I hardly know why there should be so much excitement—painful excitement—mingled with these emotions. Next to possessing genius, I would be the pleasure of living with one who possessed it.

Nov. 19th.—I have read today one canto of Dante's Inferno and eight or ten pages of Cicero de Amicitia. In this, as well as in de Senectute, which I have just finished, I am much interested. I confess I am not a little surprised to find how largely the moderns are indebted to the ancients how many wise observations on life, and death, the soul, time, eternity, etc, have been repeated by the sages of every generation since the days of Cicero.

Jan. 14th, 1836.—I spent last evening with Mr. Dana, and the conversation was, of course, of great interest. We talked of some of the leading Reviews of the day, and then of the character of our literature as connected with our political institutions. This led to a long discussion of the latter subject, but as the same views are expressed in Mr. D.'s article on Law, I shall pass it over. [2] I differed from him in regard to the French comedies, especially those of Moliere however, he allowed that they contain genuine humor, but they are confined to the exhibition of *one* ridiculous point in the character, instead of giving us the whole man as Shakespeare does.

Sept, 22nd.—This morning I have had one of the periods of *insight,* when the highest spiritual truths pertaining to the divine and human natures, become their own light and evidence, as well as the evidence of other truths. No speculations, no ridicule can shake my faith in that which I thus see and feel. I was particularly interested in thinking of the regeneration of the spirit and the part, which Faith, Hope, and Love, have in effecting it.

Sab. 23rd.—It seems to me that this truth alone, there is a God, is sufficient, rightly believed, to make every human being absolutely and perfectly happy.

Jan. 14th, 1839.—Wednesday evening attended Mr. Emerson's lecture on Genius, of which I shall *attempt* to say nothing except that it was most delightful. Thursday morning Mr. Emerson [3] called to see me and gave me a ticket for his course. Afterwards Mr. Dana called. It seems to me that I have lived *backwards* in other words, the faculties of my mind which were earliest developed, were those which in other minds come last—reflection and solidity of judgment while fancy and imagination, in so far as I have any at all, have followed.

Sat. Jan. 26th.—My occupations in the way of books at present, consist in reading "Antigone," Guizot's "History," Lockhart's "Scott," and *sundries*. I am also translating large extracts from Claudius, with a view to writing an article about him, if the fates shall so will it. [4]

Thurs. Jan. 1st.—Mr. Emerson's lecture last night was on Comedy. He professed to enter on the subject with reluctance, as conscious of a deficiency in the organ of the ludicrous—a profession, however, that was not substantiated very well by the lecture itself, which convulsed the audience with laughter. He spoke in the commencement of the silent history written in the faces of an assembly, making them as interesting to a spectator as if their lives were written in their features.

25th.—I began yesterday Schleiermacher's "Christliche Glaube"—a profound, learned, and difficult work, I am told—Jouffroy's "Philosophical Writings," Landor's "Pericles and Aspasia," and "The Gurney Papers." Considering that I was already in the midst of several books, this is rather too much, but I could not help it the books were lent me and must be read and returned speedily. I have been all the morning employed in writing an abstract of the Report of the Prison Discipline Society, and am wearied and stupefied.

Jan. 7th, 1840.—Went to Mr. Ripley's where I met Dr. Channing, and listened to a discussion of Spinoza's religious opinions. This afternoon Mr. D. came again talked about the Trinity and other theological points. This evening, heard Prof. Silliman. I have nearly finished Fichte, and like him on the whole exceedingly, though I think he errs in placing the roots of the speculative in the practical reason. It seems to me that neither grows out of the other, but that they are coincident spheres. Still, there is a truth, a great truth, in what he says. It is true that action is often the most effectual remedy against speculative doubts and perplexities. When you are in the dark about this or that point, ask what command does conscience impose upon me at this moment—obey it and you will find light.

These extracts will suffice to show the quality and extent of her reading. What sort of fruit her reading and study bore may be seen by her articles on Claudius and Goethe, in the New York Review. No abler discussion of the genius and writings of Goethe had at that time appeared in this country while the article on Claudius was probably the first to make him known to American readers.

During many of the later years of her life, Mrs. Hopkins was a martyr to ill health. The story of her sufferings, both physical and mental, as artlessly told in little diaries which she kept, is "wondrous pitiful" no pen of fiction could equal its simple pathos. Again and again, as she herself knew, she was on the very verge of insanity nothing, probably, saving her from it but the devotion of her husband, who with untiring patience and a mother's tenderness ministered, in season and out of season, to her relief. Often would he steal home from his beloved Observatory, where he had been teaching his students how to watch the stars, and pass a sleepless night at her bedside, reading to her and by all sorts of gentle appliances trying to soothe her irritated nerves. And this devotion ran on, without variableness or shadow of turning, year after year, giving itself no rest until her eyes were closed in death. [5]

Let us now resume our narrative. A portion of the summer of 1862 was passed by Mrs. Prentiss at Newport. Her season of rest was again invaded by severe illness among her children. Under date of August 3rd, she writes to Mrs. Smith:

I can see that our landlady, who has good sense and experience, thinks G. will not get well. Sometimes, in awful moments, I think so too but then I cheer up and get quite elated. Last night as I lay awake, too weary to sleep, I heard a harsh, rasping sound like a large saw. I thought some animal unknown to me must be making it, it was so regular and frequent. But after a time I found it was a dying young soldier who lives farther from this house than Miss H. does from our house in New York. His fearful cough! Oh, this war! This war! I never hated and revolted against it as I did then. I had heard someone say such a young man lay dying of consumption in this street, but until then was too absorbed with my own incessant cares to hear the cough, as the rest had done. I never realized how I felt about our country until I found the terror of losing, a link out of that little golden chain that encircles my sweetest joys, was a *kindred* suffering. Have the times ever looked as black as they do now? We seem to be drifting round without chart or pilot.

Two weeks later, August 17th, she writes to her cousin, Miss Shipman:

G. is really up and about, looking thin and white, and feeling hungry and weak but little H. has been sick with the same disease these ten days past. I got your letter and the little cat, for which G. and I thank you very much. I should think it would about kill you to cook all day even for our soldiers, but on the whole cannot blame anyone who wants to be killed in their service. I am impressed more and more with their claims upon us, who confront every danger and undergo every suffering, while we sit at home at our ease. However, the ease I have enjoyed during the last five weeks has not been of a very luxurious kind, and I have felt almost discouraged, as day after day of confinement and night after night of sleeplessness has pulled down my strength. But, what am I doing? Complaining, instead of rejoicing that I am not left unchastised.

After a careworn summer at Newport, she went with the children to Williamstown, where a month was passed with her brother-in-law, Professor Hopkins. The following letters relate to this visit:

To her Husband, Williamstown, Sept. 19, 1862.

I am glad to find that you place reliance on the reports of our late victory, for I have been in great suspense, seeing only The World, which was throwing up its hat and declaring the war virtually ended. I have no faith in such premature assertions, of which we have had so many, but was most anxious to know your opinion. Do not fail to keep me informed of what is going on. The children are all out of doors and enjoying themselves. The Professor has gone on horseback to see about his buckwheat. He took me up there yesterday afternoon, and I crawled through forty fences (more or less) and got a vast amount of exercise, which did not result in any better sleep, however, than no exercise does. Caro. H. read me yesterday a most interesting letter from her brother Henry, describing the scene at Bull Run when he went there five days after the battle. It is very painful to find such mismanagement as he deplores. He gave a most touching account of a young fellow who lay mortally wounded, where he had lain uncared-for with his companions the five days, and whom they were obliged to decline removing, as they had only room for a portion of the hopeful cases. After beseeching Mr. H. to see that he was removed, and entreating to know when and how he was ever to get home if they left him, he was told that it was not possible to make room for him in this train of ambulances. As Mr. H. tore himself away, he heard him say,

"Here, Lord, I give myself away 'tis all that I can do."

The torture of the wounded men in the ambulances was so frightful, that Mr. H. gave each of them morphine enough to kill three well men. They "cried for it like dogs and licked my hands lest they should lose a drop," he adds. As a contrast to this letter, some of the new recruits came into the Professor's grounds yesterday to get bouquets, and thought if *their* folks had a "yard" so gaily decked with flowers they would feel set up.

To Mrs. Smith, Williamstown, Sept. 25, 1862.

I have been feeling languid, or lazy, ever since I came here, and for a few days past have been miserable but I am better today. This place is perfectly lovely and grows upon me every day. But the Professor is entirely absorbed in his loss. He does not know it, or else thinks he does not show it, for he makes no complaint, but it is in every tone and word and look. It is plain that Louisa's ill health, which might have weaned a selfish man from her, only endeared her to him she was so entirely his object day and night, that he misses her and the *care* of her, as a mother does her sick child. If we ride out he says, "Here I often came with *her*" if a bird sings, "That is a note she used to love" if we see a flower, "That is one of the flowers she loved." He has an astonishing amount of journal manuscripts, and I think may in time prepare something from them…. Isn't it frightful how cotton goods have run up! I gave twenty cents for a yard of silica (is that the way to spell it?) and suppose everything else has rushed up too. I hope you are prepared to tell me exactly what to buy and instruct me in the way I should go.

To her Husband, Williamstown, Sept. 26.

I spent yesterday forenoon looking over Louisa's papers and found an enormous mass of manuscript journals, extract books, translations, and work enough planned and begun for many lifetimes. It was very depressing. One's only refuge is faith in God, and in the certainty that her lingering illness was more acceptable to Him than years of active usefulness, and such extraordinary usefulness even as she was so fitted for. I read over some of my own letters written many, many years ago and the sense this gave me of lost youth and vivacity and energy, was, for a time, most painful…. I have felt for a long while greatly discouraged and depressed, yes, weary of my life, because it seems to me that broken down and worn out as I am, and full of faults under which I groan, being burdened, I could not make you happy. But your last letter comforted me a good deal. I see little for us to do but what you suggest: to cheer each other up and wear out rather than rust out. It is more and more clear to me, that patience is our chief duty on earth, and that we cannot rest here.

I am anxious to know what you think of the President's Proclamation. [6] The Professor likes it. He seems able to think of little but his loss. Even when speaking in the most cheerful way, tears fill his eyes, and the other day putting a letter into my hands to read, he had to run out of the room. The letter stated that fifty young person's owed their conversion to Louisa's books it was written some years ago. His mother spent Saturday here. She is very bright and cheerful and full of sly humor he did everything to amuse her and she enjoyed her visit amazingly. I long to see you. Letters are more and more unsatisfactory, delusive things. M. is going to have a "party" this afternoon, and is going to one this forenoon. The others are bright and busy as bees. Goodbye.

A tinge of sadness is perceptible in most of her letters during this year. Her sister's death, the fearful state of the country, protracted sickness among her children, and her own frequent ill turns and increasing sense of feebleness, all conspired to produce this effect. But in truth her heart was still as young as ever and a touch of sympathy, or an appeal to her love of nature, instantly made it manifest. An extract from a letter to Miss Anna Warner, dated New York, December 16th, may serve as an instance: I wanted to write a book when the trunk came this afternoon that is, a book full of thanks and exclamation marks. You could not have bought with money anything for my Christmas present, which could give half the pleasure. I shut myself up in my little room up-stairs (I declare I do not believe you saw that room! did you?), and there I spread out my mosses and my twigs and my cones and my leaves and admired them till I had to go out and walk to compose myself. Then the children came home and they all admired too, and among us, we upset my big workbasket and my little workbasket, and didn't any of us care. My only fear is that with all you had to do you did too much for me. Those little red moss cups are *too* lovely! And as to all those leaves, how I shall leaf out! G. asked me who sent me all those beautiful things. "Miss Warner," quoth I absently. "Didn't Miss Anna send any of them?" he exclaimed. So you see you twain do not pass as one flesh here. I have read all the "Books of Blessing" [7] save Gertrude and her Cat—but though I like them all very much, my favorite is still "The Prince in Disguise." If you come across a little book called "Earnest," [8] published by Randolph, do read it. It is one of the few *real* books and ought to do good. I have outdone myself in picture-frames since you left. I got a pair of nippers and some wire, which were of great use in the operation. I am now busy on Mr. Bull, for Mr. Prentiss' study.

To one of her sisters-in-law she wrote, under the same date:

I do not know, as I ever was as discouraged about my health as I have been this fall. Sometimes I think my constitution is quite broken down, and that I never shall be good for anything again. However, I do not worry one way or the other but try to be as patient as I can. I have been a good deal better for some days, and if you could see our house you would not believe a word about my not being well, and would know my saying so was all a sham. To tell the truth, it does look like a garden, and when I am sick I like to lie and look at what I did when I wasn't my wreaths, and my crosses, and my vines, and my toadstools, and other fixings. Yesterday I made a bonnet of which I am justly proud tomorrow I expect to go into mosses and twigs, of which Miss Anna Warner has just sent me a lot. She and her sister were here about a fortnight. They grow good so fast that there is no keeping track of them. Does anybody in Portland take their paper? [9] The children are all looking forward to Christmas with great glee. It is a mercy there are any children to keep up one's spirits in these times. Was there ever anything as dreadful as the way in which our army has just been driven back! [10] But if we had had a brilliant victory perhaps the people would have clamored against the emancipation project, and anything is better than the perpetuation of slavery.

Our congregation is fuller than ever, but there is no chance of building even a chapel. Shopping is pleasant business now-a-days, isn't it? We shall have to stop sewing and use pins.

* * * * *

II.

Another care-worn Summer. Letters from Williamstown and Rockaway. Hymn on Laying the Cornerstone of the Church of the Covenant.

The records of 1863 are confined mostly to her letters written during the summer. In June, she went again with the younger children to Williamstown, where she remained a month. The family then proceeded to Rockaway, Long Island, and spent the rest of the season there in a cottage, kindly placed at their disposal by Mrs. William G. Bull. They passed through New York barely in time to escape the terrible riots, which raged there with such fury in the early part of July. A few extracts from her letters belonging to this period follow:

To her Husband, Troy, June 10.

I hope you will not be frightened to get a letter mailed here anyhow, I cannot resist the temptation to write, though standing up in a little newspaper office. We were routed up at half past five this morning by pounds and yells about taking the "Northern Railroad." On reaching Troy the captain bid us hurry or we should lose the train, and we did hurry, though I pretty well foresaw our fate, and after a running walk of a quarter of a mile, we had the felicity of finding the train had left and that the next one would not start till twelve. The little darlings are bearing the disappointment sweetly.

4 P.M.—After depositing my note in the Post-office, we strolled about awhile and then came across to a hotel, where I ordered a lunch-dinner. We got through at twelve and marched to the station, expecting to start at once, when M. came running up to me declaring there was no train to Williamstown until five o'clock. My heart fairly turned over however, I did not believe it, but on making inquiries, it proved to be only too true. For a minute, I sat in silent

despair. Just then, the landlord of the hotel drew nigh and said to me, "You do not look very healthy, Mrs. If you'll walk over to my house, I will give you a bedroom free of charge, and you can lie down and rest awhile." Over to his house we went, weary enough. After awhile, finding them all forlorn, I got a carriage and we drove out on coming back I ordered some ice cream, which built us all up amazingly. The children are now counting the minutes until five. One of the boys is perched on a washstand with his feet dangling down through the hole where the bowl should be the other is eating crackers the landlord is anxious I should take a glass of wine and M. is everywhere at once, having nearly worn out my watch-pocket to see what time, it was.

Monday, June 21st.—It is now going on a fortnight since we left home. Oh, if it were God's will, how I should love to get well, pay you back some of the debts I owe you, be a better mother to my children, write some more books, and make you love me so you would not know what to do with yourself! Just to see how it would seem to be well, and to show you what a splendid creature I could be, if once out of the harness! A modest little list you will say! I said to myself, Is it after all such a curse to suffer and to be a source of suffering to others? Isn't it worthwhile to pay something for warm human sympathies and something for rich experience of God's love and wisdom? And I felt, that for you to have a radiant, cheerful, health-happy wife was not, perhaps, so good for you, as a minister of Christ's gospel, as to have the poor feeble creature whose infirmities keep you anxious and off the top of the wave.

Saturday afternoon the Professor took me off strawberrying again. Can you believe that until this June I never went strawberrying in my life? I do not eat them, so the fun is in the picking. Do you realize how kind the Professor is to me? I am afraid I do not. He works very hard, too hard, I think but perhaps he does it as a refuge from his loneliness. His heart seems still full of tenderness toward Louisa. Yesterday he took me aside and told me, with much emotion, that he dreamed the night before that she floated towards him with a leaf in her hand, on which she wrote the words "Sabbath peacefulness." I love him much, but am afraid of him, as I am of all men—even of you, you need not laugh, I am.

To Mrs. Smith she writes from Rockaway, July 24th:

We were glad to hear that you were safely settled at Prout's Neck, far from riots, if not from rumors thereof. We have as convenient and roomy and closetty a cottage as possible. We are within three minutes or so of the beach, and go back and forth, bathe, dig sand, and stare at the ocean according to our various ages and tastes. I really do not know how else we spend our time. I sew a little, and am going to sew more when my machine comes read a little, doze a little, and eat a good deal. The butcher calls every morning, and so does the baker with excellent bread twice a week clams call at thirty cents the hundred we get milk, butter, and eggs without much trouble and ice and various vegetables without any, as Mrs. Bull sends them to us every day, with sprinklings of fruit, pitchers of cream, herring and whatever is going. We either sit on the beach looking and listening to the waves, every evening, or we run in to Mrs. Bull's or gather about our parlor-table reading. By ten, we are all off to bed. George does nothing but race back and forth to New York on Seminary business he has gone now. I went with him the other day. The city looks pinched and woebegone. We were caught in that tornado and nearly pulled to pieces.

27th.—You will be sorry to hear that our last summer's siege with dysentery bids fair to be repeated. Yesterday, when the disease declared itself, I must own that for a few hours I felt about heart-broken. My own strength is next to nothing, and how to face such a calamity I knew not. Ah, how much easier it is to pray daily, "Oh, Jesus Christus, wachs in mir!" than to consent to, yea rejoice in, the terms of the grant! Well, George went for the doctor. His quarters at this season are right opposite he is a German and brother of the author Auerbach. We brought G.'s cot into our room and George and I took care of him till three o'clock, when for the first time since we had children, I gave out and left the poor man to get along as nurse as he best could. I can tell you it comes hard on one's pride to resign one's office to a half-sick husband. I think I have let the boys play too hard in the sun. I long to have you see this pretty cottage and this beach.

Aug. 3rd.—The children are out of the doctor's hands and I do about nothing at all. I hope you are as lazy as I am. Today I bathed, read the paper, and finished John Halifax. I wish I could write such a book!

To Miss Gilman she writes, August 10th:

We have the nicest of cottages, near the sea. I often think of you as I sit watching the waves rush in and the bathers rushing out. I have not yet thanked you for the hymns you sent me. The traveler's hymn sounds like George Withers. Mr. P. borrowed a volume of his poems, which delights us both. I am glad you are asking your mother questions about your father. I am amazed at myself for not asking my dear mother many a score about my father, which no human being can answer now. I do not like to think of you all leaving New York. Few families would be so missed and mourned.

I can sympathize with you in regard to your present Sunday "privileges." We have a long walk in glaring sunshine, sit on bare boards, live through the whole (or nearly the whole) Prayer-book, and then listen, if we can, to a sermon three-quarters of an hour long, its length not being its chief fault. I am utterly unable to bear such fatigue, and spend my time chiefly at home, with some hope of more profit, at any rate. How true it is that our Master's best treasures are kept in earthen vessels! Humanly speaking, we should declare it to be for His glory to commit the preaching of His gospel to the best and wisest hands. But His ways are not as our ways.... I feel such a longing, when Sunday conies, to spend it with good people, under the guidance of a heaven-taught man. A minister has such wonderful opportunity for doing good! It seems dreadful to see the opportunity more than wasted. The truth is, we all need, ministers and all, a closer walk with God. If a man comes down straight from the mount to speak to those who have just come from the same place, he must be in a state to edify and they to be edified.

From New York, she writes to Miss Shipman, October 24th:

Your letter came just as we started for Poughkeepsie. The Synod met there and I was invited to accompany George, and, quite contrary to my usual habits, I went. We had a nice time. I feel that you are in the best place in the world. Next to dying and going home one's self, it must be sweet to accompany a Christian friend down to the very banks of the river. Isn't it strange that after such experiences we can ever again have a worldly thought, or ever lose the sense of the reality of divine things! But we are like little children—ever learning and ever forgetting. Still, it is well to be learning, and I envy you your frequent visits to the house of mourning. You will miss your dear friend very much. I know how you love her. How many beloved ones you have already lost for a season! Do not set me to making brackets. I am as worldly now as I can be, and my head full of work on all sorts of things. I made two cornucopias of your pattern and filled them with grasses and autumn leaves, and they were magnificent. I got very large grasses in the Rockaway marshes. The children are all well and as gay as larks.

Early in November, the cornerstone of the Church of the Covenant was laid. She wrote the following hymn for the occasion:

>A temple, Lord, we raise
>Let all its walls be praise
>To Thee alone.
>Draw nigh, O Christ, we pray,
>To lead us on our way,
>And be Thou, now and aye,
>Our corner-stone.
>In humble faith arrayed,
>We these foundations laid
>In war's dark day.
>Oppression's reign o'erthrown,
>Sweet peace once more our own,
>Do Thou the topmost stone
>Securely lay.
>And when each earth-built wall
>Crumbling to dust shall fall,
>Our work still own.
>Be to each faithful heart
>That here hath wrought its part,
>What in Thy Church Thou art—
>The Cornerstone.

* * * * *

III.

Happiness in her Children. The Summer of 1864. Letters from Hunter.
Affliction among Friends.

In the early part of 1864, she was more than usually afflicted with neuralgic troubles and that "horrid calamity," as she calls it, sleeplessness. "I know just how one feels when one cannot eat or sleep or talk. I declare, a good deal of the time pulling words out of me is like pulling out teeth."

Still (she writes to a sister-in-law, Jan. 15th), we are a happy family in spite of our ailments. I suffer a great deal and cause anxiety to my husband by it, but then I enjoy a great deal and so does he, and our younger children—to say nothing of A.—are sources of constant felicity. Do not you miss the hearing little feet pattering round the house? It seems to me that the sound of my six little feet is the very pleasantest sound in the world. Often when I lie in bed racked with pain and exhausted from want of food—for my digestive organs seem paralyzed when I have neuralgia—hearing these little darlings about the house compensates for everything, and I am inexpressibly happy in the mere sense of possession. I hate to have them grow up and to lose my pets, or exchange them for big boys and girls. I suppose your boys are a great help to you and company too, but I feel for you that you have not also a couple of girls.... Poor Louisa! It is very painful to think what she suffered. Her death was such a shock to me, I can hardly say why, that I have never been since what I was before. I suppose my nervous system was so shattered, that so unexpected a blow would naturally work unkindly.

Early in the following summer, she was distressed by the sudden bereavement of dear friends and by the death of her nephew, who fell in one of the battles of the Wilderness. In a letter to Miss Gilman, dated June 18th, she refers to this:

Your dear little flowers came in excellent condition, but at a moment when I could not possibly write to tell you so. The death of Mrs. R. H. broke my heart. I only knew her by a sort of instinct, but I sorrowed in her mother's sorrow and in that of her sisters. Death is a blessed thing to the one whom it leads to Christ's kingdom and presence, but oh, how terrible for those it leaves fainting and weeping behind! We expect to go off for the summer on next Thursday. We go to Hunter, N. Y., in the region of the Catskills. My husband's mother has been with me during the last six weeks and has just gone home, and I have now to do up the last things in a great hurry. You may not know that my A. and M. S., and a number of other young people of their age, joined our church on last Sunday. I can hardly realize my felicity. I seem to myself to have a new child. Your sister may have told you of the loss of Professor Hopkins' son. He was the first grandchild in our family and his father's *all*. We may never hear what his fate was, but the suspense has been dreadful.

Her interest in the national struggle was intense and her conviction of its Providential character unwavering. To a friend, who seemed to her a little lukewarm on the subject, she wrote at this time:

For my part, I am sometimes afraid I shall die of joy if we ever gain a complete and final victory. You can call this spunk if you choose. But my spunk has got a backbone of its own and that is deep-seated conviction, that this is a holy war, and that God himself sanctions it. He spares nothing precious when He has a work to do. No life is too valuable for Him to cut short, when any of His designs can be furthered by doing so. But I could talk a month and not have done, you wicked unbeliever.

To her Husband, Hunter, June 27, 1864.

This morning, after breakfast, I sallied out with six children to take a most charming walk, scramble, climb, etc. We put on our worst old duds, tuck up our skirts June 27, knee-high, and have a regular good time of it. If you were awake as early as eight o'clock—I do not believe you were! You might have seen us with a good spyglass, and it would have made your righteous soul leap for joy to see how we capered and laughed, and what strawberries we picked, and how much of a child A. turned into. They all six "played run" till they had counted twelve and then they tumbled down and rolled in the grass, until I wondered what their bones were made of. I do not see that we could have found a better place for the children. What with the seven calves, the cows, the sheep, the two pet lambs, the dogs, hens, chickens, horses, etc., they are perfectly happy. Just now, they have been to see the butter made and to get a drink of buttermilk. We have lots of strawberries and cream, pot cheese, Johnnycakes, and there are always eggs and milk at our service. From diplomatic motives, I advise you not to say too much about Hunter to people asking questions. It would entirely spoil its only great charm if a rush of silly city folks should scent it out. It is really a primitive place and that you can say. Mr. Coe preached an excellent sermon on Sunday morning.

To Mrs. Smith, Hunter, July 4, 1864.

I have just been off, all alone, foraging, and have come home bringing my sheaves with me: ground pine and red berries, with which I have made a beautiful wreath. I have also adorned the picture of Gen. Grant with festoons of evergreens, conjuring him the while not to disappoint our hopes, but to take Richmond. Alas! You may know, by this time, that he cannot but in lack of news since a week ago, I can but hope for the best. I've taken a pew and we contrive to squeeze into it in this wise: first a child, then a mother, then a child, then an Annie, then a child, the little ones being stowed in the cracks left between us big ones. Mr. R., the parson, looking fit to go straight into his grave, was up here to get a wagon as he was going for a load of chips. His wife was at home sick, without any servant, had churned three hours and the butter would not come, and has a pew full of little ones. Oh, my poor sisters in the ministry! My heart aches for them. Mr. R. gave us a superior sermon last Sunday.... I know next to nothing about what is going on in the world. But George writes that he feels decidedly pleased with the look of things. He has been carrying on like all possessed since I left, having company to breakfast, lunch, dinner, and finally went and had Chi Alpha all himself.

July 25th.—We went one day last week on a most delightful excursion, twenty-one of us in all. Our drive was splendid and the scenery sublime even we distinguished Swiss travelers thought so! We came to one spot where ice always is found, cut out big pieces, ate it, drank it, threw it at each other, and carried on with it generally. We had our dinner on the grass in the woods. We brought home a small cartload of natural brackets some of them beautiful.

August 1st.—You have indeed had a "rich experience." [11] We all read your letter with the deepest interest and feel that it would have been good to be there. Your account of Caro shows what force of character she possessed, as well as what God's grace can do and do quickly. This is not the first time He has ripened a soul into full Christian maturity with almost miraculous rapidity. A veteran saint could not have laid down his armor and adjusted himself to meet death with more calmness than did this young disciple. I do not wonder her family were borne, for the time, above their sorrow, but alas! Their bitter pangs of anguish are yet to meet them. Her poor mother! How much she has suffered and has yet to suffer! All the more because she bears it so heroically.

To Miss Emily S. Gilman, Hunter, Aug 1, 1864.

You must have wondered why I did not answer your letter and your book, for both of which I thank you. Well, it has been such dry, warm weather, that I have not felt like writing besides, for nurse I have only a little German girl fourteen years old, who never was out of New York before, and whom I have been so determined on spoiling that I couldn't bear to take her off from her play to mend, patch, darn, wash faces, necks, feet, etc., and unconsciously did everything there was to do for the children and a little more besides. I like the little book very much. You have the greatest knack, you girls, of lighting on nice books and nice hymns. We are right in the midst of most charming walks. Here is a grove and there is a brook here is a creek, almost a river (big enough at any rate to get on to the map) and there a mountain. As to ferns and mosses for your poetical side, and as for raspberries and blackberries for your t'other side, time would fail me if I should begin to speak of them. I think a great deal of you and your sisters when off on foraging expeditions, and wish you were here notwithstanding you are mossy and ferny there. We have as yet made only one excursion. That was delightful and gave us our first true idea of the Catskills. Before Mr. P. came, I usually went off on my forenoon walk alone, unless the children trooped after, and came home a miniature Birnam wood, with all sorts of things except creeping things and flying fowl.

I have just finished reading to M. and a little girl near her age, a little French book you would like, called "Augustin." I never met with a sweeter picture of a loving child anywhere. Well, I may as well stop writing. Remember me lovingly to all your dear household.

To Mrs. Stearns she writes, Sept. 16:

How much faith and patience we poor invalids do need! The burden of life sits hard on our weary shoulders. I think the mountain air has agreed with our children better than the seaside has done, but George craves the ocean and the bathing. He spent this forenoon, as he has a good many others, in climbing the side of the mountain for exercise, views, and blackberries. I go with him sometimes. We had a few days' visit from Prof. Hopkins. He has heard confirmation of the rumors of poor Eddy's death and burial. He means to go to Ashland as soon as the state of the country makes it practicable, but has little hope of identifying E.'s remains. It is a great sorrow to him to *lose all he had* in this horrible way, but he bears it with wonderful faith and patience, and says he never prayed for his son's life after he went into action. Some letters received by him, give a pleasant idea of the Christian stand E. took after entering the army. I believe this is Lizzie P——'s wedding day. There is a beautiful rainbow smiling on it from our mountain home, and I hope a real one is glorifying hers.

To Miss Gilman, Hunter, Sept. 17.

Oh, I wish you were here on this glorious day! The foliage has begun to turn a little, and the mountains are in a state bordering on perfection. It is wicked for me stay in-doors even to write this, but it seems as if a letter from here would carry with it a savor of mountain air, and must do you more good than one from the city could. I wish I had thought sooner to ask you if you would like some of our mosses. I *thought* I had seen mosses before, but found I had not. I will enclose some dried specimens. I thought, while I was in the woods this morning, that I never had thanked God half enough for making these lovely things and giving us tastes wherewith to enjoy them.

You ask if I have spilled ink all down the side of this white house. Yes, I have, woe be unto me. I was sick abed and got up to write to Mr. P., not wanting him to know I was sick, and one of the children came in and I snatched him up in my lap to hug and kiss a little, and he, of course, hit the pen and upset the inkstand and burst out crying at my dismay. Then might have been seen a headachy woman catching the apoplexy by leaning out of the window and scrubbing paint, sacrificing all her nice rags in the process, and dreadfully mortified into the bargain.... Yesterday we were all caught in a pouring rain when several miles from home on the side of the mountain, blackberrying. We each took a child and came rolling and tearing down through the bushes and over stones, H.'s little legs flying as little legs rarely fly. We nearly died with laughing, and if I only knew how to draw, I could make you laugh by giving you a picture of the scene. You will judge from this that we are all great walkers so we are. I take the children almost everywhere, and they walk miles every day. Well, I will go now and get you some scraps of pressed mosses.

* * * * *

IV.

The Death of President Lincoln. Dedication of the Church of the Covenant. Growing Insomnia. Resolves to try the Water-cure. Its beneficial Effects. Summer at Newburgh. Reminiscence of an Excursion to Paltz Point. Death of her Husband's Mother. Funeral of her Nephew, Edward Payson Hopkins.

Two events rendered the month of April, 1865, especially memorable to Mrs. Prentiss. One was the assassination of President Lincoln on the evening of Good Friday. She had been very ill, and her husband, on learning the dreadful news from the morning paper, thought it advisable to keep it from her for a while but one of the children, going into her chamber, burst into tears and thus betrayed the secret. Her state of nervous prostration and her profound, affectionate admiration for Mr. Lincoln, made the blow the most stunning by far she ever received from any public calamity. It was such, no doubt, to tens of thousands indeed, to the American people. No Easter morning ever before dawned upon them amid such a cloud of horror, or found them so bowed down with grief. The younger generation can hardly conceive of the depth and intensity, or the strange, unnatural character, of the impression made upon the minds of old and young alike, by this most foul murder. [12]

The other event was of a very different character and filled her with great joy. It was the dedication, on the last Sunday in April, of the new church edifice, whose growth she had watched with so much interest.

In the spring of 1865, she was induced, by the entreaty of friends who had themselves tested his skill, to consult Dr. Schieferdecker, a noted hydropathist, and later to place herself under his care. In a letter to her cousin, Miss Shipman, she writes, "I want to tell you, but do not want you to mention it to anyone, that I have been to see Dr. Schieferdecker to know what he thought of my case. He says that I might go on dieting to the end of my days and not get well, but that his system could and would cure me, only it would take a *long* time. I have not decided whether to try his process, but have no doubt he understands my disease." Dr. Schieferdecker had been a pupil and was an enthusiastic disciple of Priesnitz. He had unbounded faith in the healing properties of water. He was very impulsive, opinionated, self-confident, and accustomed to speak contemptuously of the old medical science and those who practiced it. But for all that, he possessed a remarkable sagacity in the diagnosis and treatment of chronic disease. Mrs. Prentiss went through the "cure" with indomitable patience and pluck, and was rewarded by the most beneficial results. Her sleeplessness had become too deep-rooted to be overcome, but it was greatly mitigated and her general condition vastly improved. She never ceased to feel very grateful to Dr. Schieferdecker for the relief he had afforded her, and for teaching her how to manage herself for after passing from under his care, she still continued to follow his directions. "No tongue can tell how much I am indebted to him," she wrote in 1869. "I am like a ship that after poking along twenty years with a heavy load on board, at last gets into port, unloads, and springs to the surface."

To Miss E. S. Gilman, New York, Feb. 23, 1865.

It is said to be an ill wind that blows nobody good, and as I am still idling about, doing absolutely nothing but receive visits from neuralgia, I have leisure to think of poor Miss ———. I wrote to ask her if there was anything she wanted and could not get in her region yesterday, I received her letter, in which she mentions a book, but says "anything that is useful for body or mind" would be gratefully received. Now I got the impression from that article in the Independent, that she could take next to no nourishment. Do you know what she *does* take, and can you suggest, from what you know, anything she would like? What's the use of my being sick, if it is not for her sake or that of some other suffering soul? I want, very much, to get some things together and send her nobody knows who has not experienced it, how delightfully such things break in on the monotony of a sickroom. Just yet, I am not strong enough to do anything my hands tremble so that I can hardly use even a pen yet you need not think I am much amiss, for I go out every pleasant day, to ride, and some days can take quite a walk. The trouble is that when the pain returns, as it does several times a day, it knocks my strength out of me. I hope when all parts of my frame have been visited by this erratic sprite, it may find it worthwhile to beat a retreat. Only to think, we are going to move to No. 70 East Twenty-Seventh Street, and you have all been and gone away! The rent is *enormous*, $1,000 having been just added to an already high price. Our people have taken that matter in hand and no burden of it will come on us. I received your letter and am much obliged to you for writing to Miss ———, for me the reason I did not do it was, that it seemed like hurrying her up to thank me for the little drop of comfort I sent her. Dear me! It is hard to be sick when people send you quails and jellies, and fresh eggs, and all such things—but to be sick and suffer for necessaries must be terrible.

To the Same, New York, March 9, 1865.

I thank you for the details of Miss ———'s case, as I wished to describe them to some friends. I sent her ten dollars yesterday for two of my friends. I also sent off a box by express, for the contents of which I had help. The things were such as I had persuaded her to mention a new kind of farina, figs, two portfolios (of course she didn't ask for two, but I had one I thought she would, perhaps, like better than the one I bought), a few crackers, and several books. Mr. P. added one of those beautiful large-print editions of the Psalms that will, I think, be a comfort to her. I shall also send

Adelaide Newton by-and-by I thought she had her hands full of reading for the present, and the great thing is not to heap comforts on her all at once and then leave her to her fate, but keep up a stream of such little alleviations as can be provided. She said, she had poor accommodations for writing, so I greatly enjoyed fitting up the portfolio, which was none the worse for wear, with paper and envelopes, a pencil with rubber at the end, a cunning little knife, some stamps, for which there was a small box, a few pens, etc. I know it will please you to hear of this, and as the money was furnished me for the purpose, you need not set it down to my credit.

I meant to go to see your sister, but my head is still in such a weak state that though I go to walk nearly every day, I cannot make calls. It is five weeks since I went to church, for the same reason. It is a part of God's discipline with me to keep me shut up a good deal more than the old Adam in me fancies but His way is *absolutely perfect*, and I hope I would not change it in any particular, if I could. Have you Pusey's tract, "Do all to the Lord Jesus"? If not, I must send it to you. It seems as if I had a lot of things I wanted to say, but after writing a little my hands and arms begin to tremble so that I can hardly write plainly. You never saw such a lazy life as I lead now-a-days I cannot do *any*thing. I advise you to do what you have to do for Christ *now* by the time you are as old as I am perhaps you will have the will and not the power. Well, goodbye until next time.

The summer of this year was passed at Newburgh in company with the Misses Butler—now Mrs. Kirkbride, of Philadelphia, and Mrs. Booth, of Liverpool—and the families of Mr. William Allen Butler, Mr. B. F. Butler, and Mr. John P. Crosby, to all of whom Mrs. Prentiss was strongly attached. The late Mr. Daniel Lord, the eminent lawyer, with a portion of his family, had also a cottage nearby and was full of hospitable kindness. In spite of the exacting hydropathic treatment, she found constant refreshment and delight in the society of so many dear friends. "The only thing I have to complain of" she wrote, "is everybody being too good to me. How different it is being among friends to being among strangers!"

In a letter to her husband, dated New York, Sept. 15, 1879, Mr. William Allen Butler gives the following reminiscence of an excursion to PaltzPoint and an evening at Newburgh:

From the date you, give in your note (to which I have just recurred) of our trip to Paltz Point, it seems that in writing you today I have unwittingly fallen on the anniversary of that pleasant excursion. Without this reminder I could not have told the day or the year, but of the excursion itself I have always had a vivid and delightful recollection and, if I am not mistaken, Mrs. Prentiss enjoyed it as fully as any one of the merry party. It was only on that jaunt and in our summer home at Newburgh that I had the opportunity of knowing her readiness to enter into that kind of enjoyment, which depends upon the co-operation of every member of a circle for the entertainment of all. The elements of our group were well commingled, and the bright things evoked by their contact and friction were neither few nor far between. The game to which you allude of "Inspiration" or "Rhapsody" was a favorite. The evening at Paltz Point called out some clever sallies, of which I have no record or special recollection but I know that then, as always, Mrs. Prentiss seemed to have at her pencil's point for instant use the wit and fancy so charmingly exhibited in her writings. She published somewhere an account of one of our inspired or rhapsodical evenings, but greatly to my regret failed to include in it her own contribution, which was the best of all. I distinctly remember the time and scene—the September evening—the big, square sitting-room of the old Seminary building in which you boarded—the bright faces whose radiance made up in part for the limitations of artificial light—the puzzled air which every one took on when presented with the list of unmanageable words, to be reproduced in their consecutive order in prose or verse composition within the next quarter or half hour—the stillness which supervened while the enforced "pleasures" of "poetic pains" or prose agony were being undergone—the sense of relief which supplemented the completion of the batch of extempore effusions—and the fun which their reading provoked. Mrs. Prentiss had contrived out of the odd and incoherent jumble of words a choice bit of poetic humor and pathos, which I never quite forgave her for omitting in the publication of the nonsense written by other hands. These trifles as they seemed at the time, and as in fact they were, become less insignificant in the retrospect, as we associate them with the whole character and being we instinctively love to place at the farthest remove from gloom or sadness, and as they rediscover to us in the distance the native vivacity and grace of which they were the chance expression. Since that summer of 1865, having lived away from New York, I saw little of Mrs. Prentiss, but I have a special remembrance of one little visit you made at our home in Yonkers which she seemed very much to enjoy—saying of the reunion which made it so pleasant to the members of our family and all who happened to be together at the time, that it was "like heaven." [13]

During the summer of 1865, the sympathies of Mrs. Prentiss were much wrought upon by the sickness and death of her husband's mother, who entered into rest on the 9th of August, in the eighty-fourth year of her age. On the 12th of the previous January, she with the whole family had gone to Newark to celebrate the eighty-third birthday of this aged saint. Had they known it was to be the last, they could have wished nothing changed. It was a perfect winter's day, and the scene in the old parsonage was perfect too. There, surrounded by children and children's children, sat the venerable grandmother with a benignant smile upon her face and the peace of God in her heart. As she received in birthday gifts and kisses and congratulations their loving homage, the measure of her joy was full, and she seemed ready to say her *Nunc dimittis*. She belonged to the number of those holy women of the old time who trusted in God and adorned themselves with the ornament of a meek and quiet spirit, and whose children to the latest generation rise up and call them blessed.

In the course of this year, her sympathies were also deeply touched by repeated visits from her brother-in-law, Professor Hopkins, on his way to and from Virginia. Allusion has been made already to the death of her nephew, Lieutenant Edward Payson Hopkins. He was killed in battle while gallantly leading a cavalry charge at Ashland, in Virginia, on the 11th of May, 1864. In June of the following year, his father went to Ashland with the hope of recovering the body. Five comrades had fallen with Edward, and the negroes had buried them without coffins, side by side, in two trenches in a desolate swampy field and under a very shallow covering of earth. The place was readily discovered, but it was found impossible to identify the body. The disappointed father, almost broken-hearted, turned his weary steps homeward. When he reached Williamstown his friends said, "He has grown ten years older since he went away."

Several months later, he learned that there were means of identification, which could not fail, even if the body had already turned to dust. Accordingly, he again visited Ashland, attended this time by soldiers, a surgeon, and Government officials. His search proved successful, and, to his joy, not only was the body identified, but, owing to the swampy nature of the ground, it was found to be in an almost complete state of preservation. There was something wonderfully impressive in the grave aspect and calm, gentle tone of the venerable man, as with his precious charge he passed through New York on his way home. In a letter to Mrs. Prentiss, dated January 2nd, 1866, he himself tells the story of the re-interment at Williamstown:

... After stopping a minute at my door, the wagon passed at once to the cemetery, and the remains were deposited in the tomb. This was on Thursday. After consulting with my brother and his son (the chaplain), I determined to wait until the Sabbath before the interment. Accordingly, at 3 o'clock—after the afternoon service—the remains of my dear boy were placed beside those of his mother. The services were simple, but solemn in a high degree. They were opened by an address from Harry. Prayer followed by Rev. Mr. Noble, now supplying the desk here. He prefaced his prayer by saying that he never saw Edward but once, when he preached at Williamstown at a communion and saw him sitting beside me and partaking with me. Singing then followed by the choir of which Eddy was for a long time a member. The words were those striking lines of Montgomery:

Go to the grave in all thy glorious prime, etc.

After which the coffin was lowered to its place by young men who were friends of Edward in his earlier years.

The state of the elements was exceedingly favorable to the holding of such an exercise in the open air at a season generally so inclement. The night before there was every appearance of a heavy N. E. storm. But Sabbath morning it was calm. As I went to church, I noticed that the sun rested on the Vermont mountains just north of us, though with a mellowed light as if a veil had been thrown over them. In the after part of the day the open sky had spread southward—so that the interment took place when the air was as mild and serene as spring, just as the last sun of the year was sinking towards the mountains. Almost the entire congregation were present.... Thus, dear sister, I have given you a brief account of the solemn but peaceful winding up of what has been to me a sharp and long trial, and I know to yourself and family also. In eternity, we shall more clearly read the lesson which even now, in the light of opening scenes, we are beginning to interpret.

[1] Richard H. Dana, the poet.

[2] The article referred to appeared in The Biblical Repository and Quarterly Observer for January, 1835. Vol V., pp. 1-32. It is entitled, "What form of Law is best suited to the individual and social nature of man?"

[3] Mr. Ralph Waldo Emerson.

[4] The article appeared in the New York Review for July, 1839.

[5] Some passages from the little diaries referred to, together with further extracts from her literary journal, will be found in appendix D.

[6] The Proclamation of Emancipation.

[7] By Anna Warner.

[8] By her friend, Mrs. Frederick G. Burnham.

[9] "The Little Corporal."

[10] At Fredericksburg.

[11] Referring to the sudden death of a young niece of Mrs. S.

[12] This was written before the assassination of President Garfield.

[13] The "Rhapsody," referred to by Mr. Butler was preserved by a young lady of the party, and will be found in appendix E.

CHAPTER 8 - THE PASTOR'S WIFE AND DAUGHTER OF CONSOLATION - 1866-1868.

I.

Happiness as a Pastor's Wife. Visits to Newport and Williamstown Letters. The great Portland Fire. First Summer at Dorset. The new Parsonage occupied. Second Summer at Dorset. *Little Lou's Sayings and Doings.* Project of a Cottage. Letters. *The Little Preacher.* Illness and Death of Mrs. Edward Payson and of Little Francis.

We now enter upon the most interesting and happiest period of Mrs. Prentiss's experience as a pastor's wife. The congregation of the Church of the Covenant had been slowly forming in "troublous times" it was composed of congenial elements, being of one heart and one mind some of the most cultivated families and family circles in New York belonged to it and Mrs. Prentiss was much beloved in them all. What a helpmeet she was to her husband and with what zeal and delight she fulfilled her office especially that of a daughter of consolation, among his people, will soon appear.

How ignorant we often are, at the time, of the turning points in our life! We inquire for a summer boarding-place and decide upon it without any thought beyond the few weeks for which it was engaged and yet, perhaps, our whole earthly future or that of those most dear to us, is to be vitally affected by this seemingly trifling decision. So it happened to Mrs. Prentiss in 1866. Early in May her husband and his brother-in-law, Dr. Stearns, went, at a venture, to Dorset, Vt., and there secured rooms for their families during the summer. But little did either she, or they, dream that Dorset was to be henceforth her summer home and her resting-place in death! [1]

The Portland fire, to which reference is made in the following letters, occurred on the 4th of July, and consumed a large portion of the city.

To Miss Mary B. Shipman, Dorset, July 25, 1866.

Never in my life did I live through such a spring and early summer as this! As to business and bustle, I mean. You must have given me up as a lost cause! But I have thought of you every day and longed to hear how you were getting on, and whether you lived through that dreadful weather. Annie went with the children to Williamstown about the middle of June I nearly killed myself with getting them ready to go and could see the flesh drop off my bones. George and I went to Newport on what Mrs. Bronson called our "bridal trip," and stayed eleven days. Mr. and Mrs. McCurdy were kindness personified. We came home and preached on the first Sunday in July, and then went to Greenfield Hill to spend the Fourth with Mrs. Bronson. [2] That nearly finished me, and then I went to Williamstown on that hot Friday and was quite finished on reaching there, to hear about the fire in Portland. Did you ever hear of anything so dreadful? I did not know for several days but H. and C. were burnt out of house and home most of my other friends I knew were, and can there be any calamity like being left naked, hungry and homeless, everything gone forever.... But let no one say a word that has a roof over his head. All my father's sermons were burned, the house where most of us were born, his church, etc. Fancy New Haven stripped of its shade trees, and you can form some idea of the loss of Portland in that respect. Well, I might go on talking forever, and not have said anything. [3] The heat upset G. and we have been fighting off sickness for a week, I getting wild with loss of sleep. We are enchanted with Dorset. We are so near the woods and mountains that we go every day and spend hours wandering about among them. If there is any difference, I think this place even more beautiful than Williamstown it suits us better as a summer retreat, from its great seclusion. I am, that is we are, mean enough to want to keep it as quiet and secluded as it is now, by not letting people know how nice it is a very few fashionably dressed people would just spoil it for us. So keep our counsel, you dear child.

A few days later, she writes to Mrs. Smith, then in Europe:

On the sixth, a day of fearful heat, I went to Williamstown, where I found all the children as well as possible, but heard the news of the Portland fire, which almost killed me. All my father's manuscripts are destroyed we always meant to divide them among us and ought to have done it long ago. I heard of any number of injudicious babies as taking the inopportune day succeeding the fire to enter on the scene of desolation all born in tents. I am sorry my children will never see my father's church, or the house where I was born but private griefs are nothing when compared with a calamity that is so appalling and that must send many a heart homeless and aching to the grave. I spent two weeks at Williamstown, when George came for me, and the weather cooling off, we had a comfortable journey here. We are perfectly delighted with Dorset the sweet seclusion is most soothing, and the house is very pleasant. Mr. and Mrs. F. are intelligent, agreeable people, and do all they can to make us comfortable. The mountains are so near that I hear the crows cawing in the trees. We are making pretty things and pressing an unheard-of quantity of ferns. We go to the woods regularly every morning and stay the whole forenoon. In the afternoon we rest, read, write, etc. sometimes we drive and always after tea George walks with me about two miles. I hope the war is not impeding your movements. I suppose you will call this a short letter, but I think it is as long as is good for you. All my dear nine pounds gained at Newburgh have gone by the board. *August 20th.*—I am sorry you had such hot weather in Paris, but hope it passed off as our heat did. Dr. Hamlin's two youngest daughters have been here, and came to see me they are both interesting girls, and the elder of the two really brilliant. They had never been here before, and were carried away with the beauties of their mother's birthplace. I wish you could see my room. Every pretty thing grows here and has come to cheer and beautify it. The woods are everywhere, and as for the views, oh my child! However, I do not suppose anything short of Mt. Blanc will suit you now.

In April, 1867, the parsonage on Thirty-Fifth Street was occupied. It had been built more especially for her sake, and was furnished by the generosity of her friends. Her joy in entering it was completed by a "house-warming," at the close of which a passage of Scripture was read by Prof. Smith, "All hail the power of Jesus' name" sung, and then the blessing of Heaven invoked upon the new home by that holy man of God, Dr. Thomas H. Skinner. Here she passed the next six years of her life. Here she wrote the larger portion of "Stepping Heavenward." And here the cup of her domestic joy, and of joy in her God and Savior often ran over. Here, too, some of her dearest Christian friendships were formed and enjoyed.

The summer of 1867 was passed at Dorset. In less than a month of it, she wrote one of her best children's books, *Little Lou's Sayings and Doings,* and much of the remainder was spent in discussing with her husband the project of building a cottage of their own. In a letter to her cousin, Miss Shipman, dated Sept. 21, she writes:

We have had our heads full all summer, of building a little cottage here. We are having a plan made, and have about fixed on a lot. We are rather tired of boarding George hates it, and Dorset suits us as well, I presume, as any village would. It is a lovely spot, and the people are as intelligent as in other parts of New England. The Professor is disappointed at our choosing this rather than Williamstown, but it would be no rest to us to go there. We have not decided to build it may turn out too expensive but we have taken lots of comfort in talking about it. We have been on several excursions, one of them to the top of Equinox. It is a hard trip, fully six miles walking and climbing. I have amused myself with writing some little books of the Susy sort: four in less than a month, A.'s sickness taking a good piece of time out of that period. They are to appear, or a part of them, in the Riverside next winter, and then to be issued in book-form by Hurd and Houghton. This will a good deal more than furnish our cottage and what trees and shrubs we want, so that I feel justified in undertaking that expense. We had two weeks at Newport before we came here, and Mr. and Mrs. McCurdy overwhelmed us with kindness, paying our traveling expenses, etc., and keeping up one steady stream of such favors the whole time. I never saw such people. How delightful it must be to be able to express such benevolence! Well you and I can be faithful in that which is least, at any rate.

We have all had plenty to read all summer, and have sat out of doors and read a good deal. I am going now to carry a little wreath to a missionary's wife who is spending the summer here a nice little woman this will give me a three miles walk and about use up the rest of the forenoon. In the afternoon, I have promised to go to the woods with the children, all of whom are as brown as Indians. My room is aflame with two great trees of maple I never saw such a beautiful velvety color as they have. We have just had a very pleasant excursion to a mountain called Haystack, and ate our dinner sitting round in the grass in view of a splendid prospect.... I have thus given you the history of our summer, as far as its history can be written. Its ecstatic joys have not been wanting, nor its hours of shame and confusion of face but these are things that cannot be described. What a mystery life is, and how we go up and down, glad today and sorrowful tomorrow! I took real solid comfort thinking of you and praying for you this morning. I love you dearly and always shall. Goodbye, dear child.

The "four little books" afford a good illustration of the ease and rapidity with which she composed. When once she had fixed upon a subject, her pen almost flew over the paper. Scarcely ever did she hesitate for a thought or for the right words to express it. Her manuscript rarely showed an erasure or any change whatever. She generally wrote on a portfolio, holding it upon her knees. Her pen seemed to be a veritable part of herself and the instant it began to move, her face glowed with eager and pleasurable feeling. "A kitten (she wrote to a maiden friend) a kitten without a tail to play with, a mariner without a compass, a bird without wings, a woman without a husband (and fifty-five at that) furnish faint images of the desolation of my heart without a pen." But although she wrote very fast, she never began to write without careful study and premeditation when her subject required it.

About this time *The Little Preacher* appeared. The scene of the story is laid in the Black Forest. Before writing it, she spent a good deal of time in the Astor Library, reading about peasant life in Germany. In a letter from a literary friend, this little work is thus referred to:

I want to tell you what a German gentleman said to me the other day about your "Little Preacher." He was talking with me of German peasant life, and inquired if I had read your charming story. He was delighted to find I knew you, and exclaimed enthusiastically, "I wish I knew her! I would so like to thank her for her perfect picture. It is a miracle of genius," he added, "to be able thus to portray the life of a *foreign* people." He is very intelligent, and so I know you will be pleased with his appreciation of your book. He said if he were not so poor, he would buy a whole edition of the "Little Preacher" to give to his friends.

During the autumn of this year, her sister-in-law, Mrs. Edward Payson, died after a lingering, painful illness. The following letter, dated October 28, was written to her shortly before her departure:

I have been so engrossed with sympathy for Edward and your children, that I have but just begun to realize that you are about entering on a state of felicity, which ought, for the time, to make me forget them. Dear Nelly, *I congratulate you with all my heart*. Do not let the thought of what those who love you must suffer in your loss, diminish the peace and joy with which God now calls you to think only of Himself and the home He has prepared for you. Try to leave them to His kind, tender care. He loves them better than you do He can be to them more than you have been He will hear your prayers and all the prayers offered for them, and as one whom his mother comforted, so will He comfort them. We, who shall be left here without you, cannot conceive the joys on which you are to enter, but we know enough to go with you to the very gates of the city, longing to enter in with you to go no more out. All your tears will soon be wiped away you will see the King in His beauty you will see Christ your Redeemer and realize all He is and all He has done for you and how many saints whom you have loved on earth will be standing ready to seize you by the hand and welcome you among them! As I think of these things my soul is in haste to be gone I long to be set free from sin and self and to go to the fellowship of those who have done with them forever, and are perfect and entire, wanting nothing. Dear Nelly, I pray that you may have as easy a journey homeward as your Father's love and compassion can make for you but these sufferings at the worst cannot last long, and they are only the messengers sent to loosen your last tie on earth, and conduct you to the sweetest rest. But I dare not write more lest I weary your poor worn frame with words. May the very God of peace be with you every moment, even unto the end, and keep your heart and mind stayed upon Him!

Mrs. Payson had been an intimate friend of her childhood, and was endeared to her by uncommon loveliness and excellence of character. The bereaved husband, with his little boy, passed a portion of the ensuing winter at the parsonage in New York. There was something about the child, a sweetness, and a clinging, almost wild, devotion to his father, which, together with his motherless state, touched his aunt to the quick and called forth her tenderest love. Many a page of Stepping Heavenward was written with this child in her arms and perhaps that is one secret of its power. When, not very long afterwards, he went to his mother, Mrs. Prentiss wrote to the father:

Only this morning I was trying to invent some way of framing my little picture of Francis, so as to see it every day before my eyes. And now this evening's mail brings your letter, and I am trying to believe what it says is true. If grief and pain could comfort you, you would be comforted we all loved Francis, and A. has always said he was too lovely to live. How are you going to bear this new blow? My heart aches as it asks the question, aches and trembles for you. But perhaps you loved him so, that you will come to be willing to have him in his dear mother's safe keeping will bear your own pain in future because through your anguish your lamb is sheltered forever, to know no more pain, to suffer no more for lack of womanly care, and is already developing into the rare character which made him so precious to you. Oh, do try to rejoice for him while you cannot but mourn for yourself. At the longest you will not have, long to suffer we are a short-lived race.

But while I write I feel that I want someone to speak a comforting word to me I too am bereaved in the death of this precious child, and my sympathy for you is in itself a pang. Dear little lamb! I cannot realize that I shall never see that sweet face again in this world but I shall see it in heaven. God bless and comfort you, my dear afflicted brother. I dare not weary you with words which all seem a mockery I can only assure you of my tenderest love and sympathy, and that we all feel with and for you as only those can who know what this child was to you. I am going to bed with an aching heart, praying that light may spring out of this darkness. Give love from us all to Ned and Will. Perhaps Ned will kindly write me if you feel that you cannot, and tell me all about the dear child's illness.

* * * * *

II.

Last Visit from Mrs. Stearns. Visits to old Friends at Newport and Rochester. Letters. Goes to Dorset. *Fred and Maria and Me*. Letters.

The life of a pastor's wife is passed in the midst of mingled gladness and sorrow. While somebody is always rejoicing, somebody, too, is always sick or dying, or else weeping. How often she goes with her husband from the wedding to the funeral, or hurries with him from the funeral to the wedding. And then, perhaps, in her own family circle the same process is repeated. The year 1868 was marked for Mrs. Prentiss in an unusual degree by the sorrowful experience. The latter part of May Mrs. Stearns, then suffering from an exhausting disease, came to New York and spent several weeks in hopes of finding some relief from change of scene. But her case grew more alarming she passed the summer at Cornwall on the Hudson in great pain and feebleness, and was then carried home to lie down on her dying bed.

To Mrs. Stearns, Newport, July 7, 1868.

We had a dreadful time getting here I did not sleep a wink there were 1,250 passengers on board, almost piled on each other, and such screaming of babies it would be hard to equal. There are many people here we know ever so many stopped to speak to us after church. We are in the midst of a perfect world of show and glitter. But how many empty hearts drive up and down in this gay procession of wealth and fashion!

I shall think of you a good deal today, as setting forth on your journey and reaching your new home. I do hope you will find it refreshing to go up the river, and that your rooms will be pleasant and airy. We shall be anxious to hear all about it.

It is a constant lesson to be with Mrs. McCurdy. I think she is a true Christian in all her views of life and death. Her sweet patience, cheerfulness, and contentment are a continual reproof to me. Here she is so lame that she can go nowhere—a lameness of over twenty years—restricted to the plainest food, liable to die at any moment, yet the very happiest, sunniest creature I ever saw. She says, with tears, that God has been *too good* to her and given her too much that she sometimes fears He does not love her because He gives her such prosperity. I reminded her of the four lovely children she had lost. "Yes," she says, "but how many lovely ones I have left!" She says that the long hours she has to spend alone, on account of her physical infirmities, are never lonely or sad she sings hymns and thinks over to herself all the pleasures she has enjoyed in the past, in her husband and children and devoted servants. She goes up to bed singing, and I hear her singing while she dresses. She said, the other day, that at her funeral she hoped the only services would be prayers and hymns of praise. I think this very remarkable from one who enjoys life as she does. [4]

To the Same, Newport, July 20.

George and I went to Rochester, taking M. with us, last Wednesday and got back Friday night. We had one of those visits that make a mark in one's life seeing Mr. and Mrs. Leonard, and Mrs. Randall, and Miss Deborah, [5] so fond of us, and all together we were stirred up as we rarely are, and refreshed beyond description. We rowed on Mr. Leonard's beautiful, nameless lake, fished, gathered water lilies, ate black Hamburg grapes and broiled chickens, and wished you had them in our place. Mr. L.'s mother is a sweet, calm old lady, with whom I wanted to have a talk about Christian perfection, in which she believes but there was no time. It was a great rest to unbend the bow strung so high here at Newport, where there is so much of receiving and paying visits. I have been reading a delightful French book, the history of a saintly Catholic family of great talent and culture, six of whom, in the course of seven years, died the most beautiful, happy deaths. I am going to make an abstract of it, for I want everybody I love to get the cream of it. You would enjoy it I do not know whether it has been translated.

To the Same, Dorset, July 26.

Here begins my first letter to you from your old room, whence I hope to write you regularly every week. That is the one only little thing I can do to show how truly and constantly I sympathize with you in your sore straits. It distresses me to hear how much you are suffering, and at the same time not to be near enough to speak a word of good cheer, or to do anything for your comfort. It grieves me to find how insecure my health is, for I had promised to myself to be your loving nurse, should any turn in your disease make it desirable. Miss Lyman boards here, but rooms at the Sykes', and her friend Miss Warner is also here, but rooms out. Miss W. is in delicate health, takes no tea or coffee, and is full of humor. We have run at and run upon each other, each trying to get the measure of the other, and shall probably end in becoming very good friends.

It is a splendid day, and we feel perfectly at home, only missing you and finding it queer to be occupying your room. What a nice room it is! How I wish you were sitting here with me behind the shade of these maple trees, and that I could know from your own lips just how you are in body and mind. But I suppose the weary, aching body has the soul pretty well enchained. Never mind, dear, it will not be so always by and by, the tables will be turned, and you will be the conqueror. I like to think that far less than a hundred years hence we shall all be free from the law of sin and death and happier in one moment of our new existence, than through a whole lifetime here. Rest must and will come, sooner or later, to you and to me and to all of us, and it will be glorious. You may have seen a notice of the death of Prof. Hopkins' mother at the age of ninety-five. But for this terribly hot weather, I presume she might have lived to be one hundred.

I shall not write you such a long letter again, as it will tire you, and if you would rather have two short ones a week, I will do that. Let me know if I tire you. Now goodbye, dear child may God bless and keep you and give you all the faith and patience you need.

To Miss Mary B. Shipman, Dorset, Aug. 2, 1868.

We spent rather more than two weeks at Newport, taking two or three days to run to Rochester, Mass., to see some of our old New Bedford friends. We had a charming time with them, as they took us up just where they left us nearly twenty years ago. Oh, how our tongues did fly! We left Newport for home on Tuesday night about two weeks ago. I went on board and went to bed as well as usual, tossed and turned a few hours, grew faint and began to be sick, as I always am now if I lose my sleep got out of bed and could not get back again, and so lay on the floor all the rest of the night without a pillow, or anything over me and nearly frozen. The boys were asleep, and anyhow it never crossed my mind to let them call George, who was in another stateroom. He says that when he came in, in the morning, I looked as if I had been ill six months, and I am sure I felt so. Imagine the family picture we presented driving from the boat all the way home, George rubbing me with cologne, A. fanning me, the rest crying! On Saturday more dead than alive, I started for this place and by stopping at Troy four or five hours, getting a room and a bed, I got here without much damage.

Our house is very pretty, and I suppose it will be done by next year. Oh, how they do poke! George is so happy in watching it, and in working in his woods, that I am perfectly delighted that he has undertaken this project. It may add years to his life. Imagine my surprise at receiving from Scribner a check for one hundred and sixty-four dollars for six months of Fred and Maria and Me. The little thing has done well, hasn't it? I feel now as if I should never write, any more letter writing is only talking and is an amusement, but book-writing looks formidable. Excuse this horrid letter, and write and let me know how you are. Meanwhile collect grasses, dip them in hot water, and sift flour over them. Goodbye, dear.

Fred and Maria and Me first appeared anonymously in the Hours at Home, in 1865. It had been written several years before, and, without the knowledge of Mrs. Prentiss, was offered by a friend to whom she had lent the manuscript, to the Atlantic Monthly and to one or two other magazines, but they all declined it. She herself thus refers to it in a letter to Mrs. Smith, July 13: "I have just got hold of the Hours at Home. I read my article and was disgusted with it. My pride fell below zero, and I wish it would stay there." But the story attracted instant attention. "Aunt Avery" was especially admired, as depicting a very quaint and interesting type of New England religious character in the earlier half of the century. Such men as the late Dr. Horace Bushnell and Dr. William Adams were unstinted in their praise. In a letter to Mrs. Smith, dated a few months later, Mrs. Prentiss writes, "Poor old Aunt Avery! She does not know what to make of it that folks make so much of her, and has to keep wiping her spectacles. I feel entirely indebted to you for this thing ever seeing the light." When published as a book, *Fred and Maria and Me* was received with great favor, and had a wide circulation. In 1874 a German translation appeared. [6] Although no attempt is made to reproduce the Yankee idioms, much of the peculiar spirit and flavor of the original is preserved in this version.

To Mrs. H. B. Smith, Dorset, August 4, 1868.

Miss Lyman says I have no idea of what Miss W. really is she looks as if she would drop to pieces, cannot drive out, far less walk, and every word she speaks costs her an effort. Miss Lyman is not well either and what with their health and mine, and A.'s, I see little of them. But what I do see is delightful, and I feel it to be a real privilege to get what scraps of their society I can. Our house proves to be far prettier and more tasteful than I supposed. I am writing up lots of letters, and if I ever get well enough, shall try to begin on my Katy once more. But since reading the Récit d'une Soeur, I am disgusted with myself and my writings. I ache to have you read it. Miss Lyman and Miss Warner send love to you. I do not like Miss L.'s hacking cough, and she says she does not believe Miss W. will live through the winter. Among us, we contrive to keep up a vast amount of laughter so we shall probably live forever.

August 18th.—I have enjoyed Miss Lyman wonderfully, but want to get nearer to her. I see that she is one who does not find it easy to express her deepest and most sacred feelings. I read Katy to her and Miss W., as they were kind enough to propose I should, and they made some valuable suggestions to which I shall attend if I ever get to feeling able to begin to write again. I am as well as ever save in one respect, and that is my sleep I do not sleep as I did before I left home, while I ought to sleep better, as I work several hours a day in the woods, in fact do almost literally nothing else…. But after all, we are having the nicest time in the world. I have not seen George so like himself for many years he lives out of doors, pulls down fences, picks up brushwood, and keeps happy and well. I feel it a real mercy that his thoughts are agreeably occupied this summer, as otherwise he would be incessantly worried about Anna. We work together a good deal this morning I spoiled a new hatchet in cutting down milkweed where our kitchen garden is to be and we are literally raising our Ebenezer, which we mean to conceal with vines in due season. George is just as proud of our woods as if he created every tree himself. The minute breakfast is over the boys dart down to the house like arrows from the bow, and there they are until dinner, after which there is another dart and it is as much as I can do to get them to bed I wonder they do not sleep down there on the shavings. The fact is the whole Prentiss family has got house on the brain. There, this old letter is done, and I am going to bed, all black, and blue where I have tumbled down, and as tired as tired can be.

Aug. 28th.—I made a fire in MY woods yesterday, and another today, when I melted glue, and worked at my rustic basket, and felt extremely happy and amiable.

Sept. 13th.—Miss Warner told me to-night that she thought my Katy story commonplace at the beginning, but that she changed her mind afterward. Of course I wrote a story about that marigold of G—— W——'s and I am dying to inflict it on you. Then if you like it, hurrah!

To Miss Woolsey, Dorset, Aug. 13, 1868.

I was right glad to get your letter yesterday, and to learn a little of your whereabouts and whatabouts. You may imagine "him" as seated, spectacles on nose, reading The Nation at one end of the table, and "her" as established at the other. This table is homely, but has a literary look, got up to give an air to our room books and papers are artistically scattered over it we have two bottles of ink apiece, and a box of stamps, a paper cutter and a pen-wiper between us. Two inevitable vases containing ferns, grasses, buttercups, etc., remind us that we are in the country, and a "natural bracket" regales our august noses with an odor of its own. A can of peaches without any peaches in it, holds a specimen of lycopodium, and a marvelous lantern that folds up into nothing by day and grows big at night, brings up the rear. But the most wonderful article in this room is a bookcase made by "him," all himself, in which may be seen a big volume of Fenelon, Taylor's Holy Living and Dying, the Récit d'une Soeur, which have you read? Les Soirées de Saint Petersbourg, Prayers of the Ages, a volume of Goethe, Aristotle's Ethics and some other Greek books the Life of Mrs. Fry, etc. etc. Such a queer hodge-podge of books as we brought with us, and such a bookcase! The first thing "he" ever made for "her" in his mortal life.

Our house isn't done, and what fun to watch it grow, to discuss its merits and demerits, to grab every check that comes in from magazine and elsewhere, and turn it into chairs and tables and beds and blankets! Then for "them boys," what treasures in the way of bits of boards, and what feats of climbing and leaping! Above all, think of "him" in an old banged-in hat, and "her" in a patched old gown, gathering brushwood in their woods, making it up into heaps, and warming themselves by the fires it is agoing for to make.

"Stick after stick did Goody pull!"

Mr. P. is unusually well. His house is the apple of his eye, and he is renewing his youth. Thus far, the project has done him a world of good.

To Mrs. Stearns, Dorset, September 13, 1863.

Yesterday Mr. F. and George drove somewhere to look at sand for mortar, and the horse took fright and wheeled round and pitched George out, bruising him in several places, but doing no serious harm. But I shudder when I think how the meaning might be taken out of everything in this world, for me, at least, by such an accident. He preached all day today in the afternoon at Rupert. I find my mission-school a good deal of a tax on time and strength, and it is discouraging business, too. One of the boys, fourteen years old, found the idea that God loved him so irresistibly ludicrous, that his face was a perfect study. I often think of you as these "active limbs of mine" take me over woods and fields, and remind myself that the supreme happiness of my father's life came to him when he called himself what you call yourself—a cripple. If it is not an expensive book, I think you had better buy A Sister's Story, of which I wrote to you, as it would be a nice Sunday book to last some time the Catholicism you would not mind, and the cultivated, high-toned Christian character you would enjoy.

The boys complain, as George and I do, that the days are not half-long enough. They have got their bedsteads and washstands done, and are now going to make couches for George and myself, and an indefinite number of other articles.

Sept. 20th.—I am greatly relieved, my dear Anna, to hear that you have got safely into your new home, and that you like it, and long to see you face to face. George has no doubt told you what a happy summer we have had. It has not been unmingled happiness—that is not to be found in this world—but in many ways it has been pleasant in spite of what infirmities of the flesh we carry with us everywhere, our anxiety about and sympathy with you, and the other cares and solicitudes that are inseparable from humanity. I had a great deal of comfort in seeing Miss Lyman while she was here, and in knowing her better, and now I am finding myself quite in love with her intimate friend, Miss Warner, who has been here all summer. A gentler, more tender spirit cannot exist. Mrs. F.'s brother was here with his wife, some weeks ago, and they were summoned home to the deathbed of their last surviving child. Mrs. F. read me a letter yesterday describing her last hours, which were really touching and beautiful, especially the distributing among her friends the various pretty things she had made for them during her illness, as parting gifts. I suppose this will be my last letter from Dorset and from your old room. Well, you and I have passed some happy hours under this roof. Goodbye, dear, with love to each and all of your beloved ones.

To Miss Eliza A. Warner, Dorset, Sept. 27, 1868.

I was so nearly frantic, my dear Fanny, from want of sleep, that I could not feel anything. I was perfectly stupid, and all the way home from East Dorset hardly spoke a word to my dear John, nor did he to me. [7] The next day he said such lovely things to me that I hardly knew whether I was in the body or out of it, and then came your letter, as if to make my cup run over. I longed for you last night, and it is lucky for your frail body that can bear so little, that you were not in your little room at Mrs. G.'s but not at all lucky for your heart and soul. I hope God will bless us to each other. It is not enough that we find in our mutual affection something cheering and comforting. It must make us more perfectly His. What a wonderful thing it is that coming here entire strangers to each other, we part as if we had known each other half a century!

I am not afraid that we shall get tired of each other. The great point of union is that we have gone to our Savior, hand in hand, on the supreme errand of life, and have not come away empty. All my meditations bring me back to that point or, I should rather say, to Him. I came here praying that in some way I might do something for Him. The summer has gone, and I am grieved that I have not been, from its beginning to its end, so like Him, so full of Him, as to constrain everybody I met to love Him too. Isn't there such power in a holy life, and have not some lived such a life? I hardly know whether to rejoice most in my love for Him, or to mourn over my meager love so I do both.

When I think that I have a new friend, who will be indulgent to my imperfections, and is determined to find something in me to love, I am glad and thankful. But when, added to that, I know she will pray for me, and so help my poor soul heavenward, it does seem as if God had been too good to me. You can do it lying down or sitting up, or when you are among other friends. It is true, as you say, that I do not think much of "lying-down prayer" in my own case, but I have not a weak back and do not need such an attitude. And the praying we do by the wayside, in cars and steamboats, in streets and in crowds, perhaps keeps us more near to Christ than long prayers in solitude could without the help of these little messengers, that hardly ever stop running to Him and coming back with the grace every moment needs. You can put me into some of these silent petitions when you are too tired to pray for me otherwise.

I have been writing this in my shawl and bonnet, expecting every instant to hear the bell toll for church, and now it is time to go. Goodbye, dear, till by and by.

Well, I have been and come, and—wonder of wonders!—I have had a little tiny bit of a very much needed nap. Mr. Pratt gave us a really good sermon about living to Christ, and I enjoyed the hymns. We have had a talk, my John and I, about death, and I asked him which of us had better go first, and, to my surprise, he said he thought *I* should. I am sure that was noble and unselfish in him. But I am not going to have even a wish about it. God only knows which had better go first, and which stay and suffer. Some of His children *must* go into the furnace to testify that the Son of God is there with them I do not know why I should insist on not being one of them. Sometimes I almost wish we were not building a house. It seems as if it might stand in the way, if it should happen I had a chance to go to heaven. I should almost feel mean to do that, and disappoint my husband who expects to see me so happy there. But oh, I do so long to be perfected myself, and to live among those whose one thought is Christ, and who only speak to praise Him!

I like you to tell me, as you do in your East Dorset letter, how you spend your time, etc. I have an insatiable curiosity about even the outer life of those I love and of the inner one, you cannot say too much. Goodbye. We shall have plenty of time in heaven to say all we have to say to each other.

* * * * *

III.

Return to Town. Death of an old Friend. Letters and Notes of Love and Sympathy. An Old Ladies' Party. Scenes of Trouble and Dying Beds. Fifty Years old. Letters.

Her return to town brought with it a multitude of cares. The following months drew heavily upon her strength and sympathies but for all that, they were laden with unwonted joy. The summer at Dorset had been a very happy one. While there, she had finished *Stepping Heavenward* and on coming back to her city home, the cheery, loving spirit of the book seemed still to possess her whole being. Katy's words at its close were evidently an expression of her own feelings:

Yes, I love everybody! That crowning joy has come to me at last. Christ is in my soul He is mine I am as conscious of it as that my husband and children are mine and His Spirit flows forth from mine in the calm peace of a river, whose banks are green with grass, and glad with flowers.

To Miss Eliza A. Warner, New York, Oct. 5, 1868

This is the first moment since we reached home, in which I could write to you, but I have had you in my heart and in my thoughts as much as ever. We had a prosperous journey, but the ride to Rupert was fearfully cold. I never remember being so cold, unless it was the night I reached Williamstown, when I went to my dear sister's funeral.... I have told you this long story to try to give you a glimpse of the distracted life that meets us at our very threshold as we return home. And now I am going to trot down to see Miss Lyman, whom I shall just take and hug, for I am so brimful of love to everybody that I must break somebody's bones, or burst. John preached *delightfully* yesterday I wanted you there to hear. But all my treasures are in earthen vessels he seems all used up by his Sunday and scarcely touched his breakfast. I do not see how his or my race can be very long, if we live in New York. All the more reason for running it well. And what a blessed, blessed life it is, at the worst! "Central peace subsisting at the heart of endless agitation." Goodbye, dear consider yourself embraced by a hearty soul that heartily loves you, and that soul lives in E. P.

On the 25th of October Mr. Charles H. Leonard, an old and highly esteemed friend, died very suddenly at his summer home in Rochester, Mass. He was a man of sterling worth, generous, large-hearted, and endeared to Mrs. Prentiss and her husband by many acts of kindness. He was one of the founders of the Church of the Covenant and had also aided liberally in building its pleasant parsonage.

To Miss Eliza A. Warner, New York, Oct. 26, 1868.

I am reminded as I write my date, that I am fifty years old today. My John says it is no such thing, and that I am only thirty but I begin to feel antiquated, dilapidated, and antediluvian, etc., etc.

I write to let you know that we are going to Rochester, Mass., to attend the funeral of a dear friend there. It seems best for me to risk the wear and tear of the going and the coming, if I can thereby give even a little comfort to one who loves me dearly, and who is now left without a single relative in the world. For twenty-four years, these have been faithful friends, loving us better every year, members of our church in New Bedford, Mercer Street, and then here. They lived at Rochester during the summer and we visited them there (you may remember my speaking of it) just before we went to Dorset. Mrs. Leonard was then feeling very uneasy about her husband, but he got better and seemed about as usual, until last Tuesday, when he was stricken down with paralysis and died on Saturday. Somebody said that spending so large a portion of my time as I do in scenes of sorrow, she wondered God did not give me more strength. But I think He knows just how much to give. I have been to Newark twice since I wrote you. Mrs. Stearns is in a very suffering condition I was appalled by the sight appalled at the weakness of human nature (its physical weakness). But I got over that, and had a sweet glimpse at least of the *eternal* felicity that is to be the end of what at longest is a brief period of suffering. I write her a little bit of a note every few days. I feel like a ball that now is tossed to Sorrow and tossed back by Sorrow to Joy. For mixed in with every day's experience of suffering are such great, such unmerited mercies.

Two or three of the little notes follow:

MY DEAREST ANNA,-I long to be with you through the hours that are before you, and to help cheer and sustain you in the trial of faith and patience to which you are called. But unless you need me I will not go, lest I should be the one too many in your state of excitement and suspense. We all feel anxiety as to the result of the incision, but take comfort in casting our care upon God. May Christ Jesus, our dear Savior, who loves and pities you infinitely more than any of us do, be very near you in this season of suspense. I would gladly exchange positions with you if I might, and if it were best but as I may not, and it is not best, because God wills otherwise, I earnestly commend you to His tender sympathy. If He means that you shall be restored to health, He will make you happy in living if He means to call you home to Himself, He will make you happy in dying. Dear Anna, stay yourself on Him: He has strength enough to support you, when all other strength fails. Remember, as Lizzy Smith said, you are "encompassed with prayers."

Friday Afternoon,

MY DEAR ANNA,-I send you a "lullaby" for next Sunday, which I met with at Dorset, and hope it will speak a little word and sing a little song to you while the rest are at church. How I do wish I could see you every day! I feel restless with longing but you are hardly able to take any comfort in a long visit and it is such a journey to make for-a short one! But, as I said the other day, if at any time you feel a little stronger and it would comfort you even a little bit to see me, I will drop everything and run right over. It seems hard to have you suffer so and do nothing for you. But do not be discouraged pain cannot last forever.

> "I know not the way I am going
> But well do I know my Guide!
> With a childlike trust I give my hand,
> To the mighty Friend at my side.
> The only thing that I say to Him
> As He takes it, is, 'Hold it fast.
> Suffer me not to lose my way,
> And bring me home at last!"

MY DEAR ANNA:-I feel such tender love and pity for you, but I know you are too sick to read more than a few words.

> "In the furnace God may prove thee,
> Thence to bring thee forth more bright

But can never cease to love thee:
Thou art precious in His sight!"
Your ever affectionate LIZZY.

To Mrs. Lenard, Friday, Oct. 30, 1858.

We got home safely last evening before any of the children had gone to bed, and they all came running to meet us most joyfully. This morning I am restless and cannot set about anything. It distresses me to think how little human friendship can do for such a sorrow as yours. When a sufferer is on the rack, he cares little for what is said to him though he may feel grateful for sympathy. I found it hard to tear myself away from you so soon, but all I could do for you there I could do all along the way home and since I have got here: love you, be sorry for you, and constantly pray for you. I am sure that He who has so sorely afflicted you accepts the patience with which you bear the rod, and that when this first terrible amazement and bewilderment are over, and you can enter into communion and fellowship with Him, you will find a joy in Him that, hard as it is to the flesh to say so, transcends all the sweetest and best joys of human life. You will have nothing to do now but to fly to Him. I have seen the time when I could hide myself in Him as a little child hides in its mother's arms, and so have thousands of aching hearts. In all our afflictions, He is afflicted. But I must not weary you with words. May God bless and keep you, and fully reveal Himself unto you!

To Miss. E. A. Warner, New York, Nov. 2, 1868.

I have been lying on the sofa in my room, half-asleep, and feeling rather guilty at the lot of gas I was wasting, but too lazy or too tired to get up to turn it down. Your little "spray" hangs right over the head of my bed, and it was it was slightly dilapidated by its journey hither, I have tucked in a bit of green fern with it to remind me that I was not always in the sere and yellow leaf, but had springtime once. To think of your going for to go and write verses to me in my old age! I have just been reading them over and think it was real good of you to up and say such nice things in such a nice way. I had no idea you *could!* We did not come home from Rochester through Boston if we had done so I meant to go and see you. I made it up in many loving thoughts to you on our twelve hours' journey. Poor Mrs. L. met me with open arms, and I was thankful indeed that I went, though every word I said in the presence of her terrible grief, sounded flat and cold and dead. How little the tenderest love and sympathy can do, in such sorrows! She was so bewildered and appalled by her sudden bereavement, that it was almost a mockery to say a word and yet I kept saying what I *know* is true, that Christ in the soul is better than any earthly joy. Both Mr. Prentiss and myself feel the reaction, which must inevitably follow such a strain.

You ask if I look over the past on my birthdays. I suppose I used to do it and feel dreadfully at the pitiful review, but since I have had the children's to celebrate, I have not thought much of mine. But this time, being fifty years old, did set me upon thinking, and I had so many mercies to recount and to thank God for, that I hardly felt pangs of any sort. I suppose He controls our moods in such seasons, and I have done trying to force myself into this or that train of thought. I am sure that a good deal of what used to seem like repentance and sorrow for sin on such occasions, was really nothing but wounded pride that wished it could appear better in its own eyes. God has been so good to me! I wish I could begin to realize how good! I think a great many thoughts to you that I cannot put on paper. Life seems teaching some new, or deepening the impression of some old, lesson, all the time.

You think A. may have looked scornfully at your little "spray." Well, she did not she said, "What's that funny little thing perched up there? Well, it's pretty anyhow." Among the rush of visitors today were Miss Haines and the W——s. I fell upon Miss W. and told her about you, furiously then we got upon Miss Lyman, and it did my very soul good to hear Miss Haines praise and magnify her. Never shall I cease to be thankful for being with her at Dorset, to say nothing, dear, of you! Do you know that there are twelve cases of typhoid fever at Vassar? And that Miss Lyman is not as well as she was? I feel greatly concerned about her, not to say troubled. I do not suppose I shall ever hear her pray. But I shall hear her and help her praise. I do not believe a word about there being different grades of saints in heaven. Some people think it modest to say that they do not expect to get anywhere near so and so, they are so—etc., etc. But I expect to be mixed all up with the saints, and to take perfect delight in their testimony to my Savior.

Can you put up with this miserable letter? Folks cannot rush to Newark and to Rochester and agonies in every nerve at the sufferings of others, and be quite coherent. I have sense enough left to know that I love you dearly, and that I long to see you and to take sweet counsel with you once more. Do not fail to give me the helping hand.

The following was written to Mrs. Stearns on her silver-wedding day, Nov. 15:

MY DEAREST ANNA: I have thought of you all day with the tenderest sympathy, knowing how you had looked forward to it, and what a contrast it offers to your bridal day twenty-five years ago. But I hope it has not been wholly sad. You have a rich past that cannot be taken from you, and a richer future lies before you. For I can see, though through your tears you cannot, that the Son of God walks with you in this furnace of affliction, and that He is so sanctifying it to your soul, that ages hence you will look on this day as better, sweeter, than the day of your espousals. It is hard now to suffer, but after all, the *light* affliction is nothing, and the *weight* of glory is everything. You may not fully realize this or any other truth, in your enfeebled state, but truth remains the same whether we appreciate it or not and so does Christ. Your despondency does not prove that He is not just as near to you as He is to those who see Him more clearly and it is better to be despondent than to be self-righteous. Do not you see that in afflicting you He means to prove to you that He loves you, and that you love Him? Do not you remember that it is His son—not His enemy—that He scourged?

The greatest saint on earth has got to reach heaven on the same terms as the greatest sinner unworthy, unfit, worthless but saved through grace. Do cheer and comfort yourself with these thoughts, my dearest Anna, and your sickroom will be the happiest room in your house, as I constantly pray it may be! Your ever affectionate Lizzy.

To Miss E.A.W., New York, Nov. 17, 1868

You ask how I sleep. I always sleep better at home, than elsewhere this is one great reason why we decided to have a home all the year round. I have to walk four or five miles a day, which takes a good deal of time, these short days, but there is no help for it. I do not think the time is lost when I am out of doors I suppose Christ may go with us, *does* go with us, wherever we go. But I am too eager and vehement, too anxious to be working all the time. Why, no, I do not think it *wrong* to want to be at work provided God gives us strength for work the great thing is not to repine when He disables us. I do not think, my dear, that you need trouble yourself about my dying at present it is not at all likely that I shall. I feel as if I had to be *tested* yet this sweet peace, of which I have so much, almost startles me. I keep asking myself whether it is not a stupendous delusion of Satan and my own wicked heart. How I wish I could see you tonight! There is so much one does not like to put on paper that one would love to say.

Thursday, 4 P.M.—Well, my lunch-party is over, and my sewing society is re-organized, and before I go forth to tea, let me finish and send off this epistle. We had the Rev. Mr. and Mrs. Washburn, of Constantinople, Dr. Chickering, and Prof, and Mrs. Smith gave them cold turkey, cold ham, cold ice-cream and hot coffee that was about all, for society in New York is just about reduced down to eating and drinking together, after which you go about your business.

I am re-reading Leighton on 1st Peter I wonder if you like it as much as my John and I do! I hope your murderous book goes on well then you can take your rest next summer. Now I must get ready for my long walk down and over to Ninth Street., to see a tiny little woman, and English at that. Her prayer at our meeting yesterday moved us all to tears.

To Miss Eliza A. Warner, New York, Nov. 25, 1868

Mr. Prentiss complained yesterday that no letters came, an unheard-of event in our family history, and this morning found *twelve* sticking in the top of the box among them was yours, but I was just going off to my Prayer-meeting, and had to put it into my pocket and let it go too. I am glad you sent me Mrs. Field's letter and poem she is a genius, and writes beautifully. And how glad you must be to hear about your books. I cannot imagine what better work you want than writing. In what other way could you reach so many minds and hearts? You must always send me such letters. Before I forget it, let me tell you of a real Thanksgiving present we have just had three barrels of potatoes, some apples, some dried apples, cranberries, celery, canned corn, canned strawberries, and two big chickens.

After church, Thursday.—I must indulge myself with going on with my letter, for after dinner I want to play with the children, and make this day mean something to them besides pies. For everybody spoke for pies this year (you know we almost never make such sinful things) and they all said ice-cream would not do at all, so yesterday I made fourteen of these enormities, and mean to stuff them (the children, not the pies!) so that they won't want any more for a year. I want to tell you about some pretty coincidences we went to church in a dismal rain, and Mr. Prentiss preached on the *beauty* of holiness, and every time he said anything that made sunshine particularly appropriate, the sun came in in floods, and then disappeared until the next occasion. For instance, he spoke of the sunshine of a happy home as so much brighter than that of the natural sun, and the whole church was instantly illuminated then he said that if we had each come there with ten million sorrows, Christ could give us light, when, lo, the church glowed again and so on half-a-dozen times, till at last he quoted the verse *"And the Lamb is the light thereof,"* when a perfect blaze of effulgence made those mysterious, words almost startling. And then he wound up by describing the Tyrolese custom on which Mrs. Field's poem is founded, which he had himself seen and enjoyed, and of which, it seems, he spoke at East Dorset last summer at the Sunday-school. [8] I read the poem and letter to him the instant we got home, and he admired them both. It was a little singular that her poem and his sermon came to me at almost the identical moment, wasn't it?

I must tell you about an old ladies' party given by Mrs. Cummings, wife of him who prepared my father's memoir. [9] She had had a fortune left to her and was all the time doing good with it, and it entered her head to get up a very nice supper for twenty-six old ladies, the youngest of whom was seventy-five (the Portland people rarely die until they are ninety or so). She sent carriages for all who couldn't walk, and when they all got together, the lady who described the scene to me, said it was indescribably beautiful, all congratulating each other that they were so far on in their pilgrimage and so near heaven! Lovely, wasn't it? I wish I could spend the rest of my life with such people! Then she spoke of Mrs. C.'s face during the last six months of her life, when it had an expression so blest, so seraphic, that it was a delight to look upon it—and how she had all the members of the ladies' prayer-meeting come and kiss her goodbye after she was too weak to speak.

And now the children have got together again, and I must go and stay with them until their bedtime, when, partly for the sake of the walk, partly because they asked us, we twain are going to see the Smiths. I rather think, my dear, that if, as you say, you could see all my thoughts, you would drop me as you would a hot potato. You would see many good thoughts, I won't deny that, and some loving ones but you would also see an abominable lot of elated, conceited, horrid ones self-laudation even at good planned to do, and admired before done. But God can endure what no mortal eye could He does not love us because we are so lovely, but because He always loves what He pities. I fall back upon this thought whenever I feel discouraged I was going to say *sad*, but that isn't the word, for I never do feel sad except when I've been eating something I'd no business to! Goodbye, dearie.

To the Same, New York, Dec. 3, 1868.

I think I must indulge myself, my dear, in writing to you to-night, it being really the only thing I want to do, unless it be to lie half asleep on the sofa. And that I cannot do, for there is no sofa in the room! The cold weather has made it agreeable to have a fire in the dining-room grate, and this makes it a cheerful resort for the children, especially as the long table is very convenient for their books, map drawing, etc. And wherever the rest are the mother must be I suppose that is the law of a happy family, in the winter at least. The reason I am so tired to-night is that I have been unexpectedly to Newark. I went, as soon as I could after breakfast, to market, and then on a walk of over two miles to prepare myself for our sewing circle! I met our sexton as I was coming home, and asked him to see what ailed one of the drawers of my desk that would not shut. We had a terrible time with it, and I had to take everything out, and turn my desk topsy-turvy, and your letters and all my other papers got raving distracted, and all mixed up with bits of sealing-wax, old pens, and dear knows what not, when down comes A. from the school-room, to say that Mrs. Stearns had sent for me to come right out, thinking she was dying. I knew nothing about the trains, always trusting to Mr. Prentiss about that, but in five minutes, I was off, and on reaching the depot found I had lost a train by ten minutes, and that there would not be another for an hour. Then I had leisure to remember that Mr. P. was to get home from Dorset, that I had left no message for him, had hid away all the letters that had come in his absence, where he couldn't find them that if it was necessary for me to stay at Newark all night he would be dreadfully frightened, etc., etc. Somehow, I felt very blue, but at last concluded to get rid of a part of the time by hunting up some dinner at a restaurant.

When I at last got to Newark, I found that Mrs. Stearns' disease had suddenly developed several unfavorable symptoms. She had made up her mind that all hope was over, had taken leave of her family, and now wanted to bid me goodbye. She held my hands fast in both hers, begging me to talk. I spoke freely to her about her death she pointed up once to an illumination I gave her last spring: SIMPLY TO THY CROSS I CLING. "That," she said, "is all I can do." I said all I could to comfort her, but I do not know whether God gave me the right word or not.

On my return, as I got out of the stage near the corner of our street, whom should my weary eyes light on but my dear good man, just got home from Dorset how surprised and delighted we were to meet so unexpectedly! M. rushed to meet us, and afterward said to me, "I have three great reliefs you have got home papa has got home and Aunt Anna is still alive." My children were never so lovely and loving as they are this winter, my home is almost too luxurious, and happy such things do not belong to this world. We have just heard of the death in Switzerland of Mr. Prentiss' successor at New Bedford, classmate of one of my brothers, and someone has sent a plaintive, sweet little dying song written at Florence by him. Now I am too fagged to say another word.

Dec. 4th.—"I do not get *any* time to write each day brings its own special work that cannot be done tomorrow as to letters, I scratch them off at odd moments, when too tired to do anything else. What a resource they are! They do instead of crying for me. And how many I get every week that are loving and pleasant!

What do you think of this? I hope it will make you laugh—a lady told me she never confessed her sins aloud (in prayer) lest Satan should find out her weak points and tempt her more effectually! And I want to ask you if you ever offer to pray with people? I never do, and yet there are cases when nothing else seems to answer. Oh, how many questions of duty come up every hour, and how many reasons we have every hour to be ashamed of ourselves!

Monday morning.—It was a shame to write to you, when I was so tired that I could not write legibly, but my heart was full of love, and I longed to be near you. Now Monday has come, a lowering, forbidding day, yet all is sunshine in my soul, and I hope that may make my home light to my beloved ones, and even reach you, wherever you are. I am going to run out to see how Mrs. Stearns is. Our plan is for me to make arrangements to stay with her, if I can be of any use or comfort. I literally love the house of mourning better than the house of feasting. All my long, long years of suffering and sorrow make sorrow-stricken homes homelike, and I cannot but feel, because I know it from experience, that Christ loves to be in such homes. So you may congratulate me, dear, if I may be permitted to go where He goes. I wish you could have heard yesterday's sermon about God's having as *characteristic, individual* a love to each of us as we have to our friends. Think of that, dear, when you remember how I loved you in Mrs. G.'s little parlor! Can you realize that your Lord and Savior loves you infinitely more? I confess that such conceptions are hard to attain.... Cannot you do M―― S―― up in your next letter, and send her to me on approbation? Instead of being satisfied that I have you, I want her and everybody else who is really good, to fill up some of the empty rooms in my heart. This is a rambling, scrambling letter, but I do not care, and do not believe you do. Well, goodbye thank your stars that this bit of paper does not have any arms and cannot hug you!

To Mrs. Leonard, New York, Dec. 13, 1868.

There is half an hour before bedtime, and I have been thinking of and praying for you, until I feel that I *must* write. I forgot to tell you, how the verses in my Daily Food, on the day of your dear husband's death, seem meant for you:

"Thou art my refuge and portion."—Ps. 143: 5.

> 'Tis God that lifts our comforts high,
> Or sinks them in the grave
> He gives, and blessed be His name!
> He takes but what He gave.

The Lord gave and the Lord hath taken away.—Job 1:21.

I have had this little book thirty-three years, it has travelled with me wherever I have been, and it has been indeed my song in the house of my pilgrimage. This has been our communion Sunday, and I have been very glad of the rest and peace it has afforded, for I have done little during the last ten days but fly from one scene of sorrow to another, from here to Newark and from Newark to Brooklyn.... So I have alternated between the two dying beds yesterday Jennie P. went into a convulsion just as I entered the room, and did not fully come out of it for an hour and a half, when I had to come away in order to get home before pitch dark. What a terrible sight it is! They use chloroform, and that has a very marked effect, controlling all violence in a few seconds. Whether the poor child came out of that attack alive I do not know I had no doubt she was dying until just before I came away, when she appeared easier, though still unconscious. The family seem nearly frantic, and the sisters are so upset by witnessing these turns, that I shall feel that I must be there all I can. I am in cruel doubt which household to go to, but hope God will direct.

Mr. Prentiss is a good deal withered and worn by his sister's state he had never, by any means, ceased to hope, and he is much afflicted. She and Jennie may live a week or more, or go at any moment. In my long hours of silent musing and prayer, as I go from place to place, I think often of you. I think one reason why we do not get all the love and faith we sigh for is that we try to force them to come to us, instead of realizing that they must be God's free gifts, to be won by prayer.... And now Mr. P. has come up-stairs rolled up in your afghan, and we have decided to go to both Newark and Brooklyn tomorrow, so I know I ought to go to bed. You must take this letter as a great proof of my love to you, though it does not say much, for I am bewildered by the scenes through which I am passing, and hardly fit therefore to write. What I do not say I truly feel, real, deep, constant sympathy with you in your sorrow and loneliness. May God bless you in it.

[1] Dorset is situated in Bennington County, about sixty miles from Troy and twenty-five miles from Rutland. Its eastern portion lies in a deep-cut valley along the western slope of the Green Mountain range, on the line of the Bennington and Rutland railroad. Its western part—the valley in which Mrs. Prentiss passed her summers—is separated from East Dorset by Mt. Aeolus, Owl's Head, and a succession of maple-crested hills, all belonging to the Taconic system of rocks, which contains the rich marble, slate, and limestone quarries of Western Vermont. In the north this range sweeps round toward the Equinox range, enclosing the beautiful and fertile upland region called The Hollow. Dorset belonged to the so-called New Hampshire Grants, and was organized into a township shortly before the Revolutionary War. Its first settlers were largely from Connecticut and Massachusetts. They were a hardy, intelligent, liberty-loving race, and impressed upon the town a moral and religious character, which remains to this day.

[2] Mrs. Arthur Bronson, of New York. A life of Mrs. Prentiss would scarcely be complete without a grateful mention of this devoted friend and true Christian lady. She was the centre of a wide family circle, to all of whose members, both young and old, she was greatly endeared by the beauty and excellence of her character. She died shortly after Mrs. Prentiss.

[3] While supposing that her brothers had been burnt out and had, perhaps, lost everything, she wrote to her husband with characteristic generosity, "If they did not kill themselves working at the fire, they will kill themselves trying to get on their feet again. Every cent I have I think should be given them. My father's church and everything associated with my youth, gone forever! I cannot think of anything else."

[4] Mrs. McCurdy died at her home in New York in December, 1876. A few sentences from a brief address at the funeral by her old pastor will not be here out of place. "Her natural character was one of the loveliest I have ever known. Its leading traits were as simple and clear as daylight, while its cheering effect upon those who came under its influence was like that of sunshine. She was not only very happy herself—enjoying life to the last in her home and her

friends—but she was gifted with a disposition and power to make others happy such as falls to the lot of only a select few of the race. Her domestic and church ties brought her into relations of intimate acquaintance and friendship with some of the best men of her times. I will venture to mention two of them: her uncle, the late Theodore Frelinghuysen, one of the noblest men our country has produced, eminent alike as statesman, scholar, and Christian philanthropist and the sainted Thomas H. Skinner, her former pastor. Her sick-room—if sick-room is the proper name—in which, during the last seventeen years, she passed so much of her time, was tinged with no sort of gloom it seemed to have two doors, one of them opening into the world, through which her family and friends passed in and out, learning lessons of patience and love and sweet contentment: the other opening heavenward, and ever ajar to admit the messenger of her Lord, in whatever watch he should come to summon her home. The place was like that upper chamber facing the sun rising, and whose name was *Peace*, in which Bunyan's Pilgrim was lodged on the way to the celestial city. How many pleasant and hallowed memories lead back to that room!"

[5] Old New Bedford friends.

[6] Fritz und Maria und Ich. Von Mrs. Prentiss. Deutsche autorisirte Ausgabe. Von Marie Morgenstern. Itzchoe, 1874.

[7] She gave me the pet-name of "Fanny" because she did not like mine, and there was an old joke about "John."—E. A. W.

[8] The custom related to a pious salutation, with which two *friends*, or even *strangers*, greet each other, when meeting on the mountain highways and passes in certain districts of Tyrol. *"Gelobt sei Jesu Christ!"* cries one *"In Ewigkeit, Amen!"* answers the other (*i.e.*, "Praised be Jesus Christ!" "For evermore, Amen!") The following lines are from Mrs. F.'s Poem:

> "When the poor peasant, alpenstock in hand,
> Toils up the steep,
> And finds a friend upon the dizzy height
> Amid his sheep,
> "They do not greet each other as in our
> Kind English way,
> Ask not for health, nor wish in cheerful phrase
> prosperous day
> "Infinite thoughts alone spring up in that
> Great solitude,
> Nothing seems worthy or significant
> But heavenly good
> "So in this reverent and sacred form
> Their souls outpour,—
> Blessed be Jesus Christ's most holy name!
> "For evermore!"

[9] Rev. Asa Cummings, D.D., of Portland, for many years editor of the Christian Mirror one of the weightiest, wisest and best men of his generation.

CHAPTER 9 - STEPPING HEAVENWARD - 1869.

I.

> Death of Mrs. Stearns. Her Character. Dangerous Illness of Prof. Smith.
> Death at the Parsonage. Letters. A Visit to Vassar College. Letters.
> Getting ready for General Assembly. "Gates Ajar."

A little past three o'clock on Saturday afternoon, January 2, 1869, Anna S. Prentiss, wife of the Rev. Jonathan F. Stearns, D.D., fell asleep in Jesus. The preceding pages show what strong ties bound Mrs. Prentiss to this beloved sister. Their friendship dated back thirty years it was cemented by common joys and common sorrows in some of their deepest experiences of life and it had been kept fresh and sweet by frequent intercourse and correspondence. Mrs. Stearns was a woman of uncommon attractions and energy of character. She impressed herself strongly upon all who came within the sphere of her influence the hearts of her husband's people, as well as his own and those of her children, trusted in her and the whole community where she dwelt mourned her loss. She had been especially endeared to her brother Sergeant, with whom she spent several winters in the South prior to her marriage. Her influence over him, at a critical period of his life, was alike potent and happy their relation to each other was, in truth, full of the elements of romance and some of his letters to her are exquisite effusions of fraternal confidence and affection. [1] Her letters to him, beginning when she was a young girl and ending only with his life, would form a large volume. "You excel anyone I know," he wrote to her, "in the kind and gentle art of letter-writing." In the midst of his early professional triumphs, he writes:

You do not know what obligations I am under to you I owe all my success in this country to the fact of having so kind a mother and such sweet affectionate sisters as Abby and yourself. It has been my only motive to exertion without it I should long since have thrown myself away. Even now, when, as is frequently the case, I feel perfectly reckless both of life and fortune, and look with contempt upon them both, the recollection that there are two or three hearts that beat for me with real affection, even though far away—comes over me as the music of David did over the dark spirit of Saul. I still feel that I have something worth living for.

For years, her letters helped to cherish and deepen this feeling. He thus refers to one of them:

I cannot tell how much I thank you for it. I cried like a child while reading it, and even now, the tears stand in my eyes, as I think of its expressions of affection, sympathy, and good sense.... I wish you were here now—oh, how I do wish it! But you will come next fall, won't you? And be to me

The antelope whose feet shall bless   With her light step my loneliness.

But my candle burns low, and it is past the witching hour of night. Whether sleeping or waking, God bless you and our dear mother, and all of you. Goodnight—goodnight. My love loads this last line.

To Mrs. Prentiss and her husband, the death of Mrs. Stearns was an irreparable loss. It took out of their life one of its greatest earthly blessings.

The new year opened with another painful shock—the sudden and dangerous illness of her husband's bosom friend, Henry Boynton Smith. Prof. Smith was to have made one of the addresses at the funeral of Mrs. Stearns but instead of doing so, he was obliged to take to his bed, and, soon afterwards, to flee for his life beyond the sea. To this affliction, the reader is indebted for the letters to Mrs. Smith, contained in this chapter. On the 16th of February another niece of her husband, a sweet child of seventeen, was brought to the parsonage very ill and died there before the close of the month. Her letters will show how she was affected by these troubles.

To Mrs. Leonard, New York, Jan. 9, 1869.

So many unanswered letters lie piled on my desk that I hardly know which to take up first, but my heart yearns over you, and I cannot help writing you. No wonder you grow sadder as time passes and the beloved one comes not, and comes not. I wish I could help you bear your burden, but all I can do is to be sorry for you. The peaceable fruits of sorrow do not ripen at once there is a long time of weariness and heaviness while this process is going on but I do not, will not doubt, that you will taste these fruits, and find them very sweet. One of the hard things about bereavement is the physical prostration and listlessness which make it next to impossible to pray, and quite impossible to feel the least interest in anything. We must bear this as a part of the pain, believing that it will not last forever, for nothing but God's goodness does. How I wish you were near us, and that we could meet and talk and pray together over all that has saddened our lives, and made heaven such a blessed reality!

There is not much to tell about the last hours of our dear sister. She had rallied a good deal, and they all thought she was getting well but the day after Christmas typhoid symptoms began to set in. I saw her on the Monday following, found her greatly depressed, and did not stay long. On Saturday morning, we got a dispatch we should have received early on New Year's Day, saying she was sinking. We hurried out, found her flushed and bright, but near her end, having no pulse at either wrist, and her hands and feet cold. She had had a distressing day and night, but now seemed perfectly easy knew us, gave us a glad welcome, reminded me that I had promised to go with her to the end, and kissed us heartily. Every time we went near her, she gave us such a glad smile that it was hard to believe she was going so soon. She talked incessantly, with no signs of debility, but it was the restlessness of approaching death.

At three in the afternoon, they all came into the room, as they always did at that hour. She said a few things, and evidently began to lose her sight, for as Lewis was about to leave the room, she said, "Good-night, L.," and then to me, "Why, Lizzy dear, you are not going to stay all night?" I said, "Oh yes, do not you know I promised to stay with A., who will be so lonely?" She looked pleased, but greatly surprised, her mind being so weak, and in a few seconds she laid her restless hands on her breast, her eyes became fixed, and the last gentle breaths began to come and go. "Is the doctor here?" she asked. We told her no, and then Mr. S. and the nurse, who were close each side of her, began to repeat a verse or two of Scripture then seeing she was apparently too far gone to hear, Mr. S. leaned over and whispered, "My darling!" She made no response, on which he said, "She can make no response," and she said, "But I hear," gave one or two more gentle little breaths, and was gone. I forgot to say that after her eyes were fixed, hearing Mr. S. groan, she *stopped dying*, turned, and gave a parting look! I never saw an easier death, nor such a bright face up to the very last. One of the doctors coming in, in the morning, was apparently overcome by the extraordinary smile she gave him, for he turned away immediately without a word, and left the house. I stayed, as they wished me to do, until

Monday night, when I came home quite used up. Your sorrow, and the sorrow at Brooklyn, and now this one, have come one after another until it seemed as if there was no end to it such is life, and we must bear it patiently, knowing the end will be the more joyful for all that saddened the way.

I shall always let you know if anything of special interest occurs in the church or among ourselves. After loving you so many years, I am not likely to forget you now. The addresses at Mrs. S.'s funeral will probably be published, and we will send you a copy. Mr. P. is bearing up bravely, but feels the listlessness of which I spoke, and finds sermonizing hard work. He joins me in love to you. Do write often.

To Miss Eliza A. Warner, New York, Feb. 16, 1869.

On coming home from church on Sunday afternoon I found one of the Brooklyn family waiting to tell us that another of the girls was very ill, that they were all worn out and nearly frantic, and asking if she might be brought here to be put under the care of some German doctor, as Dr. Smith had given her up. In the midst of my sorrow for the poor mother, I thought of myself. How could I, who had not been allowed to invite Miss Lyman here, undertake this terrible care? You know what a fearful disease it is—how many convulsions they have but you do not know the harm it did me just seeing poor Jennie P. in one. Yesterday I tried hard to let God manage it, but I know I wished He would manage it so as to spare me it takes so little to pull me down, and so little to destroy my health. But I was not in a good frame, could not write a Percy for the Observer, and got a letter from some house down town, asking me to write them Susy books, got a London Daily News containing a nice notice of Little Lou, but naught consoled me. [2] In fact, I dawdled so long over H.'s lessons, which I always hear after breakfast, that I had not my usual time to pray and that, of itself, would spoil any day. After dinner came two of the Prentiss sisters to say that Dr. [Horatio] Smith said Eva's one chance of getting well was to come here for change of air and scene—would I take her and her mother? Of course, I would. They then told me that Dr. Smith had said his brother's case was perfectly hopeless. This upset me. My feet turned into ice and my head into a ball of fire. As soon as they left, I had the spare room arranged, and then went out and walked until dark to cool off my head, but to so little purpose that I had a bad night the news about Prof. S. was so dreadful. Mr. Prentiss was appalled, too. I had to make this a day of rest—not daring to work after such a night. Got up at seven or so, took my bath, rung the bell for prayers at twenty minutes of eight. After breakfast heard H.'s lessons, then read the 20th chapter of Matthew and mused long on Christ's coming to minister—not to be ministered unto. Prayed for poor Mrs. Smith and a good many weary souls, and felt a little bit better. Then went down to Randolph's at the request of a lady, who wanted him to sell some books she had got up for a benevolent object. He said he would take twelve. Then to the Smiths, burdened with my sad secret. Got home tired and depressed. Tried to get to sleep and could not, tried to read and could not.

At last they came with the sick girl, and one look at the poor, half-fainting child, and her mother's "Nobody in the world but you would have let us come," made them welcome and I have rejoiced ever since that *God let* them come. One of the first things they said took my worst burden off my back the whole story about Prof. Smith was a dream! Can you conceive my relief? We had dinner. Eva ate more than she had done for a long time. We had a long talk with her mother after dinner then I went up to the sick-room and stayed an hour or so then had a call then ran out to carry a book to a widowed lady, that I hoped would comfort her then home, and with Eva till tea-time. Then had some comfort in laying all these cares and interests in those loving Arms that are always so ready to take them in. I enjoy praying in the morning best, however—perhaps because less tired but sometimes I think it is owing to a sort of night-preparation for it I mean, in the wakeful times of night and early morning.

Wednesday, 17th—While I was writing the above all the Brooklyn Prentisses went to bed, and we New York Prentisses went to the Sunday-schoolrooms next door to a church gathering. There are three rooms that can be thrown together, and they were bright and fragrant with flowers, most of which the young men sent me afterwards, exquisite things. I had a precious talk with Dr. Abbot, one of whose feet, to say the least, is already on the topmost round. I only wish he was a woman. The church was open, and we all went in and listened to some fine music. Coming out I said to a gentleman who approached me, "How is little baby?" "Which little baby?" "Why, the youngest." "Oh, we haven't any baby." And lo! I had mistaken my man! Imagine how *he* felt and how *I* felt! We got home at eleven P.M., and so ended my day of rest. I have 540 things to say, but there is so much going on that I shall defraud you of them—aren't you glad? Have you read the "Gates Ajar"? I have, with real pain. I do not think you will be so shocked at it as I am, but hope you do not like it. It is full of talent, but has next to no Christ in it, and my heaven is full of Him. I have finished Faber. How queer he is with his 3's and 5's and 6's and 7's! I feel all done up into little sums in addition, and that is about all I know of myself—he has bewildered me so. There are fine things in it, and I took the liberty of making a wee cross against some of them, which you can rub out. Miss L. sent me another of his books, which I am reading now—"All for Jesus."

To Mrs. Henry B. Smith, New York, March 22, 1869

We were gladdened early this morning by the arrival of your letter, and the good news it contained. I had a dreadful fright on the day you reached Southampton. Mr. Moore sent up a cable dispatch announcing the fact, and as it came directed to both of us, and I supposed it to be from you, I thought some terrible thing had happened. I paraded down to M. with your letter, and she, at the same time, paraded up here with the one to her and the rest. So we got all the news there was, and longed for more. I hope the worst is now over. I have just got home from a visit of four days and nights to Miss Lyman. I enjoyed it exceedingly, and wish I could tell you all about it, but cannot in a letter. She has turns of looking absolutely *aged*, and seems a good deal of the time in a perfect worry, I do not know what about. Otherwise, she is better than last summer. I never saw her when at work before and perhaps she always appears so. We had two or three good rousing laughs, however, and that did us both good. I did not know she was so fond of flowers she buys them and keeps loads of them about her parlors, library, and bedroom. What a world it is there! I only wish she was happier in her work, but perhaps if we could get behind the scenes, we should find all human workers have their sorrows and misgivings and faintings. According to her, I had an "inquiry meeting" once or twice believe it if you can and dare. It was certainly very pleasant to get into such an intelligent Christian atmosphere, and on the whole, I have been rather converted to Vassar.

I have been greatly delighted with a present of one of my father's cuff buttons (which I well remember), and a lock of his hair. I have not got anything more to say. Oh, Mrs. —— left that on her card here the other day, and we called on her this afternoon. What a jolly old lady she is! Of course, anybody could believe in perfection who was as fat and well as she!

To Mrs. Leonard, New York, April 5, 1869

If I should send you a letter every time I send you a thought, you would be quite overwhelmed with them. Now that Mrs. S. has gone away, and some of my pressing cares are over, I miss you more than ever. We have had a good deal to sadden us this winter, beginning with your sorrow, which was also ours and Eva P.'s death, occurring as it did in our house, was a distressing one. She was here about a fortnight, and the first week came down to her meals, though she kept in her room the rest of the time. On Tuesday night of the second week, she was at the tea table, and played a duet with A. after tea. Soon after she was taken with distress for breath, and was never in bed again, but sat nearly double in a chair, with one of us supporting her head. It was agonizing suffering to witness, and the care of her was more laborious than anyone can conceive who did not witness or participate in it. We had at last to have six on hand to relieve each other. She died on Saturday, after four terrible days and nights. We knew she would die here when they first proposed her coming, but did not like to refuse her last desire, and are very glad we had the privilege of ministering to her last wants…. For you I desire but one thing—a full possession of Christ. Let us turn away our eyes from everything that does not directly exalt Him in our affections we are poor without Him, no matter what our worldly advantages are rich with Him when stripped of all besides. Still I know you are passing through deep waters, and at times must well nigh sink. But your loving Savior will not let you sink, and He never loved you so well as He does now. How often I long to fly to you in your lonely hours! But I cannot, and so I turn these longings into prayers. I hope you pray for me, too. You could not give me anything I should value so much, and it is a great comfort to me to know that you love me. I care more to be loved than to be admired, do not you? I hope that by next winter you may feel that you can come and see us I want to see you, not merely to write to you and get answers. I send you a picture of our nest at Dorset. Goodbye.

To Miss E. A. Warner, New York, April 20, 1869

I opened your letter in the street, and was at once confronted with a worldly looking bit of silk! How *can* you! Why do not you follow my example and dress in sackcloth and ashes? I think however, if you *will* be worldly you have done it very prettily, and on the whole do not know that it is any wickeder than I have been in translating a "dramatic poem" in five acts from the German, only you've got your dress done and I'm only half through my play and there's no knowing how bad I shall get before I am through. I wonder if you are sitting by an open window, as I am, and roasting at that? I had a drive with A. and M. through the Park yesterday, and saw stacks of hyacinths in bloom, and tulips and violets and dandelions a willow-tree not far from my window has put on its tender green, and summer seems close at hand. I have been to an auction and got cheated, as I might have known I should and the other day I had my pocket picked. As to "Gates Ajar," most people are enchanted with it but Miss Lyman regards it as I do, and so do some other elect ladies. I have just written to see if she will come down and get a little rest, now the weather is so fine. Mr. P. has gone to Dorset to be gone all the week, and I am buying up what is to be bought, begrudging every cent! mean wretch that I am.

I have looked through and read parts of "Patience Strong's Outings"—an ugly title and a transcendental style, but beautiful in conception, and taken off the stilts, in execution. I do not like the cant of Unitarians any better than they like ours, but I like what is elevating in any sect. I have had a present of a lot of table-linen, towels, etc., for Dorset, and feel a good deal like a young housekeeper. I wonder how soon you go back to Northampton? How queer it must be to be able to float round! It is a pity you could not float to New York, and get a good hugging from this old woman. We expect 250 ministers here in May at general assembly (I ought to have spelt it with a big G and a big A). My dear child, what makes you get blue? I do not much believe in any blue devils save those that live in the body and send sallies into the mind. Perhaps I should, though, if I had not a husband and children to look after how little one can judge for another!

* * * * *

II.

How she earned her Sleep. Writing for young Converts about speaking the Truth. Meeting of the General Assembly in the Church of the Covenant. Reunion. D.D.s and Strawberry Shortcake. "Enacting the Tiger." Getting ready for Dorset. Letters.

This year was one of the busiest of her life and it were hard to say which was busiest, her body or mind her hand, heart, or brain. This relentless activity was caused in part by the increasing difficulty of obtaining sleep. Incessant work seemed to be, in her case, a sort of substitute for natural rest and a solace for the loss of it. She alludes to this constant struggle with insomnia in a letter to Miss Warner, dated May 9th:

If you knew the whole story, you would not envy my power of driving about so much. You can lie down and sleep when you please I must earn my sleep by hard work, which uses up so much time that I wonder I ever accomplish anything. I believe that God arranges our various burdens and fits them to our backs, and that He sets off a loss against a gain, so that while some seem more favored than others, the mere aspect deceives. I have to make it my steady object throughout each day, so to spend time and strength as to obtain sleep enough to carry me through the next it is thus I have acquired the habit of taking a large amount of exercise, which keeps me out of doors when I am longing to be at work within. You say I seem to be always in a flood of joy well, that too is *seems*. I think I know what joy in God means, though perhaps I only begin to know but I am a weak creature I fall into snares and get entangled—not nearly so often as I used to do, but still do get into them. I have a perfect horror of them the thought of having anything come between God and my soul makes me so restless and uneasy that I hardly know which way to turn. I have been very much absorbed of late in various interests, and am sure they have contrived to occupy me too much pressing cares do sometimes, and oh, how ashamed I am!

Do write for young inquirers, if your heart prompts you to do it. I do not know what to think of your suggestion that in writing for young converts I should impress it upon them to speak the truth. It seems to me just like telling them not to commit murder and that would be absurd. Do Christians cheat and tell lies? I have a great aversion to writing about such things if children are not trained *at home* to be upright and full of integrity, it cannot be that books can rectify that loss. You may reply that home-training is defective in thousands of cases yes, that is true, but I have a feeling that truth and honesty must spring from a soil early prepared for them, and that a young person who is in the *habit* of falsehood is not a Christian and needs to go back to first principles. I cannot endure subterfuges, misrepresentation, and the like the whole foundation looks wrong when people indulge themselves in them, and to say to a Christian, "I hope you are truthful," is to my mind as if I should say to him, "I hope you wash your face and hands every day." Now if your observation says I am wrong, let us know I am open to conviction.

To Mrs. H. B. Smith, New York, May 24, 1869.

It has just come to me that the true way to enjoy writing and to have you enjoy hearing, is to keep a sort of journal, where little things will have a chance to speak for themselves.

We are now in the midst of General Assembly. Mr. Stearns is here, and we have sprinklings of ministers to dine and to tea at all sorts of odd hours.... I cannot help loving what is Christ like in people, whether I like their natural characters or not after all, what else is there in the world worth much love? My Katy seems to be ploughing her way with more or less success, and making friends and foes. You, who helped me fashion her, would be interested in the letters I get from wives, showing that the want of demonstration in men is a wide spread evil, under which women do groan being burdened. *Entre nous*, Mrs. Dr. —— is one, and I got a letter today from Michigan to the same effect. We are having delightful weather for the meetings. Yesterday morning Dr. John Hall preached in our church, and it was crammed full to Overflowing.... Lew. S. [3] has decided to study theology. We are all glad. He and I have been quite acquainted of late and talk most learnedly together. Did I tell you I have translated a German dramatic poem in five acts? Miss Anna Nevins says I have done it extremely well. I do not know about that, but my whole soul got into it somehow, and I did not know whether I was in the body or out of it for two or three weeks. I wish I could do things decently and in order. There is to be a great party at Apollo Hall this evening for both Assemblies. I am going and expect to get tired to death.

26th—It was a brilliant scene at Apollo Hall. Everybody was there, and the hall was finely adapted to the purpose of accommodating the 2,000 people present. The speeches were very poor. I went to the prayer meeting this morning. The church was full, galleries and all, and the spirit was excellent. Many men shed tears in speaking for reunion, and, from what Mr. Stearns reports of the meeting of the Committee last night, union may be considered as good as restored. You will hear nothing else from me it is all I hear talked about. *Monday, 31.*—Hot as need be. Dr. B., of Brooklyn, dined with us said he never ate strawberry shortcake before, and was reading Katy. It is awful to think how many D.D.s are doing it (eating shortcake, I mean, of course!) Hope the Assembly will wind up to-night. *June 5.*—We are so glad you have got to La Tour and find it so pleasant there, and that you have met Dr. and Mrs. Guthrie, and that they have met you instead of the blowsy-towsy American women, who make one so ashamed of them. If I was not going to Dorset, I should wish I were going where you are but then, you see, I *am* going to Dorset! I have been to the Central Park with Mrs. ——, who talked in one steady stream all the way. I was sleepy and the carriage very noisy and take it altogether, what a farce life is sometimes! the intercourse of human beings outsides touching outsides, the heart and soul lying to all intents and purposes as dead as a doornail. Do you ever feel mentally and spiritually alone in the world? Perhaps everybody does.

To Miss E. A. Warner, New York, June 4, 1869.

I concluded you had gone and died and got buried without letting me know, when your letter reached me *via* Dorset. What possessed you to send it there when you knew, you naughty thing! that I was having General Assembly, I cannot imagine but I suppose, being a Congregationalist, you thought General Assembly wasn't nothing, and that I could entertain squads of D.D.s for a fortnight more or less, just as well at Dorset as I could here. My dear, read the papers and go in the way you should go, and behave yourself! As if 250 ministers haven't worn streaks in the grass round the church, haven't (some of 'em) been here to dinner and eaten my strawberry short-cake and cottage puddings and praised my coffee and drank two cups apiece all round, and as if I hadn't been set up on end for those of 'em to look at who are reading Katy, and as if going furiously to work, after they'd all gone, didn't use me up and send me "lopping" down on sofas, sighing like a what's-its-name. Well, well the ignorance of you country folks and the wisdom of us city folks! We hope to get to Dorset by the 17th of this month it depends upon how many interruptions I have and how many days I have to lie by. I cannot imagine why I break down so, for I do not know when I've been so well as during this spring but Mr. P. and A. say I work like a tiger, and I s'pose I do without knowing it. I am so glad you had a pleasant Sunday. No doubt, you had more bodily strength with which to enjoy spiritual things. A weak body hinders prayer and praise when the heart would sing, if it were not in fetters that cramp and exhaust it.

Monday—Today I have been enacting the tiger again, and worked furiously. A. half scolds and half entreats, but I cannot help it if I work I work, and so there it is. I have bought a dinner-set, and had a long visit from my old Mary, who wept over and kissed me, and am going out to call on Mrs. Woolsey this evening. Tomorrow A.'s scholars are to come and make an address to her and give her a picture. She is not to know it until they arrive. It is really cold after the very hot weather, and some are freezing and some have internal pains. I wish you could have seen me this forenoon at work in the attic—a mass of dust, feathers, and perplexity. I got hold of one of my John's innumerable trunks of papers, and found among them the MSS. of several of my books laid up in lavender, which I pitched into the ash-barrel. I suppose he thinks I may distinguish myself some time, and that the discerning world will be after a scratch of my gifted pen! Have you read "Gates Off the Hinges"? The next thing will be, "There ain't no Gates."

* * * * *

III.

The new Home in Dorset. What it became to her. Letters from there.

A notable incident of this year was the entering upon housekeeping at Dorset under her own roof. As is usual in such cases, the process was somewhat wearisome and trying, but the result was most happy. All the bright anticipations, with which the event had been so long looked forward to, were more than realized. For the next ten summers, the Dorset home was to her a sweet haven of rest from the agitations, cares, and turmoil of New York life. It seemed at the time a venturesome, almost a rash thing, to build it but when she left it for her home above, the building of the house seemed to have been an inspiration of Providence. While contributing greatly to her happiness, it probably added several years to her life. The four months, which she passed each season at Dorset, were spent largely in the open air, and in such varied and pleasant exercise as exerted the most healthful, soothing influence upon both body and soul. It was just this fruit her husband hoped might, by the blessing of Heaven, blossom out of the new home, and in later years he used often to say to her, that if the place should be of a sudden annihilated, he should still feel that it had paid for itself many times over.

To Mrs. Smith, Dorset, July 19, 1869.

How many times during the last month I have been reminded of your saying you had lived through the agony of getting your house ready to rent. I can sum up all I have been through by saying that almost everything has turned out the reverse of what I expected. In the first place, I broke down just as we were to start to come here, and had to be left behind to pick up life enough to undertake the journey then the car we chartered did not get here for a week, and nobody but A. had anything to wear, and all my flowers died for want of water. The car, too, was broken into and my idols of tin pans all taken, with some other things, and when it did arrive it was unpacked, and our goods brought here, in a regular deluge, the like of which has not been seen since the days of Noah. For days, everything was in dire confusion but for all that, our own home was delightful, and we had the most outrageous appetites you ever heard of. George is in ecstasies with his house, his land, his pig, and his horse…. I hope you are not sick and tired of all this rigmarole it is not in human nature to move into a house of its own and talk of anything else. I got a warm-hearted letter a few days ago from the city of Milwaukee, from an unknown western sister, beginning, "Whom not having seen I love," and going on to say that Katy describes herself and her lot exactly, only she had no Martha on hand. I get so many such testimonies. I am going to spare your eyes and brains by winding up this epistle and going to bed. I do not think your husband ought to come home until he has recovered his power of sleeping. I know how to pity him, if anybody does, and I know how loss of sleep cripples. Goodnight, dear child.

"God bless me and my wife
You and your wife,
Us four
And no more."

To Mrs. Leonard, Dorset, August 3, 1869.

Your last letter endeared you to me more than ever, and I have longed to answer it, but we have been in such a state of confusion that writing has been a task. The whole house has been painted inside and out since we entered it, and I dare say you know what endless uproar the flitting from room to room to accommodate painters, causes. We have just been admitted to our parlor, but it is in no order, and the dining room is still piled with trunks. But the house is lovely, and we shall feel well repaid for the severe labor it has cost us, when it is done and we can settle down in it. I write to ask you to send me by express what numbers of Stepping Heavenward you have on hand. I would not give you the trouble to do this if I could get them in any other way, but I cannot, as all back numbers are gone, and the copy I have has been borrowed and worn, so as to be illegible in many places. Randolph is to publish the work and says he wants it soon. I am constantly receiving testimonies as to its usefulness, and hope it will do good to many who have not seen it in the Advance.

How I do long to see you! I think of you many times every day and thank God that He enables you to glorify Him in bearing your great sorrow. Sometimes I feel as if I *must* see Mr. L.'s kind face once more, but I remind myself that by patiently waiting a little while, I shall see it and the faces of all the sainted ones who have gone before. Next to faith in God comes patience I see that more and more, and few possess enough of either to enable them to meet the day of bereavement without dismay. We are constantly getting letters from afflicted souls that cannot see one ray of light, and keep reiterating, "I am not reconciled." How fearful it must be to kick thus against the pricks, already sharp enough! I believe fully with you that there is no happiness on earth, as there is none in heaven, to be compared with that of losing all things to possess Christ. I look back to two points in my life as standing out from all the rest of it as seasons of peculiar joy, and they are the points where I was crushed under the weight of sorrow. How wonderful this is, how incomprehensible to those who have not learned Christ! Do write me oftener you are very dear to me, and your letters always welcome. I love you for magnifying the Lord in the midst of your distress you could not get so into my heart in any other way.

To Mrs. Smith, Dorset, August 8, 1869.

Half of your chickens are safely here, well and bright, and settled I hope, for the summer. A., and M., who seems as joyous as a lark, are like Siamese twins, with the advantage of untying at night and sleeping in different beds. I have not been well, and did not go to church today but Prof. Robinson of Rochester, N. Y., preached a very superior sermon, George says. They have gone to our woods together. We took tea a few nights ago at the Pratts, being invited to meet him and Mrs. R. They asked many questions about you and your husband. We find the Pratts charming neighbors in their way, modest, kind, and good. They take the Advance, read Katy, and like it.

Aug. 21st—As we have only had sixteen in our family of late, I have not had much to do. Yesterday we made up a party to the quarry and had just been seated, twenty-nine in all, to eat a very nice dinner, when it began to rain in floods. Each grabbed his plate, if he could, and rushed to a blacksmith's shop not far off twenty or thirty workmen rushed there too, and there we were, cooped up in the dirt, to finish our meal as we best could. It soon stopped pouring and we had a delightful drive home. Mr. B. F. B., with two of his boys, was with us. He is charmed with our house and its views. Katy has made her last appearance in the Advance, but I keep getting letters about her from all quarters, and the editors say they have had hundreds. [4] H. has caught up with Hal and they are exactly of a height, and I feel as if I had a dear little pair of twins. Last Sunday evening the three boys laid their heads in my lap together, all alike content.

* * * * *

IV.

Return to Town. Domestic Changes. Letters. "My Heart sides with God in everything." Visiting among the Poor. "Conflict isn't Sin." Publication of *Stepping Heavenward*. Her Misgivings about it. How it was received. Reminiscences by Miss Eliza A. Warner. Letters. The Rev. Wheelock Craig.

Early in October, she returned to town and began to make ready for the departure of her eldest daughter to Europe, where she was to pass the next year with the family of Prof. Smith. The younger children had thus far been taught by their sister, and her leaving home was fraught with no little trial both to them and to the mother.

To Mrs. Smith, New York, October 12.

I can fully sympathize with the sad toss you are in about staying abroad another year, but we feel that there is no doubt you have decided wisely and well. But the bare mention of your settling down at Vevay has driven us all wild. What hallucination could you have been laboring under? Why, your husband would go off the handle in a week! To be sure it is beautiful for situation as Mount Zion itself, but one cannot live on beauty one must have life and action, and stimulus in other words, human beings. They are all horrid (except you), but we cannot do without 'em. What I went through at lonely Genevrier!

"Oh Solitude, where are the charms That sages have seen in thy face!"

We took it for granted that you would settle in some German city, near old friends it is true, they may not be all you want, but anything is better than nothing is, and you would stagnate and molder all away at Vevay. What is there there? Why, a lake and some mountains, and you cannot spend a year staring at them. Well, I dare say light will be let in upon you. I hope A. will behave herself you must rule it over her with a rod of iron (as if you could!), and make her stand round. Her going plunges us into a new world of care and anxiety and tribulation we have thrust our children out into, or on to, the great ocean, and are about ready to sink with them. If I could sit down and cry, it would do me lots of good, but I cannot. Then how am I to spare my twin-boy, and my A. and my M.? Who is to keep me well snubbed? Who is to tell me what to wear? Who is to keep Darby and Joan from settling down into two fearful old pokes?

Your husband suggests that "if I have a husband, etc." I have had one with a vengeance. He has worked like seventeen mad dogs all summer, and I have hardly laid eyes on him. When I have, it has been to fight with him he would come in with a hoe, a rake, or a spade in his hand, and find me with a broom, a shovel, or a pair of tongs in mine, and without a word, we would pitch in and have an encounter. Of all the aggravating creatures, hasn't he been aggravating! Sometimes I thought he had run raving distracted, and sometimes I dare say, he thought I had gone melancholy mad. He persists to this day that the work did him good, and that he enjoyed his summer. Well, maybe he did I suppose he knows.

How glad I am for you that you are to have the children go to you. It seems to be exactly the right thing. I hope to get a copy of Katy to send by the girls, but cannot think of anything else. As A. is to be where you are, you will probably be kept well posted in the doings of our family. I do hope she will not be a great addition to your cares, but have some misgivings as to the effect so long absence from home may have upon her. What a world this is for shiftings and siftings!

To G. S. P. October, 1869.

I always thought George McDonald a little audacious, though I like him in the main. There is a fallacy in this cavil, you may depend. Some years ago, when I was a little befogged by plausible talk, Dr. Skinner came to our house, got into one of his best moods, and preached a regular sermon on the glory of God, which set me all right again. I am not skilled in argument, but my heart sides with God in everything, and my conception of His character is such a beautiful one that I feel that He cannot err. I do not like the expression, "He's aye thinking about his own glory" (I quote from memory) it belittles the real fact, and almost puts the Supreme Being on a level with us poor mortals. The more time we spend upon our knees, in real communion with God, the better we shall comprehend His wonderful nature, and how impossible it is to submit that nature to the rules by which we judge human beings. Every turn in life brings me back to this—*more prayer*.... I shall go with much pleasure to see Mrs. G. and may God give me some good word to say to her. I almost envy you your sphere of usefulness, but unless I give up mine, cannot get fully into it. I want you to know that next to being with my Savior, I love to be with His sufferers so that you can be sure to remember me, when you have any on your heart.... P. S. I have hunted up Mrs. G. and had such an interesting talk with her that she has hardly been out of my mind since. It is a very unusual case, and the fact that her husband is a Jew, and loves her with such real romance, is an obstacle in her way to Christ. When you can get a little spare time I wish you would run in and let us talk her case over. I am ever so glad that I am growing old every day, and so becoming better fitted to be the dear and loving friend to young people I want to be.

I wish we both loved our Savior better, and could do more for Him. The days in which I do nothing specifically for Him seem such meager, such lost days. You seemed to think, the last time I saw you, that you were not so near Him as you were last year. I think we cannot always know our own state. It does not follow that a season of severe conflict is a sign of estrangement from God. Perhaps we are never dearer to Him than when we hate ourselves most, and fancy ourselves intolerable in His sight. *Conflict is not sin.*

To Miss E. A. Warner, New York, October 11, 1869.

I hear with great concern that Miss Lyman's health is so much worse, that she is about to leave Vassar. Is this true? I cannot say I should be very sorry if I should hear she was going to be called up higher. It seems such a blessed thing to finish up one's work when the Master says we may, and going to be with Him. I can fully sympathize with the feeling that made Mrs. Graham say, as she closed her daughter's eyes, "I wish you joy, my darling!" But I should want to see her before she went that would be next best to seeing her after she got back. If you meet with a dear little book called "The Melody of the 23rd Psalm," do read it, it is by Miss Anna Warner, and shows great knowledge of, and love for, the Bible. In a few weeks, I shall be able to send you a copy of Stepping Heavenward.

We have been home rather more than a week and the house is all upside down, outwardly and inwardly. For A. sails for Europe on the 21st with M. and Hal Smith, to be gone a year, and this involves sending the other children to school, and various trying changes of the sort. Tossing my long sheltered lambs into the world has cost me inexpressible pain only a mother can understand how much and why and they, on their part, go into it shrinking and quivering in every nerve. To their father, as well as to me, this has been a time of sore trial, and we are doing our best to keep each other up amid the discouragements and temptations that confront us. For each new phase of life brings more or less of both.

Stepping Heavenward was published toward the end of October, having appeared already as a serial in the Chicago Advance. The first number of the serial was printed February 4, 1869. The work was planned and the larger part of it composed during the winter and spring of 1867-8. Referring more especially to this part of it, she once said to a friend, "Every word of that book was a prayer, and seemed to come of itself. I never knew how it was written, for my heart and hands were full of something else." By "something else" she had in mind the care of little Francis. The ensuing summer the manuscript was taken with her to Dorset, carefully revised and finished before her return to the city. In revising it, she had the advantage of suggestions made by her friends, Miss Warner and Miss Lyman, both of them Christian ladies of the best culture and of rare good sense.

Notwithstanding the favor with which the work had been received as issued in The Advance, Mrs. Prentiss had great misgiving about its success—a misgiving that had haunted her while engaged in writing it. But all doubt on the subject was soon dispelled:

The response to "Stepping Heavenward" was instant and general. Others of her books were enjoyed, praised, laughed over, but this one was taken by tired hands into secret places, pored over by eyes dim with tears, and its lessons prayed out at many a Jabbok. It was one of those books, which sorrowing, Mary-like women read to each other, and which lured many a bustling Martha from the fretting of her care-cumbered life to ponder the new lesson of rest in toil. It was one of those books of which people kept a lending copy, that they might enjoy the uninterrupted companionship of their own. The circulation of the book was very large. Not to speak of the thousands, which were sold here, it went through numerous editions in England. From England, it passed into Australia. It fell into the family of an afflicted Swiss pastor, and the comfort, which it brought to that stricken household, led to its translation into French by one of the pastor's daughters. It passed through I know not how many editions in French. [5] In Germany, it came into the hands of an invalid lady who begged the privilege of translating it. The first word of a favorite German hymn,

"Heavenward doth our journey tend We are strangers here on earth,"

furnished the title for the German translation—"Himmelan." It appeared just after the French war, and went as a comforter into scores of the homes which war had desolated, and frequent testimony came back to her of the deep interest excited by the book, and of the affectionate gratitude called out toward the author. She seemed to have inspired her translator, whose letters to her breathe the warmest affection and the most enthusiastic admiration. It would be easy to fill up the time that remains with grateful testimonies to the work of this book. From among a multitude I select only one: A manufacturer in a New England town, a stranger, wrote to her expressing his high appreciation of the book, and saying that he had four thousand persons in his employ, and a circulating library of six thousand volumes for their use, in which were two copies of "Stepping Heavenward." He adds, "I hear in every direction of the good it is doing, and a wealthy friend has written to me saying that she means to put a copy into the hand of every bride of her acquaintance." [6]

Several chapters might be filled with letters received by Mrs. Prentiss, expressing the gratitude of the writers for the spiritual help and comfort *Stepping Heavenward* had given them. These letters came from all parts of this country, from Europe, and even from the ends of the earth and they were written by persons belonging to every class in society. Among them was one, written on coarse brown grocery paper, from a poor crippled boy in the interior of Pennsylvania, which she especially prized. It led to a friendly correspondence that continued for several years. The book was read with equal delight by persons not only of all classes, but of all creeds also by Calvinists, Arminians, High Churchmen, Evangelicals, Unitarians, and Roman Catholics. [7] It was, however, wholly unnoticed by most of the organs of literary opinion in this country although abroad it attracted at once the attention of men and women well known in the world of letters, and was praised by them in the highest terms. [8]

Miss Eliza A. Warner, in the following Reminiscences, gives some interesting incidents in reference to *Stepping Heavenward*.

That summer in Dorset—the summer of 1868—is one full of bright and pleasant memories, which it is delightful to recall. I had heard much of Mrs. Prentiss from mutual friends, and been exceedingly interested in her books, so that when I found we were to be fellow-boarders for the summer I was greatly pleased yet I felt a little shy at meeting one of whose superiority in many lines I had heard so much.

How well I remember that bright morning in July on which we first met on our way to the breakfast-table! I can hear now the frank, cheery voice with which she greeted me, and see her large dark eyes, so full of animation and kindly interest, which a moment after sparkled with fun as she recalled an old joke familiar to my friends, and, it seemed, to her also. I was put at my ease at once, and from that moment onward felt the wonderful fascination of a manner so peculiarly her own it was a frank, whole-souled, sincere manner, with a certain indescribable piquancy and sprightliness blending with the earnestness which made her very individual and very charming.

For the next two months, we were a good deal together. I think it was a very happy summer to her. You were building the house in Dorset for a summer home, and the planning for this and watching its progress was a pleasant occupation. And she was such an enthusiastic lover of nature that the out-of-door life she led was a constant enjoyment. She would spend hours rambling in the woods, collecting ferns, mosses, trailing vines, and every lovely bit of blossom and greenery that met her eye—and nothing pretty escaped it—and there was always an added freshness and brightness in her face when she came home laden with these treasures, and eager to exhibit them. "Oh, you do not go crazy over such things as I do," she would say as she held them up for our admiration. She filled her room with these woodland beauties, and pressed quantities of them to carry to her city home.

In that beautiful valley among the Green Mountains, some of whose near summits rise to the height of three thousand feet, her enthusiasm for fine scenery had full scope. She would watch with delight the sunset glow as it spread and deepened along those mountain peaks, suffusing them with a glory, which we likened to that of the New Jerusalem and as we sat and watched this glory slowly fade, tint by tint, into the gray twilight, her talk, would be of heaven, holiness, and Christ.

Whatever she felt, she felt intensely, and she threw her whole heart and soul into all she said or did this was one great secret of the power of her personal presence she felt so keenly herself, she made others feel.

Those summer days were long, bright, and beautiful, but none too long for her. She was one of the most industrious persons I have ever known, and her writing, reading and sewing, and the care of her children, over the formation of whose characters she watched closely and wisely, occupied every moment of her time, except when she was out of doors, trying by exercise in the open air to secure a good night's sleep not an easy thing for her to do in those days.

Early in August, we were joined by Miss Hannah Lyman, of Vassar College, a mutual friend and a most delightful addition to our little party.

We knew Mrs. Prentiss spent a part of every day in writing, but she said nothing of the nature of her work. Do you remember coming into the parlor one morning, where Miss Lyman and I were sitting by ourselves, and telling us that she was writing a story, but had become so discouraged she threatened to throw it aside as not worth finishing? "I like it myself," you added, "it really seems to me one of the best things she has ever written, and I am trying to get her to read it to you and see what you think of it."

Of course, both Miss Lyman and I were eager to hear it, and promised to tell her frankly, how we liked it. The next morning she came to our room with a little green box in her hand, saying, with her merry laugh, "Now you've got to do penance for your sins, you two wicked women!" and, sitting down by the window, while we took our sewing, she began to read us in manuscript the work which was destined to touch and strengthen so many hearts—"which," to use the words of another, "has become a part of the soul-history of many thousands of Christian women—young and old—at home and abroad."

It was a rare treat to listen to it, with comments from her interspersed some of them droll and witty, others full of profound religious feeling. Now and then, as we queried if something was not improbable or unnatural, she would give us bits of history from her own experience or that of her friends, going to show that stranger things had occurred in real life. I need not say we insisted on its being finished, feeling sure it would do great good though I must confess that I do not think either of us, much as we enjoyed it, was fully aware of its great merits.

I was much impressed by her singleness of purpose her one great desire so evidently being that her writings should help others to know and to love Christ and His truth, that she thought little or nothing of her own reputation.

She went on with her work, occasionally reading to us what she had added. In those days she always spoke of it as her "Katy book," no other title having been given to it. But one morning she came to the breakfast-table with her face all lighted up. "I've got a name for my book," she exclaimed, "it came to me while I was lying awake last night. You know Wordsworth's Stepping Westward? I am going to call it Stepping Heavenward—do not you like it? I do." We all felt it was exactly the right name, and she added, "I think I will put in Wordsworth's poem as a preface."

Of the heart communing on sacred things that made that summer so memorable to me I cannot speak and yet, more than anything else, these gave a distinctive character to our intercourse. Her faith and love were so ardent and persuading, so much a part of herself, that no one could be with her without recognizing their power over her life. She was interested in everything about her, without a particle of cant, full of playful humor and bright fancies but the love of Christ was the absorbing interest of her life—almost a passion, it might be called, so fervent and rapturous was her devotion to Him, so great her longing for communion with Him and for a more complete conformity to His perfect will.

As I have said, all her emotions were intense and her religious affections had the same warmth and glow. Believing in Christ was to her not so much a duty as the deepest joy of her life, heightening all other joys, and she was not satisfied until her friends shared with her in this experience. She believed it to be attainable by all, founded on a complete submitting of the human to the Divine will in all things, great and small.

Truly, of her it might be said, if of any human being, "*she hath loved much.*"

To Mrs. Smith, New York, Nov. 16, 1869.

Your arrangements at Heidelberg seem to me to be as delightful as anything can be in a world where nothing is ideal. Be sure to let A. bear her full share of the expense, and be a mother to her if you can. The gayest outside life has an undertone of sadness, and I do not doubt she will have hours of unrest which she will hardly know how to account for. I am afraid Heidelberg will be rather narrow bounds for your husband, and hope he may decide to go to Egypt in case his ear gets quite well. How fortunate that he is near a really good aurist. I am always nervous about ear-troubles. Fancy your having to shout your love to him! In a letter written about two weeks ago, Miss Lyman says, "How am I? Longing for a corner in which to stop trying to live, and lie down and die," and adds that she is now too feeble to travel. I suppose she is liable to break down at any moment, but I do hope she will not be left to go abroad. I judge from what you say of Mr. H. that he is slipping off. I always look at people who are going to heaven with a sort of curiosity and envy it is next best to seeing one who has just come thence. Get all the good out of him you can there is none too much saintliness on earth. I wonder how you spend your time? Do, some time, write the history of one day what you said to that funny cook, and what she said to you what you thought and what you did and what you didn't think and didn't did.

Friday, 19th.—Thanksgiving has come and gone beautifully. It was a perfect day as to weather. Our congregation joined Dr. Murray's, and he gave us an excellent sermon. The four Stearnses came in to dinner and seemed to enjoy it. I suppose you all celebrated the day in Yankee fashion and got up those abominations—mince pies. When I told L. about ——'s fourth marriage, he said it reminded him of a place he had seen, where a man lay buried in the midst of a lot of women, the sole inscription on his gravestone being "Our Husband." Mrs. —— says the tiffs between my Katy and her husband are exactly like those she had with hers, and Mrs. —— said very much the same thing—after hearing which, I gave up.

Tell A. I had a call yesterday from Mrs. S——, who came to town to spend Thanksgiving at her father's, and fell upon my neck and ate me up three several times. I tell you what it is, it is nice to have people love you, whether you deserve it or not, and this warm-hearted, enthusiastic creature really did me good. Dr. Skinner sent us an extraordinary book to read called "God's Furnace." There is a good deal of egotism in it and self-consciousness, and a good deal of genuine Christian experience. I read it through four times, and, when I carried it back and was discussing it with him, he said he had too. It seems almost incredible that a wholly sanctified character could publish such a book, made up as it is of the author's own letters and journal and most sacred joys and sorrows but perhaps when I get sanctified I shall go to printing mine—it really seems to be a way they have. The Hitchcock's sailed yesterday, and it must have cheered them to set forth on so very fine a day. Give my love to everybody straight through from Hal up to your husband and Mr. H.

Later.—Of course, my letters to A. are virtually to you, too, as far as you can be interested in the little details of which they are made up. Randolph showed George a letter about Katy, which he says beats anything we have heard yet, which is saying a good deal. One lady said Earnest was *exactly* like her husband, another that he was *painfully* so indeed, many sore hearts are making such confessions. So I begin to think there is even more sorrowfulness and unrest in the world than I thought there was. You would get sick unto death of the book if I should tell a quarter of what we hear about it, good and bad. It quite refreshed me to hear that a young lady wanted to punch me.

Craig's Life is very touching. His delight in Christ and in close fellowship with Him is beautiful but it is painful to see that dying man wandering about Europe alone, when he ought to have been breathing out his life in the arms he loved so well. How did poor Mrs. C. live through the week of suspense that followed the telegram announcing his illness? For one must love such a man very deeply, I think. Well, he does not care now where he died or when, and he has gone where he belonged. I miss you all ever so much, and George keeps up one constant howl for your husband. It is a mystery to me what any of you find in my letters, they do seem so flat to me. What fun it would be if you would *all* write me a round letter! I would write a rouser for it. Lots of love.

The Rev. Wheelock Craig, whose Life is referred to by Mrs. Prentiss in the preceding letter, was her husband's successor in the pastorate of the South Trinitarian church, New Bedford. [9]

* * * * *

V.

Recollections by Mrs. Henry B. Smith.
The following Recollections from the pen of Mrs. Smith may fitly close the present chapter:

NORTHAMPTON, *January 2, 1879.*
MY DEAR DR. PRENTISS:—I have been trying this beautiful snowy day, which shuts us in to our own thoughts, to recall some of my impressions of your dear wife, but I find it very difficult there was such variety to her, and so much of her, and the things, which were most characteristic, are so hard to be described.

I read "Stepping Heavenward" in MS. before we went to Europe in 1869. I remember she used to say that I was "Katy's Aunt," because we talked her over with so much interest. She sent me a copy to Heidelberg, where I began at once translating it into German as my regular exercise. I was delighted to give my copy to Mrs. Prof. K. in Leipzig, as *the* American story, which I was willing to have her translate into German, as she had asked for one. There is no need of telling you about the enthusiasm which the book created. Women everywhere said, "It seems to be myself that I am reading about" and the feeling that they, too, with all their imperfections, might be really stepping heavenward, was one great secret of its inspiration. One little incident may interest you. My niece, Mrs. Prof. Emerson, was driving alone toward Amherst, and took into her carriage a poor colored woman who was walking the same way. The woman soon said, "I have been thinking a good deal of you, Mrs. E., and of your little children, and I have been reading a book which I thought you would like. It was something about walking towards heaven." "Was it 'Stepping Heavenward'?" "Yes, that was it."

How naturally, modestly, almost indifferently, she received the tributes, which poured in upon her! Yet, though she cared little for praise, she cared much for love, and for the consciousness that she was a helper and comforter to others.

On reading the book again this last summer, I was struck by seeing how true a transcript of herself, in more than one respect, was given in Katy. "Why cannot I make a jacket for my baby without throwing into it the ardor of a soldier going into battle?" How ardently she threw herself into everything she did! In friendship, love, and religion this outpouring of herself was most striking.

Her earlier books she always read or submitted to me in manuscript, and she showed so little self-interest in them, and I so much, that they seemed a sort of common property. I think that I had quite as much pleasure in their success and far more pride, than herself. The Susy books I always considered quite as superior in their way as Stepping Heavenward. They are still peerless among books for little children. "Henry and Bessie," too, contains some of the most beautiful religious teaching ever written. "Fred and Maria and Me" she used to talk about almost as if I had written it, for no other reason than that I liked it so much.

My sister says that her daughter Nettie read "Little Susy" through *twelve times*, getting up to read it before breakfast. She printed (before she could write) a little letter of thanks to your wife, who sent her the following pretty note in reply: NEW YORK, *January 10, 1854.*

MY DEAR "NETTIE":—What a nice little letter you wrote me! It pleased me very much. I shall keep it in my desk, and when I am an old woman, I shall buy a pair of spectacles, sit down in the chimney corner, and read it. When you learn to write with your own little fingers, I hope you will write me another letter.

Your friend, with love, AUNT SUSAN.

She did nothing for effect, and made little or no effort merely to please her was almost too careless of the impression, which she made upon others, and, on this account, strangers sometimes, thought her cold and unsympathetic. But touch her at the right point and the right moment, and there was no measure to her interest and warmth. She hated all pretense and display, and the slightest symptom of them in others shut her up and kept her grave and silent, and this, not from a severe or Pharisaic spirit, but because the atmosphere was so foreign to her that she could not live in it. "I pity people that have any *sham* about them when I am by," she said one day. "I am dreadfully afraid of young ladies," she said at another time. She could not adapt herself to the artificial and conventional. Yet with young ladies who loved what she loved, she was peculiarly free and playful and *forth giving* and such were among her dearest and most lovingly admiring friends.

When we met, there were no preliminaries she plunged at once into the subject which was interesting her, the book, the person, the case of sickness or trouble, the plan, the last shopping, the game, the garment, the new preparation for the table—in a way peculiarly her own. One could never be with her many minutes without hearing some bright fancy, some quick stroke of repartee, some ludicrous way of putting a thing. But whether she told of the grumbler who could find nothing to complain of in heaven except that "his halo didn't fit," or said in her quick way, when the plainness of a lady's dress was commended, "Why, I didn't suppose that anybody could go *to heaven* now-a-days without an overskirt," or wrote her sparkling impromptu rhymes for our children's games, her mirth was all in harmony with her earnest life. Her quick perceptions, her droll comparisons, her readiness of expression, united with her rare and tender sympathies, made her the most fascinating of companions to both young and old. Our little Saturday tear, with our children, while our husbands were at Chi Alpha, were rare times. My children enjoyed "Aunt Lizzy" almost as much as I did. She was usually in her best mood at these times. When you and Henry came in, on your return from Chi Alpha, you looked in upon, or, rather, you completed a happier circle than this impoverished earth can ever show us again.

Her acquisitions were so rapid, and she made so little show of them, that one might have doubted their thoroughness, which had no occasion to test them. Her beautiful translation of Griselda was a surprise to many. I remember her eager enthusiasm while translating it. The writing of her books was almost an inspiration, so rapid, without copying, almost without alteration, running on in her clear, pure style, with here and there a radiant sparkle above the full depths.

It sometimes seemed as if she were interested only in those whom she knew she could benefit. If so, it was from her ever-present consciousness of a consecrated life. She constantly sought for ways of showing her love to Christ, especially to His sick and suffering and sorrowing ones. Life with her was peculiarly intense and earnest she looked upon it more as a discipline and a hard path, and yet no one had a quicker or more admiring eye for the flowers by the wayside. I always thought that her great *forte* was the study of character. She lay bare and dissected everybody, even her nearest friends and herself, to find what was in them and what she found, reproduced in her books, was what gave them their peculiar charm of reality. The growth of the religious life in the heart was the one most interesting subject to her.

I never could fully understand the deep sadness, which was the groundwork of her nature. It certainly did not prevent the most intense enjoyment of her rich temporal and spiritual blessings, while it indicated depths, which her friends did not fathom. It was partly constitutional, doubtless, and partly, I suppose, from her keener sensitiveness, her larger grasp, her stronger convictions, her more vivid vision, and more ardent desires. Even the glowing, almost seraphic love of Christ, which was the chief characteristic of her later life, was, in her words, "but longing and seeking." She was an exile yearning for her home, "stepping heavenward," and knowing better than the rest of us what it meant.

These things come to me now, and yet how much I have omitted—her industry so varied and untiring, her generosity (so many gifts of former days are around me now), her interest in my children, her delight in flowers and colors and all beautiful things, her ready sympathy—but it is an almost inexhaustible subject. She comes vividly before me now, seated on the floor in her room, with her work around her, making something for such and such a person. What the void in your life must be those who knew most of her manifold, exalted, inspiring life can but imagine.

"Nay, Hope may whisper with the dead
By bending forward where they are
But Memory, with a backward tread,
Communes with them afar!

"The joys we lose are but forecast,
And we shall find them all once more
We look behind us for the past,
But, lo! 'tis all before!"

[1] See *Memoir of S. S. Prentiss*, edited by his Brother, and published by Charles Scribner's Sons. New Edition. 1879.

[2] The following is part of the notice in the London Daily News:

"We are, unfortunately, ignorant of *Little Suzy's Six Birthdays*, but if that book be anything like as good as the charming volume before us by the same author, ycleped *Little Lou's Sayings and Doings*, it deserves an extraordinary popularity.... *Little Lou.* is one of the most natural stories in the world, and reads more like a mother's record of her child's sayings and doings than like a fictitious narrative. Little Lou, be it remarked, is a true baby throughout, instead of being a precocious little prig, as so many good children are in print. The child's love for his mother and his mother's love for him is described in the prettiest way possible."

[3] Now Professor of Theology at Bangor.

[4] The following is an extract from a letter of one of the editors of The Advance, Mr. J. B. T. Marsh, dated Chicago, August 10,1869:—"You will notice that the story is completed this week I wish it could have continued six months longer. I have several times been on the point of writing you to express my own personal satisfaction—and more than satisfaction—in reading it, and to acquaint you with the great unanimity and *volume* of praise of it, which has reached us from our readers. I do not think anything since the National Era and 'Uncle Tom's Cabin' times has been more heartily received by newspaper readers. I am sure it will have a great sale if rightly brought before the public. A publisher from London was in our office the other day, signifying a desire to make some arrangement to bring it out there. I have heard almost no unfavorable criticism of the story—nothing which you could make serviceable in its revision. I have heard Dr. P. criticize Ernest—of course the character and not your portrayal. For myself I consider the character a natural and consistent one. Perhaps few men are found who are quite so blind to a wife's wants and yet so devoted, but—I do not know what the wives might say. We have had hundreds of letters of which the expression has been, 'We quarrel to see who shall have the first reading of the story.' I congratulate you most heartily upon its great success and the great good it has done and will yet do. I think if you should ever come West my wife would overturn almost any stone for the sake of welcoming you to the hospitality of our cottage on the Lake Michigan shore."

[5] *Marchant vers le Ciel* is the title of the French translation.

[6] *Memorial discourse* by the Rev. Marvin R. Vincent, D.D.

[7] The following is an extract from a letter, dated New Orleans, and written after Mrs. Prentiss' death:

"We called one day to see a poor dressmaker who was dying of consumption. She was an educated woman, a devout Roman Catholic, and a person whom we had long respected and esteemed for her integrity, her love of independence, and her extraordinary powers of endurance. Her husband, a prosperous merchant, had died suddenly, and his affairs being mismanaged, she was obliged, although a constant invalid, to earn a support for many years by the most unremitting labor. We found her reading 'Stepping Heavenward,' which she spoke of in the warmest terms. We told her about the authoress, of her suffering from ill health, and of her recent death. She listened eagerly and asked questions, which showed the deepest interest in the subject. Soon after she left the city, and a few weeks later we heard of her death."

[8] One of them—said to have been an eminent German theologian—used this strong language respecting it: "Schon manche gute, edle, segensreiche Gabe ist uns aus Nordamerika gekommen, aber wir stehen nicht au, diese als die beste zu bezeichnen unter allen, die uns von dort zu Gesichte gekommen."

[9] See A Memorial of the Character, Work, and Closing Days of Rev. Wheelock Craig, New Bedford.

Mr. Craig was born in Augusta, Maine, July 11, 1824. He entered Bowdoin College in 1839, and was graduated with honor in the class of 1843. He then entered the Theological Seminary at Bangor, where he graduated in 1847. After preaching a couple of years at New Castle, Me., he accepted a call to New Bedford, and was installed there December 4, 1850. In 1859, he received a call to the chair of Modern Languages in Bowdoin College, which he declined. After an earnest and faithful ministry of more than seventeen years, he went abroad for his health in May, 1868. He visited Ireland, England, Scotland, and then passing over to the Continent, travelled through Belgium, Holland, Switzerland, and so southward as far as Naples, where he arrived the last of September. Here he was taken seriously ill and advised to hasten back to Switzerland. In great weakness, he passed through Rome, Florence, Turin, Geneva, and reached Neuchatel on the 4th of November in a state of utter exhaustion. There, encompassed by newly made friends and tenderly cared for, he gently breathed his last on the 28th of November. Two names, in particular, deserve to be gratefully mentioned in connection with Mr. Craig's last hours, viz.: that of his countryman, Mr. W. C. Cabot, and that of the Rev. Dr. Godet, of Neuchatel. Of the former he said the day before his death: "He saw me coming from Geneva a perfect stranger—lying sick, helpless, wretched, and miserable in the ears—and spoke to me, inquired who I was, and took care of me. Anybody else would have gone by on the other side. He brought me to this hotel, and remained with me, and did everything for me and, fearing that I might be ill some time, and uneasy about money matters, he sent me a letter of credit for two hundred pounds. Such noble and generous conduct to an entire stranger was never heard of." To Dr. Godet he had a letter from Prof. Henry B. Smith, of New York. But he needed no other introduction to that warm-hearted and eminent servant of God than his sad condition and his love to Christ. "From the first quarter of an hour," wrote Dr. Godet to Mrs. Craig, "we were like two brothers who had known each other from infancy. He knew not a great deal of French, and I not more of English but the Lord was between him and me." "Prof. Godet and family are like the very angels of God," wrote Mr. Craig to his wife. His last days were filled with inexpressible joy in his God and Savior. Shortly before his departure, he said to Dr. Godet and the other friends who were by his bedside, *There shall be no night there, but the Lamb which is in the midst of the throne shall be their light.*"

Mr. Craig had a highly poetical nature, refined spiritual sensibilities, and a soul glowing with love to his Master. He was also a vigorous and original thinker. Some passages in his letters and journal are as racy and striking as anything in John Newton or Cecil. Mrs. Prentiss greatly enjoyed reading them to her friends. Some of them she copied and had published in the Association Monthly.

CHAPTER 10 - ON THE MOUNT - 1870.

I.

A happy Year. Madame Guyon. What sweetens the Cup of earthly Trials and the Cup of earthly Joy. Death of Mrs. Julia B. Cady. Her Usefulness. Sickness and Death of other Friends. "My Cup runneth over." Letters. "More Love to Thee, O Christ."

In every earnest life there usually comes a time when it reaches its highest point, whether of power or of enjoyment a time when it is in —the bright, consummate flower.

The year 1870 formed such a period in the life of Mrs. Prentiss. None that went before, or that followed after, equaled it, as a whole, in rich, varied, and happy experiences. It was full of the genial, loving spirit, which inspired the Little Susy books and Stepping Heavenward full, too, of the playful humor, which runs through Fred and Maria and Me, and full, also, of the intense, overflowing delight in her God and Savior that breathes in the Golden Hours. From its opening to its close she was—to borrow an expression from her Richmond journal—"one great long sunbeam." Everywhere, in her home, with her friends, by sick and dying beds, in the house of mourning, in the crowded street or among her flowers at Dorset, she seemed to be attired with constant brightness. Of course, there were not wanting hours of sadness and heart-sinking nor was her consciousness of sin or her longing to be freed from it, perhaps, ever keener and more profound but still the main current of her existence flowed on, untroubled, to the music of its own loving, grateful and adoring thoughts. Often she would say that God was too good to her that she was *satisfied* and had nothing more to ask of life her cup of domestic bliss ran over and as to her religious joy, it was at times too much for her frail body, and she begged that it might be transferred to other souls. Her letters give a vivid picture of her state of mind during this memorable year and yet only a picture. The sweet reality was beyond the power of words.

In the early part of this year, the correspondence of Madame Guyon and Fenelon fell into her hands, and was eagerly read by her. The perusal of this correspondence led, somewhat later, to a careful study of the Select Works, Autobiography, and Spiritual Letters of Madame Guyon, thus forming an important incident in her religious history. Heretofore she had known Madame Guyon chiefly through the Life by Prof. Upham and the little treatise entitled A Short and very Easy Method of Prayer and both seem rather to have repelled her. In 1867, she wrote to a friend:

There is a book I would be glad to have you read, and which I think you would wish to own 'Thoughts on Personal Religion,' by Goulburn. I never read a modern religious book that had in it so much, that really edified me. I take for granted you have Thomas à Kempis on that and on Fenelon I have feasted for years every day I like strengthening food and whatever deals a blow at this monster Self. Madame Guyon I do not understand.

But now she began to feel, as so many earnest seekers after holiness had felt before her, the strong attraction of this remarkable woman. While never becoming to her what Fenelon was, Madame Guyon for several years exerted a decided influence upon her views of the Christian life, nor is there reason to think that this influence was not, on the whole, salutary. Notwithstanding her grave errors and the extravagances that marred her career, Madame Guyon was no doubt one of the holiest, as she was certainly one of the most gifted, women of her own, or any other age. [1]

To Mrs. J Elliot Condict, New York, Jan. 2, 1870.

It has been a real disappointment not to see you. How quickly we learn to lean on earthly things! I am afraid I prize Christian fellowship too much, and that I am behaving in a miserly way about all divine gifts, shutting myself up here in this room, which often seems like the gate of heaven, and luxuriating in it, instead of going about preaching the glad tidings to other souls. Yet work for Christ, when He gives it, is sweet, too, and if answering your note is the little tiny bit, He offers me at this moment, how glad I am. Though I am not, just now, in the furnace as you are, there is no knowing how soon I shall be, and I remember well enough how the furnace feels, to have deep sympathy with you in your trials. Sympathy, but not regret I cannot make myself be very sorry for Christ's disciples when He takes them in hand—He does it so tenderly, so wisely, so lovingly and it can hardly be true, can it? that He is just as near and dear to me when my cup is as full of earthly blessings as it can hold, as He is to you whose cup He is emptying?

I have always thought they knew and loved Him best who knew Him in His character of Chastiser but perhaps one never loses the memory of His revelations of Himself in that form, and perhaps that tender memory saddens and hallows the day of prosperity. At any rate, you and I seem to be in full sympathy with each other your empty cup is not empty, and my full one would be bitter if love to Christ did not sweeten it. It matters very little on what paths we are walking, since we find Him in every one. How ashamed we shall be when we get to heaven, of our talk about our trials here! Why do not we sing songs instead? We know how, for He has put the songs into our mouths. I think I know something about the land of Beulah, but I do not quite *live* in it yet and yet what is this joy if it is not beatitude, if it is not a foretaste of that which is to come? It is not joy in what He has done for me, a sinner, but adoring joy for what He is, though I do not *begin to know* what He is. It will take an eternity to learn that lesson.

Do you really mean to say that Miss K. is going to pray for *me*? How delightful! I am *greedy* for prayer nobody is rich enough to give me anything I so long for indeed when my husband begged me to tell him what I wanted at Christmas, I couldn't think of a thing but oh, what unutterable longing I have for more of Christ. Why should we not speak freely to each other of Him? Do not apologize for it again. The wonder is that we have the heart to speak of anything else. Sometimes I am almost frightened at the expressions of love I pour out upon Him, and wonder if I am really in earnest if I really mean all I say. Is it even so with you? It is not foolish, is it? Perhaps He likes to hear our poor stammerings, when we cannot get our emotions and our thoughts into words.

To Miss E. A. Warner, New York, Jan. 7, 1870.

I find letters more and more unsatisfactory. How little I know of your real life, how little you know of mine! So much is going on all the time that I should run and tell you about if you lived here, but which it would take too long to write. I have very precious Christian friends within six months, who take, or rather to whom I give, more time than I could or would spare for any ordinary friendship one of them has spent four hours in my room with me at a time, and we had wonderful communings together. Then two dear friends have died. One of the two, of whom you have heard me speak, was the most useful woman in our church my husband and I both wept over her death. The other directed in dying that a copy of Stepping Heavenward should be given to each of her Sunday scholars a lifelong fear of death was taken away, and she declared it pleasanter and easier to die than to live her last words, five minutes before she drew her last gentle breath, came with the upward, dying look, "Wonderful love!"

You cannot think how sweet it is to be a pastor's wife to feel the *right* to sympathize with those who mourn, to fly to them at once, and join them in their prayers and tears. It would be pleasant to spend one's whole time among sufferers and to keep testifying to them what Christ can and will become to them, if they will only let Him.... No, I never "Dialed" or was transcendental. I do not think knowledge will come to us by intuition in heaven, though knowledge enough to get started there will. But I do not much care how it will be. I know we shall learn Christ there. I have read lately Prof. Phelps on the Solitude of Christ it is a suggestive little book, which I like much. Have you ever read the Life of Mrs. Hawkes? It is interesting because she records so many of Cecil's wonderful remarks—such, e.g., as these: "a humble, kind silence often utters much." "Tomorrow you and I shall walk together in a garden, when I hope to talk with you about everything but sadness." I am going to ask a favor of you, though I hate to put you to the trouble. In writing a telegram in great haste and sorrow, I accidentally used and cut into the lines you copied for me—Sabbath hymn in sickness. It was a real loss, and if you ever feel a little stronger than usual, will you make me another copy? I so often want to comfort sick persons with it.

I have half promised to write a serial for a magazine, the organ of the Young Men's Christian Association, though I know nothing of young men and hate to write serials. I wish I could hide in some hole. I get bright letters from A., who is having a very nice time. I write her every day wretched letters, which she thinks delightful, fortunately. We have a quiet time this winter, but such nice things cannot last, and I am afraid of this world anyhow. I know you pray for me, as I do for you and Miss L. every day. I have a thousand things to say that I shall have to put off until I see you. Goodbye, dearie.

To Mrs. Condict, Sunday, March 6, 1870.

I have had some really sweet days, shut up with my dear little boy. He is better, and I am comparatively at leisure again, and so happy in meditating on the character of my Savior, and in the sense of His nearness, that I *ache*, and have had to beg Him to give me no more, but to carry this joy to you and to Miss K. and to two friends, who, languishing on dying beds, need it so much. [2] If I could shed tears I should not have to tell you this, and indeed it is nothing new but one must have vent in some way. And this reminds me to explain to you why to three dear Christian friends I now and then send verses they are my tears of joy or sorrow, and when I feel most deeply it is a relief to versify, and a pleasure to open my heart to those who feel as I do. I have been in print ever since I was sixteen years old, and admiration is an old story I care very little for it but I do crave and value sympathy with those who love Christ. And it is such a new thing to open my heart thus! I have written any number of verses that no human being has ever seen, because they came from the very bottom of my heart.

I wish I could put into words all the blessed thoughts I had last week about God's dear will: it was a week of such sweet content with the work He gave me to do naturally I hate nursing, and losing the air makes me feel unwell but what cannot God do with us? I love, dearly, to have a *Master*. I fancy that those who have strong wills are the ones to enjoy God's sovereignty most. I wonder if you realize what a very happy creature I am? and how much *too good* God is to me? I do not see how He can heap such mercies on a poor sinner but that only shows how little I know Him. But then, I am learning to know Him, and shall go on doing it forever and ever and so will you. I am not sure that it is best for us, once safe and secure on the Rock of Ages, to ask ourselves too closely what this and that experience may signify. Is it not better to be thinking of the Rock, not of the feet that stand upon it? It seems to me that we ought to be unconscious of ourselves, and that the nearer we get to Christ, the more we shall be taken up with Him. We shall be like a sick man who, after he gets well, forgets all the old symptoms he used to think so much of, and stops feeling his pulse, and just enjoys his health, only pointing out his *physician* to all who are diseased. You will see that this is in answer to a portion of your letter, in which you say Miss K. interprets to you certain experiences. If I am wrong, I am willing to be set right perhaps I have not said clearly what I meant to say. I certainly mean no *criticism* on you or her, but am only thinking aloud and querying.

To Miss E. A. Warner, New York, March 27, 1870.

You ask if I revel in the Pilgrim's Progress. Yes, I do. I think it an amazing book. It seems to me almost as much an inspiration as the Bible itself. [3] I am glad you liked that hymn. I write in verse whenever I am deeply stirred, because, though as full of tears as other people, I cannot shed them. But I never showed any of these verses to any one, not even my husband, until this winter. But if I were more with you, no doubt I should venture to let you run over some of them, at least those my dear husband has seen and likes. I have felt about hymns just as you say you do, as if I loved them more than the Bible. But I have got over that I prayed myself out of it, not loving hymns the less, but the Bible more. I wonder if you sing I cannot remember if you do, I will send you, sometime, a hymn to sing for my sake, called "More love to Thee, O Christ." Only to think, our silver wedding comes next month, and A. and the Smiths away!

I have been interrupted by callers, and must have been in the parlor several hours. You cannot think what a sweet, peaceful winter this has been, or how good the children are. My cup has just run over, and at times I am too happy to be comfortable, if you know what that means not having a strong body, I suppose you do. Mrs. B. has been in a very critical state of late, but she is rallying, and I may, perhaps, have the privilege of seeing her again. I have had some precious times with her in her sickroom last Friday, a week ago, she prayed with me in the sweetest temper of mind, and came with me when I took leave, to the head of the stairs, full of love and smiles.

To a Young Friend, April 5, 1870.

I wish that hymn for the sickroom were mine, but it is not. I will enclose one that is, which my dear husband has kindly had printed perhaps you will like to sing it to the tune of "Nearer, my God, to Thee." There is not much in it, but you can put everything into it as you make it your prayer. I cannot help feeling that every soul I meet, of whom I can ask, What think you of Christ? and get the glad answer, "He is the chiefest among ten thousand, *the One* altogether lovely"—is a blessing as well as a comfort to mine and whenever you can and do say it, you will become more dear to me. Your God and Savior won you as an easy victory, but He had to fight for me. It seems to me now that He ought to have all there is of me—which, to be sure, is not much—and I hope He is taking it. His ways with me have been perfectly beautiful and infinite in long-suffering and patience.

April 11th.—Your note has reawakened a question I have often had occasion to ask myself before. Why do my friends speak of my letters as giving more pleasure or profit than anything that goes to them from me in print? Is human nature so selfish? Must everybody have everything to himself? It might seem so at first blush, but I think there are two sides to this question. May it not be possible that God sends a message directly from *one* heart to *another,* as He does not to the *many?* Does He not speak through the living voice and the pen that is that voice, as He does not do in the less unconstrained form of print? At any rate, I love to believe that He directs each word and look and tone *inspires* rather, I should say.

I should like you to offer a special prayer for us on Saturday. That day completes twenty-five years of married life to us, and, though it has its shades as well as its lights, I do not think I can do better for you than ask that you may have such years,

> "For who the backward scene hath scanned
> But blessed the Father's guiding hand?"

I can more truly thank Him for His chastisements than for His worldly indulgences the latter urge from, the former drive to Him. I am saying a great thing in a feeble way and you may multiply it by ten thousand, and it will still be weak.

The hymn, "More Love to Thee, O Christ," belongs, probably, as far back as the year 1856. Like most of her hymns, it is simply a prayer put into the form of verse. She wrote it so hastily that the last stanza was left incomplete, one line having been added in pencil when it was printed. She did not show it, not even to her husband, until many years after it was written and she wondered not a little that, when published, it met with so much favor.

* * * * *

II.

Her Silver Wedding. *"I have Lived, I have Loved."* No Joy can put her
out of Sympathy with the Trials of Friends. A Glance backward. Last
Interview with a dying Friend. More Love and more Likeness to Christ.
Funeral of a little Baby. Letters to Christian Friends.

If 1870 was the crowning year in Mrs. Prentiss' life, the 16th of April was that year's most precious jewel. As the time drew nigh, a glow of tender, grateful recollection suffused her countenance.

Her eyes are homes of silent prayer.

She talked of the past, like one lost in wonder, while the light and beauty of the vanished years appeared still to rest upon her spirit. The day itself, which had been kept from the knowledge of most of her friends, was full of sweet content, rehearsing, as it were; all the days of her married life and, at its close, the measure of her earthly joy seemed to be perfect and entire, wanting nothing.

To Mrs. Leonard, New York, April 16, 1845-1870.

Do you know that it is just twenty-five years since we first met? How gladly would I spend the day of our silver wedding with you! You will see that I am near in spirit, at all events. My thoughts have been busy the past week with reviewing the years, through which I have travelled, hand in hand, with my dear husband years full of sin, full of suffering, full of joy brimful of the loving-kindness and tender mercy that smote often and smote surely. Your last letter only confirms what I already knew, but am never tired of hearing repeated, the faithfulness of God to those whom He afflicts. When we once find out what He is to an aching, empty heart, we want to make everybody see just what we see, and, until we try in vain, think we can. I had very peculiar feelings in relation to you when your dear husband was, for a time, parted from you. I knew God would never afflict you so, if He had not something beautiful and blissful to give in place of what He took. And what can we ask for that compares for one instant with "the almost constant felt presence of our Savior's sympathy and support"? Our human nature would like to have the earthly and the divine friendship at once but, if we must choose between the twain, surely you and I would choose Christ without one moment's hesitation. I hope you mention my name every day to Him as I do yours, as I *love* to do.

I enclose, and want you, when by yourself, to sing for my sake a little hymn that I am sure is the language of your heart. My dear husband had a few copies struck off to give friends. Write soon and often. Oh, that you lived here or at Dorset. Goodbye, with warmest love, now *twenty-five* years old!

To Mrs. Condict, New York, April 20, 1870.

Last Saturday was the twenty-fifth anniversary of our marriage, and a very happy day to us both. My dear husband wrote me a letter that made me tremble, lest he should get such hold of me, as no human being must have. I have a very curious feeling about life a *satisfied* one, and as if it could not possibly give me much more than I now have. *"I have lived, I have loved."* [4] People often say they have so much to live for I cannot feel so, though I am not only willing, but glad to live while my husband and children need me and yet—and yet—to have this problem solved, and to be forever with the Lord! I want to see you. I can no longer see my dear Mrs. B. she is too ill, and that makes me miss you the more. I hope that little MS. of mine did not task your sympathies I do not want you to pity me, but to magnify Him who took such pains with me, and is carrying on just such work in thousands of hearts and lives. What goodness! What condescension! The least we can do who have suffered much is to love much.... I have been studying the Bible on the subject of giving personal testimony, and think it makes this a plain duty. There is nothing like the influence of one living soul on another. Then why should we not naturally speak to everybody who will listen, of what fills our thoughts our Savior, His beauty, His goodness, His faithfulness, His wisdom! I do not believe a full heart *can help* running over.

To a young Friend, April 21, 1870.

I was right sorry to lose your Saturday's call. It was a happy day to me, but I can conceive of no enjoyment of any sort that would put me out of sympathy with the trials of friends:

"Old and young are bringing troubles,
Great and small, for me to hear
I have often blessed by sorrows
That drew other's grief so near."

I thought I was saying a very ordinary thing when I spoke of thanking God for His long years of discipline, but very likely life did not look to me at your age as it does now. I was rather startled the other day, to find it written in German, in my own hand, "I cannot say the will is there," referring to a hymn which says, "Der Will ist da, die Kraft ist klein, Doch wird dir nicht zuwider seyn." I suppose there was some great struggle going on when this foolish heart said that, just as if God did not *invariably* do for us the very best that can be done. [5] You speak of having your love to Jesus intensified by interviews with me. It can hardly be otherwise, when those meet together who love Him, and it is a rule that works both ways acts and reacts. I should be thankful if no human being could ever meet me, even in a chance way, and not go away clasping Him the closer, and if I could meet no one who did not so stir and move me. It is my constant prayer. I have such insatiable longings to know and love Him better that I go about hungering and thirsting for the fellowship of those who feel so too when I meet them I call them my "benedictions." Next best to being with Christ Himself, I love to be with those who have His spirit and are yearning for more of His likeness. You speak of putting "deep and dark chasms between" yourself and Christ. He lets us do this that we may learn our nothingness, our weakness, and turn, disgusted, from ourselves to Him. May I venture to assure you that the "chasms" occur less and less frequently as one presses on, until finally they turn into "mountains of light." Get and keep a will for God, and everything that will is ready for will come. This is about a tenth part of what I might say.

To Miss E. A. Warner, New York, April 25, 1870.

I wish I could describe to you my last interview with Mrs. B. She had altered so in two weeks in which I had not seen her, that I should not have known her. She spoke with difficulty, but by getting close to her mouth, I could hear all she said. She went back to the first time she met me, told me her heart then knitted itself to mine, and how she had loved me ever since, etc., etc. I then asked her if she had any parting counsel to give me "No, not a word."…. Someone came in and wet her lips, gave her a sprig of citronatis, and passed out. I crushed it and let her smell the bruised leaves, saying, "You are just like these crushed leaves." She smiled, and replied, "Well, I haven't had one pain too many, not one. But the agony has been dreadful. I won't talk about that I just want to see your sunny face." I asked if she was rejoicing in the hope of meeting lost friends and the saints in heaven. She said, with an expressive look, "Oh, no, I haven't got so far as *that*. I have only got as far as Christ." "For all that," I said, "you'll see my father and mother there." "Why, so I shall," with another bright smile. But her lips were growing white with pain, and I came away.

Did I tell you it was our silver wedding-day on the 16th? We had a very happy day, and if I could see you, I should like to tell you all about it. But it is too long a story to tell in writing. I do not see but I have had everything this life can give, and have a curious feeling as if I had got to a stopping-place. I heard yesterday that two of M.'s teachers had said they looked at her with perfect awe on account of her goodness. I really never knew her to do anything wrong.

To a young Friend New York, May 1, 1870.

I could write forever on the subject of Christian charity, but I must say that in the case you refer to, I think you accuse yourself unduly. We are not to part company with our common sense because we want to clasp hands with the Love that thinks no evil, and we cannot help seeing that there are few, if any, on earth without beams in their eyes and foibles and sins in their lives. The fact that your friend repented and confessed his sin, entitled him to your forgiving love, but not to the ignoring of the fact that he was guilty…. Temptations come sometimes in swarms, like bees, and running away does no good, and fighting only exasperates them. The only help must come from Him who understands and can control the whole swarm.

You ask for my prayers, and I ask for yours. I long ago formed the habit of praying at night individually, if possible, for all who had come to me through the day, or whom I had visited but you contrive to get a much larger share than that. I love to think of your future holiness and usefulness as even in the very least linked to my prayers. Oh, I ought to know how to pray a great deal better than I do, for forty years ago, save one, I this day publicly dedicated myself to Christ. I write to you because I like to do so, recognizing no difference between writing and talking. When no better work comes to me, I am glad to give the little pleasure I can, in notes and letters. He who knows how poor we are, how little we have to give, does not disdain even a note like this, since it is written in love to Him and to one of His own dear ones.

May 23rd.—Your last letter was like a fragrant breath of country air, redolent of flowers and all that makes rural scenes so sweet. But better still, it was fragrant with love to Him who is the bond between us, in whose name and for whose sake we are friends. I wish I loved Him better and were more like Him perhaps that is about as far as we get in this world, for no matter how far we advance, we are never satisfied there is always something ahead I doubt if any one ever said, even in a whisper and to himself, "Now I love my Savior as much as a human soul can."

You speak of my having given you "counsels." Have I had the presumption to do that? Two-thirds of the time I feel as if I wanted somebody to counsel me the only thing I really know that you do not, is what it is to be beaten with persistent, ceaseless stripes, year after year, year after year, with scarcely breathing time between. I do not know whether this is most an argument against me, or for God on the whole it is most for Him, who was as good and kind as never to spare me for my writhing and groaning. Truly as I value this discipline, I want you to give yourself to Him so unreservedly that you will not need such sharp treatment. I am not going to keep writing and getting you in debt. All I ask is if you ever feel a little under the weather and want a specially loving or cheering word, to give me the chance to speak or write it.

A chapter might be written about Mrs. Prentiss' love for little children, the enthusiasm with which she studied all their artless ways, her delight in their beauty, and the reverence with which she regarded the mystery of their infant being. Her faith in their real, complete humanity, their susceptibility to spiritual influences, and, when called from earth, their blessed immortality in and through Christ, was very vivid and it was untroubled by any of those distressing doubts, or misgivings, that are engendered by the materialistic spirit and science of the age. Contempt for them shocked her as an offence against the Holy Child Jesus, their King and Savior. Her very look and manner as she took a young infant, especially a sick or dying infant, in her arms and gave it a loving kiss seemed to say:

> Sweet baby, little as thou art,
> Thou art a human whole
> Thou hast a little human heart,
> Thou hast a deathless soul. [6]

The following letter to a Christian mother, dated May 13th will show her feeling on this subject:

This morning we attended the funeral of a little baby, eight months old. My husband, in his remarks, said that though born and ever continuing to be a sufferer, it was never saddened by this fellowship with Christ and that he believed it was a partaker of His holiness, and glad through His indwelling, even though unconscious of it. During the last days of its life, after each paroxysm of coughing, it would look first at its mother, then at its father, for sympathy, and then look upward with a face radiant beyond description. I cannot tell you how it touched me to think that I had in that baby a little Christian *sister*—not merely redeemed, but sanctified from its birth—and I know it will touch and strengthen you to hear of it. I felt a reverence for that tiny, lifeless form, which I cannot put into words. And, indeed, why should it be harder for God to enter into the soul of an infant than into our "unlikeliest" ones? ... I see more and more that if we have within us the mind of Christ, we must bear the burden of other griefs than our own He did not merely *pity* suffering humanity He *bore* our griefs, and in all our afflictions He was afflicted.

To Mrs. Condict, June 6, 1870.

If you can get hold of the April number of the Bibliotheca Sacra, read an article in it called "Psychology in the Life, Work, and Teachings of Jesus." I think it very striking and very true. Praying for Dr. —— this morning, I had such a peaceful feeling that he was safe. Do you feel so about him? I had a very different experience about another man who has been to see me since I began this letter, and who said I was the first *happy* person he ever met. May God lay that to his heart! Rummaging among dusty things in the attic this forenoon with great repugnance, I found such a beautiful letter from my husband, written for my solace in Switzerland when he was in Paris (he wrote me every day, sometimes twice a day, during the two months of our enforced separation) that even the drudgery of getting my hands soiled and my back broken was sweetened. That is the way God keeps on spoiling us one good thing after another until we are ashamed. Well, let us step onward, hand in hand. I wonder which of us will outrun the other and step in first? I am so glad I am willing to live.

In the course of this spring, *The Percy's* was published. The story first came out as a serial in the New York Observer. It was translated into French under the title *La Famille Percy*. In 1876, a German version appeared under the title *Die Familie Percy*. It was also republished in London. [7]

* * * * *

III.

Lines on going to Dorset. A Cloud over her. Faber's Life. Loving Friends
for one's own sake and loving them for Christ's sake. The Bible and the

<blockquote>
Christian Life. Dorset Society and Occupations. Counsels to a young
Friend in Trouble. "Do not stop praying for your Life!" Cure for the
Heart-sickness caused by a Sight of human Imperfections. Fenelon's
Teaching about Humiliation and being patient with Ourselves.
</blockquote>

The following lines, found among her papers after her death, show in what spirit she went to Dorset:

> Once more I change my home, once more begin
> Life in this rural stillness and repose
> But I have brought with me my heart of sin,
> And sin nor quiet nor cessation knows.
> Ah, when I make the final, blessed change,
> I shall leave that behind, shall throw aside
> Earth's soiled and soiling garments, and shall range
> Through purer regions like a youthful bride.
> Thrice welcome be that day! Do thou, meanwhile,
> My soul, sit ready, unencumbered wait
> The Master bides thy coming, and His smile
> Shall bid thee welcome at the golden gate.
> DORSET, June 15, 1870.

To Mrs. Condict, Dorset, June 18, 1870.

I would love to have you here with me in this dear little den of mine and see the mountains from my window. My husband has gone back to town, and my only society is that of the children, so you would be most welcome if you should come in either smiling or sighing. I have had a cloud over me of late. Do you know about Mr. Prentiss' appointment by General Assembly to a professorship at Chicago? His going would involve not only our tearing ourselves out of the heart of our beloved church, but of my losing you and Miss K., and of our all losing this dear little home. Of course, he does not want to go, and I am shocked at the thought of his leaving the ministry but, on the other hand, there is a right and a wrong to the question, and we ought to want to do whatever God chooses. The thought of giving up this home makes me know better how to sympathize with you if you have to part with yours. I do think it is good for us to be emptied from vessel to vessel, and there is something awful in the thought of having our own way with leanness in the soul. I am greatly pained in reading Faber's Life and Letters, at the shocking way in which he speaks of Mary, calling her his mamma, and praying to her and to Joseph, and nobody knows who not. It seems almost incredible that this is the man who wrote those beautiful strengthening hymns. It sets one to praying "Hold Thou me up and I shall be safe." … I should have forgotten the lines of mine you quote if you had not copied them. God give to you and to me a thousand fold more of the spirit they breathe, and make us wholly, wholly His own! My repugnance to go to Chicago makes me feel that perhaps that is just the wrench I need. Well, goodbye at the longest we have not long to stay in this sphere of discipline and correction.

To Mr. G. S. P., Dorset, July 13, 1870.

I had just come home from a delicious little tramp through our own woods when your letter came, and now, if you knew what was good for you, you would drop in and take tea and spend the evening with us. I should like you to see our house and our mountains, and our cup that runs over until we are ashamed. Had I not known you would not come I should have given you a chance, especially as my husband was gone and I was rather lonely though to be sure he always writes me every day. On the way up here, I was glad of time to think out certain things I had been waiting for leisure to attend to. One had some connection with you, as well as one or two other friends. I had long felt that there was a real, though subtle, difference between human—and, shall I say divine?—affection, but did not see just what it was. Turning it over in my mind that day, it suddenly came to me as this. Human friendship may be entirely selfish, giving only to receive in return, or may be partially so—yet still selfish. But the love that grows out of the love of Christ, and that delights in His image wherever it is seen, claims no response loves because it is its very nature to do so, because it cannot help it, and this without regard to what its object gives. I dare not pretend that I have fully reached this state, but I have entered this land, and know that it is one to be desired as a home, an abiding place. I have thought painfully of the narrow quarters and the hot nights endured by so many in New York, during this unusually warm weather—especially of Mrs. G. with three restless children in bed with her and her poor lonely heart. I cannot but believe that Christ has real purposes of mercy to her soul. I feel interested in Mr. H.'s summer work in a hard field. In place of aversion to young men, I am beginning to realize how true work for Christ one may do by praying persistently for them, especially those consecrated to the ministry of His gospel. I do hope Christ will have the whole of you, and that you will have the whole of Him. When you write, let me know how you like my beloved Fenelon. Still, you may not like him. Some Christians never get to feeding on these mystical writers and get on without them.

To Mrs. Condict, Dorset, July 18, 1870.

I was greatly struck with these words yesterday: "As for God His way is perfect" think of reading the Bible through four times in one year, and nobody knows how many times since and never resting on these words. Somehow, they charmed me. And these words have been ringing in my ears,

"Earth looks so little and so low,"

while conscious that when I can get ferns and flowers, it does not look so "little" or so "low," as it does when I cannot. My cook, who is a Romanist, has been prevented from going to her own church seven miles off, by the weather, ever since we came here, and last Sunday said she meant to go to ours. Mr. P. preached on God's character as our Physician, and she was delighted. I think it was hearing one of his little letters to the children that made her realize, that he was a Christian man whom she might safely hear at any rate, I feel greatly pleased and comforted that she could appreciate such a subject. I fear you are suffering from the weather we never knew anything like it here. We do not suffer, but wake up every morning *bathed* in a breeze that refreshes for the day I mean we do not suffer while we keep still. I am astonished at God's goodness in giving us this place not His goodness itself, but towards *us*. If Mrs. Brinsmade [8] left much of such material as the extract you sent me, I wonder Dr. B. did not write her memoir. The more I read of what Christ said about faith, the more impressed I am. Just now, I am on the last chapters in the gospel of John, and feel as if I had never read them before. They are just wonderful. We have to read the Bible to understand the Christian life, and we must penetrate far into that life in order to understand the Bible. How beautifully the one interprets the other! I want you to let me know, without telling her that I asked you, if Miss K. could make me a visit if it were not for the expense?

To Miss E. A. Warner, Dorset, July 20, 1870.

Did you ever use a fountain pen? I have had one given me, and like it, so much that I sent for one for my husband, and one for Mr. Pratt. When one wants to write in one's lap, or out of doors, it is delightful. Mrs. Field came over from East Dorset on Sunday to have her baby baptized. They had him there in the church through the whole morning service, and he was as quiet as any of us. The next day Mrs. F. came down and spent the morning with me, sweeter, more thoughtful than ever, if changed at all. Dr. and Mrs. Humphrey, of Philadelphia, are passing the summer here at the tavern, and we spend most of our evenings there, or they come here. Mrs. H. is a very superior woman, and though I was determined not to like her, because I have so many people on hand already, I found I could not help it. She is as furious about mosses and lichens and all such things as I am, and the other day took home a *bushel-basket* of them. She is an earnest Christian, and has passed through deep waters I ought to have reversed the order of those clauses. Excuse this rather hasty letter I feared you might fancy your book lost. If you are alive, let me know it, also if you are dead.

To a young Friend, Dorset, Aug. 8, 1870.

I dare not answer your letter, just received, in my own strength, but must pray over it long. It is a great thing to learn how far our doubts and despondencies are the direct result of physical causes, and another great thing is, when we cannot trace any such connection, to bear patiently and quietly what God *permits*, if He does not authorize. I have no more doubt that you love Him, and that He loves you, than that I love Him and that He loves me. You have been daily in my prayers. Temptations and conflict are inseparable from the Christian life no strange thing has happened to you. Let me comfort you with the assurance that you will be taught more and more by God's Spirit how to resist and that true strength and holy manhood will spring up from this painful soil. Try to take heart there is more than one foot-print on the sands of time to prove that "some forlorn and shipwrecked brother" has traversed them before you, and come off conqueror through the Beloved. *Do not stop praying for your life.* Be as cold and emotionless as you please God will accept your naked faith, when it has no glow or warmth in it and in His own time, the loving, glad heart will come back to you. I deeply feel for and with you, and have no doubt that a week among these mountains would do more towards uniting you to Christ than a mile of letters would. You cannot complain of any folly to which I could not plead guilty. I have put my Savior's patience to every possible test, and how I love Him when I think what He will put up with.

You ask if I "ever feel that religion is a sham?" No, never. I *know* it is a reality. If you ask if I am ever staggered by the inconsistencies of professing Christians, I say yes, I am often made heartsick by them but heartsickness always makes me run to Christ, and one good look at Him pacifies me. This is in fact my panacea for every ill and as to my own sinfulness that would certainly overwhelm me if I spent much time in looking at it. But it is a monster whose face I do not love to see I turn from its hideousness to the beauty of His face who sins not and the sight of "yon lovely Man" ravishes me. But at your age, I did this only by fits and starts, and suffered as you do. So I know how to feel for you, and what to ask for you. God purposely sickens us of man and of self that we may learn to "look long at Jesus."

And this brings me to what you say about Fenelon's going too far, when he says we may judge of the depth of our humility by our delight in humiliation, etc. No, he does not go a bit too far. Paul says, "I will *glory* in my infirmities"—"I take *pleasure* in infirmities, in reproaches, in necessities, in persecution, in distresses for Christ's sake for when I am weak, then am I strong." I think this a great attainment but that His disciples may reach it, though only through a humbling, painful process. Then as to God's glory. We say, "Man's chief end is to glorify God and enjoy Him forever." Now, can we enjoy Him until we do glorify Him? Can we enjoy Him while living for ourselves, while indulging in sin, while prayerless and cold and dead? Does not God directly seek our highest happiness when He strips us of vainglory and self-love, embitters the poisonous draught of mere human felicity, and makes us fall down before Him lost in the sense of His beauty and desirableness? The connection between glorifying and enjoying Him is, to my mind, perfect—one following as the *necessary sequence* of the other and facts bear me out in this. He who has let self go and lives only for the honor of God, is the free, the happy man. He is no longer a slave, but has the liberty of the sons of God for "him who honors me, I will honor." Satan has befogged you on this point. He dreads to see you ripen into a saintly, devoted, useful man. He hopes to overwhelm and ruin you. But he will not prevail. You have solemnly given yourself to the Lord you have chosen the work of winning and feeding souls as your life-work, and you cannot, must not go back. These conflicts are the lot of those who are training to be the Lord's true yoke-fellows. Christ's sweetest consolations lay behind crosses and He reserves His best things for those who have the courage to press forward, fighting for them. I entreat you to turn your eyes away from self, from man, and look to Christ. Let me assure you, as a fellow traveler, that I have been on the road and know it well, and that by and by there will not be such a dust on it. You will meet with hindrances and trials, but will fight quietly through, and no human ear hear the din of battle, no human eye perceive fainting or halting or fall. May God bless you, and become to you an ever-present, joyful reality! Indeed, He will only wait patiently.

In glancing over this, I see that I have here and there repeated myself. Do excuse it. I believe it is owing to the way the flies harass and distract me.

August 17th.—I feel truly grateful to God if I have been of any comfort to you. I know only too well the shock of seeing professors of even sinless perfection guilty of what I consider sinful sin, and my whole soul was so staggered that for some days I could not pray, but could only say, "O God, if there be any God, come to my rescue." … But God loves better than He knows us, and foresaw every infidelity before He called us to Himself. Nothing in us takes Him, therefore, by surprise. Fenelon teaches what no other writer does—to be "patient with ourselves," and I think as you penetrate into the Christian life, you will agree with him on every point as I do.

August 19th.—I have had a couple of rather sickish days since writing the above, but am all right again now. Hot weather does not agree with me. I used to reproach myself for religious stupidity when not well, but see now that God Is my kind Father—not my hard taskmaster, expecting me to be full of life and zeal when physically exhausted. It takes long to learn such lessons. One has to penetrate deeply into the heart of Christ to begin to know its tenderness and sympathy and forbearance.

You cannot imagine how Miss K. has luxuriated in her visit, or how good she thinks we all are. She holds views to which I cannot quite respond, but I do not condemn or reject them. She is a modest, praying, devoted woman not disposed to obtrude, much less to urge her opinions full of Christian charity and forbearance and I am truly thankful that she prays for me and mine in fact, she loves to pray so, that when she gets hold of a new case, she acts as one does who has found a treasure.

I wish you were looking out with me on the beautiful array of mountains to be seen from every window of our house and breathing this delicious air.

September 25th.—We expect now to go home on Friday next, though if I had known how early the foliage was going to turn this year, I should have planned to stay a week longer to see it in all its glory. It is looking very beautiful even now, and our eyes have a perpetual feast. We have had a charming summer, but one does not want to play all the time, and I hope God has work of some sort for me to do at home during the winter. Meanwhile, I wish I could send you a photograph of the little den where I am now writing, and the rustic adornings which make it *sui generis*, and the bit of woods to be seen from its windows, that, taking the lead of all other Dorset woods, have put on floral colors, just because they are ours and know we want them looking their best before we go away. But this wish must yield to fate, like many another and, as I have come to the end of my paper, I will love and leave you.

* * * * *

IV.

The Story Lizzie Told. Country and City. The Law of Christian Progress. Letters to a Friend bereft of three Children. Sudden Death of another Friend. "Go on step faster." Fenelon and his Influence upon her religious Life. Lines on her Indebtedness to him.

The Story Lizzie Told was published about this time. It had already appeared in the Riverside Magazine. The occasion of the story was a passage in a letter from London written by a friend, which described in a very graphic and touching way the yearly exhibition of the Society for the Promotion of Window Gardening among the Poor. The exhibition was held at the "Dean's close" at Westminster and the Earl of Shaftesbury gave the prizes. [9]

No one of Mrs. Prentiss's smaller works, perhaps, has been so much admired as *The Story Lizzie Told*. It was written at Dorset in the course of a single day, if not at a single sitting and so real was the scene to her imagination that, on reading it in the evening to her husband, she had to stop again and again from the violence of her emotion. "What a little fool I am!" she would say, after a fresh burst of tears. [10]

To Mrs. Leonard, New York, Oct. 16, 1870.

Your letter came in the midst of the wear and tear of A.'s return to us. We were kept in suspense about her from Monday, when she was due, until, Friday when she came, and it is years since I have got so excited and wrought up. They had a dreadful passage, but she was not sick at all. Prof. Smith is looking better than I ever saw him, and we are all most happy in being together once more. I can truly re-echo your wish that you lived half way between us and Dorset, for then we should see you once a year at least. I miss you and long to see you. How true it is that each friend has a place of his own that no one else can fill! I do not doubt that the 13th of October was a silvery wedding-day to your dear husband. His loss has made Christ dearer to you, and so has made your union more perfect. I suppose you were never so much one as you are now.

We have had a delightful summer, not really suffering from the heat though, of course, we felt it more or less. All our nights were cool.... I cannot tell you how Mr. P. and myself enjoy our country home. It seems as if we had slipped into our proper nook. But if we are going to do any more brainwork, we must be where there is stimulus, such as we find here. What a mixed-up letter! I have almost forgotten how to write, in adorning my house and sowing my seeds and the like.

To Mrs. Frederick Field, New York, Oct. 19th, 1870.

I deeply appreciate the Christian kindness that prompted you to write me in the midst of your sorrow. I was prepared for the sad news by a dream only last night. I fancied myself seeing your dear little boy lying very restlessly on his bed, and proposing to carry him about in my arms to relieve him. He made no objection, and I walked up and down with him a long, long time, when some one of the family took him from me. Instantly his face was illumined by a wondrous smile of delight that he was to leave the arms of a stranger to go to those familiar to him—such a smile, that when I awoke this morning I said to myself, "Eddy Field has gone to the arms of his Savior, and gone gladly." You can imagine how your letter, an hour or two later, touched me. But you have better consolation than dreams can give in the belief that your child will develop, without spot or wrinkle or any such thing, into the perfect likeness of Christ, and in your own submission to the unerring will of God. I sometimes think that patient sufferers suffer most they make less outcry than others, but the grief that has little vent wears sorely.

"Grace does not steel the faithful heart   That it should feel no ill,"

and you have many a pang yet before you. It must be so very hard to see twin children part company, to have their paths diverge so soon. But the shadow of death will not always rest on your home you will emerge from its obscurity into such a light, as they who have never sorrowed cannot know. We never know, or begin to know, the great Heart that loves us best, until we throw ourselves upon it in the hour of our despair. Friends say and do all they can for us, but they do not know what we suffer or what we need but Christ, who formed, has penetrated the depths of the mother's heart. He pours in the wine and the oil that no human hand possesses, and "as one whom his mother comforted, so will He comfort you." I have lived to see that God never was as good to me as when He seemed most severe. Thus, I trust and believe it will be with you and your husband. Meanwhile, while the peaceable fruits are growing and ripening, may God help you through the grievous time that must pass—a grievous time in which you have my warm sympathy. I know very well all about it.

"I know my griefs but then my consolations,   My joys, and my immortal hopes I know"—

joys unknown to the prosperous, hopes that spring from seed long buried in the dust.

I shall read your books with great interest, I am sure, and who knows how God means to prepare you for future usefulness along the path of pain? "Every branch that beareth fruit He purged it, that it may bring forth more fruit."

What an epitaph your boy's own words would be—"It is beautiful to be dead"!

To the Same, New York, Nov 30th, 1870.

I thank you so much for your letter about your precious children. I remember them well, all three, and do not wonder that the death of your first-born, coming upon the very footsteps of sorrow, has so nearly crushed you. But what beautiful consolations God gave you by his dying bed! "All safe at God's right hand!" What more can the fondest mother's heart ask than such safety as this? I am sure that there will come to you, sooner or later, the sense of Christ's love in these repeated sorrows, that in your present bewildered, amazed state you can hardly realize. Let me tell you that I have tried His heart in a long storm—not so very different from yours—and that I know something of its depths. I will enclose you some lines that may give you a moment's light. Please not to let them go out of your hands, for no one—not even my husband—has ever seen them. I am going to send my last book to your lonely little boy. You will not feel like reading it now, but perhaps the 33rd chapter, and some that follow, may not jar upon you as the earlier part would.

To go back again to the subject of Christ's love for us, of which I never tire, I want to make you feel that His sufferers are His happiest, most favored disciples. What they learn about Him——His pitifulness, His unwillingness to hurt us, His haste to bind up the very wounds He has inflicted——endear Him so, that at last they burst out into songs of thanksgiving, that His "donation of bliss" included in it such donation of pain. Perhaps I have already said to you, for I am fond of saying it,

"The love of Jesus——what it is, Only His sufferers know."

You ask if your heart will ever be lightsome again. Never again with the lightsomeness that had never known sorrow, but light even to gayety with the new and higher love born of tribulation. Just as far as a heavenly is superior even to maternal love, will be the elevation and beauty of your new joy a joy worth all it costs. I know what sorrow means I know it well. But I know, too, what it is to pass out of that prison-house into a peace that passes all understanding and thousands can say the same. So, my dear suffering sister, look on and look up lay hold on Christ with *both your poor, empty hands* let Him do with you what seemeth Him good though He slay you, still trust in Him and I dare in His name to promise you a sweeter, better life than you could have known had He left you to drink of the full, dangerous cups of unmingled prosperity. I feel such real and living sympathy with you that I would love to spend weeks by your side, trying to bind up your broken heart. But for the gospel of Christ, to hear of such bereavements as yours would appall, would madden one. Yet, what a halo surrounds that word "but"!

To Miss E. A. Warner, New York, Dec 14, 1870.

I have not behaved according to my wont, and visited the sick even by way of a letter. And by this time, I hope you are quite well again, and do not need ghostly counsels…. I have felt very badly about Miss Lyman's dying at Vassar, but since Mrs. S.'s visit and learning how beloved she is there, have changed my mind. What does it matter, after all, from what point of time or space we go home how we shall smile, after we get there, that we ever gave it one moment's thought! You ask what I am doing well, I am taking a vacation and not writing anything to speak of, yet just as busy as ever not one moment in which to dawdle, though I dare say I seem to the folks here at home to be sitting round doing nothing. I must give you a picture of one day and you must photograph one of yours, as we have done before. Got up at seven and went through the usual forms had prayers and breakfast, and started off to school with M. Came home and had a nice quiet time reading, etc. at eleven went to my meeting, which was a tearful one, as one of our members who knelt with us only a week before, was this day to be buried out of our sight. She was at church on Sunday afternoon at four P.M., to present her baby in baptism, and at half-past two the following morning was in heaven. We all went together to the funeral after the meeting, and gathered round the coffin with the feeling that she belonged to us. When I got home, I found a dispatch from Miss W., saying they should be here right away. I had let one of my women go out of town to a sick sister, so I must turn chambermaid and make the bed, dust, clear out closet, cupboard, and bureau forthwith. This done, they arrived, which took the time till half-past seven, when I excused myself and went to an evening meeting, knowing it would be devoted to special prayer for the husband and children of her who had gone. Got home half an hour behind time and found a young man awaiting me who was converted last June, as he hopes, while reading Stepping Heavenward. I had just been seated by him when our doctor was announced he had lost his only grandchild and had come to talk about it. He stayed until half-past nine, when I went back to my young friend, who stayed until half-past ten and gave a very interesting history, which I have not time to put on paper. He writes me since, however, about his Christian life that "it gets sweeter and sweeter," and I know you will be glad for me that I have this joy.

Saturday Morning.—I was interrupted there, had visitors, had to go to a fair, company again, so that I had not time to eat the food I needed, went to see a poor sick girl, had more visitors, and at last, at eleven P.M., scrambled into bed. Now I am finishing this, and if nobody hinders, am going to mail it, and then go after a block of ice-cream for that sick girl (isn't it nice, we can get it now done up in little boxes, just about as much as an invalid can eat at one time). Then I am going to see a poor afflicted soul that cannot get any light on her sorrow. Here comes my dear old man to read his sermon, so goodbye.

To a young Friend, Dec. 20, 1870.

I have been led, during the last month or two, to a new love of the Holy Spirit, or perhaps to more consciousness of the silent, blessed work He is doing in and for us? and for those whose souls lie as a heavy and yet a sweet burden upon our own. And joining with you in your prayers, seeking also for myself what I sought for you, I found myself almost startled by such a response, as I cannot describe. It was not joy, but a deep solemnity, which enfolded me as with a garment, and if I ever pass out of it, which I never want to do, I hope it will be with a heart more than ever consecrated and set apart for Christ's service. The more I reflect and the more I pray, the more life narrows down to one point—What am I being for Christ, what am I doing for Him? Why do I tell you this? Because the voice of a fellow traveler always stimulates his brother pilgrim, what one finds and speaks of and rejoices over, sets the other upon determining to find too. God has been very good to you, as well as to me, but we ought to whisper to each other now and then, "Go on, step faster, step surer, and lay hold on the Rock of Ages with both hands." You never need be afraid to speak such words to me. I want to be pushed on, and pulled on, and coaxed on.

The allusion to her "beloved Fenelon," in several of the preceding letters, renders this a suitable place to say a word about him and his influence upon her religious character. "Fenelon I *lean* on," she wrote. Her delight in his writings dated back more than a quarter of a century, and continued, unabated, to the end of her days. She regarded him with a sort of personal affection and reverence. Her copy of "Spiritual Progress," composed largely of selections from his works, is crowded with pencil-marks expressive of her sympathy and approval not even her Imitation of Christ, Sacra Privata, Pilgrim's Progress, Saints' Everlasting Rest, or Leighton on the First Epistle of Peter, contain so many. These pencil-marks are sometimes very emphatic, underscoring or inclosing now a single word, now a phrase, anon a whole sentence or paragraph and it requires but little skill to decipher, in these rude hieroglyphics, the secret history of her soul for a third of a century— one side, at least, of this history. What she sought with the greatest eagerness, what she most loved and most hated, her spiritual aims, struggles, trials, joys, and hopes, may here be read between the lines. And a beautiful testimony they give to the moral depth, purity, and nobleness of her piety!

The story is not, indeed, complete her religious life had other elements, not found, or only partially found, in Fenelon elements centering directly in Christ and His gospel, and which had their inspiration in her Daily Food and her New Testament. What attracted her to Fenelon was not the doctrine of salvation as taught by him—she found it better taught in Bunyan and Leighton—it was his marvelous knowledge of the human heart, his keen insight into the proper workings of nature and grace, his deep spiritual wisdom, and the sweet mystic tone of his piety. And then the two great principles pervading his writings—that of pure love to God and that of self-crucifixion as the way to perfect love—fell in with some of her own favorite views of the Christian life. In the study of Fenelon, as of Madame Guyon, her aim was a purely practical one it was not to establish, or verify, a theory, but to get aid and comfort in her daily course heavenward. What Fenelon was to her in this respect she has herself recorded in the following lines, found, after her death, written on a blank page of her "Spiritual Progress":

> Oh wise and thoughtful words! oh counsel sweet,
> Guide in my wanderings, spurs unto my feet,
> How often you have met me on the way,
> And turned me from the path that led astray
> Teaching that fault and folly, sin and fall,
> Need not the weary pilgrim's heart appall
> Yea more, instructing how to snatch the sting
> From timid conscience, how to stretch the wing
> From the low plane, the level dead of sin,
> And mount immortal, mystic joys to win.
> One hour with Jesus! How its peace outweighs
> The ravishment of earthly love and praise
> How dearer far, emptied of self to lie
> Low at His feet, and catch, perchance, His eye,
> Alike content when He may give or take,
> The sweet, the bitter, welcome for His sake!

[1] John Wesley, after having pointed out what he considered the grand source of all her mistakes namely, the being guided by inward impressions and the light of her own spirit rather than by the written Word, and also her error in teaching that God never purifies a soul but by inward and outward suffering—then adds: "And yet with all this dross how much pure gold is mixed! So did God wink at involuntary ignorance? What a depth of religion did she enjoy! How much of the mind that was in Christ Jesus! What heights of righteousness, and peace, and joy in the Holy Ghost! How few such instances do we find of exalted love to God, and our neighbor of genuine humility of invincible meekness and unbounded resignation! So that, upon the whole, I know not whether we may not search many centuries to find another woman who was such a pattern of true holiness."

[2] See the lines MY CUP RUNNETH OVER, *Golden Hours*, p. 43.

[3] "I know of no book, the Bible excepted as above all comparison, which I, according to my judgment and experience, could so safely recommend as teaching and enforcing the whole saving truth according to the mind that was in Christ Jesus, as the Pilgrim's Progress. It is, in my conviction, incomparably the best *summa theologiæ evangelicæ* ever produced by a writer not miraculously inspired. I read it once as a theologian—and let me assure you, there is great theological acumen in the work—once with devotional feelings, and once as a poet. I could not have believed beforehand that Calvinism could be painted in such exquisitely delightful colors."—COLERIDGE.

[4] The allusion is to Thekla's song in Part I., Act 3, sc. 7 of Schiller's Wallenstein.

Du Heilige, rufe dein Kind zurück! Ich habe genossen das irdische Glück, *Ich habe gelebt und gelibet*.

[5] The hymn referred to is Paul Gerhardt's, beginning:

Wir singen dir, Immanuel, Du Lebensfürst und Gnadenquell.

It was one of her favorite German hymns. The lines she quotes belong to the tenth stanza "Ich kann nicht sagen Der Will ist da," are the words pencilled in the margin.

[6] Hartley Coleridge's Poems. Vol. II., p. 139.

[7] But greatly to Mrs. Prentiss' annoyance, with the title changed to *Ever Heavenward*—as if to make it appear to be a sequel to Stepping Heavenward.

[8] Wife of the late Rev. Horatio Brinsmade, D.D., of Newark, N. J.

[9] "Polly" was particularly happy six years old, I should say, shabby, though evidently washed up for the occasion, and very pretty and all pink with excitement. "Polly, I *knowed* you'd get a prize," I heard a young woman, tired out with carrying her own big baby, say. And then she came upon her own geranium with three blossoms on it and marked "Second Prize," and said, "I *cannot* believe it," when they told her that that meant six shillings. But the plant which my companion and myself both cried over, was a little bit of a weedy marigold, the one poor little flower on it carefully fastened about with a paper ring, such as high and mighty greenhouse men sometimes put round a choice rose in bud. That was all just this one common, very single little flower, with "Lizzie" Something's name attached and the name of her street. All the streets were put upon the tickets and added greatly to the pathetic effect just the poorest lanes and alleys in London. Nobody seemed to claim the marigold. Perhaps it was the great treasure of some sick child who could not come to look at it. It was certain not to get a prize, but the child has found something by this time tucked down in the pot and carefully covered over by F., when no one was looking, with a pinch of earth taken from a more prosperous plant alongside.

[10] Miss W. showed me a very pleasant letter of Lady Augusta Stanley, the wife of Dean Stanley, to a Miss C., through whom she received from Miss W.'s little niece a copy of *The Story Lizzie Told*. Lady Stanley is herself, I believe, at the head of the Society, which holds the annual Flower Show. She says in her letter that she had just returned from Scotland, reaching home quite late in the evening. Before retiring, however, she had read your story through. She praises it very warmly, and wonders how anybody but a "Londoner" could have written it.—*Letter to Mrs. P., dated New York, September, 1872.*

CHAPTER 11 - IN HER HOME.

The letters in the preceding chapters give a glimpse, here and there, of Mrs. Prentiss' home, but relate chiefly to the religious side of her character. What was her manner of life among her children? How were her temper and habits as a mother affected by the ardor and intensity of her Christian feeling? A partial answer to these questions is contained in letters written to her eldest daughter, while the latter was absent in Europe. These letters show the natural side of her character and although far from reflecting all its light and beauty—no words could do that!—they depict some of its most interesting traits. They are frankness itself and betray not the least respect of persons but if she speaks her mind in them without much let or hindrance, it is always done in the pleasantest way. In the portions selected for publication the aim has been to let her be seen, so far as possible, just as she appeared in her daily home-life, both in town and country.

I.

Home-life in New York.

New York, *October* 22, 1869. I have promised to walk to school with M. this morning, and while I am waiting for her to get ready, will begin my letter to you. We got home from seeing you off all tired out, and I lay on the sofa all the time till I went to bed, except while eating my dinner, and I think papa did pretty much the same. The moment we had done dinner, H. and Jane appeared, carrying your bureau drawer between them, and we had a great time over the presents you were thoughtful enough to leave behind you. My little sacque makes me look like 500 angels instead of one, and I am ever so glad of it, and the children were all delighted with their things.

Well, I have escorted M. to school, come home, and read the Advance, and Hearth and Home, and it is now eleven o'clock and the doorbell has only rung twice! Papa says you are out of sight of land, and as it is a warm day and we are comfortable, we hope you are. But it is dreadful to have to wait so long before hearing.

23rd.—Papa says this must be mailed by nine o'clock so I have hurried up from breakfast to finish it. Mr. and Mrs. S. spent most of last evening with us. They shouted over my ferrotypes. Mr.—— also called and expressed as much surprise at your having gone to Europe as if the sky had fallen. I read my sea-journal to the children last evening, and though it is very flat and meager in itself, H., to whom it was all brand new, thought it ought to be published forthwith. No time for another word but love to all the S.'s, big and little, high and low, great and small. Your affectionate Mammy.

Oct. 28th.—I can hardly believe that it is only a week today that we saw you and your big steamer disappear from view. H. said last night that it seemed to him one hundred years ago, and we all said amen. So how do you suppose it will seem ten months hence? I hope you do not find the time so long. I take turns waiting upon the children to school, which they are very strict about, and they enjoy their teachers amazingly.

I received this morning a very beautiful and touching letter from a young lady in England about the Susy books. They are associated in her mind and those of her family with a "Little Pearlie" whose cunning little photograph she enclosed, who taught herself to read in a fortnight from one of them, and was read to from it on her dying bed, and after she became speechless she made signs to have her head wet as Suzy's was. I never received such a letter among all I have had. Randolph sent me twelve copies of Stepping Heavenward, and I have had my hands full packing and sending them. M. is reading aloud to H. a charming story called "Alone in London." I am sure I could not read it aloud without crying.

The following is the letter from England:

To THE AUTHOR OF "LITTLE SUSY":

I feel as if I had a perfect right to call you "My dear friend," so much have I thought of you this last year and a half. Bear with me while I tell you why. A year ago last Christmas we were a large family—father, mother, and eight children, of whom I, who address you, am the eldest. The youngest was of course the pet, our bright little darling, rather more than five. That Christmas morning, of course, there were gifts for all and among the treasures in the smallest stocking was a copy of "Little Suzy's Six Teachers," for which I desire to thank you now. Many times, I have tried to do so, but I could not the trouble which came upon us was too great and awful in its suddenness. Little Pearl, so first called in the days of a fragile babyhood—Dora Margaret was her real name—taught herself to read from her "Little Susy," during the first fortnight she had it. And she would sit for hours, literally, amusing and interesting herself by it. She talked constantly of the Six Teachers, and a word about them was enough to quell any rising naughtiness. "Pearlie, what would Mr. Ought say?" or "Do not grieve Mrs. Love," was always sufficient. Do you know what it is to have one the youngest in a large family? My darling was seventeen years younger than I. I left school when she was born to take the oversight of the nursery, which dear mamma's illness and always-delicate health prevented her from doing. I had nursed her in her illnesses, dressed her, made the little frocks—now laid so sadly by—and to all the rest of us she had been more like a child than a sister. Friends used to say, "It is a wonder that child is not spoiled" but they could never say she *was*. Merry, full of life and fun she always was, quick and intelligent, full of droll sayings that recur to us now with *such* a pain. From Christmas to the end of February we often remarked to one another how good that child was! laughing and playing from morning to night, yet never unruly or wild. That February we had illness in the house. Jessie, the next youngest, had diphtheria, but she recovered, and we trusted all danger was passed, when one Monday evening—the last in the month—our darling seemed ill. The next day we recognized the symptoms we had seen in Jessie, and the doctor was called in. Tuesday and Wednesday, he came and gave no hint of danger, but on Wednesday night, we perceived a change and on Thursday came the sentence: No hope. Oh friend, dear friend! how can I tell you of the long hours when we could not help our darling—of the dark night when, forbidden the room from the malignity of the case, we went to bed to coax mamma to do so—of the grey February dawn when there came the words, "Our darling is *quite well* now"—quite well, forever taken from the evil to come.

The Sunday night before, she came into the parlor with "Susy" under her arm and petitioned for someone to read the "Teachers' meeting." "Why, you read it twice this afternoon," said one. "Yes, I know—but it's so nice," was the reply. "Pearlie will be six in September," said the gentle mother "we must have a Teachers' meeting for her, I think." "But perhaps I sha'n't ever be six," said the little one. "Oh Pearlie, why do you say so?" "Well, people do not all be six, you know," affirmed our darling with solemn eyes and two dimples in the rosy cheeks, which were hid forever from us before the next Sabbath day.

On the Wednesday, we borrowed from a little friend the other books of the series, thinking they might afford some amusement for the weary hours of illness, and Annie, my next sister, read four of the birthdays to her and then wished to stop, fearing she might be too fatigued. "No, read one more," was the request, and "That will do—I'm five,

~ 230 ~

read the last tomorrow," she said, when it was complied with. Ah me! with how many tears we took up that book again. That Wednesday she sat up in bed, a glass of medicine in her hand. "Mamma," she said, "Miss Joy has gone quite away and only left Mr. Pain. She cannot come back till my throat is well." "But Mrs. Love is here, is she not?" "Oh, yes," and the dear heavy eyes turned from one to another. In the night, when she lay dying, came intervals of consciousness in one of these she took her handkerchief and gave it to papa, who watched by her, asking him to wet it and put it on her head. When he told us, we recollected the incident when Susy in the favorite book was ill. And can you understand how our hearts felt very tender toward you and we said you must be thanked. I should weary you if I told you all the incidents that presented themselves of how sweet and good she was in her illness how in the agony of those last hours, when no fear of infection could restrain the passionate kisses papa was showering on her, the dear voice said with a stop and an effort between each word, "Do not kiss me on my mouth, papa you may catch it" how everything she asked for was prefaced by "please," how self was always last in her thoughts. "I'm keeping you awake, you darling." "Do not stand there—you'll be so tired—sit down or go down-stairs, if you like."

I will send you a photograph of little Pearlie it is the best we have, but was taken when she was only two years old. She was very small for her age and had been very delicate until the last year of her life.

In writing thus to thank you I am not only doing an act of justice to yourself, but fulfilling wishes now rendered binding. Often and often my dear mamma said, "How I wish we knew the lady who wrote Little Susy!" Her health, always delicate, never recovered from the shock of Pearlie's death, and suddenly, on the morning of the first of May, the Angel of Death darkened our dwelling with the shadow of his wings. Not long did he linger—only two hours—and our mother had left us. She was with her treasure and the Savior, who said so lovingly on earth, "Come unto Me."

But words cannot express such trouble as that. We have not realized it yet. Forgive me if my letter is abrupt and confused. I have only desired to tell you simply the simple tale—if by any chance it should make you thank God more earnestly for the great gift He has given you—a holy gift indeed for can you think the lessons from "Susy," so useful and so loved on earth, could be suddenly forgotten when the glories of heavens opened on our darling's view? I cannot myself. I think, perhaps, our Father's home may be more like our human ones, where His love reigns, than our wild hearts allow themselves to imagine and I think the two, on whose behalf I thank you now, may one day know you and thank you themselves.

Dear "Aunt Susan," believe me to be, your unknown yet grateful friend,

LIZZIE WRAITH L——.

Mrs. Prentiss at once answered this letter, and not long after received another from Miss L——, dated January 9, 1870, breathing the same grateful feeling and full of interesting details. The following is an extract from it:

I was so surprised, dear unknown friend, to receive your kind letter so soon. Indeed, I hardly expected a reply at all. When I wrote to you, I did not know that I was addressing a daughter of the "Edward Payson" whose name is fragrant even on this side of the Atlantic. Had I known it I think I should not have ventured to write—so I am glad I did not. If you should be able to write again, and have a carte-de-visite to spare, may I beg it, that I may form some idea of the friend, "old enough to be my mother"? Are you little and slight, like my real mother, I wonder, or stately and tall? I will send you a photograph of the monument, which the ladies of papa's church and congregation have erected to dear mamma, in our beautiful cemetery, where the snowdrops will be already peeping, and where roses bloom for ten months out of the twelve.

Nov. 3rd.—Here begins letter No. 3. We heard of your arrival at Southampton by a telegram last evening. We long to get a letter. Before I forget, it let me tell you that Alice H. and Julia W. have both got babies. We are getting nicely settled for the winter the children are all behaving beautifully.

Saturday, 6th.—Well, I have just been to see Mrs. F., and found her a bright, frank young thing, fresh and simple and very pleasing. Her complexion is like M——'s, and the lower part of her face is shaped like hers, dark eyebrows, light hair, *splendid* teeth, and I suppose would be called very pretty by you girls. Take her altogether I liked her very much. We hear next to nothing from Stepping Heavenward, and begin to think it is going to fall dead.

Monday, 14th.—Your Southampton letter has just come and we are delighted to hear that you had such a pleasant voyage, and found so many agreeable people on board.... Yesterday afternoon was devoted to hearing a deeply interesting description from Dr. Hatfield, followed by Mr. Dodge, of the re-union of the two Assemblies at Pittsburgh. Dr. H. made us all laugh by saying that as the New School entered the church where they were to be received and united to the Old School, the latter rose and sang "Return, ye ransomed sinners, home!" Oh, I do not know but it was just the other way it makes no great difference, for as Dr. H. remarked, "we're all ransomed sinners."

Nov. 30th.—Mr. Abbot dined here on Sunday. He came in again in the evening, and it would have done you good to hear what he said about the children. They are all well and happy, and give me very little trouble. I do not feel so well on the late dinner, and have awful dreams.——I was passing the C——s, after writing the above, and she called me in to see her new parlors. They are beautiful a great deal of bright, rich coloring, and various articles of furniture of his own designing. *Thursday.*——You and M. will be shocked to hear that Julia W. died last night. As Mr. W. was at church on Sunday, we supposed all danger was over. We heard it through a telegram sent to your father.

December 4, 1869.—I need not tell you that we all remember that this is your birthday, dear child, and that the remembrance brings you very near. I wish I could send you, for a birthday present, all that I have, this morning, asked God to give you. You may depend upon it, that while some people may get along through life at a certain distance from Him, *you* are not one of that sort. You may find a feverish joy, but never abiding *peace*, out of Him. Remember this whenever you feel the oppression of that vague sense of unrest, of which, I doubt not, you have a great deal underneath a careless outside this is the thirst of the soul for the only fountain at which it is worthwhile to drink. You never will be really happy until Christ becomes your dearest and most intimate friend. *7th.*—We have had a tremendous fall of snow, and Culyer says M. ought to wait an hour before starting for school, but she is not willing and I am going with her to see that she is not buried alive. Goodbye again, dearie! Will begin a new letter right away.

Dec. 9th—We went to see Mrs. W. this afternoon. Julia had typhoid fever, which ran twenty-one days, and was delirious a good deal of the time. She got ready to die before her confinement, though she said she expected to live. After she became so very ill Mrs. W. heard her praying for something "for Christ's sake," "for the sake of Christ's *sufferings*," and once asked her what it was she was asking for so earnestly. "Oh, to get well for Edward's sake and the baby's," she replied. A few days before her death she called Mrs. W. to "come close" to her, and said, "I am going to die. I did not think so when baby was born, dear little thing—but now it is impressed upon me that I am." Mrs. W. said they hoped not, but added, "Yet suppose you *should* die, what then?" "Oh I have prayed, day and night, to be reconciled, and I am, *perfectly* so. God will take care of Edward and of my baby. Perhaps it is better so than to run the risk—" She did not finish the sentence. The baby looks like her. Mrs. W. told her you had gone to Europe with M., and she expressed great pleasure but if she had known where *she* was going, and to what, all she would have done would have been to give thanks "for Christ's sake." I do not blame her, however, for clinging to life it was natural she should.

10th—We went, last evening, to hear Father Hyacinthe lecture on "Charite" at the Academy of Music. I did not expect to understand a word, but was agreeably disappointed, as he spoke very distinctly. Still I did not enjoy hearing as well as I did reading it this morning—for I lost some of the best things in a really fine address. It was a brilliant scene. The very elite of intellectual society gathered around one modest, unpretentious little man. Dr. and Mrs. Crosby were in the box with us, and she, fortunately, had an opera glass with her, so that we had a chance to study his really good face. The only book I expect to write this winter is to you I am dreadfully lazy since you left, and do not do anything but haze about. There is a good deal of lively talk at the table the children are waked up by going to school, and there is some rivalry among them, each maintaining that his and hers is the best.

Dec. 15th.—We have cards for a "Soiree musicale" at Mrs. ——'s, which is to be a great smash-up. She called here today and wept and wailed over and kissed me. I have been to see how Mrs. C. is. She is a little worse today, and he and her father scarcely leave her. He wrung my hand all to pieces, poor man. Her illness is exciting great sympathy in our church, and nobody seems willing to let her go. Dr. Adams spent last evening here. He is splendid company I really wish he would come once a week. Everybody is asking if I meant in Katy to describe myself. I have no doubt that if I should catch an old toad, put on to her a short gown and petticoat and one of my caps, everybody would walk up to her and say, "Oh, how do you do, Mrs. Prentiss, you look more like yourself than common I recognize the picture you have drawn of yourself in Stepping Heavenward and in the Percy's," etc., etc., etc., *ad nauseam*. The next book I write I will make my heroine black and everybody will say, "Oh, here you are again, black to the life!"

Dec. 18th.—You and M. will not be surprised to hear that Mrs. C.'s sufferings are over. She died this morning. Papa and I are greatly shaken. With much hesitation, I decided to go over there to see her mother and the welcome I got from her and from Mr. C. are things to remember for a lifetime. I will never hesitate again to fly to people in trouble. If you were here I would tell you all about my visit, but I cannot write it down. It seems so sad, just as they had got into their lovely new home—sad for *him*, I mean as for her I can only wish her joy that she is not weeping here below as he is. I stayed until it was time for church, and when I entered it, I was met by many a tearful face papa announced her death from the pulpit, and is going, this afternoon, to throw aside the sermon he intended to preach, and extemporize on "the first Sunday in heaven." The children are going in, this noon, to sing as to the Mission festival, that is to be virtually given up the children are merely to walk in, receive their presents, and go silently out. It is a beautiful day to go to heaven in. Mrs. C. did not know she was going to die, but that is of no consequence. Only one week ago, yesterday she was at the Industrial school, unusually bright and well, they all say. Well, I see everything double and had better stop writing.

Monday, 20th.—Your nice letter was in the letterbox as I started for school with H. I called to papa to let him know it was there and went off, begrudging him the pleasure of reading it before I did. When I got home there was no papa and no letter to be found I looked in every room, on his desk and on mine, posted down to the letterbox and into the parlor, in vain. At last, he came rushing home with it, having carried it to market, lest I should get and read it alone! So we sat down and enjoyed it together.... I take out your picture now and then, when, lo, a big lump in my throat, notwithstanding which I am glad we let you go we enjoy your enjoyment, and think it will make the old nest pleasanter to have been vacated for a while. Papa and I agreed before we got up this morning that the only fault we had to find with God was, that He was too good to us. I cannot get over the welcome I got from Mr. C. yesterday. He said I seemed like a mother to him, which made me feel very old on the one hand, and very happy on the other. If I were you, I would not marry anybody but a minister it gives one such lots of people to love and care for. Old Mrs. B. is failing, and lies there as peaceful and contented as a little baby. I never got sweeter smiles from anybody. I have got each of the servants a pretty dress for Christmas I feel that I owe them a good deal for giving me such a peaceful, untroubled home.

Dec. 23rd.—It rained very hard all day yesterday till just about the time of the funeral, half-past three, when the church was well filled, the Mission-school occupying seats by themselves and the teachers by themselves.... I thought as I listened to the address that it would reconcile me to seeing you lying there in your coffin, if such a record stood against your name. Papa read, at the close, a sort of prophetic poem of Mrs. C.'s, which she wrote a year or more ago, of which I should like to send you all a copy, it is so good in every sense. He wants me to send you a few hasty lines I scribbled off on Sunday noon, with which he closed his sermon that afternoon, and repeated again at the funeral, but it is not worth the ink. After the service, the mission children went up to look at the remains, and passed out then the rest of the congregation. One of the mission children fainted and fell, and was carried out in Mr. L.'s arms. After the rest, dispersed papa took me in, and there we saw a most touching sight a dozen poor women and children weeping about the coffin, offering a tribute to her memory, sweeter than the opulent display of flowers did. *Evening.*—The interment took place today, at Woodlawn. Mr. C. wished me to go, and I did. On the way home a gentlemanly-looking man stepped up to your father, and taking his hand said, "I never saw you till today, but I *love* you yes, there is no other word!" Wasn't it nice of him?

Dec. 24th.—Papa went in last evening, for a half hour, to see —— and his bride, at their great reception, drank two glasses of "coffee sangaree," and brought me news that overcame me quite,—namely, that —— was delighted with my book. Nesbit & Co. sent me a copy of their reprint of it. They have got it up beautifully with six colored illustrations, most of them very good little Earnest is as cunning as he can be, and the old grandpa is perfect. Katy, however, has her hair in a waterfall in the year 1835 and even after, wears long dresses, and always has on a *sontag* or something like one. She goes to see Dr. Cabot in a red sacque, and a red hat, and has a muff in her lap. Mrs. —— was here the other day to say that I had drawn her husband's portrait *exactly* in Dr. Elliot. I have been out with M. all the morning, doing up our last shopping. We came home half frozen, and had lunch together, when lo, a magnificent basket of flowers from Mrs. D. and some candy from the party papa and G. came home and we all fell to making ourselves sick.... I have bought lots of candy and little fancy cakes to put in the children's stockings. I know it is very improper, but one cannot be good always. Dr. P. is sick with pneumonia. Mrs. P. has just sent me a basket of fresh eggs, and an illustrated edition of Longfellow's "Building of the Ship."

25th.—I wish you a Merry Christmas, darling, and wonder what you are all doing to celebrate this day. We have had great times over our presents.... I got a note from Mr. Abbot saying that a friend of his in Boston had given away fourteen Katies, all he could get, and that the bookseller said he could have sold the last copy thirty times over. Neither papa nor I feel quite up to the mark today we probably got a little cold at Mrs. C.'s grave, as the wind blew furiously, and the hymn, and prayer, and benediction took quite a time.

26th.—Dr. P. is worse. Papa has been to see him since church, and Dr. B., who was there, said that Dr. Murray quoted from Katy in his sermon today, and then pausing long enough to attract everybody's attention, he said he wished each of them to procure and read it. I hope you and Mrs. Smith will not get sick hearing about it I assure you I do not tell you half I might. *Evening.*—Mr. C. has been here this evening to show us a poem by his wife, just come out in the January number of the Sabbath at Home, in which she asks the New Year what it has in store for her, and says if it is *death*, it is only going home the sooner. Neither he, nor anyone, had seen it or heard of it, and it came to them with overwhelming power and consolation as the last utterance of her Christian faith. [1]

Dec. 30th, 1869.—Your letter came yesterday morning, after breakfast, and was read to an admiring audience of Prentisses by papa, who occasionally called for counsel as to this word and that. We like the plan made for the winter, and hope it will suit all round. You had such a grand birthday that I do not see what there was left for Christmas, and hope you got nothing but a leather button. My Percy's end today, and I am shocked at the wretched way in which I ended them. I wish you would buy a copy of Griseldis for me. Why do not you tell what you are reading? I got for M. "A Sister's Bye Hours," by Jean Ingelow, and find it a delightful book such lots of quiet humor and so much good sense and good feeling you girls would enjoy reading it aloud together.

Jan. 3rd, 1870.—You will want to hear all about New Year's day, and where shall I begin unless at the end thereof, when your and Mrs. Smith's letters came, and which caused papa ungraciously to leave me to entertain, while he greedily devoured them and his dinner. In spite of rain, we had a steady flow of visitors. I will enclose a list for your delectation, for as reading a cookbook sort of feeds one, reading familiar names sort of comforts one. Mr. —— was softer and more languishing than ever, and appeared like a man who had been fed on honey off the tips of a canary bird's feather.... Papa and I agreed, talking it over last evening, that it is a bad plan for husbands and wives not to live and die together, as the one who is left is apt to cut up. He hinted that I was "so fond of admiration" that he was afraid I should, if he died. On questioning him as to what he meant by this abominable speech, he said he meant to pay me a compliment! that he thought me very susceptible when people loved me and very fond of being loved— which I am by him all other men I hate. My cousin G. dined with us on Friday and took me to the meeting held annually at Dr. Adams' church. I like him ever so much, though he *is* a man. G. has brought me in some dandelions from the churchyard. We have not had one day of severe cold yet, and there is a great deal of sickness about in consequence.

Friday.—I spent a part of last evening in writing an article about Mrs. C.'s poem for the Sabbath at Home, and have a little fit of indigestion as my reward. Have been to see my sick woman with jelly and consolation, and from there to Mrs. D., who gave me a beautiful account of Mrs. Coming's last days and of her readiness and gladness to go. I was at the meeting at Dr. Rogers' yesterday afternoon and heard old Dr. Tyng for the first time, and he spoke beautifully.... Well, Chi Alpha [2] is over we had a very large attendance and the oysters were burnt. It is dreadfully trying when Maria never once failed before to have them so extra nice. Dr. Hall came and told me he had been sending copies of Fred and Maria and Me to friends in Ireland. Martha and Jane, and M. and H. were all standing in a row together when the parsons come out to tea, and one of them marched up to the row, saying to papa, Are these your children? When Martha and Jane made a precipitate retreat into the pantry. Goodnight, darling lots of love to Mrs. Smith, and all of them. Your affectionate "Marm-er."

11th.—Yours came today, and papa and I had a brief duel with hairpins and penknives as to which should read it aloud to the other, and I beat. I should have enjoyed Eigensinn, I am sure you know I have read it in German.... The children all three are lovely, and what with them and papa and other things, my cup is running over tremendously. I have just heard that a poor woman I have been to see a few times, died this morning. I always came away from her crestfallen, thinking I was the biggest poke in a sickroom there ever was, but she sent me a dying message that quite comforted me. She had once lived in plenty, but was fearfully destitute, and I fear she and her family suffered for want of common necessaries.

Thursday.—I had an early and a long call from one of our church, who wanted to tell me, among other things, that her husband scolded her for bumping her head in the night she wept and I condoled she went away at last smiling. Then I went to the sewing circle and idled about until one then I had several calls. Then papa and I went out to make a lot of calls. Then came a note from a sick lady, whom I shall go to see in spite of my horror of strangers. Papa got a letter from Prof. Smith, which gave us great pleasure. Z. was here yesterday I asked her to stay to lunch, bribing her with a cup of tea, and so she stayed and we had a real nice time when she went away I told her I was dead in love with her.

Friday Evening.—The children have all gone to bed M. and G. have been reading all the evening M. busy on Miss Alcott's "Little Women," and G. shaking his sides over old numbers of the Riverside. Papa says our house ought to have a sign put out, "Souls cured here" because so many people come to tell their troubles. People used to do just so to my mother, and I suppose always do to parsons' wives if they will let 'em.

Monday.—Papa preached delightfully yesterday. Mr. B. took a pew and Mr. I do not know who took another. Your letter came this morning and was full of interesting things. I hope Mrs. S. will send me her own and Jean Ingelow's verses. What fun to get into a correspondence with her! I have had an interesting time today. Dr. Skinner lent me some months ago a little book called "God's Furnace" I did not like it at first, but read it through several times and liked it better and better each time. And today Mrs. —— brought the author to spend a few hours (she lives out of town), and we three black-eyed women had a remarkable time together. There is certainly such a thing as a heaven below, only it does not last, as the real heaven will. We had Mr. C. to tea last night after tea he read us three poems of his wife, and papa was weak enough to go and read him some verses of mine, which he ought not to have done until I am dead and gone. Then he played and sang with the children, and we had prayers, and I read scraps to him and papa from Faber's "All for Jesus" and Craig's Memoir. M. is lying on the sofa studying, papa is in his study, the boys are hazing about it snows a little and melts as it falls, and so, with love to all, both great and small, I am your loving "ELDERLY LADY WITH GREY PUFFS."

February 8th, 1870.—We are having a tremendous snowstorm for a wonder. I started out this morning with G., and when we got to the Fifth avenue clock he found he should be late unless he ran, and I was glad to let him go and turn back to meet M., who had heavy books besides her umbrella. The wind blew furiously, my umbrella broke and flew off in a tangent, and when I got it, it turned wrong side out and I came near ascending as in a balloon M. soon came in sight and I convoyed her safely to school. Mrs. ⸺ told a friend of ours that Mr. and Mrs. Prentiss really *enjoyed* Mrs. C⸺'s death, and they seemed destitute of natural affection and that as for Mrs. P. it was plain she had never suffered in any way. Considering the tears we both shed over Mrs. C., and some other little items in our past history, we must set Mrs. ⸺ down as wiser than the ancients.

Sunday Evening.—Yesterday Lizzy B. came to say that her mother was "in a gully" and wanted me to come and pull her out. I went and found her greatly depressed, and felt sure it was all physical, and not a case for special spiritual pulling. So I coaxed her, laughed at her, and cheered her all I could. She said she had been "a solemn pig" for a week, in allusion to some pictures Dr. P. had drawn for her and for me illustrating the solemn pig and the jolly pig. Mr. Randolph has sent up a letter from a man in Nice whose wife wants to translate Katy into French. I sent word they might translate it into Hottentot for all me. Goodnight, my dear, I am sound asleep.

Your affectionate Mother PRENTISS.

Tuesday.—On Sunday papa preached a sermon in behalf of the Mission, asking for $35,000 to build a chapel, for which Mr. Cady had made a plan. I got greatly stirred up, as I hope everybody did. Mr. Dodge will give one-quarter of the sum needed. It is Washington's birthday, and the children are all at home from school, and are at the dining-room table drawing maps. Mr. and Mrs. G. called, but I was out seeing a poor woman, whose romance of love and sorrow I should like to tell you about if it would not fill a book. She says Bishop S. has supported her and her three children for seven months out of his own pocket.

Saturday, Feb. 26th.—Your two last letters, together with Mrs. Smith's, were all in the box as I was starting with M. for her music. My children pulled in opposite directions, but I pushed on, and papa saved the letters to read to me when I got back. He reads them awfully, and will puzzle over a word long enough for me to have leisure to go crazy and recover my sanity. However, nobody shall make fun of him save myself so look out. The boys have gone skating today for the third time this winter, there has been so little cold weather.

Sunday Evening.—I did not mean to plague you with Stepping Heavenward any more, but we have had a scene today, which will amuse you and Mrs. Smith. Just before service began, an aristocratic-looking lady seated in front of Mrs. B. began to talk to her, whereupon Mrs. B. turned round and announced to the congregation that I was the subject of it by pointing me out, and then getting up and bringing her to our pew. Once there, she seized me by the hand and said, "I am Mrs. ⸺. I have just read your book and been carried away with it. I knew your husband thirty-three years ago, and have come here to see you both," etc., etc. Finding she could get nothing out of me, she fell upon M., and asked her if I was her sister, which M. declared I was not. After church I invited her to step into the parsonage, and she stepped in for an hour and told this story: She had had the book lent her, and yesterday, lunching at Mrs. A.'s, asked her if she had read it, and finding she had not, made her promise to get it. She then asked who this E. Prentiss was, and a lady present enlightened her. "What! My sister's beloved Miss Payson, and married to George Prentiss, my old friend! I'll go there to church tomorrow and see for myself." So it turns out that she was a Miss ⸺, of Mississippi that your father gallanted her to Louisville, when she was going there to be married at sixteen years of age that she was living in Richmond at the time I was teaching there, her sister boarding in the house with me. Such talking, such life, and enthusiasm you never saw in a woman of forty-eight! "Well," she winds up at last, "I've found two *treasures*, and you needn't think I'm going to let you go. I'll go home and tell Mr. ⸺ all about it." Papa and I have called each other "two treasures" ever since she went away. The whole scene worked him up and did him good, for he always loves to have his Southern friends drum him up and talk to him of your Uncle Sergeant and Aunt Anna. Mr. ⸺ is one of our millionaires, and she married him a year ago after thirteen years of widowhood. She says she still has 200 "negroes," who will not go away and will not work, and she has them to support. She talked very rationally about the war, and says not a soul at the South would have slavery back if they could…. I called at Mrs. B.'s yesterday—at exactly the right moment, she said for five surgeons had just decided that the operation had been a failure, and that she must die. Her husband looked as white as this paper, and the girls were in great distress, but Mrs. B. looked perfectly radiant.

Saturday, March 5th.—Yesterday I went to make a ghostly call on Mrs. B., and kept her and the girls screaming with laughter for an hour, which did me lots of good, and I hope did not hurt them. I have written the 403rd page of my serial today, and hope it is the last. It will soon be time to think of the spring shopping. I do not know what any of us need, and never notice what people are wearing unless I notice by going forth on a tour of observation.

Sunday Evening.—After church this afternoon Mrs. N. and Mrs. V. came in to tell us about the death of that servant of theirs, whom they nursed in their own house, who has been dying for seven months, of cancer. She died a most fearless, happy death, and I wish I knew I should be as patient in my last illness as they represent her as being. Your letters to the children came yesterday afternoon to their great delight. In an evil moment I told the boys that I had seen it stated, in some paper, that *benzole* would make paper transparent, and afterwards evaporate and leave the paper uninjured. They drove me raving distracted with questions about it, so that I had to be put in a straitjacket. The ingenuity and persistence of these questions, asked by each, in separate interviews, was beyond description.

Tuesday.—For once I have been caught napping, and have not mailed my weekly letter. But you will be expecting some irregularity about the time of your flight to Berlin. I called at Mrs. M.'s today, and ran on at such a rate that Mrs. Woolsey, who was there, gave me ten dollars for poor folks, and said she wished I would stay all day. Afterwards I went down town to get Stepping Heavenward for Mr. C., and as he wanted me to write something in it, have just written this: "Mr. C. from Mrs. Prentiss, in loving memory of one who 'did outrun' us, and stepped into heaven first." Mr. Bates showed me a half-column notice of it in the Liberal Christian, [3] of all places! By very far the warmest and best of all that have appeared. Papa is at Dr. McClintock's funeral. I declare, if it is not snowing again, and the sun is shining! Now comes a letter from Uncle Charles, saying that your Uncle H. has lost that splendid little girl of his the only girl he ever had, and the child of his heart of hearts. Mrs. W. says she never saw papa and myself look so well, but some gentleman told Mr. Brace, who told his wife, who told me, that I was killing myself with long walks. I cannot answer your questions about Mr. ———'s call. So much is all the time going on that one event speedily effaces the impression of another.

March 12th.—Julia Willis spent the evening here not long ago, and made me laugh well. She took me on Friday to see Fanny Fern, who hugged and kissed me, and whom it was rather pleasant to see after nearly, if not quite, thirty years' separation. She says nobody but a Payson could have written Stepping Heavenward, which is absurd. *March 17th.*—I went to the sewing circle [4] and helped tuck a quilt, had a talk with Mrs. W., got home at a quarter of one and ate two apples, and have been since then reading the secret correspondence of Madame Guyon and Fenelon in old French.

Saturday, 19th.—Have just seen M. to the Conservatory met Dr. Skinner on the way home, who said he had been reading Stepping Heavenward, and he hoped he should step all the faster for it. Z. has often invited us to come to see her new home, and as the 16th comes on a Saturday, we are talking a little of all going up to lunch with her. *Evening.*—It has been such a nice warm day. I had a pleasant call from Mrs. Dr. ———. She asked me if I did not get the theology of Stepping Heavenward out of my father's "Thoughts," but as I have not read them for thirty years, I doubt if I did, and as I am older than my father was when he uttered those thoughts, I have a right to a theology of my own.

Monday.—Yesterday, in the afternoon, we had the Sunday-school anniversary, which went off very well. Mr. C. came to tea after it and prayers, we sat round the table and I read scraps from Madame Guyon and Fenelon, and we talked them over. Papa was greatly pleased at the latter's saying he often stopped in the midst of his devotions to play.

Quand je suis seul, je joue quelquefois comme un petit enfant, même en faisant oraison. Il m'arrive quelquefois de sauter et de rire tout seul comme un fou dans ma chambre. Avant-hier, étant dans la sacristie et répondant à une personne qui me questionnait, pour ne la point scandaliser sur la question, je m'embarrassai, et je fis une espèce de mensonge cela me donna quelque répugnance à dire la Messe, mais je ne laissai pas de la dire.

I do not advise *you* to stop to play in the midst of your prayers, or to tell "une espèce de mensonge!" until you are as much of a saint as he was. [5]

Saturday, 26th.—Your letter and Mrs. Smith's came together this afternoon. It is pleasant to hear from papa's old friends at Halle, and he will be delighted, when he comes home from Chi Alpha, where he is now. Lizzy B. called this afternoon she wanted to open out her poor sick heart to me. She quoted to me several things she says I wrote her a few weeks ago, but I have not the faintest recollection of writing them. That shows what a harum-scarum life I lead.

March 31st.—We spent Tuesday evening at the Skinners. We had a charming visit no one there but Mrs. Sampson and her sister, and Dr. S. wide awake and full of enthusiasm. We did not get to bed until midnight. Mrs. ——— came this morning and begged me to lend her some money, as she had got behindhand. I let her have five dollars, though I do not feel sure that I shall see it again, and she wept a little weep, and went away. A lady told cousin C. she had heard I was so shy that once having promised to go to a lunch party, my courage failed at the last moment, so that I could not go. I shall expect to learn next that my hair is red.

Monday, April 4th.—Your presents came Saturday while I was out. We are all delighted with them, but I was most so, for two such darling little vases were surely never before seen. M. had Maggie to spend Saturday afternoon and take tea. She asked me if I did not make a distinction between talent and genius, which papa thought very smart of her. I read aloud to them all the evening one of the German stories by Julius Horn. Mr. and Mrs. C. came in after church and I asked them to stay to tea, which they did. After it was over, and we had had prayers, we had a little sing, Mrs. C. playing, and among other things, sang a little hymn of mine, which I wrote I know not when, but which papa liked well enough to have printed. If copies come today, as promised, I will enclose one or two. After the singing papa and I took turns, as we could snatch a chance from each other, in reading to them from favorite books, which they enjoyed very much.

~ 236 ~

April 9th.—We called on Mrs. H. M. Field yesterday, and I never saw (or rather heard) her so brilliant. In the evening, I read aloud to the children a real live, wide-awake Sunday-school book, called "Old Stories in a New Dress" Bible stories, headed thus: "The Handsome Rebel," "The Young Volunteer," "The Ingenious Mechanics."

April 16th.—I cannot go to bed, my dear chicken, until I have told you what a charming day we have had. To go back to yesterday, my headache entirely disappeared by the time the Skinners got here, and we had a pleasant cozy evening with them, and at the end made Dr. Skinner pray over us…. Everything went off nicely. The children enjoyed the trip tremendously, and hated to come away. We picked a lot of "filles avant la mère" and they came home in good condition. Mr. Woolsey and Z. gave me a little silver figure holding a cup, on blue velvet, which is ever so pretty. We got home at half-past six. Later in the evening, President Hopkins called to offer his congratulations. And now I am tired, I can tell you. It is outrageous for you and the Smiths to be away I do not see how you can have the heart. You ought to come by dispatch as telegrams.

17th.—Dr. Hopkins preached a splendid sermon [6] for us this morning, and came in after it for a call. He asked me last night if I felt conceited about my book so I said to him, "I like to give people as good as they send—do not you feel a little conceited after that sermon?" on which he gave me a good shaking.

18th.—I have been writing notes of thanksgiving, each of which dear papa reads through rose-colored spectacles and says, "You do beat all!" I have enjoyed writing them, instead of finding it a bore. We shall be curious to hear how you celebrated our wedding-day. Well, goodbye, old child. I shall begin another letter today, as like as not.

Monday, April 25th.—Friday morning, in the midst of my plans for helping Aunt E. shop, came a message from Mrs. B. that she wanted to see me. I had not expected to see her again, and of course was glad to go. She had altered so that I should not have known her, and it was hard to hear what she had to say, she is so feeble. She went back to the first time she saw me, told me what I had on, and how her heart was knitted to me. She then spoke of her approaching death said she had no ecstasies, no revelations, but had been in perfect peace, suffering agonies of pain, yet not one pain too many. I asked her if she had any parting counsel to give me. "No, not a word I only wanted to see your sunny face once more, and tell you what a comfort you have been to me in this sickness." This all came at intervals, she was so weak. She afterward said, "I feel as if I never was acquainted with Christ till now. I tell my sons to become INTIMATELY ACQUAINTED with Him." I asked her if she took pleasure in thinking of meeting friends in heaven. With a sweet, somewhat comical smile, she said, "No, I haven't got so far as that. I think only of meeting Christ." "For all that," I said, "you will soon see my father and mother and other kindred souls." Her face lighted up again. "Why, so I shall!" Her lips were growing white with pain while this bright smile was on them, and I came away, though I should gladly have listened to her by the hour, everything was so natural, sound, and-heavenly. Shopping after it did not prove particularly congenial but we must shop, as well as die.

April 29th.—Your first Dresden letter has just come yes, it was long enough, though you did not tell us how the cat did. You speak as if you were going to Paris, but papa is positive you are not. Yesterday was a lovely day, though very hot. Dr. Adams came and drove papa to the Park. Late in the afternoon, I went to see Mrs. G., the woman whose husband is in jail. She is usually all in a muss, but this time was as nice as could be, the floor clean and everything in order. The baby, a year old, had learned to walk since I was last there, and came and planted herself in front of me, and stared at me out of two great bright eyes most of the time. I had a nice visit, as Mrs. G. seems to be making a good use of her troubles. After I got home, Dr. and Mrs. C. arrived, and we had dinner and a tremendous thunder shower, after which he went out to make forty-'leven calls. He was pleased to say that he wanted his wife to see the lovely family picture we make! It is a glum, cold, lowering morning, but the C.'s are going to see the Frenches at West Point, and Miss Lyman at Vassar.

Monday.—I went to Miss C.'s (the dressmaker) again today, and found her much out of health, and about reducing her business and moving. One of the old sisters had been reading Stepping Heavenward, and almost ate me up. I got a pleasant word about it last night, from Mrs. General Upton, who has just died at Nassau. I have seen Mrs. B. today she did not open her eyes, but besought me to pray for her release. She cannot last long. The boys are off rolling hoop again, and M. is out walking with Ida. Papa informed me last night that I had got a very pretty bonnet. The bonnets now consist of a little fuss and a good many flowers. Papa has gone to Dorset, and has had a splendid day for his journey.

Thursday, May 12th.—Yesterday Miss —— came to tell me about the killing of her brother on the railroad, and to cry her very heart out on my shoulder. In the midst of it came a note from Lizzy B., saying her mother had just dropped away. I called there early this morning. We then went to the Park with your uncle and aunt after which they left and I rushed out to get cap and collar to wear at Mrs. ——'s dinner. I got back in time to go to the funeral at four P.M. Dr. Murray made an excellent, appreciative address papa then read extracts from a paper of mine (things she had said), the prayer followed, and then her sons sang a hymn. [7] I came home tired and laid me down to rest at half-past six it popped into my head that I was not dressed, and I did it speedily. We supposed we were only to meet the Rev.

Dr. and Mrs. ——, of Brooklyn, but, lo! a lot of people in full dress. We had a regular state dinner, course after course. Dr. —— sat next me and made himself very agreeable, except when he said I was the most subtle satirist he ever met (I did run him a little). Mrs. —— is a picture. She had a way of looking at me through her eyeglass until she put me out of countenance, and then smiling in a sweet, satisfied manner, and laying down her glass. We came home as soon as the gentlemen left the table, and got here just as the clock was striking twelve.

Friday.—We began this day by going at ten A.M. to the funeral of Mrs. W.'s poor little baby, and the first words papa read, "It is better to go to the house of mourning than to the house of feasting," etc., explained his and my state of mind after last night's dissipation. He made a very touching address. Later in the day we went out to see Miss ——, as we had promised to do. We went through the Park, lingered there a while, and then went on and made a long call. When we rose to come away, she said she never let people go away without lunch and made us go down to the following: buns, three kinds of cake, pies, doughnuts, cheese, lemonade, apples, oranges, pine-apples, a soup tureen of strawberries, a quart of cream, two custard puddings, one hot and one cold, home-made wine, cold corned beef, cold roast beef, and for aught I know 40 other things. We came away very tired, and papa complained of want of appetite at dinner! Goodbye, dearie. I forgot to tell you the boys have got a dog. He came of his own accord and has made them very happy. We have not let papa see him, you may depend.

Wed., May 18th.—Papa is packing his trunk for Philadelphia, and I am sitting at my new library table to write on my letter. I went yesterday to see that lady who has fits. She had one in the morning that lasted over an hour and a half. She is a very bright, animated creature and does not look older than you.

Thursday.—Papa got off yesterday at eleven for the General Assembly and I went to Mrs. D.'s and stayed four hours. She sent for Mr. S.'s baby, who does not creep, but walks in the quaintest little way. I shall write a note to Mr. S., who feels anxious at its not creeping, fearing its limbs will not be strong, to tell him that I hitched along exactly so.

Now let me give you the history of this busy day. We got up early and Miss F. called with M.'s two dresses. After prayers and breakfast, I wrote to papa, went to school with H., and marketed. Came home and found a letter from Cincinnati, urging for two hymns right away for a new hymnbook. They had several of mine already. I said, "Go to, let us make a hymn" (Prof. Smith in his Review) and made and sent them. Then I wrote to Mr. S. and to Mrs. Charles W——. [8] Then Mrs. C. came and stayed till nearly four, when she left and I went down to Twenty-second street to call on a lady at the Water Cure. Then I went to see Mrs. C. (the wife of the Rev. Mr. C.). I think I told you she had lost her little Florence. I do not remember ever seeing a person so broken down by grief she seemed absolutely heartbroken. I could not get away until five, and then I took two stages and got home as soon as I could, knowing the children would be famishing. So now, count up my various professions, chaplain, marketer, hymnist, consoler of Mr. S., Mrs. W., Mrs. C., and let me add, of Dr. B., who came and made a long call. I am now going to lie down and read until I am rested, for my brain has been on the steady stretch for thirteen hours, one thing stepping on the heels of another. [9]

May 23rd.—If your eyes were bright enough you might have seen me and my cousin George P—— tearing down Broadway this afternoon, as if mad dogs were after us. He wanted me to have a fountain pen, and the only way to accomplish it was to take me down to the place where they are sold, below the Astor House. I wanted to walk, and so did he, but he had to be on a boat for Norwich at five P.M. and pack up between while however, he concluded to risk it, hence the way we raced was a caution. I have just written him a long letter in rhyme with my new pen, and now begin one in prose to you. I have just got a letter from an anonymous admirer of Stepping Heavenward, enclosing ten dollars to give away. I wish it were a thousand! The children are in tribulation about their kitten, who committed suicide by knocking the ironing board on to herself. H. made a diagram of the position of the board that I might fully comprehend the situation, and then showed me how the corpse lay. They were not willing to part with the remains, and buried them in the yard.

Saturday.—I went to Yonkers with M. and H. to spend the day with Mrs. B. Her children are sweet and interesting as ever but little Maggie, now three years old, is the "queen of the house." She is a perfect specimen of what a child should be—gladsome, well, bright, and engaging. Her cheeks are rosy and shining, and she keeps up an incessant chatter. They are all wild about her, from papa and mamma down to the youngest child.

* * * * *

II.
Home-Life in Dorset.

DORSET, June 10, 1870. Here we are again in dear old Dorset. We got here about ten on Wednesday evening, expecting to find the house dark and forlorn, but Mrs. F. had been down and lighted it up, and put on the dining-table bread, biscuits, butter, cakes, eggs, etc., enough to last for days. Thursday was hotter than any day we had had in New York, and not very good, therefore, for the hard work of unpacking, and the yet harder work of sowing our flower-seeds in a huge bed shaped like a palm-leaf. But, with M.'s help, it was done before one o'clock today—a herculean task, as the ground had to be thoroughly dug up with a trowel stones, sticks, and roots got out, and the earth sifted in our hands. The back of my neck and my ears are nearly blistered. M. is standing behind me now anointing me with cocoa butter. Our place looks beautifully. Some of the trees set out are twelve or fifteen feet high, and when fully leaved will make quite a show. Papa is to be here about ten days, as he greatly needs the rest he will then go home until July 1st, when he will bring Jane and Martha. I told Martha I thought it very good of Maria to be willing to come with me, and she said she did not think it needed much goodness, and that *anybody* would go with me _anywhere. The boys have a little black and tan dog which Culyer gave them, and M.'s bird is a fine singer. Our family circle now consists of

Pa Prentiss, Ma "Min." Geo. "Hen." "Maria" (horse) Coco" "(cow) Sukey" "(dog) Nep" "(bird) Cherry"

We never saw Dorset so early, and when the foliage was in such perfection.

Last Tuesday I reached our door perfectly and disgracefully loaded with parcels, and said to myself, "I wonder what Mr. M. would say if he saw me with this load?" when instantly he opened the door to let me in! Account for this if you can. Why should I have thought of him among all the people I know? Did his mind touch mine through the closed door? It makes me almost shudder to think such things can be. Well, I must love and leave you. I am going to have a small basket on the table in the hall with ferns, mosses, and shells in it. They all send love from Pa Prentiss down to Sukey. What a pity you could not come home for the summer and go back again! I believe I will go to your bedroom door and say, "I wonder whether Annie would shriek out if she saw me in this old sacque, instead of her pretty one?" and perhaps you will open and let me in. Will you or won't you? Now I am going to ride.

I've been and I've got back, and I'm frozen solid, and am glad I've got back to my den. G. and H. are now in the kitchen making biscuits. Goodbye, chicken. Mamma PRENTISS.

June 12th.—Everybody is in bed save Darby and Joan. We slept last night under four blankets and a silk comforter, which will give you a faint idea of the weather. It has been beautiful today, and we have sat out of doors a good deal. Papa and the boys went out to our hill after tea last evening and picked two quarts of strawberries, so as to have shortcake today. M. took me yesterday to see a nest in the orchard which was full of birds parted into fours—not a crack between, and one of them so crowded that it filled about no space at all. The hymn says, "Birds in their little nests agree," and I should think they would, for they have no room to disagree in. They all four stared at us with awful, almost embarrassing solemnity, and each had a little yellow moustache. I had no idea they lived packed in so—no wonder they looked melancholy. The sight of them, especially of the one who had no room at all, made me quite low-spirited.

Wednesday.—Your letter reached us on Monday, and we all went out and sat in a row on the upper step, like birds on a telegraph wire, and papa read it aloud. I am lying by today—writing, reading, lounging, and enjoying the scenery. You ought to see papa eat strawberries! They are very plentiful on our hill. The grass on the lawn is pricking up like needles easy to see if you kneel down and stare hard, but absolutely invisible otherwise yet papa keeps calling me to look out of the window and admire it, and shouts to people driving by to do the same. He has just come in, and I told him what I was saying about him, on which he gave me a good beating, doubled up his fist at me, and then kissed me to make up…. *Do not sew* Isn't it enough that I have nearly killed myself with doing it? We have just heard of the death of Dickens and the sensation it is making in England.

Thursday.—This bird of ours is splendid. I have just framed the two best likenesses of you and hung them up in front of my table. You would laugh at papa's ways about coffee. He complains that he drank too much at Philadelphia, and says that with strawberries we do not need it, and that I may tell Maria so. I tell her, and lo! the next morning there it is. I ask the meaning, and she says he came down saying I did not feel very well and needed it! The next day it appears again. Why? He had been down and ordered it because it was *good*. The next day he orders it because it is his last day here but one, and tomorrow it will be on the table because it is the last! Dreadful man! and yet I hate to have him go.

Friday.—I drove papa to Manchester, and as usual, this exploit brought on a thundershower, with a much needed deluge of rain. I had a hard time getting home, and got wet to the skin. I had not only to drive, but keep a roll of matting from slipping out, hold up the boot and the umbrella, and keep stopping to get my hat out of my eyes, which kept knocking over them. Then Coco goes like the wind this summer. Fortunately, I had my waterproof with me and got home safely. The worst of it is that, in my bewilderment, I refused to let a woman get in who was walking to South Dorset. I shall die of remorse… Well, well, how it is raining, to be sure.

Monday.—I hear that papa sent a dispatch to somebody to know how I got here from Manchester. I do not wonder he is worried. I am such a poor driver, and it rained so dreadfully. M. follows me round like a little dog if I go down cellar she goes down if I pick a strawberry, she picks one if I stop picking she stops. She is the sweetest lamb that ever was, and I am the Mary that has her. I do not believe anybody else in the world loves me so well, unless it possibly is papa, and he does not follow me down cellar, and goes off and picks strawberries all by himself, and that on Sunday, too, when I had forbidden berry picking! We are rioting in strawberries, just as we did last summer. We live a good deal at sixes and sevens, but nobody cares. This afternoon I have been arranging a basket for the hall table, with mosses, ferns, shells, and white coral ever so pretty.

Wednesday.—It is a splendid day and I expect papa. The children have not said a word about their food, though partly owing to no butcher and partly to the heat, I have had for two days next to nothing picked fish one day and fish picked the next. We regarded today's dinner as a most sumptuous one, and I am sure Victoria's will not taste so good to her. Letters keep pouring in, urging papa to accept the Professorship at Chicago, and declaring the vote of the Assembly to be the voice of God. Of course, if he must accept, we should have to give up our dear little home here. But to me his leaving the ministry would be the worst thing about it. After dinner, the boys carried me off bodily to see strawberries and other plants then they made me go to the mill, and by that time, I had no hairpins on my head, to say nothing of hair. The boys are working away like all possessed. A little bird, probably one of those hatched here, has just come, and perched himself on the piazza, railing in front of me, and is making me an address that, unfortunately, I do not understand.... You have inherited from me a want of reverence for relics and the like. I would not go as far as our barn to see the fig leaves Adam and Eve wore, or all the hair of all the apostles and when people are not born hero-worshippers, they cannot even worship themselves as heroes. Fancy Dr. Schaff sending me back the MS. of a hymn I gave him, from a London printing office! What could I do with it? Cover jelly with it? He sent me a beautiful copy of his book, "Christ in Song."

Thursday, June 30th.—Papa, with J. and M., came late last night, and we all made as great a time as if the Great Mogul had come. They give a most terrific account of the heat in the city. You ask how Stepping Heavenward is selling. So far 14,000. Nidworth has been a complete failure, though the publishers write me that it is a "gem." [10]

Monday, July 4th.—M. is so absorbed in the study of Vick's floral catalogue that she speaks of seeing such a thing in the Bible or Dictionary, when she means that she saw it in Vick. I did the same thing last night. She and I get down on our knees and look solemnly at the bare ground and point out up-springing weeds as better than nothing. I had a long call this morning from Mrs. F. Field, of East Dorset. They had a dear little bright-eyed baby baptized yesterday, which sat through all the morning service and behaved even better than I did, for it had no wandering thoughts. Mrs. F. said some friends of hers in Brooklyn received letters from France and from Japan simultaneously, urging them to read Stepping Heavenward, which was the first they heard of it. We have celebrated the glorious Fourth by making and eating ice cream. Papa brought a new-fashioned freezer, which professed to freeze in two minutes. We screwed it to the wood-house floor—or rather H. did—put in the cream, and the whole family stood and watched papa while he turned the handle. At the end of two minutes we unscrewed the cover and gazed inside, but there were no signs of freezing, and to make a long story short, instead of writing a book as I said I should, there we all were from half-past twelve to nearly two o'clock, when we decided to have dinner and leave the servants to finish it. It came on to the table at last, was very rich and rather good. The boys spent the afternoon in the woods firing off crackers. M. went visiting and papa took me to drive, it being a delightful afternoon. The boys have a few Roman candles, which they are going to send off as soon as it gets dark enough.

July 13th.—This is a real Dorset day, after a most refreshing rain, and M. and I have kept out of doors the whole morning, gardening and in the woods. Dr. and Mrs. Humphrey came down and spent last evening. She is bright and wide awake, and admired everything from the scenery out of doors to the matting and chintzes within. I told her there was nothing in the house to be compared with those who lived in it. Here comes a woman with four quarts of black raspberries and a fuss to make change. Papa and the boys are getting in the last hay with Albert. M. has just brought in your letter. We are glad you have seen those remarkable scenes [at Ober-Ammergau].One would fancy it would become an old story. I should not like to see the crucifixion it must be enough to turn one's hair white in a single night.

Saturday.—Yesterday I went with the children to walk round Rupert. We turned off the road to please the boys, to a brook with a sandy beach, where all three fell to digging wells, and I fell to collecting wild grape-vine and roots for my rustic work, and fell into the brook besides. We all enjoyed ourselves so much that we wished we had our dinners and could stay all day. On the way home, just as we got near Col. Sykes', we spied papa with the phaeton, and all got in. We must have cut a pretty figure, driving through the village M. in my lap, G. in papa's, and H. everywhere in general.

July 14th.—Miss Vance was in last evening after tea, and says our lawn is getting on extremely well and that our seeds are coming up beautifully. This greatly soothed M.'s and my own uneasy heart, as we had rather supposed the lawn ought to be a thick velvet, and the seeds we sowed two weeks ago up and blooming. If vegetable corresponded to animal life, this would be the case. Fancy that what were eggs long after we came here, and then naked birds, are now full-fledged creatures on the wing, all off getting to housekeeping, each on his own hook!

July 18th.—M. and I went on a tramp this forenoon and while we were gone Mrs. M. O. R. and Mary and Mrs. Van W. called. They brought news of the coming war. Papa showed them all over the house, not excepting your room, which I think a perfect shame—for the room looks forlorn. I think men ought to be suppressed, or something done to them. Maria told me she thought papa's sermon Sunday was "ilegant." *21st.*—I feel greatly troubled lest this dreadful war should cut us off from each other. Mr. Butler writes that he does not see how people are to get home, and we do not see either. Papa says it will probably be impossible to have the Evangelical Alliance. And how prices of finery will go up!

July 27th.—M.'s and my own perseverance at our flowerbed is beginning, at last, to be rewarded. We have portulaccas, mignonette, white candytuft, nasturtiums, eutocas, etc. and the morning glories, which are all behindhand, are just beginning to bloom. Never were flowers so fought for. It is the lion and the unicorn over again. I have nearly finished "Soll und Haben," and feel more like talking German than English. The Riverside Magazine has just come and completed my downfall, as it has a syllable left out of one of my verses, as has been the case with a hymn in the hymnbook at Cincinnati and one in the Association Monthly. I am now fairly entitled to the reputation of being a jolty rhymster. It has been a trifle cooler today and we are all refreshed by the change.

Friday.—Papa read me last evening a nice thing about Stepping Heavenward from Dr. Robinson in Paris and a lady in Zurich, and I went to bed and slept the sleep of the just—till daylight, when five hundred flies began to flap into my ears, up my nose, take nips off my face and hands, and drove me distracted. They woke papa, too, but he goes to sleep between the pecks.

August 4th.—Tuesday I went on a tramp with M. and brought home a gigantic bracket. We met papa as we neared the house, and he had had his first bath in his new tank at the mill, and was wild with joy, as were also the boys. After dinner I made a picture frame of mosses, lichens, and red and yellow toadstools, ever so pretty then proofs came, then we had tea, and then went and made calls. Yesterday on a tramp with M., who wanted mosses, then home with about a bushel of ground pine. Every minute of the afternoon, I spent in trimming the grey room with the pine and getting up my bracket, and now the room looks like a bower of bliss. I was to go with M. on another tramp today, but it rains, and rain is greatly needed. The heat in New York is said to exceed anything in the memory of man, something absolutely appalling.

Friday.—Here I am on the piazza with Miss K. by my side, reading the Life of Faber. She got here last night in a beautiful moonlight, and as I had not told her about the scenery, she was so enchanted with it on opening her blinds this morning, that she burst into tears. I drove her round Rupert and took her into Cheney's woods, and the boys invited us down to their workshop so we went, and I was astonished to find that the bathhouse is really a perfect affair, with two dressing rooms and everything as neat as a pink. Miss K. is charged with everything, the cornucopias, natural brackets, crosses, etc., and her delusion as to all of us, whom she fancies saints and angels, is quite charming, only it will not last.

13th.—There is a good deal of sickness about the village. I made wine-jelly for four different people yesterday, and the rest of the morning Miss K., Mrs. Humphrey, and myself sat on a shawl in our woods, talking. We have had a tremendous rain, to our great delight, and the air is cooler, but the grasshoppers, which are like the frogs of Egypt, are not diminished, and are devouring everything. I got a letter from cousin Mary yesterday, who says she has no doubt we shall get the ocean up here, somehow, and raise our own oysters and clams.

16th.—Papa and I went to Manchester today to make up a lot of calls, and among other persons, we saw Mrs. C. of Troy, a bright-eyed old lady who was a schoolmate of my mother's. She could not tell me anything about her except that she was very bright and animated, and that I knew before. Mrs. Wickham asked me to write some letters for a fair to be held for their church tomorrow so I wrote three in rhyme, not very good.

August 20th.—After dinner papa went to Manchester, taking both boys, and I went off with M. to Cheney's woods, where we got baskets full of moss, etc., and had a good time. The children are all wild on the subject of flowers and spend the evening studying the catalogues, which they ought to know by heart. I wonder if I have told you how our dog hates to remember the Sabbath day to keep it holy? The moment the church-bell begins to ring, no matter where he is, or how soundly asleep, he runs out and gazes in the direction of the church, and as the last stroke strikes, lifts his nose high in the air and sets up the most awful wails, howls, groans, despairing remonstrances you can imagine. No games with the boys today—no romps, no going to Manchester, everybody telling me to get off their Sunday clothes—now! now! now!

Dr. Adams' house has been broken into and robbed, and so has Dr. Field's. Mrs. H. gave us the history of a conflict in Chicago between her husband and a desperate burglar armed with a dirk, who wanted, but did not get a large sum of money under his pillow also, of his being garroted and robbed, and having next day sent him a purse of $150, two pistols, a slug, a loaded cane, and a watchman's rattle. Imagine him as going about loaded with all these things! I never knew people who had met with such bewitching adventures, and she has the brightest way of telling them.

Papa has got a telegram from Dr. Schaff asking him to come on to his little Johnny's funeral. This death must have been very sudden, as Dr. Schaff wrote last Tuesday that his wife was sick, but said nothing of Johnny. He is the youngest boy, about nine years old, I think, and you will remember they lost Philip, a beautiful child, born the same day as our G., the summer we were at Hunter. When the dispatch came papa and M. thought it was bad news about you, and I only thought of Mr. Stearns! There is no accounting for the way in which the human mind works. And now for bed, you sleepy head.

Monday.—A splendid day, and we have all been as busy as bees, if not as useful,—H. making a whip to chastise the cow with, M., Nep and myself collecting mosses and toadstools of the latter I brought home 185! We were out till dinnertime, and after dinner, I changed the mosses in my baskets and jardinet, no small job, and M. spread out her treasures. She has at last found her enthusiasm, and I am so glad not only to have found a mate in my tramps, but to see such a source of pleasure opening before her as woods, fields and gardens have always been to me. We lighted this morning on what I supposed to be a horned-headed, ferocious snake, and therefore took great pleasure in killing. It turned out to be a common striped snake that had got a frog partly swallowed, and its legs sticking out so that I took them to be horns. Nep relieved his mind by barking at it. I announced at dinner that I was going to send for Vick's catalogue of bulbs, which news was received with acclamation. The fact is, we all seem to be born farmers or florists, and unless you bring us home something in the agricultural line, and I do not know that you can bring us anything we would condescend to look at. It is awful to read of the carnage going on in Europe.

Aug. 27th.—Papa got home Tuesday night. Johnny Schaff's death was from a fall he left the house full of life and health, and in a few minutes was brought in insensible, and only lived half an hour.... I take no pleasure in writing you, because we feel that you are not likely to get my letters. Still, I cannot make up my mind to stop writing. Never was a busier set of people than we. In the evening I read to the children from the German books you sent them am now on Thelka Von Grumpert's, which is a really nice book. I tell papa we are making an idol out of this place, but he says we are not.

Tuesday.—We all set out to climb the mountain near Deacon Kellogg's. We snatched what we could for our dinner, and when we were ready to eat it, it proved to be eggs, bread and meat, cake, guava jelly, cider and water. We enjoyed the splendid view and the dinner, and then papa and the boys went home, and M., Nep and myself proceeded to climb higher, Nep so affectionate that he tired me out hugging me with his "arms," as H. calls them, and nearly eating me up, while M. was shaking with laughter at his silly ways. We were gone from 10 A.M. to nearly 6 P.M., and brought home in baskets, bags, pockets and bosom, about thirty natural brackets, some very large and fearfully heavy. One was so heavy that I brought it home by kicking it down the mountain. I have just got some flower seeds for fall planting, and the children are looking them over as some would gems from the mine.

Thursday, September 1st.—Your letter has come, and we judge that you have quite given up Paris what a pity to have to do it! We spent yesterday at Hager brook with Mrs. Humphrey and her daughter's papa drove us over in the straw wagon and came for us about 6 P.M. We had lobster salad and marmalade, bread and butter and cake, and we roasted potatoes and corn, and the H.'s had a pie and things of that sort. When they saw the salad they set up such shouts of joy that papa came to see what was the matter. We had a nice time. Today I have had proofs to correct and letters to write, and berries to dry, but not a minute to sit down and think, everybody needing me at once. All are busy as bees and send lots of love. Give ever so much to the Smiths.

September 8th.—Here we are all sitting round the parlor table. The last three days have each brought a letter from you, and today one came from Mrs. S. to me, and one from Prof. S. to papa. I have no doubt that the decision for you to return is a wise one and hope you will fall in with it cheerfully. Dr. Schaff is here, and yesterday papa took him to Hager brook, and today to the quarries splendid weather for both excursions, and Dr. S. seems to have enjoyed them extremely. Last evening he read to us some private letters of Bismarck, which were very interesting and did him great credit in every way. I had a long call from M. H. today she looked as sweet as possible and I loaded her with flowers. Papa is writing Mr. B. to thank him for a basket of splendid peaches he sent us today. H. has just presented me with three pockets full of toadstools. M. walked with me round Rupert square this afternoon, and we met a crazy woman who said she wondered I did not go into fits, and asked me why I did not. In return, I asked her where she lived, to which she replied, "In the world." We are all on the *qui vive* about the war news, especially Louis Napoleon's downfall, and you may depend we are glad he has used himself up. You cannot bring anything to the children that will please them as seeds would. It delights me to see them so interested in garden work. Perhaps this will be my last letter.

Your loving Mammie.

* * * * *

III.
Further Glimpses of her Dorset Life.

The following Recollections of Mrs. Prentiss by her friend, Mrs. Frederick Field, now of San Jose, California, afford additional glimpses of her home life in Dorset. The picture is drawn in fair colors but it is as truthful as it is fair:

It was the first Sunday in September, 1866. A quiet, perfect day among the green hills of Vermont a sacramental Sabbath, and we had come seven miles over the mountain to go up to the house of the Lord. I had brought my little two-months-old baby in my arms, intending to leave her during the service at our brother's home, which was near the church. I knew that Mrs. Prentiss was a "summer-boarder" in this home, which she was the wife of a distinguished clergyman, and a literary woman of decided ability but it was before the "Stepping Heavenward" epoch of her life, and I had no very deep interest in the prospect of meeting her. We went in at the hospitably open door, and meeting no one, sat down in the pleasant family living room. It was about noon, and we could hear cheerful voices talking over the lunch-table in the dining room. Presently the door opened, and a slight, delicate-featured woman, with beautiful large dark eyes, came with rapid step into the room, going across to the hall door but her quick eye caught a glimpse of my little "bundle of flannel," and not pausing for an introduction or word of preparatory speech, she came towards me with a beaming face and outstretched hands:—

"O, have you a baby there? How delightful! I haven't seen one for such an age,—please, may I take it? The darling tiny creature!—a girl? How lovely!"

She took the baby tenderly in her arms and went on in her eager, quick, informal way, but with a bright little blush and smile,—"I'm not very polite—pray, let me introduce myself! I'm Mrs. Prentiss, and you are Mrs. F——, I know."

After a little more sweet, motherly comment and question over the baby,—"a touch of nature" which at once made us "akin," she asked, "Have you brought the baby to be christened?"

I said, No, I thought it would be better to wait till she was a little older.

"O, no!" she pleaded, "do let us take her over to the church now. The younger the better, I think it is so uncertain about our keeping such treasures."

I still objected that I had not dressed the little one for so public an occasion.

"O, never mind about that," she said. "She is really lovelier in this simple fashion than to be loaded with lace and embroidery." Then, her sweet face growing more earnest,—"There will be more of us here today than at the next communion—*more of us to pray for her.*"

The little lamb was taken into the fold that day, and I was Mrs. Prentiss' warm friend forevermore. Her whole beautiful character had revealed itself to me in that little interview,—the quick perception, the wholly frank, unconventional manner, the sweet motherliness, the cordial interest in even a stranger, the fervent piety which could not bear delay in duty, and even the quaint, original, forcible thought and way of expressing it, "There'll be more of us here to pray for her today."

For seven successive summers, I saw more or less of her in this "Earthly Paradise," as she used to call it, and once I visited her in her city home. I have been favored with many of her sparkling, vivacious letters, and have read and re-read all her published writings but that first meeting held in it for me the key-note of all her wonderfully beautiful and symmetrical character.

She brought to that little hamlet among the hills a sweet and wholesome and powerful influence. While her time was too valuable to be wasted in a general sociability, she yet found leisure for an extensive acquaintance, for a kindly interest in all her neighbors, and for Christian work of many kinds. Probably the weekly meeting for Bible-reading and prayer, which she conducted, was her closest link with the women of Dorset but these meetings were established after I had bidden goodbye to the dear old town, and I leave others to tell how their "hearts burned within them as she opened to them the Scriptures."

She had in a remarkable degree the lovely feminine gift of *home making*. She was a true decorative artist. Her room when she was boarding, and her home after it was completed, were bowers of beauty. Every walk over hill and dale, every ramble by brook side or through wildwood, gave to her some fresh home-adornment. Some shy wildflower or fern, or brilliant-tinted leaf, a bit of moss, a curious lichen, a deserted bird's-nest, a strange fragment of rock, a shining pebble, would catch her passing glance and reveal to her quick artistic sense possibilities of use that were quaint, original, characteristic. One saw from afar that hers was a poet's home and, if permitted to enter its gracious portals, the first impression deepened into certainty. There was as strong an individuality about her home, and especially about her own little study, as there was about herself and her writings. A cheerful, sunny, hospitable Christian home! Far and wide, its potent influences reached, and it was a beautiful thing to see how many another home, humble or stately, grew emulous and blossomed into a new loveliness.

Mrs. Prentiss was naturally a shy and reserved woman, and necessarily a pre-occupied one. Therefore, she was sometimes misunderstood. But those who—knew her best, and were blest with her rare intimacy, knew her as "a perfect woman nobly planned." Her conversation was charming. Her close study of nature taught her a thousand happy symbols and illustrations, which made both what she said and wrote a mosaic of exquisite comparisons. Her studies of character were equally constant and penetrating. Nothing escaped her no peculiarity of mind or manner failed of her quick observation, but it was always a kindly interest. She did not ridicule that which was simply ignorance or weakness, and she saw with keen pleasure all that was quaint, original, or strong, even when it was hidden beneath the homeliest garb. She had the true artist's liking for that which was simple and *genre*. The common things of common life appealed to her sympathies and called out all her attention. It was a real, hearty interest, too—not feigned, even in a sense generally thought praiseworthy. Indeed, no one ever had a more intense scorn of every sort of *feigning*. She was honest, truthful, *and genuine* to the highest degree. It may have sometimes led her into seeming lack of courtesy, but even this was a failing, which "leaned to virtue's side." I chanced to know of her once calling with a friend on a country neighbor, and finding the good housewife busy over a rag-carpet. Mrs. Prentiss, who had never chanced to see one of these bits of rural manufacture in its elementary processes, was full of questions and interest, thereby quite evidently pleasing the unassuming artist in assorted rags and homemade dyes. When the visitors were safely outside the door, Mrs. Prentiss' friend turned to her with the exclamation, "What tact you have! She really thought you were interested in her work!" The quick blood sprang into Mrs. Prentiss' face, and she turned upon her friend a look of amazement and rebuke. "Tact!" she said, "I despise such tact!—do you think *I would look or act a lie?*"

She was an exceedingly practical woman, not a dreamer. A systematic, thorough housekeeper, with as exalted ideals in all the affairs which pertain to good housewifery as in those matters which are generally thought to transcend these humble occupations. Like Solomon's virtuous woman, she "looked well after the ways of her household." Methodical, careful of minutes, simple in her tastes, abstemious, and therefore enjoying evenly good health in spite of her delicate constitution—this is the secret of her accomplishing so much. Yet all this foundation of exactness and diligence was so "rounded with leafy gracefulness" that she never seemed angular or unyielding.

With her children, she was a model disciplinarian, exceedingly strict, a wise lawmaker yet withal a tender, devoted, self-sacrificing mother. I have never seen such exact obedience required and given—or a more idolized mother. "Mamma's" word was indeed *Law*, but—O, happy combination!—it was also *Gospel*.

How warm and true her friendship was! How little of selfishness in all her intercourse with other women! How well she loved to be of *service* to her friends! How anxious that each should reach her highest possibilities of attainment! I record with deepest sense of obligation the cordial, generous, sympathetic assistance of many kinds extended by her to me during our whole acquaintance. To every earnest worker in any field she gladly "lent a hand," rejoicing in all the successes of others as if they were her own.

But if weakness, or trouble, or sorrow of any sort or degree overtook one she straightway became as one of God's own ministering spirits—an angel of strength and consolation. Always more eager, however, that *souls should grow than that pain should cease*. Volumes could be made of her letters to friends in sorrow. One tender monotone steals through them all,—

"Come unto me, my kindred, I enfold you
In an embrace to sufferers only known
Close to this heart I tenderly will hold you,
Suppress no sigh, keep back no tear, no moan.
"Thou Man of Sorrows, teach my lips that often
Have told the sacred story of my woe,
To speak of Thee till stony griefs I soften,
Till hearts that know Thee not learn Thee to know.
"Till peace takes place of storm and agitation,
Till lying on the current of Thy will
There shall be glorying in tribulation,
And Christ Himself each empty heart shall fill."

Few have the gift or the courage to deal faithfully yet lovingly with an erring soul, but she did not shrink back even from this service to those she loved. I can bear witness to the wisdom, penetration, skill, and fidelity with which she probed a terribly wounded spirit, and then said with tender solemnity, "*I think you need a great deal of good praying.*"

O, "vanished hand," still beckon to us from the Eternal Heights! O, "voice that is still," speak to us yet from the Shining Shore!

"Still let thy mild rebuking stand
Between us and the wrong,

                And thy dear memory serve to make
                Our faith in goodness strong."

[1] See the poem in the appendix to Golden Hours, with the "Reply of the New Year," written by Mrs. Prentiss.

[2] A clerical circle of New York.

[3] A Unitarian paper, published in New York.

[4] An association of ladies for providing garments and other needed articles in aid of families of Home and Foreign missionaries, especially of those connected in any way with their own congregation. Such a circle is found in most of the American churches.

[5] The passage occurs in a letter to Madame Guyon, dated June 9, 1689. For another extract from the same letter, see appendix F.

[6] On the Resurrection of Christ.

[7] Helen Rogers Blakeman, wife of W. N. Blakeman, M.D., was born on the 20th of December, 1811, in the city of New York. She was a granddaughter of the Rev. James Caldwell, of Elizabethtown, New Jersey, the Revolutionary patriot. The tragic fate of her grandmother has passed into history. When the British forces reached Connecticut Farms, on the 7th of June, 1780, and began to burn and pillage the place, Mrs. Caldwell, who was then living there, retired with her two children—one an infant in her arms—to a back room in the house. Here, while engaged in prayer, she was shot through the window. Two bullets struck her in the breast and she fell dead upon the floor. The infant in her arms was Mrs. Blakeman's mother. On the father's side, too, she was of an old and God-fearing family.

[8] "Your precious lamb was very near my heart few knew so well as I did all you suffered for and with her, for few have been over just the ground I have. But that is little to the purpose what I was going to say is this,— 'God never makes a mistake.' You know and feel it, I am sure, but when we are broken down with grief, we like to hear simple words, oft repeated. On this anniversary of my child's death, I feel drawn to you. It was a great blow to us because it came to hearts already sore with sorrow for our boy, and because it came so like a thunderclap, and because she suffered so. Your baby's death brought it all back."—*From the Letter to Mrs. W.*

[9] "I must tell you what a busy day I had yesterday, being chaplain, marketer, mother, author, and consoler from early morning till nine at night…. A letter came from Cincinnati from the editor of the hymnbook of the Y.M.C.A., saying he had some of my hymns in it, and had stopped the press in order to have two more, which he wanted 'right away.' I was exactly in the mood it was our little Bessie's anniversary, she had been in heaven *eighteen* years think what she has already gained by my one year of suffering! and I wanted to spend it for others, not for myself."—*Letter to her Husband, May 20.*

[10] Nidworth, and His Three Magic Wands, published by Roberts Brothers.

CHAPTER 12 - THE TRIAL OF FAITH - 1871-1872.

I.

        Two Years of Suffering. Its Nature and Causes. Spiritual Conflicts.
        Ill-health. Faith a Gift to be won by Prayer. Death-bed of Dr. Skinner.
        Visit to Philadelphia. "Daily Food." How to read the Bible so as to love
        it more. Letters of Sympathy and Counsel. "Prayer for Holiness brings
        Suffering." Perils of human Friendship.

If in the life of Mrs. Prentiss the year 1870 was marked with a white stone as one of great happiness, the two following years were marked by unusual and very acute suffering. Perhaps something of this was, sooner or later, to have been looked for in the experience of one whose organization, both physical and mental, was so intensely sensitive. Tragic elements are latent in every human life, especially in the life of woman. And the finer qualities of her nature, her vast capacity of loving and of self-sacrifice, her peculiar cares and trials, as well as outward events, are always tending to bring these elements into action. What scenes surpassing fable, scenes both bright and sad, belong to the secret history of many a quiet woman's heart! Then our modern civilization, while placing woman higher in some respects than she ever stood before, at the same time makes her pay a heavy price for her advantages. In the very process of enlarging her sphere and opportunities, whether intellectual or practical, and of educating her for their duties, does it not also expose her to moral shocks and troubles and lacerations of feeling almost peculiar to our times? Nor is religion wholly exempt from the spirit that rules the age or the hour. There is a close, though often very subtle, connection between the two just as there is between the working of nature and grace in the individual soul.

The phase of her history upon which Mrs. Prentiss was now entering cannot be fully understood without considering it in this light. The melancholy that was deep-rooted in her temperament, and her tender, all-absorbing sympathies, made her very quick to feel whatever of pain or sorrow pervaded the social atmosphere about her. The thought of what others were suffering would intrude even upon her rural retreat among the mountains, and render her jealous of her own rest and joy. And then, in all her later years, the mystery of existence weighed upon her heart more and more heavily. In a nature so deep and so finely strung, great happiness and great sorrow are divided by a very thin partition.

But spiritual trials and conflict gave its keenest edge to the suffering of these years. Such trials and conflict indeed were not wanting in the earliest stages of her religious life, nor had they been wanting all along its course but they came now with a power and in a manner almost wholly new and, while not essentially different from those which have afflicted God's children in all ages, they are yet traceable, in no small degree, to special causes and circumstances in her own case. Early in 1870 she had fallen in with a book entitled "God's Furnace," and a few months later had made the acquaintance of its author—a remarkable woman, of great strength of character, of deep religious experience, and full of zeal for God. Her book was introduced to the Christian public by a distinguished Presbyterian clergyman, and was highly recommended by other eminent divines. By means of this work, as well as by correspondence and an occasional visit, she exerted for a time a good deal of influence over Mrs. Prentiss. At first this influence seemed to be stimulating and healthful, but it was not so in the end. The points of sympathy and the points of difference between them will come out so plainly in Mrs. Prentiss' letters that they need not be indicated here. It would not be easy to imagine two women more utterly dissimilar, except in love to God, devotion to their Savior, and delight in prayer. These formed the tie between them. Miss ———'s last days were sadly clouded by mental trouble and disease.

A little book called "Holiness through Faith," published about this time, was another disturbing influence in Mrs. Prentiss' religious life. This work and others of a similar character presented a somewhat novel theory of sanctification—a theory zealously taught, and which excited considerable attention in certain circles of the Christian community. It was, in brief, this: As we are justified by faith without the deeds of the law, even so are we sanctified by faith in other words, as we obtain forgiveness and acceptance with God by a simple act of trust in Christ, so by simple trust in Christ we may attain personal holiness it is as easy for divine grace to save us at once from the power, as from the guilt, of sin.

For more than thirty years, Mrs. Prentiss had made the Christian life a matter of earnest thought and study. The subject of personal holiness in particular had occupied her attention. Whatever promised to shed new light upon it she eagerly read. Her own convictions, however, were positive and decided and, although at first inclined to accept the doctrine of "Holiness through Faith," further reflection satisfied her that, as taught by its special advocates, it was contrary to Scripture and experience, and was fraught with mischief. Certain unhappy tendencies and results of the doctrine, both at home and abroad, as shown in some of its teachers and disciples, also forced her to this conclusion. Folly of some sort is indeed one of the fatal rocks upon which all overstrained theories of sanctification are almost certain to be wrecked and in excitable, crude natures, the evil is apt to take the form either of mental extravagance, perhaps derangement, or of silly, if not still worse, conduct. But, while deeply impressed with the mischief of these Perfectionist theories, Mrs. Prentiss felt the heartiest sympathy with all earnest seekers after holiness, and was grieved by what seemed to her harsh or unjust criticisms upon them.

What were her own matured views on the subject will appear in the sequel. It is enough to say here that "Holiness through Faith" and other works, in advocacy of the same or similar doctrines, meeting her as they did when under a severe mental strain, and touching her at a most sensitive point—for holiness was a passion of her whole soul—had for a time a more or less bewildering effect. She kept pondering the questions they raised, until the native hue of her piety—hitherto so resolute and cheerful—became "sickly o'er with the pale cast of thought."

The inward conflict which has been referred to, she described sometimes, in the language of the old divines, as the want of God's "sensible presence," or of "conscious" nearness to and communion with Christ sometimes, as a state of "spiritual deprivation or aridity" and then again, as a work of the Evil One. She laid much stress upon this last point. Her belief in the existence of Satan and his influence over human souls was as vivid as that of Luther she did not hesitate to accuse him of being the fomenter and, in a sense, the author of her distress the warnings of the Bible against his "wiles" she accepted as in full force still and she could offer with all her heart, and with no doubt as to the literal meaning of its closing words, the petition of the old Litany: "That it may please Thee to strengthen such as do stand, and to comfort and help the weak-hearted, and to raise up those who fall, and finally to *beat down Satan under our feet.*"

The coming trouble seems to have cast its shadow across her path even before the close of 1870. Early in 1871, it was upon her in power. Her letters contain very interesting and pathetic allusions to this experience. But they do not explain it. Nor is it easy to explain. In the absence of certain inciting causes from without, it would never, perhaps, have assumed a serious form. But these sharp spiritual trials are generally complicated with external causes, or occasions ill health, morbid constitutional tendencies, loss of sleep, wearing cares and responsibilities, sudden calamities, worldly loss or disappointment, and the like. It is in the midst of such conditions that pious souls are most apt to be assailed by gloom and despondency. And yet distressing inward struggles and depression arise sometimes in the midst of outward prosperity and even of unusual religious enjoyment. In truth, among all the phenomena of the Christian life none are more obscure or harder to seize than those connected with spiritual conflict and temptation. They belong largely to that *terra incognita*, the dark background of human consciousness, where are the primal forces of the soul and the mustering-place of good and evil. A certain mystery enshrouds all profound religious emotion whether of the peace of God that passeth all understanding, or of the anguish that comes of spiritual desertion. Those who are in the midst of the battle, or bear its scars, will instantly recognize an experience like their own to all others it must needs remain inexplicable. Even in the natural life our deepest joys and sorrows are mostly inarticulate the great poets come nearest to giving them utterance but how much the reality always surpasses the descriptions of the poet's pen, even though it is the pen of a Shakespeare, or a Goethe!

Mrs. Prentiss never afterward referred to this "fiery trial" without strong emotion. It terrified her to think of anyone she loved as exposed to it and—not to speak of other classes—she seemed to regard those as specially exposed to it, who had just passed, or were passing, through an unusually rich and happy religious experience. One of her last letters, addressed to a dear Christian friend, related to this very point. Here are a few sentences from it:

I want to give you EMPHATIC warning that you were never in such danger in your life. This is the language of bitter, bitter experience and is not mine alone. Leighton says the great Pirate lets the empty ships go by and robs the full ones. [1] … I do hope you will go on your way rejoicing, unto the perfect day. Hold on to Christ with your teeth [2] if your hands get crippled He, alone, is stronger than Satan He, alone, knows *all* "sore temptations" mean.

This, certainly, is strong language and will sound very strange and extravagant in many ears and yet is it really stronger language than that often used by inspired prophets and apostles? or than that of Augustine, Bernard, Luther, Hooker, Fenelon, Bunyan, and of many saintly women, whose names adorn the annals of piety? Strong as it is, it will find an echo in hearts that have been assailed by the "fiery darts of the adversary," and have learned to cry unto God out of the depths of mental anguish and gloom while others still in the midst of the conflict, will, perhaps, be helped and comforted to read of the manner in which Mrs. Prentiss passed through it. Nothing in the story of her religious life is more striking and beautiful. Her faith never failed she glorified God in the midst of it all she thanked her Lord and Master for "taking her in hand," and begged Him not to spare her for her crying, if so be she might thus learn to love Him more and grow more like Him! And, what is especially noteworthy, her own suffering, instead of paralyzing, as severe suffering sometimes does, active sympathy with the sorrows and trials of others, had just the contrary effect. "How soon," she wrote to a friend, "our dear Lord presses our experiences into His own service! How many lessons He teaches us in order to make us 'sons' (or daughters) 'of consolation!'" To another friend she wrote:

I did not perceive any selfishness in you during our interview, and you need not be afraid that I am so taken up with my own affairs as to feel no sympathy with you in yours. What are we made for, if not to bear each other's burdens? And this ought to be the effect of trial upon us to make us, in the very midst of it, unusually interested in the interests of others. This is the softening, sanctifying tendency of tribulation, and he who lacks it needs harder blows.

At no period of her life was she more helpful to afflicted and tempted souls. In visits to sickrooms and dying beds, and in letters to friends in trouble, her heart "like the noble tree that is wounded itself when it gives the balm," poured itself forth in the most tender, soothing ministrations. It seemed at times fairly surcharged with love. Meanwhile she kept her pain to herself only a few intimate friends, whose prayers she solicited, knew what a struggle was going on in her soul to all others she appeared very much as in her happiest days. "It is a little curious," she wrote to a young friend, "that suffering as I really am, nobody sees it. 'Always bright!' people say to me to my amazement…. I can add nothing but love, of which I am so full that I keep giving off in thunder and lightning."

The preceding account would be incomplete without adding that the state of her health during this period, combined with a severe pressure of varied and perplexing cares, served to deepen the distress caused by her spiritual trials. Whatever view may be taken of the origin and nature of such trials, it is certain that physical depression and the mental strain that comes of anxious, care-worn thoughts, if not their source, yet tend always greatly to intensify them. In the present case the trials would, perhaps, not have existed without the cares and the ill health while the latter, even in the entire absence of the former, would have occasioned severe suffering.

To Mrs. Frederick Field, New York, Jan. 8, 1871.

'If I need make any apology for writing you so often, it must be this—I cannot help it. Having dwelt long in an obscure, oftentimes dark valley, and then passed out into a bright plane of life, I am full of tender yearnings over other souls, and would gladly spend my whole time and strength for them. I long, especially, to see your feet established on an immovable Rock. It seems to me that God is preparing you for great usefulness by the fiery trial of your faith. "They learn in suffering what they teach in song." Oh how true this is! Who is so fitted to sing praises to Christ as he who has learned Him in hours of bereavement, disappointment and despair?

What you want is to let your intellect go overboard, if need be, and to take what God gives just as a little child takes it, without money and without price. Faith is His, unbelief ours. No process of reasoning can soothe a mother's empty, aching heart, or bring Christ into it to fill up all that great waste room. But faith can. And faith is His gift a gift to be won by prayer—prayer persistent, patient, determined prayer that will take no denial prayer that if it goes away one day unsatisfied, keeps on saying, "Well, there's tomorrow and tomorrow and tomorrow God may wait to be gracious, and I can wait to receive, but receive I must and will." This is what the Bible means when it says, "the kingdom of heaven suffers violence, and the violent take it by force." It does not say the eager, the impatient take it by force, but the violent—they who declare, "I will not let Thee go except Thou bless me." This is all heart, not head work. Do I know what I am talking about? Yes, I do. But my intellect is of no use to me when my heart is breaking. I must get down on my knees and own that I am less than nothing, seek *God*, not joy *consent* to suffer, not cry for relief. And how transcendently good He is when He brings me down to that low place and there shows me that that self-renouncing, self-despairing spot is just the one where He will stoop to meet me!

My dear friend, do not let this great tragedy of sorrow fail to do *everything* for you. It is a dreadful thing to lose children but a *lost sorrow* is the most fearful experience life can bring, I feel this so strongly that I could go on writing all day. It has been said that the intent of sorrow is to "toss us on to God's promises." Alas, these waves too often toss us away out to sea, where neither sun or stars appear for many days. I pray, earnestly, that it may not be so with you.

Among Mrs. Prentiss' most beloved and honored friends in New York was the Rev. Dr. Thomas H. Skinner, the first pastor of the Mercer street church, and then, for nearly a quarter of a century, Professor in the Union Theological Seminary. His attachment to her, as also that of his family, was very strong. Dr. Skinner had been among the leaders of the so-called New School branch of the Presbyterian Church. He was a preacher of great spiritual power, an able, large-hearted theologian, and a man of most attractive personal and social qualities. He was artless as a little child, full of enthusiasm for the best things, and a pattern of saintly goodness. It used to be said that every stone and rafter in the Church of the Covenant had felt the touch of his prayers. This venerable servant of God entered into his rest on the 1st of February, 1871, in the 80th year of his age. In a letter to her cousin, Rev. George S. Payson, Mrs. Prentiss thus refers to his last hours:

You will hear at dear Dr. Skinner's funeral tomorrow his dying testimony, and I want you to know that it was whispered in my enraptured ear, that I was privileged to spend the whole of Tuesday and all he lived of Wednesday, at his side, and that mine were the hands that closed his eyes and composed his features in death. What blissful moments were mine, as I saw his sainted soul fly home how near heaven seemed and still seems!

To Miss E. S. Gilman, New York, Feb. 7, 1871.

I am glad to hear that you have such an interesting class, and yet more glad that you see how much Christian culture they need. I am astonished every day by confessions made to me by young people as to their woeful state before God, and do hope that all this is to prepare me to write something for them. I began a series of articles in the Association Monthly, called "Twilight Talks," which may perhaps prove to be in a degree what you want, but still there is much land untouched. Meanwhile I want to encourage you in your work, by letting you feel my deep sympathy with you in it, and to assure you that nothing will be so blessed to your scholars as personal holiness in yourself. We *must* practice what we preach, and give ourselves wholly to Christ if we want to persuade others to do it. I am saying feebly what I feel very deeply and constantly. You will rejoice with me that I had the rare privilege of being with dear Dr. Skinner during his last hours. If you have a copy of Watts and Select hymns, read the 106th hymn of the 2nd book, beginning at the 2nd verse, "Lord, when I quit this earthly stage," and fancy, if you can, the awe and the delight with which I heard him repeat those nine verses, as expressive of his dying love to Christ. I feel that God is always too good to me, but to have Him make me witness of that inspiring scene, humbles me greatly. In how many ways He seeks us, now smiling, now caressing, now reproving, now thwarting, and *always* doing the very best thing for us that infinite love and goodness can! Let us love Him better and better every day, and count no work for Him too small and unnoticed to be wrought thankfully whenever He gives the opportunity. I hope I am learning to honor the day of small things.

To Mrs. Humphrey, New York, March 14, 1871.

So you have at last broken the ice and made out, after almost a year, to write that promised letter! Well, it was worth waiting for, and welcome when it came, and awakened in me an enthusiasm about seeing the dear creature, of which I hardly thought my old heart was capable (that statement is an affectation my heart is not old, and never will be). Our plan now is, if all prospers, to go to Philadelphia on Friday afternoon, spend the night with you, Saturday with Mrs. Kirkbride, and Sunday and part of Monday with you. I hope you mean to let us have a quiet little time with you, unbeknown to strangers, whom I dread and shrink from....

March 28th.—What a queer way we womankind have of confiding in each other with perfectly reckless disregard of consequences! It is a mercy that men are, for the most part, more prudent, though not half so delightful! Well, I am ever so glad I have seen you in your home, only I found you more frail (in the way of health) than I found you fair. We hear that your husband preached "splendidly," as of course we knew he would, and the next exchange I shall be there to hear as well as to see.

Coming out of the cars yesterday, I picked up a "Daily Food," dropped, I suppose, by its owner, "Sarah ———," of Philadelphia, given her by "Miss H. in 1853." It has travelled all over Europe, and is therefore no doubt precious to her who thus made it her friend. Now how shall I get it to her? Can you learn her address, or shall I write to her at a venture, without one? I know how I felt—when I once lost mine it was given me in 1835, and has gone with me ever since whenever I have journeyed (as I was so happy as to find it again). [3] I think if I have the pleasure of restoring it to its owner, she will feel glad that it did not fall into profane hands. I thought it right to look through it, in order to get some clue, if possible, to its destination I fancy it was the silent comforter of a wife who went abroad with her husband for his health, and came home a widow God bless her, whoever she is, for she evidently believes in and loves Him. What sort of a world can it be to those who do not? [4] Remember me affectionately to yourself and your dear ones, and now we have got a-going, let's go ahead.

April 1st.—What a pity it is that one cannot have a separate language with which to address each beloved one! It seems so mean to use the same words to two or three or four people one loves so differently! Now about my visit to you. One reason why I did not stay longer was your looking worn out. When I am feeling so dragged, visitors are a great wear and tear to me. But I am afraid my selfishness would have got the upper hand of me if that were the whole story. I cannot put into words the perfect horror I have of being made into a somebody it fairly hurts me, and if I had stayed a week with you and the host of people you had about you, I should have shriveled up into the size of a pea. I cannot deny having streaks of conceit, but I *know* enough about myself to make my rational moments bid me keep in the background, and it excruciates me to be set up on a pinnacle. So do not blame me if I fled in terror, and that I am looking forward to your visit, when I hope to have delightful pow-wows with you all by ourselves.

I am glad that little book can be returned, and I will mail it to you. I *could not* send it without a loving word it seemed to fall so providentially into my hands and knock so at the door of my heart. In what strange ways people get introduced to each other, and how subtle are the influences that excite a bond of sympathy! What do you do with girls who fall madly and desperately in love with you? Do you laugh at them, or scold them, or love them, or what? I used to do just such crazy things, and am not sure I never do them now. Did you ever live in a queerer world than this is?

To Miss E.S. Gilman, New York, April 29, 1871.

The subject of your letter is one that greatly interests me, and I should be glad to get more light upon it myself. As far as I know, those who live apart from the world, communing with God and working for Him chiefly in prayer, have least temptation to wandering and distracted thoughts, and are more devout and spiritual than those of us who live more in the world. But it stands to reason that we *cannot* all live so. The outside work must go on, and somebody must do it. But of course, we have the hardest time, since while *in* the world we must not be of it. I have come, of late, to think that both classes are needed, the contemplative and the active, and God does certainly take the latter aside now and then as you suggest, by sickness and in other ways, to set them thinking. Holiness is not a mere abstraction it is praying and loving and being consecrate, but it is also the doing kind deeds, speaking friendly words, being in a crowd when we thirst to be alone, and so on and so on. The study of Christ's life on earth reveals Him to us as incessantly busy, yet taking *special* seasons for prayer. It seems to me that we should imitate Him in this respect, and when we find ourselves particularly pressed by outward cares and duties, break short off and withdraw from them till a spiritual tone returns. For we can do nothing well unless we do it consciously for Christ, and this consciousness sometimes gets jostled out of us when we undertake to do too much. The more perfectly He is formed in us the more light we shall get on every path of duty, the less likely to go astray from the happy medium of not all contemplation, not all activity. And to have Him thus to dwell in us we are led to pray by His own last prayer for us on earth, when He asked for the "*I in them.*" Let us pray for each other that this may be our blessed lot. Nothing will fit us for life but this. In ourselves, we do nothing but err and sin. In Him, we are complete.

* * * * *

II.

Her Husband called to Chicago. Lines on going to Dorset. Letters to young Friends, on the Christian Life. Narrow Escape from Death. Feeling on returning to Town. Her "Praying Circle." The Chicago Fire. The true Art of Living. God our only safe Teacher. An easily-besetting Sin. Counsels to young Friends. Letters.

Mrs. Prentiss' letters relating to her husband's call to Chicago require perhaps an explanatory word. She had some very pleasant associations with Chicago. It was the home of a brother and sister-in-law, to whom she was deeply attached, and of other dear relatives. There Stepping Heavenward had first appeared, and many unknown friends—grateful for the good it had done them—were eager to form her acquaintance and bid her welcome to the great city of the Interior. And yet the thought of removing there filled her with the utmost distress. Had her husband's call been to some distant post in the field of Foreign Missions, her language on the subject could hardly have been stronger. But this language in reality expresses simply the depth of her devotion to her church and her friends in New York, her morbid shyness and shrinking from the presence of strangers, and, especially, her vivid sense of physical inability to make the change without risking the loss of what health and power of sleep still remained to her. Misgiving on this last point caused her husband to hesitate long before accepting the call, and to feel in after years that his decision to accept it, although conscientiously made, had been a grave mistake.

To Mrs. Condict, New York, June 3, 1871.

I knew that you would rather hear from me than through the papers, the fact that Mr. Prentiss has been once more unanimously elected by the General Assembly to the Chicago Professorship. He has come home greatly perplexed as to his duty, and prepared to do it, at any reasonable cost, if he can only find out what it is. We built our Dorset house not as a mere luxury, but with the hope that the easy summer there would so build up our health as to increase and prolong our usefulness but going to Chicago would deprive us of that, besides cutting us off from all our friends. But we want to know no will but God's in this question, and I am sure you and Miss K. will join us in the prayer that we may not so much as *suggest* to Him what path He will lead us into. The experience of the past winter would impress upon me the fact that *place and position* have next to nothing to do with happiness that we can be wretched in a palace, radiant in a dungeon. Mr. P. said yesterday that it broke his heart to hear me talk of giving up Dorset but perhaps this heartbreaking is exactly what we need to remind us of what for many years we never had a chance to forget, that we are pilgrims and strangers on the earth. Two lines of my own keep running in my head:

Oh foolish heart, oh faithless heart, oh heart on ruin bent, Build not with too much care thy nest, thou art in banishment.

I have seen the time when the sense of being a pilgrim and a stranger was very sweet and God can sweeten whatever He does to us. So though perplexed we are not in despair, and if we feel that we are this summer living in a tent that may soon blow down, it is just what you are doing, and in this point we shall have fellowship. I am sure it is good for us to have God take up the rod, even if He lays it down again without inflicting a blow. I know we are going to pray till light comes. I feel very differently about it from what I did last summer. The mental conflicts of the past winter have created a good deal of indifference to everything. Without conscious union and nearness to my Savior I cannot be happy anywhere for years He has been the meaning of everything, and when He only *seems* gone (I know it is only seeming) I do not much care where I am. I am just trying to be patient till He makes Satan let go of me. Excuse this selfish letter, and write me one just as bad!

On the 7th of June, she went to Dorset with her husband and the younger children. The following lines, found among her papers, will show in what temper of mind she went. It is worth noting that they were written on Monday, and express a weekday, not merely a passing Sabbath feeling:

Once more at home, once more at home—
For what, dear Lord, I pray?
To seek enjoyment, please myself,
Make life a summer's day?
I shrink, I shudder at the thought
For what is home to me,
When sin and self enchain my heart,
And keep it far from Thee?
There is but one abiding joy,
Nor place that joy can give
It is Thy presence that makes home,
That makes it "life to live."
That presence I invoke naught else
I venture to entreat
I long to see Thee, hear Thy voice,
To sit at Thy dear feet.

To a young Friend, Dorset, June 12, 1871.

I trust it is an omen of good that the first letters I have received since coming here this summer, have been full of the themes I love best. I was much struck with the sentence you quote, "They cannot go back," etc., [5] and believe it is true of you. Being absorbed in divine things will not make you selfish you will be astonished to find how loving you will gradually grow toward everybody, how interested in their interests, how happy in their happiness. And if you want work for Christ (and the more you love Him the more you will *long* for it), that work will come to you in all sorts of ways. I do not believe much in duty-work I think that work that tells is the spontaneous expression of the love within. Perhaps you have not been sick enough yourself to be skilful in a sickroom perhaps your time for that sort of work has not come. I meant to get you a little book called "The Life of Faith" in fact, I went down town on purpose to get it, and passed the Episcopal Sunday-school Union inadvertently. I think that little book teaches how everything we do may be done for Christ, and I know by what little experience I have had of it, that it is a blessed, thrice blessed way to live. A great deal is meant by the "cup of cold water," and few of us women have great deeds to perform, and we must unite ourselves to Him by little ones. The life of constant self-discipline God requires is a happy one you and I, and others like us, find a wild, absorbing joy in loving and being loved but sweet, abiding peace is the fruit of steady check on affections that *must* be tamed and kept under. Is this consistent with what I have just said about growing more loving as we grow more Christ like? Yes, it is for *that* love is absolutely unselfish, it gives much and asks nothing, and there is nothing restless about it.... I have been very hard at work ever since I came here, with my darling M. as my constant, joyous comrade. We have been busy with our flowerbeds, sowing and transplanting, and half the china closet has tumbled out of doors to serve as protection from the sun. Mr. Prentiss says we do the work of three days in one, which is true, for we certainly have performed great feats. The night we got here, we found the house lighted up, and the dining table covered with good things. People seem glad to see us back. I do not know which of my Dorset titles would strike you as most appropriate one man calls me a "branch," another "a child of nature," and another "Mr. Prentiss' woman," with the consoling reflection that I sha'n't rust out.

To Mrs. Smith, Dorset, August 6, 1871.

I do not know when I have written so few letters as I have this summer. My right hand has forgot its cunning under the paralysis, under which my heart has suffered, and which is now beginning to affect my health quite unfavorably. It seems as if body and soul, joints and marrow, were rudely separating. Poor George is half-distracted with the weight of the questions concerning Chicago, and I think almost anything would be better than this crucifying suspense. But I try not to make a fuss. Mrs. D—— can tell you that I have said to her many times, during the last few years, that, according to the ordinary run of life, things would not long remain with us as they were they were too good to last.

I have read and re-read "Spiritual Dislodgments," and remember it well. I certainly wish for such dislodgments in me and mine, if we need them. George has got hold of a book of A.'s, which delights him, Letters of William Von Humboldt. [6] I suppose you recommended it to her. You *must* make your plans to come here this summer I do not seem fully to have a thing until you have seen it.

To Mrs. Humphrey, Dorset, Aug. 8, 1871.

It took you a good while to answer my last letter, and I have been equally lazy about writing since yours strayed this way. Letter writing has always been a resource and a pastime to me a refuge in headachy and rainy days, and a tiny way to give pleasure or do good, when other paths were hedged up. But this summer I have left almost everybody in the lurch, partly from being more or less unwell and out of spirits, partly because the Chicago question, remaining unsettled, has been such a damper that I hadn't much heart to speak either of it or of anything else. We are perplexed beyond measure what to do the thought of losing *my minister* and having him turn into a professor, agonizes me on the other hand, who knows but he needs the rest that change of labor and the five months' vacation would give him? *His* chief worry is the effect the attending funerals all the time has already had on my health. One day I part with and bury (in imagination!) now this friend, now that, and this mournful work does not sharpen one's appetite or invigorate one's frame. I do not know how we've stood the conflict and it seems rather selfish to allude to my part of it but women live more in their friendships than men do, and the thought of tearing up all our roots is more painful to me than to my husband, and he will not lose what I must lose in addition, and as I have said before, my minister, which is the hardest part of it.

I want you to know what straits we are in, in the hope that you and yours will be stirred up to pray that we may make no mistake, but go or stay as the Lord would have us. We have found our little home a nice refuge for us in the storm Mr. P. says he should have gone distracted in a boarding house. I do not envy you the Conway crowd. But I fancy it is a good region for collecting mosses and like treasures. I think the prettiest thing in our house is a flattish bracket, fastened to the wall and filled with flowers it looks like a graceful, meandering letter S and is one of the idols I bow down to.... I have "Holiness through Faith" the first time I read it at Mr. R——'s request, I said I believed every word of it, but this summer, reading it in a different mood, it puzzles me. The idea is plausible if God tells us to be holy, as He certainly does, is it not for Him to provide the way for our being so, and is it likely He needs our whole lives before He can accomplish His own design? I talked with Mr. Prentiss about it, and at first he rejected the thought of holiness through faith, but last night we got upon the subject again and he was interested in some sentences I read to him and said he must examine the book. When are you coming to spend that week in Dorset? Love to each and all.

To a young Friend, Kauinfels, Sept. 9, 1871.

I have had many letters to write today, for today, our fate is sealed, and we are to go. But I must say a few words to you before going to bed, for I want to tell you how very glad I am that you have been enabled to take a step [7] which will, I am sure, lead the way to other steps, increase your holiness, your usefulness, and your happiness. May God bless you in this attempt to honor Him, and open out before you new fields wherein to glorify and please Him. This has not been a sorrowful day to me. I hope I am offering to a "patient God a patient heart." I do not want to make the worst of the sacrifice He requires, or to fancy I am only to be happy on my own conditions. He has been most of the time for years "the spring of all my joys, the life of my delights." Where He is, I want to be where He bids me go, I want to go, and to go in courage and faith. Anything is better than too strong cleaving to this world. As I was situated in New York, I lacked not a single earthly blessing. I had a delightful home, freedom from care, and a circle of friends whom I loved with all my heart, and who loved me in a way to satisfy even my rapacity. Only one thing was wanting to my perfect felicity—a heart absolutely holy and was I likely to get that when my earthly cup was so full? At any rate, I am content. Now and then, as the reality of this coming separation overwhelms me, I feel a spasm of pain at my heart (I do not suppose we are expected to cease to be human beings or to lose our sensibilities), but if my Lord and Master will go with me, and keeps on making me more and more like Himself, I can be happy anywhere and under any conditions, or be made content not to be happy. All this is of little consequence in itself, but perhaps it may make me more of a blessing to others, which, next to personal holiness, is the only thing to be sought very earnestly. As to my relation to you, He who brought you under my wing for a season has something better for you in store. *That is His way.* And wherever I am, if it is His will and His Spirit dictates the prayer, I shall pray for you, and that is the best service one soul can render another.

About this time, she and her husband had an almost miraculous escape from instant death. They had been calling upon friends in East Dorset and were returning home. Not far from that village is a very dangerous railroad crossing and, as the sight or sound of cars so affrighted Coco as to render him uncontrollable, special pains had been taken not to arrive at the spot while a train was due. But just as they reached it, an "irregular" train, whose approach was masked behind high bushes, came rushing along unannounced, and had they been only a few seconds later, would have crushed them to atoms. So severe was the shock and so vivid the sense of a Providential escape, that scarcely a word was spoken during the drive home. The next morning she gave her husband a very interesting account of the thoughts that, like lightning, flashed upon her mind while feeling herself in the jaws of death. They related exclusively to her children—how they would receive the news, and what would become of them. [8]

Late in September, she returned to town, still oppressed by the thought of going to Chicago. In a letter to Mrs. Condict, dated October 2nd, she writes:

We got home on Friday night, and very early on Saturday were settled down into the old routine. But how different everything is! At church tearful, clouded faces at home, warmhearted friends looking upon us as for the last time. It is all right. I would not venture to change it if I could but it is hard. At times, it seems as if my heart would literally break to pieces, but we are mercifully kept from realizing our sorrows all the time. The waves dash in and almost overwhelm, but then they sweep back and are stayed by an almighty, kind hand…. It is like tearing off a limb to leave our dear prayer meeting. Next to my closet, it has been to me the sweetest spot on earth. I never expect to find such another.

To another friend she writes a day or two later:

My heart fairly *collapses* at times, at the thought of tearing myself away from those whom Christian ties have made dearer to me than my kindred after the flesh. And then comes the precious privilege and relief of telling my yet dearer and better Friend all about it, and the sweet peace begotten of yielding my will to His. I want to be of all the use and comfort to you and to the other dear ones He will let me be during these few months. Do pray for me that I may so live Christ as to bear others along with me on a resistless tide. Those lines you copied for me are a great comfort:

"Rather walking with Him by faith, Than walking alone in the light."

Of the little praying circle, alluded to in her letter to Mrs. C., one of its members writes:

It was unique even among meetings of its own class. Held in an upper chamber, never largely attended and sometimes only by the "two or three," it was almost unknown except to the few, who regarded it as among their chiefest religious privileges. All the other members would gladly have had Mrs. Prentiss assume its entire leadership but she assumed nothing and was no doubt quite unconscious as to how large an extent she was the life and soul of the meeting. In the familiar conversation of the hour, nothing fell from her lips but such simple words as, coming from a glowing heart, strengthened, and deepened the spiritual life of all who heard them. She had, in a degree I never knew equaled, the gift of leading the devotions of others. But there was not the slightest approach to performance in her prayers she abhorred the very thought of it. Those who knelt with her can never forget the pure devotion, which breathed itself forth in simple exquisite language, but it was something beyond the power of description.

Another member of the circle writes:

Her prayers were so simple, so earnest, and so childlike. We all felt we were in the very presence of our loving Father. One thing especially always impressed me during that sacred hour—it was her *quietness of manner*. She was very cordial and affectionate in her greetings with each one, as we assembled, and then a holy awe, a solemn hush, came over her spirit and she seemed like one who saw the Lord! O how we all miss her! There is never a meeting but we keep her in remembrance and talk together lovingly about her.

To a Friend, Oct. 21, 1871.

Mr. Prentiss sent in his resignation last evening, and the church refused unanimously to let him go. "Praise God from whom all blessings flow" penetrated the walls of the parsonage, as they sang it when the decision was made, and so we knew our fate before a whole parlorful rushed in to shake hands, kiss, and congratulate. You would have been delighted had you been here. Prof. Smith, who took strong ground in favor of his going, takes just as strong ground in favor of his staying. I feel that all this is the result of prayer. I never got any light on the Chicago question when I prayed about it never could *see* that it was our duty to go but I yielded my judgment and my will, because my husband thought that he must go. I think our very reluctance to it made us shrink from evading it we were so afraid of opposing God's will. Now the matter is taken out of our hands and we have only to resume our work here. God grant that this baptism of fire may purge and purify us and prepare us to be a great blessing to the church. It is a most awe-inspiring providence, God's burning us out of Chicago, and we feel like putting our shoes from off our feet and adoring Him in silence…. Pray that the lessons we have been learning through so many trying months may help us to be helping hands to those who may pass through similar straits. One of my brothers was burnt out, and his own and his wife's letters drew tears even down to the kitchen. For two days and a night they lost their baby, five months old, in addition to all the other horrors. But they found refuge with a dear cousin, who has filled his house to overflowing. I may have spoken of this cousin to you: he has a foundling home on Müller's trust system.

Before taking leave of the call to Chicago, a word should be added to what she says concerning it in her letters. The prospect of her husband's accepting the call rendered the summer a very trying one but it was far from being all gloom. She had a marvelous power of extracting amusement out of the most untoward situation. In 1843, she wrote from Richmond, referring to Mr. Persico's troubles, "I never spent such melancholy weeks in my life in the midst of it, however, I made fun for the rest, as I believe I should do in a dungeon." It was so in the present case. She relieved the weariness of many an anxious hour by "making fun for the rest." As an illustration, one evening at Dorset, while sitting at the parlor-table with her children and a young friend who was visiting her, she seized a pencil and wrote for their entertainment a ludicrous version of the Chicago affair in two parts. The paper which was preserved by her young friend, illustrates also another trait which she thus describes at the close of a frolicsome letter to Miss E. A. Warner: "It is one of the peculiar peculiarities of this woman that she usually carries on, when she wants to hide her feelings." Part I. begins thus:

> Where are the Prentisses? Gone to Chicago,
> Gone bag and baggage, the whole crew and cargo.
> Well, they *would* go, now let's talk 'em over,
> And see what compensation we can discover.

They are all "talked over" and then in Part II. the scene changes to Chicago itself:

> Sing a song of sixpence, a pocket full of rye,
> Here's the tribe of Prentisses just agoing by
> Dr. Prentiss he,
> Mrs. Prentiss she,
> And a lot of young ones that all begin with P.
> Well, let us view them with our eyes,
> And then begin to criticize.
> And first the doctor, what of him?

The doctor having been fully discussed, the criticism proceeds:

> Now for his wife well, who would guess
> She had set up as authoress!
> Why, she looks just like all of us,
> Instead of being in a muss
> Like other literary folks.
> They say she likes her little jokes,
> As well as those who've less to say
> Of stepping on the heavenward way.

Mrs. P. having been disposed of:

> Next comes Miss P. how she will make
> The hearts of all the students quake!
> She'll wind them round her fingers' ends,
> And find in them one hundred friends.
> They'll sit on benches in a row
> And watch her come, and watch her go
> But they'll be safe, the precious rogues,
> Since she do not care for theologues.

The other children next pass in review and the whole closes with the remark:

> Time, and Time only, will make clear   Why the poor geese came cackling here.

To a young Friend, New York, Nov., 1871.

My heart is as young and fresh as any girl's, and I am *almost* as prone to make idols out of those I love, as I ever was and this is inconsistent with the devotion owed to God. I do not mean that I really love anybody better than I do Him, but that human friendships tempt me. This easily besetting sin of mine has cost me more anguish than tongue can tell, and I deeply feel the need of more love to Christ because of my earthly tendencies. I know I would sacrifice every friend to Christ, but I am not always disentangled. How strange this is, how passing strange! In a religious way, I find myself much better off here than at Dorset. But there is yet something apparently "far off, unattained and dim" that I once thought I had caught by the wing, and enjoyed for a season, but which has flown away. I am afraid I am one who has got to be a religious enthusiast, or else dissatisfied and restless. When I give way to an impulse to the first, I care for nothing worldly, and am at peace. But I am unfitted for daily life, for secular talk and reading. Is it so with you? Does it run in our blood? I do long and pray for more light and I *will* pray for more love, cost what it may. Sometimes I long to get to heaven, where I shall not have to be curbing my heart with bit and bridle, and can be as loving as I want to be—as I *am*.

To a young Friend abroad—New York, Dec. 8, 1871.

There never will come a time in my life when I shall not need all my Christian friends can do for me in the way of prayer. I am glad you are making such special effort to oppose the icebergs of foreign life God will meet and bless you in it. Let us, if need be, forsake all others to cleave only unto Him. I do not know of any real misery except coldness between myself and Him.

I feel warm and tender sympathy with you in all your struggles, temptations, joys, hopes, and fears. As you grow older, you will *settle* more your troubles, your ups and downs, belong chiefly to your youth. Yes, you are right in saying that Mr. P—— could go through mental conflicts in silence he does not pine for sympathy as you and I do. You and I are like David, though I forget, at the moment, what he said happened to him when he "kept silence." (On the whole, I do not think he said anything!)

I think the proper attitude to take when restless and lonesome and homesick for want of God's sensible presence, is just what we take when we are missing earthly friends for whom we yearn, and whose letters, though better than nothing, do not half feed our hungry hearts, or fill our longing arms. And that attitude is patient waiting. We are such many-sided creatures that I do not doubt you are getting pleasure and profit out of this European trip, although it is alloyed by so much mental suffering. But such is life. It has in it nothing perfect, nothing ideal. And this conviction, deepened every now and then by some new experience, tosses me anew, again and again, back on to that Rock of Ages that ever stands sure and steadfast, and on whom our feet may rest. It is well to have the waves and billows of temptation beat upon us if only to magnify this Rock and teach us what a refuge He is.

I went, last night, with Mr. Prentiss and most of the children, to hear the freedmen and women in a concert at Steinway Hall. It was *packed* with a brilliant, delighted audience, and it was most interesting to see these young people, simple, dignified, earnest, full of love to Christ, and preparing, by education, to work for Him. They sang, "Keep me from sinking down" most sweetly and touchingly. I see you have the blues as I used to do, at your age, and hope you will outgrow them as I have done. I *suffer* without being *depressed* in the sense in which I used to be it is hard to make the distinction, but I am sure there is one. I do not know how far this change has come to me as a happy wife and mother, or how far it is religious.

Aunt Jane's Hero was published in 1871. It is hardly inferior to Stepping Heavenward in its pictures of life and character, or in the wisdom of its teaching. The object of the book is to depict a home whose happiness flows from the living Rock, Christ Jesus. It protests also against the extravagance and other evils of the times, which tend to check the growth of such homes, and aims to show that there are still treasures of love and peace on earth, that may be bought without money and without price.

* * * * *

III.

"Holiness and Usefulness go hand-in-hand." No two Souls dealt with exactly alike. Visits to a stricken Home. Another Side of her Life. Visit to a Hospital. Christian Friendship. Letters to a bereaved Mother. Submission not inconsistent with Suffering. Thoughts at the Funeral of a little "Wee Davie." Assurance of Faith. Funeral of Prof. Hopkins. His Character.

She entered the new year with weary steps, but with a heart full of tenderness and sympathy. A circle of young friends, living in different parts of the country, looked eagerly to her at this time for counsel, and she was deeply interested in their spiritual progress. She wrote to one of them, January 6, 1872:

Your letter has filled my heart with joy. What a Friend and Savior we have, and how He comes to meet us on the sea, if we attempt to walk there in faith! I trust your path now will be the ever brightening one that shall shine more and more unto the perfect day. Holiness and usefulness go hand in hand, and you will have new work to do for the Lord praying work especially. *Pray for me*, for one thing I need a great deal of grace and strength just now. And pray for all the souls that are struggling toward the light. O, that everybody lived only for Christ!

A few weeks later, writing to the same friend, she thus refers to the "fiery trials" through which she was passing:

This season of temptation came right on the heels, if I may use such an expression, of great spiritual illumination. Of all the years of my life, 1869-70 was the brightest, and it seems as if Satan could not endure the sight of so much love and joy, and so took me in hand. I have not liked to say much about this to young people, lest it should discourage them but I hope you will not allow it to affect you in that way, for you must remember that no two souls are dealt with exactly alike, and that the fact that many are looking up to me may have made it necessary for our dear Lord to let Satan harass and trouble me as he has done. No, let us not be discouraged, either you or I, but rejoice that we are called of our God and Savior to give Him all we have and all we are…. If we spent more time in thanking God for what He *has* done for us, He would do more.

Malignant scarlet fever and other diseases, had invaded and isolated the household mentioned in the following letter. Their gratitude to Mrs. Prentiss was most touching it was as if she had been to them an angel from heaven. The story of her visits and loving sympathy became a part of their family history.

To Mrs. Humphrey, New York, Jan. 26, 1872.

I came home half frozen from my early walk this morning, to get warm not only at the fire, but at your letter, which I found awaiting me. I am glad if you got anything out of your visit here. I rather think you and I shall "rattle on" together after we get to heaven…. You say, "How skillfully God does fashion our crosses for us!" Yes, He does. And for my part, I do not want to rest and be happy without crosses—for I cannot *do* without them. People who set themselves up to be pastors and teachers must "learn in suffering" what they teach in sermon and book. I felt a good deal reproved for making so much of mine, however, by my further visits to the house of mourning of which we spoke to you. The little boy died early on the next day, and before his funeral, his poor mother, neglected by everybody else, found it some comfort to get into my arms and cry there. It made no difference that twenty years had passed since I had had a sorrow akin to hers we mothers may cease to grieve, outwardly, but we never forget what has gone out of our sight, or ever grow unsympathetic because time has soothed and quieted us. But I need not say this to *you*. This was on Saturday all day Monday I was there watching a most lovely little girl, about six years old, writhing in agony she died early next morning. The next eldest has been in a critical state, but will probably recover a certain degree of health, but as a helpless cripple. Well, I felt that death alone was *inexorable*—other enemies we may hope and pray and fight against—and that while my children lived, I need not despair. The tax on my sympathies in the case of those half-distracted parents has been terrible, and yet I would not accept a cold heart if I had the offer of it.

To give you another side of my life, let me tell you of a pleasant dinner party one night last week, when we met Gov. and Mrs. C——, of Massachusetts, and I fell in love with her then and there…. Well, this is a queer world, full of queer things and queer people. Will the next one be more commonplace? I know not. Goodbye.

Word has come from that afflicted household that the grandfather has died suddenly of heart disease. His wife died a few weeks ago. Mr. Prentiss saw him on Saturday in vigorous health.

To Miss Rebecca F. Morse, New York, March 5, 1872.

Can you tell me where the blotting-pads can be obtained? I have got into a hospital of *spines* in other words, of people who can only write lying on their backs, one of them an authoress, and I think it would be a mercy to them if I could furnish them with the means of writing with more ease than they do now. I was sorry you could not come last Friday, and hope you will be able to join us Saturday, when the club meets here…. How you would have enjoyed yesterday afternoon with me! I went to call on a lady from Vermont, who is here for spinal treatment, and found in her room another of the patients. Two such bright creatures I never met at once, and we got a-going at such a rate that though I had never seen either of them before, I stayed nearly three hours! I mean to have another dose of them before long, and give them another dose of E. P. I have been reading a book called "The Presence of Christ" [9]—

which I liked so well that I got a copy to lend. It is not a great book, but I think it will be a useful one. It says we are all idolaters, and reminds me of my besetting sins in that direction. I feel overwhelmed when I think how many young people are looking to me for light and help, knowing how much I need both myself.... Every now and then, some Providential event occurs that wakes us up, and we find that we have been asleep and dreaming, and that what we have been doing that made us fancy ourselves awake, was mechanical.

I must be off now to my sewing society, which is a great farce, since I can earn thirty or forty times as much with my pen as I can with my needle, and if they would let me stay at home and write, I would give them the results of my morning's work. But the minute I stop going everybody else stops.

To Mrs. Condict, April 7, 1872.

How I should love to spend this evening with you! This has been our Communion Sunday, and I am sure the service would have been very soothing to your poor, sore heart. And yet why do I say *poor* when I know it is *rich*? Oh, you might have the same sorrow without faith and patience with which to bear it, and think how dreadful that would be! Your little lamb has been spending his first Sunday with the Good Shepherd and other lambs of the flock, and has been as happy as the day is long. Perhaps your two children and mine are claiming kinship together. If they met in a foreign land, they would surely claim it for our sakes why not in the land that is not foreign, and not far off? But still these are not the thoughts to bring you special comfort. "Thy will be done!" does the whole. And yet my heart aches for you. Someone, who had never had a real sorrow, told Mrs. N. that if she submitted to God's will, as she ought, she would cease to suffer. What a fallacy this is! Mrs. N. was comforted by hearing that your little one was taken away by the consequences of the fever, as her Nettie was, for she had reproached herself with having neglected her to see to Johnny, who died first, and thought this neglect had allowed her to take cold. I feel very sorry when mothers torture themselves in this needless way, as if God could not avert ill consequences, if He chose.

I have shed more than one tear today. I heard last night that my dearly loved brother, Prof. Hopkins, is on his dying-bed. I never thought of his dying, he comes of such a long-lived race. I expect to go to see him, and if I find I can be of any use or comfort, stay a week or two. His death will come very near to me, but he is a saintly man, and I am glad for him that he can go. How thankful we shall be when our turn comes! The ladies at our little meeting were deeply interested in what I had to tell them about your dear boy, and prayed for you with much feeling. May our dear Lord bless you abundantly with His sweet presence! I know He will. And yet He has willed it that you should suffer. "Himself hath done it!" Oh how glad He will be when the dispensation of suffering is over, and He can gather His beloved round Him, tearless, free from sorrow and care, and all forever at rest.

May 5th.—Yesterday, the friend at East Dorset whose three children died within a few weeks of each other, sent me some verses, of which I copy one for you:

> "The eye of faith beholds
> A golden stair, like that of old, whereon
> Fair spirits go and come
> God's angels coming down on errands sweet,
> Our angels going home."

I hope this golden stair, up which your dear boy climbed "with shout and song," is covered with God's angels coming down to bless and comfort you. One of the most touching passages in the Bible, to my mind, is that which describes angels as coming to minister to Jesus after His temptations in the wilderness. It gives one such an idea of His helplessness! Just as I was going out to church this morning, Mr. Prentiss told me of the death of a charming "baby-boy," one of our lambs, and I could scarcely help bursting into tears, though I had only seen him once. You can hardly understand how I feel, as a pastor's wife, toward our people. Their sorrows come right home. I have a friend also hanging in agonizing suspense over a little one who has been injured by a fall she is sweetly submissive, but you know what a mother's heart is. I have yet another friend, who has had to give up her baby. She is a young mother, and far from her family, but says she has "perfect peace." So from all sides I hear sorrowful sounds, but so much faith and obedience mingled with the sighs, which I can only wonder at what God can do.

To Miss Morse, May 7, 1872.

How true and how strange it is that our deepest sorrows, spring from our sweetest affections that as we love much, we suffer much. What instruments of torture our hearts are! The passage you quote is all true but people are apt to be impatient in affliction, eager to drink the bitter cup at a draught rather than drop by drop, and fain to dig up the seed as soon as it is planted, to see if it has germinated. I am fond of quoting that passage about "the peaceable fruit of righteousness" coming "afterward."

I have just come from the funeral of a little "Wee Davie" all the crosses around his coffin were tiny ones, and he had a small floral harp in his hand. I thought as I looked upon his face, still beautiful, though worn, that even babies have to be introduced to the cross, for he had a week of fearful struggle before he was released.... I enclose an extract

I made for you from a work on the baptism of the Holy Spirit. This was all the paper I had at hand at the moment. The recipe for "curry" I have copied into my recipe book and the two lines at the top of the page I addressed to M. A queer mixture of the spiritual and the practical, but no stranger than life's mixtures always are.

To a young Friend, New York, May 20th, 1872.

As to assurance of faith, I think we may all have that, and in my own darkest hours, this faith has not been disturbed. I have just come home from a brief visit to Miss ——, with whom I had some interesting discussions. I use the word *discussions* advisedly, for we love each other in constant disagreement. She believes in holiness by faith, while denying that she has herself attained it. I think her life, as far as I can see it, very true and beautiful. We spent a whole evening talking about temptation. Not long ago I met with a passage, in French, to this effect—I quote from memory only: "God has some souls whom He cannot afflict in any ordinary way, for they love Him so that they are ready for any outward sorrow or bereavement. He therefore scourges them with inward trials, vastly more painful than any outward tribulation could be thus crucifying them to self." I cannot but think that this explains Mrs. ——'s experience, and perhaps my own at any rate I feel that we are all in the hands of an unerring Physician, who will bring us, through varying paths, home to Himself.

I had a call the other day from an intelligent Christian woman, whom I had not seen for eighteen years. She said that some time ago, her attention was called to the subject of personal holiness, and as she is a great reader, she devoured everything she could get hold of, and finally became a dogmatic perfectionist. But experience modified these views, and she fell back on the Bible doctrine of an indwelling Christ, with the conviction that just in proportion to this indwelling will be the holiness of the soul. This is precisely my own belief. This is the doctrine I preached in Stepping Heavenward and I have so far seen nothing to change these views, while I desire and pray to be taught any other truth if I am wrong. I believe God does reveal Himself and His truth to those who are willing to know it.

To Miss Morse, New York, May 31, 1872.

I got home yesterday from Williamstown, where I went, with my husband, to attend the funeral of my dearly beloved brother, Professor Hopkins. He literally starved to death. He died as he had lived, beautifully, thinking of and sending messages to all his friends, and on his last day repeating passages of Scripture and even, weak as he was, joining in hymns sung at his bedside. The day of the funeral was a pretty trying one for me, as there was not only his loss to mourn, but there were traces of my darling mother and sister, who both died in that house, all over it some of my mother's silver, a white quilt she made when a girl, my sister's library, her collection of shells and minerals, her paintings, her little conservatory, the portrait of her only child, dressed in his uniform (he was killed in one of the battles of the Wilderness). Then, owing to the rain, none of us ladies were allowed to go into the cemetery, and I had thought much of visiting my sister's grave and seeing her boy lying on one side and her husband on the other. But our disappointments are as carefully planned for us as our sorrows, so I have not a word to say.

After services at the house, we walked to the church, which we entered through a double file of uncovered students. One of the most touching things about the service was the sight of four students standing in charge of the remains, two at the head and two at the foot of the coffin. His poor folks came in crowds, with their hands full of flowers to be cast into his grave. My brother said he never saw so many men shed tears at a funeral, and I am sure I never did some sobbing as convulsively as women. I could not help asking myself when my heart was swelling so with pain, whether love *paid*. Love is sweet when all goes well, but oh, how fearfully exacting it is when separation comes! How many tithes it takes of all we have and are!

A worthy young woman in our church has been driven into hysterics by reading "Holiness through Faith." I went to see her as soon as I got home from W. yesterday, but she was asleep under the influence of an opiate. There is no doubt that too much self-scrutiny is pernicious, especially to weak-minded, ignorant young people. It was said of Prof. Hopkins that he would have been a mystic but for his love to souls, and I am afraid these new doctrines tend too much to the seeking for peace and joy, too little to seeking the salvation of the careless and worldly. But I hesitate to criticize any class of good people, feeling that those who live in most habitual communion with God receive light directly and constantly from on high and of that communion we cannot seek too much. [10]

* * * * *

IV.

Christian Parents to expect Piety in their Children. Perfection. "People make too much Parade of their Troubles." "Higher Life" Doctrines. Letter to Mrs. Washburn. Last Visit to Williamstown.

Early in June she went to Dorset. The summer, like that of 1871, was shadowed by anxiety and inward conflict but her care-worn thoughts were greatly soothed by her rural occupations, by visits from young friends, and by the ever-fresh charms of nature around her.

To a Christian Friend, Dorset, June 9, 1872.

I was obliged to give up my much-desired visit to you. We went on to the funeral of Prof. Hopkins, and that took three days out of the busy time just before coming here. I particularly wanted you to know *at the time* that my three younger children united with the church on Sunday last, but had not a moment in which to write you. It was a touching sight to our people. Mr. P. looked down on his children so lovingly, and kissed them when the covenant had been read. He said ——'s face was so full of soul that he could not help it, and his heart yearned over them all. Someone said there was not a dry eye in the house. I felt not elated, not cast down, but at peace. I think it plain that Christian parents are to *expect* piety in their children, and expect it early. In mine it is indeed "first the blade," and they will, no doubt, have their trials and temptations. But it seems to me I must leave them in God's hands and let Him lead them as He will. It was very sweet to have the elements passed to me by their young hands. Offer one earnest prayer for them at least, that they may prove true soldiers and servants of Jesus Christ. No doubt, your two little sainted ones looked on and loved the children of their mother's friend.

The following testimony of one of President Garfield's classmates and intimate friends may fitly be added here:

"For him there was but one Mark Hopkins in all the world but for Professor Albert Hopkins also, or 'Prof. Al.,' as he was called in those days, the General—not only while at college, but all through life— entertained the highest regard, both as a man and a scholar. His intellectual attainments were thought by Gen. G. to be of an unusually fine order, rivaling those of his brother, and often eliciting the admiration not only of himself, but of all the other students. In speaking of his Williamstown life, Gen. Garfield always referred to Prof. Hopkins in the most affectionate manner and, both from his own statements and my personal observation. I know that their mutual college relations were of the pleasantest nature possible."

On the subject of perfection, you say I am looking for angelic perfection. I see no difference in kind. Perfection is perfection to my mind, and I have always thought it a dangerous thing for a soul to fancy it had attained it. Yet, in her last letters to me, Miss —— virtually professes to have become free from sin. She says self and sin are the same thing, and that she is entirely dead to self. What is this but complete sanctification? What can an angel say more? I feel painfully bewildered amid conflicting testimonies, and sometimes long to flee away from everybody. Miss ——'s last letter saddened me, I will own. You say, "I am in danger of becoming morbid, or stupid, or wild, or something I ought not." Why in danger? According to your own doctrine, you are safe being "entirely sanctified from moment to moment." At any rate I can say nothing "to quicken" you, for I *am* morbid and stupid, though just now not wild. Those sharp temptations have ceased, though perhaps only for a season but I have been physically weakened by them, and have got to take care of myself, go to bed early, and vegetate all I can—and this when I ought to be hard at work ministering to other souls. The fact is, I do not know anything and do not do anything, but just get through the day somehow, wondering what all this strange, unfamiliar state of things will end in. Poor M—— has gone crazy on "Holiness through Faith," and will probably have to go to an asylum…. Our little home looks and is very pleasant. I take some comfort in it, and try to realize the goodness that gives me such a luxury. But a soul that has known what it is to live to Christ can be *happy* only in Him. May He be all in all to you, and consciously so to me in His own good time.

To Miss Woolsey, Dorset, June 23, 1872.

I wish you could come and take a look at us this quiet afternoon. Not a soul is to be seen or heard the mountains are covered with the soft haze that says the day is warm but not oppressive, and here and there a brilliantly colored bird flies by, setting "Tweedle Dum," our taciturn canary, into tune. M. and I have driven at our out-door work like a pair of steam-engines, and you can imagine how dignified I am from the fact that an old fuddy-duddy who does occasional jobs for me, summons me to my window by a "Hullo!" beneath it, while G. says to us, "Where are you girls going to sit this afternoon?"

Your sister's allusion to Watts and Select Hymns reminds me of ages long past, when I used to sing the whole book through as I marched night after night through my room, carrying a colicky baby up and down for fifteen months, till I became a living skeleton. We do contrive to live through queer experiences.

To a young Friend, Dorset, Aug. 3, 1872.

The lines you kindly copied for me have the ring of the true metal and I like them exceedingly. People make too much parade of their troubles and too much fuss about them the fact is we are all born to tribulation, as we also are to innumerable joys, and there is no sense in being too much depressed or elated by either. "The saddest birds a season find to sing." Few if any lives flow in unmingled currents. As to myself, my rural tastes are so strong, and I have so much to absorb and gratify me, that I *need* a mixture of experience. Two roses that bloomed in my garden this morning, made my heart leap with delight, and when I get off in the woods with M., and we collect mosses and ferns and scarlet berries, I am conscious of great enjoyment in them. At the same time, if I thought it best to tell the other side of the story, I should want some very black ink with which to do it. We must take life as God gives it to us, without murmurings and disputing, and with the checks on our natural eagerness, that keeps us mindful of Him.

You speak of the "Higher Life people." I still hold my judgment in suspense in regard to their doctrines, reading pretty much all they send me, and asking daily for light from on high. I have had some talks this summer with Dr. Stearns on these subjects, and he urges me to keep where I am, but I try not to be too much influenced for or against doctrines I do not, by experience, understand. Let us do the will of God (and suffer it) and we shall learn of the doctrine.

To Mrs. Washburn, Kauinfels, Friday Evening, (September, 1872).

I have done nothing but tear my hair ever since you left, to think I let you go. It would have been so easy to send you to Manchester tomorrow morning, after a night here, and an evening over our little wood-fire, but we were so glad to see you both, so bewildered by your sudden appearance, that neither of us thought of it till you were gone. And now you are still within reach, and we want you to reconsider your resolution to turn your backs upon us after such a long, fatiguing journey, and eating no salt with us. I did not urge your staying because I do so hate to be urged myself. But I want you to feel what a great pleasure it would be to us if you could make up your minds to stay at least over Sunday, or if tomorrow and Sunday are unpleasant, just a day or two more, to take our favorite drives with us, and give us what you may never have a chance to give us again. I declare I shall think you are crazy, if you do not stay a few days, now that you are here. We have been longing to have you come, and only waiting for our place to be a little less naked in order to lay violent hands on you but now you have seen the nakedness of the land, we do not care, but want you to see more of it. This is the time, and *exactly* the time, when we have nothing to do but to enjoy our visitors, and next year the house may be running over. And if you do not come now, you will have the plague of having to come some other time, and it is a long, formidable journey.

Why *didn't* we just take and lock you up when we had hold of you! Well, now I have torn out *all* my hair, and people will be saying, "Go up, thou bald-head." Besides—you left them bunchberries! and do you suppose you can go home without them? Why, it would not be safe. You would be run off the track, and scalded by steam, and broken all to pieces, and caught on the cow-catcher, and get lost, and be run away with, and even struck by lightning, I should not wonder. And now if you go in tomorrow's train you will catch the smallpox and the measles and the scarlet fever and the yellow fever, and all the colors-in-the-rainbow fever, and go into consumption and have the pleurisy, and the jaundice and the toothache and the headache, and, above all, the conscience-ache. And you never ate any of our corn or our beans! You never so much as asked the receipt for our ironclads! You have not seen our cow. You have not been down cellar. You have not fished in our brook. You have not been here at all, now I come to think of it. I dreamed you flew through, but it was nothing *but* a dream. And the houses have a habit of burning down, and ours is going to do as the rest do, and then how will you feel in your minds? And when folks set themselves up against us, and will not let us have our own way, why then "I tell my daughter

What *makes* folks do as they'd ought not, And why *do not* they do as they'd ought?"

And we all pine away and die like the babes in the woods, and nobody's left to cover us up with leaves. Send all these arguments home by telegram, and your folks will shoot you if you dare to go. I could write another sheet if it would do any good. Now do lay my words to heart, and come right back.

To Miss Morse, Dorset, Oct. 7, 1872.

I sent home my servants a month ago, and they have been getting the parsonage to rights, while I have in their places two dear old souls who came to live with me twenty years ago. One stayed ten years and then got married, the other I parted with when my children died because I did not need her. It has been a green spot in the summer to have these affectionate, devoted creatures in the house. We have had only one slight frost, but the woods have been gradually changing, and are in spots very beautiful. We (you know what that word means) have been off gathering bright leaves for ourselves and the servants, who care for pretty things just as we do. Yet not a flower has gone we have had a host of verbenas and gladioli, some Japanese lilies, and so on, and have been able to give some pleasure to those who have not time to cultivate them for themselves. It has been a dreadful season for sickness here, and flowers have been wanted in many a sickroom, and at some funerals.

Since I wrote you last "we" have been to Williamstown. I wanted to get possession of my sister's private papers. Everything passed off nicely I burned a large amount and brought away a trunk full, a part of which I have been reading with deep interest. Her journals date back to the age of fifteen, though to read the early ones you would never dream of her being less than twenty or thirty. She was a wonderful woman, and as I found such ample material for a memorial of her life, I felt half tempted to carry out her husband's wishes and complete one. But on the whole, I do not think I shall. You can imagine how my soul has been stirred by the whole thing the farewell to the familiar objects of my childhood, the sense of a new race taking possession of her conservatory, her shells, her minerals, her pictures, her German, French, Italian, Spanish, Latin, Hebrew and Greek library—dear me! but I need not enlarge on it to you. And how stupid it is not to forget it all alongside of her ten years in heaven!

[1] "Especially after a time of some special seasons of grace, and some special new supplies of grace, received in such seasons, (as after the holy sacrament), then will he set on most eagerly, when he knows of the richest booty. The pirates that let the ships pass as they go by empty, watch them well, when they return richly laden so doth this great Pirate."—Archbishop Leighton, on I Peter, v. 8.

[2] "Cynegvius, a valiant Athenian, being in a great sea-fight against the Medes, espying a ship of the enemy's well manned, and fitted for service, when no other means would serve, he grasped it with his hands to maintain the fight and when his right hand was cut off, he held close with his left but both hands being taken off, he held it fast with his teeth."

[3] The following lines found on one of its blank pages were written perhaps at this time:

> Precious companion! rendered dear
> By trial-hours of many a year,
> I love thee with a tenderness
> Which words have never yet defined.
> When tired and sad and comfortless,
> With aching heart and weary mind,
> How oft thy words of promise stealing
> Like Gilead's balm-drops—soft and low.
> Have touched the heart with power of healing,
> And soothed the sharpest hour of woe.

[4] A friend writing to Mrs. Prentiss, under date of September 24, 1872, refers to Lady Stanley's high praise of The Story Lizzie Told, and then adds: "You must be so accustomed to friendly 'notices'—so almost bored by them—that I hesitate to tell you of meeting another admirer of yours in the person of Mrs. ——, of Philadelphia, who was indebted to you for the return of a little text-book. She means to call on you some day, if she is ever in New York, to thank you in person for that act of kindness of yours, and for your 'Stepping Heavenward.' She is a daughter of the late Chief Justice of Pennsylvania. Her mother, a staunch old Scotch lady over 80, has just returned from Europe. Mrs. —— is a very interesting woman, of warm religious feelings and very outspoken. She was the companion of the famous Mrs. H., of Philadelphia, all through the war,—as one of the independent workers, or perhaps in connection with the Christian Commission. She witnessed the battle of Chancellorsville—a part of it at Mary's Heights, and has told me a great deal that was thrilling—told as *she* tells it—even at this late day. She has the profoundest belief in what is called the 'work of faith' by prayer and I do not believe she would shrink from accepting Prof. Tyndall's challenge."

[5] From the "Power of the Cross of Christ."

[6] "Briefe an eine Freundin," a remarkable little book, full of light and sweetness.

[7] Praying before others.

[8] Since the warning we had the other day that we may be snatched from our children, ought we not to try to form some plan for them in case of such an emergency? I cannot account for it, that in those fearful moments I thought only of them. I should have said I ought to have had some thought of the world we seemed to be hurrying to. I suppose there was the instinctive yet blind sense that the preparation for the next life had been made for us by the Lord, and that, as far as that life was concerned, we had nothing to do but to enter it. I shudder when I think what a desolate home this might be today. Poor things! They have got everything before them, without one experience and discipline!—*From a letter to her husband, dated Dorset, Sept. 17, 1871.*

[9] The Presence of Christ. Lectures on the 23rd Psalm. By Anthony W. Thorold, Lord Bishop of Rochester. A. D. F. Randolph & Co.

[10] Albert Hopkins was born in Stockbridge, Mass., July 14, 1807. He was graduated at Williams College in the class of 1826, and three years later became Professor of Mathematics and Natural Philosophy in the same institution. Astronomy was afterward added to his chair. In 1834, he went abroad. In the summer of 1835, he organized and conducted a Natural History expedition to Nova Scotia, the first expedition of the kind in this country. Two years later, he built at his own expense, and in part by the labor of his own hands, the astronomical observatory at Williamstown. In this also, it is said, in advance of all others erected exclusively for purposes of instruction. He was a devoted and profound student, as well as an accomplished teacher, of natural science. But he was still more distinguished for his piety and his religious influence in the college. Hundreds of students in successive classes learned to love and revere him as a holy man of God—many of them as their spiritual father. The history of American colleges affords probably no instance of a happier, or more remarkable, union of true science with that personal holiness and zeal for God, by which hearts are won for Christ. Full of faith and of the Holy Ghost, he did the work of an evangelist

for more than forty years—not in the college only, but all over the town. During the last six years of his life he devoted himself especially to the White Oaks—a district in the north-east part of Williamstown-which had long before excited his sympathy on account of the poverty, vice, and degradation which marked the neighborhood. He identified himself with the population by buying and carrying on a small farm among them. He also established a Sunday school, and then he built with the aid of friends a tasteful chapel, which was dedicated in October, 1866. Later "the Church of Christ in the White Oaks" was organized, and here, as his failing strength allowed, he preached and labored the rest of his days.

Prof. Hopkins was an enthusiastic lover of nature. A few years before his death he organized a society called "The Alpine Club," composed chiefly of young ladies, with whom, as their chosen leader, he made excursions summer after summer—camping out often among the hills. He took them to many a picturesque nook and retreat, of which they had never heard, in the mountains nearby. He also explored with them other interesting and remoter portions of northern Berkshire, and interpreted to them on the spot the thoughts of God, as they appeared in the infinitely varied and beautiful details of His works. In these excursions he seemed as young as any of his young companions, with feelings as fresh and joyous as theirs. In earlier years he was a very grave man, with something of the old Puritan sternness in his looks and ways, and he bore still the aspect of a homo gravis but his gentleness, his tender devotion to the gay young companions who surrounded him, and the almost boyish delight with which he shared in their pleasures, took away all its sternness and lighted up his strongly-marked countenance with singular grace and beauty. In these closing years of his life he was, indeed, the ideal of a ripe and noble Christian manhood. His name is embalmed in the memory of a great company of his old pupils, now scattered far and wide, from the White House at Washington to the remotest corners of the earth.

P.S.—This was written soon after the inauguration of Gen. Garfield, to whom allusion is made. His high regard for the venerable ex-President of Williams College—the Rev. Dr. Mark Hopkins—he made known to the whole country, but the younger brother was also the object of his warmest esteem and love, and the feeling was heartily reciprocated. Nearly a score of years ago, when he was just emerging into public notice from the bloody field of Chickamauga, Prof. Hopkins spoke of him to the writer in terms so full of praise and so prophetic of his future career, that they seem in perfect harmony with the sentiment at once of admiration and poignant grief which today moves the heart of the whole American people—yea, one might almost say, which is inspiring all Christendom.—*Saturday, Sept. 24, 1881.*

CHAPTER 13 - PEACEABLE FRUIT - 1873-1874.

I.

Effect of spiritual Conflict upon her religious Life. Overflowing
Affections. Her Husband called to Union Theological Seminary. Baptism of
Suffering. The Character of her Friendships. No perfect Life. Prayer.
"Only God can satisfy a Woman." Why human Friendship is a Snare.
Letters.

The trouble, which had so long weighed upon her heart, crossed with her the threshold of 1873, but long before the close of the year it had in large measure passed away. Such suffering, however, always leaves its marks behind and when complicated with ill health or bodily weakness, often lingers on after its main cause has been removed. It was so in her case she was, perhaps, never again conscious of that constant spiritual delight which she had once enjoyed. But if less full of sunshine, her religious life was all the time growing deeper and more fruitful, was centering itself more entirely in Christ and rising faster heavenward. Its sympathies also became, if possible, still more tender and loving. Her whole being, indeed, seemed to gather new light and sweetness from the sharp discipline she had been passing through. Even when most tried and tempted, as has been said, she had kept her trouble to herself few of her most intimate friends knew of its existence to the world she appeared a little more thoughtful and somewhat careworn, but otherwise as bright as ever. But now, at length, the old vivacity and playfulness and merry laugh began to come back again. Never did her heart glow with fresher, more ardent affections. In a letter to a young cousin, who was moving about from place to place, she says:

I shall feel more free to write often, if you can tell me that the postmaster at C. forwards your letters from the office at no expense to you, as he ought to do. It is very silly in me to mind your paying three cents for one of my love-letters, but it's a Payson trait, and I cannot help it, though I should be provoked enough if you *did* mind paying a dollar apiece for them. There is consistency for you! Well, I know, and I am awfully proud of it, that you will get very few letters from as loving a fountain as my heart is. I have got enough to drown a small army—and sometimes when you are homesick, and cousin-Lizzy-sick, and friend-sick, I shall come to you, done up in a sheet of paper, and set you all in a breeze.

Her letters during the first half of this year were few, and relate chiefly to those aspects of the Christian life with which her own experience was still making her so familiar. "God's plan with most of us," she wrote to Mrs. Humphrey, "appears to be a design to make us flexible, twisting us this way and that, now giving, now taking but always at work for and in us. Almost every friend we have is going through some peculiar discipline. I fancy there is no period in our history when we do not *need* and *get* the sharp rod of correction. The thing is to grow strong under it, and yet to walk softly." "I do not care how much I suffer," she wrote to a friend, "if God will purge and purify me and fit me for greater usefulness. What are trials but angels to beckon us nearer to Him! And I do hope that mine are to be a blessing to some other soul, or souls, in the future. I cannot think suffering is meant to be wasted, if fragments of bread created miraculously, were not." She studied about this time with great interest the teaching of Scripture concerning the baptism of the Holy Ghost. The work of the Spirit had not before specially occupied her thoughts. In her earlier writings, she had laid but little stress upon it—not because she doubted its reality or its necessity, but because her mind had not been led in that direction. Stepping Heavenward is full of God and of Christ, but there is in it little express mention of the Spirit and His peculiar office in the life of faith. When this fact was brought to her notice, she herself appeared to be surprised at it, and would gladly have supplied the omission. To be sure, there is no mention at all of the Holy Spirit in several of the Epistles of the New Testament but a carefully-drawn picture of Christian life and progress, like Stepping Heavenward, would, certainly, have been rendered more complete and attractive by fuller reference to the Blessed Comforter and His inspiring influences.

To a young Friend, New York, Jan. 8, 1873.

I feel very sorry for you that you are under temptation. I have been led, for some time, to pray specially for the tempted, for I have learned to pity them as greater sufferers than those afflicted in any other way. For, in proportion to our love to Christ, will be the agony of terror lest we should sin and fall, and so grieve and weary Him. "One sinful wish could make a hell of heaven" strong language, but not too strong, to my mind. I can only say, suffer, but do not yield. Sometimes I think that silent, submissive patience is better than struggle. It is sweet to be in the sunshine of the Master's smile, but I believe our souls need winter as well as summer, night as well as day. Perhaps not to the end I have not come to that yet, and so do not know I speak from my own experience, as far as it goes. Temptation has this one good side to it: it keeps us *down* we are ashamed of ourselves, we see we have nothing to boast of. I told you, you will perhaps remember, that you were going to enter the valley of humiliation in which I have dwelt so long, but I trust we are only taking it in our way to the land of Beulah. And how we "pant to be there"! What a curious friendship ours has been! and it is one that can never sever—unless, indeed, we fall away from Christ, which may He in mercy forbid! I do pray for you twice every day, and hope you pray for me. I do long so to know the truth and to enter into it. Certainly, I have got some new light during the last year, in the midst of my trials, both within and without.

To another young friend she writes a few days later:

I remember when I was, religiously, at your age I was longing for holiness, but my faith staggered at some of the conditions for it. I had no conception, much as Christ was to me, what He was going to become. But I wish I could make you a birthday present of my experience since then, and you could have Him now, instead of learning, as I had to learn Him, in much tribulation.

To Mrs. Condict, Jan. 15, 1873.

I have been meaning, for some days, to write you about the Professorship. [1] It is a new one, and is called "the Skinner and McAlpine" chair, and Mr. Prentiss says there could not be a more agreeable field of usefulness. It is most likely that he will feel it to be his duty to accept. As to myself, I am about apathetic on the subject. My will has been broken over the Master's knee, if I may use such an expression, by so much suffering, that I look with indifference on such outward changes. We can be made willing to be burnt alive, if need be. For four or five years to come I shall not be obliged to leave the church I love so dearly if the Seminary is moved out to Harlem, it will be different but it is not worthwhile to think of that now. It seems to me that Mr. P. has reached an age when, never being very strong, a change like this may be salutary. *February 3rd.*—You will be sorry to hear that dear Mrs. C. is quite sick. Her daughters are all worn out with the care of her. I was there all day Saturday, but I can do nothing in the way of night watching nor much at any time. A very little over-exertion knocks me up this winter. It is just as much as I can do to keep my head above water.... Sometimes I think that the *dreadful* experience I have been passing through is God's way of baptizing me some *have* to be baptized with suffering. Certainly He has been sitting as the Refiner, bringing down my pride, emptying me of this and that, and not leaving me a foot to stand on. If it all ends in sanctification, I do not care what I suffer. Though cast down, I am not in despair.

It is an encouragement to hear Mahan compare states of the soul to house-cleaning time. [2] It is just so with me. Every chair and table, every broom and brush is out of place, topsy-turvy.... But I cannot believe God has been wasting the last two years on me I cannot help hoping that He is answering my prayer, my cry for holiness—only in a strange way. Dr. and Mrs. Abbot spent Sunday and Monday with us a week ago, and I read to them Dr. Steele's three tracts and lent them Mahan. They were much interested, but I do not know how much struck. I cannot smile, as some do, at Dr. Steele's testimony. I believe in it fully and heartily. If I do not know what it is to "find God real," I do not know anything. Never was my faith in the strongest doctrines of Christianity stronger than it is now.

Feb. 13th.—I spent part of yesterday in reading Stepping Heavenward! You will think that very strange till I add that it was in German and, as the translator has all my books, I wanted to know whether she had done this work satisfactorily before authorizing her to proceed with the rest. She has omitted so much, that it is rather an abridgment than a translation otherwise it is well done. But she has so purged it of vivacity, which I am afraid it will plod on leaden feet, if it plods at all, heavenward. And now I must hurry off to my sewing circle.

To a young Friend, April 4, 1873.

I want to correct any mistaken impression I have made on you in conversation. The utmost I meant to say was that I had got new light intellectually, or theologically, on the subject of the working of the Spirit. In the sense in which I use the words "baptism of the Holy Ghost," I certainly do not consider that I have received it. I think it means *perfect consecration*.... Thus far, no matter what people profess, I have never come into close contact with any life that I did not find more or less imperfect. I find, in other words, the best human beings fallible, and *very fallible*. The best I can say of myself is that I see the need of *immense* advances in the divine life. I find it hard to be patient with myself when I see how far I am from reaching even my own poor standard but if I do not love Christ and long to please Him, I do not love anybody or anything. And if I have talked less to you on these sacred subjects this winter, it has been partly owing to my seeing less of you, and an impalpable but real barrier between us which I have not known how to account for, but which made me cautious in pushing religion on you. Young people usually have their ups and downs and fluctuations of feeling before they settle down on to fixed *principles*, paying no regard to feeling, and older Christians should bear with them, make allowance for this, and never obtrude their own views or experiences. I think you will come out all right. Satan will fight hard for you, and perhaps for a time get the upper hand but I believe the Lord and Master will prevail. Perhaps we are never dearer to Him than when the wings on which we once *flew* to Him, hang drooping and broken at our side, and we have to make our weary way on foot.

I am always thankful to have my heart stirred and warmed by Christian letters or conversation always glad to see any signs of the presence of the Holy Spirit at work in a human soul. But never force yourself to write or talk of spiritual things try rather to get so full of Christ that mention of Him shall be natural and spontaneous.

To the Same, April 15, 1873.

I have just been reading the sermon of Dr. Hopkins on prayer you sent me. It sounds just like him. I think his brother and mine (by marriage) would have treated the subject just as logically and far more practically still, under the circumstances, that was not desirable. As to myself, I would rather have the simple testimony of some unknown praying woman, who is in the habit of "*waiting*" on God, than all the theological discussions in the world. The subject, as you know, is one of deep interest to me.

I have not answered your letter, because I was not quite sure what it was best to say. During the winter, I was not sure what had come between us, and thought it best to let time show and I have been harassed and perplexed by certain anxieties, with which it did not seem necessary to trouble you, to a degree that may have given me a preoccupied manner. There have been points where I wanted a divine illumination, which I did not get. I wanted to hear, "This is the way, walk in it" but that word has not come yet, and almost all my spiritual life has been running in that one line, keeping me, necessarily, out of sympathy with everybody. As far as this has been a fault, it has reacted upon you, to whom I ought to have been more of a help. But I can say that it delights me to see you even trying to take a step onward, and to know that while still young, and with the temptations of youth about you, you have set your face heavenward. Your temptations, like mine, are through the affections. "Only God can satisfy a woman" and yet we try, every now and then, to see if we cannot find somebody else worth leaning on. *We never shall*, and it is a great pity we cannot always realize it. I never deliberately make this attempt now, but am still liable to fall into the temptation. I am *sure* that I can never be really happy and at rest out of or far from Christ, nor do I want to be. Getting new and warm friends is all very well, but I emerge from this snare into a deepening conviction that I must learn to say, "None but Christ."... Now, dear ———, it is a dreadful thing to be cold towards our best Friend' a calamity if it comes upon us through Satan a sin and folly if it is the result of any fault or omission of our own. There is but one refuge from it, and that is in just going to Him and telling Him all about it. We cannot force ourselves to love Him, but we can ask Him to *give* us the love, and sooner or later, He *will*. He may seem not to hear, the answer may come gradually and imperceptibly, but it will come. He has given you one friend at least who prays for your spiritual advance every day. I hope you pray thus for me. Friendship that does not do that is not worth the name. *April 17th.*—Of course, I will take the will for the deed and consider myself covered with "orange blossoms," like a babe in the wood. And it is equally of course that I was married with lots of them among my lovely auburn locks, and wore a veil in point lace twenty feet long.

I have had several titles given me in Dorset—among others, a "child of nature"—and last night I was shown a letter in which (I hope it is not wicked to quote it in such a connection) I am styled "a Princess in Christ's Kingdom." Can you cap this climax?

* * * * *

II.

Goes to Dorset. Christian Example. At Work among her Flowers. Dangerous Illness. Her Feeling about Dying. Death an "Invitation" from Christ. "The Under-current bears *Home*." "More Love, More love!" A Trait of Character. Special Mercies. What makes a sweet Home. Letters.

Early in June, accompanied by the three younger children, she went to Dorset. This change always put her into a glow of pleasurable emotion. Once out of the city, she was like a bird let loose from its cage. In a letter to her husband, dated "Somewhere on the road, five o'clock P.M.," she wrote, "M. is laughing at me because, Paddy-like, I proposed informing you in a P. S. that we had reached Dorset as if the fact of mailing a letter there could not prove it. So I will take her advice and close this now. I feel that our cup of mercies is running over. We ought to be ever so good! And I *am* ever so loving!" "We are all as gay as larks," she wrote a few days later and in spite of heat, drought, over-work and sickness, she continued in this mood most of the summer. But while "gay as a lark," she was also grave and thoughtful. Her delight in nature seemed only to increase her interest in divine things and her longing to be like Christ. In a letter to one of her young friends, having spoken of prayer as "the greatest favor one friend can render another," she adds:

But perhaps I may put one beyond it—Christian example. I ought to be so saintly, so consecrated, that you could not be with me and not catch the very spirit of heaven never get a letter from me that did not quicken your steps in the divine life. But while I believe the principle of love to Christ is entrenched in the depths of my soul, the emotion of love is hot always in that full play I want it to be. No doubt, He judges us by the principle He sees to exist in us, but we cannot help judging ourselves, in spite of ourselves, by our feelings. At church this morning my mind kept wandering to and fro I thought of you about twenty times thought about my flowers thought of 501 other things and then got up and sang

"I love Thy kingdom, Lord," as if I cared for that and nothing else. What He has to put up with in me! But I believe in Him, I love Him, I hate everything in my soul and in my life that is unlike Him. I hope the confession of my shortcomings won't discourage you it is no proof that at my age you will not be far beyond such weakness and folly as often carry me away captive.... As far as earthly blessings go I am as near perfect happiness as a human being can be everything is *heaped* on me. What I want is more of Christ, and that is what I hope you pray that I may have.

To another young friend she writes, June 12th:

We have varied experiences, sick or well, and the discipline of a heart not perfectly satisfied with what it gets from God, often alternates with the peace of which you speak as just now yours. What a blessed thing this "very peace of God" is! There is no earthly joy to be compared with it. But to go patiently on without it, when it is not given, is, I think, a great achievement for instance, if I held no communication with you for a year, would it not be a wonderful proof of your love to and faith in me, if you kept on writing me and telling me your joys and trials? To go back—I have been a good deal confused by the contradictory testimony of different Christians, and am driven more and more to a conviction that human beings, *at the best*, are very fallible. We must get our light directly from on high. At the same time we influence each other for right or for wrong, and one who is thoroughly upright and true, will, unconsciously, influence and help those about him.... I am enjoying, as I always do, having the three younger children close about me here, and all sleeping on my floor. We are really like *four* children, continually frolicking together. We are all crowded now into my den, and I wish you were here with us to be the "*fifth* kitten." Did you ever read that story?

To Mrs. Catherine G. Leeds, Dorset, July 12, 1873.

It was ever so kind in you to let us share in your relief and pleasure, and we unite in affectionate congratulations to you all. I do hope this new and precious treasure will be spared to his dear mother, and grow up to be her stay and staff years hence. It is the nicest thing in the world to have a baby. What marvels they are in every respect, but especially in their royal power over us!

In spite of the dry weather, we have had a pleasant summer, so far. Just before we entirely burned up and turned to tinder, showers came to our relief, and our gardens are putting on some faint smiles and making some promises. I did not allow a drop of water to be wasted for weeks dish-water, soap-suds, dairy water, everything went to my flower-beds, and each night, after Mr. Prentiss came, a barrel-full was carted up from the pond for me how many the rest used I do not know. Disposing of such a load has not been blessed to my health, and I have had to draw in my horns a little, but M. and I work generally like two day-laborers for the wages we get, and those wages are flowers here, there and everywhere, to say nothing of ferns, brakes, mosses, scarlet berries, and the like. And when flowers fail, we fall back on different shades of green the German ivy being relieved by a background of dark foliage, or light grasses against grave ones and when we hit on any new combination, each summons the other to be lost in admiration. And when we are too sore and stiff from weeding, grass-shearing or watering, we fall to framing little pictures, or to darning stockings, which she does so beautifully that it has become a fine art with her, or I betake myself to the sewing-machine and stitch for legs that seem to grow long by the minute.

What the rest of the family is about meanwhile, I can not exactly say. Mr. Prentiss sits in a chair with an umbrella over his head, and pulls up a weed now and then, and then strolls off with a straw in his mouth he also drives off sometimes on foraging expeditions, and comes back with butter, eggs, etc., and on hot days takes a bath where a stream of cold water dashes over him "splendid" he says, and "horrid" I say. The boys are up to everything they are carpenters, and plumbers, and trouters, and harnessers, and drivers H. has just learned to solder, and saves me no little trouble and expense by stopping leakages heretofore every holey vessel had to be sent out of town. Both boys have gardens and sell vegetables to their father at extraordinary prices, and they are now filling up a deep ditch 500 feet long at a "York shilling" an hour—men get a "long shilling" and do the work no better. With the money thus made they buy tools of all sorts, seeds and fruit trees, but no nonsense. Three happier children than these three cannot be found.

You may be interested, too, to know what are the famous works of art we are framing, as above referred to. Well, photographs of our kindred and friends for one thing: my brothers, my husband's mother and other relatives of his, Prof. and Mrs. Smith, Mr. and Mrs. B. B., and so on, a good deal as it has happened, for everybody hasn't been photographed and some bodies have not given us their pictures—you, for instance, and if you want to be hung as high as Haman in my den, nine feet square, where I write, why, you can. Last summer I had a mania for illuminating, and made about a cord of texts and mottoes I cannot paint, so I cut letters out of red, blue and black paper, and deceived thereby the very elect, for even Mrs. Washburn was taken in, and said they were painted nicely.

Your little note has drawn large interest, hasn't it? Well, it deserved its fate.

Hardly had she finished this letter when she was taken very ill. For a while, it seemed as if the time of her departure had come. At her request the children were called to her bedside, and she gave them in turn her dying counsels, bade them live for Christ as the only true, abiding good, and then kissed each of them goodbye. She was much disappointed on finding that her sickness, after all, was not an "invitation" from the Master. "You do not get away *this* time," said her husband to her, half playfully, half exultingly, referring to her eagerness to go.

And here it may not be amiss to say a word as to her state of mind respecting death. After her release, her husband thus described it to a friend:

Her feeling about dying seemed to me to be almost unique. In all my pastoral experience, at least, I do not recall another case quite like it. Her faith in a better world, that is, a heavenly, was quite as strong as her faith in God and in Christ she regarded it as the true home of the soul and the tendency of a good deal of modern culture to put *this* world in its place as man's highest sphere and end, struck her as a mockery of the holiest instincts at once of humanity and religion. Death was associated in her mind with the instant realization of all her sweetest and most precious hopes. She viewed it as an invitation from the King of Glory to come and be with Him. During the more than three-and-thirty years of our married life I doubt if there was ever a time when the summons would have found her unwilling to go rarely, if ever, a time when she would not have welcomed it with great joy. On putting to her the question, "Would you be ready to go *now?*" she would answer, "Why, yes," in a tone of calm assurance, rather of visible delight, which I can never forget. And during all her later years her answer to such a question would imply a sort of astonishment, that anybody could ask it. So strong, indeed, was her own feeling about death as a real boon to the Christian, that she was scarcely able, I think, fully to sympathize with those who regarded it with misgiving or terror. The point may be illustrated, perhaps, by referring to her perfect fearlessness and repose in the midst of the most terrific thunderstorm. No matter how vivid the lightning's flashes or how near and loud the claps that followed, they affected her nerves as little as any summer breeze—scarcely ever awaking her if asleep, or hindering her from going to sleep if awake. And so it was with regard to the terrors of death. But not merely was there an absence of all apparent dread of death, but an exulting joy in the thought of it. There is a passage in The Home at Greylock, which was evidently inspired by her own experience. It is where old Mary, when her first wild burst of grief was over, said:

Sure, she has got her wish and died sudden. She was always ready to go, and now she is gone. Often is the time I have heard her talk about dying, and I mind a time when she thought she was going, and there was a light in her eye, and "What d'ye think of that?" says she. I declare it was just as she looked when she says to me, "Mary, I'm going to be married, and what d'ye think of that?" says she.

This feeling about death is the more noteworthy in her case because of her very deep, poignant sense of sin and of her own unworthiness.

To a Friend, Dorset, July 27, 1873.

This is my third Sunday home from church. I have been confined to my bed only about a week, but it took me some days to run down to that point, and now it is taking some to run me up again. I had two or three very suffering days and nights, and the doctor was here nearly all of one day and night, but was very kind, understood my case and managed it admirably. He is from Manchester and is son of a missionary. [3]

You speak in your letter of being oppressed by the heat, and wearied by visitors, and say that prayer is little more than uttering the name of Jesus. I have asked myself a great many times this summer how much that means.

"All I can utter sometimes is Thy name!"

This line expresses my state for a good while. Of course getting out of one house into another and coming up here, all in the space of one month, was a great tax on time and strength, and all my regular habits *had* to be broken up. Then before the ram was put in I over-exerted myself, unconsciously, carrying too heavy pails of water to my flowerbeds, and so broke down. For some hours, the end looked very near, but I do not know whether it was stupidity or faith that made me so content to go. I am afraid that a good deal of what passes for the one is really the other. Fortunately, for us, our faith does not entitle us to heaven any more than our stupidity shuts us out of it when we get there it will be through Him who loved us. But if I may judge by the experience of this little illness, our hearts are not so tied to or in love with this world, as we fear. We make the most of it as long as we *must* stay in it but the undercurrent bears *home*.

The following extract from a letter to a young relative, dated Sept. 23rd, furnishes at once a key to several marked traits of her character and a practical comment upon her own hymn, "More love to Thee, O Christ!"

I had no right to leave my friend undefended. I prayed to do it aright. If I did not I am not ashamed to say I am sorry for it, and ask you to forgive me. And if I were twice as old as I am, and you twice as young, I would do it. I will not tolerate anything wrong in myself. I hate, I hate sin against my God and Savior, and sin against the earthly friends whom I love with such a passionate intensity that they are able to wring my heart out, and always will be, if I live to be a hundred.... People who feel strongly express themselves strongly vehemence is one of my faults. Let us pray for each other. We have great capacities for enjoyment, but we suffer more keenly than many of our race. I have been an intense sufferer in many ways the story would pain you nobody can go through this world with a heart and a soul, and jog along smoothly long at a time.... I do not remember ever having a discussion on paper with my husband we should not dare to run the risk. But I know I said something once in a letter, I forget what, that made him snatch the first train and rush to set things right, though it cost him a two days' journey. We are tremendous lovers still. Write and tell me we have kissed and made up! We both mean well we do not want to hurt each other but each has one million points that are very vulnerable. And neither can know these points in the other by intuition a cry of pain will often be the first intimation that the one can hurt the other just there. We must touch each other with the tips of our fingers.... To love Christ more—this is the deepest need, the constant cry of my soul. Down in the bowling-alley, and out in the woods, and on my bed, and out driving, when I am happy and busy, and when I am sad and idle, the whisper keeps going up for more love, more love, more love!

To a Christian Friend, Dorset, Oct. 3, 1873.

I do hope you will be in New York this winter and your mother, too. What a blessing to have a mother with whom one can hold Christian communion! You need some trials as a set-off to it. You say few live up to what light they have it is true I think we get light just as fast as we are ready for it. At the same time, I must own that I have not all the light I need. I am still puzzled as to the true way to live how far to cherish a spirit that makes one sit very lightly to all earthly things, when that spirit unfits one, to a great extent, to be an agreeable, thoroughly sympathizing companion to one's children, for instance. My children have a real horror of Miss ———, because she thinks and talks on only one subject of course, it never would do for me to do as she does, as far as they are concerned. Perhaps the problem may be solved by a resort to the fact that we are not called to the same experience. And yet an experience of as perfect love and faith as is ever vouchsafed to a soul on earth, is what I long for. At times, my heart dies within me when I realize how much I need. As you say, no doubt the mental strain I had been passing through prepared the way for my breakdown in health as I lay, as I thought, dying, I said so to myself. That strain is over I am in a sense at rest but not satisfied. I have been too near to Christ to be *happy* in anything else I do not mean by that, however, that I never *try* to be happy in other things—alas, I do.

As to the minor trials, no life is without them. But what mercies we get every now and then! The other day three letters came to me by one mail, each of which was important, and came from exactly the quarter where I was troubled, and dispersed the trouble to a great degree. In fact, I am overwhelmed with mercies, and dreadfully stupid and unthankful for them. I have had also some experiences of late of the smallness and meanness, of which you have had specimens. One has to betake oneself to prayer to get a sight of One, who is large-hearted and noble and good and true. Oh, how narrow human narrowness must look to Him! I do not know how many times I have smiled at your remark about Miss ——: "She seems to have such a hard time to learn her lessons." I feel sorry for her in one sense, but if she belongs to Christ, isn't He home enough for her? I think it *always* a very doubtful experiment to offer other people a home with you and equally doubtful whether such an offer is wisely accepted. Being a saint does not, I am sorry to say, necessarily make one an agreeable addition to the family circle as God has formed it if His hand *sends* this new element into the house, of course one may expect grace to bear it but voluntarily to seek it argues either want of experience or an immense power of self-sacrifice. I should prefer Miss ——'s friends agreeing to give her an independent home, as far as a boarding house can furnish a home. And if it provides a place in which to pray, as sweet a home may be found there as anywhere.

We go to town on the ninth of this month. Mr. Prentiss has been gone some time, and has entered upon his new duties with great delight. I must confess that if I were going to choose my work in life, I could think of nothing more congenial than to train young Christians. It has come over me lately that *all* those whom he now instructs, have more or less of the new life in them. I am sorry, however, to add that some young theological friends of mine deny this. They say that many young men preparing for the ministry give no other sign of piety. Young people judge hastily and severely. As soon as I get over my first hurry, after reaching home, I hope you will come and see me.... You speak of my experience on my sickbed as a precious one. To tell you the truth, it does not seem so to me I mean, nothing extraordinary. Not to want to go, if invited, would be a contradiction to most of my life. But as I was *not* invited, I realize that I am needed here and I am afraid it was selfish to be so delighted to go, horribly selfish.

* * * * *

III.

Change of Home and Life in New York. A Book about Robbie. Her Sympathy with young People. "I have in me Two different Natures." What Dr. De Witt said at the Grave of his Wife. The Way to meet little Trials. Faults in Prayer-Meetings. How special Theories of the Christian Life are formed. Sudden Illness of Prof. Smith. Publication of *Golden Hours*. How it was received.

Her return from Dorset brought with it a new order of life. The transfer of her husband to a theological chair was almost as great a change to her as to him. In ceasing to be a pastor's wife she gave up a position, which for more than a quarter of a century had been to her a spring of constant joy, and which, notwithstanding its cares, she regarded as one of the most favored on earth. While in the parsonage, too, she was in the midst of her friends the removal to Sixty-first street left the most of them at a distance and distance in New York is no slight hindrance to the full enjoyment of social intimacy and fellowship. Several weeks after the return to town were devoted to the congenial task of fitting-up and adorning the new home. Then for the first time in many years, she found herself at leisure and one of its earliest fruits was a selection of stray religious verses for publication that, however, soon gave way to a volume of her own. She was able also to give special attention to her favorite religious reading.

The sharp trials and suffering of the previous years showed their effect in deepened spiritual convictions, humility, and tenderness of feeling, but not in repressing her natural playfulness. At times, her spirits were still buoyant with fun and laughter. An extract from a letter to her youngest daughter, who with her sister was on a visit at Portland, will give a glimpse of this gay mood. Such mishaps as she recounts are liable to occur in the best-regulated households, especially on a change of servants but they were rare in her experience and so the more amused her:

I undertook to get up a nice dinner for Dr. and Mrs. V——, about which I must now tell you. First, I was to have raw oysters on the shell. *Blunder 1st*, small tea-plates laid for them. Ordered off, and big ones laid. *Blunder 2nd*, five oysters to be laid on each plate, instead of which five were placed on platters at each end, making ten in all for the whole party! Ordered a change to the original order. Result, a terrific sound in the parlor of rushing feet and bombardment of oyster-shells. Dinner was announced from Dr. P., who asked, helplessly, where he should place Mrs. V——. *Blunder 4th* by Mrs. P., who remarked that she had got fifty pieces of shell in her mouth. *Blunder 5th* by Dr. P., who failed to perceive that the boiled chickens were garnished with a stunning wine-jelly and regarding it as gizzards, presented it only to the boys! *Blunder 6th*. Cranberry-jelly ordered. Cranberry as a dark, inky fluid instead gazed upon suspiciously by the guests, and tasted sparingly by the family.—And now prepare for *blunder No. 7*, bearing in mind that it is the third course. *Four* prairie hens instead of two! The effect on the Rev. Mrs. E. Prentiss was a resort to her handkerchief, and suppression of tears on finding none in her pocket. *Blunder 8th*. Iauch's biscuit glacé stuffed with hideous orange-peel. *Delight 1st*, delicious dessert of farina smothered in custard and dear to the heart of Dr. V——. *Blunder 9th*. No hot milk for the coffee, delay in scalding it, and at last serving it in a huge cracked pitcher. *Blunder 10th*. Bananas, grapes, apples, and oranges forgotten at the right moment and passed after the coffee and of course declined. But hearing that Miss H. V. was fond of bananas, I seized the fruit-basket and poured its contents into one napkin, and a lot of chocolate-cake into another, and sent them to the young princesses in the parsonage, who are, no doubt, dying of indigestion, this morning. Give my love to C. and F., and a judicious portion to the old birds.

To a young Friend, Oct. 19, 1873.

I am sorry that we played hide-and-go-seek with each other when you were in town. I have seen all my most intimate friends since I came home I mean all who live here. There are just eight of them, but they fill my heart so that I should have said, at a guess, there were eighty! Try the experiment on yourself and tell me how many such friends you have. It is very curious.

I have just got hold of some leaves of a journal rescued from the flames by my (future) husband, written at the age of 22, in which I describe myself as "one great long sunbeam." It recalled the sweet life in Christ I was then leading, and made me feel that if I had got so far on as a girl, I ought to be *infinitely* farther on as a woman. Still, in spite of all shame and regrets, I had a long list of mercies to recount at the communion-table today. Among other things, I feel that I know and love you better than heretofore, and it is pleasant to love. I must not forget to answer your little niece's questions. I remember her father's calling with your sister, but I do not remember any little girl as being with them, much less "kissing her because she liked the Susy books." As to writing more about Robbie, I cannot do that till I get to heaven, where he has been ever so many years. Give my love to the wee maiden, and tell her I should love to kiss her.

No trait in Mrs. Prentiss was more striking than her sympathy with young people, especially with young girls, and her desire to be religiously helpful to them. But her interest in them was not confined to the spiritual life. She delighted to join them in their harmless amusements, and to take her part in their playful contests, whether of wit or knowledge. Her friend, Miss Morse, thus recalls this feature of her character:

In Mrs. Prentiss' life the wise man's saying, *A merry heart doeth good like a medicine*, was beautifully exemplified. Yet few were thoroughly acquainted with this phase of her character. Those who knew her only through her books, or her letters of Christian sympathy and counsel—many even who came into near and tender personal relations to her—failed to see the frolicsome side of her nature which made her an eager participant in the fun of young people—in a merry group of girls the merriest girl among them. In contests where playful rhymes were to be composed at command, on a moment's notice, she sharpened the wits of her companions by her own zest, but in most cases, herself bore off the palm.

She always entered into such contests with an unmistakable desire to win. I remember one evening in her own home in Dorset, when four of us were engaged in a game of verbarium, two against two—the opposite party was gaining rapidly. She suddenly turned to her partner with a comical air of chagrin and exclaimed "Why is it they are winning the game? You and I are a great deal brighter than they!"

The first time I ever saw Mrs. Prentiss was through an invitation to her home to meet about half a dozen young persons of my own age. She was in one of her merriest moods. Games of wit were played and she took part with genuine interest. She at once impressed me with the feeling that she was one of us, and that this arose from no effort to be sympathetic, but was simply part of her nature.

This brightness wonderfully attracted young people to her, and gave her an influence with them that she could not otherwise have exercised. She recognized it in herself as a power, and used it, as she did all her powers, for the service of her Master. Young Christians, seeing that her deeply religious life did not interfere with her keen enjoyment of all innocent pleasures, realized that there need be no gloominess for them, either, in a life consecrated to God.

Just as her line of thought would often lie absorbingly in some one direction for quite a period of time, so her fun ran "in streaks," as she would have been likely to express it. One winter she amused herself and her friends by a great number of charades and enigmas, many of which I copied and still possess. They were dashed off with an ease and rapidity quite remarkable. And I believe the same thing was true of most of her books. I have watched her when she was writing some funny piece of rhyme, and as her pen literally flew over the paper, I could hardly believe that she was actually composing as she wrote. One day two young girls were translating one of Heine's shorter poems. They had agreed to send their several versions to an absent friend, who on his part was to return his own to them. Mrs. Prentiss entered heartily into the plan and in an hour had written as many as a dozen translations, all in English rhyme and differing entirely one from the other. The stimulating effect on the genius of her companions was such that over thirty translations were produced in that one afternoon.

In thinking of the ease with which Mrs. Prentiss would suddenly turn from grave to gay and the reverse, I often recall her answer when I one day remarked on this trait in her.

"Yes, I have in me two very different natures. Did you ever hear the story of the dog, which by an accident was cut in two, and was joined together by a wonderful healing salve? Unfortunately, the pieces were not put together properly, so two of his legs stood up in the air. At first his master thought it a great misfortune, but he found that the dog, when a little accustomed to his strange new form, would run until tired on two legs, and then by turning himself over he would have a fresh unused pair to start with, and so he did double duty! I am like that dog. When I am tired of running on one nature, I can turn over and run on the other, and it rests me." [4]

I want to spend a few minutes of this my birthday in talking with you in reply to your letter.

To a Christian Friend, New York, Oct. 26, 1873.

I want to tell you how I love you, because you "learn your lessons" so easily, and how thankful I am that in your great trials and afflictions you have been enabled to glorify God. How small trouble is when set over against that! Is not Christ enough for a human soul? Does it really need anything else for its happiness? You will remember that when Madame Guyon was not only homeless, but deprived of her liberty, she was perfectly happy. "A little bird am I." [5] It seems to me that when God takes away our earthly joys and props, He gives Himself most generously and is there any joy on earth to be compared for a moment with such a gift?... My husband has just come in and described the scene at Mrs. De Witt's funeral, [6] when her husband said, *Goodbye, dear wife, you have been my greatest blessing next to Christ* and he added, "and that I can say of you." This was very sweet to me, for *I* have faults of manner that often annoy him—I am so vehement, so positive, and lay down the law so! But I believe the grace of God can cure faults of all sorts, be they deep-seated or external. And I ought to be one of the best women in the world, if I am good in proportion to the gifts with which I am overwhelmed. I count it not the least of your and my mercies, which we have been permitted to add four little children to the happy company above. No wonder you miss your darling boy, but I am sure you would not call him back. Have you any choice religious verses not in any book, that you would like to put into one I am going to get up?

To the Same, Nov. 12th.

I want you and your mother to know what I am now busy about, hoping it may set you to praying over it. When I asked you for bits of poetry, I meant pieces gleaned from time to time from newspapers. My plan was to make a compilation, interspersing verses of my own anonymously. But Mr. Randolph has convinced me that it is my duty and privilege to have the little book all original, and to appear as mine and in unexpected ways my will about it has been broken, and I have ceased from all morbid shyness about it, and am only too thankful that God is willing thus to use me for His own glory. Of course, I shall meet with a good deal of misapprehension and disgust from some quarters, but not from you or yours. It is a comfort, on the other hand, to think of once more ministering to longing or afflicted souls, as I hope to do in these lines, written for no human eye. You say Jesus is pained when His dear ones suffer. I hardly think that can be. Tender sympathy He no doubt feels, but not pain. If He did, He would be miserable all the time, the world is so full of misery.

When I look back over my own life, the precious times were generally seasons of great suffering so much so, that the idea of discipline has become a hobby. But one can only learn all this by experience. Mrs. —— says she never sings the verse containing "E'en though it be a cross that raiseth me," and that little children never talk in that way to their mothers, and, therefore, we ought not to talk so to God! I did not argue with her about it, but I felt thankful that I could sing and say that line very earnestly, and had been taught to do so by the Spirit of God.

To a Friend in Texas, New York, Dec. 1, 1873.

I am glad you like Faber better on a closer acquaintance. He certainly has said some wonderful things among many weak and foolish ones. What you quote from him about thanksgiving is very true. Our gratitude bears no sort of comparison with our petitions or our sighs and groans. It is contemptible in us to be such thankless beggars. As to domestic cares, you know Mrs. Stowe has written a beautiful little tract on this subject—"Earthly Care a Heavenly Discipline." God never places us in any position in which we cannot grow. We may fancy that He does. We may fear we are so impeded by fretting, petty cares that we are gaining nothing but when we are not sending any branches upward, we may be sending roots downward. Perhaps in the time of our humiliation, when everything seems a failure, we are making the best kind of progress. God delights to try our faith by the conditions in which He places us. A plant set in the shade shows where its heart is by turning towards the sun, even when unable to reach it. We have so much to distract us in this world that we do not realize how truly and deeply, if not always warmly and consciously, we love Christ. But I believe that this love is the strongest principle in every regenerate soul. It may slumber for a time, it may falter, it may freeze nearly to death, but sooner or later it will declare itself as the ruling passion. You should regard all your discontent with yourself as negative devotion, for that it really is. Madame Guyon said boldly, but truly, "O mon Dieu, plutot pecheur que superbe," and that is the consoling word I feel like sending you today. I know all about these little domestic foxes that spoil the vines, and sympathize with you in yours. But if some other trial would serve God's purpose, He would substitute it.

To a young Friend, New York, Dec. 3, 1873. I was interested in what you wrote about Miss G. and of Dr. C.'s meeting. You say she spends her time in young works of benevolence. This shows that her piety is of the genuine sort. It is hard to have faith in mere talk. It is a great mystery to me, that, while we meet with negative faults in ordinary prayer meetings, we find so many positive faults in more earnest ones. Perhaps there is less of self in those who conduct them than we imagine. I always regret to see talk to each other supplant address to God in such meetings—always. As to Miss —— and others making a "creed" as you say out of their experience, I think it may be accounted for in this way:

They come suddenly into possession of thoughts and emotions to which others are led gradually they are startled and overwhelmed by the novelty of the revelations, and at once form a theory on the subject and, having formed the theory, they fall to so interpreting the Bible as to support it. Those who reach the point they have reached more slowly are not startled, and do not need to form theories or seek for unscriptural expressions with which to declare what they have learned. They are probably less self-conscious, because they have not been aiming to enter any school formed by man, but have been simply following after Christ hardly knowing what they expect will be the result, but getting a great deal of sweet peace on the way. And they also acquire, gradually, a certain kind of heaven-taught wisdom, whose access comes not with observation blessed truths revealed by the Holy Spirit, full of strength and consolation.

At any rate, this is as far as I have come to there may be oceans of knowledge I have yet to acquire, which will modify or wholly change my range of thought. And, according to what light I have, I am inclined to advise you not to confuse yourself with trying to believe in or experience this or that because others do, but to get as close to Christ as you can every day of your life feeling sure that if you do, He by His Spirit will teach you all you need to know. There has been to my mind, during the last few weeks, something awe-inspiring in the sense I have had of the way in which God instructs His ignorant, forgetful, stupid children. Such goodness, such patience, such love! And, on the other hand, our *amazing* coldness and ingratitude.

To Mrs. Smith, New York, Dec. 21, 1873.

I wanted to see you before you left, but it would have been cruel to add to the cares and distractions amid which you were hurrying off. [7] ... I am reading, with great interest, the letters of Sara Coleridge. What strikes me most in her is, that knowing so much of her, one still feels what *lots* there is more to her one does not know. *22nd.*—Strangely enough, in writing you last evening, I forgot to tell you how much prayer is being offered for you and your husband, and what intense sympathy is expressed. Dr. Vincent said he could not bear to hear another word about his sufferings. Mrs. L—— said, "I do love that man." Mrs. D., herself all knotted up with rheumatism, would hardly speak of herself when she heard he was so ill and this is only a specimen of the deep feeling expressed on all sides.... I am glad you find anything to like in my poor little book. I hear very little about it, but its publication has brought a blessing to my soul, which shows that I did right in thus making known my testimony for Christ. My will in the matter was quite overturned.

The "poor little book" appeared under the title of *Religious Poems*, afterwards changed to *Golden Hours Hymns and Songs of the Christian Life*. In a letter of Mrs. Prentiss to a friend, written in 1870, occurs this passage:

Most of my verses are too much my own personal experience to be put in print now. After I am dead, I hope they may serve as language for some other hearts. After I am dead! That means, oh ravishing thought! That I shall be in heaven one day.

Until the fall of 1873, her husband and two or three friends only knew of the existence of these verses, and their publication had not crossed her mind. But shortly after her return from Dorset, she was persuaded to let Mr. Randolph read them. She soon received from him the following letter:

The poems *must* be printed, and at once! "We"—that is, the firm living at Yonkers—read aloud all the pieces, except those in the book, at one sitting, and would have gone on to the end but that the eyes gave out. Out of the lot, three or four pieces were laid aside as not up to the standard of the others. The female member of the firm said that Mrs. Prentiss would do a wrong if she withheld the poems from the public. This member said *he* should give up writing, or trying to write, religious verses.

I am not joking. The book must be printed. We were charmed with the poems. Some of them have all the quaintness of Herbert, some the simple subjective fervor of the German hymns, and some the glow of Wesley. They are, as Mrs. R. said, out of the beaten way, *and all true*. So they differ from the conventional poetry. If published, there may be here and there some sentimental soul, or some soul without sentiment, or some critic who dotes on Robt. Browning and do not understand him, or on Morris, or Rossetti, because *they* are high artists, who may snub the book. Very well, for compensation you will have the fact that the poems will win for you a living place in the hearts of thousands—in a sanctuary where few are permitted to enter.

A day or two later Mr. Randolph wrote in reply to her misgivings:

If I had the slightest thought that you would make even a slight mistake in publishing, I would say so. As I have already said, I am *sure* that the book would prove a blessing in ten thousand ways, and at the same time add to your reputation as a writer.

She could not resist this appeal. The assurance that the verses would prove a blessing to many souls disarmed her scruples and she consented to their publication. The most of them, unfortunately, bore no date. But all, or nearly all of them, belong to the previous twenty years, and they depict some of the deepest experiences of her Christian life during that period they are her tears of joy or of sorrow, her cries of anguish, and her songs of love and triumph. Some of them were hastily written in pencil, upon torn scraps of paper, as if she were on a journey. Were they all accompanied with the exact time and circumstances of their composition, they would form, in connection with others unpublished, her spiritual autobiography from the death of Eddy and Bessie, in 1852, to the autumn of 1873. [8]

As she anticipated, the volume met in some quarters with anything but a cordial reception the criticisms upon it were curt and depreciatory. Its representation of the Christian life was censured as gloomy and false. It was even intimated that in her expressions of pain and sorrow, there was more or less poetical affectation. Alluding to this in a letter to a friend, she writes:

I have spoken of the deepest, sorest pain not of trials, but of sorrow, not of discomfort, but of suffering. And all I have spoken of, I have felt. Never could I have known Christ, had I not had large experience of Him as a chastiser.... You little know the long story of my life, nor is it necessary that you should but you must take my word for it that if I do not know what suffering means, there is not a soul on earth that does. It has not been my habit to say much about this it has been a matter between myself and my God but the *results* I have told, that He may be glorified and that others may be led to Him as the Fountain of life and of light. I refer, of course, to the book of verses. I never called them poems. You may depend upon it the world is brimful of pain in some shape or other it is a "*hurt*" world." But no Christian should go about groaning and weeping though sorrowing, he should be always rejoicing. During twenty years of my life my kind and wise Physician was preparing me, by many bitter remedies, for the work I was to do I can never thank or love Him enough for His unflinching discipline.

Even the favorable notices of the volume, with two or three exceptions, evinced little sympathy with its spirit, or appreciation of its literary merits. [9] But while failing to make any public impression, the little book soon found its way into thousands of closets and sickrooms and houses of mourning, carrying a blessing with it. Touching and grateful testimonies to this effect came from the East and the farthest West and from beyond the sea. The following is an extract from, a letter to Mr. Randolph, written by a lady of New York eminent for her social influence and Christian character:

The book of heart-hymns is wonderful, as I expected from the specimens, which you read to me from the little scraps of paper from your desk. Do you know that I *lived* on them ("The School" and "My Expectation is from Thee") and was greedy to get the book that I might read them again and again. And behold, the volume is full of the things I have felt so often, *expressed* as no one ever expressed them before. I am overwhelmed every time I read it. Mr. —— and the children have quite laughed at "Mamma's enthusiasm" over a book of poems, as I am considered very prosaic. I made C. read two or three of them and he *surrenders*. N. too, who is full of appreciation of poetry as well as of the *best things*, is equally delighted. I carried the volume to a sick friend and read to her out of it. I wish you could have seen how she was comforted! I do not know Mrs. Prentiss, but if you ever get a chance, I would like you to tell her what she has done for me.

A highly cultivated Swiss lady wrote from Geneva:

What a precious, precious book! and what mercy in God to enable us to understand, and say Amen from the heart to every line! It was He who caused you to send me a book I so much needed—and I thank Him as much as you.

* * * * *

IV.

Incidents of the Year 1874. Prayer. Starts a Bible-Reading in Dorset.
Begins to take Lessons in Painting. A Letter from her Teacher.
Publication of *Urbane and his Friends*. Design of the Work. Her views
of the Christian Life. The Mystics. The Indwelling Christ. An Allegory.

During the winter and early spring of 1874, Mrs. Prentiss found much delight in attending a weekly Bible-reading, held by Miss Susan Warner. She was deeply impressed with the advantages of such a mode of studying the Word of God, and in the course of the summer was led to start a similar exercise in Dorset. Her letters will show how much satisfaction it gave her during all the rest of her life.

Another incident, that left its mark upon this year, was the sudden and dangerous illness of her husband. His life was barely saved by an immediate surgical operation. He convalesced very slowly and it was many months before she recovered from the shock.

To a Christian Friend, Jan. 25, 1874.

I do not perfectly understand what you say about prayer, but it reminds me of Mrs.——'s expressing surprise at my praying. She said she did not, because Christ was all round her. But it is no less a fact that Christ Himself spent hours in prayer, using language when He did so. That does not prove, however, that He did not hold silent, mystical communion with the Father. It seems to me that communion is one thing, and intercessory prayer another my own prayers are chiefly of the latter class the sweet sense of communion of which I have had so much, has been greatly wanting I dare not ask for it I must pray as the Spirit gives me utterance. No doubt, your experience is beyond mine I can conceive of a silence that unites, not separates, as existing between Christ and the soul. As to her of whom we sadly spoke, I am so absolutely lost in confusion of thought that I feel as if chart and compass had gone overboard. I believe there can be falls from the highest state of grace, and that sometimes a fall is the best thing that can happen to one but it is an appalling thought. How wary all this should make you and me! Though I have felt the greatest respect for Miss ———, I have often wondered why I did not *love* her more. Well, we have a new reason for fleeing to Christ in this perplexity and disappointment. I had let her be in many things my oracle, and perhaps no human being ought to be that. Shall we ever learn to put no confidence in the flesh? My husband thinks Miss ——— insane.

To a young Friend, Jan 27, 1874.

The comfort I have had as the fruit of close acquaintance with a sickroom! I see more and more how *wise* God was, as well as how good, in hiding me away during all the years that might have been very tempting, had I had my freedom. My publishing this book [10] was a sort of miracle I *never* meant to do it, but my will was taken away and it was done in one short month. I should not expect a girl as young as yourself to respond to much of it, but I am glad you found anything to which you could.... When I received my own great blessing thirty-five years ago, I was younger than you are now, and had not half the light you have, nor did I know exactly what to aim at, but blundered and suffered not a little.... It seems to me that it is eminently fitting that we should go to the throne of grace together, and expect, in so doing, a different kind of blessing from that sought alone, in the closet. I never feel any embarrassment in praying with those older and better than myself the better they are, the less disposed they will be to look down upon me. The truth is, we are all alike in being poor and needy, and it is a good thing to get together and confess this to our Father, in each other's hearing. I can unite cordially with anyone, man, woman or child, who really *prays*. A very illiterate person could win my heart if I knew he truly loved the Lord Jesus, no matter how clumsily he expressed that love and his prayers would edify me. Perhaps you cannot look at this matter exactly as I do. I know I *suffered* for years, whenever I prayed with others, old or young but I persevered in what I believed to be a duty, until, not so very long ago, the duty became a pleasure, all fear of man being taken away. I never think anything about what sort of a prayer I make in fact *I* make no prayer we have to speak as the Spirit gives us utterance.

To Mrs. Condict, Kauinfels, [11] *Aug. 16, 1874.*

Yesterday Miss H. came down and asked me if I would start a Bible-reading at her house. I told her I would with pleasure. This morning I decided to open with the Sermon on the Mount, and have been studying the first promise. Do take your Bible and study that verse by reading the references. I am *delighted* that our dear Lord has at last pointed out my mission to this village. I have long prayed that He would open a way of access to hearts here. Pray next Wednesday afternoon that I may be a witness for Him. There are a number of families boarding in town, who will join the reading. Miss H. wanted to give notice from the pulpit, but I could not consent to that.... You say your mother asks about my book. It is a queer one, and I am not satisfied with it but my husband is, and thinks it will do good. God grant it may. I entitle it Paths of Peace or, Christian Friends in Council. [12] After the most earnest prayer for light, I cannot preach sinless perfection. I think God has provided a way to perfection, and that that is, "looking unto Jesus." If the "higher life" means utter sinlessness then I shall have to own that I have never had any experience of it. Mr. P. has given me a world of anxiety. He will go round everywhere, even on jolting straw-rides his wound is nearly healed, however. He is *looking* the picture of health, but feels uncomfortable and sleeps restlessly. I went up to the tavern lately as a great piece of self-denial to call on a lady boarding there, and found I had thus stumbled on to fine gold the gold you and I love. She is the wife of the Rev. Mr. R., of Flushing.

Soon after returning to town, she began to take lessons in oil painting. Her teacher was Mrs. Julia H. Beers—now Mrs. Kempson—a lady gifted with much of the artistic power belonging to her distinguished brothers, William and James M. Hart. In this new pursuit, Mrs. Prentiss passed many very busy and happy hours. The following letter to her husband gives Mrs. Kempson's recollections of them:

FIRTREE COTTAGE, METUCHEN, *Jan. 27, 1880.*

My dear Dr. Prentiss:—When the news came of Mrs. Prentiss' death, I felt that I had lost a friend whose place could not be filled. I never had a pupil in whom I was so much interested, or one that I loved so dearly. She has told me many times that "the days spent with me were red-letter days in her life." They certainly were in my own. I shall never forget her first visit to my studio on the corner of Fifth avenue and Twenty-sixth street. We had not met before, and I felt somewhat awed in the presence of an authoress. But in a few minutes, we were fast friends. Taking one of my portfolios in her arms she asked, "May I sit down on the floor and take this in my lap?" Of course, I assented. She pored over the contents with the delight of a child. Then turning to me she said, "This is what I have had a craving for all my life. There has always been a want unsupplied I knew not what it was but now I know. It was a reaching out for the beautiful. Look at my white hair and tell me if it would be possible for me to learn." I replied, "Yes, if you desire to do so." "Will you take me for a pupil?" she asked. "I do not know which end of the brush to use." "No matter," I said, "I can teach you."

She became my pupil and you know the result. But you cannot know, as I do, the delight she took in her studies. My ordinary pupils were limited to two hours. But I said to her, "Come at ten and stay as long as you please." Punctual to the moment she came, seated herself at her easel, and rarely left it while the light lasted. I never saw such enthusiasm or such appreciation. At first, her progress was slow, but as she gained knowledge of the materials, it became very rapid. In my opinion, she had remarkable talent, and, if spared, might even have made herself a name as an artist. I have had hundreds of pupils, but not one of them ever made such progress. What a delight it was to teach her! All her quaint sayings and her beautifully expressed thoughts I treasured up as precious things. She always brought brightness to the studio with her. I can see her so plainly this moment as she came in one morning. "Well," she said, "I thought when I commenced painting if ever I painted a daisy that did not need to be labeled, I should be proud, and I have done it." I wish, dear Dr. Prentiss, I could recall the thousand and one pleasant things that every now and then have occurred to me, while I was thinking of her. I tried to write to you when I heard of your great loss, but my heart failed me. I could not, nor can I, imagine you living without her. In her last letter to me, she says, speaking of my daughter's marriage:

I hope thirty years hence the twain will be as much in love with each other as two old codgers of my acquaintance, who go on talking heavenly nonsense to each other after the most approved fashion.

How little I then dreamed that we should never meet again! I should much like to see you all. I have not forgotten that pleasant summer at Dorset in 1875, nor the great pan of blackberries you picked for me with your own hands.

With kindest regards, very sincerely,
JULIA H. KEMPSON.

To Mrs. Humphrey, New York, Dec. 1874.

After learning how to manage a "Bible-reading" by attending Miss Warner's once a week for four or five months, I got my tongue so loosed that I have held one by request at Dorset. The interest in it did not flag all summer, and ladies, young and old, came from all directions, not only to the readings, but with tears to open their hearts to me. Some hitherto worldly ones were among the number. I have also helped to start one at Elizabeth, another at Orange, another at Flushing. My husband says if one were held in every church in the land, the country would be revolutionized. It is just such work, as you would delight in. Do forgive the blots I am tearing away on this letter so that I forget myself and dip up too much ink. I have been urged to hold three readings a week in different parts of the city, but that is not possible. You cannot imagine how thankful I am that I have at last found a sphere of usefulness in Dorset.

We had a great shock last spring when Mr. Prentiss was stricken down I do not dare to think how hard it would have been to become husbandless and homeless at one blow. But I well know that no earthly circumstances need really destroy our happiness in that which is, after all, *our Life*. Even if it is only for the few years before our boys leave home, never to return permanently to it, I shall be thankful to have it left as it is—if that is best. If I had not known what my husband's trouble was, and summoned aid in the twinkling of an eye, Dr. Buck says he would have died. He would certainly have died if he had been at Dorset. He has never recovered his strength, but is able to give his lectures. Although I did very little nursing, I got a good deal run down, especially from losing sleep, and have had to go to bed at half-past eight or nine all summer and thus far in the winter.

I am taking lessons this winter in oil painting with A. She has the advantage of me in having had lessons in drawing, while I have had none. My teacher says she never had a beginner do better than I, so I think beginners very awkward mortals, who get paint all over their clothes, hands and faces, and who, if they get a pretty picture, know in the secrecy of their guilty consciences it was done by a compassionate artist who would fain persuade one into the fancy that the work was one's own.

What you say about my having done you good surprises me. Whatever treasure God has in me is hidden in an earthen vessel and unseen by my own eyes.... I feel every day how much there is to learn, how much to unlearn, and that no genuine experience is to be despised. Some people roundly berate Christians for want of faith in God's word, when it is want of faith in their own private interpretation of His word. I think that when the very best and wisest of mankind get to heaven, they will get a standard of holiness that might make them blush only it is not likely they *will* blush.

In the latter part of this year *Urbane and His Friends* appeared. Urbane is an aged pastor and his Friends are members of his flock, whom he had invited to meet him from week to week for Christian counsel and fellowship. Some of their names, Antiochus, Hermes, Junia, Claudia, Apelles and the like, sound rather strange, but, together with those more familiar, they are all borrowed from the New Testament.

Urbane and His Friends is the only book of a didactic sort written by Mrs. Prentiss. It is not, however, wholly didactic, but contains also touches of narrative and character that add to its interest. Among the topics discussed are, The Bible, Temptation, Faith, Prayer, the Mystics, "The Higher Christian Life," Service, Pain and Sorrow, Peace and

Joy, and the Indwelling Christ. She was dissatisfied with the work and required some persuasion before she would consent to its being published. But its spiritual tone, its tenderness, its "sweet reasonableness," and the bright little pictures of Christian truth and life, which enliven its pages, have led some to prize it more than any other of her writings.

And here it may not be out of place to insert the following letter of her husband, written several months after her death. It gives her matured views on certain points relating to the Christian life, about which there has been no little difference of opinion:

NEW YORK, *April 16, 1879.*

MY DEAR FRIEND:—Many thanks for your kind words about Urbane and His Friends. So far, at least as the aim and spirit of the book are concerned, no praise could exceed its merits. It was written with a single desire to honor Christ by aiding and cheering some of His disciples on their way heavenward. At that time, as you know, there was a good deal of discussion about "the Higher Christian Life" and "Holiness through Faith." She herself had felt some of the difficulties connected with the subject, and was anxious to reach out a helping hand to others similarly perplexed. I do not think her mind was specially adapted to the didactic style, nor was it much to her taste. When writing in that style her pen did not seem to be entirely at ease or to move quite at its own sweet will. Careful statement and nice theological distinctions were not her forte. And yet her mental grasp of Christian doctrine in its vital substance was very firm, and her power of observing, as well as depicting, the most delicate and varying phenomena of the spiritual life was like an instinct. A purer or more whole-hearted love of "the truth as it is in Jesus," I never witnessed in any human being. At the same time, she was very modest and distrustful of her own judgment when opposed to that of others whom she regarded as experienced Christians. I wish you could enjoy a tithe of the happiness that was mine during the winter and spring of 1873-4, as, evening after evening, she talked over with me the various points discussed in her book, and then read to me what she had written. Those were golden hours indeed—hours in which was fulfilled the saying that is written—*And it came to pass that while they communed together and reasoned, Jesus Himself drew near.* As I look back to the Sabbath evenings passed with her in such converse, they seem to me radiant still with the glory of the risen Christ. Nor am I able to imagine what else than His presence could have rendered them, at the time, so soothing and blissful.

You refer to her fondness for the mystics. She thought that Christian piety owes a large debt of gratitude to such writers as Thomas à Kempis, Madame Guyon, Fenelon, Leighton, Tersteegen, and others like them in earlier and later times, to whom "the secret of the Lord" seemed in a peculiar manner to have been revealed, and who with seraphic zeal trod as well as taught the paths of peace and holiness. While she was writing the chapter on the Mystics, I showed her Coleridge's tribute to them in his Biographia Literaria, which greatly pleased her. It is her own experience that she puts into the mouth of Urbane, where he says, after quoting Coleridge's tribute, "I have no recollection of ever reading this passage till today, but had *toiled out* its truth for myself, and now set my hand and seal to it." [13] It is for her, too, as well as for himself, that Urbane speaks, where, in answer to Hermes' question, "Who are the Mystics?" he says:

They are the men and women known to every age of the Church, who usually make their way through the world completely misunderstood by their fellow men. Their very virtues sometimes appear to be vices. They are often the scorn and contempt of their time, and are even persecuted and thrown into prison by those who think they thus do our Lord service. But now and then one arises who sees, or thinks he sees, some clue to their lives and their speech. Though not of them, he feels a mysterious kinship to them that makes him shrink with pain when he hears them spoken of unjustly. Now, I happen to be such a man. I have not built up any pet theory that I want to sustain I am not in any way bound to fight for any school but I should be most ungrateful to God and man if I did not acknowledge that I owe much of the sum and substance of the best part of my life to mystical writers—aye, and mystical thinkers, whom I know in the flesh.... I use Christ as a magnet, and say to all who cleave to Him—even when I cannot perfectly agree with them on every point of doctrine: You love Christ, therefore I love you.

Closely allied to her fondness for the Mystics was her delight in the doctrine of the indwelling Christ. For more than thirty years, it was a favorite subject of our Sunday and weekday talk. The closing chapters of the Gospel of John, the Epistle to the Ephesians, and other parts of the New Testament, in which this most precious truth is enshrined, were especially dear to her. So too, and for the same reason, was Lavater's hymn beginning,

O Jesus Christus, wachs in mir—

a hymn with which we became acquainted soon after our marriage, and which I do not doubt she repeated to herself many thousands of times. [14]

The surest way, as she thought, of rising above the bondage of "frames" and entering into the glorious liberty of the sons of God, is to become fully conscious of our actual union to Christ and of what is involved in this thrice-sacred union. It is not enough that we trust in Him as our Savior and the Lord our Righteousness He must also dwell in our hearts by faith as our spiritual life. The union is indeed mystical and indescribable, but nonetheless real or less joy inspiring for all that. We want no metaphor and no mere abstraction in our souls we want Christ Himself. We want to be able to say in sublime contradiction, "I live, yet not I, but Christ lives in me." And this, too, is the way of sanctification, as well as of rest of conscience. For just in proportion as Christ lives in the soul, self goes out and with it sin. Just in proportion as self goes out, Christ comes in, and with Him righteousness, peace, and joy in the Holy Ghost.

But as, in her view, the doctrine of an indwelling Christ did not supplant the doctrine of an atoning and interceding Christ, so neither did it supplant that of Christ as our Example or annul the great law of self-sacrifice by which, following in His steps, we also are to be made perfect through suffering.

Such is a brief outline of her teaching on this subject in Urbane and His Friends. And from its publication until her death, her theory of the way of holiness reduced itself more and more to these two simple points: Christ in the flesh showing and teaching us how to live, and Christ in the Spirit living in us. And this presence of Christ in the soul she regarded, I repeat, as an actual, as well as actuating, presence mediated indeed, like His sacrifice upon the cross, by the Holy Ghost. But, as "through the Eternal Spirit He offered HIMSELF without spot unto God," even so in and through the same Eternal Spirit, He HIMSELF comes and takes up His abode in the hearts of His faithful disciples. His indwelling is not a mere metaphor, not a bare moral relation, but the most blessed reality—a veritable union of life and love. She thought that much of the meaning and comfort of the doctrine was sometimes lost by not keeping this point in mind. In a letter written not long before her death, she reiterated very strongly her conviction on this subject, appealing to our Lord's teaching in the seventeenth chapter of John. [15]

And this brings me to what you say about the chapter entitled The Mystics of Today or, "The Higher Christian Life and to your inquiry as to her later views on the question. You are quite right in supposing that while writing this chapter she had a good deal of sympathy with some of the advocates of the "Higher Life" doctrine. She heartily agreed with them in believing that it is the privilege of Christ's disciples to rise to a much higher state of holy love, assurance, and rest of soul than the most of them seem ever to reach in this world and further, that such a spiritual uplifting may come, and sometimes does come, in the way of a sudden and extraordinary experience. But it is never without a history. She gives a beautiful picture of such an experience in the case of Stephanas, who was "as gay as any boy," and then adds, "Now, the descent of the blessing was sudden and lifted him at once into a new world, but the preparation for it had been going on ever since he learned to pray."

But while agreeing with the advocates of the Higher Life doctrine in some points, she was far from agreeing with them in all. And her disagreement increased and grew more decided in her later years. The subject is often alluded to in her letters to Christian friends and should these letters ever be published, they will answer your inquiry much better than I can do. The points in the "Higher Life" and "Holiness through Faith" views, which she most strongly dissented from, related to the question of perfection. The Christian life—this was her view—is subject to the great law of growth. It is a process, an education, and not a mere volition, or series of volitions. Its progress may be rapid, but ideally considered, each new stage is conditioned by the one that went before *first the blade, then the ear, after that the full corn in the ear*. It embraces the whole spirit and soul and body and its perfect development, therefore, is a very comprehensive thing, touching the length and breadth, the depth and height of our entire being. It is also, in its very nature, conflict as well as growth the forces of evil must be vanquished, and these forces, whether acting through body, soul, or spirit, are very subtle, treacherous, and often occult, as well as very potent the best man on earth, if left to himself, would fall a prey to them. No fact of religious experience is more striking than this, that the higher men rise in real goodness—the nearer they come to God, the more keen-eyed and distressed are they to detect evil in themselves. Their sense of sin seems to be in a sort of inverse ratio to their freedom from its power. And we meet with a similar fact in the natural life. The finer and more exalted the sentiment of purity and honor, the more sensitive will one be to the slightest approach to what is impure or dishonorable in one's own character and conduct. Such is substantially her ground of dissent from the "Higher Life" theory. Her own sense of sin was so profound and vivid that she shuddered at the thought of claiming perfection for herself and it seemed to her a very sad delusion for anybody else to claim it. True holiness is never self-conscious it does not look at itself in the glass and if it did, it would see only Christ, not itself, reflected there. This was her way of looking at the subject and she came to regard all theories, still more all professions, of entire sanctification as fallacious and full of peril—not a help, but a serious hindrance to real Christian holiness. For several years, she not only read but carefully studied the most noted writers who advocated the "Higher Life" and "Holiness through Faith" doctrines, and her testimony was that they had done her harm. "I find myself spiritually injured by them," she wrote to a friend less than two years before her death. "How do you explain the fact," she added, "that truly good people are left to produce such an effect? Is it not to shut us up to Christ? What a relief it will be to get beyond our own weaknesses, and those of others! I long for that day."

I have just alluded to her deep, vivid consciousness of sin. It would have been an intolerable burden, had not her feeling of God's infinite grace and love in Christ been still more vivid and profound. The little allegory in the ninth chapter of Urbane and His Friends expresses very happily this feeling.

There are several other points in her theory of the Christian life, to which she attached much importance. One is the close connection between suffering in some form and holiness, or growth in grace. The cross the way to the crown—this thought runs, like a golden thread, through all the records of her religious history. She expressed it while a little girl, as she sat one day with a young friend on a tombstone in the old burying-ground at Portland. It occurs again and again in her early letters in one written in 1840 she says: "I thought to myself that if God continued His faithfulness towards me, I shall have afflictions such as I now know nothing more of than the name" in another written four years later, in the midst of the sweetest joy: "I know there are some of the great lessons of life yet to be learned I believe I must *suffer* as long as I have an earthly existence." And in after years, when it formed so large an element in her own experience, she came to regard suffering, when sanctified by the word of God and by prayer, as the King's highway to Christian perfection. This point is often referred to and illustrated in her various writings—more especially in Stepping Heavenward and Golden Hours. Possibly she carried her theory a little too far perhaps it does not appear to be always verified in actual Christian experience but, certainly, no one can deny that it is in harmony with the general teaching of inspired Scripture and with the spirit of catholic piety in all ages. [16]

Another point, which also found illustration in her books, is the vital connection between the habit of devout communion with God in Christ and all the daily virtues and charities of religion another still is the close affinity between depth in piety and the highest, sweetest enjoyment of earthly good.

Her own Christian life was to me a study from the beginning. It had heights and depths of its own, which awed me and which I could not fully penetrate. Jonathan Edwards' exquisite description of Sarah Pierrepont at the age of thirteen, Mrs. Edwards' own account of her religious exercises after her marriage, and Goethe's "Confessions of a Beautiful Soul," always reminded me of some of its characteristic features. If my pastoral ministrations gave any aid and comfort to other souls, I can truly say it was all largely due to her. And as for myself, my debt of gratitude to her as a spiritual helper and friend in Christ was, and is, and ever will be, unspeakable. The instant I began to know her, I began to feel the cheering influence and uplifting power of her faith. For more than a third of a century, it was the most constant and by far the strongest human force that wrought in my religious life. Nor was it a human force alone for surely faith like hers is in real contact with Christ Himself and is an inspiration of His Spirit. She longed so to live and move and have her being in love to Christ, that nobody could come near her without being straightway reminded of Him. She seemed to be always saying to herself, in the words of an old Irish hymn: [17] Christ with me, Christ before me, Christ behind me, Christ within me, Christ beneath me, Christ above me, Christ at my right, Christ at my left, Christ in the heart of every man who thinks of me, Christ in the mouth of every man who speaks to me, Christ in every eye that sees me, Christ in every ear that hears me. Such was her constant prayer and it was answered in the experience of many souls, whose faith was kindled into a brighter flame by the intense ardor of hers. So long and so closely, in my own mind, was she associated with Christ, that the thought of her still reminds me of Him as naturally as does reading about Him in the New Testament.

The allegory referred to above is here given:

A benevolent man found a half-starved, homeless, blind beggar-boy in the streets of a great city. He took him, just as he was, to his own house, adopted him as his own son, and began to educate him. But the boy learned very slowly, and his face was often sad. His father asked him why he did not fix his mind more upon his lessons, and why he was not cheerful and happy, like the other children. The boy replied that his mind was constantly occupied with the fear that he had not been really adopted as a son, and might at any moment learn his mistake.

Father. But can you not believe me when I assure you that you are my own dear son?

Boy. I cannot, for I can see no reason why you should adopt me. I was a poor, bad boy you did not need any more children, for you had a house full of them, and I never can do anything for you.

Father. You can love me and be happy, and as you grow older and stronger, you can work for me.

Boy. I am afraid I do not love you that is what troubles me.

Father. Would you not be very sorry to have me deny that you are my son, and turn you out of the house?

Boy. Oh, yes! But perhaps that is because you take good care of me, not because I love you.

Father. Suppose, then, I should provide someone else to take care of you, and should then leave you.

Boy. That would be dreadful.

Father. Why? You would be taken good care of, and have every want supplied.

Boy. But I should have no father. I should lose the best thing I have. I should be lonely.

Father. You see you love me a little, at all events. Now, do you think I love you?

Boy. I do not see how you can. I am such a bad boy and try your patience so. And I am not half as thankful to you for your goodness as I ought to be. Sometimes, for a minute, I think to myself, He *is* my father and he really loves me then I do something wrong, and I think nobody would want such a boy, nobody can love such a boy.

Father. My son, I tell you that I do love you, but you cannot believe it because you do not know me. And you do not know me because you have not seen me, because you are blind. I must have you cured of this blindness.

So the blind boy had the scales removed from his eyes and began to see. He became so interested in using his eyesight that, for a time, he partially lost his old habit of despondency. But one day, when it began to creep back, he saw his father's face light up with love as one after another of his children came to him for a blessing, and said to himself: *They* are his own children, and it is not strange that he loves them, and does so much to make them happy. But I am nothing but a beggar-boy he cannot love me. I would give anything if he could. Then the father asked why his face was sad, and the boy told him.

Father. Come into this picture gallery and tell me what you see.

Boy. I see a portrait of a poor, ragged, dirty boy. And here is another. And another. Why, the gallery is full of them!

Father. Do you see anything amiable and lovable in any of them?

Boy. Oh, no.

Father. Do you think I love your brothers?

Boy. I know you do!

Father. Well, here they are, just as I took the poor fellows out of the streets.

Boy. Out of the streets as you did me? They are all your adopted sons?

Father. Every one of them.

Boy. I do not understand it. What made you do it?

Father. I loved them so that I could not help it.

Boy. I never heard of such a thing! You loved those miserable beggar-boys? Then you must be made of Love!

Father. I am. And that is the reason I am so grieved when some such boys refuse to let me become their father.

Boy. Refuse? Oh, how can they? Refuse to become your own dear sons? Refuse to have such a dear, kind, patient father? Refuse *love*?

Father. My poor blind boy, do not you now begin to see that I do not wait for these adopted sons of mine to wash and clothe themselves, to become good, and obedient, and affectionate, but loved them *because* they were such destitute, wicked, lost boys? I did not go out into the streets to look for well-dressed, well-cared-for, faultless children, who would adorn my house and shine in it like jewels. I sought for outcasts I loved them as outcasts I knew they would be ungrateful and disobedient, and never love me half as much as I did them but that made me all the more sorry for them. See what pains I am taking with them, and how beautifully some of them are learning their lessons. And now tell me, my son, in seeing this picture gallery, do you not begin to see me? Could anything less than love take in such a company of poor beggars?

Boy. Yes, my father, I do begin to see it. I do believe that I know you better now than I ever did before. I believe you love even me. And now I *know* that I love you!

Father. Now, then, my dear son, let that vexing question drop forever, and begin to act as my son and heir should. You have a great deal to learn, but I will myself be your teacher, and your mind is now free to attend to my instructions. Do you find anything to love and admire in your brothers?

Boy. Indeed I do.

Father. You shall be taught the lessons that have made them what they are. Meanwhile I want to see you look cheerful and happy, remembering that you are in your father's heart.

Boy. Dear father, I will! But oh, help me to be a better son!

Father. Dear boy, I will.

[1] In Union Theological Seminary, New York.

[2] The Baptism of the Holy Ghost, by Rev. Asa Mahau, D.D., p. 118.

[3] Dr. L. H. Hemenway.

[4] Some of the charades referred to will be found in appendix E.

[5] Referring to the following hymn composed by Madame Guyon in prison:

> A little bird I am,
> Shut out from fields of air,
> And in my cage I sit and sing
> To Him who placed me there.
> Well-pleased a prisoner to be,
> Because, my God, it pleaseth Thee.
> Naught have I else to do
> I sing the whole day long
> And He, whom most I love to please,

> Doth listen to my song.
> He caught and bound my wandering wing,
> But still He bends to hear me sing.

[6] Mrs. De Witt was the wife of the Rev. Thomas De Witt, D.D., a man of deep learning, an able preacher in the Dutch language as well as the English, and universally revered for his exalted Christian virtues. He was a minister of the Collegiate Church, New York, for nearly half a century. He died May 18, 1874, in the eighty-third year of his age. Here are other sentences uttered by him at the grave of his wife: "Farewell, my beloved, honored, and faithful wife! The tie that united us is severed. Thou art with Jesus in glory He is with me by His grace. I shall soon be with you. Farewell!"

[7] Prof. Smith had been suddenly stricken down by severe illness and with difficulty removed to the well-known Sanitarium at Clifton Springs.

[8] Referring to the book in a letter to a friend, written shortly after its publication, she says, "Of course it will meet with rough treatment in some quarters, as indeed it has already done. I doubt if any one works very hard for Christ who does not have to be misunderstood and perhaps mocked."

[9] One of the best notices appeared in The Churchman, an Episcopal newspaper then published at Hartford, but since transferred to New York. Here is a part of it:

"For purity of thought, earnestness, and spirituality of feeling, and smoothness of diction, they are all, without exception, good—if they are not great. If no one rises to the height, which other poets have occasionally reached, they are, nevertheless, always free from those defects, which sometimes mar the perfectness of far greater productions. Each portrays some human thirst or longing, and so touches the heart of every thoughtful reader. There is a sweetness running through them all which comes from a higher than earthly source, and which human wisdom can neither produce nor enjoy."

[10] *Golden Hours*.

[11] The name given to the Dorset home.

[12] Afterwards changed to *Urbane and His Friends*.

[13] The passage from Coleridge is as follows: "The feeling of gratitude which I cherish towards these men has caused me to digress further than I had foreseen or proposed but to have passed them over in an historical sketch of my literary life and opinions, would have seemed like the denial of a debt, the concealment of a boon for the writings of these mystics acted in no slight degree to prevent my mind from being imprisoned within the outline of any dogmatic system. They contributed to keep alive the *heart* in the *head* gave me an indistinct, yet stirring and working presentiment that all the products of the mere *reflective* faculty partook of DEATH, and were as the rattling of twigs and sprays in winter, into which a sap was yet to be propelled from some root to which I had not penetrated, if they were to afford my soul either food or shelter. If they were too often a moving cloud of smoke to me by day, yet they were always a pillar of fire throughout the night, during my wanderings through the wilderness of doubt, and enabled me to skirt, without crossing, the sandy desert of utter unbelief."

[14] See her translation of the hymn in *Golden Hours*, p. 123. The original will be found in appendix C.

[15] I in them and Thou in me, that they may be made perfect in one.—V. 23.

[16] There should be no greater comfort to Christian persons, than to be made like unto Christ, by suffering patiently adversities, troubles, and sicknesses. For He himself went not up to joy, but first He suffered pain He entered not into His glory, before He was crucified. So truly, our way to eternal joy is to suffer here with Christ.—(The Book of Common Prayer.)

[17] Ascribed to St. Patrick, on the occasion of his appearing before King Laoghaire.

CHAPTER 14 - WORK AND PLAY - 1875-1877.

I.

A Bible reading in New York. Her Painting. "Grace for Grace." Death of a young Friend. The Summer at Dorset. Bible-readings there. Encompassed with Kindred. Typhoid Fever in the House. Watching and Waiting. The Return to Town. A Day of Family Rejoicing. Life a "Battlefield."

Her time and thoughts during 1875 were mostly taken up by her Bible-readings, her painting, the society of kinsfolk from the East and the West, getting her eldest son ready for college, and by the dangerous illness of her youngest daughter. Some extracts from the few letters belonging to this year will give the main incidents of its history.

To a young Friend, Jan. 13, 1875.

I have had two Bible-readings, and they bid fair to be more like those of last winter than I had dared to hope. There are earnest, thoughtful, praying souls present, who help me in conducting the meeting, and you would be astonished to see how much better I can do when not under the keen embarrassment of delivering a lecture, as at Dorset…. I have a young friend about your age who is dying of consumption, and it is very delightful to see how happy she is. She used to attend the Bible-readings last winter.

About the painting? Well, I have dug away, and Mrs. Beers painted out and painted in, till I have got a beautiful great picture almost entirely done by her. Then I undertook the old fence with the clematis on it here at home, and made a *horrid* daub. She painted most of that out, and is having me do it at the studio. Meanwhile, I have worked on another she lent me, and finished it today, and they all say that it is a success. In my last two lessons, Mrs. B. contrived to let some light into my bewildered brain, and says that if I paint with her this winter and next summer I shall be able to do what I please. My most discouraging time, she says, is over. Not that I have been discouraged an atom! I have great faith in a strong will and a patient perseverance, and have had no idea of saying die…. Some lady in Philadelphia bought forty copies of Urbane. It was very discriminating in you to see how comforting to me would be that passage from Robertson. God only fully knows how I have got my "education." The school has at times been too awful to talk about to any being save Him. [1]

To Mrs. Humphrey, New York, April 6, 1875.

My point about "Grace for Grace" [2] is this: I believe in "growth in grace," but I also believe in, because I have experienced it and find my experience in the Word of God, a work of the Spirit subsequent to conversion (not necessary in all cases, perhaps, but in all cases where Christian life begins and continues feebly), which puts the soul into new conditions of growth. If a plant is sickly and drooping, you must change its atmosphere before you can cure it or make it grow. A great many years ago, *disgusted* with my spiritual life, I was led into new relations to Christ to which I could give no name, for I never had heard of such an experience. When we moved into this house, I found a paper that had long been buried among rubbish, in which I said, "I am one great long sunbeam" and I do not know any words that, on the whole, could better cover most of my life since then. I have been a great sufferer, too but that has, in the main, nothing to do with one's relation to Christ, except that most forms of pain bring Him nearer. Now, one cannot read "Grace for Grace" without loving and sympathizing with the author, because of his deep-seated longing for, and final attainment of, holiness but it seemed to me there was a good deal of needless groping, which more looking to Christ might have spared him. It is, as you say, curious to see how people who agree in so many points differ so in others. I suspect it is because our degrees of faith vary the one who believes most gets most.

The subject of sin *versus* sinlessness is the vexed question, on which, as fast as most people get or think they get light, somebody comes along and snuffs out their candles with unceremonious finger and thumb. A dearly beloved woman spent a month with me last spring. She thinks she is "kept" from sin, and certainly the change from a most estimable but dogmatic character is absolutely wonderful…. There was this discrepancy between her experience and mine, with, on all other points, the most entire harmony. She had had no special, joyful revelations of Christ to her soul, and I had had them till it seemed as if body and soul would fly apart. On the other hand, she had a sweet sense of freedom from sin, which transcended anything I had ever had consciously although I really think that when one is "looking unto Jesus," one is not likely to fall into much noticeable sin. Talking with Miss S. about the two experiences of my dear friend and myself, she said that it could be easily explained by the fact that *all* the gifts of the Spirit were rarely, if ever, given to one soul. She is very (properly) reticent as to what she has herself received, but she behaved in such a beautiful, Christ like way on a point where we differed, a point of practice, that I cannot doubt she has been unusually blest.

Early in May of this year, she was afflicted by the sudden death in Paris of a very dear friend of her eldest daughter, Miss Virginia S. Osborn. [3] During the previous summer Miss Osborn had passed several weeks at Dorset and endeared herself, while there, to all the family. The following is from a letter of Mrs. Prentiss to the bereaved mother:

I feel much more like sitting down and weeping with you than attempting to utter words of consolation. Nowhere out of her own home was Virginia more beloved and admired than in our family we feel afflicted painfully at what to our human vision looks like an unmitigated calamity. But if it is so hard for us to bear, to whom in no sense she belonged, what a heartrending event this is to you, her mother! What an amazement, what a mystery. But it will not do to look upon it on this side. We must not associate anything so unnatural as death with a being so eminently formed for life. We must look beyond, as soon as our tears will let us, to the sphere on which she has been honored to enter in her brilliant youth to the society of the noblest and the best human beings earth has ever known to the fullness of life, the perfection of every gift and grace, to congenial employment, to the welcome of Him who has conquered death and brought life and immortality to light. If we think of her as in the grave, we must own that hers was a hard lot but she is not in a grave she is at home she is well, she is happy, she will never know a bereavement, or a day's illness, or the infirmities and trials of old age she has got the secret of perpetual youth.

But while these thoughts assuage our grief, they cannot wholly allay it. We have no reason to doubt that she would have given and received happiness here upon earth, had she been spared and we cannot help missing her, mourning for her, longing for her, out of the very depths of our hearts. The only real comfort is that God never makes mistakes that He would not have snatched her from us, if He had not had a reason that would satisfy us if we knew it. I cannot tell you with what tender sympathy I think of your return to your desolate home the agonizing meeting with your bereaved boys the days and nights that have to be lived through, face to face with a great sorrow. May God bless and keep you all.

To Mrs. Condict, Dorset, July 11, 1875.

I have been sitting at my window, enjoying the clear blue sky, and the "living green" of the fields and woods, and wishing you were here to share it all with me. But as you are not, the next best thing is to write you. You seem to have been wafted into that strange seaside spot, to do work there, and I hope you will have health and strength for it. One of the signs of the times is the way in which the hand of Providence scatters "city folks" all about in waste places, there to sow seed that in His own time shall spring up and bear fruit for Him. I was shocked at what you said about Miss —— —— not recognizing you. It seemed almost incredible. Mr. Prentiss has persuaded me to have a family Bible-reading on Sunday afternoon, as we have no service, and studying up for it this morning I came to this proverb, which originated with Huss, whose name in Bohemian signifies goose. He said at the stake: "If you burn a goose a swan will rise from its ashes" and I thought—Well, Miss ——'s usefulness is at an end, but God can, and no doubt will, raise up a swan in her place. About forty now attend my Bible-reading.

We have my eldest brother here and he is a perfect enthusiast about Dorset, and has enjoyed his visit immensely. He said yesterday that he had laughed more that afternoon than in the previous ten years. We expect Dr. Stearns and his daughter on the 20th, and when they leave Mr. P. intends to go to Maine and try a change of air and scene. I hate to have him go his trouble of last year keeps me uneasy, if he is long out of my sight.

To the Same, Dorset, Aug., 1875.

I have just written a letter to my husband, from whom I have been separated a whole day. He has gone to Maine, partly to see friends, partly to get a little sea air. He wanted me to go with him, but it would have ended in my getting down sick. This summer I am encompassed with relatives two of my brothers, a nephew, a cousin, a second cousin, and in a day or two one brother's wife and child, and two more second cousins are to come not to our house, but to board next door. There is a troop of artists swarming the tavern all ladies, some of them very congenial, cultivated, excellent persons. They are all delighted with Dorset, and it is pleasant to stumble on little groups of them at their work. A. has been out sketching with them and succeeds very well. I have given up painting landscapes and taken to flowers. I have just had a visit here in my room from three humming-birds. They are attracted by the flowers… One of the cousins is just now riding on the lawn. Her splendid hair has come down and covers her shoulders and with her color, always lovely, heightened by exercise and pleasure, she makes a beautiful picture. What is nicer than an unsophisticated young girl? I have no time for reading this summer among the crowd but one cannot help thinking wherever one is, and I have come to this conclusion: happiness in its strictest sense is found only in Christ at the same time there are many sources of enjoyment independently of Him. It is getting dark and I cannot see my lines. I am more and more puzzled about good people making such mistakes. Dr. Stearns says that the Rev. Mr. —— has been laying his hands on people and saying, "Receive the Holy Ghost." Such excesses give me great doubt and pain.

To the Same, Sept. 3, 1875.

Your letter came to find me in a sorrowful and weary spot. My dear M. lies here with typhoid fever, and my heart and soul and body are in less than a fortnight of it pretty well used up, and my husband is in almost as bad a case with double anxiety, he and A. expecting every hour to see me break down. It has been an awful pull for us all, for not one of us has an atom of health to spare, and only keep about by avoiding all the wear and tear we can. Dr. Buck has sent us an excellent English nurse she came yesterday and insisted on sitting up with M. all night and we all *dropped* into our beds like so many shot birds. I heard her go down for ice three times, so I knew my precious lamb was not neglected, and slept in peace. We are encompassed with mercies the physician who drives over from Manchester is as skilful as he is conscientious this house is admirably adapted to sickness, the stairway only nine feet high, plenty of water, and my room, which I have given her, admits of her lying in a draught as the doctor wishes her to do. While the nurse is sleeping, as she is now, A. and I take turns sitting out on the piazza, where there is a delicious breeze almost always blowing.

The ladies here are disappointed that I can no longer hold the Bible-readings, but it is not so much matter that I am put off work if you are put on it the field is one, and the Master knows whom to use and when and where. We have been reading with great delight a little book called "Miracles of Faith." I am called to M., who has had a slight chill, and of course high fever after it. It seems painfully unnatural to see my sunbeam turned into a dark cloud, and it distresses me so to see her suffer that I do not know how I am going to stand it. But I will not plague you with any more of this, nor must I forget how often I have said, "Thy will be done." You need not doubt that God's will looks so much better to us than our own, that nothing would tempt us to decide our child's future.

To her eldest Son, Dorset, Sept. 19, 1875.

Your letters are a great comfort to us, and the way to get many is to write many. M.'s fever ran twenty-one days, as the doctor said it would, and began to break yesterday. On Friday it ran very high her pulse was 120 and her temperature 105—bad, bad, bad. She is very, very weak. We have sent away Pharaoh and the kitten Pha *would* bark, and Kit *would* come in and stare at her, and both made her cry. The doctor has the house kept still as the grave he even brought over his slippers lest his step should disturb her. She is not yet out of danger so you must not be too elated. We four are sitting in the dining-room with a hot fire papa is reading aloud to A. and H. it is evening, and M. has had her opiate, and is getting to sleep. I have not much material of which to make letters, sitting all day in a dark room in almost total silence. The artists are rigging up the church beautifully with my flowers, etc., Mr. Palmer and Mr. Lawrence lending their aid. Your father is reading about Hans Andersen you must read the article in the Living Age, No. 1,631 it is ever so funny.

I had such a queer dream last night. I dreamed that Maggie plagued us so that your father went to New York and brought back *two* cooks. I said I only wanted one. "Oh, but these are so rare," he said, "come out and see them." So he led me into the kitchen, and there sat at the table, eating dinner very solemnly, two *ostriches*! Now what that dream was made of I cannot imagine. Now I must go to bed, pretty tired. When you are lonely and blue, think how we all love you. Goodnight, dear old fellow.

Sept. 21st.—It cuts me to the heart, my precious boy, which your college life begins under such a shadow. But I hope you know where to go in both loneliness and trouble. You may get a telegram before this reaches you if you do not you had better pack your valise and have it ready for you to come at a minute's warning. The doctor gives us hardly a hope that M. will live she may drop away at any moment. While she does live, you are better off at Princeton but when she is gone, we shall all want to be together. We shall have her buried here in Dorset otherwise I never should want to come here again. A. said this was her day to write you, but she had no heart to do it. The only thing I can do while M. is asleep, is to write letters about her. Goodnight, dear boy.

22nd—The doctor was here from eight to nine last night and said she would suffer little more and sleep her life away. *She* says she is nicely and the nurse says so. Your father and I have had a good cry this morning, which has done us no little service. Dear boy, this is a bad letter for you, but I have done the best I can.

To Mrs. George Payson, New York, Oct. 31, 1875

I hope you received the postal announcing our safe arrival home. I have been wanting to answer your last letter, but now that the awful strain is over I begin to flag, am tired and lame and sore, and any exertion is an effort. But after all the dismal letters I have had to write, I want to tell you what a delightful day yesterday was to us all G. home from Princeton, all six of us at the table at once, "eating our meat with gladness" the pleasantest *family* day of our lives. M.'s recovery during the last week has been little short of miraculous. We got her home, after making such a bugbear of it, in perfect comfort. We left Dorset about noon in a close carriage the doctor and his wife were at the station and weighed M., when we found she had lost thirty-six pounds. The coachman took her in his arms and carried her into the car, when who should meet us but the Warners. On reaching the New York depot, George rushed into the car in such a state of wild excitement that he took no notice of anyone but M. he then flew out and a man flew in, and without saying a word snatched her up in his arms, whipped her into a reclining-chair, and he and another man scampered with her to the carriage and seated her in it I had to run to keep up with them, and nearly knocked down a gigantic policeman who was guarding it. The Warner's spent the night here and left next morning before I was up, so afraid of making trouble…. A friend has put a carriage at our disposal, and M. is to drive every day when and where and as long as she pleases. And now I hope I shall have something else to write about…. As to the Bible-readings, I do not find commentaries of much use. Experience of life has been my chief earthly teacher, and one gains that every day. You must not write me such long letters it is too much for you. How I do wish you would do something desperate about getting well! At any rate, *do not*, any of you, have typhoid fever. It is the very meanest old snake of a fox I ever heard of, making its way like a masked burglar.

To Mrs. Condict, New York, Nov 7, 1875.

We came home on the 27th of October M. bore the journey wonderfully well, and have improved so fast that she drives all round the Park every day, Miss W. having put a carriage at our disposal. How delightful it is to get my family together once more no tongue can tell, nor did I realize all I was suffering till the strain was over. I am longing to get physical strength for work, but my husband is very timid about my undertaking anything…. Dr. Ludlow [4] was here one day last week to ask me to give a talk, in his study, to some of his young Christians but my husband told him it was out of the question at present. I shall be delighted to do it much of my experience of life has cost me a great price, and I want to use it for the strengthening and comforting of other souls. No doubt you feel so too. Whatever may be said to the contrary by others, to me life has been a battlefield, and I believe always will be but is the soldier necessarily unhappy and disgusted because he is fighting? I know not. I am reading the history of the Oxford Conference [5] there is a great deal in it to like, but what do you think of this saying of its leader? "Did it ever strike you, dear Christian, that if the poor world could know what we are in Christ, it would worship us?" [6] *I say Pshaw!* What a fallacy! *Why* should it worship us when it rejects Christ? Well, we have to take even the best people as they are.

A few weeks later she met, a company of the young ladies of Dr. Ludlow's church and gave them a familiar talk on the Christian life. The following letter from Dr. L. will show how much they were interested:

DEAR MRS. PRENTISS:—I find that you have so taken hold of the young ladies of my church that it will be hard for you to relieve yourself of them. They insist on meeting you again. The hesitancy to ask you questions last Thursday was due to the large number present. I have asked *only the younger ones* to come this week—those who are either "seeking the way," or are just at its beginning. *Five* of those you addressed last week have announced their purpose of confessing Christ at the coming Communion.

Several questions have come from those silent lips, which I am requested to submit to you:

"What is it to believe?"

"How much feeling of love must I have before I can count myself Jesus' disciple?"

"I am troubled with my lack of feeling. I know that sin is heinous, but do not feel deep abhorrence of it. I know that Jesus will save me, but I have no enthusiasm of gratitude. Am I a Christian?"

"I am afraid to confess Christ lest I should not honor Him in my life, for I am naturally impulsive and easily fall into religious thoughtlessness. Should I wait for an inward assurance of strength, or begin a Christian life trusting Him to help me?"

Any of these topics will be very pertinent. I trust that nothing will prevent you from being present on Thursday afternoon. I will call for you. The limited number who will be present will give you a better working basis than you had last week. The *older young* ladies have assented to their exclusion this week on the condition that at some time they too can come.

Very gratefully yours, JAMES M. LUDLOW.

In a letter dated May 3, 1880, Dr. Ludlow thus refers to these meetings:

I regret that I cannot speak more definitely of Mrs. Prentiss' conversations with the young ladies of my charge, as it was my custom to withdraw from the room after a few introductory words, so that she could speak to them with the familiarity of a mother. I know that all that group felt the warmth of her interest in them, the charm of her character, which was so refined by her love of Christ and strengthened by her experience of needed grace, as well as the wisdom of her words. I was impressed, from so much as I did hear of her remarks, with her ability to combine rarest beauty and highest spirituality of thought with the utmost simplicity of language and the plainest illustrations. Her conversation was like the mystic ladder, which was "*set up on the earth,* and the top of it *reached to heaven.*" Her most solemn counsel was given in such a way as never to repress the buoyant feeling of the young, but rather to direct it toward the true "joy of the Lord." She seemed to regard the cheer of today as much of a religious duty as the hope for tomorrow, and those with whom she conversed partook of her own peace. I shall always remember these meetings as among the happiest and most useful associations of my ministry in New York.

* * * * *

II.

The Moody and Sankey Meetings. Her Interest in them. Mr. Moody.
Publication of *Griselda*. Goes to the Centennial. At Dorset again. Her
Bible-reading. A Moody-Meeting Convert. Visit to Montreal. Publication
of *The Home at Greylock*. Her Theory of a happy Home. Marrying for
Love. Her Sympathy with young Mothers. Letters.

The early months of 1876 were very busily spent in painting pictures for friends, in attendance upon Mr. Moody's memorable services at the Hippodrome, and in writing a book for young mothers. Before going to Dorset for the summer, she passed a week at Philadelphia, visiting the Centennial Exhibition. Her letters during the winter and spring of this year relate chiefly to these topics.

To a Christian Friend, Feb. 22, 1876.

You gave me a good deal of a chill by your long silence, and I find it a little hard to be taken up and dropped and then taken up still, almost everybody has these fitful ways, and very likely I myself among that number. Your little boy must take a world of time, and open a new world of thought and feeling. But do not spoil him the best child can be made hateful by mismanagement. I am trying to write a book for mothers and find it a discouraging work, because I find, on scrutiny, such awfully radical defects among them. And yet such a book would have helped me in my youthful days.

You ask if I have been to hear Moody yes, I have and am deeply interested in him and his work. Yesterday afternoon he had a meeting for Christian workers, in which his sound common sense created great merriment. Some objected to this, but I liked it because it was so genuine, and, to my mind, not un-Christ like. So many fancy religion and a long face synonymous. How stupid it is! I wonder they do not object to the sun for shining. I am glad you think Urbane may be useful, for I hear little from it. Junia's story is true as far as the laudanum and the blindness go it happened years ago. I do not know what religious effect it had. As to the friend of whom you speak, she would not love you as you say she does if her case was hopeless at least I do not think so. I am oppressed with the case of one who wants me to help him to Christ, while unwilling to confide to me his difficulties. How little they know how we care for their souls!

To Mrs. George Payson, Feb 28, 1876.

I have been trying to do more than any mortal can, and now must stop to take breath and write to you. In the first place, M.'s illness cut out three months then fitting up G.'s room at Princeton took a large part of the next three then ever so many people wanted me to paint them pictures then I began a book then Moody and Sankey appeared, and I wanted to hear them, and was needed to work in co-operation with them. I do not know how you feel about Moody, but I am in full sympathy with him, and last Friday the testimony of four of the cured "gin-pigs" (their own language) was the most instructive, interesting language I ever heard from human lips. In talking to those he has drawn into the inquiry rooms, I find the most bitterly wretched ones are back-sliders they are not without hope, and expect to be saved at last but they have been trying what the world could do for them and found it a failure. Their anguish was harrowing one after another tried to help them, and gave up in despair.

I had a vase given me at Christmas somewhat like yours, but a trifle larger, and shaped like a fish. The flowers never fell out but once. I had two little tables given me on which to set my majolica vases, with India-rubber plants, which will grow where nothing else will also a desk and bookcase, and two splendid specimens of grass which grew in California, and had been bleached to a creamy white. They are more beautiful than Pampa, or even feather grass.

A. is driven to death about a fair for the Young Women's Christian Association. I have given it a German tragedy, which I translated a few years ago. [7] They expect to make $1,600 on it, but Randolph says if they make half that they may thank their stars. I have spent all my evenings of late in revising it, and it goes to the printers today. George is going to deliver a literary lecture for the same object this evening, this being the age of obedient parents. No, I never saw and never painted any window-screens. The best things I have done are trailing arbutus and apple-blossoms. A. invited me to do apple-blossoms for her, and said she should have to own that I had more artistic power than herself. I do not agree with her, but it is a matter of no consequence, anyhow. It is a shame for you to buy Little Lou I meant to send you one and thought I had done so. The bright speeches are mostly genuine, made by Eddy Hopkins and Ned and Charley P.

How came you to have blooming hepaticas? It is outrageous. My plants do better this winter than ever before. I have had hyacinths in bloom, and a plant given me, covered with red berries, has held its own. It hangs in a glass basket the boys gave me and has a white dove brooding over it. Let me inform you that I have lost my mind. A friend dined with us on Sunday, and I asked him when I saw him last. "Why, yesterday," he said, "when I met you at Randolph's by appointment."

There, I must stop and go to work on one of my numerous irons.

The "German tragedy" referred to fell into her hands in the spring of 1869, and her letters, written at the time, show how it delighted her. It is, indeed, a literary gem. The works of its author, Baron Münch-Bellinghausen—for Friederich Halm is a pseudonym—are much less known in this country than they deserve to be. He is one of the most gifted of the minor poets of Germany, a master of vivid style and of impressive, varied, and beautiful thought. *Griselda* first appeared at Vienna in 1835. It was enthusiastically received and soon passed through several editions.

The scene of the poem is laid in Wales, in the days of King Arthur. The plot is very simple. Percival, count of Wales, who had married Griselda, the daughter of a charcoal burner, appears at court on occasion of a great festival, in the course of which he is challenged by Ginevra, the Queen, to give an account of Griselda, and to tell how he came to wed her. He readily consents to do so, but has hardly begun when the Queen and ladies of the court, by their mocking air and questions, provoke him to such anger that swords are at length drawn between him and Sir Lancelot, a friend of the Queen, and only the sudden interposition of the King prevents a bloody conflict. The feud ends in a wager, by which it is agreed that if Griselda's love to Percival endure certain tests, the Queen shall kneel to her otherwise, Percival shall kneel to the Queen. The tests are applied, and the young wife's love, although perplexed and tortured in the extreme, triumphantly endures them all. The character of Griselda, as maiden, daughter, wife, mother, and woman, is wrought with exquisite skill, and betokens in the author rare delicacy and nobility of sentiment, as well as deep knowledge of the human heart.

The following extract gives a part of Percival's description of Griselda:

PERCIVAL.

Plague take these women's tongues!

GINEVRA (*to her party*).

Control your wit and mirth, compose your faces,
That longer yet this pastime may amuse us!
Now, Percival, proceed!

PERCIVAL.

What was I saying?
I have it now! Beside the brook she stood
Her dusky hair hung rippling round her face.
And perched upon her shoulders sat a dove
Right home-like sat she there, her wings scarce moving.
Now suddenly she stoops—I mean the maiden—
Down to the spring, and lets her little feet
Sink in its waters, while her colored skirt
Covered with care what they did not conceal
And I within the shadow of the trees,
Inly admired her graceful modesty.
And as she sat and gazed into the brook,
Plashing and sporting with her snow-white feet,
She thought not of the olden times, when girls
Pleased to behold their faces smiling back
From the smooth water, used it as their mirror
By which to deck themselves and plait their hair
But like a child she sat with droll grimaces,
Delighted when the brook gave back to her
Her own distorted charms so then I said:
Conceited is she not.

KENNETH.

The charming child!

ELLINOR.

What is a collier's child to you! By heaven!
Do not make me fancy that you know her, Sir!

PERCIVAL.

And now resounding through the mountain far,
From the church-tower rang forth the vesper-bell,
And she grew grave and still, and shaking quickly
From off her face the hair that fell around it,
She cast a thoughtful and angelic glance
Upward, where clouds had caught the evening red.
And her lips gently moved with whispered words,
As rose-leaves tremble when the soft winds breathe.
O she is saintly, flashed it through my soul
She marking on her brow the holy cross,
Lifted her face, bright with the sunset's flush,
While holy longing and devotion's glow,
Moistened her eye and hung like glory round her.
Then to her breast the little dove she clasped,
Embraced, caressed it, kissed its snow-white wings,
And laughed when, with its rose-red bill, it pecked,
As if with longing for her fresh young lips.

    How she'd caress it, said I to myself,
    Were this her child, the offspring of her love!
    And now a voice resounded through the woods,
    And cried, "Griselda," cried it, "Come, Griselda!"
    While she, the distant voice's sound distinguished,
    Sprang quickly up, and scarcely lingering
    Her feet to dry, ran up the dewy bank
    With lightning speed, her dove in circles o'er her,
    Till in the dusky thicket disappeared
    For me the last edge of her flutt'ring robe.
    "Obedient is she," said I to myself
    And many things revolving, turned I home.

GINEVRA.

    By heaven! You tell your tale so charmingly,
    And with such warmth and truth to life, the hearer
    Out of your words can shape a human form.
    Why, I can see this loveliest of maidens
    Sit by the brook-side making her grimaces
    They are right pretty faces spite of coal-smut.
    Is it not so, Sir Percival?

Mrs. Prentiss' translation is both spirited and faithful—faithful in following even the irregularities of meter, which mark the original. It won the praise and admiration of some of the most accomplished judges in the country. The following extract from a letter of the late Rev. Henry W. Bellows, D.D., may serve as an instance:

I read it through at one sitting and enjoyed it exceedingly. What a lovely, pure, and exalting story it is! I confess that I prefer it to Tennyson's recent dramas or to any of the plays upon the same or kindred themes that have lately appeared from Leighton and others. The translation is melodious, easy, natural, and hardly bears any marks of the fetters of a tongue foreign to its author. How admirable must have been the knowledge of German and the skill in English of the translator!

To Mrs. Condict, New York, May 2, 1876.

I do not know but I have been on too much of a drive all winter, for besides writing my book I have been painting pictures for friends, and am now at work on some wild roses for Mrs. D.'s golden wedding next Monday, and yesterday I wrote her some verses for the occasion. The work at the Hippodrome took a great deal of my time, and there is a poor homeless fellow now at work in my garden, whom it was my privilege to lead to Christ there, and who touched me not a little this morning by bringing me three plants out of his scanty earnings. He has connected himself with our Mission and has made friends there.

I do not know what Faber says about the silence of Christ, but I know that as far as our own consciousness goes, He often answers never a word, and that the grieved and disappointed heart must cling to Him more firmly than ever at such times. We live in a mystery, and shall never be satisfied till we see Him as He is. I am enjoying a great deal in a great many ways, but I am afraid I should *run* in if the gates opened. If I go to the Centennial, it will be to please some of the family, not myself. You ask about my book it is a sort of story had to be to get read I could finish it in two weeks if needful. When I wrote it, no mortal knows I should *say* that about all I had done this winter was to hold my Bible-reading, paint, and work in the revival. I have so few interruptions compared with my previous life that I hardly have learned to adjust myself to them.

To Miss E. A. Warner, Philadelphia, May 30, 1876.

We came here on a hospitable invitation to spend a week in the Centennial grounds, and yesterday passed several hours in wandering about, bewildered and amazed at the hosts of things we saw, and the host we did not see. We found ourselves totally ignorant of Norway, for instance, whose contributions are full of artistic grace and beauty and I suppose we shall go on making similar discoveries about other nations. As to the thirty-two art galleries, we have only glanced at them. What interested me most was groups of Norwegians, Lapps and other Northerners, so life-like that they were repeatedly addressed by visitors—wonderful reproductions. The extent of this Exhibition is simply beyond description. The only way to get any conception of it is to make a railroad circuit of the grounds.

I have had a *very* busy winter held a Bible-reading once a week, written a book, painted lots of pictures to give away, and really need rest, only I hate rest…. We find out where our hearts really are when we get these fancied invitations homeward. I look upon Christians who are, at such times, reluctant to go, with unfeigned amazement. The spectacle, too often seen, of shrinking from the presence of Christ, is one I cannot begin to understand. I should think it would have been a terrible disappointment to you to get so far on and then have to come back but we can be made willing for anything.

I am glad you liked Griselda I knew you would. [8]

The extreme heat and her unusually enfeebled state rendered the summer a very trying one but its discomfort was in a measure relieved by the extraordinary loveliness of the Dorset scenery this season. There was much in this scenery to remind her of Chateau d'Oex, where she had passed such happy weeks in the summer and autumn of 1858. If not marked by any very grand features, it is pleasing in the highest degree. In certain states of the atmosphere the entire landscape—Mt. Equinox, Sunset Mountain, Owl's Head, Green Peak, together with the intervening hills, and the whole valley—becomes transfigured with ever-varying forms of light and shade. At such times, she thought it unsurpassed by anything of the kind she had ever witnessed, even in Switzerland. The finest parts of this enchanting scene were the play of the cloud-shadows, running like wild horses across the mountains, and the wonderful sunsets and both were in full view from the windows of her "den." Her eyes never grew weary of feasting upon them. The cloud-shadows, in particular, are much admired by all lovers of nature. [9]

To Mrs. George Payson, Kauinfels, July 8, 1876.

We have been here four weeks, and ought to have been here six, for I cannot bear heat it takes all the life out of me. Last night when I went up to my room to go to bed, the thermometer was 90°.... Are you not going to the Centennial? George and I went on first and stayed at Dr. Kirkbride's. They were as kind as possible, and we all enjoyed a great deal. What interested me most were *wonderful* life-like figures (some said wax, but they were no more wax than you are) of Laplanders, Swedes, and Norwegians, dressed in clothes that had been worn by real peasants, and done by an artistic hand. Next to these came the Japanese department amazing bronzes, amazing screens ($1,000 a pair, embroidered exquisitely), lovely flowers painted on lovely vases, etc., etc., etc., ad infinitum. The Norwegian jewelry was also a surprise and delight I do not care for jewelry generally, but these silvery lace-like creations took me by storm. Among other pretty things were lots of English bedrooms, exquisitely furnished and enormously expensive. The horticultural department was very poor, except the rhododendrons, which drove me crazy. I only took a chair twice. You pay sixty cents an hour for one with a man to propel it, but can have one for three hours and make your husband (or wife!) wheel you. You do not pay entrance fee for children going in your arms, and I saw boys of eight or nine lugged in by their fathers and mothers. We think everybody should go who can afford it. Several countries had not opened when we were there Turkey and Spain, for instance and if Switzerland was ready, we did not see it. The more I think of the groups I spoke of, the more I am lost in admiration. A young mother kneeling over a little dead baby, and the stern grief of the strong old grandfather, brought a lump into my throat the young father was not capable of such grief as theirs, and sat by, looking subdued and tender, but nothing more. The artist must be a great student of human nature. I went, every day, to study these domestic groups at first they did not attract the crowd but later it was next to impossible to get at them. Everyone was taken from life, and you see the grime on their knuckles. Almost every face expressed strong and agreeable character. There were very few good and a great many had pictures. Of statuary "The Forced Prayer" was very popular the child has his hands folded, but is in anything but a saintly temper, and two tears are on his cheeks. I should like to own it. If I had had any money to spare, I should have bought something from Japan and something from Denmark. I do not think anyone can realize, who has not been there, what an education such an Exposition is. China's inferiority to Japan I knew nothing about.

A. goes out sketching every day. The other day I found her painting a white flower which she said she got from the lawn it was something like a white lockspur, only very much prettier, and was, of course, not a wild flower, as she supposed, or, at any rate, not indigenous to this soil. She declared it had no leaves, but I made her go out and show me the plant it grew about ten inches high, with leaves like a lily, and then came the pure, graceful flowers.

To Mrs. Condict, Dorset, July 9, 1876.

There has been a great change here in religious interest, the foundation of which is thought to have been laid in the Bible-readings. I am ashamed to believe it, all I say and do seems so flat but our Lord can overrule incompetence. The ladies are eager to have the readings resumed, but I cannot undertake it unless I get stronger. The Rev. Mr. and Mrs. Reed are doing a quiet work among non-churchgoers at the other end of the village. She has been to every house in the neighborhood and "compelled them to come in," having meetings at her own house. *Of course, the devil is on hand.* He reminds me of a slug that sits on my rose bushes watching for the buds to open, when he falls to and devours them instantly. I am sure it is as true of him as of the Almighty, that he never slumbers or sleeps. His impertinences increase daily.

One of the last things I did before leaving home was to decide to bring here one of the Hippodrome converts, about whom I presume I wrote you. We knew next to nothing about him, and I could ill afford to support him but I was his only earthly friend. He had no home, no work, and I felt I ought to look after him. We gave him a little room in the old mill, and he is perfectly happy calls his room his "castle," does not feel the heat, takes care of my garden, enjoys haying, has put everything in order, is as strong as a horse, and a comfort to us all being willing to turn his hand to anything. In the evenings, he has made for me a manila mat, of which I am very proud. He has been all over the world and picked up all sorts of information. He went to hear Mr. Prentiss' centennial address on the Fourth at a picnic, and I was astonished when he came back at his intelligent account of it. Everybody likes him, and he has proved a regular institution. I would not have had a flower but for him, for I cannot work out in such a blazing sun as we have had. [10]

My book is to be called, I believe, "The Home at Greylock" but I do not know. My husband and Mr. Randolph fussed so over the title that I said it would end in being called "Much Ado about Nothing." *They*, being men, look at the financial question, to which I never gave a thought. Even Satan has never so much as whispered, Write to make money do not be too religious in your books. Still he may do it, now I have put it into his head. How little any of us know what he will not make us do! I enjoyed the Centennial more than I expected to do, but got my fill very soon, and was glad to go home.

No account of the Dorset home would be complete without some reference to "the old mill." It had been dismantled during the war, but, at the request of the neighbors, was now restored to its original use. It also contained the boys' workshop, a bathing room, an icehouse, a ram, and a bowling alley formed, indeed, together with the pond and the boat, part and parcel of the Dorset home itself.

To Mrs. James Donaghe, Dorset, July 15, 1876.

I have hardly put pen to paper since I came here. I never could endure heat it always laid me flat. Yesterday there was a let-up to the torrid zone, and today it is comparatively cool. Yesterday the mother of our pastor here got her release. I cried for joy, for she has been a great sufferer, and had longed to die. What a mystery death is! I went in to see how she was, and she had just breathed her last, and there lay her poor old body, eighty-two years old, looking as rent and torn as one might suppose it would after a fight of thirty years between the soul and itself. I have wondered if the heat, so dreadful to many, had not been good for you. A rheumatic boy, who works for us off and on, says it has been splendid for him. We heard yesterday that Dr. Schaff had lost his eldest daughter after a ten days' illness with typhoid fever. He has been greatly afflicted again and again and again by such bereavements, but this must be hardest of all. [11] There is a different religious atmosphere here now from anything we have ever known. The ladies hoped to begin the Bible-readings right off, but it was out of the question. I expect such a number of guests this week that I dare not undertake it. I wish you were coming, too. How you would enjoy sitting on the piazza watching the shadows on the mountains! We have had some magnificent sunsets this season. Mr. Prentiss and I drive every night after tea, a regular old Darby and Joan. Generally, I prefer working in the garden to driving, but this time it has been too hot, and we have next to no flowers. It quite grieves me that I have nothing to lay on Grandma Pratt's coffin. However, *she will not care!* Won't it be nice to get rid of these frail, troublesome bodies of ours, and live without them! I hope I shall see you in heaven, with plenty of room and no rheumatism. How could you make such a time over that doggerel! [12] Such things are a drug in this house. I thought I had a long letter from you, and it was that stuff! My last book is all printed. My husband kindly corrected the proof sheets for me a thing I hate to do. He likes the book better than I do. I always get tired of my books by the time they are done. I read very little only some few devotional books over and over. I wonder if you have read "Miracles of Faith"? It is a remarkable little book. Do write and let me know how you and your husband are. We make great account of our afternoon mail.

She alludes in the preceding letter to the guests she was expecting. The entertainment of friends formed a marked feature of her Dorset life and it called into play the brightest traits of her character. Her visitors always went away feeling like one who has been gazing upon a beautiful landscape or listening to sweet music, so charming was her hospitality. One of them, writing to her husband a year after her death, thus refers to it:

I seem to see the Dorset hills now with their beautiful cloud-shadows and lovely blue. I can see in my mind your pleasant home and all the faces, including the dear one you miss this summer. What a delightful home she made! The "good cheer" she furnished for the minds, hearts, and bodies of her guests was something remarkable. I shall never forget my visits I was in a state of high entertainment from beginning to end. What entertaining stories she told! What practical wisdom she gave out in the most natural and incidental way! And what housekeeping! Common articles of food seemed to possess new virtues and zest. I always went away full of the marvels of the visit, as well as loaded down with many little tokens of her kindness and thoughtfulness.

To Mrs. Condict, Dorset, Sept. 9, 1876.

What interested me most at the Centennial was in the Main Building, and two things stand out, prominently, in my memory. The first is groups of Swedish figures, dressed in national costume, and all done by the hand of a real artist. Especially examine the dead baby and its weeping mother and rugged old wounded grandfather it will remind you of the words, "A little child shall lead them." Next in interest to me were the Japanese bronzes and screens next wares from Denmark, butterflies and feathers from Brazil. In the art department, a picture called "Betty" in the British division, up in a corner, and in statuary "The Forced Prayer." Both my girls agreed with me in the main the boys cared most for Machinery hall, and my husband for Queensland, for which I did not care a fig.

Last Sunday was as perfect here as with you. My husband preached at Pawlet, about six miles from here, and I went with him. He preached a very earnest sermon on prayer. My Bible-reading is thronged, and I cannot but hope the Holy Spirit is helping my infirmities and blessing souls. My heart yearns over these women, many of whom have faces stamped with care. There is a class here that nobody has any idea how to get at. To meet their case, apostolic work needs to be done. Do you know that Irishmen are buying up the New England farms at a great rate?

To Mrs. Donaghe, Dorset, Sept. 10, 1876.

The extraordinary heat has worked unfavorably on both my husband and myself he has been under medical treatment most of the time, forlorn and depressed. I have just pushed through as I could my Bible-reading, which has been wonderfully attended, being the only work I have done. The weather is cool now and I feel stronger.

A party of young people, who were coming to call on A., were upset just above us two had broken legs, others bruises and cuts, and one had both knee-pans seriously injured. We got her here and put her to bed, and then I started off to get the rest but the surgeon, on arriving, decided they should be removed at once, and got them all safely back to Manchester.

To Mrs. Condict, New York, Oct. 16, 1876.

Since my last letter, I have been to Montreal, fled from and settled down here. My book is out in England, and my husband sat up till midnight, reading an English copy of it, although he had heard me read it aloud when written, and read it twice in proof sheets. He thinks it will be a useful book. I feel sure you will agree with me in its main points. God grant it may send many a bewildered mother to her knees! Miss S. called here a few days ago she has written a book called "The Fullness of the Blessing,"—one object of which is to prove that sanctification is not, cannot be instantaneous.... I do hope the book will do good. It seems timely to me, for I shudder when I hear that A. and B. "professed sanctification" on such and such a day. My visit to Montreal gave me indignant pain when I saw crowds kneeling to the Virgin, and not to Christ, in those costly churches and cathedrals.

As to Miss ——— I do not know enough of her to form an opinion of her state I incline, however, to think that demoniac possession is sometimes permitted. Fenelon, you know, thinks we should not be too eager for spiritual delight. He is entirely right when he says that the "night of faith" may witness a faith dearer to God than that of sensible delight. I love Job when he says, "Though He slay me, yet will I trust in Him," more than I do David when he is in green pastures and beside still waters it does not require much faith to be happy there.

Nov. 12th.—I am glad Greylock reached you in safety, and sorry I could not correct its numerous misprints. Your question about Kitty I do not quite understand I did not mean to say that her parents had no more trouble with her, but they had no more fights growing out of self-will on both sides. I know that there is no end to trouble with obstinate or otherwise naughty children, only if the mother lives close to Christ the fault will be on their side, not hers. You speak, by the bye, of my using the word Christ rather than the word Jesus. I do so because it means more to my mind, and because the apostles use it much more frequently. I do hope my book will be a comfort and help to many well-meaning but inexperienced mothers. And I wish I practiced more perfectly, what I preach. But I have my infirmities and find it hard to be always on my guard.... A. and I are taking drawing-lessons of a very superior French teacher, who offers us the privilege of spending our whole time in her studio, with "conceal."

The Home at Greylock was published the latter part of October. It embodied, as she said, the results of thirty years of experience and reflection. Its views of marriage and of the office of a Christian mother found frequent expression in her other writings and in her correspondence. She placed religion and love alike at the foundation of a true home the one to connect it with heaven above, the other to make it a heaven upon earth. She enjoined it upon her young friends, as they desired enduring domestic felicity, to marry first of all for love. To one of them, who was tempted, as she feared, to marry out of gratitude rather than from love, she wrote:

We women are exacting creatures and you cannot please us unless we have the whole of you. Oh, if you knew the sacredness, the beauty, the sweetness of married life, as I do, you would as soon think of entering heaven without a wedding garment, as of venturing on its outskirts even, save by the force of a passionate, overwhelming power that is stronger than death itself!

How warmly she sympathized with mothers, especially with young mothers, in their peculiar experiences and how great she thought their privilege to be, her writings testify. The same trait is brought out still more fully in her letters. "Only a mother," she wrote, "knows the varied discipline of hopes and fears and joys and sorrows through which a mother passes to glory—for this is the mother's pathway, and she rarely walks on a higher road or one that may so lead to perfection." Some of her letters addressed to bereaved mothers have already been given. But if her heart was always touched with grief by the death of an infant, it seemed to leap for joy whenever she heard that in the home of a friend a child was coming or had just arrived. Here are samples of her letters on such occasions.

To Mrs. ——, Jan 10, 1874.

You little know into what a new world you are going to be introduced! I would not be a bit frightened, if I were you it is ever so much more likely that you'll get through safely, than that you will not and then what joy! You will be a very loving, devoted mother, and I hope this little one will only be the beginning of a houseful. I spoke for ten, but only had six and our dear Lord had to take two of them back…. I have just run over your letter again, and want to reiterate my charge to you to feel no fear about your future. If you live and have a child, your joy will be wonderful, but if you do not live (here) it will be because you are going to dwell with Christ, which is better than having a thousand children. So I see nothing but bright sides for you.

To the Same, April 18 10, 1874.

By this time, you ought to be able to receive letters at any rate. I am going to write one and you can do as you please about reading it. Well, isn't a baby an institution? I am sure you had no idea what a delightful thing it is to be a mother, and that you have had a most bewildering experience of both suffering and joy. I shall want to hear all about the young gentleman when you get strong enough to write an enthusiastic letter about him nor have I any objection to hear how his mother is behaving under these new circumstances.

What does your husband think of the upsetting of all home customs and the introduction of this young hero therein? Thank him for sending me the news in good season. I should not have liked it from a stranger. And by the bye, do not let your children say parp-er and marm-er, as nine children out of ten do. I daresay you never meant they should, having a little mite of sense of your own. Now this is all a new mother ought to read at once, so with lots of congratulations and thanksgivings, goodbye.

The following is an extract from a letter to another friend, dated Feb. 20, 1875:

Your last letter was so eloquent in its happiness that in writing an article for a magazine on the subject of education, I could not help beginning "The King is coming," and depicting his heralds… I am indeed rejoicing in your joy, and hope the little queen will long sit on the right royal throne of your heart. Keep me posted as to Miss Baby's progress. I know a family where the first son was called "Boy" for years, the servants addressing him as "Master Boy."

Here are the opening sentences of the article referred to:

The King is at hand. Heralds have been announcing his advent in language incomprehensible to man, but which woman understands as she does her alphabet. A dainty basket, filled with mysteries half hidden, half displayed soft little garments, folded away in ranks and files here delicate lace and cambric there down and feathers and luxury. The King has come. Limp and pink, a nothing and nobody, yet welcomed and treasured as everything and everybody, his wondrous reign begins. His kingdom is the world. His world is peopled by two human beings. Yesterday, they were a boy and a girl. Today, they are man and woman, and are called father and mother.

Their new King is imperious. He has his own views as to the way he shall live and move and have his being. He has his own royal table, at which he presides in royal pomp. His waiting-maid is refined and educated—his superior in every way. He takes his meals from her when he sees fit if he cannot sleep, he will not allow her to do so. His treasurer is a man whom thousands look up to, and reverence, but, in this little world, he is valued only for the supplies he furnishes, the equipages he purchases, the castle in which young royalty dwells. The picture is not unpleasing, however the slaves have the best of it, after all.

The reign is not very long. Two years later, there is a descent from the throne, to make room for the Queen. She is a great study to him. He puts his fingers into her eyes to learn if they are little blue lakelets. He grows chivalrous and patronizing. So the world of home goes on. The King and Queen give place to new Kings and Queens, but, though dethroned, they are still royal their wants are forestalled, they are fed, clothed, instructed, but above all, beloved. When did their education begin? At six months? A year? Two years? No, it began when *they* began the moment they entered the little world they called theirs. Every touch of the mother's hand, every tone of her voice, educates her child. It never remembers a time when she was not its devoted lover, servant, vassal, and slave. Many an ear enjoys, is soothed by music, while ignorant of its laws. So the youngest child in the household is lulled by uncomprehended harmonies from its very birth. Affections group round and bless it, like so many angels, it could not analyze or comprehend an angel, but it could feel the soft shelter of his wings. [13]

The following was addressed to a friend, whose home was already blessed with six fine boys:

DORSET, *Sept. 16, 1868.*

Dear Mr. B.:—I am just as glad as I can be! I *said* it was a girl, and I *knew* it was a girl, and that is the reason it *is* a girl. Give my best love to Mrs. B., and tell her I hope this little damsel will be to her like a Sabbath of rest, after the six week and workdays she has had all along. It is hard to tell which one loves best, one's girls or one's boys, but it is pleasant to have both kinds… I hope your place has as appropriate a name as ours has had given to it—"Saints' Rest"!—and that you will fill it full of saints and angels only let them be girls, you have had boys enough.

* * * * *

III.

The Year 1877. Death of her Cousin, the Rev. Charles H. Payson. Illness and Death of Prof. Smith. "Let us take our Lot in Life just as it comes." Adorning one's Home. How much Time shall be given to it? God's Delight in His beautiful Creations. Death of Dr. Buck. Visiting the sick and bereaved. An Ill-turn. Goes to Dorset. The Strangeness of Life. Kauinfels. The Bible-reading. Letters.

During the early months of 1877, Mrs. Prentiss' sympathies were much excited by sickness and death among her friends.

"I spend a deal of time," she wrote, "at funerals and going to see people in affliction, and never knew anything like it." And wherever she went, it was as a daughter of consolation. The whole year, indeed, was marked by a very tender and loving spirit, as also by unwonted thoughtfulness. But it was marked no less by the happiest, most untiring activity of both hands and brain. During the month of January she wrote the larger portion of a new serial for The Christian at Work. It would seem as if she foresaw the end approaching and was pressing toward it with eager steps and a glad heart.

To her eldest Son, New York, Jan. 28, 1877.

The great event of last week was cousin Charles' unexpected death. [14] Your father and I attended the funeral, in his church, which was crowded to overflowing with a weeping audience. Most of the ministers we know were there. Cousin G. came on Friday night and said nothing would comfort him like hearing your father preach and he promised to do so. I went with him to Inwood, and we have just got back. Your father preached a beautiful sermon and paid a glowing tribute to cousin Charles in it, and I am very glad I went. After the funeral yesterday I came home and put up some chicken-jelly I had made for Prof. Smith, and carried it down to him there, I met Dr. Gould, of Rome, who had seen him, and said he considered his case a very critical one. *Feb. 4th.*—Your father was invited to repeat his lecture on Recollections of Hurstmonceux and Rydal Mount, and did so, yesterday morning, in our lecture-room, which was filled with a fine audience, mostly strangers. What have you on your natural bracket? And have you put up your leaves on your windows? Mine are looking splendidly. H. is burning one of them with a magnifying glass your father gave me at Christmas. The sun does lie delightfully in this room. I must now go to the Smiths. All send love.

Prof. Smith passed away peacefully in the early morning on the 7th of February. One of his last conscious utterances was addressed to Mrs. Prentiss: "I have ceased to cumber myself with the things of time and sense, and have had some precious thoughts about death." Henry Boynton Smith was one of those men who enrich life by their presence, and seem to render the whole world poorer by their absence. He was strongly attached to Mrs. Prentiss for more than forty years the relation between him and her husband resembled that of brothers Mrs. Smith was one of her oldest and most beloved friends, and for a quarter of a century the two families had dwelt together in unity. And, then, with one of the saddest and one of the happiest events of her domestic history—the burial of her little Bessie, at which he ministered with Christ like sympathy, and at the baptism of her Swiss boy who bore his name—he was tenderly associated. It is not strange, therefore, that his death, as well as the wearisome years of invalidism which preceded it, touched her deeply. What manner of man he was how gifted, wise and large-hearted how devoted to the cause of his Lord and Savior what a leader and master-workman in sacred science and in the Church of Christ how worthy of love and admiration—all this may be seen and read elsewhere. [15]

To Mrs. Condit, Feb. 14, 1877.

Before I go down to the meeting at Mrs. D.'s I must have a little chat with you, in reply to your last two letters. I felt like shrieking aloud when you contrasted your life with mine. But it is impossible to state fully why. Yet I may say one thing I have had to learn what I teach in loneliness, suffering, conflict, and dismay, which I do not believe you have physical strength to bear. The true story of my life will never be written. But whatever you do, do not envy it. And I do not mean by that, that I am a disappointed, unhappy woman *far from it*. But I enjoy and suffer intensely, and one insulting word about Greylock, for instance, goes on stinging and cutting me, amid forgetfulness of hundreds of kind ones. [16] Let us take our lot in life just as it comes, courageously, patiently, and faithfully, never wondering at anything the Master does. I am concerned just as you are about my interest in things of time and sense. But I have not the faintest doubt that if we could have all we want in Christ, inferior objects would fade and fall. But we live in a strange world, amid many claims on time and thought we can not dwell in a convent, and must dwell among human beings, and fall more or less under their influence. We shall get out of all this by and by. *Feb. 27th.*—This winter I am drawing in charcoal under an accomplished teacher she has so large a class that I had to withdraw from it and take private lessons. She has invited A. to assist her in teaching little ones twice a week, which materially curtails her bill. A. was introduced to one youth, aged five, as *Monsieur* So and So he had his easel, his big portfolio, and charcoal, in great style, but only took one lesson, he hated it so. I do not see what his mother was made of. I sympathize with your fear of spending too much time adorning your home, etc., etc. It is a nice question how far to go and how far to stay. But I honestly believe that a bare, blank, prosaic house makes religion appear dreadfully homely. We enjoy seeing our children enjoy their work and their play is our Father unwilling to let us enjoy ours? In a German book [17] I translated, a little boy is very happy in making a scrapbook for a little friend, and God is represented as being glad to see him so happy. And I do not believe He begrudged your making me that pretty picture, or did not wish me to make yours. (By the bye, when you have time, tell me how to do it.) It seems to me we are meant to use *all* the faculties God gives us to abuse them is another thing. I feel that I am having a vacation, and wonder how long it is going to last. I do not know how I should have stood the *tremendous* change in my life, through my husband's change of profession, if I had not had this resource of painting. O, how I do miss his preaching! How I miss my pastoral work! Dr. Buck is on his dying bed, and longing to go. [18]

To her eldest Son, New York, March 11, 1877.

We had an excellent sermon from Dr. Vincent this morning, which he repeated by request. Last evening we had Chi Alpha, and as I saw this body of men enter the dining room, I wondered whether I had borne any minister to take up your father's and my work when we lay it down.

18th.—I thought within myself, as I listened to a sermon on the union of Christ and the believer, whether I should have the bliss of hearing you preach. Let me see how old should I have to be, at soonest? Sixty-two the age at which my ancestors died, unless they died young. I got a beautiful letter, a few days ago, from a minister in Philadelphia, the Rev. Mr. Miller, who has 1,300 members in his church, and says if he could afford it, he would give a copy of Greylock to every young mother in it.

I went to Mrs. P.'s funeral on Friday. She wanted to die suddenly, and had her wish. She ate her breakfast on Tuesday then went into the office and arranged papers there her husband went out at ten, and shortly after, she began to feel sick and the girls made her go to bed. One of them went out to do some errands, and the other sat in the room she soon heard a sound that made her think her mother wanted something, and on going to her found her dead. Dr. P. got home at twelve, long after all was over. He told me it was the most extraordinary death he ever heard of, but his theory was that a small clot of blood arrested the circulation, as she had no disease. I had a talk with C. about his wife's sudden death. I had already written him and sent him a note. I cut from the Evening Post the slip I enclose about Mr. Moody's question-drawer. I wish I could hope for as sudden a death as Mrs. P.'s.

To Mrs. Condict, April 16, 1877.

I am glad you liked the picture. Did you know that you too can get leaves and flowers in advance of spring, by keeping twigs in warm water? I had forsythia bloom, and other things leafed beautifully. It is said that apple and pear blossoms will come out in the same way, if placed in the sun in glass cans. I have been thinking, lately, that if I enjoy my imperfect work, how God, who has made so many beautiful, as well as useful, things, must enjoy His faultless creations. My work is still to go from house to house where sickness and death are so busy. Mrs. F. G. has just lost her two only children within a day of each other. Neither her mother nor sister could go near her during their illness or after their death, because of the flock of little ones in their house, and it was not safe to have a funeral. Dr. Hastings made a prayer he said the scene was heart-rending.

May 3rd.—Dr. Storrs preached for us last Sunday, and said one striking thing I must tell you on the passage, "They were stoned, were sawn asunder, they were tempted," etc. He said many thought the word *tempted* out of place amid so many horrors, but that it held its true position, since few things could cause such anguish to a Christian heart as even a suggestion of infidelity to its Lord. To this à Kempis adds the *hell* of not knowing whether one had yielded or not.

May 17th.—"Misery loves company" and so I am writing to you. Perhaps it will be some consolation to you that I too have been knocked up for two weeks, one of which I spent in bed. Nothing serious the matter, only put down and kept down not agreeable, but necessary. How *astounded* we shall be when we wake up in heaven and find our hateful old bodies could not get in! M. is making, and H. has made, a picture scrapbook for a hospital in Syria. Your mother might enjoy that. We all *crave* occupation. "Imprisonment with hard labor" never seems to me so frightful as imprisonment and nothing to do, does. Did you ever hear the story of the man who spent years in a dark dungeon, idle, and then found some pins in his coat, which he spent years in losing, and crawling about and finding?

Well, I have got rid of a wee morsel of this weary day in writing this, and you will get rid of another morsel in reading it. So we will patch each other up, and limp along together, and by and by go where there is no limping and no patching.

The new serial, her Bible-readings, and painting, with visits to sick-rooms and to the house of mourning, during the early half of this year, left little time for correspondence. Her letters were few and brief but they are marked, as was her life, by unusual quietness and depth of feeling. Her delight was still to speak in them a helpful and cheering word to souls struggling with their own imperfections, or with trials of the way. A single extract will illustrate the gentle wisdom of her counsels:

I think there is such a thing as peace of conscience even in this life. I do not mean careless peace, or heedless peace I mean calm consciousness of an understanding, so to speak, between the soul and its Lord. A wife, for instance, may say and do things to her husband that show she is human yet, at the same time, the two may live together loyally, and be happy. And unless a Christian is aware of having on hand an idol, dearer than God, I see no reason why he should not live in peace, even while aware that he is not yet finished (perfect). We love God more than we are aware when He slays us we trust in Him, when He strikes us, we kiss His hand.

Her own mood at this time was singularly grave and pensive. She felt more and more keenly the moral puzzle and contradictions of existence. "From beginning to end, in every aspect," she wrote to a friend, "life grows more mysterious to me, not to say queer—for that is not what I mean. Such strange things are all the time happening, and even good people doing and saying things that nearly drive one wild.... We live in a mixed state, in a kind of see-saw: we go up and then we go down go down and then fly up." Still this strange, ever-changing mystery of life, although it sometimes perplexed her in the extreme, did not make her unhappy. "I have great sources of enjoyment," she adds, "and do enjoy a good deal infinitely more than I deserve."

Early in June, she and the younger children went to Dorset. On reaching there, she wrote to her husband:

Here we are, sitting by the fire in our dear little parlor. We made a very comfortable journey to Manchester, but the ride from there here was rather cheerless and cold, as they forgot to send wraps. The neighbors had sent in various good things, and the strawberries looked very nice. It rains, but M. and I have surveyed the garden, and she says it is looking better than usual.

I only wish you were here. Your love is intensely precious to me, as I know mine is to you. How thankful we ought to be that we have loved each other through thick and thin! This is God's gift. I cannot write legibly with this pencil, nor see very well, as it is a dark day, and yet too early for a lamp.

The latter part of June she made a short visit with her husband to Montreal. A pleasant incident of this journey was an excursion to Quebec, where two charming days were spent in seeing the Falls of Montmorency, the Plains of Abraham, and other objects of interest in and about that remarkable city. During the ride in the cars from Montreal to St. Albans, she called the attention of her husband to a paragraph from an English newspaper containing an account of the death of a miner by an explosion, on whose breast was found a lock of hair inscribed with the name of "Jessie." She remarked that the incident would serve as an excellent hint for a story. This was the origin of *Gentleman Jim*, the pathetic little tale published shortly after her death.

Soon after her return from Montreal, she began painting in watercolors, which afforded her much delight during the rest of her life. The following note to Mrs. Ellen S. Fisher, of Brooklyn, dated July 2nd, will show how her lessons were taken:

Will you kindly inform me as to your method of teaching your system of watercolors by mail, and as to terms? I have not had time to do anything in that line, as I had to go to Canada (by the bye, you can get delightful Chinese white paint there in tubes). My daughter says she thinks she heard you say that you would paint a little flower-piece reasonably, or perhaps you have one to spare now. I should like a few wild flowers against a blue sky. I got half a dozen Parian vases at Montreal—each a group of three—and filled with daisies and a few grasses, they are exquisite. Some of them are in imitation of the hollow toadstools one finds in the woods.

To Mrs. Condict, Kauinfels, July 23, 1877.

Kauinfels is a word we invented, after spending no little time, by referring to a spot in a favorite brook as "the place where the old cow fell in" it looked so German and pleased us so much that we concluded to give our place that name. We are fond of odd names. We have a dog Pharaoh and a horse Shoo Fly. Then we had Shadrach, Meshach, and Abednego for cats. We had a dog named Penelope Ann—a splendid creature, but we had to part with her. My Bible-reading began two weeks ago, and neither rain nor shine keeps people away. For a small village the attendance is very large. I do not know how much good they do, but it is a comfort to try.

I cannot get over Miss ——'s tragic end. She must have suffered dreadfully. I do not doubt her present felicity, nor that she counts her life on earth as anything more than a moment's space. I do not feel sure that she did me any good. I saw so much that was morbid when she visited me here, that I never enjoyed her as I did when I knew her less. But there is nothing morbid about her now.

To Mrs. James Donaghe, Dorset, Aug. 20, 1877.

Yesterday was the first fine day we have had in a long time, and, as I sat enjoying it on the front porch, how I wished I could transport you here and share these mountains with you! Today is equally fine, and how gladly would I bottle it up and send it to you! A score of times I have asked myself why I do not bring you here, and then been reminded that you cannot leave your husband.

I do not write many letters this summer. We have three or four guests nearly all the time. This uses up what little brain I have left, and by half-past eight or nine, I have to go to bed. I am unusually well, but work hard in the garden all the forenoon and get tired. Yesterday the Rev. Mr. Reed, of Flushing, preached a most impressive sermon on the denial of self. In the afternoon, he preached to a neighborhood meeting at his own house, to which we three girls go, namely, M., her friend Hatty K., and myself. I give Thursdays pretty much up to my Bible-reading—studying for it in the morning and holding it at three in the afternoon. Utter unfitness for this or any other work for the Master makes me very dependent on Him. The service is largely attended, and how I get courage to speak to so many, I know not.

A. is gone to Portland and Prout's Neck. Mr. P. is unusually well this summer, and has actually worked a little in my garden. He is going to Saratoga this week to visit Mrs. Bronson.... M. is a kind of supplement to her father I love in her what I love in him, and she loves in me what he loves we never had a jar in our lives, and are more like twin-sisters than mother and daughter. Hatty K. is like a second M. to me. At this moment, they are each painting a plate. They work all the morning in the garden, and in the afternoon sit in my room sewing "for the poor" like two Dorcases, or drive, or row on the pond. They also study their Greek Testament together like a pair of twins. Just here, Mr. P. came driving up to take me out to make calls. We made three together, and then I made three alone. Now we are going to have tea, and should be glad if you could take it with us.

To Mrs. Condict, Kauinfels, Sept. 13, 1877.

Since you left, I have been very busy in various ways among other things, helping Hatty collect her last trophies, pack her various plants, and the like. Then there is a woman, close by, who is very sick and very poor, and the parson and his wife (meaning himself and myself) must needs pack a big basket of bread, butter, tea, apples, etc., for her watchers and family, with extract of beef for her. That was real fun, as you may suppose. I mean to devote Thursdays to such doings, including the Bible-readings. I took for my Bible-reading this afternoon, the subject of confession of sin, and should really like to know what perfectionists would say to the passages of Scripture relating to it. However, I know they would explain them away or throw them under the table, as they do all the Bible says about the discipline of life. Our bad Pharaoh lifted up his voice in every hymn at Mrs. Reed's last Sunday, and little Albert fairly shrieked with laughter. If next Sunday is pleasant, we are to go to Pawlet to preach. Goodnight. [19]

To Mrs. Fisher, Kauinfels, Sept. 15, 1877.

Excuse my keeping your pictures so long. It is owing to my having so much company. We feel it a duty to share our delightful home here with friends.

Will you send me some more pictures, and in your letter please tell me how to make the light green in the large arbutus leaf I tried all sorts of experiments, but failed to get such a toned-down tint. My copy is pretty, as I have improved a good deal on the whole but my work looks parvenu. I had to use a powerful magnifying glass to puzzle out your delicate touches, and your work bore the test, it is so well done. My work, viewed in the same way, is horrid. A. has been to Portland and found there some exquisite plaques some of them of a *very* delicate cream color others of a least suspicion of pink. She began to paint thorn apples on one but a day or two later, found some of the foliage we had thrown away, turned to most delicious browns so she painted the leaves in those shades, only—and the effect is richly and gravely autumnal. I hope your eyes are better.

* * * * *

IV.

Return to Town. Recollections of this Period. "Ordinary" Christians and spiritual Conflict. A tired Sunday Evening. "We may make an Idol of our Joy." Publication of *Pemaquid*. Kezia Millet.

She returned to town early in October and began at once to prepare for the winter's work. Her industry was a marvel. The following references to this period are from reminiscences, written by her husband after her death:

She lost not a day, scarcely an hour. The next eight months were among the busiest of her life and in some respects, I think, they were also among the happiest. She resumed her painting with new zeal and delight. It was a never-failing resource, when other engagements were over. Hour after hour, day after day, and week after week she would sit near the western window of her sunshiny chamber, absorbed in this fascinating occupation. Rarely did I fail to find her there, on going in to kiss her goodbye, as I started for my afternoon lecture. How often the scene comes back again! Were I myself a painter I could reproduce it to the life. Her posture and expression of perfect contentment, her quick and eager movements, all are as vividly present to my mind, as if I saw and parted from her there yesterday! One morning each week was devoted to her Bible-reading the others, when pleasant, were generally spent in going down town with M. in quest of painting materials, shopping, making calls, etc., etc.

She was much exercised in the early part of the winter by a burglary, which robbed her of a beautiful French mantel clock given her on our silver wedding-day by a dear friend and by the loss of my watch, stolen from me in the cars on my way home from the Seminary—a beautiful watch with a chain made of her hair and that which once "crowned little heads laid low." She had ordered it of Piguet, when we were in Geneva in 1858, and given it to me in memory of our marriage. But *her* grief over the loss of the watch was small compared with mine, then and even since.

What precious memories can become associated with such an object! One of the books that she read during the winter was "Les Miserables" by Victor Hugo. She read it in the original in a copy given her by Miss Woolsey. She was quite captivated by this work, and some of its most striking scenes and incidents she repeated to me, during successive mornings, before we got up. Her power of remembering and reproducing, in all its details, and with all the varying lights and shades, any story that she had read was something almost incredible. It always seemed to me like magic. Her father possessed the same power and perhaps she inherited it from him. [20]

The following letter will show that while her mind was still exercised about the doctrines taught by writers on the "Higher Life" and "Holiness through Faith," it was in the way of a deepening conviction that these doctrines are not in harmony with the teaching of Scripture or with Christian experience. Referring to some of these writers, she says:

To a Christian Friend, Oct. 21, 1877.

I have not only no unkind feeling towards them, but have no doubt they have lived near to Christ. But this I believe to have been their state of mind for years, though perhaps not consciously: Most Christians are "ordinary." Nearly all are a set of miserable doubters. Most of them believe the Christian life a warfare. Most of them imagine it is also a state of discipline, and make much of chastening, even going so far as to thank God for His strokes of Fatherly love! Strange love, to be sure! They also fancy they can work out their own salvation.

Now we are not "ordinary" Christians. We understand God's Word perfectly and when He says, "Work out your own salvation," He means nothing by it except this, that *He* will work it in you to will and to do, and you are to do nothing, but *let* Him thus work. And furthermore, we know His mind beyond dispute we cannot err in judgment. Therefore, if you doubt our doctrine, it is the same as doubting God, and you should fall on your knees and pray to read Scripture as we do.

As to the Christian life being a conflict, why, you "ordinary" Christians are all wrong. Satan never tempts us, though he tempted our Lord it comes natural to us to go into Canaan with one bound the old-fashioned saints were ridiculous in "fighting the good fight of faith." Look at the characters in the Bible, "resisting unto blood, striving against sin" what blunderers they were to do that! In our enlightened day nobody is "chastened" it used to be done to every son the Father received and it was a token of His love. He knows better now. He chastens no one or if He does, we will cover it up and ignore it religion is all rapture, and this is not a scene of probation. Still if you insist that you have been smitten, it only shows how very "ordinary" you are, and how angry God is with you.

Now you may ask why I have taken time to write this, since you are not led away by these errors. Well, they are pleasant and very plausible writers, and it has puzzled me to learn just where they were wrong. So I have been thinking aloud, or thinking on paper, and perhaps you may find one or more persons entangled in this attractive web, and be able to help them out. How a good man and a good woman ever fell into such mischievous mistakes, I cannot imagine….

As to you and me, I see nothing strange in the weaning from self God is giving us. It is natural to believe that He weans us from the breast of comfort in which we had delighted, because He has strong meat in store for us. I know I was awfully selfish about my relation to Christ, and went about for years on tiptoe, as it were, for fear of disturbing and driving Him away but I do not know that I should *dare* to live so again. And how better can He show us our weakness than by making it plain that we, who thought we were so strong in prayer, are almost "dumb before Him"! My dear friend, I believe more and more in the *deep* things of God.

"STRENGTH is born
In the deep silence of long-suffering hearts,
Not amid joy."

Imagine soldiers getting ready for warfare, being told by their commander that they had no need to drill, and had nothing to do but drink nectar! As to being brought low, I will own that I have not been entirely left of God to my own devices and desires if I had been, I should have gone overboard. He had such a grip of me that He *couldn't* let go. I saw a man apply a magnet to steel pens the other day, and that is the way I clung to God there was no power in me to hold on, the magnetism was in Him, and so I hung on. Wasn't it so with you?

And now to change the subject again if you have any faded ferns, vines, leaves on hand, you can paint and make them beautiful again. For a light wall, paint them with Caledonian brown, and they will have a very rich effect. I expect a patent-right for this invention.

The vivid sense of human weakness and of the sharp discipline of life, which she expresses in this letter, was deepened by hearing what a sea of trouble some of her friends had been suddenly engulfed in. Early in October, she wrote to one of them:

For some time before I left Dorset, your image met me everywhere I went, and I felt sure something was happening to you, though not knowing whether you were enjoying or suffering. And since then there has been nothing I could do for you but to pray that your faith may bear this test and that you may deeply realize that—

God is the refuge of His saints, When storms of sharp distress invade.

The longer I live the more conscious I am of human frailty, and of the constant, overwhelming need we *all* have of God's grace.... I cannot but hope things will turn out better than they seem. But if not, there is God nothing of this sort can take Him from you. You have longed and prayed for holiness this fearful event may bring the blessing. May God tenderly bless and keep you, dear child.

But vivid as was her sense of human weakness and of the imperfections cleaving to the best of men, while yet in the flesh, she still held fast to the conviction, uttered so often in "Urbane and His Friends" and in her other writings, that it is the privilege of every disciple of Jesus to attain, by faith, to high degrees of Christian holiness, and that, too, without consuming a whole lifetime in the process. In a letter to a young friend, she says:

Your letter shows me that I have expressed my views very inadequately in Urbane, or that you have misunderstood what I have said there.... "There *is* a shorter way" a better way God never meant us to spend a lifetime amid lumbering machinery by means of which we haul ourselves laboriously upward the work is His, not ours, and when I said I believed in "holiness through faith," I was not thinking of the book by that title, but of utterances made by the Church ages before its author saw the light of day. We *cannot* make ourselves holy. We are born sinners. A certain school believes that they are "kept" by the grace of God from all sin. I do not say that they are not. But I do say that I think it requires superhuman wisdom to *know* positively that one not only keeps all God's law, but leaves no single duty undone. Think a minute. Law proceeds from an infinite mind can finite mind grasp it so as to know, through its own consciousness, that it comes up to this standard? On the other hand, I do believe that a way has been provided for us to be set free from an "evil conscience" that we may live in such integrity and uprightness as to be at peace with God not being afraid to let His pure eye range through and through us, finding humanity and weakness, but also finding something on which His eye can rest with delight—namely, His own Son. Every day I live, I see that faith is my only hope, as perhaps I never saw it before.... Read over again the experience of Antiochus he got in early life what dear Dr. —— only found on his deathbed, and so may you.

To Miss E. A. Warner, New York, Oct. 28, 1877.

I am too tired on Sunday evenings to find much profit in reading, and have been sitting idle some minutes, asking myself how I should spend the hour until bedtime, if I could pick and choose among human occupations. I decided that if I had just the right kind of a neighbor, I should like to have her come in, or if there were the right kind of a little prayer meeting round the corner, I would go to that. Then I concluded to write to you, in answer to your letter of July 24. I write few letters during the summer, because it seems a plain duty to keep out of doors as much as I possibly can then we have company all the time, and they require about all the social element there is in me. We feel that we owe it to Him who gives us our delightful home to share it with others, especially those who get no mountain breezes save through us of some I must pay travelling expenses, or they cannot come at all. Their enjoyment is sufficient pay. My Bible-reading takes all the time of two days not spent in outdoor exercise, as I have given up almost everything of help in preparation for it but that which is given me in answer to prayer and study of the Word. I am kept, to use a homely expression, with my nose pretty close to the grindstone in other words, am kept low and little. But God blesses the work exactly as if I were a better woman. Sometimes I think how poor He must be to use such instruments as He does.

How is the niece you spoke of as so ill and so happy? For my part I am *confounded* when I see people hurt and distressed when invited home. How a loving Father must feel when His children shrink back crying, "I have so much to live for!" or, in other words, so little to die for. It frightens me sometimes to recall such cases.

And now I am going to tote my old head to bed. It is 59 years old and has to go early.

To Mrs. Fisher, Oct. 31, 1877.

With young children, and artistic work to do, the wonder is not that you have to neglect other things, but that you ever find time to attend to anyone outside of house and home. I do not want you to make a care and trouble of me I feel it a privilege to *try* even to copy anything from your hand, and am willing to bide my time. It is shocking to think of your summer's work being burned up no money can compensate for such a loss—I hate to think of it. I have had your landscape framed, and it is the finest thing in the house.

Nov. 9th.—I have your apple-blossoms ready to mail with this. I found the subject very difficult, and at one time thought I should have to give it up but your directions are so clear and to the point that I have succeeded in getting a picture we all think pretty, though wanting in the tender grace of yours.

The picture, which is a gentle blaze of beauty, has just reached me. We have had burglars in the house, and one of my songs of praise is that they did not take the little gem I got from you last summer. Glad you are a *woman* and not all artist.

To Mrs. Condict, Nov. 24, 1877

As to the running fern, I paint it the color of black walnut, and round plaques it looks like carving. Emerald green I hate, but it is a popular color, and A. was obliged to put it into the flower pictures she painted on portfolios. I am glad you are still interested in your painting. I have just finished the second reading of Miss Smiley's book, and marked passages, which I am sure you will like. I will mail my copy to you. As to joy—"the fruits of the Spirit" come naturally to those in the Spirit, and joy is one. But we may make an idol of our joy, and so have to part with it. There may come a period when God says, virtually, to the soul, "You clung to Me when I smiled upon and caressed you let Me see how you will behave when I smile and speak comfortably no more." Fenelon says, "To be constantly in a state of enjoyment that takes away the feeling of the cross, and to live in a fervor of devotion that keeps Paradise constantly open—this is not dying upon the cross and becoming nothing." [21]

When I look at the subject at a distance, as it were, remembering that this life is mere preparation for the next, it seems *likely* that we shall have religious as well as other discipline if we ascend the mount of Transfiguration it is not that we may *dwell* there, though it is natural to wish we could. And the fact is, no matter what professions of rapture people make, if they believe in Christ and love Him as they ought to do, what they have enjoyed will be nothing when compared with going to live *with* Him forever, surrounded by sanctified beings all united in adoring Him. When I think of this my courage grows apace, and I say to myself, I may never live in heaven again here below but I certainly shall, above and cannot I be patient till then? I wonder if you know that I am going to begin a Bible-reading on the first Wednesday in December? I have a very kind letter from Mr. Peter Carter, who says Kezia would make the fortune of any book.

Kezia is one of the characters in *Pemaquid or, a Story of Old Times in New England*, then recently published. She had written it with "indescribable ease and pleasure," to use her own words, mostly during the previous January. The pictures of New England life—especially its religious life—in old times are vivid and faithful and the character of Kezia Millet for originality, quiet humor, and truth to nature, surpasses any other in her writings, with the exception, perhaps, of Aunt Avery in "Fred and Maria and Me."

The following is an extract from a letter of Mr. Hallock, the publisher of "The Christian at Work," dated Aug. 25, 1877, in which he begged her to gratify its readers by telling them more about Ruth and Juliet. She accordingly added some pages to the last chapter, although not quite enough to satisfy the curiosity about Juliet:

Let me express to you my *personal* thanks for your most excellent serial. I feel that it has done a real good to thousands. You need to be placed in my position, receiving hundreds of letters daily from your readers, to be able to fully appreciate how intensely interested they are in the story. It does not seem to satisfy them to feel assured of Ruth's marriage, but they want *to be there* and see it. Juliet, too, is not with them, as with you, a mere impersonation, but a living reality, and they will never rest until they hear from her. If I were a betting man, I would bet five to one that what your husband struck out, is just exactly what is wanted. What do we men know about such things, anyhow?

A lady friend, well qualified to judge, writes to her:

I have read "Pemaquid," and have laughed until I cried, then cried and laughed together. In my humble opinion, it is the brightest book you have written. You know how to make a saint and how to make a sinner. As for old Kezia Millet, with her great loving heart, if she is not a model of Christian "*consistency*" and a natural born poet, where will you find one? She is perfectly fascinating. How do you keep your wit so ready and so bright? I suppose you will answer, "by using it." The chapter, which contains Mrs. Woodford's interview with Rev. Mr. Strong (the dear old saint) in her penitential mood, is very, very admirable.

To Mrs. George Payson, Dec. 20, 1877.

Before the year quite departs, I must tell you, my dear Margaret, how glad I am that you appreciate my dear, good bad Kezia. It is nineteen years since I read Adam Bede, but I remember Mrs. Poysen in general. Kezia is not an imitation of her the main points of her character were written out long before Adam Bede appeared I destroyed the book in which I trotted her out, but kept *her*, and once in a while tried her on my husband, but as he did not seem to see it, put her away in her green box, biding my time. As to Juliet, my good man *loathes* so to read about bad people that he almost made me cut out all my last mention of her. I was in an unholy frame when I did it, and with reason, for they who like Pemaquid best, say it was a mistake not to dispose of her in some way. But as to Mrs. Woodford being a model mother, I did not aim to make her a model anything. All I wanted of her was to bring out the New England peculiarities, as they would appear to a worldly stranger. As to all parties *seeming* indifferent about Juliet, you may be right I was behind the scenes and knew they were not but as I say, what I thought the best part of her, George made me cut out. No, I never knew any one sing exactly like Kezia, but there are such cases on record. There was "the Singing Cobbler," whose wife complained of him in court, and he defended himself so wittily in verse, that everybody sided with him, and his wife forgave his offence, whatever it might be.

[1] The following is the passage referred to: "If you aspire to be a son of consolation if you would partake of the priestly gift of sympathy if you would pour something beyond commonplace consolation into a tempted heart if you would pass through the intercourse of daily life with the delicate tact that never inflicts pain if to that most acute of human ailments—mental doubt, you are ever to give effectual succor, you must be content to pay the price of the costly education. Like Him, you must suffer, being tempted."

[2] By the late Rev. William James, D.D.

[3] See appendix G.

[4] Then pastor of the Collegiate Reformed Church, Fifth avenue and Forty-Eighth Street, now of Brooklyn.

[5] "Account of the Union Meeting for the Promotion of Scriptural Holiness, held at Oxford, August 29 to September 7, 1874."

[6] "Account of the Union Meeting for the Promotion of Scriptural Holiness, held at Oxford, August 29 to September 7, 1874." P. 59.

[7] GRISELDA A Dramatic Poem in Five Acts. *Translated from the German of* FRIEDERICH HALM (Baron Münch-Bellinghausen), *by Mrs. E. Prentiss.*

[8] How glad I was to see Griselda's fair face! She is a gem, and I am sure will prove a blessing as she moves about the world in her nobleness and purity, so exceedingly womanly and winning. The book is full of poetry, and held me spellbound to the close. It is very musical, too, in its rich, pure English. I do not know how much of its poetic charm lies in the original or in your rendering, but as it is, it is "just lovely," as the girls say.—*Letter from Miss Warner.*

[9] In a letter written in 1879, just after a visit to Dorset, Dr. Hamlin thus refers to them:

"Now that I have seen again those lights and shadows of the Green Mountains, as they lie around your Dorset home, I must tell you why they awakened such deep emotions. Forty-one years ago, I was married to Miss Henrietta Jackson, the youngest daughter of the venerated and beloved pastor of Dorset, and we left that lovely valley for our oriental home. I had heard from her lips a glowing description of the magic work of light and shade upon those uplands and heights that lie west of the valley, before I had seen the place. The first morning of my first visit I recognized the truth and accuracy of her description, and was forced to confess that, although I had always admired cloud-shadows, I had never seen them in such rich display and constant recurrence. There were certain days, which we called field days, when all their resources were called out, and they seemed hurrying in swift battalions to some great contest or grand coronation scene. But at other times they rested in calm repose as though the pulse of nature had ceased to beat… In our home upon the Bosporus, we were sometimes reminded of these scenes of her native valley. When, occasionally, the Black Sea clouds floated down in broken masses, and floods of light here and there poured through the darkly shadowed landscape, lighting up fragments of hill and vale to the very summits of Alem Dagh, her soul took flight to her beloved Dorset and all other thoughts vanished."

[10] On hearing of Mrs. Prentiss' death, the "poor, homeless fellow" wrote to her husband a touching letter of sympathy. The following is an extract from it:

It was, I must acknowledge, a cherished desire of your dear departed lady that I should walk in the footsteps of the Lord Jesus, and, to obtain that grace, I must invoke God's Power that I may accomplish that great Result. Dear Sir, I would like to suggest to you that I am disgusted with a wandering life would like to see Dorset next summer and look on the grave of my greatest friend. Nothing could give me greater Pleasure than to be under the Influence of your Christian family now, if I had any Employment, no matter how simple, in that locality for the winter, then I would feel Happy to go next season to your country Residence and offer my services free.

[11] Meeta Sophia Schaff died July 14, 1876, in the twenty-first year of her age. She had just returned from the Centennial. She was a young lady of unusual loveliness of character, and was deeply lamented by a wide circle of friends, both young and old.

[12] A printed copy of Lines on her Golden Wedding, written by Mrs. Prentiss.

[13] The article is entitled *Educated while Educating*, and appeared in the Brooklyn Journal of Education for March, 1875.

[14] The Rev. C. H. Payson. See the interesting Memoir of him, entitled "All for Christ," edited by his brother George, and published by the American Tract Society.

[15] See HENRY BOYNTON SMITH His Life and Work. Edited by his Wife. A. C. Armstrong & Son. 1880.

[16] His biographer, Mr. Moore, relates of Lord Byron that in all the plenitude of his fame, he confessed, "the depreciation of the lowest of mankind was more painful to him than the applause of the highest was pleasing."

[17] *Peterchen and Gretchen.* She translated it at Genevrier during the illness of her children.

[18] Dr. Gurdon Buck. He died shortly afterwards. For more than a quarter of a century be had been a faithful friend of Mrs. Prentiss, and as their family physician had made both her and her husband his debtors alike by his kindness and his skill. With a generosity so characteristic of his profession, he refused, during all these years, to receive

any compensation for his services. As a surgeon he stood in the front rank, some of the operations, performed by him, attracted wide attention for then—novelty and usefulness. He published an account of them, with illustrations, which greatly interested Mrs. Prentiss. She was almost as fond of reading about remarkable eases in surgery as about remarkable criminal trials.

Dr. Buck was one of the founders and first ruling elders of the Church of the Covenant. His gratuitous labors in connection with the New York Hospital and other public institutions were very great. He was a man of solid worth, modest, upright, and devoted to his Lord and Master.

[19] "One of my brightest recollections of this season at Dorset is our last Sunday before returning to town. We went in the phaeton to Pawlet, where I preached for the Rev. Mr. Aiken. The morning was pleasant, the road lay through a lovely mountain valley, and the beauty of nature was made perfect by the sweet Sabbath stillness and our thoughts were in unison with the scene and the day. I preached on Rest in Christ, and the service was very comforting to us both. How well I recall the same drive and a similar service early in September of 1876, when prayer was my theme! What sweet talks and sweeter fellowship we had together by the way, going and coming!"—*Recollections of* 1877-8.

[20] Recollections of 1876-7

[21] "Better is it sometimes to go down into the pit with him, who beholding darkness and bewailing the loss of consolation, cried from the bottom of the lowest hell, My God, my God, why hast Thou forsaken me? than continually to walk arm in arm with angels, to sit, as it were, in Abraham's bosom, and to have no thought, no cogitation but this, '*I thank my God it is not with me as it is with other men.*'"—HOOKER.

CHAPTER 15 - FOREVER WITH THE LORD - 1878.

"But a bound into home immortal, And blessed, blessed years."

I.

Enters upon her last Year on Earth. A Letter about The Home at Greylock. Her Motive in writing Books. Visit to the Aquarium. About "Worry." Her Painting. Saturday Afternoons with her. What she was to her Friends. Resemblance to Madame de Broglie. Recollections of a Visit to East River. A Picture of her by an old Friend. Goes to Dorset. Second Advent Doctrine. Last Letters.

Mrs. Prentiss crossed the threshold of her last year on earth with hands and thoughts still unusually busied. Her weekly Bible-reading, painting in oils and in watercolors, needlework, and other household duties, left her no idle moment. "My fire is so full of irons," she wrote, "that I do not know which one to take out." Nor was her heart less busy than her hands and brain. Twice in January, once in February, and again in April, death invaded the circle of her friends and when her friends were in trouble, she was always in trouble, too. [1] These deaths led to earnest talk with her husband on the mystery of earthly existence, and on the power of faith in Christ to sustain the soul in facing its great trials. "I am filled with ever fresh wonder at this amazing power," she said. Such subjects always interested her deeply never more so than at this time, when, although she knew it not, her feet were drawing so near to the pearly gates.

The keynote of her being throughout this last winter was one of unwonted seriousness. A certain startling intensity of thought and feeling showed itself every now and then. It was painfully evident that she was under a severe strain, both physical and mental. Again and again, as spring advanced, the anxiety of her husband was aroused to the highest pitch by what seemed to him indications that the unresting, ever-active spirit was fast wearing away the frail body. At times, too, there was a light in her eye and in her face an "unearthly, absolutely angelic expression"—to use her own words about her little Bessie, six and twenty years before—that filled him with a strange wonder, and which, after her departure, he often recalled as prophetic of the coming event and the glory that should follow.

But while to his ear an undertone of unusual seriousness, deepening ever and anon into a strain of the sweetest tenderness and pathos, ran through her life during all these early months of 1878, there was little change in its outward aspect. She was often gay and full as ever of bright, playful fancies. Never busier, so was she never more eager to be of service to her friends—and never was she more loving to her children, or more thoughtful of their happiness. She proposed for their gratification and advantage to write four new books, one for each of them, provided only they and their father would furnish her with subjects. The plan seemed to please her greatly, and, had she been spared, would probably have been carried into effect—for it was just the sort of stimulus she needed to set her mind in action. Once furnished with a subject, her pen, as has been said before, always moved with the utmost ease and rapidity. But while she wrote very easily, she did not write without reflection. 'She had a keen sense of character in all its phases, and her individual portraits, like those of Katy, Mrs. Grey and Margaret, Aunt Avery and Kezia Millet, were worked out with the utmost care, the result of years of observation and study being embodied in them.

And here, in passing, it may not be out of place to dwell for an instant upon her motives and experience as an author. From first to last she wrote, not to get gain or to win applause, but to do good and herein she had her reward, good measure, pressed down and running over. But of that kind of reward that gratifies literary taste and ambition, she had almost none. Her books, even those most admired by the best judges, and which had the widest circulation, both at home and abroad, attracted but little attention from the press. The organs of literary intelligence and criticism scarcely noticed them at all. Nor is it known that any attempt was ever made to analyze any of her more striking characters, or to point out the secret of her power and success as a writer. To be sure, she had never sought or counted upon this sort of recognition and yet that she was keenly alive to a word of discriminating praise, will appear from a letter to Mrs. Condict, dated Jan. 20th:

The burglary was on this wise, as far as we know. One man stood on the front steps, and another slipped the hasp to one of the parlor windows, stepped in, took a very valuable French clock, given me on my silver- wedding day, and all the hats and overcoats from the hall. This was all they had time to do before our night watchman came round they left the window wide open, and at 4 A.M. Pat rang the bell and informed Mr. Prentiss that such was the case. We feel it a great mercy that we were not attacked and maltreated. Poor A. was sitting up in bed, hearing what was going on, but being alone on the third floor, did not dare to move.

I have just finished a short story called Gentleman Jim, which I am going to send to Scribner's very likely it will get overlooked and lost. I received, not long ago, a letter from Mr. Cady [2] about Greylock, which he had just read. It was a gratification to both my husband and myself, as the most discriminating letter I ever received and after the first rush of pleasure, the Evil One troubled me, off and on, for two or three hours, but at last I reminded him that I long ago chose to cast in my lot with the people of God, and so be off the line of human notice or applause, and that I was glad I had been enabled to do it, since literary ambition is unbecoming a Christian woman. There are 500 other things I should say, if you were here!

The following is a part of the letter referred to: The day after "New Year's" I was visited with a severe cold and general prostration that has kept me in my bed—*giving me time!* As soon as I was strong enough to read I had "The Home" brought. After reading it, I felt I ought to tell you how deeply I was impressed with the usefulness, excellence, and spirit of the book. As to its usefulness, you are to be envied to have brought light, as I believe you have, to a large number of people upon the most precious and vital interests of life, is something worth living and suffering for. The good sense, wisdom, experience, and Christian faith embodied in it must make it a strong helper and friend to many a home in trouble and to many perplexed and discouraged hearts, who will doubtless rise up some day to call you "blessed."

Though you cared less about the manner than the matter, I was impressed by its literary qualities. The scene at the death of Mrs. Grey and parting of herself and Margaret is as highly artistic and beautiful as anything I can think of. The contrast of good and bad, or good and indifferent, is common enough but the contrast of what is noble and what is "saintly" is something infinitely higher and subtler. I cannot imagine anything more exquisitely tender and beautiful than Mrs. Grey's departure, but it is the more realized by the previous action of Margaret. The few lines in which this is told bring their whole character—in each case—vividly before you. But I see that if the book had previously to this point been differently written it would have been impossible to render this scene so remarkably impressive. The story of "Eric" is extremely quaint and charming it is a vein I am not familiar with in your writings. It is a little classic. This quaint child's story and the death of Mrs. Grey affect me as a fine work of art affects one, whenever I recall them. The trite saying is still true, "A thing of beauty is a joy forever."

You know children complain of some sweets that they leave a bad taste—and works of fiction often do with me. I feel tired and dissatisfied after I have passed out of their excitements but the heavenly atmosphere of this book left me better I know that the Blessed Spirit must have influenced you in the writing of it, and I doubt not His blessing will accompany its teachings.

Now will you excuse this blotty letter—written in bed—and accept my thanks for all the good your book has done me.

The following is her reply:

DEAR MR. CADY:—Your letter afforded me more satisfaction than I know how to explain. It is true that I made up my mind, as a very young girl, to keep out of the way of literary people, so as to avoid literary ambition. Nor have I regretted that decision. Yet the human nature is not dead in me, and my instincts still crave the kind of recognition you have given me. I have had heaps of letters from all parts of this country, England, Scotland, Ireland, Germany, and Switzerland, about my books, till I have got sick and tired of them. And the reason I tired of them was, that in most cases there was no discrimination. People liked their religious character, and of course, I wanted them to do so. But you appreciate and understand everything in Greylock, and have, therefore, gratified my husband and myself. Not a soul out of this house, for instance, has ever so much as alluded to my little Eric, except one friend who said, "We thought that part of the book forced, and supposed A. wrote it." Nobody has ever alluded to Margaret, save yourself. I hoped a sequel to the book might be called for, when I meant to elaborate her character. Still, it would have been very hard.... I am not sorry that I chose the path in life I did choose. A woman should not live for, or even desire, fame. This is yet more true of a Christian woman. If I had not steadily suppressed all such ambition, I might have become a sour, disappointed woman, seeing my best work unrecognized. But it has been my wish to

"Dare to be little and unknown, Seen and loved by God alone."

Your letter for a few hours, did stir up what I had always trampled down but only for that brief period, and then I said to myself, God has only taken me at my word I have asked Him, a thousand times, to make me smaller and smaller, and crowd the self out of me by taking up all the room Himself. There is so much of that work yet to be done, that I wonder He ventures to make so many lines fall to me in pleasant places, and that I have such a goodly heritage. I trust He will bless you for your labor of love to me.

I do not like the idea of your buying my books. Greylock being for mothers, I never dreamed of men reading it. Have you had The Story Lizzie Told, Six Little Princesses, The Little Preacher, and Nidworth? Neither of these is really a child's book, and the next time you are sick, if you have not read them, I shall love to send them to you. If this is conceit, I have the effrontery not to be a mite ashamed of it!

The following notes to Mrs. Fisher show how pleasantly she sympathized with her teacher as a young mother, while taking lessons of and admiring her as an artist:

NEW YORK, *February 4, 1878.*

What a relief to have the days come long again! On Saturday, I found in A.'s portfolio a study you lent her exquisite ferns behind the fallen trunk of a tree, and a tiny group of orange-colored toadstools. I will send it with its two lovely sisters, when I get through with them. I wish you could get time to come to see me, or that I could get time to go to see you. But it is my unlucky nature to have a great many irons in the fire at once. I am glad your baby keeps well, and hope he will grow up to be a great comfort to you.

Feb. 23rd.—I have just received your letter. I have my hands full and there is no need to hurry you.

As to "worry" not being of faith, I do not suppose it is. But a young mother cannot be *all* faith. I do not envy people who love so lightly that they have no wringing out of the heart when they lose their dear ones nor can I understand her who says she can sit and read the newspaper, while her babies are crying. "None are so old as they who have outlived enthusiasm" and who should be enthusiastic if a mother may not? I do not think God has laid it up against me that I nearly killed myself for the sake of my babies, because when He took two away within three months of each other, my faith in Him did not falter.... Dear Mrs. Fisher, if you love God nothing but His best things will ever come to you. This is the experience of a very young, old woman, and I hope it will comfort you.

April 21st.—Such a fight as I have had with your exquisite studies, and how I have been beaten! I failed entirely in the golden-rod, and do not get the brilliant yellow of the mullein flower one could not easily fail on the saggitarius, and the clover was tolerable. I think I will take no more lessons at present, as I have much to do in getting another boy fitted for college. After I get settled at Dorset, I want to make a desperate effort to paint from nature, and if I have any success, send to you for criticism. "Fools rush in where angels fear to tread," and I am afraid you will be disgusted with my work, which will be in the dark, since I have had no instruction in copying nature.... Perhaps you may put alongside of the rejection of your picture a lady's telling me about one of my books into which I had thrown an experience of the last thirty years of my life, "There was nothing in it." "Il faut souffrir pour etre belle." As long as memory lasts, I shall rejoice that I have seen and studied your work.

I remember what a splendid fellow your baby was a year ago. It will depend on your maternal prayers and discipline whether he grows up to be your comfort.

A few extracts from her letters will give further glimpses of the manner in which she passed these closing months of her life in New York— especially of her delight in the weekly Bible reading. One of the ladies, who attended it, thus refers to that exercise:

You remember that for one or two years she was a member of a small circle that met weekly for Bible-study. When the leader of this circle removed from the city, Mrs. Prentiss was urgently requested to become its teacher, and she consented to do so. For the last four years of her life, she threw her whole soul into this exercise. Every week the appointed morning found her surrounded by a little group of from eight to fifteen, each with an open Bible and all intent less to analyze the word of God than to feed upon it and "grow thereby." And what a wonderful teacher she was! Not neglectful of any helps that dictionary or commentator might give, her chief source of light was none of these, but was received in answer to the promise, "If any man will do the will of God he shall know of the doctrine." She wished the service to be entirely informal, and that each one present should do her part to aid in the study. This brought out diverse views and different standards of opinion. Here her keen intellect, her warm heart, the rich stores of her experience and her "sanctified common sense" all found play, and many of the words that fell from her lips dwell in the memory as little less than inspired. The last winter of this service showed some marked differences from previous years. As eager as ever to have questions asked and answered by others, yet from the moment she commenced to speak she scarcely paused until the hour was finished, her eyes sparkling and her whole manner intensely earnest. Often those words of the Psalmist passed through my mind, *the zeal of Thy house hath eaten me up*. Her love for her work and zeal in doing it were visibly consuming her. At the last meeting, I asked her if she should commence the Bible reading at Dorset immediately. She said no, she must rest a little she would wait until her garden was made. When next I heard from her, flowers and her Bible study she had made the "bound into home immortal." And all who loved her must rejoice with her else have we failed to learn one of the clearest lessons of her life: *For me to live is Christ, and to die is gain*.

To Mrs. Condit, Feb. 14, 1878.

Is it possible I had portiére on the brain when I wrote you last? I thought I had just caught the disease. I am very fond of needlework, but for years have nearly abandoned it, because I could not thread my needle. But the portiére is made with a large worsted needle and will give me pleasant work for the evening. I am getting my hand in on a contumacious closet door that will not stay open in my bedroom....

Imitation Macaroni,

By the author of Pemaquid:

Boil hominy overnight. Next day's dinner prepare like macaroni, with a little milk and grated cheese and bake. Good for a change and cheaper.

March 9th.—What an improvement on the old fashion of *reading* the Bible is the present *search* of the Word! It is, as you say, fascinating work. I have just given M. an admirable book called "Emphatic Diaglott," being the Greek Testament with a literal translation still even that can be misunderstood by one who has a false theory to sustain. The spiritual conflicts I have passed through have been a blessing, as I am beginning to see I can understand better *how* such conflicts may prepare one for work. This afternoon I have, as usual, been getting ready for the Wednesday reading, and as I was requested to speak of the Holy Spirit, have been poring over the Bible and am astonished at the frequency and variety of passages in which He is spoken of. But I feel painfully unfit to guide even this little circle of women, and would be so glad to sit as a learner.

Some of the children were going, last Friday night, to see the Aquarium, and some educated horses and dogs there, and they persuaded me to go. The performance was wonderful, but I could not help thinking of all these poor animals had gone through in learning all these incredible feats each horse responding to his own name, each dog barking in response to his two dogs hanging a third, cutting him down, when he lay apparently dead, other dogs driving in, in a cart, and carrying away the body others waltzing on their hind legs, and others jumping the rope. Two horses played seesaw, and one rolled a barrel up an inclined plane with his fore legs he *hated* to do it. But the marvelous fishes and sea-flowers charmed me most.

To Mrs. Reed, New York, March 13, 1878.

... I have had a busy winter. We had a variety of losses, and I undertook, therefore, to manufacture Reed, most of my Christmas gifts, which were, chiefly, umbrella racks this took time. Then my Bible-reading uses up pretty much one day. I never felt so unfit for it, or more determined to keep it up as long as one would come. Besides that, I have read and painted more or less and sewed a good deal on the whole, have had more vacation than work, at least one looking on would say so. But we all lead two lives, and one of them is penetrated and understood by no mortal eye. I heard such a sermon from Dr. Bevan last Sunday night on the text, "They saw God and did eat and drink." He divided mankind into four classes: Those who do eat and drink and do not see God those who do not see Him and do not eat and drink those who see Him and do not eat and drink (he handled them tenderly) and those who see Him and yet eat and drink. I hope I have made its outline plain to you. It took hold of me.

To Mrs. Donaghe, New York, April 26, 1878.

I am living my life among breakings-up you gone, Mrs. Smith about to flee to Northampton, and our neighbor Miss W. storing her furniture and probably leaving New York for good. On the other hand, M. spends most of her time in helping Mr. and Mrs. Talbot get to rights in apartments they have just taken. Mr. T., as I suppose you know, is pastor of our Mission and as good as gold. God has been pleased greatly to bless two ladies, who attend the Bible-reading, and I am sure He loves to have us study His Word. The more I dig into it the richer I find it, and I have had some delightful hours this winter in preparing for my Wednesday work.

There is to be a Women's Exchange in this city, where everything manufactured by them (except underclothing) will be exposed for sale embroidery, pickles, preserves, confectionery, and articles rejected by the Society of Decorative Art. I hope it will be a success, and help many worthy women, all over the land, to help themselves.... I find it hard to consent to your having, at your age, to flit about from home to home, but a loving Father has a mansion for you beyond all the changes and chances of this strange complicated life. If He gives you His presence, that will be a home. I wish you could visit us at Dorset.

A visit to Dorset was afterward arranged, and one of Mrs. Prentiss' last letters was addressed to this old friend, giving her directions how to get there. [3]

To Mrs. Condict, New York, May 6, 1878. My last Bible-reading, or rather one of the last, was on prayer as I could not do justice to it in one reading, I concluded to make a resumé of the whole subject. Though I devoted all the readings to this topic last summer, yet it loomed up wonderfully in this resumé. Last week the subject was "the precious blood of Christ," and in studying up the word "precious" I lighted on these lovely verses, Deut. 33. 13-16. Since I began to *study* the Bible, it often seems like a new book. And that passage thrilled the ladies, as a novelty. I am to have but one more reading. The last sermon I heard was on lying. That is not one of my besetting sins, but, on the other hand, I push the truth too far, haggling about evils better let alone. A. has just finished a splendid plaque to order a Japanese figure, with exquisite foliage in black and grey as background. I have a widow lady every Saturday to paint with me she has a large family, limited means, and delicate health and I want to aid her all I can. She enjoys these afternoons so much, and is doing so well.

The lady herself thus recalls these afternoons:

How dearly I should love to add but one little flower to her wreath of immortelles! I cherish memories of her as among the pleasantest of my life. I recall her room so bright and cheery, just like herself, and all the incidents of those Saturday afternoons. When she first asked me to paint with her, I thought it very kind, but with her multiplicity of cares, felt it must be burdensome to her, and that possibly she would even forget the invitation, and so I hesitated about going. But when the week came round everything was made ready to give me a cordial welcome. Again and again I found my chair, palette and other materials waiting for me, while she sat in her little nook, busy as a bee over some painting of her own.

One day, passing about the room, I saw on her bookshelves, arranged with order and precision, nine little butter plates in the form of pansies. I uttered an exclamation of delight, and she from her corner, with the artlessness of a child, said, "I *put* them there for you to see." Another time she sprang up with her quick, light step, and ran to the yard to fetch a flower for me to copy, apparently thoughtless of two flights of stairs to tax her strength. Sometimes she would read to me verses of poetry that pleased her. Once I remember her throwing herself at my feet, and when I stopped to listen to the reading, she said, "Oh, go right on with your painting." Now she would relate some amusing anecdote that almost convulsed me with laughter, and then again speak of some serious theme with such earnestness of feeling! She was eager to give of her store of strength and cheer to others, but the store seemed inexhaustible. The more she gave, the more one felt that there was enough and to spare. I looked forward to my little weekly visit as to an oasis in the desert not that all else was bleak, but that spot seemed to me so very refreshing and attractive.

Little did I think, when she loaded me down that last day with all I could carry, then ran down to the parlor to show me some choice articles there which she knew would give me pleasure—little did I think that I should see her again no more! Not a day passed after leaving her that she was not an inspiration to me. While painting a wayside flower I would think, "Mrs. Prentiss would like this"—or, "In the fall I must show that to Mrs. Prentiss." Even in my dreams she was present with me, and one morning, only a little while before she passed from us, I waked with a heavy burden upon my spirits—for it seemed to me as if she were gone. The impression was so strong that I spoke of it at the time, and for days could not throw it off. But at last, saying to myself, "Oh, it is only a dream," I answered her little note, making, of course, no reference to my strange feelings in regard to her. Her letter, by a singular mistake, is dated "Kauinfels, *October* 10, 1878," nearly two months after she had fallen asleep. How just like her is this passage in it: "I wish you could leave your little flock, and take some rest with us. It would do you good, I am sure. Is it impossible? You do look so tired." My letter in reply must have been one of the very last received by her. In it, I spoke of having just re-read Stepping Heavenward and Aunt Jane's Hero, and of having enjoyed them almost as much as at the first. This was, perhaps, one reason why she had been so constantly in my thoughts. When the news came that she had left us, I was at first greatly shocked and grieved—for I felt that I had lost no ordinary friend—but when I considered how complete her life had been in all that makes life noble and beautiful, and how meet it was that, having borne the burden and heat of the day, she should now rest from her labors, it seemed selfish to give way to sorrow and not rather to rejoice that she had gone to be with Christ.

Scores of such grateful testimonies as this might be given. To all who knew and loved her well, Mrs. Prentiss was "an inspiration." They delighted to talk about her to each other and even to strangers. They repeated her bright and pithy sayings. They associated her with favorite characters in the books they read. The very thought of her wrought upon them with gracious and cheering influence. An extract from a letter of one of her old and dearest friends, written to her husband after her death, will illustrate this:

On the very morning of her departure I had been conversing with my physician about her. He spoke in admiration of her published works, and I tried to give him a description of her personal characteristics. The night before, in my hours of sleeplessness, I recounted the names of friends who I thought had been most instrumental in molding my character, and Mrs. Prentiss led the list. How little did I dream that already her feet had safely touched "the shining shore"! In all the three and thirty years of our acquaintance I loved her DEARLY and reverenced her most deeply but between us there was such a gulf that I always felt unworthy to touch even the hem of her garment. Whenever I did touch it, strength and comfort were imparted to me. How much I was indebted to her most tender sympathy and her prayers in my own great sorrow, only another world will reveal. Is it not a little remarkable that her last letter to me, written only a few weeks before her death, closed with a benediction? I could go on talking about her without end for I have often said that there was more of her, and to her, and in her, than belonged to any five women I ever knew. How exceedingly lovely she was in her own home! I remember you once said to me, "The greatest charm of my wife is, after all, her perfect naturalness." All who knew her must have recognized the same winning characteristic. She was always fresh and always new—for she had "the well-spring of wisdom as a flowing brook." ... Were you not struck, in reading Thomas Erskine's letters on the death of Madame de Broglie, by the wonderful likeness between her and dear Mrs. Prentiss? Twin sisters could scarcely have resembled each other more perfectly. Such passages as the following quite startled me:

Her friendship has been to me a great gift. She has been a witness to me for God, a voice crying in the wilderness. She has been a warner and a comforter. I have seen her continually thirsting after a spiritual union with God. I have heard the voice of her heart crying after God out from the midst of all things, which make this life pleasant, and satisfying.... She had all the gifts of mind and character—intelligence, imagination, nobleness, and thoughts that wandered through eternity. She had a heart fitted for friendship, and she had friends who could appreciate her but God suffered her not to find rest in these things, her ear was open to His own paternal voice, and she became His child, in the way that the world is not and knows not. I see her before me, her loving spirit uttering itself through every feature of her beautiful and animated countenance.... There was an unspeakable charm about her. She had a truth and simplicity of character, which one rarely finds even in the highest order of men. I know nobody like her now. I hope to pass eternity with her. It is wonderful to think what a place she has occupied in my life since I became acquainted with her.

You know it is my belief that we become better acquainted with our friends after they have passed on "within the veil." And may it not be that they become better acquainted with us, too, loving us more perfectly and forgiving all that has been amiss? [4]

To her eldest son, New York, May 12, 1878.

This is your father's birthday, and I have given him, to his great delight, a Fairbanks postal scale. His twenty-years-old one would not weigh newspapers or books, and it is time for an improvement on it. On Thursday evening, there was a festival at our church in aid of sick mission children. Everybody was there with their children, and it was the nicest affair we ever had. M. and I went and enjoyed it ever so much. I took between four and five dollars to spend, though I had given between twenty and thirty to the mission, but did not get a chance to spend much, as Mr. M. took me in charge and paid for everything I ate. Your father and I rather expect to go to East River, Conn., tomorrow to help Mrs. Washburn celebrate her seventieth birthday but the weather is so cold he doubts whether I had better go. A. went on a long drive on Friday and brought back a host of wild flowers, which I tried with some failure and some success to paint.

May 19th.—We went to East River on Monday afternoon and came home on Thursday, making a delightful visit. On Tuesday Mrs. W. and I went to Norwich to see the Gilmans. I was very tired when we got back, and had to go to bed at half-past seven. The next day it rained so Mrs. W. and I fell to painting. She became so interested in learning Mrs. Fisher's system that she got up at five the next morning and worked two hours. In the evening, your father gave his lecture at a little clubroom, got up chiefly by Mr. and Mrs. Washburn at their own expense. It is just such a room, as I should like to build at Dorset. On Thursday morning, Mrs. W. took me out to drive through their own woods and dug up some wild flowers for me. A. has a Miss Crocker, an artistic friend from Portland, staying with her—a very nice, plucky girl. She wants me to let her take my portrait. [5] H. is full of a story of a pious dog, who was only fond of people who prayed, went to church regularly, and, when not prevented, to all the neighborhood prayer-meetings, which were changed every week from house to house his only knowledge of where they would be held being from Sunday notices from the pulpit! I believe this the more readily because of Pharaoh's always going to my Bible reading at Dorset and never barking there, whereas if I went to the same house to call he barked dreadfully.

We are constantly wondering what you boys will be. Good men, I hope, at any rate. Goodnight, with a kiss from your affectionate mother.

The substance of the following letter of Mrs. Washburn, giving an account of the visit to East River, as also her impressions of Mrs. Prentiss, was written in response to one received by her from an old friend in Turk's Island: [6]

I am most thankful that we had that last visit from dear Mrs. Prentiss. It was a rare favor to us that she came. Her health was very delicate, and a slight deviation from the regular routine of home life was apt to give her sleepless nights. Dr. P. had sent us word that he was going to be in New Haven, and would give us a call before returning to New York. We' were overjoyed at the prospect of seeing him, and wrote immediately begging Mrs. Prentiss to come with him. She, ever ready to sacrifice her own ease for the sake of giving pleasure to others, and knowing that the 15th of May would be my 70th anniversary, and that I perfectly longed to see her, took the risk of personal suffering upon herself to satisfy my earnest desire, and came. They arrived on the 13th in the late afternoon train. She was so bright and cheerful it was difficult to notice any traces of the weariness that she must have felt.

We passed a delightful evening, and as Dr. P. was to spend a part of the next day in New Haven, we formed a plan for Mrs. Prentiss and me to go to Norwich at the same time and make a brief visit to our mutual friends, the Misses Gilman. Mr. Washburn telegraphed to them that we were coming. On arriving at New London we found, to our dismay, that we had been misinformed in regard to the trains, and that the one we had taken did not connect with the one to Norwich, which had been gone two hours. So there we were, left alone on the platform, strangers in the place, with no means of either going on or returning. What should we do? Our first thought was to procure, if possible, some conveyance to take us to Norwich and back but this we found could not be done, for want of time, the distance between the two cities being fourteen miles or more. Fortunately, for us, a young lad appeared who promised to take us to our friends in Norwich, allow us half an hour to spend with them, and drive to the station there in time for the return train to New London and East River. He looked so honest and true that we felt we could trust him, and we acceded to his terms at once. As soon as he could get his carriage ready, we started off on our untried way.

It began at the foot of a long hill, and continued up and down over a succession of the same kind, with very rare exceptions of a level space between them, through the whole distance. But the scenery was so varied and beautiful, we thought if our only object in setting out had been a drive, we could not have chosen one more charming. The weather was fine, and dear Mrs. Prentiss in her happiest mood. As for me, nothing marred my enjoyment but fear that the fatigue would be too much for her, and an undercurrent of anxiety lest by some mishap we should fail to re-arrive at the home-station in time to meet our husbands who would be waiting for us. But if she had any such misgivings, nothing in word or manner betrayed it. So entire was her self-control, and so delicate her tact, not to throw the faintest shadow across the wisdom of my precipitate arrangements. She was as happy as a bird all the way, and talked delightfully.

We found our friends had been in a state of great excitement on our account, having received the telegram, and knowing that we had taken the wrong train so that our unexpected arrival was greeted with even more than their usual cordiality and they were especially gratified to see Mrs. Prentiss, who almost without looking, discovered a hundred beauties in and around their lovely home, which it would have taken the eyes of an ordinary guest a week to notice. The very shortness of our time to stay intensified our enjoyment while it lasted. Our half hour was soon over, and we came away with our hands full of flowers and our hearts as full of love.

We arrived in good time and met our husbands waiting for us at the station. Dear Mrs. Prentiss did not appear to be very much fatigued while recounting in her inimitably pleasant manner the various experiences of the day. A restful night prepared her for the quiet enjoyments of the next day, which we spent mostly at home, merely making short calls in the morning on my two sisters, and slowly driving, or rather, as I call it, "taking a walk in the buggy," through the woods, stopping every few minutes to look at, or gather ferns or mosses or budding wild flowers that could not escape her beauty-loving eye. The afternoon we remained in the house, occupied with our pencils. She painted a spray of trailing arbutus, talking while she was doing it, as nobody else could, about things beloved and fair. Our darling Julia was with us, completely charmed with her, and as busy as we, trying with her little hands to make pictures as pretty as ours.

In the evening Dr. P. gave his most interesting lecture on "Recollections of Hurstmonceaux" in our reading room but Mrs. Prentiss was not able to go, which I regretted the more because I knew many ladies would be there who came almost as much to see her as to hear him. They were greatly disappointed, but enjoyed every word of the lecture, as well they might. The next day was all too short. It seemed to me that I *could not* let them go. But she had more than enough for her ever busy hands and mind and heart to do in preparation for going to her summer home, and we *had* to say goodbye.

A few short, characteristic, loving notes came from the city, before she left, and I did not hear from her at Dorset until the overwhelming news came of her death. I could not control my grief. Little Julia tried to comfort me with her sweet sympathy. "Dear grandma," she said, "I am sorry too. I cannot feel so bad as you do, because you loved her so much, and you loved her so long but *I* loved her too, and I can think just how she looked when she sat right there by that little table talking, and painting those beautiful flowers. Oh! I am very sorry." And here the poor child's tears flowed again with mine. So will all the children who knew her say, "We remember just how she looked." Yes, there was no mistaking or forgetting that kindly, loving "look." Julia's mother had felt its influence from her own early childhood until she left her precious little one to receive it in her stead. To each of these half-orphaned ones in turn, I had to read "Little Susy's Six Birthdays," and both always said to me when I finished, "Please read it again."

She could read and understand the heart of children through and through, as indeed she could everybody's. And that was, perhaps, her chiefest charm a keen eye to see and a true heart to sympathize and love. She was absolutely sincere, and no one could help feeling that she was so. We felt ourselves fairly imaged when standing before her, as in a clear plate-glass mirror. There were no distorted lines caused by her own imperfections for although she considered herself "compassed with infirmity," no one else could take such a view of her, but only saw the abundant charity which could cover and forgive a multitude of failings in others. We felt that if there was any good in us, she knew it, and even when she saw them "with all our faults she loved us still," and loved to do us good.

You would like me to tell you "how she looked." You can form some idea from her picture, but not an adequate one. Her face defied both the photographer's and the painter's art. The crayon likeness, taken shortly before her death by Miss Crocker, a young artist from Maine, is, in some respects, excellent. The eyes and mouth—not to speak of other features—are very happily reproduced. She was of medium height, yet stood and walked so erect as to appear taller than she really was. Her dress, always tasteful, with little or no ornament that one could remember, was ever suited to the time and place, and seemed the most becoming to her that could have been chosen. She was perfectly natural, and, though shy and reserved among strangers, had a quiet, easy grace of manner, that showed at once deference for them and utter unconsciousness of self. Her head was very fine and admirably poised. She had a symmetrical figure, and her step to the last was as light and elastic as a girl's.

When I first knew her, in the flush and bloom of young maternity, her face scarcely differed in its curving outlines from what it was more than a quarter of a century later, when the joys and sorrows of full-orbed womanhood had stamped upon it indelible marks of the perfection they had wrought. Her hair was then a dark-brown her forehead smooth and fair, her general complexion rich without much depth of color except upon the lips. In silvering her clustering locks, time only added to her aspect a graver charm, and harmonized the still more delicate tints of cheek and brow. Her eyes were black, and at times wonderfully bright and full of spiritual power but they were shaded by deep, smooth lids, which gave them when at rest a most dove-like serenity. Her other features were equally striking the lips and chin exquisitely molded and marked by great strength as well as beauty. Her face, in repose, wore the habitual expression of deep thought and a soft earnestness, like a thin veil of sadness, which I never saw in the same degree in any other. Yet when animated by interchange of thought and feeling with congenial minds, it lighted up with a perfect radiance of love and intelligence, and a most beaming smile that no pen or pencil can describe—least of all in my hand, which trembles when I try to sketch the faintest outline.

Hundreds of heart-stirring memories crowd upon me as I write, but it is impossible to give them expression. Her books give you the truest transcript of herself. She wrote, as she talked, from the heart. To those who knew her, a written page in almost any one of them recalls her image with the vividness of a portrait and they can almost hear her musical voice as they read it themselves. But, alas! in reality—

> No more her low sweet accents can we hear
> No more our plaints can reach her patient ear.
> O! loved and lost, oh! trusted, tried, and true,
> O! tender, pitying eyes forever sealed
> How can we bear to speak our last adieu?
> How to the grave the precious casket yield,
> And to those old familiar places go
> That knew thee once, and never more shall know?
> I hear from heaven a voice angelic cry,
> "Blessed, thrice blessed are the dead who lie
> Beneath the flowery sod and graven stone."
> "Yea," saith the answering Spirit, "for they rest
> Forever from the labors they have done.
> Their works do follow them to regions blest
> No stain hereafter can their lustre dim
> The dead in Christ from henceforth live in Him."
> O! doubly dear transfigured friend on high,
> We, through our tears, behold thine eyelids dry.

> By Him who suffered once, and once was dead,
> But liveth evermore through endless days,
> God hath encircled thy redeemed head
> With rays of glory and eternal praise,
> And with His own kind hand wiped every trace
> Of tears, and pain and sorrow from thy face.
> C. W.,   WILDWOOD, March 7, 1880.

One of the notes referred to is as follows:

DEAR MRS. WASHBURN:—If you judge by my handwriting, you will have to conclude that I am 100 years old. But it all comes of my carrying a heavy bag too long, and is all my own fault for trying to do too many errands in one trip. Your dear little chair, the like of which I should love to give to 540 people, only cost $2.50, so I enclose my check for the rest of your $10. We sent off Mrs. Badger's parcel early this morning. I hope digging and driving and packing and climbing in my behalf, has not quite killed you. A lot of flowers in two boxes came to me from Matteawan while I was gone, and as my waitress fancied I had been shopping—as if I *should* shop at East River!—she did not open the boxes or inform the children, so the spectacle of withered beauty was not very agreeable. A. and M. send love and thanks. The flowers you gave me look beautifully. Give our love to Mr. W. and Julia, and write about her. We shall not soon forget our charming visit to East River!

In acknowledging this note, Mrs. Washburn alludes to one of Mrs. Prentiss' most striking traits—the eager promptitude with which she would execute little commissions for her friends. It was as if she had taken a vow that there should not be one instant's delay.

I do hope you have not been made sick by doing so many errands in such a short time. The little chair has come and Mr. W. is much pleased with it. Nobody is so punctual as you. We were all amazed at receiving the picture so soon. How could you possibly have gotten home and packed it and marked the catalogues and bought the chair and written the check and sent me the little package of Japanese corn-seed and written me the note and have had a moment even to look at A.'s portrait? It is a mystery to me. You are a wonder of a woman! You are a genius! You are a *beloved friend!* I thank you again and again. Just think of the good you have done us. Shall I send you some more daisies? I have written in the greatest haste. That is the reason I have done no better and not because I am seventy years old.

Here is her last note to Mrs. Washburn, dated June 3:

The box of daisies, clover, and grass came on Saturday. We set the plants out in the box in which they came, and mixed the grass with what cut flowers we had, in the very prettiest receptacle for flowers I ever saw, just given M. The plants look this morning like a piece of Wildwood and a piece of you, and will gladden every spring we live to see.... We are packing for Dorset, though we do not mean to go if this weather lasts. I wonder if you have a "daily rose"? I have just bought one first heard of it at the Centennial. It is said to bloom every day from May to December.

I am going out, now, to do ever so many errands for H.'s outfit for college. Give our dear love to Mr. Washburn and Julia. O, what a mercy it is to have somebody to love. [7]

On the 6th of June Mrs. Prentiss went to Dorset for the last time. Her husband, after her departure, thus referred to this period:

For four or five weeks after coming here, she was very much occupied about the house, and seemed rather weary and care-worn. But the pressure was then over and she had leisure for her flowers and her painting, for going to the woods with the girls, and for taking her favorite drives with me. She spoke repeatedly of you and other friends. On the 23rd of July I started for Monmouth Beach. The week preceding this little journey was one of the happiest of our married life. No words can tell how sweet and loving and bright—in a word, how just like herself—she was. The impassion of that week accompanied me to the seaside and continued with me during my whole stay there. As day after day I sat looking out upon the ocean, or walked alone up and down the shore, she was still in all my thoughts. The noise of the breakers, the boundless expanse of waters, the passing ships, going out and coming in, recalled similar scenes long ago on the coast of Maine, before and after our marriage—scenes with which her image was indissolubly blended. Then I met old friends and found new ones, who talked to me with grateful enthusiasm of "Stepping Heavenward," "More Love to Thee, O Christ," and other of her writings. In truth, my feelings about her, while I was at Monmouth Beach, were quite peculiar and excite my wonder still. I scarcely know how to describe them. They were at times very intense, and, I had almost said, awe-struck, seemed bathed in a sweet Sabbath stillness, and to belong rather to the other world than to this of time and sense. How do you explain this? Was my spirit, perhaps, touched in some mysterious way by the coming event? Certainly, had I been warned that she was so soon to leave me, I could hardly have passed those days of absence in a mood better attuned to that in which I now think of her as forever at home with the Lord.

The following are two of her last letters:

To Mrs. Condict, Kauinfels, July 22, 1878.

To begin with the most important part of your letter. I reply that neither Mr. Prentiss or myself have ever had any sympathy with Second Adventists. All the talk about it seems to us mere speculation and probable doom to disappointment. I do not see that it is as powerful a stimulant to holiness as the uncertainty of life is. Christ may come any day but He may not come for ages but we must and *shall* die in the merest fragment of an age, and see Him as He is. It will be a day of unspeakable joy, when we meet Him here or there. I shrink from unprofitable discussion of points that, after all, can only be tested by time and events. I do not think our expecting Christ will bring Him a minute sooner, for the early church expected Him, yet He came not. There has been so much wildness in theories on this subject that I am sore when I hear new ones advanced none of these theories have proved to be correct, and I do not imagine any of them will.

I have been busy indoors, upholstering not only curtains and couches, but ever so many boxes, as our bureaus are shallow and our closets small. I made one for A. large enough for her to get into, and she uses it as she would a room, suspending objects from the sides and keeping all her artistic implements in it. I began my Bible reading last Thursday, the hottest day we have had, but there was a good attendance. My G. met with an accident from the circular saw, which alarmed and distressed me so that his father had to fan me, while the girls did what they could for G. until the doctor could be got from Factory Point. His eyebrow was cut open and his forehead gashed, but all healed wonderfully, and we have reason to be thankful that he did not lose an eye, as he was so near doing. At any time when you must have change, let me know, as there are often gaps between guests, and sometimes those we expected, fail. Mr. Prentiss is, apparently, benefited by hot weather, and is unusually well. Thanks for the needles, which will be a great comfort. Have you painted a horseshoe? I had one given me black ground and blue forget-me-nots, and hung by a blue ribbon. I am going to paint one for M. and Hatty. I feel as if I had left out something I wanted to say.

To Mrs. George Payson, Kauinfels, Aug. 1, 1878.

I am all alone in the house, this evening, and as this gives me room at the table, I am going to begin to answer your letter. George is out of town, and all the rest, including the servants, have gone to see the Mistletoe Bough. It is astonishing how slowly you get well and yet with such heat and such smells as you have in Chicago, it is yet more astonishing that you live at all. I thought it dreadful to have the thermometer stand at 90° in my bedroom, three weeks running, and to sniff a bad sniff now and then from our pond, when the water got low, but I see I was wrong. We have next to no flowers this summer white flies destroyed the roses, frost killed other things, and then the three weeks of burning heat, with no rain, finished up others. Portulacca is our rear-guard, on which we fall back, filling empty spaces with it, and I grow more fond of it every year. A good many verbenas sowed themselves, but came up too late to be of any use. We have a splendid bed of pansies, sown by a friend here.

I have not done much indoors but renovate the house, but that has been a great job. I brought up a Japanese picture book to use as a cornice in my den, but A. persuaded me to get some wallpaper, and use the pictures as a dado for the dining room. The effect is very unique and pretty. I expect George home tomorrow he has been spending a delightful week at Monmouth Beach, visiting friends. I wish I could send you some of our delicious ice cream. We have it twice a week, with the juices of what fruit is going peaches being best. We have not had much company yet. Last Saturday a friend of A.'s came and goes with her to Prout's Neck tomorrow. We do not count Hatty K. as company, but as one of us. She gets the brightest letters from Rob S., son of George. I should burst and blow up if my boys wrote as well. They have telephone and microphone on the brain, and such a bawling between the house and the mill you never heard. It is nice for us when we want meal, or to have a horse harnessed. Have you heard of the chair, with a fan each side that fans you twenty-five minutes from just seating yourself in it? It must be delightful, especially to invalids, and ought to prolong life for them…. The clock is striking nine, my hour for fleeing to get ready for bed, but none of the angels have come home from the Mistletoe Bough, and so I suppose I shall have to make haste slowly in undressing. Love to all.

Aug. 3rd.—I am delighted that you enjoyed the serge so much I knew you would. I forgot to answer your question about books. Have you read "Noblesse Oblige"? We admire it extremely. There are two works by this title one poor. I read "Les Miserables" last winter, and got greatly interested in it whether there is a good English translation, I do not know. "That Lass o' Lowrie's" you have probably read. I saw a Russian novel highly praised the other day "Dosea," translated from the French by Mary Neal (Sherwood) "Victor Lascar" is said to be good. I have, probably, praised "Misunderstood" to you. "Strange Adventures of a Phaeton" we liked also "The Maid of Sker" and "Off the Skelligs" its sequel is "Fated to be Free."

Two tongues are running like mill-clappers, so goodnight.

* * * * *

II.

Little Incidents and Details of her last Days on Earth. Last Visit
to the Woods. Sudden Illness. Last Bible-reading. Last Drive to
Hager-Brook. Reminiscence of a last Interview. Closing Scenes. Death.
The Burial.

Her last days on earth were now close at hand. Such days have in themselves, of necessity, no virtue above other days and yet a tender interest clings to them simply as the last. Their conjunction with death and the Life beyond seems to invest whatsoever comes to pass in them—even trifles light as air—with unwonted significance. Soon after her sudden departure, her husband noted down, for the satisfaction of absent friends, such little incidents and details as could be recalled of her last ten days on earth. The following is a part of this simple record:

Sunday, Aug. 4, 1878.— Today she went to the house of God for the last time and, as would have been her wish, had she known it was for the last time, heard me preach. There was much in both the tone and matter of the sermon that made it seem, afterwards, as if it had been written in full view of the approaching sorrow. A good deal of the day at home was spent in getting ready for her Bible-reading on the ensuing Thursday. At four o'clock in the afternoon she and the girls, M. and H., usually drove in the phaeton over to the Rev. Mr. Reed's, on the West road, to attend a neighborhood prayer meeting but today, on account of a threatening thunder-shower, they did not go. She enjoyed this little meeting very much.

Monday, Aug. 5th.—Soon after breakfast, she and the girl—"we three girls," as she used to say—started off, carrying each a basket, for the Cheney woods in quest of ferns it having been arranged that at ten o'clock I should come with the phaeton to fetch her and the baskets home. The morning, although warm, was very pleasant and all three were in high spirits. Before leaving the house, she ran up to her "den"—so she called the little room where she wrote and painted—to get something and on passing out of it through the chamber, where just then I was shaving, she suddenly stopped, and pointing at me with her forefinger, her eye and face beaming with love and full of sweet witchery, she exclaimed in a tone of pretended anger: "How dare you, sir, to be shaving in my room?" and in an instant she was gone! A minute or two later I looked after her from the window and saw her, with her two shadows, hurrying towards the woods. At the time appointed, I went for her. She awaited me sitting on the ground on the further side of the woods, near the old sugarhouse. The three baskets, all filled with beautiful ferns, were placed in the phaeton and we drove home.

The Cheney woods, as we call them, form one of the attractions of Dorset. They are quite extensive, abound in majestic sugar-maples, some of which have been "tapped," it is said, for more than sixty successive seasons, and at one point in them is a water-shed dividing into two little rivulets, one of which, after mingling with the waters of the Battenkill and the Hudson, finds its way at last into the Atlantic Ocean while the other reaches the same ocean through Pawlet River, Lake Champlain and the St. Lawrence River. These woods and our own, together with the mountain and waterfall and groves beyond Deacon Kellogg's, where she often met her old friend "Uncle Isaac," [8] were her favorite resorts.

A little while after returning home, I found her in her little room, looking well and happy, and busy with her brush. The girls, also, on reaching the house found her there. But somewhat later, without our knowledge, she went out and worked for a long time on and about the lawn. There was a breeze, but the rays of the sun were scorchingly hot and she doubtless exerted herself, as she was always tempted to do, beyond her strength. I was occupied until noon at the mill and later, in the field, watching the men cradling oats. On coming in to dinner, a little past one, I was startled not to find her at the table, "Where is mamma?" said I to M. "She is not feeling very well," M. answered, "and said she would not come down, as she did not want any dinner." I ran up-stairs, found her in her little room, and asked her what was the matter. She replied that she had been troubled with a little nausea and felt weak, but it was nothing serious. I went back to the table, but with a worried, anxious mind. Somewhat later, she lay down on the bed and the prostration became so great, that I rubbed her hands vigorously and administered hartshorn. It occurred to me at once that she had barely escaped sunstroke. After rallying from this terrible fit of exhaustion, she seemed quite like herself again, and listened with much interest while the girls read to her out of Boswell's Johnson. She was in a sweet, gentle mood all the afternoon. "I prayed this morning," she said, "that I might be a comfort today to everybody in the house."

Tuesday, Aug.6th.—She passed the day in bed feeble, but otherwise seeming still like herself. In the course of the morning we persuaded her to let Margaret, Eddy's old nurse, make her some milk-toast, which she enjoyed so much that she said, "I wish, Margaret, you were well enough to come and be our cook." M. had taken the place of our two servants, who were gone to East Dorset to a Confirmation, at which their bishop was to be present. Throughout the day, she was in a very tender, gentle mood, as she had been on the previous afternoon. She was much exercised by the sudden death of the mother of one of our servants, the news of which came while they were away. Had the case been that of a near relative, she could hardly have shown warmer sympathy, or administered consolation in a more considerate manner.

During the day there was more or less talk about the Bible reading and I begged her to give it up. We finally agreed that the girls should drive over to Mrs. Reed's and ask her to take charge of it. They did so but at Mrs. R.'s suggestion it was decided not to give up the meeting, but to convert it, if needful, into a little service of prayer and praise. This arrangement seemed to please her. Although feeling very weak, she did not appear at all depressed and was alive to everything that was going on in the room. The girls having written to a friend who was to visit us the next week, she asked if they had mentioned her illness. They both replied no—for each supposed the other had done it. "Then (said she) you had better add a postscript, telling her that I lie at the point of death."

Wednesday, Aug. 7th.—A beautiful day. She got up, put on a dressing gown, and sat most of the day in the easy chair, or rather the *sea*-chair, given us by my dear friend, Mr. Howland, when we went to Europe in 1858. She looked very lovely and we all enjoyed sitting and talking with her in her chamber. The girls arranged her hair to please their own taste, and then told her how very charming she was! She liked to be petted by them and they were never so happy as in petting and "fussing" about her. She spent an hour or two in looking over a package of old Agriculturists that had belonged to her brother-in-law Prof. Hopkins, of Williams College. She delighted in such reading, and nothing curious and interesting, or suggestive, escaped her notice. She called my attention to an article on raising tomatoes, and cut it out for me and also cut out many other articles for her own use.

Towards night, she dressed herself and came down to tea. She remained in the parlor, talking with me and the boys, and reading the paper, until the girls returned from the Wednesday evening meeting. Something had occurred to excite their mirth, and they came home in such a "gale" that she playfully rebuked them for being so light-minded. But at the same time, she could not help joining in their mirth. In truth, she was quite as much a girl as either of them and her laugh was as merry.

Thursday, Aug. 8th.—She seemed to feel much better this morning. Before getting up we talked about her Bible reading, and she asked me various questions concerning the passage that was to be its theme, namely, John xv. 27. She referred particularly to our Lord's sayings, at the beginning of the sixteenth chapter, on the subject of persecution, and told me how very strange and impressive they seemed to her, coming, as they did, in the midst of His last conversation with His disciples—a conversation so full of divine tenderness and love. This was almost the last of innumerable and never-to-be-forgotten talks, which we had had together, during more than a third of a century, upon passages of Holy Scripture.

After breakfast, she went to her workshop and painted six large titles and then went down to the piazza and painted a chair for Hatty. She also assisted the girls in watering her flowers. "She came round to the back stoop Thursday morning (one of the servants told me afterwards) and I said to her, 'Mis Prentiss, and how d'ye feel?' and she said, 'Ellen, I feel *weak*, but I shall be all right when I get my strength.'" I still felt troubled about her holding the Bible-reading and tried to dissuade her from attempting it. She had set her heart upon it, however, and said that the disappointment at giving it up would be worse than the exertion of holding it. Her preparation was all made the ladies would be there, some of them from a distance, expecting to see her, and she could not bear to lose the meeting. So I yielded. We were expecting Dr. Vincent by the afternoon train and I was to go to the station for him. Just as I was seated in the carriage and was about to start, she came out on the porch, already dressed for the Bible-reading, and with an expression of infinite sweetness, half playful and half solemn, pointing at me with her finger, said slowly: "*You pray—one—little—prayer for me.*" Never shall I forget that arch expression—so loving, so spiritual, and yet so stamped with marks of suffering—the peculiar tones of her voice, or that dear little gesture!

Of her last Bible reading, the following brief account is prepared from the recollections kindly furnished me by several of the ladies who were present:

HER LAST BIBLE READING. There was something very impressive in Mrs. Prentiss' Bible-readings. She seemed not unlike her gifted father in the power she possessed of captivating those who heard her. Her manner was perfectly natural, quiet, and even shy it evidently cost her considerable effort to speak in the presence of so many listeners. She rarely looked round or even looked up but a sort of magnetic influence attracted every eye to *her* and held all our hearts in breathless attention. Her style was entirely conversational her sentences were short, clear as crystal, full of happy turns, and always fresh and to the point. The tones of her voice were peculiar I scarcely know how to describe them they had such a fine, subtle, *womanly* quality, were touched—especially at this last reading—with such tenderness and depth of feeling I only know that as we heard them, it was almost as if we were listening to the voice of an angel! And they are, I am sure, echoing still in all our memories.

The first glance at her, as she entered the room, a little before three o'clock on the 8th of August, showed that she was not well. Her eyes were unusually bright, but the marks of recent or approaching illness were stamped upon her countenance. It was lighted up, indeed, with even unwonted animation and spiritual beauty but it had also a pale and wearied look. The reading was usually opened with a silent prayer and closed with two or three short oral prayers. The subject this afternoon was the last verse of the fifteenth chapter of the Gospel according to John: *And ye also shall bear witness, because ye have been with me from the beginning.* Witnessing for Christ, this was her theme. She began by giving a variety of Scripture references illustrative of the nature and different forms of Christian witness bearing. It was her custom always to unfold the topic of the reading, and to verify her own views of it, by copious and carefully prepared citations from the Word of God. A Bible-reading, as she conducted it, was not merely a study of a text, or passage of Scripture, by itself, but study of it in its vital relations to the whole teaching of the Bible on the subject in hand. In the present instance, her references were all written out and were so numerous and so skillfully arranged that they must have cost her no little labor. Feeling, apparently, too feeble to read them herself, she turned to her daughter, who sat by her mother's side, and requested her to do it.

After the references had been given and the passages read, she went on to express her own thoughts on the subject. And, surely, had she been fully conscious that this was the last opportunity she would ever have of thus bearing witness for Christ, her words could not have been more happily chosen. Would that they could be recalled just as they issued from her own lips! But it is not possible so to recall them. One might as well try to reproduce the sunset scene on the evening of her burial. For even if the exact words could be repeated, who could bring back again her tender, loving accents, or that strange earnestness and "unction from the Holy One" with which they were uttered? Or who could bring back again the awe-struck, responsive emotions that thrilled our hearts? The simplest outline of this farewell talk is all that is now practicable. Had we known what was coming, our memories would, no doubt, have been rendered thereby sevenfold more retentive, and little that fell from her lips would have been lost.

Her first point was the great variety of ways in which we can bear witness for Christ. We can do it in private as well as in public and it is in the private spheres and familiar daily intercourse of life that most of us are called to give this testimony, and to give it by manifesting in this intercourse and in these retired spheres the spirit of our Master. What an opportunity does the family, for example, afford for constant and most effective witness bearing! How a mother may honor Christ in what she says to her children about Him and especially by the manner in which she fulfils her every-day home duties! How a wife may thus testify of Christ to her worldly, unconverted husband! And here she spoke of one form of *public* testimony, which everybody might and ought to give. "I cannot (she said) see all the faces in this room but there may be those here who have never confessed Christ before men by uniting with His visible church. Let me tell any such who may be present that they are grieving their Savior by refusing to give Him this testimony of their love and devotion."

In referring to this subject, she remarked that young persons, after having united with the church, sometimes felt greatly disheartened and thought themselves the worst Christians in the world. But this was often a very wrong feeling. Their sense of their own weakness and unworthiness might come from the Holy Comforter and we should be very careful how we treat Him. His influence is a very tender, sacred thing, and, like the sensitive plant, recoils at the touch of a rude hand. I have wanted, she said, to speak *cheerful, comforting* words to you today. It was the particular desire of my husband this morning that I should do so. He thought that young Christians, especially, needed much encouragement on this point. It was a great thing to lead them to feel that they could please their Master and be witnesses for Him in quiet, simple ways, and that, too, every day of their lives. Our Lord, to be sure, does not really *need* our services. He could quite easily dispense with them. But He lets us work for Him somewhat as a mother lets her little child do things for her—not because she needs the child's help, but because she loves to see the child trying to please her. "And yet, Mrs. Prentiss (asked one of the ladies), does there not come a time when the child is really of service to the mother?" "I thank you for the suggestion (she replied) I left my remark incomplete. Yes, it is true such a time does come. And so, in a certain sense, it may be said, perhaps, that God needs the services of His children. But how easily He can dispense with the best and most useful of them! One may seem to have a great task to perform in the service of the Master, but in the midst of it, he is taken away, and, while he is missed, the work of God goes right on. God does not see such a difference as we do, she said, between what we call great and small services rendered to Him. A cup of cold water given in Christ's name, if that is all one can give, is just as acceptable as the richest offering and so is a teaspoonful, if one has no more to give. Christ loves to be loved and the smallest testimony of real love is most pleasing to Him. And love shown to one of His suffering disciples He regards as love to Himself. So a little child, just carrying a flower to some poor invalid, may thus do Christ honor and become more endeared to Him. There is no one, old or young, who has not the power of blessing other souls. We all have far more influence, both for good and evil, than we dream of."

In the course of her talk, she alluded to the trials of life and the shortness of them at the longest. We are all passing away, one after another. Our intimate friends will mourn for us when we are gone, but the world will move on just the same. And we should not allow ourselves to be troubled lest when our time comes we may be afraid to die. Dying grace is not usually given until it is needed. Death to the disciple of Jesus is only stepping from one room to another and far better room of our Father's house. And how little all the sorrows of the way will seem to us when we get to our home above! I suppose St. Paul, amidst the bliss of heaven, fairly *laughs* at the thought of what he suffered for Christ in this brief moment of time. And as she said this, she gently waved her hand in the way of emphasis. No one of us who saw it will soon forget that little gesture!

In one part of her remarks, she cautioned us against hasty and harsh judgments. We should cover with our charity the faults and imperfections of those about us, as nature hide with her mossy covering the unsightly stone.

She referred to the case of children: a child often has a sweet disposition until five or six years of age and then becomes very irritable and cross, causing the parents much anxiety—and, perhaps, much impatience. And yet it may not be the child's fault at all but only the effect of ill health, too much study and confinement, or pure mismanagement. A large portion of the disobedience and wrong temper of children comes from improper food or loss of sleep, or something of that sort. And it is not cross and fretful *children* alone that need to be judged tenderly. A consumptive friend of hers, rendered nervous and weak by long sickness, upon being asked one morning, as usual, about her health, replied: "Do not ask me again—*I feel as if I could throw this chair at you.*" Now I do not think, said Mrs. Prentiss, that this speech was a sin in the sight of God. He saw in it nothing but the poor invalid's irritable nerves, God judges us according to the thoughts and intentions of the heart and we ought, as far as possible, to judge each other in the same way. And when we ourselves are the ones really at fault, we ought to confess it. I never shall forget how humiliated I felt when my mother once came to me and asked my forgiveness—but I loved her ten times as much for it.

Prayer was another point touched upon in this last Bible-reading. She almost always had something fresh and striking to say about prayer. It was one of her favorite topics. I recall two or three of her remarks at this time. "Always move the lips in prayer. It helps to keep one's thoughts from wandering." "A mother can pray with a sick child on her lap more acceptably than to leave it alone in order to go and pray by herself." "Accustom yourself to turn all your wants, cares, and trials into prayer. If anything troubled or annoyed my mother, she went straight to the 'spare room,' no matter how cold the weather, and we children knew it was to pray. I shall never forget its influence over me." "When a question as to duty comes up, I think we can soon settle it in this way: 'Am I living near to Christ? Am I seeking His guidance? Am I renouncing self in what I undertake to do for Him?' If we can say yes to these questions, we may safely go into any path where duty lies." "We never dread to hear people pray who pray truly and in the Spirit. They may be unlearned. They may be intellectually weak. But if they pray habitually in the closet, they will edify out of it."

Such is a poor, meager account of this last precious Bible-reading. Possibly some of the things here recorded belonged to previous readings—though Mrs. Prentiss occasionally repeated remarks on points to which she attached special importance. "Some good (she said) will come of these meetings, I feel sure. It is impossible that you should take so many pains, and some of you put yourselves to so much inconvenience, in order to come here and study together God's Word—and His blessing not follow." The blessing has already followed, good measure, pressed down and running over, and it will continue to follow in days to come especially the blessings of this last meeting, when, in a strain so sweet and tender—as though she had a new glimpse of heaven and the heart of God—our beloved and now sainted teacher urged us to bear witness for Christ and showed us so plainly how to do it.

At the close of the meeting, she looked very pale and seemed much exhausted. "You are ill, Mrs. Prentiss," said one of the ladies, distressed by her appearance. "Yes," she said, "I *am*." Still, it seemed a great pleasure to her to have met us once more. Nor can I help thinking that, even if she herself had no presentiment of what was coming, she was yet led of the Spirit, the blessed Comforter, to hold this last Bible reading. It was itself just such a testimony for Christ as fitly crowned her consecrated and beautiful life.

Upon my return from the station with Dr. Vincent she met us on the porch, bade him welcome to Dorset, told him with what extraordinary care the girls had made ready his room, and appeared in excellent spirits all the rest of the day. While at tea, she expressed to Dr. V. our regret that Dr. Poor could not have made his visit at the same time although, to be sure, they might, if together, have "brought the house down" upon our heads by the explosions of their mirth. She then related some amusing anecdotes of a queer, crotchety old domestic of ours in New Bedford a third of a century ago, and of her delight when Dr. Poor (then settled at Fair Haven, opposite New Bedford) got married, because "*now*, it was to be hoped, he would stay at home with his wife and not be coming over all the time and drinking up our tea!"

On my asking her about the Bible-reading, she said she got through with it very well, expressed surprise at the large attendance, and spoke of the deep interest manifested. After tea she sat with us in the parlor for some time and then, kissing M. goodnight, omitted Hatty and the boys (a most unusual thing), remarking, as she left for her chamber, "Well, I'm not going to kiss all this roomful."

Friday, Aug. 9th—A severe thunderstorm had set in early last night and continued at short intervals throughout the day. She was very anxious that Dr. Vincent should enjoy his visit, and on his account was disturbed by the weather otherwise, a thunderstorm seemed to exhilarate her, as is said to have been the case with her father. She spent most of Friday in her "den," finishing a little picture and chatting from time to time with the girls who were busy in the adjoining room. Dr. Vincent and I sat a part of the forenoon on the piazza under her window and whiled away the time, he in telling and I in listening to any number of amusing stories. She called the attention of M. and H. to our unclerical behavior: "Just hear those doctors of divinity giggling like two schoolgirls!" But nobody enjoyed more an amusing story, or told one with more zest than she did herself.

I forget whether it was on Friday, or an earlier day, that she showed me a remarkable letter she had received, during my absence at the seaside, from London. It was written by a young wife and mother nearly related to two of the most honored families of England, and sought her counsel in reference to certain questions of duty that had grown out of special domestic trials. "Stepping Heavenward," the writer said, had formed an era in her religious life she had read it through *from fifty to sixty times* it had its place by the side of her Bible and no words could express the good it had done her, or the comfort she had derived from its pages. "The Home at Greylock" had also been of great help to her as a wife and mother and she could not but hope that one whose books had been such a blessing to her, might be able to render her still greater and more direct aid by personal counsel. The letter, which was beautifully written and was full of the most grateful feelings, appealed very strongly to her sympathy. But it was never answered.

Saturday, Aug. 10th—She had a tolerable night, but on coming down to breakfast said, in reply to Dr. Vincent's question, How she felt? "I feel like bursting out crying." After prayers, however, when the plans for the day were arranged and a drive to Hager brook—a picturesque mountain glen and waterfall—was made the order of the forenoon, she proposed to go with us. I had almost feared to suggest it, and yet was greatly relieved to find that she felt able to take the ride. It was decided, therefore, that she, Hatty K., Dr. Vincent and I should form the party. As we drove toward the village, I noticed that Dr. Wyman was just stopping at our next neighbor's. Dr. Hemenway, our old physician, had removed to St. Paul's, and Dr. W. had taken his place. I was rejoiced to see him, both on her account and my own. I had not been well myself during the week, and although I had repeatedly proposed to call in the doctor for her, she stoutly refused. So, after getting a prescription for myself, I said, "And now, doctor, I want you to do something for my wife," relating to him her ill turn on Monday. "Certainly (the doctor replied) she needs some *arsenicum*," which he gave her, promising to call and see us on the next Monday. As we rode on Dr. Vincent suggested, laughingly, what a strange story might be based upon Dr. W.'s prescription. "I might report, for example, that I myself saw the author of 'Stepping Heavenward' eating arsenic!" She joined heartily in the laugh and during all the rest of the drive conversed with great animation. She related several anecdotes of her early life, talked with admiration of the writings and genius of Mrs. Stowe—one of whose New England stories she had just been reading—and seemed exactly like herself. Upon reaching the brook in East Rupert and starting with Dr. Vincent for the glen, I said to her, "Now do not walk off out of sight, where I cannot see you when we come back." "Oh yes, I shall," she replied in her pleasant way.

"After we were left alone that Saturday morning (Hatty writes) Mrs. Prentiss gathered quite a bunch of the wild ageratum, and then dug up the roots of three wild clematis vines with her scissors. She then called my attention to the thimbleberry bushes along the edge of the brook, admiring the foliage of the plant and expressing the determination to have one or more in her garden next year."

On coming down from the glen I found her sitting on the ground near the brook. Taking her by the hand—for she seemed very tired—I helped her to rise and walked back with her toward the carriage. Just before reaching the road, she saw some clusters of clematis on the side of the brook, which at her desire I gathered. It was the last service of the kind ever performed for her, and I am so thankful that no hands but mine were privileged to perform it! During the drive home she said almost nothing and was, evidently, feeling very much wearied. We returned by the West road and on passing in at our gate I observed that Dr. Wyman's gig was still in front of Miss Kent's. "Why, Lizzy, Dr. Wyman is still here," said I. "Then, I would like to see him now rather than wait till Monday," she said, to my surprise. I went immediately and asked him to call. It was, I think, between eleven and twelve o'clock. He came very soon and she received him in the parlor. I noticed at once that she was extremely nervous and agitated, while explaining to him her symptoms and not being able to recall some point, she remarked that her mind had been much confused all the week. Just then, she rose hastily, excused herself, and went up to her room. "*She is very ill* (said the doctor, turning to me) and must go to bed instantly." While he was preparing her medicines Judge M. and family from New York, who were sojourning at Manchester, called but learning of her illness, soon left. Later in the day I told her who had called and how much Mrs. M. and the young ladies admired her flowers, especially the portulacas. She seemed pleased and said to me, "You had better, then, prepare two little boxes of portulacas and send them over to Mrs. M. to keep in her windows while she stays at the Equinox House." A few days after her death I did so and received a touching note of thanks from Mrs. M.

As the doctor directed, she at once took to her bed. For an hour or two, her prostration was extreme, and she nearly fainted. Her head shook and her condition verged on a collapse. I rubbed her hands vigorously, gave her a restorative, and gradually her strength returned. In speaking of the attack, she said the sense of weakness was so terrible that she would gladly have died on the spot. In the course of the afternoon, however, she was so much easier that the girls read to her again out of Boswell's Johnson and she seemed to listen with all the old interest. It pleased her greatly to have them read to her and she loved to talk with them about the books read and especially to discuss the characters depicted in any of them.

Toward evening, George brought in some trout, which he had caught for her out of our brook. Her appetite was exceedingly poor, but she was very fond of trout and G. often caught a little mess for her supper. Our brook never seemed so dear to me, nor did its rippling music ever sound so sweet, as when I did the same thing, before he came home from Princeton and took the privilege out of my hands. When he brought in the trout, Ellen went to his mother's chamber and asked if they should not be kept for breakfast? "No, they are very nice and you had better have them for supper." "Shan't I save some for your breakfast?" asked Ellen, knowing how fond she was of them. "No," said she, "the doctor says I must take nothing but beef-tea." "And d'ye feel better, Mis' Prentiss?" continued Ellen. "Oh I feel better, Ellen, but I'm very weak—I shall be all right in a few days."

After tea, she insisted on sending for Mrs. Sarah C. Mitchell, of
Philadelphia, whom she had been unable to see on the previous Monday.
Mrs. M. was the last person out of the family, with whom she conversed,
excepting the doctors and nurse. [9]

Sunday, Aug. 11th.—She slept better than I feared, but awoke very feeble, taking no nourishment except a little beef tea. She lay quiet a part of the time but the quiet intervals grew shorter and were followed by most distressing attacks. M. and I sat by her bed, but could do nothing to relieve her. My fears had now become thoroughly aroused and I awaited the arrival of the doctor with the most intense anxiety. Hour after hour of the morning, however, passed slowly away and he did not come. At length a messenger brought word from the "West road," where he had been called at midnight, that an urgent telegram had summoned him to Arlington and that he should not be able to reach Dorset before one or two o'clock P.M. The anguish of the suspense during the next three or four hours was something dreadful. When the bell rang for church, she desired that M. should go, as Dr. Vincent was to preach, and it would give a little relief from the strain that was upon her.

Soon after M. had left, during an interval of comparative ease, she fixed her eyes upon me with a most tender, loving expression, and in a sort of beseeching tone, said, "Darling, do not you think you could ask the Lord to let me go?" Perceiving, no doubt, how the question affected me, she went on to give some reasons for wishing to go. She spoke very slowly, in the most natural, simple way, and yet with an indescribable earnestness of look and voice, as if aware that she was uttering her dying words. I cannot recall all that she said, but its substance, and some of the exact expressions, are indelibly impressed upon my memory. For my and the children's sake she had been willing and even desired to live and for several years had made extraordinary efforts to keep up, although much of the time the burden of ill-health, as I well knew, had been well-nigh insupportable. So far as this world was concerned, few persons in it had such reasons for wishing to live, or so much to render life attractive. But the feeling in her heart had become overpowering that no earthly happiness, no interest, no distraction, could any longer satisfy her, or give her content, away from Christ and she longed to be with Him, where He is. During the past three months especially, she had passed through very unusual exercises of mind with reference to this subject and it seemed to her as if she had now reached a point beyond which she could not go. She evidently had in view the dreadful *sleeplessness*, to which she had been so in bondage for a quarter of a century, whose grasp had become more and more relentless, and the effects of which upon her nervous system were such as words can hardly describe. No human being but myself had any conception of her suffering, both physical and mental, from this cause.

To return to her conversation… In answer to a question which I put to her later, about her view of heaven and of the relation of the saints in glory to their old friends there and here, she replied, in substance, that to her view *heaven is being with Christ and to be with Christ is heaven*. By this she did not mean, I am sure, to imply any doubt respecting the immortality of Christian love and friendship, or that our individual human affections will survive the grave. Often had she delighted herself in the thought of meeting her sainted father and mother in heaven, of meeting there Eddy and Bessie and other dear ones who had gone before and certain I am, too, she believed that those who are gone before retain their peculiar interest in those who are toiling after, only her mind was so absorbed in the thought of the presence and beatific vision of Christ in His glory that, for the moment, it was lost to everything else.

She then said that, in the event of her death, she would like to be buried in Dorset, where we could easily visit her grave. "But I do not expect to go now," she added. This meant, as I interpret it, that she regarded so speedy a departure to be with Christ as something *too good to be true*. Repeatedly, when very ill, she had thought herself on the verge of heaven and had been called back to earth, and she feared it would be so now.

Hardly had this never-to-be-forgotten conversation come to a close when her feet entered "the swelling of Jordan," and found no rest until they walked the "sweet fields beyond." Her disease (gastro-enteritis) returned with great violence the medical appliances seemed to have little or no effect and the paroxysms of pain were excruciating. A chill, also, began to creep over her. About two o'clock, to my inexpressible relief, the doctor arrived. Her first thought was that he should rest a little and that some ice cream should be brought to him. In answer to his inquiries, she told him that she had never known agony such as she had endured that forenoon, and he immediately applied remedies adapted to the case. But they afforded only temporary relief. A terrible restlessness seized upon her and would not let go its hold. Towards evening, she got into the sea-chair, and remained in it near the open window until morning. On leaving for the night, Dr. Wyman entrusted her to the care of Dr. Slocum, who had recently come to Dorset. Dr. S. remained with her all night and was indefatigable in trying to alleviate her sufferings. "How kind he is!" she said to me once when he had left the room. M. sat up with me till towards morning and assisted in giving the medicines. Her distress could only be assuaged by inhaling chloroform every few minutes and by the constant use of ice. As from time to time, going down for the ice, I stepped out on the piazza, the scene that met my eye was in strange contrast to the one I had just left. Within the sick chamber, it was a night dark with suffering and anxiety as the hours passed slowly away, my heart almost died in the shadow of the coming event all was gloom and agitation except the sweet patience of the sufferer. But the beauty and stillness of the night out of doors was something marvelous. The light of the great harvest moon was like the light of the sun. It flooded hills and valley with its splendor. The outlines of each mountain, of every tree, and of all visible objects, far or near, were as distinct as those of the stars, or of the moon itself. As I stood and gazed upon the infinite beauty of the scene, I felt, as never in my life before, how helpless is Nature in the presence of a great trouble. The beauty of the night was fully matched by that of the morning. As the first rays of the sun crossed the mountains and shone down upon the valley, I said to myself, even while my heart was racked with anxious foreboding—"How wonderful! How wonderful!"

Monday, Aug. 12th.—For some hours she seemed much more comfortable, and, in the course of the morning, of her own accord, was removed from the chair to the bed. "On Monday morning (writes Dr. Wyman) I found her with temperature nearly normal, pulse less than 100, and other symptoms improved. This gave us hope that the worst was passed, but it was only the lull before the storm." She was for the most part quiet and took little notice of anything that was going on. During the forenoon, M. tried to get some rest in the sea-chair by the window, while Hatty kept her place by the bed. Several times Lizzy looked round the room as if in quest of some one. Hatty perceiving this and guessing what it meant, stepped aside (she was between the bed and the chair so as to intercept the view), when she fixed her eyes upon M. and rested as if she had found what she sought. Having been up most of the night, I also tried to get a little rest in another room, and later went out in search of a nurse and engaged an excellent one, Mrs. C., who came early in the afternoon.

Notwithstanding my deep anxiety, I was deceived by the more favorable symptoms, and did not allow myself, during the day, to think she would not recover. In the early evening, I wrote to A., who was absent, in Maine:

I am sorry to say that your mother had a very trying day yesterday and has been extremely weak and exhausted today.... Nervous prostration appears to be the great trouble. She has rested quietly much of the time today and the medicines seem to be doing their work and in a couple of days, I trust, she may be greatly improved. You know how these ill turns upset her and how quickly she often rallies from them. She is very anxious you should not shorten your visit on her account.

Soon after this letter was written, the whole aspect of the case suddenly changed. The unfavorable symptoms had returned with renewed violence. Dr. W. asked her, during one of the paroxysms, about the pain. She answered that it was not a pain—it was a distress, an *agony*. But from first to last she never uttered a groan—not during the sharpest paroxysms of distress. She seemed to say to herself, in the words of two favorite German mottoes, which she had illumined and placed on the wall over her bed, *Geduld, Mein Herz!* (Patience, My Heart!)—*Stille, Mein Wille!* (Still, My Will!) "The patient and uncomplaining manner," writes Dr. Wyman, "in which the most agonizing pains which it has ever been my lot to witness were borne—with no repining, no murmur, no fretfulness, but quiet, peaceful submission to endure and suffer—will not soon be forgotten." At eleven o'clock, when the doctor left, I sent the nurse away for a couple of hours rest and took her place by the sickbed. Lizzy, who had already begun to feel the effects of the morphine, lay motionless and breathed somewhat heavily, but not alarmingly so.

Tuesday, Aug. 13th.—Shortly after one o'clock I called the nurse and, directing her to summon me at once in the event of any change, retired to the greenroom for a little rest. The girls had been persuaded before the doctor left, to throw themselves on their bed. Everything was quiet until about three o'clock, when Hatty knocked at my door with a message from the nurse. I hurried down and saw at the first glance as I entered the room, that a great change had taken place. It seemed as if I heard the crack of doom and that the world was of a sudden going to pieces. I went to G.'s room, woke him, told him what I feared, and desired him to go for Dr. Slocum as quickly as possible. He was dressed in an instant, as it were, and gone. In the meantime, I woke H., and told him his mother, I feared, was dying. When Dr. Slocum arrived, he felt her pulse, looked at her and listened to her breathing for a minute or two, and then, turning slowly to me, said, *It is death!* This was not far from four o'clock. I asked if I had better send at once for Dr. Wyman? "He can do nothing for her," was the reply, "but you had better send." I requested G. to call Albert, and tell him to go for Dr. W. as fast as possible. "I will saddle Prince and go myself," G. said and in a few minutes, he was riding rapidly towards Factory Point. I then knocked at Dr. Poor's door. Upon opening it and being told what was coming, he was so completely stunned that he could with difficulty utter a word. He had arrived the previous afternoon on the same train by which Dr. Vincent left. I had tried by telegraph to *prevent* his coming but a kind Providence so ordered it that my message reached Burlington, where he had been on a visit, just after he had started for Dorset.

The night, like that of Sunday, was as day for brightness. Never shall I forget its wondrous beauty, although it seemed only a mockery of my distress. Soon after the first rays of the sun appeared, Dr. Wyman came, but only to repeat, *It is death*. I asked him how long she might be a dying. "Perhaps several hours but she may drop away at any moment." We all gathered about her bed and watched the ebbing tide of life. The girls were already kneeling together on the left side. They never changed their posture for more than four hours they wept, but made no noise. The boys stood at the foot of the bed, deeply moved, but calm and self-possessed. The strain was fearful and yet it was relieved by blessed thoughts and consolations. Although the chamber of death, it was the chamber of peace, and a light not of earth shone down upon us all. He who was seen walking, unhurt, in the midst of the fire and whose form was like the Son of God, seemed to overshadow us with His presence.

As the end drew near, we all knelt together and my old friend, Dr. Poor, commended the departing spirit to God and invoked for us, who were about to be so heavily bereaved, the solace and support of the blessed Comforter.... The breathing had now grown slower and less convulsive, and at length became gentle almost like that of one asleep the distressed look changed into a look of sweet repose the eyes shut the lips closed and the whole scene recalled her own lines:

> Oh, where are words to tell the joy unpriced
> Of the rich heart, that breasting waves no more,
> Drifts thus to shore,
> Laden with peace and tending unto Christ!

About half-past seven it became evident that the mortal struggle was on the point of ending. For several minutes, we could scarcely tell whether she still lived or not and at twenty minutes before eight, she drew one long breath and all was over.

Again we knelt together, and in our behalf Dr. Poor gave thanks to Almighty God for the blessed saint now at rest in Him—and for all she had been to us and all she had done for Him, through the grace of Christ her Savior.

The following account of the burial was written by the Rev. Dr. Vincent and appeared in the New York Evangelist: DORSET, VT. *August 16, 1878.*

This lovely valley has been, for the past few days, "a valley of the shadow." It is not the least significant tribute to one so widely known as Mrs. Prentiss, that her death has affected with such real sorrow, and with such a deep sense of loss, this little rural community which has been her home during a large part of the last ten years. It would have been hard to find among all who gathered at the funeral services on Wednesday, a face which did not bear the marks of true sorrow and of tender sympathy while from the groups of sunburned farmers gathered round the door or walking towards the cemetery, were often heard the words "a great loss."

* * * * *

The funeral took place at the house on Wednesday afternoon, and was conducted by the Rev. P. S. Pratt, pastor of the old Congregational Church of Dorset assisted by Dr. Vincent, and Dr. D. W. Poor. Mr. Pratt read the twenty-third Psalm and a part of the fourteenth chapter of John, which was followed by the hymn, "O gift of gifts, O grace of faith," after which Dr. Poor delivered a most appropriate, tender, and interesting address. Dr. Vincent then offered prayer, and the hymn "Nearer, my God, to Thee," was sung, closing the services at the house. The large assemblage passed in succession by the casket, where lay such an image of perfect rest as one is rarely favored to see. All traces of struggle and pain had faded from the expressive face, and nothing was left but the sweetness of eternal repose.

It was now a little after six o'clock, and the shadows were lengthening in the valley at the close of one of those rare days of the ripe summer, which only the hill-countries develop in their perfect loveliness. The long procession moved from the house, and at the distance of about a quarter of a mile entered the little cemetery and as it mounted the slope on which was the grave, the scene was one of most pathetic beauty. Standing in the shadow of the hills which bound the valley on the east, the eye ranged southward to the long, undulating outline of the Green Mountain, coming round to the Equinox range on the west, "muffled thick" to its very crest with the green maples and pines, and still farther round to the bold hills and sloping uplands on the north. Below lay the quiet village, at our feet "God's acre," with the train of mourners winding among the white stones. Who could stand there, compassed about by the mountains, and in the shadow of that great sorrow, and not whisper the words of the Pilgrim Psalm, "I will lift up mine eyes unto the hills. Whence should help come to me? My help cometh from Jehovah, who made heaven and earth."

As the casket was borne to the grave, the setting sun, which for the last half hour had been hidden by a mass of clouds, burst out in full splendor, gilding the mountain-tops and shedding his parting rays upon the group around the tomb, the stricken family, the weeping neighbors and friends, especially the women whom for some years past she had been in the habit of meeting at her weekly Bible-reading, and some of whom had walked each week for miles along the mountain roads, through storm and heat, to drink of the living waters which flowed at her touch.

Dr. Vincent, holding in his hand a little, well-worn volume, and standing at the foot of the grave, spoke substantially as follows:

I am glad, my friends, that I am not one of those who know God only as they find Him identified with the woods and fields and streams. If this were so, I should turn from the grave of this beloved friend, and go my way in utter heart-sickness and hopelessness for Nature would but mock me today with her fullness of summer life. These forest-clad mountains, that waving grain, those woods, pulsating with the hum of insects and with the song of birds, all speak of life, while we stand here at the close of a precious and useful human life, to lay in the dust all that remains of what was so dear, and so fruitful in good.

But, thanks to God, we are not here as those who face an insoluble riddle. We believe in the Lord Jesus Christ, and in the resurrection of the dead and with this key in our hand, we stand here at the grave's mouth, and looking backward, interpret the lesson of this closed life and looking forward, gaze with hope into the future. Thus, Nature becomes our consoler instead of our mocker a type, and not a contradiction of human immortality. Thus, and only thus, do we find ourselves at the standpoint from which Christ viewed nature when He said, "Except a corn of wheat fall into the ground and die it abides alone but if it die, it bringeth forth much fruit" the standpoint from which Paul viewed nature when he wrote, "That which thou sows is not quickened except it die and that which thou sows, thou sows not that body which shall be, but bare grain, it may chance of wheat, or of some other grain but God giveth it a body as He willed, and to every seed his own body. So also is the resurrection of the dead. It is sown in corruption, it is raised in incorruption. It is sown in dishonor, it is raised in glory. It is sown in weakness, it is raised in power. It is sown a natural body, it is raised a spiritual body."

And thus too we can understand the words which I read from this little volume, the daily companion of our friend for many years, containing a passage of Scripture for every day in the year, and marked everywhere with her notes of special anniversaries and memorable incidents. Was it merely an accidental coincidence that, on the morning of the thirteenth of August, on which she exchanged earth for heaven, the passage for the day was, "I heard a voice from heaven saying unto me, Write, Blessed are the dead which die in the Lord, from henceforth, yea, saith the Spirit, that they may rest from their labors, and their works do follow them."

There are two thoughts in this verse that seem to me to be fraught with comfort and hope to us as we gather round this grave. There is the thought of rest. "They rest from their labors." Bethink you of the long life marked by the discipline of sorrow, and by those unwearied labors for others. Bethink you of the racking agony of the last two days and how blessed, how soothing the contrast introduced by the words—"She rests from her labors." Still is the busy hand at rest the active brain completed the discipline the pain ended forever.

The other thought is that her work is not done, so far as its results are concerned. "Their works do follow them." Think you that because she will no longer meet you in her weekly Bible-readings, because her pen will no more invite the thoughts which have made so many patient under life's burdens, and helped so many to make of their burdens steps on which to mount heavenward—think you her work is ended? Nay. Go into yonder field, and pluck a single head of wheat, and plant the grains, and you know that out of each grain which falls into the ground and dies, there shall spring up one hundred-fold. Shall you recognize so much multiplying power in a corn of wheat, and not discern the infinitely greater power of multiplication enfolded in a holy life and in a holy thought? No. Through the long years in which her mortal remains shall be quietly resting beneath this sod, the work of her tongue and pen shall be reproducing itself in new forms of power, of faith, and of patience.

And yet we seem to want something more than these two thoughts give us. It does not satisfy us to contemplate only rest from labor and the perpetuated fruits of labor. And that something this same little volume gives us in the words appointed for this day, on which we commit her mortal part to the grave: "For God is not unrighteous to forget your work and labor of love, which ye have showed toward His name, in that ye have ministered to the saints and do minister. Be not slothful, but followers of them who, through faith and patience, inherit the promises." Here the veil is lifted, and we get the glimpse we want of her inheritance and reward in heaven. She has inherited the promises such promises as these: "If children, then heirs, heirs of God, and joint-heirs with Christ if so be that we suffer with Him, that we may be also glorified together." "They shall hunger no more, neither thirst any more, neither shall the sun light on them, nor any heat for the Lamb which is in the midst of the throne shall feed them, and shall lead them to living fountains of waters, and God shall wipe away all tears from their eyes." "They shall see His face, and His name shall be in their foreheads." "To him that overcomes will I grant to sit with me in my throne, even as I also overcame, and am set down with my Father in His throne."

Thus, we commit this mortal body to the ground in hope, and with assurances of victory. Oh, it is one of the most wonderful of facts, that at the grave's very portal, amid all the tears and desolation which death brings, we can stand and sing hymns of triumph—even that song which, from the morning when the angels met Mary at the Lord's empty sepulcher, has been sounding over the graves of the dead in Christ—"O death, where is thy sting? O grave, where is thy victory? The sting of death is sin and the strength of sin is the law but thanks be to God, who giveth us the victory through our Lord Jesus Christ."

How sweet, how impressive, is this scene! No wonder that we linger here while Nature, at this evening hour, speaks to us so tenderly and beautifully of rest. Even as yonder clouds break from the setting sun, and are tinged with glory by its parting beams, so our sorrow is illumined by this truth of the Resurrection. There is no terror in death, and relieved by such a faith and hope, our thoughts are all of peace, and flow naturally into the mould of those familiar lines:

"So fades a summer cloud away,
So sinks the gale when storms are o'er,
So gently shuts the eye of day,
So dies a wave along the shore."

But this scene is adapted also to kindle aspiration in our hearts— aspiration to be followers of them who, through faith and patience, inherit the promises. Her victory over death is the victory of love to Christ and that same victory may be yours through the same Christ in whose name she conquered. Shall we not pray that His love may be shed abroad in all our hearts in richer measure? And can we better frame that prayer than in those lines that she wrote out of her own heart? Let us then sing

MORE LOVE TO THEE, O CHRIST.

More love, O Christ, to Thee!
Hear Thou the prayer I make
On bended knee:
This is my earnest plea,—
More love, O Christ, to Thee!
More love, O Christ, to Thee!
More love to Thee.
Once earthly joy I craved,
Sought peace and rest
Now Thee alone I seek
Give what is best!
This all my prayer shall be,—
More love, O Christ, to Thee!
More love to Thee.
Let sorrow do its work,
Send grief and pain
Sweet are Thy messengers,
Sweet their refrain,
When they can sing with me
More love, O Christ, to Thee!
More love to Thee.
Then shall my latest breath
Whisper Thy praise!
This be the parting cry
My heart shall raise,

> This still its prayer shall be,
> More love, O Christ, to Thee!
> More love to Thee!

After the singing of these words, Mr. Pratt, according to the old country custom, returned thanks to the assembled friends in the name of the family, for their sympathy and aid in the burial of their dead. The several members of the household each laid a floral offering upon the casket lid, and the body was lowered into the grave. Dr. Vincent uttered the solemn words of committal to the dust, and Dr. Poor pronounced the parting blessing in the words, "The God of peace who brought again from the dead our Lord Jesus, that Great Shepherd of the sheep, through the blood of the Everlasting Covenant, make you perfect in every good work to do His will, working in you that which is well-pleasing in His sight, through Jesus Christ, to whom be glory forever and ever. Amen."

Thus, the valley of the shadow has been irradiated. To those who have been permitted to participate in these closing scenes, it has seemed like standing at heaven's gate. The valley of the shadow has become a transfiguration mountain, where we have seen the Lord.

* * * * *

Hardly had the news of her death left Dorset when there began to pour in upon its stricken household a stream of the tenderest Christian sympathy nor did the stream cease until it had brought loving messages from the remotest parts of the land. Her friends seemed overcome with special wonder that she could have died, so vividly was she associated in their thoughts with life and sunlight. For months, too, after the return of the family to their city home, letters from far and near continued to bear witness to the mingled emotions of sorrow and of thanksgiving excited by her sudden departure from earth—sorrow for a great personal loss thanksgiving that she had gone to be forever with the Lord. A little volume of selections from these varied testimonies would form a very touching and precious tribute to her memory.

"The human heart," to use her own words, "was made by so delicate, so cunning a hand that it needs less than a breath to put it out of tune and an invisible touch, known only to its own consciousness, may set all its silvery bells to ringing out a joyous chime. Happy he, thrice blessed she, who is striving to hush its discords and to awaken its harmonies by never so imperceptible a motion!" Surely, the triple benediction belonged to her. Already tens of thousands, both young and old, who never saw her face, but have been aided and cheered by her writings, gladly call her "thrice blessed." May this story of her life serve to increase their number and so to render her name dearer still. Above all, may it help to inspire some other souls with her own impassioned and adoring love to our Lord Jesus Christ.

[1] She was specially touched by the sudden decease of Mrs. Harriet Woolsey Hodge, of Philadelphia, to whom both for her mother's and her own sake she was warmly attached.

[2] J. Cleveland Cady, the distinguished architect.

[3] Mrs. Antoinette Donaghe died at Staunton, Va., April 14, 1882. Her last years were passed amid great bodily sufferings, which she bore with the patience of a saint. She was a woman of uncommon excellence, a true Christian lady, and much endeared to a wide circle of friends in New Haven, New York, and elsewhere. Her husband, Mr. James Donaghe, a most worthy man, for many years a prominent citizen of New Haven, died on the 1st of January, 1878. He and Mrs. Donaghe were among the original members of the Church of the Covenant.

[4] The book alluded to is Letters of Thomas Erskine of Linlathen. From 1800 till 1840. Edited by Dr. Hanna, and republished by G. P. Putnam's Sons. The Duchess de Broglie was born in Paris, in 1797, and died in September, 1838, at the age of forty-one. She was the only daughter of the celebrated Madame de Stael. Some pleasant glimpses of her are given in the Life, Letters, and Journals of George Ticknor. Vol. I., pp. 128-139. Vol. II., pp. 103-139.

[5] The portrait in this volume is from a drawing by Miss Crocker, engraved by A. H. Ritchie. Miss C., after pursuing her studies for some time in Paris, has opened a studio in New York.

[6] In this letter, she told me how much good Stepping Heavenward had done her and how sorry she felt on hearing of Mrs. P.'s death, that she had never written, as she longed to do, to thank her for it. "Dear soul! (she added) perhaps she knows now how many hearts she has lifted up and comforted by her wonderful words."—*From a letter of Mrs. W.*

[7] Mr. Washburn died on Sunday, the 18th of September, 1881, aged 80 years. He was born in Farmington, Conn. His father, the Rev. Joseph Washburn, pastor of the Congregational Church in F., was cut off in the prime of a beautiful and saintly manhood. He inherited some of his father's most attractive traits and was a model of Christian fidelity and uprightness. In a notice which appeared in the New York Evangelist, shortly after his death, President Porter, of Yale College, whose father succeeded the Rev. Mr. Washburn as pastor of the church in Farmington, thus refers to his life at Wildwood: "Some twenty years since he retired for a part of eight years to the singularly beautiful

house which was selected and prepared by the taste of himself and wife, near East River, a district in Madison, which he has for several years made his permanent residence. His life was singularly even in its course and happy in its allotments a blessing to himself and a blessing to the world. His memory will long be cherished by the many who knew him as one whom to know was to love and honor."

[8] Mr. Isaac Farwell, or "Uncle Isaac," as everybody called him, was the most remarkable man in Dorset. He died in 1881 in the 102nd year of his age. His centennial was celebrated on the 14th of July, 1879 the whole town joining in it. He was full of interest in life, retained his mental powers unimpaired, and would relate incidents that occurred in the last century, as if they had just happened. Mrs. Prentiss was fond of meeting him: and after her departure he delighted to recall his talks with her and to tell where he had seen her creeping through fences, laden with rustic trophies, as she and her daughter came home from their tramps in the fields and over the hills.

[9] The following is an extract from a letter of Mrs. M. giving an account of the interview: It was of her I thought, as an hour before sunset, on that day, I passed through the grounds to the door of her beautiful home. I thought of her as I had seen her busy at work among her flowers on the morning of the day when the fatal illness began, wearing a straw hat, with broad brim to protect her from the heat of the sun. Several of her family were standing around her, and the pleasant picture we saw as we drove by the lovely lawn is fresh and green in my memory now. Once, after this, I had seen her, at our last precious Bible-reading (though little thought we then it would be our last), when she so earnestly urged us to be true "witnesses" for our Master and Lord and gently bade us God-speed, "*encouraging*" us also, as she expressed it, "by the particular desire of my husband today," in the heavenward path. I knew that she was not quite well, and as I entered the house was invited to her chamber.

I found her attired as usual, but reclining on the bed, apparently only for quiet rest. Her greeting was warm, her eyes bright, she was very cheerful, and, I think, was not then suffering from pain. To my inquiries after her health, she replied, that she had been at first prostrated by the heat of the sun, remaining at work in it too long, with no idea of danger from the exposure "but now," she said, "I do not think much is the matter with me"—though afterwards she added, "The doctor has said something to my husband which has alarmed him about me, and he is anxious, but I cannot perceive any reason for this." We talked of many familiar things, even of home-like methods of cookery, and she kindly sent for a small manuscript receipt-book of her own to lend me, looking it over and turning down the leaves at some particular receipts which she approved, and "those were my mother's," she said of several. She spoke of her engagements and the guests she loved to entertain, adding that she thought God had given this pleasant home, surrounded by such beautiful things in nature, that others too might be made happy in enjoying them. All the time while listening to her remarks, and deeply interested in every one she made, the strong desire was in my heart to speak to her of her works, of my appreciation of their great usefulness, and how God had blessed her in permitting her to do so much to benefit others. I longed to say to her, "O had you only written the books for the little ones, 'Little Susy's Six Birthdays,' and its companions, it would have been well worth living for! Had you never written anything but 'The Flower of the Family,' it was a blessing for you to have lived! And 'Stepping Heavenward'—what a privilege to have lived to write only that volume!" I could scarcely refrain from pouring out before her the thoughts that warmed my heart, but I had been told that she preferred not to be spoken to of her works, and I refrained. Only once, when we were alone, I said, with some emotion, "I am so glad to have seen you it was because *you* were here that I wished to come to this village this was the strong attraction." ... Thus, I parted from her. I shall not look upon her again until the day when "those who sleep in Jesus shall God bring with Him."

APPENDIX

A.

The allusion is to a young officer of the navy, James Swan Thatcher—a grandson of General Knox, the friend of Washington, and a younger brother of Lieutenant, afterwards the gallant Rear Admiral, Henry Knox Thatcher. He had become deeply interested in Miss Payson, and at length solicited her hand. The story of his hopeless attachment to her, as disclosed after his death, is most touching. He would spend hours together late into the night in walking about the house, which, to borrow his brother's expression, "his love had placed on holy ground." He was a young man of singular purity and nobleness of character—"one of a thousand," to use her own words—and, although she could not accept him as a lover, she cherished for him a very cordial friendship. Not long after, he was lost at sea. In later years, she often referred to him and his tragic end with the tenderest feeling. The following is an extract from a letter of Rear Admiral Thatcher to her husband, written several months after her death and shortly before his own:

I have read with great interest your reference to my dear and only brother, James Swan Thatcher. It carried me back to one of the saddest afflictions of my life. We had both been stationed at Portland for the purpose of recruiting some of the hardy sons of Maine as seamen for the U. S. naval service. The wife of the Rev. Dr. Dwight had advised my calling upon Mrs. Payson, Cumberland Street, to obtain quarters. I did so, and with my wife removed from a noisy hotel to the quiet of that most desirable retreat. My brother made frequent visits to us, and, by invitation of Mrs. Payson, dined with us on Sundays, and passed the hours between meetings, accompanying the ladies to church in the afternoons. This led to an acquaintance between Miss Payson and himself. As they were both highly intellectual and were both "stepping heavenward," they naturally fancied each other's conversation and formed a mutual friendship. Until after my dear brother's death I never imagined that it was more than a fondness for Miss Payson's conversational gifts that induced him to call so frequently at Cumberland street.... James was unexpectedly ordered to join the U. S. schooner Grampus at Norfolk, Va., for a winter cruise on the Southern coast for relief of distressed merchant vessels. The cruise continued for some weeks without entering any port, but about the 20th of March, 1843, the Grampus appeared off the bar of Charleston, S. C., and sent in a letter-bag for mailing. That night there came on a terrible gale and the Grampus disappeared forever—no vestige of her ever having been seen. She was commanded by Lt.-Commander Albert E. Downes, a good man and a fine seaman, and who as a midshipman had sailed with me three years before in the Pacific. My brother was educated for the law, and studied his profession with the Hon. John Holmes, and, after completing his studies, became Mr. Holmes' law-partner. But he being my only brother, I was very desirous that he should obtain a commission as a purser in the navy, in order that we might be associated on duty and, at Mr. H.'s request, he was appointed by General Harrison soon after his inauguration. My brother then joined me in Portland. It is a consolation to know that he lived and died in the exercise of those Christian sentiments which were deeply instilled into his mind by the society of your angelic wife, who has preceded you to our home of rest. God grant that we may all meet there!

* * * * *

B.

S. S. PRENTISS.

One of the best informed writers on the history of the Revolutionary times and of the war for the Union thus introduces a notice of Mr. Prentiss:

Small in stature limping in gait broad-chested a high intellectual forehead manly beauty in every feature a voice of remarkable sweetness and flexibility a mild but deeply penetrating eye a most retentive memory endowed with varied knowledge by extensive reading unrivaled in power of oratory frank in thought, speech, and manner patient and forbearing in temper powerfully governed by the affections, and with unbounded generosity of disposition, Sergeant Smith Prentiss was one of the most remarkable characters in our history. Living persons who were adults a generation ago will remember how the newspapers between 1835 and 1850 were filled with his praises as a citizen unapproachable in oratory, whether he spoke as an advocate at the bar, a debater in the halls of legislation, or at occasional public gatherings. [1]

S. S. Prentiss was born at Portland, Maine, September 30, 1808. While yet an infant, he was reduced by a violent fever to the verge of the grave and deprived for several years of the use of his limbs, the right leg remaining lame and feeble to the last. For his partial recovery he was indebted to the unwearied care and devotion of his mother, herself in delicate health.

During the war of 1812, his father removed to Gorham. At the academy in this town, then one of the best in Maine, Sergeant was fitted for Bowdoin College, where he was graduated in the class of 1826, at the age of seventeen. After studying law for a year with Judge Pierce, of Gorham, he set out for what was at that day the Far West, in quest of fortune. Having tarried a few months at Cincinnati, he then made his way down the Mississippi to Natchez, where he obtained the situation of tutor in a private family. Here he completed his legal studies was admitted to the bar in

June, 1829, soon afterwards became the law-partner of Gen. Felix Huston, and almost at a bound stood in the front rank of his profession in the State. "Boundless good-nature," to use the language of Dr. Lossing "keen logic quickness and aptness at repartee overflowing but kindly wit an absolute earnestness and sincerity in all he undertook to do, made him a universal favorite in every circle." In 1832, Mr. Prentiss removed to Vicksburg. John M. Chilton, a leading member of the bar of that place, thus describes his first appearance in the Circuit Court of Warren county:

There arrived, with other members of the bar, from Natchez, a limping youth in plain garb, but in whose bearing there was a manly, indeed almost a haughty, mien in whose cheek a rich glow, telling the influence of more northern climes in whose eye a keen but meditative expression and in whose voice and conversation a vivacity and originality that attracted every one, and drew around him, wherever he appeared, a knot of listeners, whose curiosity invariably yielded in a few moments to admiration and delight. There was then a buzz of inquiry, succeeded by a pleased look of friendly recognition, and a closer approach, and in most instances an introduction, to the object of this general attraction, so soon as it was told that the stranger was S. S. Prentiss, of Natchez. His fame had preceded him, and men were surprised to see only beardless youth in one whose speeches, and learning, and wit, and fine social qualities, had already rendered him at Natchez "the observed of all observers."

Society in the Southwest at that day was full of perils to young men, especially to young men of talent and generous, impressionable natures. Drinking, dueling, and gambling widely prevailed. It was a period of "flush times," and wild, reckless habits. Mr. Prentiss did not wholly escape the contagion but his faults and errors were very much exaggerated in many of the stories that found currency concerning him. One of his friends wrote after his death, "I have heard many anecdotes of him, which I considered of doubtful authority for he is a traditional character all over Mississippi—their Cid, their Wallace, their Coeur de Lion, and all the old stories are wrought over again, and annexed to his name." Another of his friends, who knew him long and intimately, the late Balie Peyton, of Tennessee, testified: "No man ever left a purer fame than Sergeant S. Prentiss, in all that constitutes high honor and spotless integrity of character. His principles remained as pure, and his heart continued as warm and fresh, as at the instant he bade farewell to his mother."

From his settlement at Vicksburg his career as a lawyer was one of remarkable success and it were hard to say in what department of his profession he most excelled, whether in the varied contests of the *Nisi Prius* courts, in an argument on a difficult question of legal construction, or in discussing a fundamental principle of jurisprudence. In 1833, at the age of 24, he appeared before the Supreme Court at Washington, where, in spite of his youth, he at once attracted the notice of Chief Justice Marshall. "I made a speech three or four hours long (he wrote to his mother) and I suppose you will say I have acquired a great deal of brass since I left home, when I tell you that I was not at all abashed or alarmed in addressing so grave a set of men as their Honors the Judges of the Supreme Court of the United States." In attending the circuit courts of Mississippi, he had experiences of the roughest sort and many a hairbreadth escape. He wrote:

I travel entirely on horseback and have had to swim, on my horse, over creeks and bayous that would astonish you Northerners. Beyond Pearl river I had to ride, and repeatedly to swim, through a swamp four miles in extent, in which the water was all the time up to the horse's belly. What do you think of that for a lawyer's life?

In the winter of 1836-7 he won the great "Commons" suit, which involved a considerable portion of the town of Vicksburg. This made him, as was supposed, one of the richest men in the State.

About this time he was induced to run for the legislature of Mississippi. He was elected, and at once took a foremost position as leader of his party.

The next summer he visited his home, and by a speech at a Whig political meeting in Portland, on the Fourth of July, he so electrified his hearers by his eloquence that he was pronounced, in the East, the most finished orator of his time as he really was. He became a candidate for a seat in Congress, and made the most remarkable electioneering canvass ever recorded. Traveling on horseback, he visited forty-five counties in a sparsely settled country. For ten weeks he traveled thirty miles each weekday, and spoke each day two hours. He had announced his engagements beforehand, and never missed one. Mississippi was a strong "Jackson State," but Mr. Prentiss carried it for the Whigs. His seat was contested by his Democratic opponent, and his speech in the House of Representatives at Washington in favor of his claim gained for him a national reputation as the greatest orator of the age. It occupied three days in its delivery. He had not spoken long before intelligence of his wonderful oratory reached the Senate chamber and drew its members to the other House. Rumors of his speech ran through the city, and before it was concluded the anxiety to hear him became intense. The galleries of the House became densely packed, chiefly with ladies, and the lobbies were crowded with foreign ministers, heads of departments, judges, officers of the army and navy, and distinguished citizens. Among the charmed auditors were the best American statesmen of the time who then occupied seats in both branches of Congress—John Quincy Adams leading those of the Representatives, and Daniel Webster and Henry Clay of the Senate. The entire self-possession of Mr. Prentiss, then only twenty-nine years of age, never forsook him in such an august presence. There was no straining for effect, no trick of oratory but from the first to the last sentence, everything in manner, as in matter, seemed perfectly natural, as if he were addressing a jury on an ordinary question of law. This feature of his speech—this evidence of sincerity in every word—with the almost boyish beauty of his face, bound his distinguished audience as with a magic spell. When, at the conclusion of the speech, Mr. Webster left the hall, he remarked to a friend, with his comprehensive brevity, "Nobody can equal that!" [2]

Mr. Prentiss was rejected by the casting vote of the Speaker, Mr. Polk, and the election sent back to the people when, after another extraordinary canvass, he was triumphantly returned. After the adjournment of Congress, he visited his mother in Portland. About this time, a great reception was given to Mr. Webster, as defender of the Constitution, in Faneuil Hall, and Mr. Prentiss was invited to be present and address the assemblage. His speech on the occasion is still fresh in the memory of all who heard it. He was called upon late in the evening, and after a succession of very able speakers but hardly had the vast audience heard the tap of his cane, as he stepped forward, and caught the first sound of his marvelous voice, when he held them, as it were, spell-bound. Before he had uttered a word, indeed, he had taken possession of his audience by his very look—for, when aroused by a great occasion, his countenance flashed like a diamond. Gov. Everett, who presided at the banquet, himself an orator of classic power, thus referred to Mr. Prentiss' address, in a letter written more than a dozen years later:

It seemed to me the most wonderful specimen of sententious fluency I had ever witnessed. The words poured from his lips in a torrent, but the sentences were correctly formed, the matter grave and important, the train of thought distinctly pursued, the illustrations wonderfully happy, drawn from a wide range of reading, and aided by a brilliant imagination. That it was a carefully prepared speech, no one could believe for a moment. It was the overflow of a full mind, swelling in the joyous excitement of the friendly reception, kindling with the glowing themes suggested by the occasion, and not unmoved by the genius of the place. Sitting by Mr. Webster, I asked him if he had ever heard anything like it? He answered, "Never, except from Mr. Prentiss himself."

Political life was exceedingly distasteful to Mr. Prentiss and he soon abandoned it and returned with fresh zeal to the practice of his profession. The applauses of the world seemed never for an instant to deceive him. He wrote after a great speech at Nashville, addressed, it was estimated, to 40,000 people: "They heap compliments upon me till I am almost crushed beneath them." And yet in the midst of such popular ovations he wrote to his sister:

I laugh at those who look upon the uncertain, slight, and changeable regards of the multitude, as worthy even of comparison with the true affection of one warm heart. I have ever yearned for affection I believe it is the only thing of which I am avaricious. I never had any personal ambition, and do not recollect the time when I would not have exchanged the applause of thousands for the love of one of my fellow-beings.

In 1842, his yearning for affection was satisfied by his marriage to Miss Mary Jane Williams, of Natchez and henceforth his life was full of the sweetest domestic peace and joy. From the moment of first leaving home, he had carried on a constant correspondence with his mother, sisters, and brothers, in the North and he kept it up while he lived. He took a special interest in the education of his youngest brother, and at one time had planned to join him in Germany for purposes of study and travel. All the later years of his life were years of unwearied toil and struggle.

In 1845 a case involving the validity of his title to the "Commons" property, was decided against him in the Supreme Court of the United States thus wresting from him at a blow that property and the costly buildings that he had erected upon it. In consequence of this misfortune and of his abhorrence of repudiation, which, in spite of his determined opposition, had, unhappily, been foisted upon his adopted State, he removed to New Orleans in 1846. Here, notwithstanding that he had to master a new system of law, he at once took his natural position as a leader of the bar and but for failing health, would no doubt have in the end repaired his shattered fortunes and made himself a still more brilliant name among the remarkable men of the country. He died at Natchez, July 1, 1850, in the forty-second year of his age, universally beloved and lamented. He left a wife and four young children, three of whom still survive.

Mr. Prentiss was a natural orator. Even as a boy, he attracted everybody's attention by the readiness and charm of his speech. But all this would have contributed little toward giving him his marvelous power over the popular mind and heart, had he not added to the rare gifts of nature the most diligent culture, a deep study of life and character, and a wonderful knowledge of books. The whole treasury of general literature—more especially of English poetry and fiction—was at his command Shakespeare, Milton, and Byron he almost knew by heart with the Bible, Pilgrim's Progress, and Sir Walter Scott, he seemed to be equally familiar and from all these sources he drew endless illustrations in aid of his argument, whether it was addressed to a jury, to a judge, to the people, or to the legislative assembly. When, for example, he undertook to show the wrongfulness of Mississippi repudiation, he would refer to Wordsworth as "a poet and philosopher, whose good opinion was capable of adding weight even to the character of a nation," and then expatiate, with the enthusiasm of a scholar, upon the noble office of such men in human society. He had corresponded with Mr. Wordsworth and knew that members of his family had suffered heavily from the dishonesty of the State and perhaps no passages in his great speeches against repudiation were more effective than those in which he thus brought his fine literary taste and feeling to the support of the claims of public honesty. This feature of his oratory, together with the large ethical element, which entered into it, was, no doubt, a principal source of its extraordinary power. It would be hard to say in what department of oratory he most excelled. On this point, the following is the testimony of Henry Clay, himself a great orator as well as a great statesman, and one of Mr. P.'s most devoted and admiring friends:

Mr. Prentiss was distinguished, as a public speaker, by a rich, chaste, and boundless imagination, the exhaustless resources of which, in beautiful language and happy illustrations, he brought to the aid of a logical power, which he wielded to a very great extent. Always ready and prompt, his conceptions seemed to me almost intuitive. His voice was fine, softened, and, I think, improved, by a slight lisp, which an attentive observer could discern. The great theatres of eloquence and public speaking in the United States are the legislative hall, the forum, and the stump, without adverting to the pulpit. I have known some of my contemporaries eminently successful on one of these theatres, without being able to exhibit any remarkable ability on the others. Mr. Prentiss was brilliant and successful on them all.

Of the attractions of his personal and social character, the testimonies are very striking. Judge Bullard, in a eulogy pronounced before the bar of New Orleans, thus refers to his own experience:

What can I say of the noble qualities of his heart? Who can describe the charms of his conversation? Old as I am, his society was one of my greatest pleasures—I became a boy again. His conversation resembled the ever-varying clouds that cluster round the setting sun of a summer evening—their edges fringed with gold, and the noiseless and harmless flashes of lightning spreading, from time to time, over their dark bosom.

In a similar strain, Gov. J. J. Crittenden, of Kentucky, wrote of him shortly after his death:

It was impossible to know him without feeling for him admiration and love. His genius, so rich and rare his heart, so warm, generous, and magnanimous and his manners, so graceful and genial, could not fail to impress these sentiments upon all who approached him. Eloquence was a part of his nature, and over his private conversations as well as his public speeches it scattered its sparkling jewels with more than royal profusion.

* * * * *

C.

Here are the first stanzas of some of her favorite German hymns, referred to in this letter:

Jesus, Jesus, nichts als Jesus
Soll mein Wunsch sein und mein Ziel
Jetzund mach ich ein Verbündniss,
Dass ich will, was Jesus will
Denn mein Herz, mit ihm erfüllt,
Rufet nur Herr, wie du willt.

Written by Elizabeth, Countess of Schwartzburg, 1640-1672.

Gott ist gegenwärtig! Lasset uns anbeten,
Und in Erfurcht vor ihn treten
Gott ist in der mitten! Alles in uns schweige
Und sich innig vor ihm beuge
Wer ihn kennt, wer ihn nennt,
Schlagt die Augen nieder,
Kommt, ergebt euch wieder.

By Gerhard Tersteegen, 1697-1769.

Zum Ernst, zum Ernst ruft Jesu Geist inwendig
Zum Ernst ruft auch die Stimme seiner Braut
Getreu und ganz, und bis zum Tod beständig.
Ein reines Herz allein den reinen schaut.

By the Same.

Wir singen dir, Immanuel,
Du Lebensfürst und Gnadenquell,
Du Himmelsblum und Morgenstern,
Du Jungfrausohn, Herr aller Herrn.

Paul Gerhard, 1606-1676.

Such, wer da will, ein ander Ziel
Die Seligkeit zu finden,
Mein Herz allein bedacht soll sein

Auf Christum sich zu gründen:
Sein Wort ist wahr, sein Werk ist klar,
Sein heilger Mund hat Kraft und Grund,
All Feind zü überwinden.
George Weissel, 1590-1635.

Gott, mein einziges Vertrauen,
Gott, du meine Zuversicht,
Deine Augen zu mir schauen,
Deine Hülf versage mir nicht
Lass mich nicht vergeblich schreien,
Sondern hör und lass gedeihen
So will ich, Gott, halten still,
Gott, dein Will ist auch mein Will.
Elizabeth Eleonore, Duchess of Sax-Meiningen, 1658-1729.

O Durchbrecher aller Bande,
Der du immer bei uns bist,
Bei dem Shaden, Spott und Schande
Lauter Lust und Himmel ist,
Uebe femer dein Gerichte
Wider unsern Adamssinn,
Bis dein treues Angesichte
Uns führt aus dem Kerken hin.
Gotter. Arnold, 1666-1714.

* * * * *

Lavater's Hymn.
HE MUST INCREASE, BUT I MUST DECREASE.
—John 3:30.

O Jesus Christus, ivachs in mir,
Und alles andre schwinde!
Mein Herz sei täglich näher dir,
Und ferner von der Sünde.
Lass täglich deine Huld und Macht
Um meine Schwachheit schweben!
Dein Licht verschlinge meine Nacht,
Und meinen Tod dein Leben!
Beim Sonnenstrahle deines Lichts
Lass jeden Wahn verschwinden!
Dein Alles, Christus, und mein nichts,
Lass täglich mich empfinden.
Sei nahe mir, werf ich mich hin,
Wein ich vor dir in stillen
Dein reiner gottgelassner Sinn
Beherrsche meinen Willen.
Blick immer herrlicher aus mir
Voll Weisheit Huld und Freude,
Ich sei ein lebend Bild von dir
Im Gluck, und wenn ich leide.
Mach alles in mir froh und gut,
Dass stets ich minder fehle
Herr, deiner Menschen-Liebe Glut
Durchglühe meine Seele.
Es weiche Stolz, und Trägheit weich
Und jeder Leichtsinn fliehe,

> Wenn, Herr, nach dir und deinem Reich
> Ich redlich mich bemühe.
> Mein eignes, eitles, leeres Ich
> Sei jeden Tag geringer.
> O rd ich jeden Tag durch dich
> Dein würdigerer Junger.
> Von dir erfüllter jeden Tag
> Und jeden von mir leerer!
> O du, der uber Flehn vermag,
> Sei meines Flehns erhörer!
> Der Glaub an dich und deine Kraft
> Sei Trieb von jedem Triebe!
> Sei du nur meine Leidenschaft,
> Du meine Freud und Liebe!

* * * * *

D.

A few extracts from the little diaries referred to are here given:

May 15, 1857.—Box came from Mrs. Bumstead—my dear, kind friend— containing *everything* salmon, tomatoes, oranges, peaches, prunes, cocoa and ham, tea and sugar from her father.[3] How pleasant the kindness of friends! *21st.*—Worked at planting aster seeds and putting in verbena cuttings—all in my room, of course. *23rd.*—First hepaticas in garden. Sweet peas coming up. Brownie hatched—*one* chicken. *June 1st.*—Books from dear Lizzy. "Sickness," may it do me good. [4] *28th.*—Sent flowers to the B.'s, flowers and strawberries to Mrs. N., green peas to E. M., and trout to Mother Hopkins. *July 2nd.*—Continue to send strawberries—yesterday to the B.'s—today to A. B. and Miss G., with rosebuds.

Oct. 11th.—A beautiful autumn day. Could not leave my bed till near noon. Then Albert drove me down the lane and carried me into the woods in his arms. Eddy has collected $30 for Kansas. [5] *25th.*—My whole time, night and day, is spent in setting traps for sleep. Today the money was sent for Kansas—$55, of which $9 was from us. *Nov. 4th.*—Election Day. Great excitement. *5th.*—Wretched news it is feared that Buchanan is elected. *Nov. 17th.*—The anniversary of my dear mother's death. My own cannot be far distant. *I earnestly entreat that none of my friends will wear mourning for me.*

January 1, 1858.—Outwardly all looks dark—health at the lowest—brain irritated and suffering inexpressibly—but *underneath all*, thank God, some patience, some resignation, some quiet trust. If it were not for wearing out my friends! But this care, too, I must learn to cast on Him.

5th.—Albert is reading Miss Bronte's Life to me, and oh, how many chords vibrate deep in my soul as I hear of her *shyness* her dread of coming in contact with others her morbid sensitiveness and intense suffering from lowness of spirits her thirst for knowledge, her consciousness of personal defects, etc., etc., etc.

9th.—Storms today "like mad." Present from Julia Willis. Each day seems a week long, but let me be thankful that I have a chair to sit in, limbs free from palsy, books of all sorts to be read, and kind friends to read. Oh, yes let me be *thankful*. A. brought "School-days at Rugby." *22nd.*—Eddy began to wear his coat! A. read to me Tom Brown's "School-days." *23rd.*—LOVE is the word that fills my horizon today. God is Love I must be like Him. *Feb. 3rd.*—How lovely seem the words DUTY and RIGHT! How I long to be spotless—all pure within and without!... Albert read from Adolph Monod. What a precious book! *23rd.*—Tomorrow I shall be forty-six years old. If I said one hundred, I should believe it as well. *24th.*—My birthday.... I feel disposed to take as my motto for this year, "I will hope continually, and will yet praise Thee *more and more*" Eddy began Virgil today. *27th.*—Woke with a strong impression that I am Christ's, His servant, and as such have nothing to do for myself—no separate interest. Oh, to feel this and *act* upon it always. And not *only* a servant, but a *child* and therefore entitled to feel an interest in the affairs of the *Family*. Albert read from the Silent Comforter the piece called "Wearisome Nights," which is an exact expression of my state and feelings. Long to do some good, at least by praying for people. A note from Mrs. C. Stoddard to my husband and myself, which was truly refreshing. *26th.*—This morning God assisted me out of great weakness to converse and pray with my beloved child. He also prayed. I cannot but entertain a trembling hope that he is indeed a Christian. So great a mercy would fill me with transport.

April 6th.—"I love the Lord because He hath heard my voice and my supplication" (Ps. 66:1). Albert read this psalm to me nearly fifteen years ago, the morning of the day succeeding that on which God had delivered me out of great danger and excruciating sufferings and had given us a *living child*. Our hearts swelled with thankfulness then now we have received our child a second time—anew *gift*. *June 8th.*—A.'s holiday. First strawberry! and first rose! (cinnamon).

July 3rd.—Oh, my dear, dear sister Lizzy! Shall I never see you again in this world? I fancied I was familiar with the thought and reconciled to it, but now it agonizes me. [6]

Dec. 26th.—I do long to submit to—no, to accept joyfully—the will of God in everything to see only Love in every trial. But to be made a whip in His hand with which to scourge others—I, who so passionately desire to give pleasure, to give only pain—I, who so hate to cause suffering, to inflict nothing else on my best friends—oh, this is *hard*!... I write by feeling with eyes closed. It is midnight and, as usual, I am and have been sleepless. I am full of tossings to and fro until the dawn. All temporal blessings seem to be expressed by one word—*Sleep*.... Disease is advancing with rapid strides many symptoms of paralysis that or insanity certain, unless God in mercy to myself and my friends takes me home first.

31st.—"Here then to Thee Thine own I leave—
    Mould as Thou wilt Thy passive clay
  But let me all Thy stamp receive,
  But let me all Thy words obey.
  Serve with a single heart and eye,
  And to Thy glory live or die."

Jan. 26, 1859.—Cars ran through from Adams to Troy *first time*. Eddy studying Greek, Latin, etc., at school Geology at home. *Feb. 3rd.*—Much of the day in intense bodily anguish, but have had lately more of Christ in my heart. Albert is reading me a precious sermon by Huntingdon on "a life hid with Christ in God." Oh, to learn more of Christ and His love! *5th.*—O God, who art *rich* in mercy, if Thou art looking for some creature on whom to bestow it, behold the poorest, neediest, emptiest of all Thou hast made, and *satisfy* me with Thy mercy. *Sunday, 6th.*—How thankful I am for the many good books I have! And oh, how I stand *amazed* at the faith and patience of God's dear children (Mrs. Coutts, *e.g.*), to *read* of whose sufferings makes my heart bleed and almost murmur on their account. *March 17th.*—"So foolish was I and ignorant, I was as a *beast* before Thee." Oh, how it comforts me that there is such a verse in the Bible as this! It comes *near* describing my folly, stupidity, ignorance, and blindness.... Quite overcome today by a most unexpected favor from my dear friends the Jameses, [7] who I thought had forgotten me. *April 12th.*—My love to my dear, dear sister. I shall never see her, never write to her, but we will spend eternity together.

Dec 1st.—Albert opened the *piano*, and, for the first time in *six years*, I touched it. Beautiful flower-pictures from Lizzy. [8]

Sunday, Jan. 1, 1860.—"Out of weakness we are made strong." This is the verse that has been given me as a motto for the year. May it be fulfilled in my experience! But should it not be so to my apprehension, may I be able to say, "Most gladly, therefore, will I glory in my infirmities, that the power of Christ may rest upon me."

March 26th.—For several days I have been led to pray that the indwelling Spirit may invite my petitions. Today He leads me to pray for the annihilation of self. My whole soul cries out for this—to forget my own sorrows, wants, sins even, and lose myself in Christ.... O precious Savior, let me see Thee let me behold Thy beauty let me hear Thy voice let me wash Thy feet with tears let me gaze on Thee forever.

March 31st.—A remarkable day. 1st. Weather like Indian summer. 2nd. after a very poor night, expecting to spend the day in bed, I was so strengthened as to ride up to the mountain with Albert and to enjoy seeing the mosses. In the P.M. rode again with Eddy.

June 30th.—For years I have been constantly fearing insanity or palsy. Now I hear of Mrs. ——— struck with paralysis and my dear friend ——— with mental alienation, while I am spared.

June 27th.—Let a person take a delicately strung musical instrument and strike blows on it with a hammer till nearly every string is broken and the whole instrument trembles and shrieks under the infliction—that is what has been done to me. Words are entirely inadequate to paint what I suffer.

June 30th.—Another great mercy. A letter from N. P. W. [9] Under date of June 4th, I wrote, "May God bless," etc., and God has blessed him. Oh, praise, praise to Him who hears even before we ask.

April 26, 1861.—"Hangs my helpless soul on Thee." Oh, how many thousand times do I repeat this line during the sleepless hours of my wretched nights!

As the year advanced, the entries became fewer and fewer some of them, by reason of extreme weakness and suffering, having been left unfinished. But no weakness or suffering could wholly repress her love of Nature. Imprisoned within the same pages that record her nights and days of anguish are exquisite bits of fern, delicate mosses, roseleaves, and other flowers pressed and placed there by her own hand. But far more touching than these mementoes of her love of Nature are the passages in this diary of her last year on earth, which express her love to Christ and testify to His presence and supporting grace in what she describes as "the fathomless abyss of misery" in which she was plunged. They remind one of the tints of unearthly light and beauty that adorn sometimes the face of a thundercloud. They are such as the following:

June 11, 1861.—Blessed be God for comfort. I see my sins all gone—all set down to Christ's account and not only so, but—oh, wonder!—all His merits transferred to me. Well may it be said, "Let us come boldly to the throne of grace." Why not be bold with such—just like presenting an order at a bank.

Nov. 6th.—Come, O come, dear Lord Jesus! Come to this town, this church, this family, and oh, come to this poor longing famished heart.

Sunday, Nov. 10th.—A better night and some peace of mind. But O my Savior, support me let not the fiery billows swallow me up! And O let me not fail to be thankful for the mercies mingled in my cup of suffering—a pleasant room adorned with gifts of love from absent friends, and just now with beautiful mosses brought from the woods by my dear husband.

The next entry contains directions respecting parting gifts to be sent to her sister and other absent friends after her death. Then comes the last entry, which is as follows:

"I need not be afraid to ask to be—first, 'holy and without blame before Him in love' second, 'filled with all the fullness of God' third—."

Here her pen dropped from her hand, and a little later her wearisome pilgrimage was over, and she entered into the saint's everlasting rest.

* * * * *

Further extracts from her literary journal:

Tuesday, Jan. 11, 1836.—Last meeting of the class. Mr. Dana made some remarks intended as a sort of leave-taking. He spoke of the importance of having some fixed *principles* of criticism. These principles should be obtained from within—from the study of our own minds. If we try many criticisms by this standard, we shall turn away from them dissatisfied. Addison's criticisms on Milton are often miserable, and, where he is right, it seems to be by a sort of accident. He constantly appeals to the French critics as authorities. Another advantage will result from establishing principles of judging—we shall acquire self-knowledge. We cannot ask ourselves, Is this true? Does it accord with my own consciousness? etc., without gaining an acquaintance with ourselves. And then, in general, the more the taste is cultivated and refined, the more we shall find to like. Critics by rule, who have one narrow standard by which they try everything, may find much to condemn and little to approve but it is not so in nature, nor with those who judge after nature. The great duty is to learn to be happy in ourselves.... I am surprised (said Mr. Dana) to find how much my present tastes and judgments are those of my childhood. In some respects, to be sure, I have altered but, in general, the authors I loved and sympathized with then, I love and sympathize with now. When I was connected with the North-American, I wrote a review of Hazlitt's British Poets, in which I expressed my opinion of Pope and of Wordsworth. The sensation it excited is inconceivable. One man said I was mad and ought to be put in a straitjacket. However, I did not mind it much, so long as they did not put me in one—that, to be sure, I should not have liked very well. Public opinion has changed since then. Many of the old *prose* writers are very fine. Jeremy Taylor, though I admire him exceedingly, has been, I think, rather indiscriminately praised.... To come to the poets again, Young should be read and thought upon. He is often antithetical, but is a profound thinker. I was quite ashamed the other day on taking up his works to find how many of my thoughts he had expressed better than I could express them. I am convinced there is nothing new under the sun. Collins has written but little, but he is a most graceful and beautiful creature. For faithfulness of portraiture and bringing out every-day characters, Crabbe is unrivalled in modern days. And Wordsworth—he and Coleridge have been obliged to make minds to understand them. Who equals Wordsworth in purity, in majesty, in tranquil contemplation, in childlikeness? Coleridge is exerting a great influence in this country, especially over the minds of some of the young men.

Friday. — Today by invitation I attended the first meeting of the new class and heard the introductory lecture. Mr. D. began by speaking of the object of the formation of the class. I shall adopt the first person in writing what he said, though I do not pretend to give his words. I have not invited you here to amuse an idle hour, or to afford you a topic of conversation when you meet. One great design has been to cherish in you a love of home and of solitude. Yet this is not all, for of what advantage is it to be at home, unless home is a place for the unfolding of warm affections? And of what use is solitude, unless it be improved by patient thought, self-study, and a communion with those great minds who became great by thinking. But it is not merely thinking as an operation of the intellect that is necessary it must be affectionate thinking there must be heartfelt love, and this can be attained only by a *habit* of loving.... I would not impart sternness to the beautiful countenance of English literature. Beautiful indeed it is, but not like the beauty of the human face, that may be discovered by all who have eyes to look upon it the heart as well as the head must engage, or as Coleridge says, *the heart in the head*. Let us not approach with carelessness or light-mindedness. Poetry requires a peculiar state of mind, a peculiar combination of mental and moral qualifications to be feelingly apprehended. But there—I will not write a word more. It is a shame to spoil anything so beautiful. Poor Mr. Dana! I hope he will never know to what he has been subjected.

Wednesday.—Everybody has set out to invite me to visit them. I made two visits last evening, one to Mrs. Robinson, where I had a fine opportunity to settle some of my Hebrew difficulties with Prof. R., and saw De Wette's translations of Job. This evening I am to make two more, and tomorrow I spend the day out and receive company in the evening. So much for dissipation, and for study.

PORTLAND, March 1, 1836.

I believe there is scarcely any branch of knowledge in which I am so deficient as history, both ecclesiastical and profane. I have never been much interested *facts*, considered simply as facts, and that is about all that is to be found in most historical works. The relations of facts to each other and of all to reason, in other words, the philosophy of history, are not often to be found in books, and I have not hitherto been able to supply the want from my own mind. *April 16, 1836.*—If my bump of combativeness does not grow it will not be for want of exercise. I have had another dispute of two hours' length today with another person. Subjects, Cousin—Locke—innate ideas—idea of space—of spirit-life, materialism—phrenology—Upham—wine—alcohol—etc.

June.—My patience has been sorely tried this afternoon. I was visiting and Coleridge was dragged in, as it seemed for the express purpose of provoking me by abusing him—just as anybody might show off a lunatic.... But I did not and never will dispute on such subjects with those who seek not to know the truth.

Feb. 6, 1837.—Why is it that our desires so infinitely transcend our capacities? We grasp at everything—do so by the very constitution of our natures and seize—less than nothing. We cannot rest without perfection in *everything*, yet the labor of a life devoted to *one thing*, only shows us how unattainable it is. I am oppressed with gloom—oh, for light, light, light! *Feb. 20th.*—Alas! My feelings of discouragement and despondency, instead of diminishing, strengthen every day. I have been ill for the last fortnight and possibly physical causes have contributed to shroud my mind in this thick darkness. Yet I cannot believe that conviction so clear, conclusions so irresistible as those which weigh me down, are entirely the result of morbid physical action. In order to prove that they are not, and to have the means of judging hereafter of the rationalness of my present judgments, I will record the grounds of my despondency. As nearly as I can recollect, the thought, which oftenest pressed itself upon me, when these feelings of gloom began, was that I was living to no purpose. I was conscious, not only of a conviction that I *ought* to live to do good, but of an *intense desire* to do good—to *know* that I was living to some purpose and I felt perfectly certain that this knowledge was essential to my happiness. I began to wonder that I had been contented to seek knowledge all my life for my own pleasure, or with an indefinite idea that it might contribute in some way to my usefulness,—without any distinct plan.... I then began to inquire what results I had of "all my labor which I have taken under the sun" and these are my conclusions:

1. I have not that mental discipline, or that command of my own powers, which is one of the most valuable results of properly directed study. I cannot grasp a subject at once, and view it in all its bearings.

2. I have not that self-knowledge which is another sure result of proper study. I do not know what I am capable of, nor what I am particularly fitted for, nor what I am most deficient in. I am forever pouring into my own mind, and yet never find out what is there.

3rd. I have no principle of arrangement or assimilation, which might unite all my scattered knowledge. Oh, how different if I had had one definite object which, like the lens, should concentrate all the scattered rays to one focus. I met with this remark of Sir Egerton Bridges today it applies to me exactly: "I have never met with one who seemed to have the same overruling passion for literature as I have always had. A thousand others have pursued it with more principle, reason, method, fixed purpose, and effect mine I admit to have been pure, blind, unregulated love."

4th. I have lost the power of thinking for myself. My memory, which was originally good, has been so washed away by the floods of trash which have been poured into it, that now it scarcely serves me at all.

A pleasant pictures this of a mind, which ought to be in the full maturity of its powers. And much reason have I to hope that with such an instrument I shall leave an impress on other minds! How I envy the other sex! They have certain fixed paths marked out for them—regular professions and trades—between which they may make a choice and know what they have to do. A friend, to whom I had spoken of some of these feelings, tried last night to convince me that they are the result of physical derangement, and not at all the expression of a sane mind in a sound body. I laughed at him, but have every now and then a suspicion that he was right.

Feb. 25th.—Last evening we had the company of some friends who are interested in the subjects, which I love most to talk about. We had a good deal of conversation about books, authors, the laws of mind and spirit, etc. My enthusiasm on these subjects revived I felt a genial glow resulting from the action of mind upon mind, and the delight of finding sympathy in my most cherished tastes and pursuits. Whether it is owing to this or not, I cannot say but I must confess to a new change of mood, and, consequently, of opinion. I mean that my studies have not only regained their former attractions in my eyes, but that it seems unquestionably right and proper to pursue them (when they interfere with no positive duty) as a means of expanding and strengthening the mind— even when I cannot point out the precise *use* I expect to make of such acquisition....

One of my friends tried to convince me last night that I was not deficient in invention, because I assigned the fact that I am so, as a reason for attempting translation rather than original writing. Several others have labored to convince me of the same thing. Strange that they can be so mistaken! I know that I have no fancy, from having tried to exert it and, as this is the lower power and implied in imagination, of course I have none of the latter faculty. The only two things that look like it are my enthusiasm and my relish for works of a high imaginative order.

Feb. 28th.—... Oh, how transporting—how infinite will be the delight when *all* truth shall burst upon us as ONE beautiful and perfect whole—each distinct ray harmonizing and blending with every other, and all together forming one mighty flood of radiance!... I cannot remember all the thoughts which have given so much pleasure this evening I only know that I have been very happy, and wondered not a little at my late melancholy. I believe it must have been partly caused by looking at myself (and that, too, as if I were a little, miserable, isolated wretch), instead of contemplating those things which have no relation to space and time and matter—the eternal and the infinite—or, if I thought of myself at all, feeling that I am part of a great and wonderful whole. It seems as if a new inner sense had been opened, revealing to me a world of beauty and perfection that I have never before seen. I am filled with a strange, yet sweet astonishment.

Sept. 24, 1837.—I have been profoundly interested in the character of Goethe, from reading Mrs. Austin's "Characteristics" of him. Certainly, very few men have ever lived of equally wonderful powers. A thing most remarkable in him is what the Germans call Vielseitigkeit, many-sidedness. There was no department of science or art of which he was wholly ignorant, while in very many of both classes his knowledge was accurate and profound. Most men who have attained to distinguished excellence, have done so by confining themselves to a single department—frequently being led to the choice by a strong, original bias. Even when this is not the case, there is some *class* of objects or pursuits, towards which a particular inclination is manifested one loves facts, and devotes himself to observations and experiments another loves principles and seeks everywhere to discover a *law*. One cherishes the Ideal, and neglects and despises the Real, while another reverses his judgment. We have become so accustomed to this one-sidedness that it occasions no wonder, and is regarded as the natural state of the mind. Thus, we are struck with astonishment on finding a mind like Goethe's equally at home in the Ideal and the Real equally interested in the laws of poetical criticism, and the theory of colors, equally attentive to a drawing of a new species of plants, and to the plan of a railroad or canal. In short, with the most delicate sense of the Beautiful, the most accurate conception of the mode of its representation, and the most intense longing for it (which alone would have sufficed to make him an Idealist) he united a fondness for observation, a love of the actual in nature, and a susceptibility to deep impressions from and interest in the objects of sense, which would have seemed to mark him out for a Realist. But is not this the true stale of the mind, instead of being one, which should excite astonishment? Is it not one-sidedness rather than many-sidedness that should be regarded as strange? Is it not as much an evidence of disease as the preponderance of one element or function in the physical constitution?

26th.—I have been thinking more about this many-sidedness of Goethe. It is by no means that *versatility* which distinguishes so many second-rate geniuses, which inclines to the selection of many pursuits, but seldom permits the attainment of distinguished excellence in one. It was one and the same principle acting throughout, the striving after unity. It was this that made him seek to idealize the actual, and to actualize the Ideal. The former he attempted by searching in each outward object for the law which governed its existence and of which its outward development was but an imperfect symbol, the latter by giving form and consistency to the creations of his own fancy. Thus, *the one* was ever-present to him, and he sought it not in one path, among the objects of one science alone, but everywhere in nature and out. In all that was genuine nature, he knew that it was to be found that it was *not* to be found in the acquired and the artificial was perhaps the reason of his aversion for them. This aversion he carried so far that even acquired virtue was distasteful to him. Whatever may be thought of such distaste esthetically, we must think that, morally, it was carrying his principle rather to an extreme. I have just come across a plan of study, which I formed some months ago and I could not but smile to see how nothing of it has been accomplished. I was to divide my attention between philosophy, language (not languages), and poetry. The former I was to study by topics e.g., take the subject of perception, write out my own ideas upon it, if I had any, and then read those of other people. In studying language, or rather ethnography, I intended—1. To take the Hebrew roots, trace all the derivatives and related words first in that language, then in others. 2. To examine words relating to the spiritual, with a view to discover their original picture meaning. 3. Search for a type or symbol in nature of every spiritual fact. Under the head of poetry, I mean, to study the great masters of epic and dramatic poetry, especially Shakespeare and Milton, and from them make out a science of criticism. Alas!

April 5, 1838.—I have been thinking about myself—what a strange, wayward, incomprehensible being I am, and how completely misunderstood by almost everybody. Uniting excessive pride with excessive sensitiveness, the greatest ardor and passion of emotion with an irresolute will, a disposition to *distrust*, in so far only as the affection of others for me is concerned, with the extreme of confidence and credulity in everything else—an incapability of expressing, except occasionally as it were in gushes, any strong feeling—a tendency to melancholy, yet with a susceptibility of enjoyment almost transporting—subject to the most sudden, unaccountable and irresistible changes of mood—capable of being melted and molded to anything by kindness, but as cold and unyielding as a rock against harshness and compulsion—such are some of the peculiarities which excellently prepare me for un-happiness. It is true that sometimes I am conscious of none of them—when for days together I pursue my regular routine of studies and employments, half mechanically—or when completely under the influence of the outward, I live for a time in what is around me. But this never lasts long. One of the most painful feelings I ever know is the sense of an unappeasable craving for sympathy and appreciation—the desire to be understood and loved, united with the conviction that this desire can never be gratified. I feel *alone*, different from all others and of course misunderstood by them. The only other feeling I have more miserable than this is the sense of being *worse* than all others, and utterly destitute of anything excellent or beautiful. Oh! What mysteries are wrapped up in the mind and heart of man! What a development will be made when the light of another world shall be let in upon these impenetrable recesses!

BOSTON, *Jan. 7, 1839.*—I came here on the last day of the last year, and have since then been very much occupied in different ways. Yesterday, I heard President Hopkins all day, and in the evening, a lecture from Dr. Follen on Pantheism. The most abstract of all pantheistic systems he described to be that of the Brahmans, as taught in the Vedas and Vedashta, and also at *first* by Schelling, viz., that the *absolute* is the first principle of all things and this absolute is not to be conceived of as possessing any attribute at all—not even that of existence. A system a little less abstract is that of the Eleatics, who believed in the absolute as existing. Then that of Giordano Bruno, who made *soul* and *matter* the formative principle and the principal recipient of forces—to be the ground of the universe. Then Spinoza, who postulated *thought* as the representative of the spiritual, and *extension* as that of the material principle and these together are his *originaux*. From thence sprang the spiritual pantheists—such as Schelling, Fichte, and Hegel—and the material pantheists.

Wednesday, April 10th.—Tomorrow I go to Andover. Have been indescribably hurried of late. Have finished Claudius—am reading Prometheus and Kant's Critique. *April 19th.*—Am reading Seneca's Medea and Southey's Life of Cowper.

ANDOVER, *May 13th.*—Dr. Woods was remarking today at dinner on the influence of *hope* in sustaining under the severest sufferings. It recalled a thought that occurred to me the other day in reading Prometheus that, regarded as an example of unyielding determination and unconquerable fortitude he is not equal to Milton's Satan. For he has before him not only the *hope*, but the *certainty* of ultimate deliverance, whereas Satan bears himself up, by the mere force of his will, unsustained by hope, "which comes to all," but not to him. *15th.*—It has just occurred to me that the doctrine of the soul's mortality seems to have *no* point of contact with humanity. It surely cannot have been entertained as being agreeable to man's *wishes*. And what is there in the system of things, or in the nature of the mind, to suggest it? On the contrary, everything looks in an opposite direction. How is it *possible* to help seeing that the soul is not here in its proper element, in its native air? How is it possible to escape the conviction that all its unsatisfied yearnings, its baffled aims, its restless, agonizing aspirings after a *something*, clearly perceived to exist, but to be here unattainable—that all these things point to *another* life, the *only* true life of the soul? There is such a manifest disproportion between all objects of earthly attainment and the capacities of the spirit, that, unless man is immortal, he is vastly more to be pitied than the meanest reptile that crawls upon the earth. So I thought as I was walking this morning and saw a frog swimming in a puddle of water. I could hardly help envying him when I considered that *his* condition was suited to his nature, and that he has no wants, which are not supplied.

June 17th.—I am reading Goethe's Conversations with Eckermann. One thing I remark is this—he does not, as most men do, make the degree of sympathy he finds in others the measure of his interest in them and attention to them. Goethe looked at all as specimens of human nature, and, therefore, all worthy of study. But, after all, this way of looking at others seems to be more suited to the *artist* than to the man and I cannot conceive of any but a very passionless and immobile person who could do it.... Does all nature furnish one type of the soul? If so, it might be the ocean the rough, swelling, fluctuating, unsounded ocean. Shall it ever *rest*? Rest? What an infinite, mournful sweetness in the word! How perfectly sure I feel that my soul can never rest in *itself*, nor in anything of earth if I find peace, it must be in the bosom of God.

July 2nd.—The vulgar proverb, "It never rains but it pours," is fully illustrated in my case. Last week I would have given half the world for a new book yesterday and today have overflooded me. Mr. Hubbard has sent me Prof. Park's "German Selections," Pliny, Heeren's Ancient Greece, two volumes of the Biblical Repository, and two of his own magazines Mr. Judd has sent me two volumes of Carlyle, and Mr. Ripley four of Lessing—all of these must be dispatched *à la hâte*. *July 5th.*—Last evening we spent upon the Common witnessing a beautiful exhibition of fireworks. This morning I have been to Union wharf to see the departure of some missionaries. For a few minutes, time seemed a speck and eternity near—but how transient with me are such impressions! I am indulging myself too much of late in a sort of sentimental reverie. Life and its changes, the depths of the soul, the fluctuations of passion and feeling—these are the subjects that attract my thoughts perpetually.... We spent last evening at Richard H. Dana's. *He* does not separate his intellectual and sentimental tastes from his moral convictions as I do—I mean that neither in books nor men does he find pleasure unless they are such as his conscience approves. *Tuesday, 9th.*—Have visited the Allston gallery and seen Rosalie for the last time before going home. I could not have believed that I should feel such a pang at parting from a picture. I did not succeed in getting to the gallery before others—but, no matter. I forgot the presence of everybody else and sat for an hour before Rosalie without moving. I took leave of the other pictures mentally, for I could not look. Farewell, sweet Beatrice, lovely Inez, beautiful Ursulina—dear, dear Rosalie, farewell!

Monday, 15th.—Yesterday I was happy today I am not exactly unhappy, but morbid and anxious. I feel continually the pressure of obligation to write something, in order to contribute toward the support of the family—and yet, I cannot write. Mother wants me to write children's books Lizzy wants me to write a book of Natural Philosophy for schools. I wish I had a "vocation." *Sabbath.*—Stayed at home on account of the rain and read one of Tholuck's sermons to Julia. Wrote in my other journal some account of my thoughts and feelings. Burned up part of an old diary.

Thursday, July 25th.—"My soul is dark." What with the sin I find within me, and the darkness and error, disputes and perplexities around me, I well nigh despair. Whether I seek to *discover* truth or to *live* it, I am *equally* unsuccessful. "I grope at noon-day as in the night." But there is a God, holy and changeless. He *is*. From eternity to eternity, He IS. On this Rock will I rest——. I stopped a moment and my eye was caught by the waving trees. What do they say to me? How silent they are! And yet how *eloquent!* And here I sit—to myself the center of the world, wondering, and speculating about this same little self. Do the trees so? No they wave and bend and bloom for *others*. I am ready to join with Herbert in wishing that I were a tree then

"At least some bird would trust Her household to me, and I should be just."

Evening.—I read today another of Lessing's tragedies—"Miss Sarah Sampson,"—which I do not like nearly as well as Mina von Barnhelm. We were engaged to take tea with "the Mayor," and went with many tremblings and hesitations on account of the rain. Very few there, and a most uncommonly stupid time.

Saturday Evening.—I have been alone for a little while, and, as usual, this time brings with it thronging remembrances of absent friends. Their forms flit before me their spirits are around me I feel their presence—almost dear friends, almost I clasp you in my arms. My soul yearns for love and sympathy. I do bless and praise my God for all His goodness to me in this respect, for my *many* tender and faithful and devoted friends. Part of the day I spent in arranging shells in my cabinet of drawers. This afternoon I went to Mr. Prentiss' library and obtained Schlegel's Lectures on Dramatic Art and Literature.

Monday Morning.—Have been trying to rouse myself to write Lessing, but cannot. It looks so little. When it is all done, what will it amount to? Why, I shall get a few dollars for mother, which will go to buy bread and butter—and that is the end of it.

Evening.—S. W. and M. W. made a call on us and the former played and sang. Then we sat up till after eleven naming each of our acquaintances after some flower. *Aug. 8th,*—Oh, what a happy half hour I had last evening, looking at the sky after sunset! We went down to the water—it was smooth as a crystal lake. The horizon was all in a glow—the softest, mellowest, warmest glow, and above dark, heavy clouds of every variety of form—the clouds and the glow alike reflected in the answering heaven below—I was almost *too* happy but—it *faded*. *Evening.*—I had something to wake me up this afternoon, viz., the arrival of the July No. of the New York Review, containing "Claudius." This led to some conversation about writing, its pecuniary profitableness, and subjects for it, etc. Julia wished I would take some other topics besides German authors, but when I told her the alternative would be metaphysics, she laughed and retracted the wish. We then laughed over several schemes such as these—that one of us should write a review and another make the book for it afterward that I should review some book, which did not exist and give professed extracts from it, etc. Soon after Mrs. D. came in and began to talk about "Undine," which she and her husband have just been reading—the new translation. I was amused at their opinion of it. The most absurd, ridiculous story, she said—with no *rationality*, nothing that one can *understand* in it—and so on, showing that she had not the slightest idea of a work of fancy merely. I have been wishing, as I often do, for some records of my past life. What could I not give for a daily journal as minute as this, beginning from my childhood! My past life is mostly a blank to me. *Aug. 15th.*—I am beginning to see dimly some new truths—such I believe them to be—in theology. I am inclined to think, but do not feel sure, that Redemption, instead of being merely a necessary *remedy* for a great evil, is in itself the highest positive good, and that the state into which it brings man, of union with God, is a far nobler and better condition than that of primitive innocence, and at the same time a condition attainable in no other way than through redemption, and, of course, through sin. In this case the plan of redemption, instead of being an *afterthought* of the divine mind (speaking anthropomorphically), is that in reference to which the whole world-system was contrived. These thoughts were partly suggested by reading Schleiermacher, who, if I understand him, has some such notions. If there is any truth in them, do they not throw light on the much-vexed question why God permitted the introduction of moral evil? Another point which I feel confident is misunderstood by our theologians is the nature of the redemptive act. The work of Christ in redemption is generally explained to be His incarnation, sufferings, and death, by which He made *atonement* to justice for the sins of the world. This, it is true, is a part of what He did it is that part which He performed in reference to God and His law, but it is not what Coleridge calls the "spiritual and transcendent act" by which He made us one with Himself, and thus secured the possibility of our restoration to spiritual life. *Aug. 17th.*—Have devoted almost the whole day to Coleridge's Literary Remains, which Mr. Davenport brought me. My admiration, even veneration, for his almost unequalled power is greater than ever, but I cannot help thinking that his studies—some of them—exerted an unfavorable influence upon him, especially, perhaps, Spinoza. *Aug. 22nd*—Mr. Park sent me the Life of Mackintosh by his son. I rejoiced much too soon over it, for it proves very uninteresting. This is partly to be accounted for from my want of interest in politics, etc. In great measure, however, it is the fault of the biographer, who has shown us the man at a distance, on stilts, or at best only in his most outward circumstances, never letting us know, as Carlyle says, what sort of stockings he wore, and what he ate for dinner. I do not think Sir James himself has much *inwardness* to him, but certainly his son has shown us only the outermost shell. Have read the Iliad and Schleiermacher today. *Aug. 24th.*—A queer circumstance happened this evening. Col. Kinsman and Mr. C. S. Davies called. I was considering what unusual occurrence could have brought Mr. D. here, when he increased my wonder still more by disclosing his errand. He had received, he said, a letter from Prof. Woods, requesting that I, or a "lady whose taste was as correct in dress as in literature," would decide upon the fashion of a gown to be worn by him at his inauguration as President of Bowdoin College, and forthwith procure such a gown to be made. *Aug. 25th.*—I have been reading the second volume of Mackintosh, which is much better than the first, and gives a higher opinion of him. He is certainly well described by Coleridge as the "king of men of talent." It is curious, by the way, to compare what M. says of C.: "It is impossible to give a stronger example of a man, whose talents are beneath his understanding, and who trusts to his ingenuity to atone for his ignorance…. Shakespeare and Burke are, if I may venture on the expression, above talent but Coleridge is not!" Ah, well—*de gustibus*, etc.

I have been as busy as a bee all day wrote notes, prepared for leaving home, read Schleiermacher, and Philip von Artevelde, which delighted me, walked after tea with Lizzy, then examined my papers to see what is to be burned. I wish I knew what I was made for—I mean, in *particular*—what I *can* do, and what I *ought* to do. I cannot bear to live a life of literary self-indulgence, which is no better than another self-indulgence. I *do want* to be of some use in the world, but I am infinitely perplexed as to the *how* and the *what*. *Aug. 26th.*—Hurried through the last 200 pages of Mackintosh today. On the whole, there is much to *like* as well as to admire in him. One thing puzzles me in his case as in others: How men who give no signs through a long life of anything more than the most cold and distant *respect* for religion—the most infrequent and uninterested remembrance, if any at all—of the Savior, all at once become so devout—I mean it not disrespectfully—on their death-beds. What strange doubts this and other like mysteries suggest!

After tea, I carried a bouquet to Mrs. French. Saw all the way a sky so magnificent that words can do no justice to it—splendors piled on splendors, till my soul was fairly sick with admiration. Mrs. French asked me if life ever looked sad and wearisome to me. *Ever!*

BOSTON, *Saturday morning, Sept. 8th*—The rain keeps me home from church, but I still have the more time for reading and reflection. At every change in my outward situation I find myself forming new purposes and plans for the future…. I *will* trust that, by the grace of God, the ensuing winter shall be a period of more vigorous effort and more persevering self-culture than any previous season of my life. Above all, let me remember that intellectual culture is worthless when dissociated from moral progress that true spiritual growth embraces both and the latter as the basis and mould of the former. Let me remember, too, that in the universe *everything* may be had for a price, but nothing can be had without price. The price of successful self-culture is unremitted toil, labor, and self-denial am I willing to pay it? I feel that I need light and strength and life may I find them in *Christ!* As to studies, I mean to study the Bible *much* also dogmatic theology—which of late has an increasing interest for me—and ecclesiastical history. To the Spirit of all Truth I surrender my mind.

Monday.—I have fallen in with Swedenborg's writings. Wonder whether the destiny, which seems to bring to us just what we chance to be interested in is a real ordinance of fate or only a seeming one—because interest in a subject makes us observant. Am reading Greek with Julia. We began the sixth book of the Iliad. *Tuesday.*—Fifty lines in Homer Companion proofs Schleiermacher the prologue and first scene of Terence's comedy of Andria two Nos. of N. Nickleby, and walked round the Common with Julia twice. *Wednesday.*—Studies the same as yesterday, except that I read less of Schleiermacher and spent an hour or so upon Lessing. Read "Much Ado about Nothing," and disliked Beatrice less than ever before. But I am not satisfied with Claudio he is not *half* sorry and remorseful enough for the supposed death of Hero—and then to think of his being willing to marry another right off! Oh, it is abominable! Walked over *four miles* in the morning, and out again before tea.

Tuesday, Sept. 17th—Well. The family is off—Mr. and Mrs. Willis, and Julia too—and the Recorder and Companion [10] are left for a fortnight in my charge. I have been much interested in what I have read today in Schleiermacher. It is his evolution of the idea of God—if I may so say—from holy, human consciousness. It recalls some thoughts which I had on this subject once before, and which I began to write about. My notion was this—that an absolutely perfect idea of man implies, contains an idea of God. I have a great mind to try and make something out of it, only I am so hurried just now. They keep sending me papers to make selections for the Recorder, and I have just been writing an article for the Companion. I spend half my time looking over newspapers. Double, double toil and trouble most wearisome and profitless. Would not edit a paper for the world.

No truth can be said to be seen *as it is* until it is seen in its relation to all other truths. In this relation only is it true…. No *error* is understood till we have seen all the truth there is in it, and, therefore, as Coleridge says, you must "understand an author's ignorance, or conclude yourself ignorant of his understanding."

Monday, 30th.—I have been very happy this afternoon—writing all the time with a genial flow of thought and without effort. How I love to feel that for this I am indebted to God. He is my intellectual source, the Father of my spirit, as well as the author of everything morally good in me.

Friday, Oct. 4th.—I have been too busy reading and writing for the last few days to find time for my journal. I go on with Schleiermacher and have resumed Lessing. I am reading the Memoir of Mrs. S. L. Smith and Tappan's "Review of Edwards on the Will." Fifty lines in the Iliad with Julia. Finished the Andria and today began the Adelphi. I am amused at comparing the comedy of that day with the modern French school. Davus in Andria is but a rough sketch of Moliere's valet, and the whole plot is so bungling in comparison. Have had very few attacks of melancholy lately because, I suppose, my health is good and I am constantly employed.

Evening.—I never came nearer losing my wits with delight than this afternoon. Went to call on Mr. and Mrs. Ripley, and saw his fine library of German books. The sight was enough to excite me to the utmost, but to be told that they were all at my service put me into such an ecstasy that I could hardly behave with decency. I selected several immediately and promised myself fuller examination of the library very soon…. Mr. R. proposed to me to translate something for his series. Shall I? [11]

Sabbath Evening, Oct. 13th.—I have just been writing to my dear brother G., for whom as well as for my other brothers, I feel the greatest solicitude. I have separate sources of anxiety for each of them, and hope that the intenseness of this anxiety will make me more earnest in commending them to God. *Oct. 14th.*—Gave up the time usually devoted to Lessing to writing two articles for the Mother's Magazine. Read Homer, and the 149th and 150th Psalms and the first chapter of Genesis in Hebrew. Read or rather *studied* Schleiermacher. Corrected proof. Read several articles in the Biblical Repository—one by Prof. Park—aloud to Julia. On the whole, I have been pretty industrious. Oh, how many reasons I have for gratitude! Health, friends, books—nothing is wanting but the heart to enjoy God in all. Wrote to mother.

Oct. 17th.—This morning dear Lizzy came of course the day has been given up to *miscellanies*.

Oct. 21st.—Mr. Albro [12] called and stayed until dinnertime. After dinner read Greek with Julia and then wrote a notice of Gesenius' Hebrew Grammar, and then set off for Lucy's, where the others were already gone. Mr. Albro has concluded to read Schleiermacher with me—that is, to keep along at the same rate, that we may talk about it. Letter from mother, and notes from Mr. Condit and Mr. Hamlin, with a copy of "Payson's Thoughts" in Armenian. Have just finished reading Mr. Ripley's Reply to Mr. Norton. Mr. Willis is forming a Bible class for me to teach on the Sabbath—am very glad.

Nov. 14th.—Finished Lessing yesterday, and hope for a little rest from hurry. Shall resume Schleiermacher and take up Fichte on the Destination of Man.

Nov. 22nd.—I am afraid that I may have to be resigned to a very great misfortune namely, to the partial loss of eyesight—for a time at least so yesterday I resolved to give them a holiday, though sorely against my will, by not opening a book the whole day. Whether I should have succeeded in observing such a desperate resolution without the aid of circumstances is quite problematical, but Mr. Gray opportunely came with a request that I should take a ride with him to Cambridge, and visit the libraries there. This occupied four or five hours, and a lyceum lecture provided for the evening. I have always congratulated myself on being so little dependent on *others* for entertainment—but never considered how entirely I am dependent on *books*. If I should be deprived of the use of my eyes, I should be a most miserable creature.

Thanksgiving, Nov. 29th.—A very pleasant and delightful day—our hearts full of gladness and, I hope, of gratitude. I hope dear mother and all at home are as happy.

Dec. 25th.—How plain that all the creations of the ancient mythology are but representations of something in the heart of man! What is the end of man? Infinite contradictions—all opposites blended into one—a mass of confused, broken parts, of disjointed fragments—such *is* he. The circumstances that surround him—the events that happen unto him, are no less strange. What shall be the end? Oh then, abyss of futurity, declare it! Unfold thy dark depths—let a voice come up from thy cloudy infinite—let a ray penetrate thy unfathomable profound. If we could but *rest* till the question is decided! If we could but float softly on the current of time till we reach the haven! But no, we must *act*. We must *do* something. *I* must do something *now*—WHAT?

Evening. But as the morning. In the afternoon, I was talking with L. W. [13] with as much eagerness and vivacity as if I had never known a cloud. This evening I was going to a *dance* at the *Insane* Hospital. For me truly it has been a day of opposites—all the elements of life have met and mingled in it.

Wednesday, 26th.—The end of man, says Carlyle, is an action, not a thought. This is partly true, though all noble action has its root in thought. Thought, indeed, in its true and highest sense, *is* action. It is never lost. If uttered, it may breathe inspiration into a thousand minds and become the impulse to ten thousand good actions. If unuttered, and terminating in no single outward act, it yet has an emanative influence it impregnates the man and makes itself felt in his life. A man cannot do so noble and godlike a thing as to think, without being the better for it. Indeed, the distinction between thought and action is not always an accurate one. Many thoughts deserve the name of activities much better than certain movements of the muscles and changes of the outward organization that we denominate actions. In this sense, it is better of the two to think without acting than to act without thinking.

Mrs. Hopkins was the author of the following works, intended mostly for the young. Some of them have had a wide circulation. They are written in an attractive style and breathe the purest spirit of Christian love and wisdom: 1. The Pastor's Daughter. 2. Lessons on the Book of Proverbs. 3. The Young Christian Encouraged. 4. Henry Langdon or, What Was I Made For? 5. The Guiding Star or, The Bible God's Message a Sequel to Henry Langdon. 6. The Silent Comforter a Companion for the Sick room. A Compilation.

* * * * *

E.

The following is the rhapsody referred to by Mr. Butler: (The words to be used were *Mosquito, Brigadier, Moon, Cathedral, Locomotive, Piano, Mountain, Candle, Lemon, Worsted, Charity,* and *Success*).

A wounded soldier on the ground in helpless languor lay,
Unheeding in his weariness the tumult of the day
In vain a pert *mosquito* buzzed madly in his ear,
His thoughts were far away from earth—its sounds he could not hear
Nor noted he the kindly glance with which his *brigadier*
Looked down upon his manly form when chance had brought him near.
It was a glorious autumn night on which the *moon* looked down,
Calmly she looked and her fair face had neither grief nor frown.
Just as she gazed in other lands on some *cathedral* dim,
Whose aisles resounded to the strains of dirges or of hymn.
But now with *locomotive* speed the soldier's thoughts took wing:
Back to his home they bore him, and he heard his sisters sing—
Heard the softest-toned *piano* touched by hands he used to love.
Was it home or was it heaven? Was that music from above?
Oh, for one place or the other! In his mountain air to die,
Once more upon his mother's breast, as in infancy, to lie!
The scene has changed. Where is he now? Not on the cold, damp ground.
Whence came this couch? and who are they who smiling stand around?
What friendly hands have borne him to his own free *mountain* air?
And father, mother, sisters—every one of them is there.
Now gentle ministries of love may soothe him in his pain
Water to cool his fevered lips he need not ask in vain.
His mother shades the *candle* when she steals across the room
A face like hers would radiant make a very desert's gloom.

> The fragrant *lemon* cools his thirst, pressed by his sister's hand—
> Not one can do enough for him, the hero of their band.
> Oh, happy, convalescing days! How full of pleasant pain!
> How pleasant to take up the old, the dear old life again!
> Now, sitting on the wooden bench before the cottage door,
> How many times they make him tell the same old story o'er!
> How he fought and how he fell how he longed again to fight
> And how he would die fighting yet for the triumph of the right.
> His good old mother sits all day so fondly by his side
> How can she give him up again—her first-born son, her pride?
> His sisters with their *worsted* his stockings fashion too,
> In patriotic colors—the red, the white, the blue.
> If he should never wear them, a *charity* 'twill be
> To give them to some soldier-lad as brave and good as he.
> They're dreadful homely stockings one cannot well say less,
> But whosoever wears 'em—why, may he have *success*!

Here are samples of the charades referred to by Miss Morse:
ON RETURNING A LOST GLOVE TO A FRIEND.
MARCH, 1873.

> A hand I am not, yet have fingers five
> Alive I am not, yet was once alive.
> Am found in every house and by the dozen,
> And am of flesh and blood a sort of cousin.
> Now cut my head off. See what I become!
> No longer am I lifeless, dead, and dumb.
> I am the very sweetest thing on earth
> Royal in power and of royal birth.
> I in the palace reign and in the cot—
> There is no place where man is and I'm not.
> I am too costly to be bought and sold
> I cannot be enticed by piles of gold.
> And yet I am so lowly that a smile
> Can woo and win me—and so free from guile,
> That I look forth from many a gentle face
> In tenderness and truthfulness and grace.
> Say, do you know me? Have you known my reign?
> My joy, my rapture, and my silent pain?
> Beneath your pillow have I roses placed—
> Your heart's glad festival have I not graced?
> Ah me! To mother, lover, husband, wife
> I am the oil and I the wine of life.
> With you, my dear, I have been hand and *glove*.
> Shall I return the first and keep the *Love*?

CHARADE.

> My *first* was born to rule before him stand
> The potentates and nobles of the land.
> He loves his grandeur—hopes to be more grand.
> My second you will find in every lass—
> Both in the highest and the lowest class,
> And even in a simple blade of grass.
> But add it to my *first*, and straightway he
> Becomes my *whole*—loses identity
> Parts with his manhood and becomes a *She*.
> (Prince, *ss.*, Princess).

* * * * *

F.

Here is another extract from the same letter:

J'ai peine à me mettre à l'oraison, et quelquefois quand j'y suis il me tarde d'en sortir. Je n'y fais, ce me semble, presque rien. Je me trouve même dans une certaine tiédeur et une tâcheté pour toutes sortes de biens. Je n'ai aucune peine considérable ni dans mon intérieur, ni dans mon extérieur, ainsi je ne saurois dire que je passe par aucune épreuve. Il me semble que c'est un songe, ou que je me moque quand je cherche mon état tant je me trouve hors de tout état spirituel, dans la voie commune des gens tiedes qui vivent à leur aise. Cependant cette languor universelle jointe à l'abandon qui me fait acceptes tout et qui m'empêche de rien rechercher, ne laisse pas de m'abattre, et je sens que j'ai quelquefois besoin de donner à mes sens quelque amusement pour m'égayer. Aussi le fais—je simplement, mais bien mieux quand je suis seul que quand je suis avec mes meilleurs amis. Quand je suis seul, je joue quelquefois comme un petit enfant, etc., etc.

The letter may be found in Vol. 5, of Madame Guyon's
LETTRES CHRÉTIENNES ET SPIRITUELLES *sur divers Sujets qui regardent*
La Vie Intérieure, ou L'esprit du vrai Christianisme—enrichie de la
Correspondance secrete de MR. DE FENELON avec l'Auteur. London, 1768.
The whole work is extremely interesting.

* * * * *

G.

[From The Evangelist of May 27, 1875.]

IN MEMORIAM.

Died in Paris, France, May 8, 1875, VIRGINIA S. OSBORN, only daughter of William H. and Virginia S. Osborn, of this city, and granddaughter of the late Jonathan Sturges.

The sudden death of this gifted young girl has overwhelmed with grief a large social and domestic circle. Last February, in perfect health and full of the brightest anticipations, she set out, in company with her parents and a young friend, on a brief foreign tour. After passing several weeks at Rome and visiting other famous cities of Italy, she had just reached Paris on the way home when a violent fever seized upon her brain, and, in defiance of the tenderest parental care and the best medical skill, hurried her into the unseen world.

And yet it is hardly possible to realize that this brilliant young life has forever vanished away from earth, for she seemed formed alike by nature and Providence for length of days. Already her character gave the fairest promise of a perfect woman. It possessed a strength and maturity beyond her years. Although not yet twenty-one, her varied mental culture and her knowledge of almost every branch of English literature, history, poetry, fiction, even physical science, were quite remarkable nor was she ignorant of some of the best French and German, not to speak of Latin, authors. We have never known one of her age whose intellectual tastes were of a higher order. She seemed to feel equally at home in reading Shakespeare and Goethe Prescott, Motley, and Froude Mrs. Austin, Scott, and Dickens Taine, Huxley, and Tyndall or the popular biographies and fictions of the day. And yet her studious habits and devotion to books did not render her any the less the unaffected, attractive, and whole-hearted girl. Her friends, both old and young, greatly admired her, but they loved her still more. As was natural in one of so much character, she was very decided in her ways but she was also perfectly frank, truthful, and conscientious—resembling in this respect, as she did in some other excellent traits, her honored grandfather, Mr. Sturges.

Several years before her death she was enrolled among the disciples of Jesus. How vividly the writer recalls her earnest look and tones of voice when she declared to him her desire publicly to confess her Savior and to remember Him at His table! When from beneath the deep sea the news that she was dangerously ill and then soon after that she was dead stole upon her friends here like a thief in the night, almost stunning them with grief their first feeling was one of tender sympathy for the desolate, sorely-smitten parents, and of prayer that God would be pleased to comfort and uphold them in their affliction.

From many hearts, we are sure, that prayer has been offered up oftentimes since. If it were not for the relief which comes of faith and prayer, what a cloud of hopeless gloom would enshroud such an event! Blessed be God for this exceeding great and precious relief. The dark cloud is not indeed dispersed even by faith and prayer, but with what a silver lining they are able to invest it! If we really believed that such tragic events are solely the effects of chance or mere natural law—if we did not believe that the hand of infinite wisdom and love is also in them, surely the grass would turn black beneath our feet. *The Lord gave the Lord hath taken away and blessed be the name of the Lord.*

G. L. P.

* * * * *

H.
Extracts from Dr. Vincent's Memorial Discourse.

The men and women, who know how to comfort human sorrow, and to teach their fellows to turn it to its highest uses, are among God's best gifts to the world. The office and the name of Comforter have the highest and purest associations. It is the Holy Spirit of God who calls Himself by that name, and to be a true comforter is to be indeed a co-worker with God. But even as the *word* "comfort" goes deeper than those pitying commonplaces which even nature teaches us to utter to those who are in any trouble, so the *office* of a true comforter requires other qualifications than mere natural tenderness of heart, or even the experience of suffering. One must know how to *interpret* as well as how to *feel* sorrow must know its *lessons* as well as its *smart*. Hence, it is that God makes His comforters by processes of His own by hard masters ofttimes, and by lessons not to be found in books.

It is in illustration of this truth that I bring to you today some memorials of the experience, character, and life work of one widely known, deeply beloved, and greatly honored by God as an instrument of Christian instruction and of Christian comfort. It would, indeed, be possible to strike some other keynote. A character presenting so many points of interest might be studied from more than one of those points with both pleasure and profit but, on the whole, it seems to me that the thought of a *Christian comforter* best concentrates the lessons of her life, and best represents her mission to society so that we might aptly choose for our motto those beautiful words of the Apostle: "Blessed be God, even the Father of our Lord Jesus Christ, the Father of mercies, and the God of all comfort, who comforted us in all our tribulation, that we may be able to comfort them which are in any trouble by the comfort wherewith we ourselves are comforted of God."

In endeavoring to depict a life which was largely shaped by sorrow, I am not going to open the record of a sorrowful life, but rather of a joyful one not of a starved and meager life, but of a very rich one, both in itself and in its fruits yet it may be profitable for us to see through what kind of discipline that life became so rich, and to strike some of the springs where arose the waters which refreshed so many of the children of pain and care.

The daughter of Edward Payson might justly have appropriated her father's words: "Thanks to the fervent, effectual prayers of my righteous parents, and the tender mercies of my God upon me, I have reason to hope that the pious wishes breathed over my infant head are in some measure fulfilled." She might have said with Cowper:

> "My boast is not that I deduce my birth
> From loins enthroned and rulers of the earth
> But higher far my proud pretensions rise
> The child of parents passed into the skies."

The life and work of that devoted minister of Jesus Christ have passed into the religious history of New England—not to say of our whole country—and no student of that history is unfamiliar with that character so tried, yet so exalted by suffering with that ministry so faithful, so unselfish, marked by such yearning for souls, and with such persistence, tact, and success in leading them to Christ with that intellect so richly endowed and so well trained that devotional spirit so rapt, that conscience so acutely sensitive with that life so fruitful and that death so triumphant....

* * * * *

In the summer of 1869, she found a lovely and peaceful retreat among the hills of Vermont. There arose that tasteful home with which, perhaps more than any other spot, memory loves to associate her. There, for ten happy summers, she enjoyed the communion with Nature's "visible forms," and heard her "various language," and felt her healing touch on the wearied brain and overstrung nerves there, as I think she would have wished, she took leave of earth amid the pomp and flush of the late summer, and gladly ascended to the eternal sunshine of heaven and there, in the shadow of the giant hills which "brought peace" to her, and the changing moods of which she so loved to study, her ashes await the morning of the Resurrection.

In reviewing this life of nearly sixty years, we find its keynote, as was said at the outset, in the thought of the Christian comforter. We see in her one whom God commissioned, so far as we can judge, to bring light and comfort to multitudes, and whom He prepared for that blessed work by peculiar and severe discipline.

There is nothing in which ordinary minds are more commonly mistaken than in their estimate of *suffering*. They seem often unable to conceive it except in its association with appreciable tragedies, in those grosser forms in which it waits upon visible calamity. Such do not know that the heart is often the scene of tragedies, which cannot not be written, and that there are sufferings more subtle and more acute than any which torture the nerve or wring the brow.

Take a character like this with which we are dealing combine the nature to which love was a necessity of being with those high and pure ideals of character which culled cautiously the objects of affection add the intense sensitiveness without the self- esteem which so often serves as a rock of refuge to the most sensitive add the sharply-cut individuality which could only see and do and express in its own way, and which, therefore, so frequently exposed its subject to the misunderstanding of strangers or of unappreciative souls crown all with the stern conscientiousness which would not compromise the truth even for love's sake, and the exquisite self reverence, if you will allow the expression, which held the region of religious emotion as holy ground, and which regarded the attempt to open or to penetrate the inner shrines of Christian feeling as something akin to sacrilege—and blend all these in a delicate, highly-strung, nervous organization, and you have the elements of a fearful capacity for suffering.

Besides this *capacity* for suffering, Mrs. Prentiss had a very clear cognition of the sacred *office* of suffering, and of its relation to perfection of character. There were two ideas, which pervaded her whole theory of religious experience. The one was that whenever God has special work for His children to do, He always fits them for it by suffering. She had the most intense conviction of any one I ever knew of the necessity of suffering to perfection of character or of work. Doubtless there have been others who have learned as well as she its value as a purifying and exalting power, but very few, I think, who have so early and so uncompromisingly taken that truth into their theory of Christian education. She quoted with approval the words of Madame Guyon, that "God rarely, if ever, makes the educating process a painless one when He wants remarkable results." Such must drink of Christ's cup and be baptized with His baptism. Along with this went another and a complementary thought, viz., that as God prepares His workmen for great work by suffering, so there is another class of His children whom He does not find competent to this preparation who escape much of the conflict and suffering, but never attain the highest enjoyments or fight the decisive battles of time…. In a volume of Fenelon's Christian Counsel, which was one of her favorite closet companions, this passage is scored: God "attacks all the subtle resources of self-love within, especially in those souls who have generously and without reserve delivered themselves up to the operations of His grace. The more He would purify them, the more He exercises them interiorly." And she has added a special note at the foot of the page: "He never forces Himself on ungenerous souls for this work."

Along with this went the thought that God's discipline was intended to make not only *models*, but *ministers* that one who had passed through the furnace with Christ was to emerge from the fiery baptism not merely to be *gazed* at, but to go down to his brethren telling with power the story of the "form of the Fourth." This is the sentiment of some lines addressed by her to an afflicted friend:

> "O that this heart with grief so well acquainted
> Might be a fountain, rich and sweet and full,
> For all the weary that have fallen and fainted
> In life's parched desert—thirsty, sorrowful.
> "Thou Man of Sorrows, teach my lips that often
> Have told the sacred story of my woe,
> To speak of Thee till stony griefs I soften—
> Till those that know Thee not, learn Thee to know."

At a comparatively early period of her Christian experience, the theme of her prayer was, "I beseech Thee, show me Thy glory" for in the answer to that prayer there seemed, as she said, to be summed up everything that she needed or could desire. In a paper in which she recorded some of her aspirations, she wrote, "Let my life be an all-day looking to Jesus. Let my love to God be so deep, earnest, and all pervading, that I cannot have even the passing emotion of rebellion to suppress. There is such a thing as an implicit faith in, and consequent submission to, Christ. Let me never rest till they are fully mine."

I do not know the precise date, but I think it could not have been very late when she received a mighty answer to the prayer to behold God's glory. New views of Christian privilege and of the relation of Christ to believing souls came with prayerful searching of the Scriptures. She entered, to use her own words, upon "a life of incessant peace and serenity—notwithstanding it became, by degrees, one of perpetual self- denial and effort." The consciousness of God never left her. The whole world seemed holy ground. Prayer became a perpetual delight. The pride and turbulence of nature grew quiet under these gentle influences, and anything from God's hand seemed just right and quite good.

The secret of her peace and of her usefulness lay very largely in the prayerfulness of her life. From her early years, prayer was her delight. In describing the comforts of her chamber in the school at Richmond, she noted as its crowning charm the daily presence of the Eternal King, who condescended to make it His dwelling-place. With the deeper experiences of which we have spoken came a fresh delight in prayer. "It was very delightful," she says, "to pray all the time all day long not only for myself, but for the whole world—particularly for all those who loved Christ." Her views of prayer were Scriptural, and, therefore, discriminating. She fully accepted Paul's statement that "we know not what we should pray for as we ought" without the help of the Spirit and, therefore, she always spoke of prayer as something to be *learned*. If she believed that a Christian "learns to pray when first he lives," she believed also that the prayer of the infant Christian life was like the feeble breath of infancy. She understood by prayer something far more and higher than the mere preferring of petitions. It was *communion* God's Spirit responding harmoniously to our own. With Coleridge she held, that the act of praying with the total concentration of the faculties is the very highest energy of which the human heart is capable. Hence, she was accustomed to speak of *learning* the mysterious art of prayer by an apprenticeship at the throne of grace. She somewhere wrote, "I think many of the difficulties attending the subject of prayer would disappear if it could be regarded in early life as an art that must be acquired through daily, persistent habits with which nothing shall be allowed to interfere." She saw that prayer is not to be made dependent on the various emotive states in which one comes to God. "The question," she said, "is not one of mere delight." The Roman Catholic poet accurately expressed her thought on this point:

> "Prayer was not meant for luxury,
> Nor selfish pastime sweet
> It is the prostrate creature's place
> At the Creator's feet."

She illustrated in her own quaint way the truth that moods have nothing to do with the duty of prayer. When one of your little brothers asks you to lend him your knife, do you inquire first what is the state of his mind? If you do, what reply can he make but this: "The state of my mind is, I want your knife."

With her natural temperament and inherited tendencies she might, perhaps, under other influences have been drawn too far over to the emotional, or at least to the contemplative side of religious life. But she saw and avoided the danger. She discerned the harmony and just balance between the contemplative and the active Christian life, and felt that they ought to co-exist in every genuine experience. She attached as little meaning to a life of mere raptures as to one of bare, loveless duty. "Christian life," she wrote, "is not all contemplation and prayer it is not all muscle and sinew. It is a perfect, practicable union of the two. I believe in your joyful emotions if they result in self-denying, patient work for Christ—I believe in your work if it is winged by faith and prayer." She had scored this passage in her copy of Fenelon: "To be constantly in a state of enjoyment that takes away the feeling of the cross, and to live in a fervor of devotion that continually keeps Paradise open—this is not dying upon the cross and becoming nothing."

Such experience and such views were behind the active side of her life, as represented by her personal ministries and by the work of her pen. The one book in which she endeavored to embody *formally* her views of Christian doctrine and experience did not, as might have been expected, find the same reception or the same response that were accorded to other productions. It was a book that appealed to a smaller and higher class of readers. But, when she wrought these same truths into pictures of living men and women—when she illustrated them at the points where they touched the drudgery and commonplace of thousands of lives—when she opened outlooks for hundreds of discouraged souls upon the roads where hundreds more were bearing the very same burdens, and yet stepping heavenward under their pressure—when she, who had walked in the fire herself, went to her sisters in the same old furnace and told them of her vision of the form of the Fourth—when she went down to the many who were sadly working out the mistakes of ill-judged alliances, and lifted the veil from sorrows which separate their subject from human sympathy because they must be borne in silence—when she told such how heaven might come even into their life—when she, with her hands yet bleeding from the grasp of her own cross, came to other sufferers, not to mock them by the show of an unattainable beauty and an impossible peace, but to *offer* them *divine* peace and the beauty of the Lord in the name of her Savior—then she spoke with a power which multitudes felt and confessed.

I am sure that hers is, in an eminent degree, the blessing of them that were ready to perish. Weary, overtaxed mothers misunderstood and unappreciated wives, servants, pale seamstresses, delicate women forced to live in an atmosphere of drunkenness and coarse brutality, widows and orphans in the bitterness of their bereavement, mothers with their tears dropping over empty cradles—to thousands of such she was a messenger from heaven.

Of all her seventeen or eighteen published volumes, "Stepping Heavenward" is the one which best represents her and her life-work—not that she produced nothing else of value, nor that many of her other books were not widely read, greatly enjoyed, and truly useful but "Stepping Heavenward" seemed to meet so many real, deep, inarticulate cravings in such a multitude of hearts, that the response to it was instant and general….

She wrote for readers of all ages. Not the least fruitful work of her pen was bestowed upon the little ones and in the number of copies circulated, the Susy Books stand next to Stepping Heavenward. Through those little half allegories, she initiated the children into the rudiments of self-control, discipline, and consecration, and taught eyes and hands and tongue and feet the noble uses of the kingdom of God. Even from these children's stories, the thought of the discipline of suffering was not absent, and *Mr. Pain*, as many mothers will remember, figures among Little Susy's Six Teachers. With the same pure and wholesome lessons, and with the same easy vivacity she appealed to youth through "The Flower of the Family," "The Percys," and "Nidworth," and it would be hard to say by readers of what age was monopolized the interest in "Aunt Jane's Hero," "Fred and Maria and Me," and those two little gems—"The Story Lizzie Told," and "Gentleman Jim."

While all her writings were *religious* in the best sense, they were in nothing more so than in their *cheerfulness*. They were not only happy and hopeful in their general tone, but sparkled with her delicate and sprightly humor. The children of her books were not religious puppets, moving in time to the measured wisdom of their elders, but real children of flesh and blood, acting and talking out their impish conceits, and in nowise conspicuous by their precocious goodness.

I think that those who knew her best in her literary relations, will agree with me that no better type of a consecrated literary talent can be found in the lists of authors. She received enough evidences of popular appreciation to have turned the heads of many writers. Over 200,000 bound volumes of her books have been sold in this country alone, to say nothing of the circulation in England, France, and Germany. She was not displeased at success, as I suppose no one is—but success to her meant doing good. She did not write for popularity, and her aversion to having her own literary work mentioned to her was so well known by her friends, that even those who wished to express to her their gratitude for the good they had received from her books were constrained to be silent. "While," says her publisher, "she was very sensitive to any criticism based on a misconception or a perversion of her purpose, never, in all my intercourse with her, did I discover the slightest evidence of a spirit of literary pique, or pride, or ambition."

In attempting to sum up the characteristics of her writings, time will suffer me only to state the more prominent features without enlarging upon details.

First, and most prominent, was their *purpose*. Her pen moved always and only under a sense of *duty*. She held her talent as a gift from God, and consecrated it sacredly to the enforcement and diffusion of His truth. If I may quote once more the words of her publisher in his tribute to her memory—"her great desire and determination to educate in the highest and best schools was never overlooked or forgotten. She never, like many writers of religious fiction, caught the spirit of sensationalism that is in the air, or sought for effects in unhealthy portraiture, corrupt style, or unnatural combinations."

Second, she was *unconventional*. Her writings were not religious in any stereotyped, popular sense. Her characters were not stenciled. The holiest of them were strongly and often amusingly individualized. She did not try to make automatons to repeat religious commonplaces, but actual men and women, through whose very peculiarities the Holy Spirit revealed His presence and work.

Third, I have already referred to her *sprightliness*. She had naturally a keen sense of humor, which overflowed, both in her conversation and in her books. She saw nothing in the nature of the faith she professed which bade her lay violent hands on this propensity and she once said that if her religion could not stand her saying a funny thing now and then it was not worth much. But, whatever she might say or write of this character, one never felt that it betrayed any irreverent lightness of spirit. The undertone of her life was so deeply reverential, so thoroughly pervaded with adoring love for Christ that it made itself felt through all her lighter moods, like the ground swell of the sea through the sparkling ripples on the surface.

Fourth, her style was easy, colloquial, never stilted or affected, marked at times by an energy and incisiveness that betrayed earnest thought and intense feeling. She aimed to impress the truth, not her style, and therefore aimed at plainness and directness. Her hard common sense, of which her books reveal a goodly share, was offset by her vivid fancy that made even the region of fable tributary to the service of truth.

Fifth, her books were intensely *personal* expressions, I mean, of her own experience. Many of her characters and scenes are simple transcripts of fact, and much of what she taught in song, was a repetition of what she had learned in suffering.

To go back once more to her office of consoler. She exercised this not only through her books, but also through her personal ministries in those large and widening circles, which centered in her literary and pastoral life. Those who were favored with her friendship in times of sorrow found her a comforter indeed. Her letters, of which, at such times, she was prodigal, were too many sore hearts as leaves from the tree of life. She did not expect too much of a sufferer. She recognized human weakness as well as divine strength. But in all her attempts at consolation, side by side with her deep and true sympathy, went the *lesson* of the *harvest* of sorrow. She was always pointing the mourner *past* the floods, to the high place above them—teaching him to sing even amid the waves and billows—"the Lord will command His loving-kindness" "I shall yet praise Him for the help of His countenance." "I knew," she wrote to a bereaved friend, "that God would never afflict you so, if He had not something beautiful and blissful to give in place of what He took." The insight which her writings revealed into many and subtle aspects of sorrow, made her the recipient of hosts of letters from strangers, opening to her their griefs, and asking her counsel and to all she gave freely and joyfully as far as her strength and time and judgment would allow. There was a tonic vein mingling with her comforts. Her touch was firm as well as tender. She knew the shoals of morbid sentimentality, which skirt the deeps of trouble, and sought to pilot the sorrowing past the shoals to the shore.

And now, having thus spoken of her preparation for God's work, the work itself, and its fruits, how can we gather up and depict the many personal traits and associations that crowd upon the memory? Of such things how many are incapable of reproduction, their fine flavor vanishing with the moment. How often that which most commends them to remembrance lies in the glance of an eye, an inflection of the voice, an expression of the face, which neither pen nor pencil can put on record.

How many such recollections, for example, group themselves round that beautiful home among the hills. How it bore her mark and was pervaded with her presence, and seemed, more than any other spot, the appropriate setting of her life. Now she was at her chamber window studying the ever shifting lights and shadows on the hills now rambling over the fields and through the woods and returning with her hands laden with flowers and grasses now busy with her ferns in her garden again beguiling the hours with her pencil, or stealing away to develop some happy fancy or fresh thought on which her mind had been working for days. And how pleasant her talk. How she would dart off sometimes from the line of the gravest theme into some quaint, mirth-provoking conceit. How many odd things she had seen of how many strange adventures she had partaken, and how graphically and charmingly she told them. With what relish she would bring forth some good thing saved up to tell to one who would appreciate it yet, on the other hand, how earnestly, how intelligently, with what simplicity, with what eager delight would she pursue the discussion of the deep things of God. Nor was her home merely a place of rest and retirement. Its doors were ever wide open to congenial spirits, and also to some of Christ's poor, to whom the healing breath of the mountains and the rare sights and sounds of country life were as gifts from heaven. In that little community, she was not content to be a mere summer idler. There, too, she pursued her ministry of comfort and of instruction. Eternity alone will reveal the fruitage of the seeds she sowed in her weekly Bible-reading, to which the women came for miles over the mountain roads, through storm and through sunshine.

And here the end came. Death, if a surprise at all to her, could only be a pleasant surprise. In one of her stories an old family servant says of her departed mistress: "Often's the time I've heard her talk about dying, and I mind a time when she thought she was going, and there was a light in her eye, and it was just as she looked when she said, 'Mary, I'm going to be married.'" It was a leaf out of her own life. She had marked in one of her books of devotion a passage that, I imagine, summed up her view of the whole matter: "A true Christian is neither fond of life nor weary of it." She had no sentimental disgust with life, but her overmastering desire was to see and be like her Lord, and death was the entrance gate to that perfect vision. Only the opening of that portal could bring the full answer to her prayer of years, "I beseech Thee, show me Thy glory." In this attitude, the messenger found her. I will not dwell on the closing scenes…. It is pleasanter to turn from that long, weary Sabbath, when nature in its perfect beauty and repose seemed to mock the bitter agony of the death-chamber, to the hour when, with the first full brightness of the morning, the silver cord was loosed, and she was present with the Lord. Surely it was something more than an accidental coincidence that, in the little "Daily Food," which for nearly forty years had been her closet companion, the passage for the 13th of August was: "I heard a voice from heaven saying unto me, Write, blessed are the dead which die in the Lord from henceforth: yea, saith the Spirit, that they may rest from their labors and their works do follow them." That summer afternoon when she was laid to rest had a brightness that was not all of the glories of the setting sun, as he burst forth from the encircling clouds, and touched with his parting splendor the gates of the grave. Nature, with its fullness of summer life, was set in the key of the resurrection by the assurance of her victory over death, and it was with a new and mighty sense of their truth that we spoke over her ashes the words of the Apostle: "It is sown in corruption, it is raised in incorruption it is sown in dishonor, it is raised in glory it is sown in weakness, it is raised in power it is sown a natural body, it is raised a spiritual body. O death, where is thy sting? O grave, where is thy victory?"

So now, as then, *more* even than then, since these months have given us time to study the lesson of that life and the sources of its power, we give thanks to God through Jesus Christ our Lord thanks for the divine processes which molded a daughter of consolation thanks for the fountains of comfort opened by her along life's highways and which continue to flow while she sleeps in Jesus thanks for a good and fruitful life ended "in the communion of the Holy Catholic Church, in the confidence of a certain faith, in the comfort of a reasonable, religious, and holy hope, in charity with all mankind, and in peace with God."

* * * * *

[1] B. J. Lossing, L.L.D., in the Christian Union of Oct. 15, 1879.

[2] B. J. Lossing in The Christian Union.

[3] Mr. Nathaniel Willis, then in his 76th year. He died at Boston, May 26, 1870, in the 90th year of his age.

[4] Sickness: its Trials and Blessings. A very wise and comforting book. She bequeathed it back to Mrs. Prentiss at her death.

[5] To aid in defending it against the "Border-Ruffians."

[6] Mrs. Prentiss was on her way to Europe. Before sailing, she went to Williamstown to say goodbye to her sister, but the latter was too ill to see her. They never met again on earth.

[7] Referring to the family of Rev. Wm. James, D.D., of Albany.

[8] Sent from Genevrier.

[9] N. P. Willis.

[10] The Boston Recorder and The Youth's Companion.

[11] The late George Ripley, the eminent scholar and critic, is referred to. In a letter, dated New York, Nov. 20, 1879, Mr. Ripley writes:

"I beg you to accept, dear Dr. Prentiss, my most cordial thanks for your kindness in sending me the extract from Miss Payson's journal. I remember perfectly the visits of the young German enthusiast to my house in Boston and the great pleasure they always gave to my wife and myself. My acquaintance with her, I think, was through Mr. Tappan's family, of which your former parishioner and my dear friend and classmate, Thomas Denny, afterward became a member. With my infatuation for New England people and New England biography and genealogy and literary endeavor, it would give me great delight to be permitted to see Miss Payson's journal."

The journal was sent to Dr. Ripley and read by him with great pleasure. The incident led to the renewal of an old acquaintance and to repeated visits at his residence—one shortly before his death—which left upon the writer a strong impression of his deep interest in theological and religious truth, as well as of his genial temper and remarkable literary accomplishments.

[12] The late Rev. John Adams Albro, D.D., of Cambridge.

[13] Leonard Woods, Jr., D.D., then President of Bowdoin College.

[14] Allgemeiner literarischer Anzeiger für das evangelische Deutschland, Jan., 1873.

Also available from Woodbine Cottage Publications
E-mail us for special discount pricing at awcpublications@aol.com

Lex Rex - The Law, The King
ISBN: 1-4505-9240-6
Samuel Rutherford's Lex Rex for the modern reader.
by Thomas Adamo

The ideas in Lex Rex predate modern concepts of nationalism and politics. They are older than the United States Constitution, as well as the American Revolution – where many modern ideas of liberty originated. Lex Rex is even older than the Enlightenment that receives so much credit for concepts such as popular sovereignty, limited government, separation of powers, and individual liberty. Nevertheless, Samuel Rutherford's Lex Rex – written at a time that viewed kings as vessels of divine power – raised a Scriptural standard arguing for the dignity of the people and the accountability of earthly governments. Although some would seek to pigeonhole the book as merely a tract on civil resistance, Lex Rex contains a comprehensive examination of a Christian view of civil government. In doing so, Lex Rex actually formulates a blueprint for freedom applicable for any time and place. Rutherford hoped to demonstrate the need for government based on law instead of the arbitrary decisions of fallible humanity. Throughout this process, the Bible is the final authority and basis for law. This Scriptural base was a primary reason for both the great support and opposition that met Lex Rex.

Mrs. Beeton's Book of Household Management
ISBN: 1-4818-1526-1

by Mrs. Isabella Mary Beeton

Published in 1861, Mrs. Beeton's Book of Household Management has been a benchmark guide for all aspects of running the middle class Victorian household. Written in the midst of the Industrial Revolution, Mrs. Beeton addressed a variety of issues relating to this historically transitional period. This included advice about cooking, child rearing, hygiene, servant's pay, and much more. While certainly not a modern book on these topics, this guide provides great insights into the daily tasks of the 19th century. From the preface, "I must frankly own, that if I had known, beforehand, that this book would have cost me the labor that it has, I should never have been courageous enough to commence it. What moved me, in the first instance, to attempt a work like this, was the discomfort and suffering which I had seen brought upon men and women by household mismanagement. I have always thought that there is no more fruitful source of family discontent than a housewife's badly cooked dinners and untidy ways. Men are now so well served out of doors,—at their clubs, well-ordered taverns, and dining-houses, that in order to compete with the attractions of these places, a mistress must be thoroughly acquainted with the theory and practice of cookery, as well as be perfectly conversant with all the other arts of making and keeping a comfortable home."

Our Muslim Sisters
ISBN: 1-4818-1531-8
A cry of need from lands of darkness.
by Annie Van Sommer & Samuel M. Zwemer

Islam. Has a religion of peace been hijacked by modern radicals? Our Muslim Sisters documents Muslim beliefs and practices relating to women from across a broad spectrum of the Islamic world. First published in 1906, these first-hand case studies and testimonies demonstrate how the oppression of women, in a myriad of forms, is a fundamental tenet of the Muslim system. From the Introduction, "This book - with its sad, reiterated story of wrong and oppression - is an indictment and an appeal. It is an indictment of the system, which produces such pathetic results. It is an appeal to Christians to right these wrongs and enlighten this darkness by sacrifice and service. At the recent Islamic Educational Conference in Bombay [1906], the president of the gathering, the Agha Khan, himself a leading Muslim, spoke very vigorously of the chief barriers to progress in the Muslim world. The first and greatest of these barriers in his opinion was "the seclusion of women, which results in keeping half the community in ignorance and degradation and this hinders the progress of the whole." Surely, the ignorance and degradation of one-half of a community, which has a world population of over 233 million, is a question that concerns all who love humanity." Has Islam been hijacked? In fact, nothing has changed.

Creeds, Confessions, & Catechisms
ISBN: 1-4818-1536-9

Why study creeds? Isn't the Bible enough? The Bible is everything we need for salvation and living, yet it is a large work of great complexity. Developing an accurate understanding of Biblical concepts is essential to a thriving Christian. Even so, not everyone has the time or inclination to "reinvent the wheel" – so to speak. This is where tools such as creeds, confessions, and catechisms can help. These tools can serve as guides that can develop systematic ideas for biblical beliefs with specific focus. Believers seeking to plume, with accuracy and cohesion, the depths of Scripture, while bringing together a consensus of understanding and interpretation, developed these statements of faith. Even when examining a variety of creeds, confessions, and catechisms, what is striking is not the disagreements in details. Rather, the vast areas of agreement across the millennia demonstrate that the consistency of biblical truth is timeless. Why study creeds? Confessions? Catechisms? They can help you to maximize you Bible study focus, in a systematic way, to know the Word of God better and more effectively.

The Imitation of Christ & The Practice of the Presence of God
ISBN: 1-4818-1541-5
A modern rendering
by Thomas à Kempis & Brother Lawrence

Do not pick up this book unless you want to be changed! What good is it to "know" God if that knowledge does not influence your attitudes and behavior. For hundreds of years, The Imitation of Christ and The Practice of the Presence of God have served as remedies to this dilemma. Going beyond dead formalities and vainly exalting doctrine over the needs of people's souls, both of these works demonstrate what the Christian life should look like by example. With Jesus Christ as the ultimate point of reference, these two works display the Christian life filled with awe, reverence, love, mercy, and compassion – a faith that is not alone. This modern rendering of these devotional classics will stir your conscience, move your soul, and change your life.

Printed in Great Britain
by Amazon